Opera Companies and Houses
of the United States

In memory of my father
Dr. Bernard Kopelman

Opera Companies and Houses of the United States

A Comprehensive, Illustrated Reference

by

KARYL LYNN ZIETZ

McFarland & Company, Inc., Publishers
Jefferson, North Carolina, and London

British Library Cataloguing-in-Publication data are available

Library of Congress Cataloguing-in-Publication Data

Zietz, Karyl Lynn.
     Opera companies and houses of the United States : a comprehensive,
illustrated reference / by Karyl Lynn Zietz.
        p.   cm.
     Includes bibliographical references and index.
     ISBN 0-89950-955-X (lib. bdg. : 50# alk. paper) ∞
     1. Opera companies—United States—Directories.   2. Theaters—
United States—Directories.   3. Opera—United States.   I. Title.
ML13.Z54   1995
782.1′06′073—dc20   94-943
                                                            CIP
                                                            MN

Manufactured in the United States of America

McFarland & Company, Inc., Publishers
  Box 611, Jefferson, North Carolina 28640

Acknowledgments

A book of this kind would not be possible without the cooperation of the opera companies and houses, and I want to express my deep appreciation to those who assisted with information and photographs.

At the opera companies: Charlotte Shockley, Alfreda Irwin, Jack Belsom, Lisa Jardanhazy, Jon Finck, Stein Bujan, Ray Delia, Dean Shapiro, Timothy Dunn, Gerald Farrar, Barbara Smith, Cris Stravinsky, Robert Jimenez, Charles Blazek, Elena Park, Ernesto Alorda, Linda Shockley, Joan Fox, Debra Ayers, JoAnn Sims, Elizabeth Lilly, Gail Billingsley, Eric Skelly, Walt Stevens, Larry Hancock, Diana Hossack, Kathy Graves, Judith Frisbie-Goins, Daryl Friedman, Suzanne Stephens, Todd Schultz, Allison van Kirk, Kathleen Kirkman, Leslie Paliyenko, Donna Noblitt, Marilyn Porcino, James Fullan, Marietta Hedges, Lynn Allen, Leslie Findlen, Edward Denny, Michael Connor, Marilyn Altman, Catherine Lucas, Kathy Bumgardner, Kay Pierson, Barbara Johnson, Sue Stout, Norman Johnson, Claudia Snowden-Rawley, Jim Jaye, Jill Johnson-Danielson, Barbara Seckler, Dayna Booth, Pam Goodyn, Janice Mackay, Susan Threadgill, Bill Wiemuth, Judith Clark, Anne Farrell, and Ann Stanke.

And at the opera houses: Philip Procter, Al Brown, John Vogt, Arthur Bustamante, Stacey Grimaldi, Barry Steinman, Michael Thomson, Laura Longley, Robert Pomory, Paula Yudelevit, Stephen Martin, Rodney Smith, Carol Minter, Molly Paradiso, Sally Baker, Shannon Lenoir, Frank Mlyniec, Shirley Cowles, Susan Apthorp, JoAnn Barry, Carmela Fanelli, John van Zandt, Charles Kuba, Marilyn Settergren, Kathleen Southworth, and Michael Sandy.

A special word of thanks goes to those general, artistic, and music directors that took time out from their busy schedules to discuss with me their philosophy and plans: Sarah Caldwell, Plato Karaynis, Lotfi Mansouri, Thomson Smillie, David DiChiera, Marvin David Levy, Paul Kellogg, Peter Russell, Ian Campbell, Peter Hemmings, Robert Heuer, Martin Feinstein, Peter Mark, Tito Capobianco, Stephen Lord, Linda Jackson, Judith Walker, Donald Jenkins, Dan Andrews, Kyle Ridout, Mary Robert, Victor de Renzi, Irene Dalis, Robert Swedberg, Jane Nelson, Donald Rule, Michael Harrison, Eric Kjellmark, Robert Larsen, Nathaniel Merrill, and Russell Patterson.

My deepest thanks go to Joachim, whose support, advice, and assistance helped make *Opera Companies and Houses of the United States* possible.

Karyl Lynn Zietz

Table of Contents

List of Photographs
and Credits

Introduction

Opera came of age in the United States during the 1980s and 1990s, with the number of active professional companies proliferating. A few decades ago, one could practically count them on one hand. Little is known about most of these companies and almost nothing has been written on them, outside of their home territories. With this reference book, I hope to rectify the situation, and increase awareness of the wealth of operatic activity in the United States.

The difficulty in compiling a reference book on opera is that so much contradictory and unreliable information has been published. The problem is compounded because someone else then uses this unreliable material, with a footnote as verification. Theaters that never existed had nevertheless already burned down and been rebuilt! A case in point is the first Théâtre d'Orléans (New Orleans), which opened in 1815. Several sources had the theater opening in 1809, burning down and being rebuilt, all before 1815. Other sources placed premieres in theaters that had not even opened or had already been destroyed. I could fill more than a few chapters with all the conflicting and inaccurate information I encountered while researching this book. Therefore, I have made every effort not to contribute to this perpetuation of error. I have verified all information, especially conflicting material, with original sources (programs, newspaper accounts, and other historic memorabilia) and relied only on books that used original sources as references. Secondary sources were avoided whenever possible. Unverifiable conflicting information was omitted.

This problem manifests itself most when researching premieres and their dates. In my text I noted the erroneous attribution of American premieres to Philadelphia and New York that had been staged previously in New Orleans. But the problem also extends to current companies in the United States that have referred to performances of rare or obscure operas as American or even world premieres. Consequently the premieres were all thoroughly checked and rechecked before they were listed. If there was doubt as to where a premiere took place, the information was omitted. If I could not verify a date or time period, I placed a question mark after it. Because of the enormous variety of spellings and translations to which opera titles are subjected, all titles are in their original language and follow the grammatical rules of that language. (Russian titles use a standard transliteration.)

At the end of each chapter the reader will find, in the following order, a list of the general or artistic directors of the current opera company, chronological listings of world and American premieres, and finally, the early repertory at

1

selected theaters, and the repertory of the current opera companies. In major early operatic centers, the premieres are grouped according to the opera house in which the performances took place. Otherwise, early premieres are grouped by city, and the rest by opera company. If a house or company staged no world or American premieres, the heading was omitted. When the term "American premiere" is used, the performance was the first in North, South or Central America; the term "United States premiere" is used when an opera was previously performed in Canada, Mexico, or South or Central America. The list was restricted to those performances by professional companies.

In compiling these lists, I made extensive use of the following sources: Julius Mattfeld's *A Handbook of American Operatic Premieres, 1731–1962*, Oscar Sonneck's *Early Opera in America*, Henry Kmen's *Music in New Orleans: The Formative Years, 1791–1841*, Quaintance Eaton's *The Boston Opera Company*, Ronald Davis's *Opera in Chicago*, John Frederick Cone's *Oscar Hammerstein's Manhattan Opera Company*, Arthur Bloomfield's *The San Francisco Opera, 1922–1978*, Mary Voelz Chandler's *The Greater Miami Opera: From Shoestring to Showpiece 1941–1985*, Edwin S. Lindsey's *Achievements of the Chattanooga Opera Association, 1943–1978*, Frank Merkling & John W. Freeman's *The Golden Horseshoe: The Life and Times of the Metropolitan Opera House*, and Martin Sokol's *The New York City Opera*. Other good source books are John Francis's *Within These Walls: A History of the Academy of Music in Philadelphia*, Ralph Becker's *Miracle on the Potomac: The Kennedy Center from the Beginning*, Toni Young's *The Grand Experience: A History of the Grand Opera House*, Albert Coote's *Four Vintage Decades*, Charles A. Johnson's *Opera in the Rockies: A History of the Central City Opera House Association, 1932–1992*, Eleanor Scott's *The First Twenty Years of the Santa Fe Opera*, Claudia Cassidy's *Lyric Opera of Chicago*, and Martin Mayer's *The Met*.

Alabama

• *Mobile Opera* •

The birth of the Mobile Opera came in 1947 with an unusual pairing of operas, Pietro Mascagni's *Cavalleria rusticana* with Ermanno Wolf-Ferrari's *Il segreto di Susanna*. These were the sole offerings for the inaugural season. Czech Hungarian soprano Rose Palmai-Tenser founded the Mobile Opera, which was an outgrowth of her students' performances. The previous year, her students, accompanied by two pianos, performed Engelbert Humperdinck's *Hänsel und Gretel* in the Murphy High School Auditorium.

Opera was seen in Mobile as early as 1830. Gioachino Rossini's *La Cenerentola* was the first work performed. Because of Mobile's proximity to New Orleans, many traveling opera troupes and well-known singers passed through the port city on their way to or from Louisiana, offering similar fare as given in New Orleans. The *bel canto* repertory, Giuseppe Verdi's new works, and an occasional novelty predominated. By 1860, a European-style opera house was built in Mobile. The theater boasted a horseshoe-shaped auditorium with parquet boxes, proscenium boxes, and a gallery. Here Adelina Patti sang Zerlinda in Wolfgang Amadeus Mozart's *Don Giovanni* on January 11, 1861, the night Alabama seceded from the Union. After the Civil War, Jake Tannenbaum organized an outdoor operetta performance at Monroe Park. A decade later, the Stevens company staged Jacques Offenbach's *La Périchole*. Emma Abbott sang Marguerite in Charles Gounod's *Faust*. The Galton Opera Company offered opera in English, and a New Orleans troupe presented French works. When Mobile's opera house burned to the ground in 1917, all opera came to a standstill until the founding of the Mobile Opera.

Although the second season of the newly formed company also offered a unique double bill, Douglas Moore's *The Devil and Daniel Webster* and Ruggero Leoncavallo's *I pagliacci*, the repertory quickly turned to standard fare. Works like Giacomo Puccini's *La bohème*, *Madama Butterfly*, and *Tosca*, Verdi's *La traviata* and *Rigoletto*, and Mozart's *Le nozze di Figaro* comprised the one-opera season. Every spring the company imported conductor Frederick Kurzweil and director Elemer Nagy from the North to mount their performances in the Murphy High School Auditorium, their home for nineteen years. Mobile's first production of a Russian opera, Modest Mussorgsky's *Boris Godunov*, took place in 1961. Three years later, Figaro cleverly outmaneuvered Dr. Bartolo to win Rosina's hand for a disguised Count Almaviva, and Rossini's *Il barbiere di Siviglia*, sung in English, became the swan song for the high school auditorium stage. In 1965, the company celebrated its move into the newly built Civic Center Theater with a grand production of Verdi's *Aida*. The 1980s ushered in a permanent season expansion to two operas, and with it the opportunity to mount an occasional novelty. The 1985-86 season witnessed Claude Debussy's *L'enfant prodigue* on a double-bill with Leon-cavallo's *I pagliacci* and the 1989-90 season saw Moore's *The Ballad of Baby Doe*. The Mobile Opera has developed from a community opera into a professional regional company, showcasing the talents of young American singers.

The two-opera season offers standard repertory in a *stagione* system. Recent productions include Jules Massenet's *Manon*, Georges Bizet's *Carmen*, and Rossini's *Il barbiere di Siviglia*. The company performs in the Civic Center Theater.

Civic Center Theater

The Civic Center Theater opened it doors in 1965. Housed in a huge brick building that is also home to a 10,000-seat arena, the theater is part of a $10 million com-plex. With an orchestra level and one tier, the Civic Center theater seats 1,937.

Practical Information. The Mobile Civic Center Theater is at 401 Civic Center Drive. The Mobile Opera box office is reached by telephoning 205-460-2900 be-tween 9:00 A.M. and 5:00 P.M. weekdays or writing Mobile Opera, Inc., P.O.B. 8366, Mobile, AL 36689. If you go, stay at the Radisson Admiral Semmes Hotel, 251 Government Street, Mobile, AL 36602; telephone 205-432-8000. (You may fax to the same number, but it is necessary to call the hotel operator prior to your transmission.) For reservations call 1-800-333-3333. The Admiral Semmes is a luxurious historic hotel located only two blocks from the Mobile Civic Center.

REPERTORY

1947: Cavalleria rusticana/Il segreto di Susanna. **1948**: The Devil and Daniel Webster/I pagliacci. **1949**: La bohème. **1950**: La traviata. **1951**: Les contes d'Hoffmann. **1952**: Madama Butterfly. **1953**: Le nozze di Figaro. **1954**: Il trovatore. **1955**: Carmen. **1956**: Faust. **1957**: Tosca. **1958**: Rigoletto. **1959**: Don Pasquale. **1960**: Roméo et Juliette. **1961**: Falstaff. **1962**: Boris Godunov. **1963**: La bohème. **1964**: Il barbiere di Siviglia. **1965**: Aida. **1966**: La traviata. **1967**: Turandot. **1968**: Un ballo in maschera. **1969**: Lucia di Lammermoor. **1970**: Andrea Chénier. **1971**: Faust. **1972**: Carmen. **1973**: Tosca. **1974**: Le nozze di Figaro. **1975**: Manon. **1976**: Susannah. **1977**: La bohème. **1978**: Rigoletto. **1978-79**: Don Pasquale, Madama Butterfly. **1979-80**: La traviata. **1980-81**: Don Giovanni, Les contes d'Hoffmann. **1981-82**: Il barbiere di Siviglia, Die Fledermaus. **1982-83**: L'elisir d'amore, Carmen. **1983-84**: Die lustige Witwe, Tosca. **1984-85**: La fille du régiment, Faust. **1985-86**: Lucia di Lammermoor, L'enfant prodigue/I pagliacci. **1986-87**: La bohème, Die Zauberflöte. **1987-88**: Rigoletto, The Mikado. **1988-89**: La Cenerentola, Madama Butterfly. **1989-90**: The Ballad of Baby Doe, La traviata. **1990-91**: Turandot, Don Pasquale. **1991-92**: Manon, Carousel. **1992-93**: Il bar-biere di Siviglia, Carmen. **1993-94**: Tosca, L'elisir d'amore.

Alaska
ANCHORAGE

• *Anchorage Opera* •

Engelbert Humperdinck's *Hänsel und Gretel* inaugurated the Anchorage Opera in 1962. Opera was brought to Anchorage by Marita Ferrell, a former soprano with

the Metropolitan Opera in New York City. The singers are local talent. The repertory is primarily traditional. Anchorage Opera anticipates its first world premiere
in 1994 when it will present John Luther Adams's *Earth and the Great Weather*.
The three-opera season is presented in the Discovery Theater. The Theater seats
700.

    Practical Information. The Discovery Theater is located at 619 West 6th
Street. Tickets can be purchased by calling (907) 263-2787 or writing the Anchorage Opera, 1507 Spar Avenue, Anchorage, AK 99501.

Arizona ———————————————— TUCSON

• *Arizona Opera* •

Gioachino Rossini's *Il barbiere di Siviglia* inaugurated the Arizona Opera on April
7, 1972. A second performance followed April 8. It was a modest production
mounted on a tiny budget, but well-received. The company had been founded in
November 1971 by a group of local opera lovers.

    The second season offered Giuseppe Verdi's *La traviata*, and Giacomo Puc-
cini's *Tosca*. By the third season, the number of productions had risen to three,
but the repertory remained traditional. The eleventh season, however, saw a
Phoenix novelty, Sergey Prokofiev's *Lyubov' k tryom apel'sinam* (Love for Three
Oranges). The company's first American opera, Douglas Moore's *The Ballad of
Baby Doe*, graced the stage the following year.

    Glynn Ross, who had founded the Seattle Opera (see Seattle entry) arrived
in October 1983 to take the helm. Three years later, Ross increased the number
of productions to four. Beginning in 1988, the company began staging one
unusual work. Léo Delibes's *Lakmé* initiated the effort. Verdi's rarely performed
Giovanna d'Arco and *Nabucco* followed. Ross, who founded the Wagner Festival
in Seattle, introduced a similar festival to Arizona. Richard Wagner's *Die Walküre*
initiated the Cycle during the 1992-93 season. *Siegfried* followed the next season.
Götterdämmerung and *Das Rheingold* were mounted during the 1994-95 season.
The company staged the entire Ring as a separate Festival following the regular
season.

    The four-opera season offers a standard repertory with one lesser-known work
in a *stagione* system. Young artists "approaching their prime" sing alongside
established artists. Recent productions include Puccini's *La bohème* and *Turandot*,
Rossini's *Il barbiere di Siviglia* and *La donna del lago*, and Verdi's *Don Carlo*. The
company performs in the Music Hall, which is part of the Tucson Convention
Center. The Hall seats 2,277.

    Practical Information. The Music Hall is at 260 South Church Avenue. Tickets
are purchased from the Arizona Opera box office at 3501 North Mountain. Tickets
can be ordered by telephoning 602-293-4336, faxing 602-293-5097, or writing
P.O.B. 42828, Tuscon, AZ 85733. If you go, stay at The Westin La Paloma, 3800
East Sunrise Drive, Tucson, AZ 85718; telephone 602-724-6000, fax 602-577-5878,
reservations 1-800-228-3000. The La Paloma is a wonderful resort only a short
distance from the Music Hall.

COMPANY STAFF AND REPERTORY

General/Artistic Director. Glynn Ross (1983–present).
Repertory. **1972:** Il barbiere di Siviglia. **1972-73:** La traviata, Tosca. **1973-74:** Un ballo in maschera, Die Zauberflöte, Madama Butterfly. **1974-75:** Le nozze di Figaro, Hänsel und Gretel, La bohème. **1975-76:** Carmen, Cavalleria rusticana/I pagliacci, Così fan tutte. **1976-77:** Faust, Rigoletto, La Cenerentola. **1977-78:** Lucia di Lammermoor, Otello, Don Giovanni. **1978-79:** Il trovatore, Madama Butterfly, Rigoletto, Die Zauberflöte. **1979-80:** Macbeth, Die Fledermaus, Tosca, Il barbiere di Siviglia. **1980-81:** La traviata, Lohengrin, Turandot. **1981-82:** L'italiana in Algeri, Cavalleria rusticana/I pagliacci, Lyubov' k tryom apel'sinam (Love for Three Oranges). **1982-83:** The Ballad of Baby Doe, Carmen, L'elisir d'amore. **1983-84:** Madama Butterfly, Lucia di Lammermoor, Le nozze di Figaro. **1984-85:** Aida, Boris Godunov, Die lustige Witwe, Carmen. **1985-86:** Tosca, Il trovatore, Manon. **1986-87:** Pikovaya dama, La bohème, Manon Lescaut, Il barbiere di Siviglia. **1987-88:** Roméo et Juliette, Rigoletto, Così fan tutte, Turandot. **1988-89:** La traviata, Lakmé, Carmen, Il tabarro/Gianni Schicchi. **1989-90:** Faust, La forza del destino, Madama Butterfly, Lucia di Lammermoor, Giovanna d'Arco. **1990-91:** Cavalleria rusticana/I pagliacci, Otello, L'elisir d'amore, Don Giovanni. **1991-92:** La sonnambula, Tosca, Aida, La Cenerentola, Nabucco. **1992-93:** Don Carlo, Die Walküre, La bohème, Le nozze di Figaro, La donna del lago. **1993-94:** Die Fledermaus, Siegfried, Turandot, Il barbiere di Siviglia.

California
COSTA MESA
• *Opera Pacific* •

George Gershwin's *Porgy and Bess*, the company's first production, was staged in the Orange County Performing Arts Center on February 11, 1987. Leonard Bernstein's *West Side Story* and a Carlo Menotti–directed Giacomo Puccini's *La bohème* completed the inaugural season. David DiChiera, general director of the Michigan Opera Theater (see Detroit entry) was invited to take the helm of the newly established company.

Opera Pacific had its roots in the Festival of Opera Association, founded in 1962. Supported by the Lyric Opera Association of Laguna Beach, the Festival presented opera each summer at the Irvine Bowl. Works like Giuseppe Verdi's *La traviata* with Kathryn Grayson, Wolfgang Amadeus Mozart's *Così fan tutte* with Marni Nixon, and Georges Bizet's *Carmen* with Joan Grillo entertained the region's opera-lovers. With the arrival of a new performing arts center in Orange County, the Festival of Opera merged with an existing Opera Society of Orange County, and Opera Pacific was the result. The company calls the Orange County Performing Arts Center home.

Verdi's *Aida* with Leona Mitchell and Dolora Zajic opened the company's second season. John Mauceri was on the podium. The final presentation of the season, Johann Strauß's *Die Fledermaus*, marked the first time that Opera Pacific produced all its own sets and costumes. Joan Sutherland in Vincenzo Bellini's *Norma* was the high point of the third season. The fourth season saw Diana Soviero in a John Conklin–designed Verdi's *La traviata*, Johanna Meier in Puccini's *Turandot*, and the company's first Mozart production. Other highlights have been Emmerich

Kálmán's *Czárdásfürstin* and a Beni Montresor–designed Camille Saint-Saëns's *Samson et Dalila* with Ludmilla Schemtschuk and Vladimir Atlantov. The artists are established singers.

DiChiera, who built the Michigan Opera Theater into one of the top ten companies in the country (in budget size), has similar ambitions for Opera Pacific. He intends to expand the season by increments, first with additional performances, then with more productions and novelties. He envisions an Opera Center where the company can rehearse year round, and where there will be a library and museum. He plans to launch a summer festival in the cozy 800-seat theater at the University of California, Irvine. The summer festival will become the venue for expansion of the season to seven or eight productions.

The five-opera season offers the standard repertory with one unusual piece in a *stagione* system. Recent productions include Verdi's *Il trovatore*, Charles Gounod's *Faust*, Donizetti's *Lucia di Lammermoor*, Richard Wagner's *Die Walküre*, and Penella's *El Gato Montés*. The company performs in the Orange County Performing Arts Center.

Orange County Performing Arts Center

The Orange County Performing Arts Center opened its doors on September 29, 1986. The inaugural celebration featured the Los Angeles Philharmonic and a special guest appearance by Leontyne Price. The New York City Opera Company presented the first opera on January 13, 1987, and Opera Pacific made its debut two weeks later. Caudill Rowlett Scott architectural firm with Charles Lawrence as the chief architect designed the facility. It was built entirely with private funds at a cost of $72.8 million.

The center is an imposing modern structure of Napoleon red granite and glass. A massive grand portal soars in front of the glass façade and frames an enormous red, gold, and silver aluminum and steel sculpture called Fire Bird. The lobby is teak- and rosewood-panelled. Segerstrom Hall, named after its principal benefactor, is a vast auditorium, asymmetrical in shape. The three tray-like seating clusters appear as space ships that hover over a sea of red plush orchestra seats. The maroon-painted hall was designed to emulate the acoustics of a shoe box–shaped room, but offer the sight-lines of a fan-shaped one. The auditorium seats 2,903.

Practical Information. The Orange County Performing Arts Center is at 600 Town Center Drive. The Center's box office is open 10:00 A.M. to 6:00 P.M., Monday through Saturday, 12:00 noon to 6:00 P.M., Sunday, and 10:00 A.M. to 8:30 P.M. on performance days. The Opera Pacific ticket office is at 650 Town Center Drive, Suite 400, and is open between 10:00 A.M. and 5:00 P.M. weekdays. You can order tickets by telephoning 714-979-7000 or 1-800-346-7372 during office hours, or by writing Opera Pacific Tickets, 650 Town Center Drive, Suite 400, Costa Mesa, CA 92626- 1925. If you go, stay at the Ritz-Carlton, 33533 Ritz-Carlton Drive, Laguana Niguel, CA 92677; telephone 714-240-2000, fax 714-240-0829, reservations 1-800-241-3333. The Ritz-Carlton is perched on a 150-foot bluff overlooking the Pacific Ocean with a magnificent view and accommodations. It is convenient to the Orange County Performing Arts Center.

Orange County Performing Arts Center (Costa Mesa, California).

COMPANY STAFF AND REPERTORY

General/Artistic Director. David DiChiera (1986–present).
Repertory. **1986-87:** Porgy and Bess, West Side Story, La bohème. **1987-88:** Aida, Kismet, Die Fledermaus. **1988-89:** Norma, Il barbiere di Siviglia, My Fair Lady. **1989-90:** La traviata, Show Boat, Don Giovanni, Turandot. **1990-91:** Madama Butterfly, Les pêcheurs des perles, Un ballo in maschera. **1991-92:** Cavalleria rusticana/I pagliacci, Tosca, Die Czárdásfürstin, Samson et Dalila. **1992-93:** La bohème, Il trovatore, Roméo et Juliette, Le nozze di Figaro. **1993-94:** Faust, El Gato Montés, Die lustige Witwe, Die Walküre, Lucia di Lammermoor.

——————————————————— LONG BEACH

• *Long Beach Opera* •

Giuseppe Verdi's *La traviata* with Benita Valente inaugurated the Long Beach Grand Opera, the original name of the Long Beach Opera, in 1979. It was the sole offering of the inaugural season. Jeanette Pilou sang the title role in Giacomo Puccini's *Madama Butterfly* the following year. Again there was only one offering. Initially there was skepticism that the company would survive, since opera at that time could not even take root in Los Angeles.

Although the company offered the standard repertory in ordinary productions with has-been Met stars for the first few seasons, hints that Long Beach wanted to be different began to emerge in 1983, when the company dropped "grand" from its name and mounted the Southern California premiere of Benjamin Britten's *Death in Venice*. When the Los Angeles Music Center Opera opened in 1986, the Long Beach company adopted a totally unconventional repertory—Ernest Křenek's *Jonny spielt auf*, Wolfgang Amadeus Mozart's *Lucia Silla*, and the United States premiere of Karol Szymanowski's *Król Roger* among its offerings.

Michael Milenski, who founded the company and is still the general director, presents the works in a theatrically provocative way, offering a different product than the larger, more established opera companies in Southern California. He frequently updates the productions. Although the company eschews the star system, several well-known artists sang in Long Beach early in their careers—Richard Stilwell in Pyotr Il'yich Tchaikovsky's *Eugene Onegin*, Catherine Malfitano in Claudio Monteverdi's *L'incoronazione di Poppea*, James Morris in Charles Gounod's *Faust*, and Jerry Hadley in Puccini's *La bohème*.

The opera season offers two or three works (depending on the budget) in a *stagione* system. The repertory consists of lesser-known works in unusual productions. Recent operas include Arnold Schönberg's *Die Jakobsleiter* and Jacques Offenbach's *Barbe-Bleue*. The company performs in the Center Theater.

Practical Information. The Center Theater is at 300 East Ocean. Tickets are purchased at the Long Beach Opera Box Office, 6372 Pacific Coast Highway, Monday through Friday between 10:00 A.M. and 5:00 P.M., or by telephoning 213-596-5556, faxing 213-596-8380, or writing Long Beach Opera, 6372 Pacific Coast Highway, Long Beach, CA 90803. If you go, stay at the Ritz-Carlton, 33533 Ritz-Carlton Drive, Laguana Niguel, CA 92677; telephone 714-240-2000, fax 714-240-0829, reservations 1-800-241-3333. The Ritz-Carlton is perched on a 150-foot bluff overlooking the Pacific Ocean with a magnificent view and accommodations. It is a pleasant drive to the Center Theater.

COMPANY STAFF AND REPERTORY

General/Artistic Director. Michael Milenski (1979–present).

United States Premiere. Szymanowski's *Król Roger* (first stage performance, in English as King Roger, January 24, 1988).

Repertory. **1979:** La traviata. **1980:** Madama Butterfly. **1981:** Don Pasquale, Faust. **1982:** La bohème, Il barbiere di Siviglia. **1983:** Carmen, Death in Venice, Rigoletto. **1984:** Hänsel und Gretel, L'incoronazione di Poppea. **1985:** Die Entführung aus dem Serail, La Grand Duchesse de Gérolstein, Il barbiere di Siviglia, Eugene Onegin. **1986:** Jonny spielt auf, Les contes d'Hoffmann, Don Carlo. **1987:** The Ballad of Baby Doe, Ariadne auf Naxos. **1988:** Il ritorno di Ulisse in patria, Król Roger. **1989:** Il barbiere di Siviglia (Paisiello), Le nozze di Figaro, The Guilty Wife (play with incidental music). **1991:** Pelléas et Mélisande, Lucia Silla. **1992:** Simon Boccanegra, Barbe-Bleue. **1993:** Die Jakobsleiter, Ich wandte mich und sah an Alles Unrecht das geschah unter der Sonne.

--------------------------------- LOS ANGELES

• *Los Angeles Music Center Opera* •

Giuseppe Verdi's *Otello* inaugurated the Los Angeles Music Center Opera in October 1986. The company was born "fully mature," with a first season budget of $6 million and four additional productions, including Giacomo Puccini's *Madama Butterfly*, Camille Saint-Saën's *Samson et Dalila*, Georg Friedrich Händel's *Alcina*, and George Gershwin's *Porgy and Bess*. Peter Hemmings was appointed general director.

Although the Los Angeles Music Center Opera is less than a decade old, opera has been heard in the city since the early 1880s, when a lumber yard worker named L.E. Behymer gave the city Adelina Patti in concert at Mott's Hall. After the city's mayor Henry Hazard built Hazard's Pavilion in 1884, Behymer had a place to present grand opera, and he offered Los Angeles its first taste. In 1891, he brought the National Opera Company to Hazard's Pavilion. With a loan of $2500 from a Mrs. Hancock, the National brought stars like Édouard and Jean de Reszke, Emma Abbott, and Nellie Melba, and mounted productions of Giacomo Meyerbeer's *L'Africaine* and *Les Huguenots*, Georges Bizet's *Carmen*, Gaetano Donizetti's *Lucia di Lammermoor*, Verdi's *Rigoletto*, and Anton Rubinstein's rarely performed *Nero*. Behymer discovered another troupe in Mexico City, the Del Conti Opera, and Los Angeles experienced its first premiere on October 14, 1897, Puccini's *La bohème* with Linda Montanari and Giuseppe Agostini. The Los Angeles Theater hosted the performance. Eight years earlier, Los Angeles opera-lovers were treated to two Emmas and two operas on the night of December 24, 1889. Emma Abbott was finishing her Los Angeles season with Michael Balfe's *The Rose of Castile* in the Los Angeles Theater, and in the early morning hours, Emma Juch materialized at the Grand Opera House in Meyerbeer's *Les Huguenots*, opening her season.

The Metropolitan Opera paid its first visit in 1900, offering Richard Wagner's *Lohengrin*, Charles Gounod's *Roméo et Juliette*, and Puccini's *La bohème* at Hazard's Pavilion. The Met returned to the Pavilion on November 8, 1901, and presented Bizet's *Carmen* with Emma Calvé. Meyerbeer's *Les Huguenots* and Wagner's *Lohengrin* followed. On their 1905 visit, the company brought Donizetti's *Lucia di Lammermoor* and Wagner's *Parsifal*. They did not return again until April 13, 1948. In 1911, the Lombardi Opera Company (called the San Carlo Grand Opera when Fortune Gallo took it over) and the Boston National Opera Company visited. Three years later, the Chicago Opera came to town. The company returned eleven times featuring artists such as Titta Ruffo, Claudio Muzio, and Edward Johnson. Los Angeles also hosted Henry W. Savage's English Grand Opera, Henry W. Russell's Boston Grand Opera, the Melba Opera Company, the Grazzi Company, and the Leoncavallo Opera, which the composer conducted. The American La Scala Opera Company visited in 1916, with two Alices—Nielsen and Gentle, and the Scotti Opera Company ushered in the 1920s with Geraldine Farrar, Florence Easton, and Mario Chamlee. Nineteen twenty-two was a special year. The Russian Grand Opera Company visited, giving Los Angeles the first American staging in Russian of Nikolay Rimsky-Korsakov's *Snegurochka* (February 13, 1922) and Rubinstein's *The Demon* (February 18, 1922) in Mason Opera House.

The world premiere of Horatio William Parker's *Fairyland* inaugurated outdoor opera in the Hollywood Bowl on July 1, 1915. The "Bowl" was actually a shed surrounded by a few benches, with most of the audience sitting on the grass. Seven years later, Bizet's *Carmen* with Marguerite Sylva was mounted on July 8, 1922. The next year saw Verdi's *Aida* with Lawrence Tibbett, and 1926 witnessed Charles Wakefield Cadman's *Shanewis*. The world premiere of the first Japanese language opera in the United States, Claude Lapham's *Sakura*, took place on June 24, 1933. Three years later, Bizet's *Carmen*, Ruggero Leoncavallo's *Pagliacci*, and Bedřich

Smetana's *Prodaná nevěsta* (The Bartered Bride) graced the stage. Wagner's *Die Walküre*, with Maria Jeritza, Grete Stückgold, Paul Althouse, and Freidrich Schorr, highlighted the 1938 season. Verdi's *Aida* was mounted the next year, followed by Bizet's *Carmen* in 1940. Conducted by Pietro Cimini and starring Gladys Swarthout, the opera drew a record 24,900 spectators.

Homegrown efforts appeared when the Los Angeles Grand Opera Association was formed in 1924 with Gaetano Merola, who had established the San Francisco Opera (see San Francisco entry), as general director. The next season Merola changed allegiance and organized a rival company with Behymer, the California Grand Opera Company. Both the California Grand and the Los Angeles Grand offered one week seasons. The Los Angeles Grand performed in the Philharmonic Auditorium and the California Grand constructed a stage in the Olympic Auditorium. The California Grand presented Italo Montemezzi's *L'amore dei tre re*, Gioachino Rossini's *Il barbiere di Siviglia*, Puccini's *Madama Butterfly* and *Tosca*, and Saint-Saëns's *Samson et Dalila* among its offerings. The Los Angeles Grand mounted not only the standard fare—Puccini's *Manon Lescaut* and *Turandot*, Verdi's *Falstaff*, and Gounod's *Romeo et Juliette*, but less-familiar works like Henri Rabaud's *Mârouf, Savetier du Caire*. The company moved into the Shrine Auditorium in 1926, and Merola returned to the company a few years later. It died in the depression. Another homegrown effort, the Columbia Opera, survived one season—1929.

The Ring Cycle appeared during the 1930-31 season when the German Opera Company visited. They also staged Eugen d'Albert *Tiefland*. The world premiere of Mary Carr Moore's *David Rizzio* was mounted on May 26, 1932, the same year, Lily Pons made her West Coast debut with the Los Angeles Grand Opera. The following year witnessed Louis Gruenberg's *Emperor Jones*, with Lawrence Tibbett. In 1937, the San Francisco Opera, two hundred strong, boarded a train and headed for Los Angeles. The company performed five operas in the Shrine Auditorium—Wagner's *Tristan und Isolde* and *Lohengrin*, Léo Delibes's *Lakmé*, Verdi's *Aida*, and Puccini's *Tosca*. The company continued to make annual visits until 1965.

Homegrown opera was attempted again in 1979 with the formation of the Los Angeles Opera Theater. Founded by Johanna Dordick, it presented a three-opera season at the 1,200-seat Wilshire-Ebell Theater with up-and-coming talent. One such young artist was Susan Quittmeyer. Along with Richard Strauss's *Der Rosenkavalier* and *Ariadne auf Naxos*, Puccini's *Madama Butterfly* and *Tosca*, Verdi's *La traviata*, and Donizetti's *L'elisir d'amore*, the company boasted the American premiere of Iain Hamilton's *Anna Karenina* on March 16, 1983. After several years, the company quietly expired.

The Los Angeles Music Center Opera Association was founded in 1966, but opera was a low priority for the Association founders. Although a few attempts were made in producing opera, they ended in disarray. One such undertaking was Rossini's *L'italiana in Algeri* with a young Marilyn Horne. Instead the Association entered the opera presenting business. The New York City Opera paid regular visits between 1967 and 1982, funded primarily by a group of Beverly Sills fans. When she retired, the visits ceased. The Los Angeles Philharmonic also tried its hand at opera productions. Strauss's *Salome* was mounted in 1965 with Zubin Mehta on the podium. But it was the 1982 production of Verdi's *Falstaff* that revealed the large latent Los Angeles opera audience.

The Los Angeles Music Center Opera is the first new major resident opera company since 1932, and is also one of the largest in the United States. As one might expect in star-struck Hollywood, big name stars are necessary for success, so Plácido Domingo is the company's artistic consultant. The casts offer international artists alongside rising young talent and resident singers. In the company's short history, there have been some noteworthy events — Hector Berlioz's epic *Les Troyens*, a David Hockney–designed Wagner's *Tristan und Isolde*, Sergey Prokofiev's shocking *Ognenniy angel* (The Fiery Angel), and the company's first world premiere, Aulis Sallinen's *Kullervo* (February 25, 1992).

Opera in Los Angeles is primarily a social event. Since the audience has had little exposure to opera, it is an unsophisticated opera group for one of the country's largest cities. The advantage is that they have no preconceived notions and little for comparison. They accept not only the innovative productions, but also the hackneyed, outdated ones. This results in a wide variety and range of quality of operas presented. A new home for the symphony, the Walt Disney Concert Hall, is under construction. When it is completed, the opera will not have to share the Pavilion with the symphony, and Hemmings then plans to expand the season to twelve operas, staging four operas a week for twenty-five weeks.

The seven- (sometimes eight-) opera season offers an interesting repertory mixture of standard, twentieth-century, and unusual works performed in a repertory block-system. Recent operas included Benjamin Britten's *A Midsummer Night's Dream* and *Turn of the Screw*, Leoš Janáček's *Věc Makropulos* (The Makropulos Affair), Puccini's *La bohème* and *Tosca*, Verdi's *La traviata* and *Un ballo in maschera*, and Wolfgang Amadeus Mozart's *Die Zauberflöte* and *Le nozze di Figaro*. The company performs in the Los Angeles Music Center.

Los Angeles Music Center

The Chandler Pavilion was inaugurated on December 6, 1964, with a gala program, played by the Los Angeles Philharmonic. Works by Richard Strauss, Robert Schumann, Ottorino Respighi, and Ludwig van Beethoven were offered, with Jascha Heifetz as the featured violinist. Designed by Welton Becket & Associates, the Music Center cost $34.5 million. Three theaters housed in separate buildings comprise the Center. There had been three unsuccessful attempts to build a music hall dating back to 1945. The first was by a group called the Greater Los Angeles Plans that envisioned an auditorium, a conventional hall, and an opera house, funded by a $31.5 million bond issue. The voters rejected the proposition. The group tried a new approach, but were again rebuffed. Another group called Forward Los Angeles proposed a 15,000-seat auditorium, an exhibition hall, and a small music hall that carried a $19.5 million price tag. They were also rejected. Finally a private offer of $4 million got the ball rolling and the Center was constructed.

Overlooking downtown Los Angeles, the Pavilion is a rectangular concrete, glass, and charcoal granite structure. A broad roof overhang is supported by a ring of white, tapered, fluted columns. The grand lobby is of honey-toned onyx, and forms a U around the auditorium. The large, square auditorium holds three tiers that curve gently around the hall. Deep coral velvet plush seats stretch across in unbroken rows. Rich butternut wood panelling and silk textured vinyl cover the

Dorothy Chandler Pavilion (Los Angeles, California).

walls. The stage curtain is woven in a huge sunburst pattern. An enormous gold acoustic shell extends out from the plain proscenium. The ambiance fits "Tinseltown." The Pavilion seats 3,250.

Practical Information. The Dorothy Chandler Pavilion is at 1st and Hope streets. The ticket window is outside to the left of the main entrance. The hours are 10:00 A.M. to 5:00 P.M., Monday through Saturday. You can order tickets by telephoning 213-972-7211 during the above hours, or writing Los Angeles Music Center Opera Box Office, P.O.B. 2237, Los Angeles, CA 90051. If you go, stay at The Biltmore, 506 South Grand Avenue, Los Angeles, CA 90071; telephone 213-624-1011, fax 213-612-1545, reservations 1-800-245-8673. Designed by Earl Heitschmidt, The Biltmore opened in 1923. Recently restored to its original splendor, the hotel is an architectural treasure. It has been designated a Historic Cultural Monument. Plácido Domingo is counted among its illustrious guests.

COMPANY STAFF AND REPERTORY

General/Artistic Director. Peter Hemmings (1986–present).

World Premieres (before the Los Angeles Music Center Opera). Parker's *Fairyland* (July 1, 1915); Breil's *The Asra* (November 24, 1925); Moore's *Los Rubios* (September 10, 1931); Moore's *David Rizzio* (May 26, 1932); Lapham's *Sakura* (June 24, 1933); Pemberton's *The Painter of Dreams* (USC, May 1934); Alderman's *Bombastes Furioso* (USC, April 30, 1938); Ruger's *Gettysburg* (September 23, 1938); Villa-Lobos's *Magdalena* (July 26, 1948); Ruger's *The Fall of the House of Usher* (April 15, 1953); Clarke's *The Loafer and the Loaf* (UC, May 1, 1956); Leginska's *The Rose and the Ring* (February 23, 1957); Kanitz's *Room No. 12* (UC, February 26, 1958); Milhaud's *Fiesta* (UC, in English, March 16, 1959).

United States Premieres (before the Los Angeles Music Center Opera). Puccini's *La bohème* (October 14, 1897); Rimsky-Korsakov's *Snegurochka* (in Russian, February 13, 1922); Rubinstein's *The Demon* (February 18, 1922); Zador's *X-Mal Rembrandt* (UC, in English as Forever Rembrandt, January 16, 1955); Thomas's *Hazila* (second performance, October 27, 1936); Milhaud's *David* (first performance in English, September 22, 1956). Shimizu's *The Mask Maker* (UC, April 6, 1962); Hamilton's *Anna Karenina* (March 16, 1983).

World Premiere (Los Angeles Music Center Opera). Sallinen's *Kullervo* (February 25, 1992).

United States Premiere. Offenbach's *Les contes d'Hoffmann* (Kaye version, October 7, 1988)

Repertory. **1986-87:** Otello, Madama Butterfly, Samson et Dalila, Alcina, Porgy and Bess. **1987-88:** La bohème, Ognenniÿ angel (The Fiery Angel), La Cenerentola, Tristan und Isolde, Macbeth, A Midsummer Night's Dream, The Mikado. **1988-89:** Les contes d'Hoffmann, Kát'a Kabanová, Così fan tutte, Wozzeck, Tancredi, Orphée aux Enfers. **1989-90:** Tosca, Aufstieg und Fall der Stadt Mahagonny, Le nozze di Figaro, Falstaff, Don Carlo, Oklahoma!, Where the Wild Things Are/Higglety Pigglety Pop! **1990-91:** Fidelio, Nixon in China, Idomeneo, Orfeo ed Euridice, Elektra, Così fan tutte, La fanciulla del West, The Turn of the Screw. **1991-92:** Madama Butterfly, Les Troyens, Don Giovanni, Il barbiere di Siviglia, Carmen, Kullervo, Albert Herring. **1992-93:** La traviata, Věc Makropulos, A Midsummer Night's Dream, Tosca, Ariadne auf Naxos, Die Zauberflöte, Rigoletto, Lucia di Lammermoor. **1993-94:** La bohème, Un ballo in maschera, Die Frau ohne Schatten, El Gato Montés, Madama Butterfly, Le nozze di Figaro, Der Rosenkavalier.

SACRAMENTO
• *Sacramento Opera* •

Giacomo Puccini's *La bohème* inaugurated the Sacramento Opera at the Community Center Theater. Marianne Oaks founded the company and is still running it. The 1993-94 season offered the West Coast premiere of David Carlson's *The Midnight Angel*. The singers are up-and-coming talent.

The two-opera season offers primarily traditional fare in a *stagione* system. Recent productions include Puccini's *Madama Butterfly* and Giuseppe Verdi's *Un ballo in maschera*. The company performs in the 2,480-seat Community Center Theater.

Practical Information. The Community Center Theater is at 14th and L Streets. Tickets can be purchased at the Center box office at the above address or by writing Community Center Box Office, 1301 L Street, Sacramento, CA 95814. The Sacramento Opera is at 2131 Capitol Avenue, Suite 307, Sacramento, CA 95816, telephone 916-264-5181.

SAN DIEGO
• *San Diego Opera* •

Giacomo Puccini's *La bohème* inaugurated the San Diego Opera on May 6, 1965, with Walter Herbert on the podium. The opera was the sole offering of the inaugural season. Herbert, the driving force behind the New Orleans Opera and the Houston Grand Opera, also headed the newly formed San Diego Opera.

Opera in San Diego goes back to the late-nineteenth century, when touring companies began visiting. The San Diego Civic Grand Opera staged the first homegrown efforts. Established in 1919, the company mounted forty productions, mainly of a French and Italian nature. Its demise took place in 1932.

The San Diego Opera Guild was founded on January 20, 1950, with the mission to bring opera to the city. Two years later, the San Francisco Opera extended their annual Los Angeles season to San Diego and Puccini's *La bohème*, with Dorothy Kirsten and Jan Peerce, graced the stage of the Russ Auditorium. (The San Francisco Opera moved into the Fox Theater in the third year.) The company visited for fourteen seasons bringing stellar sopranos and mezzo-sopranos (Licia Albanese, Victoria de los Angeles, Giulietta Simionato, Gabriella Tucci, and Joan Sutherland), and renowned tenors (James McCracken, Giuseppe di Stefano, and Jon Vickers) and basses (Jerome Hines and Salvatore Baccaloni). The productions were equally outstanding. The San Francisco Opera's last season was the first season of the San Diego Opera. For their swan song, San Francisco brought their best: Franco Corelli in Puccini's *La fanciulla del West*, Jess Thomas in Richard Wagner's *Lohengrin*, and Johann Strauß's sparkling *Die Fledermaus*.

The completion of the Civic Theater in 1965 and the cessation of the San Francisco Opera's visits were the catalysts that changed the Guild from a presenting organization to a producing one. On May 19, 1966, the fledgling company mounted Charles Gounod's *Faust* in English. The production appeared doomed. Mallory Walker, scheduled for the title role, canceled, and an unknown Spanish tenor, who knew the role only in French, replaced him. But the tenor was Plácido Domingo, and the bass (Méphistophélès) was Norman Treigle. The results were electrifying. The "pop-art" production, however, generated controversy. There were semi-naked muscle men threatening Marguerite during her prayer scene, and her apotheosis took place through blinking Times Square lights. William Adams, famous for his stage feats, was the company's stage director. (He resigned in December 1971, after refusing to remove a falling ceiling and exploding cannons from Wolfgang Amadeus Mozart's *Il barbiere di Siviglia*.)

The Herbert era defined the company's first decade. The inaugural production was Puccini's *La bohème*, and the final production of the 1974-75 season was again Puccini's *La bohème*. Herbert lost no time in placing the young company on the operatic map. His third season witnessed the American premiere of Hans Werner Henze's *Der junge Lord* (February 13, 1967), which was a hit with both the critics and the public. San Diego then slowly gained a reputation as a company that mounted major productions of unusual operas. The novelties continued with Jules Massenet's *Don Quixote*, Carl Orff's *Der Mond*, and Gian Carlo Menotti's *Help, Help the Globolinks*. Then a financial crisis struck in the 1970-71 season, and only two productions were launched—Verdi's *La traviata* and Puccini's *Madama Butterfly*. The company recovered by the next season, which Treigle highlighted with his Boris. San Diego's first world premiere, Alva Henderson's *Medea*, followed on November 29, 1972, with Irene Dalis creating the title role. Herbert's last novelty was Frederick Delius's *A Village Romeo and Juliet*. The tenth season witnessed the company's first incursion into *Ring* territory when Wagner's *Das Rheingold* was mounted. Wagner's *Die Walküre*, *Siegfried*, and *Götterdämmerung* followed in successive seasons.

Many illustrious singers appeared with the company during Herbert's reign. Treigle sang most seasons, and Beverly Sills was a frequent visitor. Of particular note were their portrayals in Jacques Offenbach's *Les contes d'Hoffmann* with Sills singing all three of Hoffmann's loves. In addition, Lucine Amara (*Aida*), Gilda Cruz-Romo (*La traviata*), Janis Martin and John Reardon (*Tannhäuser*), and Joan Sutherland (*Lucia di Lammermoor*) sang in San Diego. The critics noted that Sutherland's Lucia appeared anchored to the stage, but her voice more than compensated. Most operas were sung in English.

When Herbert died suddenly of a stroke in 1975, Tito Capobianco, hired originally as artistic advisor, took the reins. His first planned season offered eight productions, including the novelty, Sergey Prokofiev's *Lyubov' k tryom apel'sinam* (The Love for Three Oranges). Ambroise Thomas's *Hamlet* was revived the following season as a vehicle for Sherrill Milnes. The season also witnessed the company's second world premiere, Gian Carlo Menotti's *Juana, La Loca* (June 3, 1979) with Sills in the title role. On August 4, 1978, Verdi's *Aida* was presented as the Prologue to a Verdi Festival. Conceived by Capobianco as an experimental study and performance center for Verdi's operas, the festival survived only six seasons. Although it was critically acclaimed, it was a financial disaster. The two-opera summer festival paired one Verdi favorite with one of his rarely performed works. Counted among the latter were *I Lombardi*, *Giovanna d'Arco*, *Un giorno di regno*, *I masnadieri*, and the American premiere of *Il corsaro* (June 18, 1982). The festival gasped its last breath on June 30, 1984, when Joan Sutherland starred in Verdi's *Il masnadieri*. Sutherland and Sills also treated San Diego to Johann Strauß's *Der Fledermaus*. The company mounted other novelties: Riccardo Zandonai's *Giulietta e Romeo*, Emmanuel Chabrier's *Gwendoline* (in English), and Saint-Saëns's *Henry VIII* with Sherrill Milnes.

Capobianco's departure from San Diego in March 1983 was described as bitter and hasty. It concerned artistic control and the cancellation of "his baby," the Verdi Festival. His reign was summed up by John Willett in the *San Diego Magazine*. "Capobianco's tenure became one of autocracy and of too much too soon — too much experimentation, too much unfamiliar operatic fare, and a Verdi Festival with great international critical acclaim but poor local audiences that bled the opera's coffers."

Ian Campbell arrived in May 1983 and retrenchment began. His first planned season trimmed the schedule to five operas of a more familiar nature and one new production. Emerging young talent replaced the superstars. Campbell, however, has introduced several twentieth-century works to San Diego: Francis Poulenc's *Les dialogues des Carmélites*, Benjamin Britten's *Albert Herring* and *The Rape of Lucretia*, and Carlisle Floyd's *The Passion of Jonathan Wade* among them. He has also updated productions, one of which generated much controversy. Ludwig van Beethoven's *Fidelio* was updated to modern-day Latin America. At the finale, American troops staged an invasion. The audience accepted the transposition and updating. It was the soldiers handing out American flags at the finale that caused an uproar. Since the company has returned to a solid financial base, the casts have included some excellent voices — James Morris, Richard Leech, Jeffrey Wells, Hei-Kyung Hong, and Ashley Putnam. Campbell has commissioned the company's third world premiere for the year 2000, and he continues to offer twentieth-century works, to attract and keep younger audiences. He markets opera in terms non-opera-lovers can understand. "You've seen *Miss Saigon*, now see the real thing—

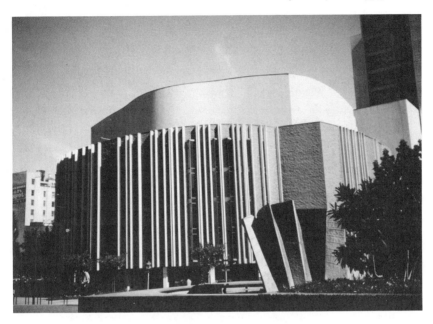

Civic Theater (San Diego, California).

Madama Butterfly." This is how Campbell is facing the challenge of keeping opera growing and expanding in a city that has no operatic heritage.

The five-opera season offers a well-mixed repertory, performed in the *stagione* system. Recent productions include Verdi's *Rigoletto*, Georges Bizet's *Les pêcheurs de perles*, Wolfgang Mozart's *Don Giovanni*, Rossini's *Il barbiere di Siviglia*, Catán's *La Hija de Rappaccini*, Vincenzo Bellini's *La sonnambula*, and Pyotr Il'yich Tchaikovsky's *Eugene Onegin*. The company performs in the Civic Theater.

Civic Theater

The Civic Theater opened in March 1965. Part of an urban redevelopment plan to revitalize the downtown area, the Civic is an impressive, modern structure, set in the San Diego Convention & Performing Arts Center. A series of vertical aluminum stripes adorn the concrete, glass, and steel building. The gently curving façade sits on large pillars. The foyer mixes red and walnut panel with glass and gray terrazzo. A bronze bust of Giuseppe Verdi, commissioned for the opening of the Verdi Festival in 1978 resides in the Grand Salon, where there is also a lithograph of Beverly Sills. The auditorium is acoustically treated, with no dead spots. Red acoustic fabric covers the continental-style seats, maroon acoustic fabric covers the side walls, and beige acoustic fabric is on the rear wall. Rectangular acoustic panels blanket the ceiling. The hall holds two glossy-white tiers. The Civic Theater seats 2,992.

Practical Information. The Civic Theater is at Third Avenue and B Street. Tickets are sold at the Center Box Office window across from the theater at the

Golden Hall entrance. The ticket office hours are 9:00 A.M. to 5:30 P.M., Monday through Friday. On performance days, the Civic Theater box office opens two hours before curtain time. To order tickets call 619-236-6510, between 9:00 A.M. and 5:00 P.M., Monday through Friday, or write Center Box Office, 202 "C" Street MS-57, San Diego, CA 92101. If you go, stay at the U.S. Grant Hotel, 326 Broadway, San Diego, CA 92101; telephone 619-232-3121, fax 619-232-3626, reservations 1-800-237-5029. The U.S. Grant Hotel opened in 1910 and has become San Diego's historic center piece. An architectural masterpiece, the hotel is furnished with Queen Anne reproductions. The Civic Theater is only a block away.

COMPANY STAFF AND REPERTORY

General/Artistic Directors. Walter Herbert (1965–1975); Tito Capobianco (1975–1984); Ian Campbell (1984–present).

World Premieres. Henderson's *Medea* (November 29, 1972); Menotti's *La Loca* (June 3, 1979).

American/United States Premieres. Henze's *Der junge Lord* (in English as The Young Lord, February 13, 1967); Zandonai's *Giulietta e Romeo* (April 23, 1982); Verdi's *Il Corsaro* (first stage performance, June 18, 1982); Chabrier's *Gwendoline* (October 2, 1982); Catán's *La Hija de Rappaccini* (March 5, 1994).

Repertory. **1965:** La bohème. **1966:** Faust, Il barbiere di Siviglia. **1966-67:** Aida, Der junge Lord, Tosca. **1967-68:** Salome, Carmen, Die Zauberflöte. **1968-69:** Rigoletto, La bohème, Don Quichotte. **1969-70:** I pagliacci, Der Mond, Tannhäuser, Faust, Les contes d'Hoffmann. **1970-71:** La traviata, Madama Butterfly. **1971-72:** Turandot, Il barbiere di Siviglia, Boris Godunov, Gianni Schicchi, Help, Help, The Globolinks. **1972-73:** Aida, Medea, Roméo et Juliette, La fille du régiment. **1973-74:** Mefistofele, Carmen, Le nozze di Figaro, Das Rheingold, Tosca. **1974-75:** Manon, Lucia di Lammermoor, A Village in Romeo and Juliet, Die Walküre, La. bohème. **1975-76:** Il trovatore, Rusalka, Siegfried, Der Rosenkavalier, Norma. **1976-77:** Otello, The Saint of Bleecker Street, Die Fledermaus, Götterdämmerung, La traviata, The Medium. **1977-78:** Die lustige Witwe, Don Giovanni, Carmen, Falstaff, Madama Butterfly, Lyubov' k tryom apel'sinam (The Love for Three Oranges), La Cenerentola; Verdi Festival: Aida. **1978-79:** Hamlet, Rigoletto, Così fan tutte, Manon Lescaut, Cavalleria rusticana/I pagliacci, La. Loca; Verdi Festival: I Lombardi, La traviata. **1979-80:** Don Carlo, Die Entführung aus dem Serail, Les contes d'Hoffmann, Mefistofele, Don Pasquale, La bohème; Verdi Festival: Giovanna d'Arco, Il trovatore. **1980-81:** Elektra, Die Fledermaus, Werther, Tosca, Lucia di Lammermoor, Lyubov' k. tryom apel'sinam (The Love for Three Oranges); Verdi Festival: Nabucco, Un giorno di regno. **1981-82:** Andrea Chénier, Susannah, Faust, Giulietta e Romeo, Il barbiere di Siviglia, Turandot; Verdi Festival: Il corsaro, Un ballo in maschera. **1982-83:** Gwendoline, Madama Butterfly, La Périchole, Henry VIII, Aida, Adriana Lecouvreur. **1983-84:** Lohengrin, Hamlet, La Cenerentola, Anna Bolena, Don Giovanni, Carmen; Verdi Festival: Simon Boccanegra, I masnadieri. **1984-85:** Peter Grimes, La traviata, Hänsel und Gretel, Die lustige Witwe, La bohème, Oberto. **1985-86:** Les contes d'Hoffmann, Eugene Onegin, Le nozze di Figaro, Otello, The Lighthouse. **1986-87:** Tosca, Norma, Die fliegende Holländer, Il barbiere di Siviglia, The Telephone/The Medium, Porgy and Bess. **1987-88:** Rigoletto, L'elisir d'amore, Faust, Il trovatore, Messa da Requiem. **1988-89:** Lucia di Lammermoor, Fidelio, Don Pasquale, Madama Butterfly. **1989-90:** Boris Godunov, La bohème, Dialogues des Carmélites, La fille du régiment, Die Zauberflöte. **1991:** Così fan tutte, Albert Herring, Die Fledermaus, The Passion of Jonathan Wade, La traviata. **1992:** Der Rosenkavalier, Le nozze di Figaro, The Rape of Lucretia, Die lustige Witwe, Carmen. **1993:** Il barbiere di Siviglia, Madama Butterfly, Don Giovanni, Les pêcheurs des perles, Werther. **1994:** Eugene Onegin, Rigoletto, La Hija de Rappaccini, La sonnambula, Les contes d'Hoffmann.

————————————————— SAN FRANCISCO

• *The San Francisco Opera* •

The San Francisco Opera was born on September 26, 1923, with a gala performance of Giacomo Puccini's *La bohème*. Five thousand people crowded into the Civic Auditorium on Grove Street to hear Giovanni Martinelli, Queena Mario, and Anna Young. Gaetano Merola, who founded the company, was on the podium. His dream of a permanent opera company in San Francisco had become a reality.

Opera in San Francisco dates back to the mid-1800s, when the Pellegrini Opera Troupe first visited. Pellegrini, who had previously been a court singer to the King of Denmark, was the lead tenor and manager of the company. The company performed at the Adelphi Theater, which had opened on October 16, 1850. Pellegrini staged Vincenzo Bellini's *La sonnambula* on February 12, 1851, and *Norma* on February 27, 1851, and Giuseppe Verdi's *Ernani* on April 8, 1851. Less than a month later, fire devoured the theater on May 4. The Adelphi, also known as the French Theater, was rebuilt, reopening on August 1, 1851. Pellegrini returned to the Adelphi two years later with another opera season. The Planet French Opera Company also visited in 1853, staging François Boieldieu's *La dame blanche*, Gaetano Donizetti's *La fille du régiment* and *La favorite*, and works by Albert Grisar. D.G. Robinson managed the Adelphi in direct competition with another impresario, Tom Maguire.

Maguire opened his opera house in 1856. Although Maguire's Opera House was erected as a home for his San Francisco Minstrels, it also saw farce, burlesque, melodrama, and beginning in 1859, grand opera. That year Maguire organized an opera company. The season opened on March 18, 1859, with Verdi's *Il trovatore*, featuring the Bianchis, Alfredo Roncovieri, Stephen Leach, and Madame Feret. Verdi's *Ernani*, *La traviata*, and *Attila*, Donizetti's *Lucrezia Borgia*, and Bellini's *Norma* followed. The Planet French Opera Company, Kate Hayes Opera, and Lyster's English Opera Company all visited Maguire's. Operas by Bellini, Donizetti, and Verdi were the most often staged, but works by Gioachino Rossini, Wolfgang Amadeus Mozart, and Michael Balfe were not neglected. The most frequently performed operas were Donizetti's *Lucia di Lammermoor* and *La fille du régiment*, and Bellini's *Norman* and *La sonnambula*. In 1864, Maguire presented Caroline Ritchings in Balfe's *The Enchantress*, and the Bianchis returned the next year for Charles Gounod's *Faust*. The year 1866 witnessed the California premiere of John Gay's *The Beggar Opera*. Another troupe, featuring Signorina Souncia and Signori Orlandino and Sbriglia, gave the California premiere of Verdi's *Un ballo in maschera*. Although Maguire lost $20,000 with this troupe's visit, he continued staging opera. Next the Howson English and Italian Opera Troupe arrived. In 1871, the Smocchia Opera Bouffe Company presented a short season of works by Jacques Offenbach, including *Orphée aux Enfers*. The following year, Aimée Opera Bouffe Company mounted additional Offenbach works—*La Périchole*, *Barbe-Bleue*, and *La belle Hélène*. Maguire's Opera House was razed in 1873.

The Metropolitan Theater also saw opera. Constructed by Joseph French, the Metropolitan opened in 1853. Catherine Sinclair, who managed the theater, harbored a fondness for grand opera and brought the Thillon English Opera Troupe in 1854. She then launched an ambitious operatic season with Bishop's Opera

War Memorial Opera House (San Francisco, California).

Company, which opened with Giacomo Meyerbeer's *Robert le Diable*. Herr Mengis sang the title role and Anna Bishop sang the role of Alice. The performance attracted "the largest audience ever gathered within the walls of any theatre in this state" according to the newspaper *Alta*. Bishop also assayed an outstanding Agathe in Carl Maria von Weber's *Der Freischütz*. Then the Barili-Thorne's Italian Company arrived, creating a partnership with Bishop's Company. Bishop's Company and the Barili-Thorne Italian Company returned the next year, but Sinclair's operatic ventures were at an end. During a run, the troupe refused to perform Verdi's *I Lombardi* because of "insufficiency of attendance." Sinclair had lost around $4,000 in her first sixteen opera presentations, and almost $10,000 on her next sixteen! She could not continue.

The Tivoli Opera House first opened as the Tivoli Gardens, a beer garden, where San Franciscans drank beer while being serenaded to the tunes of the Vienna Ladies' Orchestra. Joe Kreling ran the Garden, and when his brother John joined him from New York, they built the Tivoli Opera House. The Tivoli became a home for moderately-priced and locally-produced opera and operetta. Arthur Sullivan's *H.M.S. Pinafore* inaugurated the opera house on July 3, 1879, and continued to play for eighty-four consecutive nights. Sullivan's *The Mikado*, *Patience*, *Pirates of Penzance*, and *Trial by Jury* followed. Works by Offenbach, Johann Strauß, Charles Lecocq, and Franz von Suppé also graced the stage. Gounod's *Faust* was offered in 1880 (for forty-two consecutive nights), followed by Verdi's *Otello*. The era ended with Kreling's death in 1887. Kreling's widow, Ernestine, then ran the theater with William "Doc" Leahy, introducing Offenbach's *La voyage dans la lune* in English as *A Trip to the Moon* on January 2, 1888. More novelties followed, including the world premiere of W.W. Furst's *Theodora* and the American premiere of Ruggero Leoncavallo's *Zazà*. The theater then underwent extensive renovation and in 1905, hosted the United States debut of Luisa Tetrazzini. (Tetrazzini had been stranded in Mexico while on tour and was only too happy to accept a singing engagement in San Francisco.) Although the Tivoli succumbed to the 1906 earthquake-fire, it was resurrected. The Chicago Opera Company with Tetrazzini and Mary Garden reopened the house on March 12, 1913, and Leoncavallo's *Zingari* was introduced to America on October 30, 1913. The chronicle ended the following year when the theater was transformed into a movie house.

In 1876, a local dentist, Dr. Thomas Wade, built Wade's Opera House on Mission and Third streets at a cost of $750,000. Described as a blending of Italian and Romanesque architecture, the theater originally seated 2,500. (It was later enlarged and known as the Grand Opera House.) A play entitled *Snowflake* opened the Wade on January 17, 1876. Although drama was the theater's primary fare until 1884, the Wade witnessed its first world premiere in 1877, Gustav Hinrichs's *Der vierjährige Posten*. Colonel James Henry Mapleson brought Her Majesty's Opera Company in 1884, opening the season on March 10 with Etelka Gerster in Donizetti's *L'elisir d'amore*. Three days later Mapleson introduced Adelina Patti to San Francisco in Verdi's *La traviata*. Patti's final performance came on March 29 in Luigi Ricci's *Crispino e la comare*. Lillian Nordica also sang with the company, and Verdi's *Il trovatore* and *Rigoletto*, Bellini's *I Puritani* and *La sonnambula*, and Donizetti's *Linda di Chamounix* and *Lucia di Lammermoor* were in the repertoire as well. The Grand hosted a novelty on August 27, 1884, Antonio Gomes's *Il Guarany*. Ten days later, the Pappenheim-Fabbri German-Italian Opera Company opened with Fromental Halévy's spectacular French grand opera, *La Juive*. The top ticket price was $3, when ticket prices ranged from 10¢ to 50¢. The turnout was so poor that Giacomo Meyerbeer's *Les Huguenots*, also scheduled during the run, had to be "postponed indefinitely." Only stars the caliber of Patti, Gerster, Emma Albani, Francesco Tamagno, and Enrico Caruso could command such high ticket prices during that era. After that debacle, plays occupied the stage until Her Majesty's Opera Company returned on March 2, 1885. The company opened with Rossini's *Semiramide*. The season included Rossini's *Il barbiere di Siviglia*, Bellini's *Norma* and *La sonnambula*, Verdi's *Ernani*, *Rigoletto*, *Il trovatore*, *La traviata*, and *Aida*, Gounod's *Faust*, Friedrich von Flotow's *Martha*, Weber's *Der Freischütz*, and Donizetti's *Lucia di Lammermoor*. *Lucia* was the vehicle for Emma Nevada's debut on March 23. Charles E. Locke's National Opera Company paid a visit in May 1887, bringing Emma Juch and Jessica Bartlett. The company performed Verdi's *Aida* and Léo Delibes's *Lakmé*. Conried's English Opera Company offered Adolph Müller's *The King's Fool* in February 1890. Tamagno made his first appearance in Rossini's *Guillaume Tell*. Verdi's *Otello* and *Il trovatore*, Meyerbeer's *Les Huguenots* and *L'Africaine*, and Boïto's *Mefistofele* were also staged. Juch returned in 1892 for Richard Wagner's *Tannhäuser* and *Lohengrin*, Pietro Mascagni's *Cavalleria rusticana*, and Ludwig van Beethoven's *Fidelio*. On March 13, 1899, Nellie Melba came to San Francisco with the Ellis Opera Company, appearing in Gounod's *Faust*. The repertory included Ruggero Leoncavallo's *I pagliacci*, Mascagni's *Cavalleria rusticana*, Donizetti's *Lucia di Lammermoor*, Meyerbeer's *Les Huguenots*, Verdi's *Aida*, Gounod's *Roméo et Juliette*, Puccini's *La bohème*, and Rossini's *Il barbiere di Siviglia*. Other company artists included Johanna Gadski and Angelica Pandolfini. Southwell Opera Company provided the popular repertory with Strauß's *Der Zigeunerbaron*, Sullivan's *Pirates of Penzance*, Karl Millöcker's *Der Bettelstudent*, and Georges Bizet's *Carmen*.

The Metropolitan Opera began annual visits in 1890, bringing Tamagno for Meyerbeer's *L'Africaine* and Verdi's *Otello* and *Il trovatore*, and Patti for Bellini's *La sonnambula*, Verdi's *La traviata*, and Donizetti's *Lucia di Lammermoor*. The company mounted a complete *Der Ring des Nibelungen* in 1900. The next year Wagner's *Lohengrin* opened the Met's tour on November 11, 1901, with Emma Eames, Ernestine Schumann-Heink, Édouard de Reszke, and Ernest van Dyck. Five days later Puccini's *Manon Lescaut* trod the boards. San Francisco also saw Melba in Puccini's *La bohème*, Emma Calvé in Georges Bizet's *Carmen*, and Walter Damrosch conducting Wagner's *Die Meistersinger von Nürnberg*. The following January, the Grand Opera Stock Company brought lighter works. The catastrophic earthquake struck on April 17, 1906, when the Met was two days into its visit. A few hours earlier, Enrico Caruso had sung in Bizet's *Carmen*. The company lost all of its costumes, instruments, and sets for nineteen operas. The golden era of opera in San Francisco came to a sudden and ruinous end.

Visiting companies began to trickle back by 1909. W.A. Edwards International Opera Company, whose conductor was Gaetano Merola, was among them. The seeds for a permanent company were planted in November 1921, when Merola attended a football game in Stanford Stadium. He was impressed with the superb acoustics of the stadium and got permission for a short opera season the following June, raising the funds from the city's large Italian community. The season opened on June 3 with Leoncavallo's *I pagliacci*. Bizet's *Carmen* followed four days later, and Gounod's *Faust* was performed on June 10. Six thousand people attended the opening *Pagliacci*, and 10,000 showed up for *Carmen*. Since the stadium held 17,000, Merola ended the season with a huge deficit, but he was not discouraged. He had lofty ambitions—to set up a permanent company with imported first-rate performers from New York and Chicago. His goal was accomplished the next year.

Merola's first regular season boasted nine operas— Puccini's *La bohème*, *Tosca*, and *Il tabarro/Suor Angelica/Gianni Schicchi*, Umberto Giordano's *Andrea Chénier*, Boïto's *Mefistofele*, Gounod's *Roméo et Juliette*, and Verdi's *Rigoletto*—and superstars Beniamino Gigli and Giovanni Martinelli. The third season witnessed a novelty to San Francisco, Franco Vittadini's *Anima allegra*. Only four years earlier, the opera had received its *novità assoluta* at Teatro Costanzi in Rome on April 15, 1921. San Francisco's first American premiere took place on September 19, 1930, Maurice Ravel's *L'enfant et les sortilèges*. Although the decade saw other rarities, including Daniel Auber's *Fra Diavolo*, Giordano's *La cena delle beffe*, and Henri Rabaud's *Mârouf, Savetier du Caire*, the repertory was predominately standard Italian fare, with an occasional French and German work. Merola scheduled San Francisco's season before the Met opened, so its leading artists, including Maria Jeritza, Tito Schipa, Gigli, Martinelli, Ezio Pinza, Giuseppe de Luca, and Giacomo Lauri-Volpi could also sing in San Francisco.

On October 15, 1932, Puccini's *Tosca* inaugurated the long awaited opening of the War Memorial Opera House, the San Francisco Opera's new permanent home. The cast included Claudio Muzio, Dino Borgioli, and Alfredo Gandolfi, and was under the baton of Merola. Warm applause welcomed Merola onto the podium, and before the curtain went up, he led a lively rendition of the national anthem. The company's first season in its new home featured twelve operas including Gounod's *Faust*, Verdi's *La traviata* and *Rigoletto*, Wagner's *Lohengrin*, and Donizetti's *Lucia di Lammermoor*. Its inaugural season was successful, notwithstanding a few mishaps that sometimes befall opera performances. Wagner's *Lohengrin* was especially vulnerable, suffering from a falling trumpeter, a swan that would not leave, and an Elsa who almost outweighed the choristers who had to lift her. The next season opened with Camille Saint-Saëns's *Samson et Dalila* on November 3, 1933, followed three days later by Nikolay Rimsky-Korsakov's *Zolotoy petushok* (sung in English as The Golden Cockerel). *Zolotoy petushok* was presented as "pantomime-cum-vocal accompaniment in a new and expensive production with a light scenic touch" as described by critic Arthur Bloomfield. Two other operas were presented in English in 1933 — Ermanno Wolf-Ferrari's *Il segreto di Susanna,* and a provocative new work, Louis Gruenberg's *Emperor Jones* featuring Lawrence Tibbett. It was a somber and emotionally-charged piece that did not please everyone, even eliciting some boos. But the unhappy patrons were soon compensated with a splendid new production of Wagner's *Tristan und Isolde*. The 1934 season saw Bedřich Smetana's *Prodaná nevěsta* (The Bartered Bride) sung in German, Lotte Lehmann in Puccini's *Tosca* and *Madama Butterfly*, and Lauritz Melchior in Wagner's *Tannhäuser* and Verdi's *Otello*. The complete Ring cycle highlighted the 1935 season with a cast headed by Kirsten Flagstad and Melchior. The sets and costumes were traditional, but an intermission after the second scene in *Das Rheingold* — it was Opening Night — caused dismay among the purists. For the non-Wagnerian operas, Martinelli, Schipa, Richard Bonelli, and Pinza kept the audience satisfied. Halévy's *La Juive* opened the 1936 season, which saw the first Wolfgang Amadeus Mozart opera — *Le nozze di Figaro*. Fritz Reiner began his three year association with the company conducting Wagner's *Tristan und Isolde*. Two year later, another fine conductor who was only twenty-six at the time, Erich Leinsdorf, led a single performance of Claude Debussy's *Pelléas et Mélisande*. The season had opened with Gigli in the title role of Giordano's *Andrea Chénier*. His appearance five days later as Lionel in Flotow's *Martha* resulted in one of the company's few encores. His "M'appari" was so extraordinary that the audience demanded an encore. Jussi Bjoerling made his San Francisco debut in 1940 in Puccini's *La bohème*. (It was rumored that he filled his Café Momus mug with genuine beer.) He also sang Riccardo in Verdi's *Un ballo in maschera*.

After the war, Helen Traubel headed the return to Wagner operas. The following season witnessed Astrid Varnay as Elsa in the opening-night *Lohengrin*. But the scheduling of Flagstad in Wagner's *Tristan und Isolde* and *Die Walküre* in 1949 almost caused the cancellation of the season. Flagstad's sympathies during World War II were not with the Allies and consequently quite distasteful to the American Legion, which played a large role in the building of the opera house. The Legion felt "her appearances would desecrate the War Memorial and the ideals it stands for." The Opera Association directors told the War Memorial trustees that they would cancel the season if Flagstad's appearance was banned. It looked as if that would be the case until a couple of months before opening night, when a compromise was reached.

Merola had led his company for almost thirty years. On a chilly August 30, 1953, when he was conducting an afternoon Stern Grove concert and soprano Brunetta Mazzolini was singing "Un bel di" from Puccini's *Madama Butterfly*, the orchestra suddenly stopped. Merola lurched forward and collapsed onto the stage. A stunned silence swept over the auditorium. Then the orchestra and audience arose as if they were paying their last respects. Merola had been struck down by a massive heart attack. Opening night was sixteen days later, but no eulogy was given for Merola. None was necessary. Merola's company was his legacy, and his choice for opening night, Boïto's *Mefistofele*, was one of his great successes.

The following year Kurt Herbert Adler, who had been Merola's assistant for the past decade, was named artistic director. He ushered in a new era: adventurous repertory, revolutionary stage designs, and American debuts of prominent artists. He raised the San Francisco Opera to its highest *niveau*. Adler's first novelty took place on October 7, 1955, William Walton's *Troilus and Cressida*. The American debut of Birgit Nilsson, one of the great Wagnerian sopranos of the twentieth century, in Wagner's *Die Walküre*, and Leonie Rysanek in Wagner's *Der fliegende Holländer* highlighted the next season. Adler was named general director in 1957, the season that Maria Callas canceled in Donizetti's *Lucia di Lammermoor* and Verdi's *Macbeth* shortly before the performances. It was her revenge for an unsuccessful audition back in the mid-1940s. Antonietta Stella also canceled that season because of an appendectomy. Rysanek, who was scheduled in Puccini's *Turandot* and Richard Strauss's *Ariadne auf Naxos*, gallantly took over the roles of both Callas and Stella. That turned Verdi's *Un ballo in maschera* into an Italian-German affair, since Rysanek only knew the role of Amelia in German. All was not bad during 1957. The American premiere of Francis Poulenc's *Dialogues des Carmélites* took place on September 20, 1957, only eight months after the world premiere at Teatro alla Scala. In the opera, Leontyne Price made her debut as Madame Lidoine, and Dorothy Kirsten portrayed Blanche de la Force, with Erich Leinsdorf conducting. Price also assayed two Aidas. The double bill of Carl Orff's *Die Kluge* and *Carmina Burana* was introduced to America on October 3, 1958, followed by another novelty, Strauss's *Die Frau ohne Schatten*. This challenging opera presented more obstacles than usual at its premiere—three of the original four principal singers had canceled.

The 1961 season saw two novelties: Norman dello Joio's *Blood Moon* and Benjamin Britten's *A Midsummer Night's Dream*. Joio's *Blood Moon* was not successful, and died a peaceful death. Britten's *A Midsummer Night's Dream* fared substantially better. The season closed with one of the great operatic disasters of all times, the shooting of Tosca instead of Cavaradossi in Puccini's *Tosca*. The execution squad consisted of young college boys, instructed to shoot when the officer lowered his sword. But no one told them whom to shoot. They were also told to exit with the principals. The execution squad marched on the stage and were startled to see two singers. When the officer lowered his sword, they aimed their rifles at Tosca (after all, the opera was called *Tosca*) but Cavaradossi collapsed. At this point Scarpia's men had discovered his death, so Tosca, to elude her pursuers, jumped from the battlements, shouting "O Scarpia, avanti a Dio." One by one, the entire execution squad followed!

For the company's fiftieth anniversary, Adler offered a spectacular season. Joan Sutherland opened in Bellini's *Norma* on September 15, followed by Kiri Te Kanawa in Mozart's *Le nozze di Figaro*. Jean Pierre Ponnelle staged a controversial (nontraditional) Puccini's *Tosca* and Francis Ford Coppola directed his first opera, Gottfried von Einem's *Der Besuch der alten Dame*. The most splendid production of the season, Meyerbeer's *L'Africaine*, opened on November 7 with Plácido Domingo and Shirley Verrett. The performance marked the first major production of a Meyerbeer opera in the United States in thirty-eight years. Someone was apparently offended since the opera drew a bomb threat, but Adler informed the audience of a "ten minute delay due to technical problems" and the opera continued until almost midnight. Beverly Sills and Luciano Pavarotti regaled the opera crowd next with Donizetti's *Lucia di Lammermoor*. The 1976 season saw Ponnelle's controversial production of Mascagni's *Cavalleria rusticana* followed by the world premiere of Andrew Imbrie's *Angle of Repose*. Adler retired at the end of 1981, but before leaving he launched a five-opera summer festival which included the American premiere of Aribert Reimann's emotionally-draining *Lear* and Claudio Monteverdi's *L'incoronazione di Poppea*. His last fall season witnessed the revised version of Dmitry Shostakovich's *Ledi Makbet Mtsenskovo uyezda* (Lady Macbeth of the Mtsensk District).

Terence McEwen took the helm in 1982. During his brief (compared to Merola and Adler) and troubled tenure, he introduced Michael Tippett's *The Midsummer Marriage* and mounted a spectacular *Ring Cycle* Festival in the summer of 1985, removing the *Ring Cycle* as the exclusive domain of the Seattle Opera during the summer. (see Seattle entry) Nevertheless, there was a steady decline in the San Francisco Opera during his reign that culminated in the cancellation of the festival after 1986. He resigned a short time later, ostensibly for health reasons. Adler was asked to return to lead the company but died unexpectedly.

On January 1, 1989, Lotfi Mansouri became the fourth general director of the San Francisco Opera. The first season completely planned by him was the impressive 1991 fall season, highlighted by a spectacular production of Sergey Prokofiev's epic, *War and Peace*, the rarely-performed Verdi's *Attila*, and the American premiere of Hans Werner Henze's chilling *Das verratene Meer*. The fall of 1992 saw the West Coast premiere of John Adams's *The Death of Klinghoffer*, co-commissioned with several opera companies. To continue the flow of new works, Mansouri introduced "Pacific Visions" a program to grant opera commissions. The first fruits appeared in the fall of 1994 with Conrad Susa's *Dangerous Liaisons*. The second commissioned work, Bobby McFerrin's *Gethsemane* coincides with the 50th anniversary of the signing of the United Nations Charter in the opera house. The company is committed to stage rarely-performed and unusual operas, including the lesser-known versions of "war horses" (if they exist). A recent Verdi's *Don Carlo* was the five-act Italian revision first seen in Modena in 1886, plus the third act duet for Don Carlo and Philip "Chi rende a me quest'uom?", which was eliminated from the original French version and not sung in the Modena version.

Mansouri resurrected the summer opera season as a festival devoted to one composer. In 1991, it was a Mozart Festival, celebrating the bicentennial of the composer's death. The following summer commemorated the bicentennial of Rossini's birth with a festival devoted to his works. An all Strauss schedule defined the 1993 program that included *Salome*, *Der Rosenkavalier*, *Capriccio*, and *Daphne*. The 1994 scheduled festival devoted to French opera, however, was canceled.

Mansouri's philosophy of opera as an active art form that makes you "think, feel and get involved" is reflected in his wide-ranging repertory and evocative productions. He has four criteria for running the company: "Opera should be food for thought, controversy is healthy, the audience must never be bored, and the company must dare to try new things, even if they fail or are wrong." He quotes Adler's response when the Board chides him for occasional mistakes. "If I did not have failures, you could not afford me." His long-term ambition for the company will revolutionize operagoing in San Francisco: he plans to replace the fall season with a year-round *stagione* system. Ensemble casting and finely tuned productions are the mark of the Mansouri era and will carry opera in San Francisco into the twenty-first century.

The nine-opera fall season presents a splendid mix of mainstream and unusual works with both international artists and outstanding newcomers. Recent fall season operas include Verdi's *I vespri siciliani* and *Don Carlo*, Leoš Janáček's *Věc Makropulos*, Puccini's *La bohème*, Mozart's *La clemenza di Tito*, Bellini's *I Puritani*, Donizetti's *La fille du régiment*, and Modest Mussorgsky's *Boris Godunov*. The company performs in the War Memorial Opera House.

War Memorial Opera House

The earthquake of 1906 destroyed all of San Francisco's opera houses. Several attempts were made to build San Francisco a new, proper shrine of the Muses, before a small group of prominent San Franciscans joined with some veterans groups to gain the necessary funds. The result was twin buildings, one for the Muses, and one for the veterans. Designed by Arthur Brown, Jr., who had designed City Hall, with Albert Lansburgh responsible for the interior, the structures cost $5.5 million. Puccini's *Tosca* inaugurated the opera house on October 15, 1932.

The War Memorial Opera House is a Beaux Arts building. Its off-white stone and granite façade bears a resemblance to several great European opera houses. A peristyle boasting coupled monumental granite Doric columns rests above the arched-glass portals. Gargoyles inhabit in the keystones. The courtyard entrance faces its near-twin, the Veterans Building. A blue- and-gold wrought iron fence that stretches across the courtyard links the two buildings. The inner lobby, with walls of cast stone, is rung with pairs of Doric columns. The gilded, coffered ceiling soars thirty-eight-feet. Bronze lamp posts and Doric columns flank the entrance into the auditorium. Three tiers soar in regal splendor across the red raspberry velvet plush seats of the gold and cream-colored room. Fluted pilasters restrain the gilded hexagonal coffers embellishing the proscenium arch. Masks of comedy and tragedy flank the proscenium. Gilded relief figures — Amazons riding horses — reside in the spandrels. The War Memorial seats 3,252.

Practical Information. The War Memorial Opera House is at 301 Van Ness Avenue. The box office, on the right side of the outer lobby, is open 10:00 A.M. to 6 P.M. daily, and through the first intermission on performance days. Tickets can be ordered by calling 415-864-3330, faxing 415-621-7508, or writing Opera Box Office, 301 Van Ness Avenue, San Francisco, CA 94102-4509. If you visit, stay at the Inn at the Opera, 333 Fulton Street, San Francisco, CA; telephone 415-863-8400, fax 415-861-0821, reservations 1-800-325-2708. This treasured hideaway has hosted some of opera's important personalities — like Luciano Pavarotti and Philip Glass. It is a quaint, cozy place located across the street from the opera house.

COMPANY STAFF AND REPERTORY

General/Artistic Directors. Gaetano Merola 1923-1953; Kurt Herbert Adler 1954-1981; Terence McEwen 1982-1988; Lotfi Mansouri 1989 to present.

World Premieres (before the San Francisco Opera). Hinrichs's *Der vierjährige Posten* (April 15, 1877); Furst's *Theodora* (September 16, 1889); Moore's *The Oracle* (1894); Stewart's *The Oracle* (November 12, 1910).

American/United States Premieres (before the San Francisco Opera). Strauß's *Die Fledermaus* (in English, July 1880); Strauß's *Prinz Methusalem* (August 29, 1880); Gomes's *Il Guarany* (August 27, 1884); Offenbach's *La voyage dans la lune* (second performance, in English as A Trip to the Moon, January 2, 1888); Chapi's *La Tempestad* (1888); Barbieri's *Jugar con Fuego* (March 22, 1889); Leoncavallo's *Zazà* (November 27, 1903); Zandonai's *Conchita* (September 28, 1912); Leoncavallo's *Zingari* (October 30, 1913); Rimsky-Korsakov's *The Czar's Bride* (January 9, 1922); Mussorgsky's *Boris Godunov* (first performance in Russian, January 15, 1922).

World Premieres (San Francisco Opera). Dello Joio's *Blood Moon* (September 18, 1961); Imbrie's *Angle of Repose* (November 9, 1976); Susa's *The Dangerous Liaisons* Fall 1994; McFerrin's *Gethsemane* Summer 1995. Opera Center: Mechem's *Tartuffe* (1980); Fine's *The Women in the Garden* (1982); Harbison's *Full Moon in March* (1982).

American/United States Premieres (San Francisco Opera). Strauss's *Salome* (first performance in German, September 12, 1930); Ravel's *L'enfant et les sortilèges* (September 19, 1930); Cherubini's *L'hôtellerie portugaise* (September 24, 1954); Honegger's *Jeanne d'Arc au bûcher* (in English as Joan of Arc at the Stake, first stage performance, October 15, 1954); Walton's *Troilus and Cressida* (October 7, 1955); Poulenc's *Dialogues des Carmélites* (September 20, 1957); Cherubini's *Medée* (first stage performance, September 12, 1958); Orff's *Die Kluge* (first professional performance, in English as The Wise Maiden, October 3, 1958); Orff's *Carmina Burana* (first stage performance, October 3, 1958); Strauss's *Die Frau ohne Schatten* (September 18, 1959); Britten's *A Midsummer Night's Dream* (October 10, 1961); Shostakovich's *Katerina Izmaylova* (October 23, 1964); Janácek's *Věc Makropulos* (in English as The Makropulos Affair, November 22, 1966); Schuller's *The Visitation* (November 3, 1967); Weill's *Royal Palace* (October 8, 1968); Milhaud's *Christophe Colomb* (in English as Christopher Columbus, first stage performance, October 8, 1968); Donizetti's *Maria Stuarda* (first stage performance, November 16, 1971); Von Einem's *Der Besuch der alten Dame* (in English as The Visit of the Old Lady, October 25, 1972); Tippett's *The Midsummer Marriage* (October 15, 1983); Reimann's *Lear* (June 12, 1981); Rossini's *Maometto II* (September 17, 1988); Henze's *Das verratene Meer* (November 8, 1991). Opera Center: Harbison's *A Winter* (first stage performance, 1979), Titus's *Rosina* (1988), Händel's *Giustino* 1989, Reimann's *The Ghost Sonata* (1990).

Repertory. 1923: La bohème, Andrea Chénier, Il tabarro/Suor Angelica/Gianni Schicchi, Mefistofele, Tosca, Roméo et Juliette, I pagliacci, Rigoletto. **1924:** Andrea Chénier, La bohème, Madama Butterfly, Rigoletto, Manon, Tosca, L'amico Fritz, La traviata. **1925:** Manon, Samson et Dalila, Il barbiere di Siviglia, Anima Allegra, La traviata, Martha, L'amore dei tre re, Aida, Tosca. **1926:** Martha, Faust, Il barbiere di Siviglia, Samson et Dalila, Manon Lescaut, Rigoletto, Aida, Fra Diavolo, La bohème, Tosca, Lucia di Lammermoor, Il trovatore. **1927:** Manon Lescaut, Tristan und Isolde, Tosca, Turandot, Roméo et Juliette, Il trovatore, Cavalleria rusticana/ I pagliacci, Falstaff, Aida, La cena delle beffe, La bohème, Carmen. **1928:** Aida, La cena delle beffe, Tosca, Madama Butterfly, Turandot, L'amore dei tre re, Fedora, Andrea Chénier, Faust, Carmen, Cavalleria rusticana/I pagliacci. **1929:** Rigoletto, L'elisir d'amore, Il trovatore, Il barbiere di Siviglia, La bohème, Gianni. Schicchi/I pagliacci, Martha, Aida. Don Pasquale, Faust, Manon. **1930:** Manon, Salome, La traviata, La fanciulla del West, La bohème, L'enfant et les sortilèges, Hänsel und Gretel, Cavalleria rusticana/I pagliacci, Mignon, Tannhäuser, Faust, Lucia di Lammermoor. **1931:** Mârouf, Aida, Lohengrin, Andrea Chénier, Madama Butterfly, Un ballo in maschera, Tosca, Tannhäuser, La bohème, Il trovatore, Die Meistersinger, Carmen. **1932:** Tosca, Lucia di Lammermoor, Die Meistersinger, Rigoletto, Hänsel und Gretel, Cavalleria rusticana/I pagliacci, Lucia di Lammermoor, Lohengrin, Faust, Il trovatore, La traviata. **1933:** Samson et Dalila, Zolotoy petushok (The Golden Cockerel), Aida, Tristan und Isolde, Manon, Il segreto di Susanna, The Emperor Jones, Cavalleria rusticana/I pagliacci, La traviata,

La bohème, La forza del destino. **1934:** Prodaná nevěsta (The Bartered Bride), Tosca, Carmen, Manon, Madama Butterfly, Tannhäuser, La traviata, La rondine, Lakmé, Otello, Mignon. **1935:** Das Rheingold, Die Walküre, Siegfried, Götterdämmerung, Aida, Martha, La Juive, Werther, Il barbiere di Siviglia, La bohème, Rigoletto, Suor Angelica/Zolotoy petushok (The Golden Cockerel). **1936:** La Juive, Tristan und Isolde, Carmen, Rigoletto, Götterdämmerung, Il nozze di Figaro, I pagliacci/Gianni Schicchi, Die Walküre, La forza del destino, Tosca, Otello. **1937:** Aida, La bohème, Un ballo in maschera, Tristan und Isolde, Madama Butterfly, Lakmé, Roméo et Juliette, Lohengrin, Fidelio, Manon, Norma. **1938:** Andrea Chénier, Don Giovanni, Martha, Die Meistersinger, Cavalleria rusticana/ Don Pasquale, Pelléas et Mélisande, Lucia di Lammermoor, Elektra, La forza del destino, La bohème, Zolotoy petushok (The Golden Cockerel). **1939:** Manon, Die Walküre, Madama Butterfly, Tristan und Isolde, Rigoletto, Lucia di Lammermoor, Otello, La traviata, Il barbiere di Siviglia, Fidelio. **1940:** Le nozze di Figaro, Lakmé, Der Rosenkavalier, La bohème, Don Giovanni, Un ballo in maschera, Carmen, Rigoletto, Aida, Manon. **1941:** Don Pasquale, Der Rosenkavalier, La fille du régiment, Tosca, Madama Butterfly, Il barbiere di Siviglia, Tannhäuser, Carmen, L'amore dei tre re, Simon Boccanegra. **1942:** Aida, La fille du régiment, La traviata, Prodaná nevěsta (The Bartered Bride), Carmen, Faust, L'amore dei tre re, Die Fledermaus, Un ballo in maschera, Zolotoy petushok (The Golden Cockerel). **1943:** Samson et Dalila, La forza del destino, Cavalleria rusticana/I pagliacci, La fanciulla del West, Lucia di Lammermoor, La bohème, Il trovatore, Rigoletto, Don Giovanni, Don Pasquale. **1944:** Aida, Martha, Lakmé, Manon, Il segreto di Susanna, Falstaff, Faust, Un ballo in maschera, Les contes d'Hoffmann, Carmen. **1945:** Carmen, La bohème, Der Rosenkavalier, Tristan und Isolde, Die Walküre, Boris Godunov, Don Giovanni, Lucia di Lammermoor, L'heure espagnole/Salome, Rigoletto. **1946:** Lohengrin, La traviata, Roméo et Juliette, Boris Godunov, Lakmé, La forza del destino, Der Rosenkavalier, Fidelio, Madama Butterfly, Le nozze di Figaro. **1947:** La traviata, Don Giovanni, Madama Butterfly, Götterdämmerung, La gioconda, Louise, Otello, Pelléas et Mélisande, L'amore dei tre re, Lucia di Lammermoor. **1948:** Falstaff, Manon, Die Meistersinger, La forza del destino, Cavalleria rusticana/I pagliacci, Boris Godunov, Carmen, Madama Butterfly, L'elisir d'amore, Siegfried. **1949:** Tosca, Faust, Don Giovanni, Tristan und Isolde, Aida, Manon Lescaut, Die Walküre, Les contes d'Hoffmann, Samson et Dalila, Lucia di Lammermoor. **1950:** Aida, Le nozze di Figaro, Tristan und Isolde, Andrea Chénier, Otello, Die Zauberflöte, Il barbiere di Siviglia, Suor Angelica/Salome, Manon Lescaut, Parsifal. **1951:** Otello, Roméo et Juliette, Der Rosenkavalier, La forza del destino, Boris Godunov, La traviata, La bohème, Tosca, Manon, Fidelio. **1952:** Tosca, Mefistofele, Aida, Il tabarro/Suor Angelica/Gianni Schicchi, Der Rosenkavalier, Il trovatore, La fille du régiment, La bohème, Don Giovanni, L'amore dei tre re. **1953:** Mefistofele, Werther, La traviata, Elektra, Boris Godunov, Tristan und Isolde, Turandot, Il barbiere di Siviglia, Die Walküre, Un ballo in maschera. **1954:** Rigoletto, La forza del destino, L'hôtellerie portugaise/Salome, Manon, Tosca, Der Fliegende Holländer, Turandot, Le nozze di Figaro, Il tabarro/Jeanne d'Arc au bûcher, Fidelio. **1955:** Aida, Der Rosenkavalier, Louise, Macbeth, Don Giovanni, Andrea Chénier, Troilus and Cressida, Zolotoy petushok (The Golden Cockerel)/I pagliacci, Lohengrin, Faust. **1956:** Manon Lescaut, Der fliegende Holländer, Falstaff, Boris Godunov, Francesca da Rimini, Così fan tutte, Die Walküre, Simon Boccanegra, L'elisir d'amore, La bohème. **1957:** Turandot, Dialogues des Carmélites, Un ballo in maschera, Lucia di Lammermoor, Der Rosenkavalier, Ariadne auf Naxos, Macbeth, Tosca, Aida, Così fan tutte. **1958:** Medée, Don Carlo, La bohème, Il trovatore, Prodaná nevěsta (The Bartered Bride), Die Kluge/Carmina Burana, La forza del destino, Gianni Schicchi/Elektra, Tannhäuser, Manon, Le nozze di Figaro. **1959:** Aida, Die Frau ohne Schatten, Madama Butterfly, Andrea Chénier, Carmen, Die Meistersinger, L'amore dei tre re, Ariadne auf Naxos, Otello, Don Giovanni. **1960:** Tosca, Die Frau ohne Schatten, La fanciulla del West, Simon Boccanegra, Wozzeck, Der Rosenkavalier, la sonnambula, La bohème, Così fan tutte, Lohengrin, La traviata. **1961:** Lucia di Lammermoor, Blood Moon, Madama Butterfly, Turandot, Le nozze di Figaro, Nabucco, A Midsummer Night's Dream, Boris Godunov, Die Meistersinger, Un ballo in maschera, Fidelio. **1961:** (spring) Roméo et Juliette, La bohème, Martha, La traviata, Die Zauberflöte, Carmen. **1962:** La bohème, Don Carlo, Wozzeck, Faust, Il trovatore, Carmen, Otello, Der Rosenkavalier, Don Giovanni, The Rake's Progress, Falstaff. **1962:** (spring) Manon, Il barbiere di Siviglia, Les pêcheurs des perles, Die Entführung aus dem Serail, Tosca, La traviata. **1963:** Aida, La sonnambula, Il barbiere di Siviglia, Mefistofele, Pikovaya dama, La traviata, La forza del destino, Samson et Dalila, Die Walküre, Dialogues des Carmélites, Capriccio, Così fan tutte. **1963:** (spring) Les contes d'Hoffmann, Rigoletto, Die Zauberflöte, Don Pasquale, Madama Butterfly, L'heure espagnole/A Kékszakállú herceg vára (Duke Bluebeard's Castle). **1964:** Otello, Carmen, Parsifal, Der Rosenkavalier, Il trovatore, Gianni Schicchi/Carmina Burana, Nabucco, Fidelio, Turandot, Katerina Izmaylova, Die Frau ohne Schatten, La traviata. **1964:** (spring) Der Freischütz, Susannah, La bohème, Les pêcheurs des perles, Faust, Die Entführung aus dem Serail, L'italiana in Algeri. **1965:** Andrea Chénier, Die Fledermaus, Die Meistersinger, La fanciulla del West, La forza del destino, Lulu, Il barbiere di Siviglia, Lohengrin, Don Giovanni,Un ballo in maschera, Ariadne auf Naxos, Pelléas et Mélisande. **1965:** (spring) A Kékszakállú herceg vára (Duke Bluebeard's Castle), Madama Butterfly, Così fan tutte, Rigoletto, The Crucible. **1966:** I puritani, Don Carlo, Elektra, L'amore dei tre re, Boris Godunov, Tannhäuser, Madama Butterfly, Le nozze di Figaro, Les Troyens, Falstaff, Carmen, Věc Makropulos. **1966:** (spring) Mignon, Lucia di Lammermoor, L'italiana in Algeri, Carry Nation, Il trovatore, The Turn of the Screw. **1967:** La gioconda, Die Zauberflöte, Louise, Der Rosenkavalier, Macbeth, Manon Lescaut, Tristan und Isolde, The Visitation, Faust, Un ballo in maschera, Das Rheingold, La bohème. **1967:** (spring) La traviata, Les pêcheurs des perles, Cavalleria rusticana/I pagliacci, Les contes d'Hoffmann. **1968:** Ernani, Il barbiere di Siviglia, Les Troyens, Die Walküre, Madama Butterfly, Royal Palace/Erwartung/Christophe Colomb, Il trovatore, Wozzeck, Lucia di Lammermoor, Salome, Don Giovanni, Turandot, Fra Diavolo. **1968:** (spring) Die Entführung aus dem Serail, Carmen, La rondine, Rigoletto. **1969:** La traviata, La bohème, Ariadne auf Naxos, Fidelio, L'elisir d'amore, Götterdämmerung, Aida, Die Zauberflöte, La forza del destino, La Cenerentola, Pelléas et Mélisande, Jenůfa. **1969:** (spring) La rondine, The Consul, Le nozze di Figaro, Roméo et Juliette. **1970:** Tosca, Siegfried, Falstaff, Carmen, Nabucco, Così fan tutte, Salome, Faust, Tristan und Isolde, The Rake's Progress, Otello. **1971:** Manon, Der Rosenkavalier, Madama Butterfly, Midsummer Night's Dream, Die Meistersinger, Eugene Onegin, Il trovatore, Un ballo in maschera, Lulu, Maria Stuarda, Il tabarro/Carmina Burana. **1971:** (spring) Titus, Rigoletto, Don Pasquale, Faust Counter Faust. **1972:** Norma, Le nozze di Figaro, Das Rheingold, Die Walküre, Siegfried, Götterdämmerung, Der Besuch der alten Dame, L'Africaine, Lucia di Lammermoor, Aida, Tosca. **1972:** (spring) Il barbiere di Siviglia, La favola d'Orfeo, Aufstieg und Fall der Stadt Mahagonny. **1973:** La favorita, Die Fledermaus, Rigoletto, Così fan tutte, Tannhäuser, Boris Godunov, Elektra, Peter Grimes, Don Carlo, La bohème, La traviata. **1973:** (spring) The Passion According to Saint Matthew, Carmen, La Grande Duchesse de Gérolstein, A Postcard from Morocco. **1974:** Manon Lescaut, Parsifal, Salome, Madama Butterfly, Tristan und Isolde, La Cenerentola, Esclarmonde, Otello, Don Giovanni, Luisa Miller, La fille du régiment. **1974:** (spring) Don Pasquale, Ormindo, Of Mice and Men, La Grande Duchesse de Gérolstein. **1975:** Il trovatore, L'incoronazione di Poppea, Der fliegende Holländer, L'elisir d'amore, Norma, Pikovaya dama, Werther, Simon Boccanegra, Andrea Chénier, Il tabarro/Gianni Schicchi, Die Zauberflöte. **1975:** (spring) Les pêcheurs des perles, Death in Venice, Die Entführung aus dem Serail, Le convenienze e le inconvenienze teatrali. **1976:** Thaïs, Die Walküre, La forza del destino, Tosca, Peter Grimes, Die Frau ohne Schatten, Věc Makropulos, Angle of Repose, Cavalleria rusticana/I pagliacci, Il barbiere di Siviglia. **1976:** (spring) La Périchole, L'amico Fritz, Meeting Mr. Ives, The Passion According to Saint Matthew. **1977:** Adriana Lecouvreur, Idomeneo, Kát'a Kabanová, Das Rheingold, Faust, Aida, Ariadne auf Naxos, Turandot, I Puritani, Un ballo in maschera. **1977:** (spring) Carmen, Titus, Il combattimento di Tancredi e Clorinda/Savitri, The Emperor of Atlantis, Le convenienze e le inconvenienze teatrali. **1978:** Otello, Norma, Billy Budd, Lohengrin, Don Giovanni, Tosca, Werther, Der Rosenkavalier, La bohème, Fidelio. **1978:** (spring)

La rondine, Julius Caesar, L'italiana in Algeri, Elegy for Young Lovers. **1979:** La gioconda, Pelléas et Mélisande, Don Carlo, Elektra, Il prigioniero/La voix humaine/gianni Schicchi, Der fliegende Holländer, La fanciulla del West, Roberto Devereux, La forza del destino, Così fan tutte, Tancredi. **1980:** Samson et Dalila, Simon Boccanegra, Die Frau ohne Schatten, Don Pasquale, Jenůfa, Die. Zauberflöte, La traviata, Arabella, Tristan und Isolde, Cavalleria rusticana/I pagliacci, Madama Butterfly. **1981:** (summer) Lear, Don Giovanni, Die Meistersinger, Rigoletto, L'incoronazione di Poppea. **1981:** Semiramide, Manon, Ledi Makbet Mtsenskovo uyezda (Lady Macbeth of Mtsensk), Die lustige Witwe, Carmen, Le Cid, Wozzeck, Lucia di Lammermoor, Aida, Die Walküre, Il trovatore. **1982:** (summer) Julius Caesar, Turandot, Il barbiere di Siviglia, Nabucco, The Rake's Progress. **1982:** Un ballo in maschera, Norma, Salome, Le nozze di Figaro, La Cenerentola, Dialogues des Carmélites, Pikovaya dama, Cendrillon, Lohengrin, Tosca. **1983:** (summer) Das Rheingold, Die Walküre, La bohème, Carmen, Così fan tutte. **1983:** Otello, Ariadne auf Naxos, Kát'a Kabanová, La traviata, Midsummer Marriage, Samson et Dalila, La Grande Duchesse de Gérolstein, La gioconda, Manon Lescaut, Boris Godunov. **1984:** (summer) Don Pasquale, Siegfried, Aida, Die Fledermaus. **1984:** Ernani, Carmen, La sonnambula, L'elisir d'amore, Madama Butterfly, Elektra, Anna Bolena, Khovanshchina, Rigoletto, Don Giovanni. **1985:** (summer) Der Ring des Nibelungen: Das Rheingold, Die Walküre, Siegfried, Götterdämmerung; Der Freischütz (concert). **1985:** Adriana Lecouvreur, Lear, Orlando, Turandot, Werther, Falstaff, Tosca, Un ballo in maschera, Billy Budd, Der Rosenkavalier. **1986:** (summer) Il trovatore, Lucia di Lammermoor, Cavalleria rusticana/I pagliacci, The Medium/La voix humaine. **1986:** Don Carlos, Le nozze di Figaro, Jenůfa, La forza del destino, Faust, Die Meistersinger, La bohème, Eugene Onegin, Manon, Macbeth. **1987:** Il barbiere di Siviglia, Salome, Die Zauberflöte, Tosca, Fidelio, La traviata, Nabucco, Les contes d'Hoffmann, Roméo et Juliette, Pikovaya dama. **1988:** L'Africaine, The Rake's Progress, Maometto II, Der fliegende Holländer, Così fan tutte, Manon Lescaut, Parsifal, Ledi Makbet Mtsenskovo uyezda (Lady Macbeth of Mtsensk), La bohème, La gioconda. **1989:** Falstaff, Lulu, Mefistofele, Otello, Idomeneo, Aida, Madama Butterfly, Lohengrin, Orlando furioso, Die Frau ohne Schatten. **1990:** (summer) Der Ring des Nibelungen: Das Rheingold, Die Walküre, Siegfried, Götterdämmerung. **1990:** Suor Angelica/I pagliacci, Wozzeck, Rigoletto, Die Entführung aus dem Serail, Don Quichotte, Capriccio, Un ballo in maschera, Die Fledermaus, Khovanshchina, Il ritorno di Ulisse in patria. **1991:** (summer) Die Zauberflöte, Le nozze di Figaro, Così fan tutte, Lucio Silla (concert version), La finta giardiniera (Opera Center). **1991:** La traviata, War and Peace, I Capuleti e i Montecchi, Don Giovanni, Carmen, Tristan und Isolde, Das verratene Meer, Elektra, Attila. **1992:** (summer) Guillaume Tell, Il barbiere di siviglia, L'italiana in Algeri, Ermione (concert version). **1992:** Tosca, Boris Godunov, L'elisir d'amore, Fidelio, La forza del destino, Don Carlo, The Death of Klinghoffer, Andrea Chénier, A Midsummer Night's Dream, Christophe Colomb (concert version). **1993:** (summer) Salome, Der Rosenkavalier, Capriccio, Daphne (concert version). **1993:** I vespri siciliani, La fille du régiment, La bohème, Turandot, Věc Makropulos, Die Meistersinger von Nürnberg, La clemenza di Tito, I Puritani, Pikovaya dama.

───────────────────── SAN JOSÉ

• *Opera San José* •

Wolfgang Amadeus Mozart's *Die Zauberflöte* inaugurated the San José Opera on October 6, 1984. The company's origins were in the San José State University Studio Opera Workshop, known as the San José Community Opera Theater, founded by mezzo-soprano Irene Dalis. The company's purpose was to offer

Montgomery Theater (San José, California).

training and experience to new American talent. Dalis, like other singers of her generation, went to Europe for training and experience. In establishing the company, she wanted to offer rising American talent an alternative to training in Europe. When Dalis was appointed Professor of Music at San José State University, she was able to turn her ambitions into practice. Her goal was a year-round resident company similar to the resident-singer system in place in Germany.

The San José's Community Opera Theater's first performances took place on December 2 and 3, 1977. Giacomo Puccini's *Gianni Schicchi* and Virgil Thomson's *The Mother* followed in May. The second season added Gian Carlo Menotti's *The Medium* and *The Telephone*. The students mounted their first world premiere on June 17, 1979, Alva Henderson's *The Last Leaf*. (*The Last Leaf* became Act I of *West of Washington Square*.) During the next few seasons, the student-company mounted rarely performed eighteen- and twentieth-century works, Henry Purcell's *Dido and Aeneas*, Paul Hindemith's *Hin und Zurück*, and Giovanni Pergolesi's *La serva padrona* among them.

By 1984, Dalis felt she had a large enough pool of talented singers to establish a professional regional company, and the Opera San José was born. The first season offered four operas, including Benjamin Britten's *Albert Herring* and Giuseppe Verdi's *La traviata*. Subsequent seasons witnessed Puccini's *Madama Butterfly*, Gaetano Donizetti's *L'elisir d'amore*, Gioachino Rossini's *Il barbiere di Siviglia*, and Franz Lehár's *Die lustige Witwe* among others. The company has also tackled neglected seventeenth-century pieces (Francesco Cavalli's *Ormindo*) and new works: the world premieres of Henderson's *West of Washington Square* (November 26, 1988), Henry Mollicone's *Hotel Eden* (November 25, 1989), and George Roumanis's *Phaedra* (November 14, 1992). Mollicone's *Hotel Eden* is a jazzy comic opera sung primarily in traditional operatic form that incorporated several musical styles, including rock. The work is a musical farce with serious undertones that address an important contemporary problem: wife-beating. Several biblical couples check into a "seen-better-days" hotel where they experience the joys and problems of martial love: Adam's first wife Lilith appears when he is on his honeymoon with his second wife, Eve and informs Eve that Adam is a wife-abuser. Roumanis's *Phaedra* draws its characters and situations from the classic Greek play by Euripides, *Hippolytus.*

Resident artists sing the leading roles, and talented young singers perform as comprimario. There are currently six resident singers. Dalis's goal is ten, and she hopes other regional companies copy her year-round resident program. The resident company's long rehearsal time minimizes inevitable mishaps, but cannot prevent printing errors. In October 1986, Puccini's *Suor Angelica* almost greeted the audience as *Sour Angelica*!

The four-opera season offers an eclectic repertory — a mixture of contemporary and repertory favorites, mostly from the Italian repertory. There are some French and English works. One opera is a new production. The Montgomery Theater's toy-sized stage (twenty-five feet) and tiny orchestra pit partially determine the operas. The other determining factor is the availability of a reduced orchestration. The company only reduces scores that retain the composer's original intent. Recent productions include Britten's *The Turn of the Screw*, Puccini's *La bohème*, Mozart's *Die Zauberflöte*, and Verdi's *Un ballo in maschera*. The company performs in the Montgomery Theater.

Montgomery Theater

The Montgomery Theater was a WPA project, built during the Depression. Constructed on land donated by Mr. Montgomery, it opened in the 1930s. Defined by Spanish style, the theater is beige stucco with wrought iron and a terra cotta tile roof. MONTGOMERY THEATER in large black letters extends across the top part of the façade. Mustard-colored seats alleviate the blackness of the auditorium. Pillars and arches embellish the room. Four large white glass and wrought-iron light fixtures hang from the ceiling. The black stucco proscenium is unadorned. The theater seats 554.

Practical Information. The Montgomery Theater is on West San Carlos & South Market Street. Tickets are available at the San José Ticket Center, 29 North San Pedro Street, Monday through Friday, between 9:00 A.M. and 5:30 P.M. Tickets can be ordered by telephoning 408-288-7077, by faxing 408-279-2432, or by writing Opera San José, 12 South First Street, Suite 207, San José, CA 95113-2404. If you go, stay at the Fairmont Hotel, 170 South Market Street, San José, CA 95113; telephone 408-998-1900, fax 408-280-0394, reservations 1-800-223-6800. The Fairmont Hotel is the focal point of the city and three blocks from the Montgomery Theater.

COMPANY STAFF AND REPERTORY

General/Artistic Director. Irene Dalis (1984–present).

World Premieres. Henderson's *West of Washington Square* (November 26, 1988); Mollicone's *Hotel Eden* (November 25, 1989); Roumanis's *Phaedra* (November 14, 1993).
Repertory (San José Community Opera Theater). **1977-78:** Opera Comes Alive, Gianni Schicchi, The Mother. **1978-79:** The Last Leaf, Gianni Schicchi, The Mother, The Medium, The Telephone, Così fan tutte (scenes), Le nozze di Figaro (scenes). **1979-80:** Dido and Aeneas, Chanticleer, Signor Deluso, Der Schauspieldirektor. **1980-81:** Amahl and the Night Visitors, Il matrimonio segreto, Many Moons, Trouble in Tahiti, The old Maid and the Thief. **1981-82:** Amahl and the Night Visitors, Rita, Suor Angelica, La Canterina, The Little Harlequin, Hin und Zurück. **1982-83:** Amahl and the Night Visitors, The Scarf, Harrison Loved his Umbrella, Così fan tutte. **1983-84:** La bohème, Amahl and the Night Visitors, La serva padrona/The old Maid and the Thief, Die Fledermaus.
Repertory (San José Opera). **1984-85:** Die Zauberflöte, Amahl and the Night Visitors, Albert Herring, La traviata. **1985-86:** Madama Butterfly, Hänsel und Gretel, Tartuffe, L'elisir d'amore. **1986-87:** Suor Angelica/Gianni Schicchi, Le nozze di Figaro, Die lustige Witwe, Amahl and the Night Visitors. **1987-88:** Tosca, Hänsel und Gretel, The Medium, Don Pasquale. **1988-89:** La bohème, West of Washington Square, Il barbiere di Siviglia, Die Fledermaus. **1989-90:** La traviata, Hotel Eden, Les pêcheurs des perles, Così fan tutte. **1990-91:** Madama Butterfly, Vanessa, L'elisir d'amore, Ormindo. **1991-92:** Lucia di Lammermoor, The Turn of the Screw, Il tabarro/Gianni Schicchi, Un ballo in maschera. **1992-93:** Die Zauberflöte, Phaedra, Die lustige Witwe, La bohème.

Colorado ———————————————— A S P E N

• *Aspen Music Festival* •

The Goethe Bicentennial Convocation and Music Festival marked the beginning of the Aspen Music Festival on June 7, 1949. Walter Paepcke launched the celebration for the bicentennial of Johann Wolfgang von Goethe's birth, an event that attracted more than two thousand people during the inaugural season, including Dmitry Mitropoulos and Arthur Rubinstein. The Institute of Music was established in 1951. Three years later, the Institute and Festival were united as the Music Associates of Aspen. Opera plays an important role in the Festival, and several prominent operatic conductors and singers are alumni of the Institute — James Levine, James Conlon, Leonard Slatkin, Barbara Hendricks, and Dawn Upshaw among them.

In 1878 silver was discovered in Aspen and a "silver rush" was on. Two years later, Jerome B. Wheeler was lured to the area by a mine broker named Henry Gillespie. Wheeler had married the niece of Macy's founder and was flush with money. He soon made fortunes more in silver. Since Aspen had become a minimetropolis in the Rockies, it was deemed appropriate that a grand hotel and opera house be built. Wheeler agreed to finance both, lending his first name to the hotel, Hotel Jerome, and his last name to the opera house, Wheeler Opera House.

Conried's English Comic Opera Company inaugurated the Wheeler with Adolph Müller's *The King's Fool*, on April 23, 1889. White satin programs were handed to the gala opening night crowd, and the ladies received perfume vials.

Although the Wheeler was called an opera house, opera played a small part in the total number of performances. The inaugural year offered no additional opera besides opening night. The next year, the Wheeler hosted six operas by three different companies: the Grau Comic Opera performed Jacques Offenbach's *Les brigands* and *Amorita* on January 13 and 14, 1890; the California Opera Company staged Arthur Sullivan's *H.M.S. Pinafore* and Daniel-François Auber's *Said Pasha* and *Fra Diavolo*, on April 14 and 15, 1890, and the Carleton Opera Company mounted Richard Genée's *Nanon* on November 18, 1890. Michael Balfe's *The Bohemian Girl*, performed by the Abbott English Opera Company, was scheduled to usher in 1891 on January 6, but the performance was canceled. Emma Abbott had died the day before in Salt Lake City. The end of January saw the Kimball Opera Comique and Burlesque Company present a burlesque of *Carmen*, and the Bostonians presented Franz von Suppé's *Fatinitza* on March 14, 1891. The first opera in 1892 did not appear until July 11, when the Eckert Opera Company staged a twelve-day season. Edmond Audran's *Les noces d'Olivette*, Robert Planquette's *Les cloches de Corneville*, and Sullivan's *H.M.S. Pinafore* trod the boards. When the silver standard died in 1893, Aspen became a ghost town overnight. The Calhoun Opera Company mounted the last operas seen in Aspen — Auber's *Said Pasha* on April 17, 1893, and von Suppé's *Boccaccio* the following evening — until the founding of the Festival. Wheeler declared bankruptcy a decade later, and lost both his hotel and opera house.

Paepcke discovered Aspen during the 1940s while looking for "an intellectual and physical utopia where overworked business leaders could revitalize body and soul." He leased the Jerome Hotel and made it the site of the founding of the Aspen Institute, Music Festival and School. Opera composer-in-residence, Darius Milhaud, founded the Conference on Contemporary Music in 1951. Milhaud integrated contemporary music into the festival, giving it an international flair. The Wheeler hosted the premieres of several of his works. Unable to walk, Milhaud was carried up the three flights of stairs to the Wheeler auditorium by his students, so he could attend the premieres. Other opera composers-in-residence have been Igor Stravinsky, Hans Werner Henze, Benjamin Britten, and Philip Glass. Britten, who received the first Aspen Award in 1962, attended a production of his *Albert Herring* at the opera house.

The Aspen Opera Theater, the Festival's opera company, celebrated its opening night in the restored Wheeler Opera House on July 28, 1984, with Wolfgang Amadeus Mozart's *Le nozze di Figaro*. The Aspen Opera workshop staged Britten's *Paul Bunyan* in August. The company mounted Mozart's *Die Zauberflöte*, Britten's *A Midsummer Night's Dream*, and Maurice Ravel's *L'enfant et les sortilèges* the following summer. The repertory emphasizes twentieth-century and rarely-performed works alongside the popular operas. Among the former are Aaron Copland's *Tender Land*, Stravinsky's *The Rake's Progress*, Giacomo Rossini's *Mosè in Egitto*, Britten's *The Rape of Lucretia* and *Owen Wingrave*, and Thomson's *Four Saints in Three Acts*. The Festival boasts more than 150 American and world premieres, including several operas. Among them are Henri Sauguet's *La contrebasse*, William Walton's *The Bear* with Slatkin making his debut, Thomas Pasatieri's *The Penitentes*, and László Vidovsky's *Narcissus and Echo*.

The Festival originally took place in an Eero Saarinen-designed tent situated on a former dairy farm along the Roaring Fork River. Herbert Bayer's larger Music Tent, with unreserved bench seating for 1,700, has been the main performance

Wheeler Opera House (Aspen, Colorado).

venue since 1964. Lack of adequate rehearsal space has hampered expansion, but this is changing. Ground breaking took place in August 1992 for a new, $12 million, year-round, 500-seat performance/rehearsal hall, adjacent to the summer-only Music Tent.

The three-opera festival season offers one familiar work and two unusual pieces. The Aspen Opera Theater stages modest productions in the *stagione* system. Opera is sung in the original language and there are no surtitles. Singers-in-training, culled from national auditions, make up the case. Recent productions include Milhaud's *Le pauvre matelot/Les malheurs d'Orphée*, Manuel de Falla's *El Retablo de Maese Pedro*, and Rossini's *Il barbiere di Siviglia*. The company performs under the Festival Tent and in the Wheeler Opera House.

Wheeler Opera House

Nestled in the Rocky mountains, 8,000 feet above sea level, the Wheeler Opera House is one of the few gems remaining from Aspen's silver heyday. The opera house was named after Wheeler, the silver king who paid the $100,000 price tag. W.J. Edbrooke, architect of the Horace Tabor Grand Opera House in Denver, designed the theater. It took ten months to build. Müller's *The King's Fool* inaugurated the house on April 23, 1889. In 1912, a disgruntled worker splashed kerosene on the scenery, causing a large fire. The auditorium was boarded up and forgotten. Although the opera house was renovated in 1960 under the direction of Herbert Bayer, decline set in during the mid-1970s, and the Wheeler was used exclusively as a movie theater. Beginning in the summer of 1981, under the direction of William Kessler and Associates, the opera house was restored to its original glory. The Wheeler reopened on May 22, 1984, with "curtain raising ceremonies" and open house tours. A gala week that offered a variety of entertainment followed.

The Wheeler Opera House is a distinctive building of native peachblow sandstone and brick. Rows of both rectangle and arched windows break up the massive façade. WHEELER OPERA HOUSE in large white letters blazons from a center awning. A claret-red-carpeted grand staircase with a honey-colored, faux-wood balustrade leads to a modern, second floor lobby. The gently curving horseshoe-shaped Victorian auditorium inhabits the third and fourth floors. The single balcony, supported by gilded Corinthian cast iron coral columns, sweeps gracefully around a room filled with crimson red plush seats. The maroon-and-gold-bordered proscenium originally framed a curtain painted with the Brooklyn Bridge in the moonlight. The curtain is now crimson. The Wheeler seats 488.

Practical Information. The Wheeler Opera Houses is at 320 East Hyman. The Festival box office is located in the Gondola building at the foot of Aspen Mountain on Durant Avenue. Tickets can be ordered by telephoning 303-925-9042 or by writing Music Associates of Aspen, P.O.B. AA, Aspen, CO 81612. For a Festival brochure, call 303-925-3254. If you go, stay at the Hotel Jerome, 330 East Main Street, Aspen, CO 81611; telephone 303-920-1000, fax 303-925-2784, reservations 1-800-331-7213. The Hotel Jerome is historically linked to the opera house, since Jerome Wheeler financed both. Conceived by Messrs. Bixby and Phillips, The Jerome has been restored to its original Victorian splendor and is furnished with authentic period-pieces. It is three blocks from the Wheeler Opera House.

COMPANY STAFF AND REPERTORY

Music Directors. Dmitry Mitropoulos (1949); Joseph Rosenstock (1950–53); William Steinberg (1954); Hans Schwieger (1955); Izler Solomon (1956–61); Walter Susskind (1962); Szymon Goldberg (1963); Walter Susskind (1964–68); Jorge Mester (1970–90); Lawrence Foster (1990–present).

World Premieres. Tcherepnin's *La fée et le cultivateur* (in English as The Farmer and the Fairy, August 13, 1952); Barab's *Chanticleer* (August 4, 1956); del Tredici's *Pop-pourri* (summer 1970); Pasatieri's *The Penitentes* (August 3, 1974); Legg's *The Wife of Bath's Tale* (workshop, summer 1986); Neikrug's *Los Alamos* (concert, July 24, 1992).

American/United States Premieres. Henri Sauguet's *Le contrebasse* (July 27, 1962); Humphrey Searle's *Diary of a Madman* (August 17, 1967); Walton's *The Bear* (August 15, 1968); Goehr's *Naboth's Vineyard* (July 30, 1970); Davies's *The Martyrdom of St. Magnus* (July 29, 1978); Schat's *Houdini* (August 2, 1979); László Vidovsky's *Narcissus and Echo* (July 12, 1988).

Repertory (1984–1993). **1984:** Le nozze di Figaro, Paul Bunyan. **1985:** Die Zauberflöte, A Midsummer Night's Dream, L'enfant et les sortilèges. **1987:** La Cenerentola, Tender Land, The Rake's Progress. **1988:** Don Giovanni, Salome (concert), Falstaff. **1989:** Mosè in Egitto, Turn of the Screw, The Rape of Lucretia. **1990:** Così fan tutte, Noyes Fludde, Four Saints in Three Acts. **1991:** Die Zauberflöte, Let's Make an Opera: The Little Sweep, Owen Wingrave. **1992:** El retablo de Maese Pedro/Pauvre Matelot/Les malheurs d'Orphée, Le nozze di Figaro, Los Alamos (concert). **1993:** Il barbiere di Siviglia, Carmen, Mass (concert).

CENTRAL CITY

• *Central City Opera* •

Opera was reborn in Central City on August 5, 1933, with Franz Lehár's *Die lustige Witwe* featuring Gladys Swarthout and Richard Bonelli. A year earlier, Lillian Gish in *Camille* had inaugurated the Central City Opera Festival, originally called the Performing Arts Festival. Founded by Ida Kruse McFarlane and Anne Evans, the Central City Opera Association launched the highest (8,450 feet) and one of the oldest opera festivals in the United States.

On May 6, 1859, John Gregory discovered gold in what later was to be known as Gregory Gulch. Within weeks, thousands of German, Welsh, and Cornish miners flocked to the area. They brought with them their love for music, especially choral concerts, and the following year erected a log theater called the Montana Theater. The Montana hosted plays and light opera until a downtown firestorm on May 21, 1874, destroyed it. Before the conflagration, various opera troupes had added Central City to their tours. One of the first to visit, the Hawson Opera Troupe, arrived in 1869, staging Jacques Offenbach's *La Grande Duchesse de Gérolstein*. Five years later, the Ware-Linton Company arrived, followed by the Oates Comic Opera Company. Oates offered operettas by Charles Lecocq and Arthur Sullivan, with piano and violin as accompaniment. The Richings-Bernard Company visited in 1878, mounting Giuseppe Verdi's *Il trovatore*, Friedrich von Flotow's *Martha*, and Vincent Wallace's *Maritana*. The company then went broke and left its members stranded in Central City!

Homegrown opera also thrived. The Choral Union and Amateur Company jointly staged Michael Balfe's *The Bohemian Girl* on April 17, 1877. Originally scheduled for one weekend, the opera was so successful that it ran for two weekends. Then Jack Langrishe, a theater manager, staged a world premiere "of sorts." He presented a work called *Pat Casey's Night Hands*, an unflattering piece about Pat Casey. When the real Casey threatened to disrupt the performance, half the seats were reserved for security guards. The performance took place without disturbance. Decline set in during the 1880s, and the opera companies stopped visiting. The theater slowly fell into a state of disrepair.

The Central City Opera Association rescued the opera house and launched the festival. The festival grew very slowly at first with only one production a season for the first nine years. Robert Edmond Jones was the first artistic director, guiding the festival with the following tenets: singers were cast according to type, productions reflected an ensemble approach, and performances were sung in English. These principals were considered uncommon back in the 1930s, although most regional opera companies and festivals follow at least one of them today. The repertory expanded to two offerings in 1941, but World War II caused cancellation of the festival for the next three summers. In the post-war years, the Festival experienced rapid growth, offering opera and operetta each season along with spoken drama. It became known as the Central City Opera Festival. Some early Festival highlights were Jerome Hines in Wolfgang Amadeus Mozart's *Die Entführung aus dem Serail* (1946), Eleanor Steber in Verdi's *La traviata* (1946), Judith Raskin in Gaetano Donizetti's *Lucia di Lammermoor* (1950), and Beverly Sills and Rosalind Elias in Verdi's *Aida* (1950).

Central City Opera House (Central City, Colorado).

During the 1950s and 1960s, the Festival commissioned two operas with plots that unfold in Colorado. The first was Douglas Moore's *The Ballad of Baby Doe* (July 7, 1956). The opera is based on the true story of Horace Tabor and his two wives, Augusta Tabor and Elizabeth "Baby" Doe Tabor. Highly acclaimed, it has entered the repertories of numerous opera companies. Eight years later, to celebrate its 33rd anniversary, the festival opened with Robert Ward's *The Lady from Colorado*. It was not as fortunate as "Baby Doe," and the Lady has not been seen since. The festival continued to expand and pursue an adventurous course during the 1970s and early 1980s, and Central City saw two more world premieres— Garland Anderson's *Soyazhe* (July 28, 1979) and Henry Mollicone's *Face on the Barroom Floor* (July 22, 1978). Anderson's *Soyazhe* played as a companion piece to Gian Carlo Menotti's *The Medium*. Taking place on a Navaho reservation, the opera contains all the elements of a successful opera—murder, revenge, and witchcraft. But the piece only lasted forty-five minutes, not leaving the composer sufficient time to develop the conflicts musically. Mollicone's work was of a different ilk. It concerns a face actually painted on the floor in the Teller House Bar, and some performances take place there. The repertory also saw long-neglected works alongside contemporary pieces—Francesco Cavalli's *Scipio Africanus*, Carlisle Floyd's *Of Mice and Men*, and Dominick Argento's *Postcard from Morocco* among others. The experiment was artistically significant and box office poison. The Festival ran up a $600,000 debt and was forced to cancel the 1982 season.

When opera graced the stage the following season, it was the standard repertory in traditional productions sung in English. This conservative formula has proved successful and the Festival has remained in the black since 1983. In November 1991, however, another problem developed: legalized gambling. Although there is discussion of a fourth production and a possible winter season due to the rapid population increase, the company has adopted a "wait and see" attitude before committing to anything. Central City's goal is to find and develop American talent, so the casts are young artists perfecting their craft. The small size of the theater requires that the singers both look and act the part. During the more than six decades of the festival's existence, many future stars of the opera have performed in the Central City Opera House. According to general manager Daniel Rule, over twenty-nine singers on the Met roster are veterans of Central City. Among them are Samuel Ramey, Catherine Malfitano, Charles Anthony, Justino Díaz, Sherrill Milnes, and Paul Plishka.

The three-opera season offers two standard operas and one operetta, performed in repertory. Recent productions include Jules Massenet's *Manon*, Gounod's *Faust*, Puccini's *La bohème*, Georges Bizet's *Carmen*, and Friml's *Rose-Marie*. The company performs in the Central City Opera House.

Central City Opera House

In 1877, Henry Teller and Henry Wolcott formed the Gilpin County Opera Association to raise money by popular subscription to build an opera house. Architect Robert S. Roeschlaub of Denver designed the theater and Will and Peter McFarlane were in charge of the construction. The opera house cost $23,000. Ground breaking took place on June 14, 1877, and less than eight months later, the Central City Opera House opened. Located over Eureka Creek, the house was cool in the summer and freezing in the winter. Flotow's *Martha* was scheduled to inaugurate the house, but several parties objected. They felt a program representing the mixed national origins of Central City residents was more appropriate, and a "Grand Vocal and Instrumental Concert" was selected. The opera house opened on March 4, 1878, with "The Poet and Peasant Overture" by Franz von Suppé, with music by Verdi, Richard Wagner, and Carl Maria von Weber following. Fifty kerosene lamps provided the footlights across the stage front. The auditorium's centerpiece was a massive chandelier holding one hundred kerosene lamps. The ladies sat in the orchestra, and the miners were in the balcony. Special trains carried visitors from as far away as Denver, Boulder, and Idaho Springs.

The glory was short-lived. Gold, to which the opera house's fortunes were tied, soon crashed. Silver was now king and Horace Tabor of Leadville wore the crown. When his opulent Tabor Grand Opera House was opened in Denver on September 5, 1881, the fate of the Central City Opera House was sealed. The theater then hosted wrestling matches, minstrel shows, graduation exercises, and even funerals. Eventually one of the original builders, McFarlane, converted it into a movie house. The theater's doors were shut on January 1, 1927. The Central City Opera House Association was formed to save the building, and after extensive renovation, the opera house was ready for its second life as home to a summer festival.

The Central City Opera House is an austere, imposing building of locally-quarried granite. OPERA HOUSE in large cream-colored letters is affixed to the beige stone façade. Large posters announce the season's fare. The rectangular auditorium holds a single balcony. Maroon-cushioned hickory seats with the names of Colorado pioneers carved on the back inhabit the tan, brown, and turquoise hall.

Multi-colored frescoes decorate the proscenium arch and ceiling. The theater seats 756.

Practical Information. The Opera House is on Eureka Street. The Central City Opera ticket office is in Denver at 621 Seventeenth Street, Suite 1625. It is open between 10:00 A.M. and 5:00 P.M., Monday through Friday. During the summer opera season, you can also buy tickets at the opera house in Central City at the following times: Tuesday, Thursday, Friday, and Saturday from 6:00 P.M. to 9:00 P.M., Wednesday through Friday from 12:30 P.M. to 3:30 P.M., and Saturday and Sunday from 11:00 A.M. to 3:30 P.M. Tickets can be ordered by telephoning 303-292-6700 between 9:00 A.M. and 5:00 P.M., or writing Central City Opera Box Office, 621 17th Street, Suite 1625, Denver, CO 80293. Tickets go on sale in mid-April for the season. If you go, stay at the Denver Marriott West, 1717 Denver West Blvd, Golden, CO 80401; telephone 303-279-9100, fax 303-271-0205, reservations 1-800-228-9290. The Marriott is the most convenient hotel to the Central City Opera House.

COMPANY STAFF AND REPERTORY

General/Artistic Directors. Robert Edmond Jones (1932–35). Frank Saint Leger (music director, 1935–41). John Evans (president, 1942–1943). Frank Ricketson (president, 1943–1964). Donald Carney (president, 1964–1969). Myron Neusteter (president, 1970–1977). Robert Darling (1977–1982). John Moriarty (1982–present).

World Premieres. Moore's *The Ballad of Baby Doe* (July 7, 1956). Ward's *The Lady from Colorado* (July 1964). Mollicone's *The Face on the Barroom Floor* (July 22, 1978). Anderson's *Soyazhe* (July 28, 1979).

Repertory (Opera, Operetta, Music Theater). **1933:** Die lustige Witwe. **1936:** The Gondoliers. **1938:** Ruy Blas. **1939:** The Yeoman of the Guard. **1940:** Prodaná nevěsta (The Bartered Bride). **1941:** Il barbiere di Siviglia, Orpheus. **1942-1945:** No performances: World War II. **1946:** La traviata, Die Entführung aus dem Serail. **1947:** Martha, Fidelio. **1948:** Les contes d'Hoffmann, Così fan tutte. **1949:** Die Fledermaus. **1950:** Don Pasquale, Madama Butterfly. **1951:** Amelia al ballo, Roméo et Juliette, Die schöne Galatea. **1952:** La bohème, Le nozze di Figaro. **1953:** Carmen, Die lustigen Weiber von Windsor. **1954:** Faust, Ariadne auf Naxos. **1955:** The Mikado, H.M.S. Pinafore, Trial by Jury, Yeoman of the Guard Iolanthe. **1956:** The Ballad of Baby Doe, Tosca. **1957:** Rigoletto, Der Zigeunerbaron. **1958:** Cavalleria rusticana/I pagliacci, la Périchole. **1959:** Die Fledermaus, The Ballad of Baby Doe. **1960:** Lucia di Lammermoor, Aida. **1961:** L'elisir d'amore, La traviata. **1962:** La fanciulla del West, La bohème. **1963:** Don Giovanni, Il trovatore. **1964:** Madama Butterfly, Lady from Colorado. **1965:** Manon, Il barbiere di Siviglia, Lakmé. **1966:** Carmen, L'italiana in Algeri, The Ballad of Baby Doe. **1967:** Die lustige Witwe, Don Pasquale, Un ballo in maschera. **1968:** H.M.S. Pinafore, Yeoman of the Guard, The Mikado, The Pirates of Penzance, Iolanthe. **1969:** Die Fledermaus, Tosca. **1970:** La bohème, Of Mice and Men. **1971:** I Do! I Do! **1972:** Le nozze di Figaro, Falstaff, 1776. **1972:** Twentieth Century Program: Curlew River, The Wandering Scholar, La voix humaine, Il gabbiano, the Queen and the Rebels. **1973:** Falstaff, Il barbiere di Siviglia. **1974:** A Midsummer's Night Dream, Rigoletto, Gigi. **1975:** Don Giovanni, Aida, Scipio Africanus, I quattro rusteghi. **1976:** The Ballad of Baby Doe, Capriccio, La bohème. **1977:** Prodaná nevěsta (The Bartered Bride), A Midsummer's Night Dream, Die Fledermaus. **1978:** Salome, The Bohemian Girl, Don Pasquale, The Boor, Sunday Excursion, The Face on the Barroom Floor. **1979:** Die lustige Witwe, Il barbiere di Siviglia, Soyazhe, The Medium, The Face on the Barroom Floor. **1980:** Candide, Lucia di Lammermoor, Der Vampyr, Postcard from Morocco, The Boor, The Face on the Barroom Floor. **1981:** The Ballad of Baby Doe, Madama Butterfly, Fables, The Face on the Barroom Floor. **1982:** no performances. **1983:** La traviata, L'elisir d'amore, The Face on the Barroom Floor. **1984:** Rigoletto, La Cenerentola, The Student Prince, The Face on the Barroom Floor. **1985:** Carmen, La fille du régiment, The Desert Song, The Face on the Barroom Floor. **1986:** La bohème, Il barbiere di Siviglia, Naughty Marietta, The Face on the Barroom Floor. **1987:** Madama Butterfly, Don Pasquale, The Vagabond King, The Face on the Barroom Floor. **1988:** The Ballad of Baby Doe, Macbeth, The New Moon, The Face on the Barroom Floor. **1989:** Die Zauberflöte, Lucia di Lammermoor, The Desert Song, The Face on the Barroom Floor. **1990:** La traviata, Così fan tutte, Die lustige Witwe, The Face on the Barroom Floor. **1991:** Tosca, Roméo et Juliette, Die Fledermaus, The Face on the Barroom Floor. **1992:** Faust, The Student Prince, L'italiana in Algeri, The Face on the Barroom Floor. **1993:** Carmen, Rose Marie, Falstaff, The Face on the Barroom Floor. **1994:** La bohème, Manon, The Vagabond King, The Face on the Barroom Floor.

———————— COLORADO SPRINGS

• *Colorado Opera Festival* •

When a festival makes its debut with a work that had not been performed for two hundred years, one knows this festival strives to be different. The American premiere of Tommaso Traetta's *Il cavaliere errante* inaugurated the Colorado Opera Festival on June 23, 1971. Performed in the Armstrong Theater at Colorado College, the opera featured Virginia Starr, Bill Beck, and DeRos Hogue. Donald Jenkins, general director and co-founder of the festival, was on the podium. Jenkins, a professor of music at Colorado College, originally conceived a summer workshop in which six operas would be performed. Gilbert Johns, the dean of summer sessions at Colorado College, told Jenkins, "That's nuts. Let's start a professional company and do four instead." And they did. In addition to the debut opera, Claudio Monteverdi's *Il combattimento di Tancredi e Clorinda*, Igor Stravinsky's *L'histoire du soldat*, and Giuseppe Verdi's *Otello* graced the stage the summer of 1971.

The festival was originally under the auspices of Colorado College, so it could afford to be adventurous. While under the College's umbrella, several twentieth-century works entered the repertory, including Sergey Prokofiev's *Lyubov' k tryom apel'sinam* (The Love for Three Oranges), Benjamin Britten's *The Turn of the Screw*, Kurt Weill's *Aufstieg und Fall der Stadt Mahagonny*, and Maurice Ravel's *L'enfant et les Sortilèges*. Grand opera and repertory favorites, however, were not forgotten. Some of the most outstanding productions from the 1970s were of that ilk: Verdi's *Otello*, *Aida*, and *Macbeth*, Wolfgang Amadeus Mozart's *Die Zauberflöte* and *Don Giovanni*, and Modest Mussorgsky's *Boris Godunov*. The festival also offered Georg Friedrich Händel's *Xerxes*. Three works were featured every season until 1978, when the festival left the college's sponsorship. Then the number of offerings dropped to two.

When the Pikes Peak Center opened in 1982, the festival dramatically changed its course. Big productions and major fund-raising and marketing efforts defined its new direction. Unfortunately, the cost of the productions outpaced the fund-raising and marketing efforts, and large deficits resulted. It reached the nadir in 1986. All full-time staff were eliminated and only a concert was offered in 1987.

Pikes Peak Center (Colorado Springs, Colorado).

Opera performances resumed the following season, but only one opera is scheduled each season.

The Festival's debt was completely eliminated in December 1991, and Jenkins is slowly expanding the season. The year 1992 saw an increase in the number of performances. Eventually, Jenkins hopes to reintroduce the type of repertory on which the festival was founded—one centerpiece jewel, complemented by an avant-garde/contemporary piece and an unusual early work. Jenkins's philosophy is one of living theater. He strives for productions that involve the audience in the performance. "The repertory should not be confined to museum pieces. Unfamiliar important works that opened the door to our current great operas must be performed, so that we may discover anew what opera is all about," states Jenkins. He inaugurated the Festival with a Traetta work because "Traetta was the source from which Mozart and Verdi drew their inspiration." Above all, Jenkins believes that opera must be a "spectacle." The Festival concentrates its limited budget on purchasing lavish costumes and attracting young, promising singers. (Timothy Nobel sang his first *La traviata* and *Rigoletto*, with the company in 1981 and 1982.) The scenery is minimal, but striking.

The one-opera season offers a popular opera. The past few festivals have seen Verdi's *Aida*, Mozart's *Die Zauberflöte*, and Jacques Offenbach's *Les contes d'Hoffmann*. The company performs in the Pikes Peak Center.

Pikes Peak Center

The Pikes Peak Center opened on October 16, 1982. The Colorado Springs Symphony, with Roberta Peters singing, played an inaugural symphonic program. John

James Wallace designed the Center in association with Clifford Nakata & Associates. The citizens of El Paso County built the facility to serve as a regional multipurpose cultural and entertainment center. Both private and public funds paid for the construction. The Center carried a $13.4 million price tag.

Nestled in a valley of the Rocky Mountains, with the backdrop of Pikes Peak, the Center is an imposing modern structure. The beige fluted-concrete building is shaped into rectangles of varying sizes. PIKES PEAK CENTER in large black letters is affixed to the façade. Glass and concrete define a lobby with white walls and gray fluted columns. The two-tier auditorium is horseshoe-shaped, with chocolate-brown walls, orange velour seats, and maroon box seats. Boxes shaped like tug boats float from the side walls. The hall can be acoustically adjusted according to the needs of the performance with the forward section divided into acoustic canopies that can be raised or lowered. Along the sides, acoustic velour banners hang, burnishing the colors of autumn—amber, rust, maroon. The Hall has 1,775 permanent seats. Additional wooden boxes can be rolled into the auditorium.

Practical Information. Pikes Peak Center is at 190 South Cascade Avenue. Tickets are available at the Center's box office the beginning of May, Monday through Friday, 10:00 A.M. to 6:00 P.M., Saturday, 10:00 A.M. to 5:00 P.M., and 45 minutes before curtain. Tickets can be reserved by telephoning 719-520-7469 or writing Colorado Opera Festival, P.O.B. 1484, Colorado Springs, CO 80901. If you go, stay at the Antlers Doubletree Hotel, Four South Cascade, Colorado Springs, CO 80903; telephone 719-473-5600, fax 719-389-0259, reservations 1-800-528-0444. The Antler dates from 1883, and is a historically significant hotel with fantastic views. It is only two blocks from the Pikes Peak Center.

COMPANY STAFF AND REPERTORY

General/Artistic Director. Donald Jenkins (1971–present).

American/United States Premieres. Traetta's *Il cavaliere errante* (June 23, 1971).

Repertory. **1971:** Il cavaliere errante, Il combattimento di Tancredi e Clorinda, L'histoire du soldat, Otello. **1972:** Don Giovanni, Lyubov' k tryom apel'sinam (The Love for Three Oranges), L'enfant et les sortilèges, L'heure espagnole. **1973:** Die Zauberflöte, L'italiana in Algeri, Aufstieg und Fall der Stadt Mahagonny. **1974:** Iolanthe, Le nozze di Figaro, Macbeth. **1975:** Turn of the Screw, Die Entführung aus dem Serail, Les contes d'Hoffmann. **1976:** Don Pasquale, Boris Godunov, Gianni Schicchi, L'histoire du soldat. **1977:** Così fan tutte, The Rake's Progress, Aida. **1978:** Carmen, Xerxes, La Cenerentola. **1979:** L'elisir d'amore, Faust. **1980:** Regina, La bohème, Die Fledermaus. **1981:** La traviata. **1982:** Rigoletto. **1983:** Carmen, Il barbiere di Siviglia. **1984:** Die lustige Witwe, Tosca. **1985:** Così fan tutte, Madama Butterfly. **1986:** The Ballad of Baby Doe, Requiem (Mozart). **1987:** Messa da Requiem. **1988:** La traviata. **1989:** Die Fledermaus. **1990:** Il trovatore. **1991:** Die Zauberflöte. **1992:** Les contes d'Hoffmann. **1993:** Aida.

———————————————— DENVER

• *Opera Colorado* •

The inaugural performance of Opera Colorado, Giuseppe Verdi's *Otello*, with James McCracken, Pilar Lorengar, and Cynthia Munzer, took place in Boettcher

Boettcher Hall (Denver, Colorado).

Hall on April 4, 1982. Nathaniel Merrill established the company to introduce grand opera to the Rocky Mountain region.

Opera was performed in Denver in the 1870s at the Governor's Guard Hall. Opened in 1873, the Guard Hall was designed for military drill purposes, but also served as a public hall for concerts, lectures, plays, and opera. Six years later, the Denver Choral Union presented Arthur Sullivan's *H.M.S. Pinafore*, only six months after the American premiere in Boston. Then a most important event occurred on September 5, 1881: the opening of the Tabor Grand Opera House. The Colorado pioneer Horace Tabor, whose love affair with Elizabeth "Baby Doe" inspired Douglas Moore's opera, *The Ballad of Baby Doe* (see Central City, Colorado, entry) erected the opera house. It cost more than $800,000, a staggering amount in those days. W. J. Edbrooke designed the Tabor Grand, which had a seating capacity of 1,500. With the opening of this elegant opera house, several traveling opera troupes added Denver to their tours. The Tabor Grand also hosted the premiere of *Brittle Silver*, the first opera composed about Colorado.

A decline in opera activity set in during the early 1900s. Except for a visit by the Metropolitan Opera in 1900, little significant opera took place. It was rumored that numerous opera companies bypassed Denver because of the Eastern Theater syndicate. This led to the construction of the Denver City Auditorium. Financed by a $400,000 bond issue, the auditorium opened in 1908. Twelve years later, Enrico Caruso gave a sold-out concert there. He was guaranteed $12,000, the largest sum ever guaranteed an artist performing in Denver. The Tuesday Musical Club presented operas and operettas during the 1920s. Among the performances were Charles Gounod's *Faust*, an old English light opera, *Dorothy*, and the operetta

Miss Cherryblossom. Minimal additional opera activity took place until the founding of Opera Colorado.

Although Opera Colorado offers mainly standard Italian fare, the company can boast two rarely-performed operas and one world premiere during its short existence: Benjamin Britten's *Curlew River* (February 17, 1990) and *The Burning Fiery Furnace* (February 22, 1991), and Thomas Downard's *Martin Avdēich: The Christmas Miracle* (December 15, 1985). Downard's *Martin Avdēich* featured Stephen West, Stuart Steffen, Sara Bardill, and Eileen Farrell. Merrill's association with the Metropolitan Opera initially brought star-studded casts to his opera-in-the-round productions. The first season saw Plácido Domingo and Catherine Malfitano in Giacomo Puccini's *La bohème*. The 1983/84 season offered James Morris, Ruth Welting, Ashley Putnam, Rosalind Elias, and Susan Quittmeyer in Jacques Offenbach's *Les contes d'Hoffmann*. Jon Vickers was an outstanding Samson, Eva Marton a memorable Turandot, and Aprile Millo assayed Aida. Quittmeyer and Morris returned for Wolfgang Amadeus Mozart's *Don Giovanni*. The casts are not as star-studded as in the early years, although Sherrill Milnes recently sang Macbeth. The singers, as in most regional American companies, are young up-and-coming talent, with only an occasional "name-star" appearing.

The tenth anniversary season was celebrated with a repeat of the inaugural-season productions of Verdi's *Otello* and Puccini's *La bohème*, and the Colorado premiere of Richard Wagner's *Die Meistersinger von Nürnberg*. It was the first *Die Meistersinger* performed "in-the-round." The company's "Vision of the Nineties" program calls for a season expansion to four works, with Russian and additional German works entering the repertory. Every season witnesses a Verdi or Puccini opera.

The three-opera season offers two standard Italian works and one Denver "novelty" in a *stagione* system. Recent productions include Verdi's *Macbeth*, Puccini's *Madama Butterfly*, Gaetano Donizetti's *Lucia di Lammermoor*, Mozart's *Le nozze di Figaro*, and Richard Strauss's *Der Rosenkavalier*. The company performs in Boettcher Hall and Buell Theater in the Denver Performing Arts Complex.

Boettcher Hall

A concert by the Denver Symphony inaugurated Boettcher Hall on March 4, 1978. Designed by Hardy, Holtzman and Pfeiffer Associates as a home for the Denver Symphony, the Hall cost $13 million. Ground breaking took place on December 19, 1974, and the facility was completed in under four years.

An integral part of the Complex, Boettcher exhibits a glass and aluminum façade lined with teal metal columns. The lobby exudes the feeling of a subterranean basement with its exposed ducts. The auditorium is circular. Pomegranate-colored acoustic-velour seats swirl around the stage. The taupe facias are hand-molded plaster. An acoustical canopy of plexiglass disks is suspended over the audience. These "clouds" can be raised or lowered to tune the hall for different types of performances. Super-titles are projected at different levels in five locations around the room. The hall accommodates 2,628 people.

Buell Theater

The ticket lobby joins Buell Theater to Boettcher Hall. Buell was inaugurated on November 1, 1991, with a gala program which included Opera Colorado presenting Verdi's *Otello*. Designed by Beyer Blinder Belle of New York (exterior) and Van Dijk Johnson of Cleveland (interior), the theater cost $33 million. Constructed over a two year period, the Buell lies within the shell of the old Denver Arena.

The building's glass and sea-green metal façade rises to meet the curved, glass roof of the galleria. A cream-colored lobby soars six stories to an open jagged ceiling. The two-tier auditorium is constructed of Colorado sandstone. The parapets shimmer with blue and lavender neon lights. A red sandstone proscenium frames a brown curtain. The seats are bluish green. Side boxes are suspended at different levels on silver steel columns. The auditorium seats 2,830.

Practical Information. Boettcher Hall and Buell Theater are reached through the galleria at 14th and Curtis. The Colorado Opera box office is at 695 South Colorado Boulevard, Suite 20. It is open Monday through Friday, 10:00 A.M. to 5:00 P.M. Tickets can be ordered by telephoning 303-778-6464, from 10:00 A.M. to 6:00 P.M. Monday through Friday, 10:00 A.M. to 4:00 P.M. Saturday, or by writing to Opera Colorado, P.O.B. 9721, Denver, CO 80209. If you go, stay at the Westin Hotel, Tabor Center, 67 Lawrence Street, Denver, CO, 80202; telephone 303-572-9100, fax 303-572-7288, reservations 1-800-228-3000. The hotel is the focal point of downtown. It is four blocks from the Performing Arts Complex, with a free shuttle provided between the hotel and the Complex.

***

COMPANY STAFF AND REPERTORY

General/Artistic Director. Nathaniel Merrill (1982–present).

World Premieres (before Colorado Opera). Freeman's *The Martyr* (September 1893). Houseley's *Narcissus and Echo* (January 30, 1912). Antheil's *The Brothers* (July 28, 1954). Lockwood's *Early Dawn* (August 7, 1961).

World Premieres (Colorado Opera). Downard's *Martin Avdéich* (December 15, 1985).

Repertory. **1982-83:** Otello, La bohème. **1983-84:** Un ballo in maschera, Les contes d'Hoffmann, Turandot. **1984-85:** Tosca, Il trovatore. **1985-86:** Martin Avdéich/Amahl and the Night Visitors, Aida, Don Giovanni, Die. Fledermaus (Acts I, II). **1986-87:** Amahl and the Night Visitors, Manon Lescaut, Samson et Dalila. **1987-88:** Gianni Schicchi/I pagliacci, Carmen. **1988-89:** La traviata, Falstaff. **1989-90:** Curlew River, Faust, Un ballo in maschera. **1990-91:** The Burning Fiery Furnace, Don Carlo, L'elisir d'amore. **1991-92:** Otello, Der Meistersinger, La bohème. **1992-93:** Rigoletto, Macbeth, Le nozze di Figaro. **1993-94:** Madama Butterfly, Der Rosenkavalier, Lucia di Lammermoor.

Connecticut
─────────────────── EAST HADDAM

• *Goodspeed Opera House* •

Jerome Kern's *Oh, Lady! Lady!!* opened the Goodspeed Opera House on June 18, 1963, as the only theater in America "dedicated to the heritage of the American

Goodspeed Opera House (East Haddam, Connecticut).

musical and the development of new works to add to the repertoire." Albert Selden, whose parents donated much of the funds that restored the opera house, was the theater's first director.

A repertory group's performance of the comedy *Charles II* and the farces *Box and Cox* and *Turn Him Out* inaugurated the Goodspeed Opera House on October 24, 1877. Built by William Goodspeed, the opera house hosted the finest in plays and comedy. The New York actors and actresses were brought to East Haddam by steamboats. Amy Stone performed in the melodrama *Pearls of Savoy or a Mother's Prayer*, Effie Ellsler played the leading role of her New York hit, *Hazel Kirk*, and Minnie Maddern Fiske offered her repertoire. The Goodspeed also saw vaudeville and costume balls. For five memorable years, the Goodspeed dominated the cultural life of the area. When Goodspeed died in 1882, the theater's golden years died with him. Two decades later, the theater was closed. More than six decades passed before the building served again as a theater.

The Goodspeed's first season in its new role saw the gamut, from Nikolay Rimsky-Korsakov's *Mozart and Salieri*, to Arthur Sullivan's *H.M.S. Pinafore*. Under the guidance of Selden, it was groping for a "mission." The next season saw a curious pairing of Sullivan's *Ruddigore* with Wolfgang Amadeus Mozart's *Die Entführung aus dem Serail*. Within a few years, however, the theater became a home for musical theater, and more than one hundred works have been produced, both new and revivals. Around ten percent have gone on to Broadway, including the fourth longest-running musical in Broadway history, Mitch Leigh's *Man of La Mancha*. Other successful Broadway shows like Charles Strouse's *Annie* and Gard Geld's *Shenandoah* were also born at Goodspeed.

In 1982, the owner of a former knitting-needle factory donated its abandoned building to the Goodspeed Foundation, which transformed the structure into an intimate 200-seat theater. Known as the Goodspeed-at-Chester/Norma Terris Theatre, it opened in July 1984. This theater serves as a try-out space, and it is here that Goodspeed launches its new musical theater pieces. More than a dozen have been introduced.

The six musical-theater season offers a mixture of new works and revivals. Three musicals are performed at the Goodspeed Opera House, and three are offered at Goodspeed-at-the-Chester. Recent works include Burt Bacharach's *Promises, Promises*, Andrew Lippa's *John & Jen*, Amanda McBroom's *Heartbeats* and Leonard Bernstein's *On the Town*.

Goodspeed Opera House

William Goodspeed had shipping, banking, and other mercantile interests in East Haddam when he decided to erect a structure to house them all—and an opera house. Construction began in 1876 and was finished the following year. The first two levels faced the river, and housed a steamboat passenger terminal, and a bar. The third level faced the street and boasted a general store. The offices for his shipping business were situated above. The icing on the cake was the exquisite opera house that occupied the top two floors. After Goodspeed's death, the theater was reduced to hosting traveling minstrel shows and amateur productions until 1902, when it closed. During World War I, it was reopened as a military base. Later it served as a general store, insurance office, and post office. By the 1940s, it was reduced to being a storage depot for the State Highway Department. In 1958, the building was slated for demolition, but a Goodspeed Opera House Foundation was formed to restore the theater to its former glory.

The Goodspeed Opera House rises majestically from the banks of the Connecticut River, conjuring up the days of a by-gone era. It is a six-story, white Victorian jewel crowned with a Mansard roof and tower. The tallest wooden structure ever built along the banks of the Connecticut River, the Goodspeed hosts its shows on the top floors. The grand staircase with a green-and-gold marbleized balustrade leads up to the rectangular auditorium. A slim lyre-shaped balcony gently curves around a small blood red and cream-colored room, housing royal blue seats. Portraits of young girls embellish the facia. The theater seats 398.

Practical Information. Goodspeed Opera House is at Goodspeed Landing, on route 82 in East Haddam. The box office is inside the opera house on the left. During the season it is open Monday through Saturday from 9:00 A.M. to 5:00 P.M. and until the first intermission on performance days. You can also order tickets by telephoning 203-873-8668 or by writing Goodspeed Opera House, East Haddam, CT 06423. If you go, stay at the Riverwind Inn, 209 Main Street, Deep River, CT 06417; telephone 203-526-2014. A treasury of antiques, the Inn captures the flavor of William Goodspeed's days. It is a short drive to the opera house.

COMPANY STAFF AND REPERTORY

General/Artistic Directors. Albert Selden (1963–1967); Michael Price (executive, 1968–present).

Premieres. (year opened, and year went to Broadway); Man of La Mancha (1965, 1966); Something's Afoot (1973, 1976); Shenandoah (1974, 1974); Very Good Eddie (1975, 1975); Going Up (1976, 1976); Annie (1976, 1977); Whoopee (1978, 1979); The Five O'Clock Girl (1979, 1981); Little Johnny Jones (1980, 1982); Take Me Along (1984, 1985); Harrigan 'n Hart (1984, 1985); Oh, Kay! (1989, 1990); The Most Happy Fella (revival, 1991, 1992).

Repertory. **1963:** Oh Lady! Lady!!, Mozart & Salieri, The Marriage Contract, Vaudeville, The Fantasticks, Gaslight Flickers, Fiesta of American Music, H.M.S. Pinafore, The Mikado. **1964:** Naughty-Naught, Oh, Boy!, A Connecticut Yankee, You Never Know, Vaudeville, Ruddigore, Die Entführung aus dem Serail. **1965:** Man of La Mancha, Purple Dust, Mr. Gilbert, Mr. Sullivan, Mr. Green. **1966:** Beyond the Fringe, Engaged, New Faces of 1966, What Every Woman Knows. **1967:** By Jupiter, Coach with the Six Insides, Room Service, Iolanthe, Anatomy of Burlesque. **1968:** After You, Mr. Hyde, Allegro, On Time, Peter Pan. **1969:** The Boy Friend, Tom Piper, Lock Up Your Daughters, Peter Pan. **1970:** Little Mary Sunshine, I Do! I Do!, The King of Schnorrers. **1971:** Bloomer Girl, Crazy Girl, Hubba Hubba. **1972:** Good News, Sunny, Where's Charley. **1973:** El Capitan, 45 Minutes from Broadway, Something's Afoot. **1974:** Lady Be Good!, DuBarry was a Lady, Shenandoah. **1975:** Louisiana Purchase, Very Good Eddie, Cowboy. **1976:** Dearest Enemy, Going Up, Annie. **1977:** Sweet Adeline, Hit the Deck, The Red Blue-Grass Western Flyer Show. **1978:** Tip-Toes, Whoopee, She Loves Me. **1979:** Babes in Arms, The Five O'Clock Girl, A Long Way to Boston. **1980:** The Happy Time, Little Johnny Jones, Zapata. **1981:** Noel, Funny Face, Bloomer Girl. **1982:** Lock Up Your Daughters, High Button Shoes, The Great American Backstage Musical. **1983:** Gay Divorce, Miss Liberty, Oh, Boy! **1984:** The Boys from Syracuse, Follow Thru, Take me Along. **1985:** You Never Know, Fiorello! Leave It to Jane, The Dream Team, Georgia Avenue. **1986:** Irma La Douce, Fanny, Carnival!. **1987:** One Touch of Venus, Lady, Be Good!, The Little Rascals. **1988:** The Wonderful Town, Ankles Aweigh, Mr. Cinders. **1989:** A Connecticut Yankee, Madama Sherry, Oh, Kay! **1990:** The Chocolate Soldier, Pay Joey, Bells are Ringing. **1991:** The Most Happy Fella, Arthur: The Musical, Here's Love (Miracle on 34th Street). **1992:** It's a Bird, It's a Plane, It's Superman, Paint Your Wagon, Animal Crackers. **1993:** On the Town, Heartbeats, Promises, Promises.

Repertory. (Goodspeed-at-Chester/The Norma Terris Theater, all are premieres). **1984:** Harrigan 'n Hart, Mrs. McThing, A Broadway Baby. **1985:** The Dream Team, Georgia Avenue. **1986:** Jokers, A House in the Woods. **1987:** Kaleidoscope, Abyssinia, Butterfly. **1988:** Abyssinia . **1989:** A Fine and Private Place, The Real Life Story of Johnny de Facto. **1990:** Annie 2, Blanco!, Arthur: The Musical. **1991:** Woody Guthrie's American Song, Conrack. **1992:** Heartbeats, Some Sweet Day, Good Sports. **1993:** Jack, Das Barbecü (1991, premiered in Seattle), John & Jen.

——————————————————— HARTFORD

• *Connecticut Opera* •

Georges Bizet's *Carmen*, with Winifred Heidt and Eugene Conley, inaugurated the Connecticut Opera in the Horace Bushnell Memorial Auditorium on April 14, 1942. Frank Pandolfi, who was a Hartford music teacher and tenor, founded the company to give his students a stage on which to practice their artistry. The previous year, Pandolfi had rented the Avery Memorial, presenting his pupils in abbreviated versions of Giuseppe Verdi's *La traviata*, Ruggero Leoncavallo's *Cavalleria rusticana*, and Giacomo Puccini's *La bohème*. These performances had impressed the Bushnell management enough to invite Pandolfi present his next opera season at the Bushnell. It included eight popular operas: Giuseppe Verdi's *Aida*, *Rigoletto*, *La traviata*, and *Il trovatore*, Giacomo Puccini's *La bohème* and *Tosca*, Donizetti's *Lucia di Lammermoor*, and Bizet's *Carmen*.

Opera in Hartford dates back to the late 1700s, before the act of May 1800 "forbade theatrical representations." The Old American Company made Hartford one of their main performance centers and mounted productions there every summer until the end of the century except 1798. John Hodgkinson managed the large troupe, which turned a small town of 3,000 into an operatic summer resort for five seasons. Other companies from Boston and Charleston visited as well. Initially the performances took place in Frederick Bull's Long Room. Then in 1795, a "New Theater" began hosting the shows. With the prohibition against "theater" at the turn of the century, everything came to an abrupt halt. Hartford's glorious days as an operatic summer resort had ended.

Visits by traveling operatic troupes, including the Metropolitan Opera, provided the operatic fare until the early 1940s. During the Met's 1931 visit, the company staged Ambroise Thomas's *Mignon* and Verdi's *La traviata*. Excessively high costs forced the Bushnell, which hosted the visits for more than a decade, to terminate them. But the theater was interested in continuing operatic performances, and Pandolfi was delighted to have such an excellent performing venue. For his second season, he presented Jan Kiepura and Dorothy Kirsten in Puccini's *La bohème*. It was Kirsten's first leading role. That same season Robert Merrill sang his first operatic role with Giovanni Martinelli in Ruggero Leoncavallo's *I pagliacci*. Adriana Maliponte tackled her first Vincenzo Bellini's *I Puritani* in Hartford.

From its inception, the company concentrated on "war horses," and many productions were "star vehicles." The Connecticut Opera was fortunate. Located only 111 miles from New York City, it was able to attract Met stars. They arrived by train or limousine for their one-night appearances between performances at the Met. Franco Corelli made the journey in 1966 for Verdi's *Aida*. Two years later, Renata Tebaldi and Plácido Domingo came for Puccini's *Manon Lescaut*. Magda Olivero stopped in town for Francesco Cilèa's *Adriana Lecouvreur* in 1969. The year 1973 was especially glorious. Richard Tucker and Gwendolyn Killebrew appeared in Verdi's *Il trovatore*, and Domingo sang in Pietro Mascagni's *Cavalleria rusticana*. The following year, two *prima donne* visited, Joan Sutherland for Donizetti's *Maria Stuarda* and Beverly Sills for Donizetti's *La fille du régiment*. Grace Bumbry assayed Salome in 1982, and James McCracken was Otello four years later.

Bushnell Memorial Auditorium (Hartford, Connecticut)

Eventually the high fees put an end to this glamorous era and the company began concentrating on "total theatrical opera" with better sets, costumes, lighting, and staging. There was also an expansion to "arena opera." The company opened it fiftieth anniversary on October 3, 1991, with a spectacular production of Verdi's *Aida* that played to over 42,000 spectators. The repertory remains mainstream. The two "adventurous" (for Hartford) offerings scheduled during the 1990-91 season — Puccini's *La rondine* and Verdi's *Macbeth* — were replaced with perennial favorites: Puccini's *Madama Butterfly* and Donizetti's *Don Pasquale*.

The four-opera season offers a standard "popular" repertory of comic and tragic works in a *stagione* system. Recent productions include Verdi's *Rigoletto* and *Un ballo in maschera*, Puccini's *Tosca*, Donizetti's *L'elisir d'amore*, and Franz Lehár's *Die lustige Witwe*. The Connecticut Opera performs in the Horace Bushnell Memorial Auditorium.

Horace Bushnell Memorial Auditorium

The Horace Bushnell Memorial Auditorium first opened its doors on January 13, 1930, with a musical evening featuring Moshe Paranov conducting the Hartford Choral Club, the Oratorio Society, and the Cecilia Club, accompanied by fifty members of the Boston Symphony Orchestra. Designed by the architectural firm of Corbett, Harrison, and MacMurray, the Auditorium was built by Horace Bushnell's daughter, Dotha Bushnell Hillyer, as a living memorial to her father. It cost over $3 million.

The Bushnell is a neo-classical brick and Indiana limestone building. The façade features a monumental arcaded recessed gallery above the main entrance. The building's sides are embellished with six Ionic columns supporting tympanums inscribed with quotes from Horace Bushnell. Limestone and beige marble define the lobby. The cream-and-cranberry auditorium is intricately designed in a striking art-deco fashion. Turquoise lyres embellish the parapets and rest above the proscenium arch. Acoustic panels extend out from the proscenium to the audience. A ceiling mural decorates overhead. Two balconies curve over golden olive seats. The Auditorium seats 2,722.

Practical Information. The Bushnell Memorial Hall is at 166 Capitol Avenue. Tickets are available at the Connecticut Opera Box Office, 226 Farmington Avenue, or by telephoning 203-527-0713, or writing Connecticut Opera, 226 Farmington Avenue, Hartford, CT 06105. If you go, stay at the Goodwin Hotel, One Haynes Street, Hartford, CT 06103; telephone 203-246-7500, fax 203-247-4576, reservations 1-800-922-5006. The Goodwin Hotel is part of the Goodwin Building, erected in 1881, and historically significant. John Pierpont Morgan lived there for several years. A focal point of downtown, it is a few blocks to the Auditorium.

COMPANY STAFF AND REPERTORY

General/Artistic Directors. Frank Pandolfi (1942–1974). William Warden (1974–1979). George Osborne (1979–present).

World Premieres. (before the Connecticut Opera). Siegmeister's *Sing Out Sweet Land!* (November 9, 1944).

American/United States Premieres. (before the Connecticut Opera). Shield's *The Lock and Key* (July 7, 1796).

Repertory (Old American Company). 1794: Harlequin's Cook (pantomime), Love in a Village, No Song, no Supper, Rosina. 1795: Agreeable Surprise, Children in the Wood, Columbus, Elopement (pantomime), Farmer, Forêt noire (pantomime), Harlequin Gardener (pantomime), Harlequin Restored, Haunted Tower, Highland Reel, Highland Wedding (pantomime), Mountaineers, Old Sergeant, Poor Soldier, Poor Vulcan, Prize, Purse, Quaker, Rival Candidates, Romp, Rosina, Sophia (pantomime), Two Philosophers (pantomime). 1796: Adopted Child, Agreeable Surprise, Battle of Hexham, Children in the Wood, Farmer, Flitch of Bacon, Harlequin Restored (pantomime), Highland Reel, Inkle and Yarico, Lock and Key, My Grandmother, Padlock, Poor Soldier, Prisoner, Purse, Quaker, Romp, Rosina, Waterman. 1797: Adopted Child, Children in the Wood, Deserter, Double Disguise, Flitch of Bacon, Inkle and Yarico, Launch, Lock and Key, Milliners (pantomime), Mountaineers, Padlock, Purse, Siege of Belgrade, Siege of Quebec, Tom Thumb the Great, Virgin Unmasked, Waterman, Zorinski. 1798: no season. 1799: Agreeable Surprise, Daphne and Amintor, Double Disguise, Enchanted Island. (pantomime), Harlequin in Hartford (pantomime), Highland Reel, Lock and Key, Padlock, Prize, Purse, Rosina, Shipwreck, Smugglers.

Repertory. 1942-43: Carmen, Rigoletto, Aida, La traviata, La bohème, Il trovatore, Lucia di Lammermoor, Tosca. 1943-44: Carmen, Cavalleria rusticana/I pagliacci, Faust, Rigoletto, La traviata, La bohème. 1944-45: Aida, Il barbiere di Siviglia, Tosca, Madama Butterfly. 1945-46: Il trovatore, Carmen, La traviata, Rigoletto, La bohème. 1946-47: Faust, Aida, Madama Butterfly. 1947-48: La bohème, La traviata, Lucia di Lammermoor. 1948-49: Cavalleria rusticana/I pagliacci, Il barbiere di Siviglia. 1949-50: Il trovatore, Rigoletto, Un ballo in maschera. 1950-51: Tosca, Madama Butterfly, La bohème, Carmen. 1951-52: La traviata, Faust, Aida, L'elisir d'amore. 1952-53: Il trovatore, La bohème, Rigoletto, Otello. 1953-54: Tosca, Carmen, Madama Butterfly, Cavalleria rusticana/Gianni Schicchi. 1954-55:

La traviata, Il barbiere di Siviglia, Aida, La bohème. **1955-56:** Tosca, La forza del destino, Rigoletto, Le nozze di Figaro, Lucia di Lammermoor. **1956-57:** Turandot, Carmen, Il trovatore, La traviata. **1957-58:** Andrea Chénier, Faust, Aida, La bohème. **1958-59:** Cavalleria rusticana/I pagliacci, Rigoletto, Madama Butterfly, Lucia di. Lammermoor. **1959-60:** Manon, Tosca, Il barbiere di Siviglia, La traviata. **1960-61:** La gioconda, Carmen, Lucia di Lammermoor, La bohème. **1961-62:** Norma, Aida, Turandot, Il trovatore. **1962-63:** Otello, Madama Butterfly, L'elisir d'amore, La traviata. **1963-64:** Un ballo in maschera, Samson et Dalila, Tosca, Rigoletto. **1964-65:** Les pêcheurs des perles, Manon, La bohème, Faust, Il barbiere di Siviglia. **1965-66:** Don Carlo, Carmen, I Puritani, Aida, Il trovatore. **1966-67:** La gioconda, La sonnambula, La bohème, La traviata, La fille du régiment. **1967-68:** Tosca, Madama Butterfly, Roméo et Juliette, Manon, Otello, Cavalleria rusticana/I pagliacci. **1968-69:** Boris Godunov, Lucia di Lammermoor, Andrea Chénier, Rigoletto, Die Walküre, Turandot. **1969-70:** Adriana Lecouvreur, Un ballo in maschera, Salome, Carmen, Il barbiere di Siviglia, Faust. **1970-71:** Aida, La traviata, La bohème,Il trovatore, Madama Butterfly. **1971-72:** Tosca, Tristan und Isolde, Norma, Don Pasquale, I pagliacci, Gianni Schicchi, Die Fledermaus. **1972-73:** Lucia di Lammermoor, Rigoletto, Otello, Samson et Dalila, Cavalleria rusticana/Il tabarro, Le nozze di Figaro. **1973-74:** Carmen, Il trovatore, I Puritani, Un ballo in maschera, Maria Stuarda, La fille du régiment. **1974-75:** Aida, La forza del destino, La bohème, Manon Lescaut, L'elisir d'amore. **1975-76:** La fanciulla del West, Tosca, Madama Butterfly, La traviata, Der fliegende Holländer. **1976-77:** Don Carlo, Il barbiere di Siviglia, Rigoletto, Otello. **1977-78:** Faust, Lohengrin, La bohème, Norma. **1978-79:** Il trovatore, Don Pasquale, Die Zauberflöte. **1979-80:** La traviata, Madama Butterfly, Die lustige Witwe. **1980-81:** Carmen, Tosca, Macbeth, Porgy and Bess. **1981-82:** Aida, Die Fledermaus, Salome, Nabucco. **1982-83:** Turandot, Les contes d'Hoffmann, Lucia di Lammermoor, Rigoletto. **1983-84:** La bohème, Il trovatore, Madama Butterfly. **1984-85:** La traviata, Il barbiere di Siviglia, Samson et Dalila. **1985-86:** Un ballo in maschera, La sonnambula, Otello, Die lustige Witwe. **1986-87:** Tosca, Così fan tutte, Trouble in Tahiti/I pagliacci, Hänsel und Gretel. **1987-88:** Madama Butterfly, L'elisir d'amore, Rigoletto, Die Fledermaus. **1988-89:** Roméo et Juliette, Porgy and Bess (La bohème, Die Zauberflöte canceled). **1989-90:** La bohème, Nabucco, Die Zauberflöte, Lucia di Lammermoor. **1990-91:** Carmen, Le nozze di Figaro, Madama Butterfly, Don Pasquale. **1991-92:** Aida, Il barbiere di Siviglia, Norma, La traviata. **1992-93:** Rigoletto, La Cenerentola, L'elisir d'amore, La bohème. **1993-94:** Barbe-Bleue, Un ballo in maschera, Tosca, Die lustige Witwe.

Delaware
WILMINGTON

• *OperaDelaware* •

OperaDelaware was born as the Wilmington Opera Singers in the mid-1945. The Wilmington Opera Singers were a community choral group under the guidance of W.W. Laird. Their first opera was Georges Bizet's *Carmen*, performed once during the inaugural season. The second season also offered only one opera, Giuseppe Verdi's *La traviata*.

During the 1700s and 1800s, there were strong prejudices against "theatre" in Wilmington, and constant attacks from the clergy and Puritan leaders limited its activity. Except for a brief visit by the Charleston Comedians in 1798, returning to Charleston from a tour in the north through Wilmington, almost no opera was performed. When the Grand Opera House opened on December 22, 1871, the

Grand Opera House (Wilmington, Delaware).

situation changed, although opera played only a minor role in the theater's repertory. For the inaugural gala, representatives from the Philadelphia Academy of Music offered a first-rate opera, but their offer was refused. The only opera seen during the inaugural season was Friedrich von Flotow's *Martha*, performed by the Parepa Rosa Grand English Opera Company. The opera reportedly attracted a sizable crowd. The remainder of the 1870s saw the number of performances, usually of *opéra bouffe*, fluctuate between one and eight per season. Twice, however, the management had to cancel performances because no one showed up for the Hyer Sisters and their Operatic troupe in 1873, and the Kellogg Troupe in 1874.

Opera grew in popularity in the 1880s with the 1882-83 season boasting seventeen performances. Between 1884 and 1887, twenty-five performances graced the stage annually. The Bennett & Moulten's Comic Opera Company presented Robert Planquette's *Les cloches de Corneville* and Edmond Audran's *La mascotte* and *Les noces d'Olivette* between September 22 and 27, 1884. The Boston Ideal Opera Company offered Daniel Auber's *Fra Diavolo* and Michael Balfe's *The Bohemian Girl* between February 26 and 28, 1885. The Amy Gordon Comic Opera Troupe performed Edward Solomon's *Billie Taylor*, Franz von Suppé's *Fatinitza*, Charles Lecocq's *Giroflé-Girofla*, and Audran's *La mascotte* and *Les noces d'Olivette* between April 20 and 25, 1885. The Standard Opera Company followed with Audran's *Les noces d'Olivette* and *La mascotte*, Arthur Sullivan's *H.M.S. Pinafore*, and Planquette's *Les cloches de Corneville* on April 27 through 30, 1885. The Harris Opera Company staged Audran's *La mascotte* and *Les noces d'Olivette*, Sullivan's *H.M.S. Pinafore*, and Planquette's *Les cloches de Corneville* between May 25 and 30, 1885. The Harris Opera was one of Wilmington's favorites. A September 1885 performance of Audran's *La mascotte* attracted a record crowd of 1,957. The Bennett & Moulten's Comic Opera Company mounted Sullivan's *The Mikado* on Wednesday, October 28, 1885. Two years later, the National Opera Company staged Léo Delibes's *Lakmé* before 1,600 spectators who included the city's most socially prominent. The Lyceum Opera Company and Wilbur Opera Company visited toward the end of the decade with more popular operas. The American Opera Company, Dugg Opera Company, and Juch Perotti's Troupe brought grand opera, which was not well received.

The 1890s saw a continuation of operatic performances by visiting companies. Comic operas still dominated the repertory, but the operas and troupes changed. The Digby Bell Comic Opera Company visited, performing *Tar and Tartar* in September 1893. This opera was later staged by the Waite Comic Opera and Bijou Opera Companies. The Waite also presented Vincent Wallace's *Maritana* and Planquette's *Paul Jones* to enthusiastic audiences. The most popular comic opera at the Grand was *Wang*. At a 1896 performance of *Wang*, Albert Hart was the King of Siam, and the chorus used over one hundred costumes. The Grand English Opera Company brought grand opera, mounting Pietro Mascagni's *Cavalleria rusticana* and Ruggero Leoncavallo's *I pagliacci*. Milton Aborn's New England Opera Company also visited.

With opera increasing in popularity, it was no surprise that a home-grown opera company momentarily blossomed. Under the leadership of T. Leslie Carpenter, talented local artists formed the Wilmington Opera Club. They gave two performances of Sullivan's *Mikado* on May 22 and 23, 1895, at the Grand Opera House, then quietly disappeared. Wilmington did not hear home-grown opera again until the birth of the Wilmington Opera Singers. In 1947, the Singers changed their name to Wilmington Opera Society and mounted Verdi's *Aida* and Giacomo Puccini's *La bohème* in the Playhouse inside the duPont Hotel. The Society moved to Breck's Mill in 1952, their home for the next twelve years. In 1964, the company reorganized and returned to the Playhouse, where they stayed until 1976. Four years earlier, the Opera Society had hired their first professional singers for Verdi's *Un ballo in maschera*, Mascagni's *Cavalleria rusticana*, and Leoncavallo's *I pagliacci*.

A new era dawned in 1976. The company moved into the Grand Opera House and presented their first world premiere, Alva Henderson's *The Last of the Mohicans*, in celebration of the American Bicentennial. For the Quincentennial of Columbus's discovery of America, Kate Waring's *America Before Columbus* was commissioned, arriving on October 26, 1992. OperaDelaware celebrated its fiftieth anniversary with an opera on Vietnam, *Tonkin*, by Conrad Cummings (November 27, 1993). The company has reached into the rarely performed repertory and staged Gaetano Donizetti's *Il furioso all'isola di San Domingo* during the 1982-83 season. That same year, to reflect its new role as a regional opera company, the Society changed its name to OperaDelaware. The American stage premiere of Verdi's *Stiffelio* highlighted the 1988 season. (The Italians had difficulty identifying with a story that concerned adultery of the wife of a clergyman, so Verdi reworked the opera, renaming it *Aroldo*. This is the version that is usually performed.)

OperaDelaware emphasizes children's operas with its Family Opera Theater and has presented several novelties for children—Charles Strouse's *Charlotte's Web*, Libby Larsen's *A Wrinkle in Time*, and Evelyn Swensson's *The Enormous Egg* among them. The company is semi-professional, hiring professional singers for the principal roles. The productions are modest but clever. The artists sing in English, but a recent questionnaire suggested that the company is considering converting to original language productions with surtitles.

The three-opera season offers one grand opera, one unusual/contemporary work (recently premieres), and one children's opera for the Family Opera Theater. Recent operas include Verdi's *La traviata* Puccini's *La bohème*, Donizetti's *La fille du régiment*, Cummings's *Tonkin*, and Strouse's *Charlotte's Web*. The company performs in the Grand Opera House.

Grand Opera House

The opening of the Grand Opera House on December 22, 1871, was "the event of the decade" in the city. The festivities began precisely at nine. The musical program offered eight selections and lasted two hours. Afterward, trumpets drew the gala crowd to the dance floor where they tarried until the wee hours of the morning. The Delaware Lodge of Ancient Free and Accepted Masons built the Grand Opera House, incorporating the theater into their Temple. Designed by Thomas Dixon, the Grand took two years and cost $100,000 to construct. Comedies, tragedies, melodramas, burlesque, and vaudeville appeared on the stage. In 1910, movies displaced live entertainment, starting the Grand Opera House's fall from grace. It hit rock bottom in the 1960s.

A centennial gala on December 22, 1971, proved strong interest existed to restore the opera house to its former glory. Four and a half years later, on May 7, 1976, the world premiere of Stephan Kozinski's *American Rhapsody for Piano and Orchestra*, performed by the Delaware Symphony under the baton of Van Lier Lanning, inaugurated the splendidly restored opera house.

The Grand is on the first floor of the Masonic Temple. Constructed of brick, the building boasts a white-painted, cast-iron façade that imitates chiseled marble. Topped by a Mansard roof, the façade incorporates important Masonic principles. Pairs of white Doric columns flank the entrance doors, above which GRAND OPERA HOUSE is etched in the glass transom. The chocolate-brown and cream-colored lobby transports back to the Victorian era. The maroon, brown, and gold horseshoe-shaped auditorium holds velvet plush seats. Eight Corinthian columns support a single balcony. The Muse-inhabited frescoed ceiling is painted like a dome. The Grand Opera House seats 1,150.

Practical Information. The Grand Opera House is at 818 North Market Street, in the middle of the pedestrian mall. Tickets can be purchased at OperaDelaware, St. Andrews Annex, 719 North Shipley Streets, between 9:30 A.M. and 5:00 P.M. weekdays. The Opera House box office, on the right side of the entrance foyer, opens one and a half hours before curtain time. Tickets can be ordered by telephoning 302-658-8063 during office hours, or writing OperaDelaware, c/o St. Andrews, 719 North Shipley Street, Wilmington, DE 19801. If you go, stay at the Hotel duPont, 11th & Market streets, Wilmington, DE 19801; telephone 302-594-3100, fax 302-656-2145, reservations 1-800-323-7500. Built in the Italian Renaissance style, the hotel opened in 1913. It features a museum quality art collection that includes three generations of Wyeth paintings and mixed media works by local artists. The duPont offers complimentary limousine service to the Grand Opera House.

COMPANY STAFF AND REPERTORY

General/Artistic Directors. Eric Kjellmark (1985–present).

World Premieres (before OperaDelaware). Stothart & Gershwin's *Song of the Flame* (December 10, 1925); Romberg's *The Desert Song* (October 21, 1926).

World Premieres (OperaDelaware). Henderson's *The Last of the Mohicans* (American Bicentennial, 1976); Waring's *America Before Columbus* (October 26, 1992); Cummings's *Tonkin* (November 27, 1993).

World Premieres (Family Opera Theater). Menotti's *The Boy Who Grew Too Fast* (September 24, 1982); Strouse's *Charlotte's Web* (February 17, 1989); Larsen's *A Wrinkle in Time* (March 27, 1992); Swensson's *The Enormous Egg* (March 5, 1993).

American/United States Premieres (Family Opera Theater). McCabe's *The Lion, the Witch and the Wardrobe* (March 9, 1990).

Repertory. 1945: Carmen. 1946: La traviata. 1947: Aida, La bohème. 1948: Cavalleria rusticana/I pagliacci. 1949: Carmen. 1950: Faust. 1952: Pastia's Tavern. 1953: Lohengrin. 1954: King Canute, Bottle, Bullet, Blade. 1955: Trial by Jury, Cavalleria rusticana. 1956: Princess Ida, Die Fledermaus. 1957: Martha, Comet Feather. 1958: Carmen, The Vagabond King. 1959: La traviata, Prodaná nevěsta (The Bartered Bride) . 1960: Faust, Die lustige Witwe. 1961: Aida, La Périchole. 1962: Un ballo in maschera, Die Fledermaus. 1963: Il trovatore, Der Zigeunerbaron. 1964: Cavalleria rusticana/I pagliacci, Naughty Marietta. 1965: Martha, Carmen. 1966: Madama Butterfly, Die lustige Witwe. 1967: La bohème, Tosca. 1968: Faust, Rigoletto. 1969: La traviata, Hänsel und Gretel, The Partisans, Le nozze di Figaro. 1970: Aida, Madama Butterfly. 1971: Carmen, L'elisir d'amore. 1972: Un ballo in maschera, Cavalleria rusticana/I pagliacci. 1973: Lucia di Lammermoor, Die Fledermaus. 1974: Tosca, Il trovatore. 1975: Il barbiere di Siviglia, La traviata. 1976: The Last of the Mohicans, Rigoletto. 1977: Aida, Faust. 1978: Otello, Le nozze di Figaro. 1979: Turandot, L'elisir d'amore. 1980: Carmen, Madama Butterfly. 1981: Così fan tutte, Il trovatore, La bohème. 1982: Tosca, Lucia di Lammermoor, Il barbiere di Siviglia. 1983: La traviata, La Périchole, Il furioso all'isola di San Domingo. 1984: Aida, La Cenerentola. 1985: Don Pasquale, Die Zauberflöte, Macbeth. 1986: Cavalleria rusticana/I pagliacci, Die Fledermaus, Hänsel und Gretel. 1987: Don Giovanni, Fidelio. 1988: Stiffelio, Un ballo in maschera, Harriet, The Woman called Moses. 1989: Madama Butterfly, Carmen. 1990: Il barbiere di Siviglia, Die Entführung aus dem Serail. 1991: The Ballad of Baby Doe, Les contes d'Hoffmann, Rigoletto. 1992: America Before Columbus, La bohème, Die lustige Witwe. 1993: Tonkin, La fille du régiment. 1994: La traviata. Family Opera Theater. 1970: Help, Help, The Globolinks! 1971: Little Sweep. 1972: Oliver. 1973: Pinocchio, Little Red Riding Hood. 1974: Wizard of Oz, Little Red Riding Hood. 1975: Peter Pan. 1976: Help, Help, The Globolinks! 1977: Sleeping Beauty. 1978: Sound of Music. 1979: Amahl and the Night

Visitors. **1980**: Babes in Toyland. **1981**: Peter Pan. **1982**: The Boy Who Grew Too Fast. **1984**: The Bewitched Boy. **1987**: Help, Help, The Globolinks!. **1988**: Nightingale. **1989**: Charlotte's Web. **1990**: The Lion, the Witch and the Wardrobe. **1991**: Charlotte's Web. **1992**: A Wrinkle in Time. **1993**: The Enormous Egg. **1994**: Charlotte's Web.

———————— W A S H I N G T O N ,   D. C.

• *The Washington Opera* •

The Opera Society of Washington, the original name of The Washington Opera, presented Wolfgang Amadeus Mozart's *Die Entführung aus dem Serail* on January 31, 1957, in Lisner Auditorium as its inaugural opera. Gian Carlo Menotti's *The Old Maid and the Thief* and *The Unicorn, The Gorgon, and the Manticore* concluded the first season on April 25, 1957. Day Thorpe founded the Opera Society and was its first general director. Thorpe, who also presided over the National Symphony Orchestra, hired its music director Paul Callaway to conduct the performances. Behind the scenes, Hobart Spalding was the prime catalyst. His creative input and financial backing helped shape the company's early years.

Traveling opera companies offered Washington its first opera when in 1800 Thomas Wignell and Alexander Reinagle added the nation's capital to its touring agenda. They remodelled Blodgett's Inn, renaming it the United States Theatre, and brought their Philadelphia company for several seasons. The troupe performed the usual English ballad opera fare and pantomimes (see Philadelphia entry). In 1836, Washington saw its first European opera, Gioachino Rossini's *Il barbiere di Siviglia*, performed in English by the Walton Opera. Near the end of the 19th century, the 2,000-seat Albaugh's Opera House hosted grand opera. The Lafayette Square Opera House (built in 1907 and later called Shubert-Belasco) saw opera after the turn of the century, and the Savage Opera Company presented Washington's first premiere, Giacomo Puccini's *Madama Butterfly* (in English) on October 15, 1906, in the Columbia Theater.

There were also attempts at home-grown opera. A black opera company was established in 1872, performing both in Washington and Philadelphia. The Washington National Opera Association was founded in 1918 as the Washington Community Opera. It survived a decade. Mary Cardwell Dawson formed the National Negro Opera Company, making Washington its home-base from the late 1940s until 1962. The company presented traditional repertory with the occasional rarity, such as Clarence Cameron White's *Ouanga*. During the 1950s and 1960s, the Washington Civic Opera, subsidized by the city government, offered free performances.

The Opera Society of Washington was established to present unusual repertoire in innovative productions with emerging young artists. The emphasis was on twentieth-century operas, introducing new works and resurrecting neglected pieces from the distant past. The company productions reflected this mission with Richard Strauss's *Ariadne auf Naxos*, Igor Stravinsky's *The Rake's Progress*, and Claudio Monteverdi's *La favola d'Orfeo*. Within the first decade, the company had staged Claude Debussy's *Pelléas et Mélisande*, Maurice Ravel's *L'heure espagnole* and *L'enfant et les sortilèges*, Benjamin Britten's *The Rape of Lucretia*, Samuel Barber's *Vanessa*, Lee Hoiby's *Natalia Petrovna*, Manuel de Falla's *El Retablo de Maese Pedro*, and Stravinsky's *Le rossignol* and *Oedipus Rex*. The latter two works were conducted by the composer himself. In addition, the first ten years boasted four novelties: Arnold Schoenberg's *Erwartung*, Paul Hindemith's *The Long Christmas Dinner*, Hector Berlioz's *Béatrice et Bénédict*, and Menotti's *Maria Golovin*. During the early years, several young artists who went on to international careers performed with the company—James McCracken, John Reardon, Judith Raskin, Charles Anthony, Reri Grist, John Alexander, Morley Meredith, Shirley Verrett, George Shirley, Donald Gramm, Justino Díaz, and James Morris.

The second United States production of Monteverdi's *L'infedelta delusa* on November 25, 1966, welcomed the Opera Society into its second decade. Jules Massenet's *Werther* followed on January 13, 1967, and a few months later, the world premiere of Alberto Ginastera's *Bomarzo* took place. A dark season ensued. When the Society resumed operations, Menotti directed his *The Medium* with Regina Resnick and Judith Blegen, and his *Amahl and the Night Visitors* with Julian Patrick. Next came Giacomo Puccini's *Manon Lescaut* followed by the professional premiere of Francesco Cavalli's *Ormindo* on May 22, 1969. The 1969-70 season balanced Rossini's rarely-performed *Le Comte Ory* with Britten's *The Turn of the Screw*. The company's last season before moving into the newly built Kennedy Center featured the United States premiere of Frederick Delius's *Koanga* as its sole offering.

The world premiere of Alberto Ginastera's *Beatrix Cenci* on September 10, 1971, welcomed the company into its new home, the John Fitzgerald Kennedy Center for the Performing Arts. The inaugural cast featured Arlene Saunders as Beatrix Cenci and Díaz as Count Francesco Cenci. The United States premiere of Delius's *A Village Romeo and Juliet* with Patricia Wells and Reardon was the season's other highlight. The emphasis on neglected masterpieces and twentieth-century works continued during the first few seasons at the Kennedy Center when Kurt Weill's *Aufstieg und Fall der Stadt Mahagonny*, Stravinsky's *The Rake's Progress*, and Monteverdi's *L'incoronazione di Poppea* and *Il ritorno di Ulisse in patria* graced the stage. Talented young artists still populated the casts: Alan Titus, Paul Plishka, Frederica von Stade, Maria Ewing, Richard Stilwell, Catherine Malfitano, Leona Mitchell, and Neil Shicoff. As the 1970s progressed, the company's repertory turned more mainstream and its cast more "star" oriented. "War horses" began to grace the stage, and internationally-known artists began to decorated the roster— Evelyn Lear, Ermanno Mauro, Nicolai Gedda, Carol Neblett, Cornell MacNeil, and Tatiana Troyanos. A few unusual works remained in the repertory, including Massenet's *Thaïs*, Verdi's *Attila*, Thomas Pasatieri's *The Seagull*, and Vincenzo Bellini's *I Capuleti ed i Montecchi*.

In 1975, George London, formulating ambitious plans for the company's expansion, was appointed general director. Two years later he suffered a stroke, bringing his ambitions to a sudden halt. The burden fell to Gary Fifield, managing director, and Francis Rizzo, artistic administrator, to carry out London's plans. The company's name was changed to The Washington Opera in 1977, because it was felt that "Opera Society" perpetrated elitism. When Martin Feinstein took charge in 1980, he expanded the season to seven productions, utilizing the Opera House for "grand opera" and the 475-seat Terrace Theater for the twentieth-century works and eighteenth-century revivals. Among the Opera House productions were

Richard Wagner's *Tristan und Isolde*, Verdi's *Un ballo in maschera*, *Falstaff*, *La forza del destino*, *La traviata*, and *Aida*, Italo Montemezzi's *L'amore dei tre re*, and Pyotr Il'yich Tchaikovsky's *Pikovaya dama*. The Terrace Theater saw Georg Friedrich Händel's *Semele*, Dominick Argento's *Postcard from Morocco*, Stravinsky's *The Rake's Progress*, Johann Strauß's *Wiener Blut*, and Britten's *The Turn of the Screw*. The small size of the Terrace Theater did not prove financially viable, and since the 1987-88 season, the 1,142-seat Eisenhower Theater has been the company's second performing venue. The Eisenhower has hosted Pietro Mascagni's *L'amico Fritz*, Stephen Paulus's *The Postman Always Rings Twice*, Argento's *The Aspern Papers*, Otto Nicolai's *Die lustigen Weiber von Windsor*, and Menotti's *The Consul* among its offerings. The company's only world premiere during the 1980s, Menotti's *Goya* with Plácido Domingo creating the title role, took place on November 15, 1986. Menotti had also directed Washington's productions of his *The Telephone*, *The Medium*, and *The Consul*, as well as Puccini's *La bohème* and *Tosca*, Rossini's *La Cenerentola*, and Tchaikovsky's *Eugene Onegin*.

Strauss's *Salome* with Ewing in the title role ushered in the 1990s. Highlights in the Opera House included Leoš Janáček's *Příhody Lišky Bystroušky* (The Cunning Little Vixen), Eugen d'Albert's *Tiefland*, and the company's first world premiere of decade, Argento's *The Dream of Valentino* (January 15, 1994). Revivals of neglected masterpieces and twentieth-century works inhabited the Eisenhower Theater: Henry Purcell's *King Arthur*, Händel's *Agrippina*, Menotti directing his *The Saint of Bleecker Street*, and the American premiere of Jin Xiang's *The Savage Land*. The casts combine established singers with what Feinstein labels "youth and beauty" artists. (What they lack in voice and experience, they make up for with youth and beauty.) Feinstein considers The Washington Opera sandwiched between "star-power dependent" companies (The Met and Lyric Opera of Chicago) and the companies whose mission is to showcase young aspiring American singers (New York City Opera). Feinstein has two goals: to expand the season to eight operas and to offer twentieth-century, avant-garde pieces performed by young singers in the Terrace Theater with a top ticket price of $15.

Feinstein characterizes himself as a Broadway producer and runs the company like an old-style impresario. His word is the final word, and he attends every rehearsal and every performance. If he does not like something, he changes it, and if the person does not agree, he fires him. He could not do that with Monteverdi's *L'incoronazione di Poppea*, which he feels is his only "disaster." So he did something he rarely does, compromise, resulting in what for him was a controversial and unsatisfying outcome. Another major problem occurred with Aprile Millo. He had signed her to sing Aida before she hit stardom—and star fees. By the time Millo arrived in Washington to sing her opening night Aida, she was a "big name" artist. Although she appeared for opening night, by the second performance, she merely walked on stage, said she did not feel like singing, and walked off. After canceling several performances, she returned for the final Verdi's *Aida*.

The productions are conservative, although there have been exceptions. In one case, an updated production of Jacques Offenbach's *Les Contes d'Hoffmann* bore no relationship to the opera or the composer's intent. Set in a 1920s Parisian cafe with the "students" implausibly dressed in white tie and tails, the opera held Olympia's "coming-out" party in a post-Bauhaus sterile environment, and Giulietta's "business" in a Trump Tower apartment. The most unbelievable part was the casting in the non-singing part of Stella, a "woman-of-a-certain-age" whose primary qualification was donating money to the Washington Opera. Even opera is not immune to perks and politics in Washington! And purists should also be warned. Feinstein sometimes economizes his effects and endings. Strobe lights are frequently employed for storm scenes and other special effects, temporarily blinding the audience to all stage activity. In Mozart's *Don Giovanni*, the lecher simply jumped into the orchestra pit, and in Wagner's *Der fliegende Holländer*, the doomed couple sank with the ship, never rising to heaven. In Puccini's *Turandot*, he subscribed to an (inappropriate) trumpet fanfare ending written by a young American conductor/composer and disapproved of by Ricordi, among others. Recently, however, the company has upgraded its productions. Leoš Janáček's *Příhody Lišky Bystroušky* (The Cunning Little Vixen) was technically as sophisticated and exhilarating as anything staged at the major houses, and the sets for Puccini's *Turandot* were as monumental as those in the top Italian opera houses. The Washington Opera is on the verge of joining the international circuit, especially with the appointment of Placído Domingo as Artistic Director beginning in 1996.

The seven-opera season offers a mixed repertory of standard and unusual works, with at least one contemporary piece, in a repertory block system. Recent productions include Verdi's *Un ballo in maschera*, Giacomo Puccini's *Madama Butterfly*, Donizetti's *Le fille du régiment*, Georges Bizet's *Les pêcheurs de perles*, Strauss's *Ariadne auf Naxos*, and d'Albert's *Tiefland*. The company performs in the Opera House and Eisenhower Theater in the Kennedy Center for the Performing Arts.

Kennedy Center for the Performing Arts

On September 8, 1971, Leonard Bernstein's *Mass*, (a theater piece for singers, players, and dancers) written in memory of President Kennedy, formally opened the Opera House. The following evening, Isaac Stern and the National Symphony under the baton of Antal Dorati opened the Concert Hall. Henrik Ibsen's *A Doll's House* starring Claire Bloom dedicated the Eisenhower Theater on October 18, 1971. The story of the Kennedy Center began on September 2, 1958, when President Dwight David Eisenhower signed the National Cultural Center Act. Thirteen years passed between the signing of the Act and the Center's inauguration. Problems plagued the project from the outset. The favored location for the Center was the site where the Air and Space Museum was slated to be built, so Foggy Bottom was chosen instead. Then the architect Edward Durell Stone designed an extremely impractical and outrageously expensive ($75 million) building. Shaped like a clamshell, the Center was to be entered from the Potomac River with the patrons arriving by barge! Eventually Stone reshaped the building into a rectangle, planted the entrance firmly on the ground, and cut the price by half. The original funding was private, but after President John Kennedy was assassinated, the Center was turned into a living memorial to the slain President. President Lyndon Baines Johnson broke ground for the Kennedy Center on December 2, 1964. Almost seven years passed before the Center was completed. Stone had underestimated the cost of construction by almost fifty percent.

The Kennedy Center is not only home to the Washington Opera, but also hosts some of the great opera companies of the world. Teatro alla Scala, Paris Opéra, Staatsoper Wien, Peking Opera, and Deutsche Oper have all paid visits. The Center's crowning operatic achievement came in June 1989, when it produced

Götz Friedrich's "tunnel" Ring, brought by the Deutsche Oper. A visit by Andrew Lloyd Weber's *Phantom of the Opera* demonstrated the versatility of the Opera House. The show recreated the Paris Opéra of 1896, complete with the crystal chandelier that plummets into the orchestra.

The Kennedy Center looms over the Potomac, an enormous rectangular box of white travertine marble. THE JOHN F. KENNEDY MEMORIAL CENTER FOR THE PERFORMING ARTS in brass letters is affixed to the middle of the building. Slender gold columns ring the structure which boasts two fifty-foot high glass entrances, one leading into the Hall of States, and the other into the Hall of Nations. Anchored to the marble on the right of the Hall of States entrance is EISENHOWER THEATER in bronze letters. OPERA HOUSE in bronze letters is to the left. The cream-colored, red and gold Opera House lobby rises in three levels. Open to the Grand Foyer, it overlooks the bust of John Fitzgerald Kennedy. The auditorium swims with panels of red plush fabric separated by large brass buttons that radiate like rays of sun from the center ceiling dome. A red-and-gold curtain hangs in the proscenium. The huge center dome houses a crystal sunburst chandelier. The opera house seats 2,250.

A bust of Eisenhower inhabits the red-and-white lobby of the Eisenhower Theater. The auditorium boasts two plain black tiers rising above red velvet plush seats. The ceiling is covered with red plush cloth. Vertical strips of gold balls wind around the proscenium, and separate the dark wood panels covering the side walls. A red-and-black, geometric-patterned curtain covers the stage. The Eisenhower Theater seats 1,150.

Practical Information. The Kennedy Center is located on its own plaza at the end of New Hampshire Avenue N.W. The box office for the Opera House and Eisenhower Theater is in the Hall of States and is open 10:00 A.M. to 9:00 P.M., Monday through Saturday, and 12:00 noon to 9:00 P.M., Sunday and holidays. Tickets can be ordered by telephoning 202-416-7800 or 1-800-876-7372, Monday through Friday between 9:00 A.M. and 5:00 P.M., by faxing 202-416-7857 anytime, or by writing The Washington Opera, Kennedy Center, Washington D.C. 20566. If you go, stay at the Four Seasons, 2800 Pennsylvania Avenue, N.W., Washington D.C. 20007; telephone 202-342-0444, fax 202-944-2076, reservations 1-800-332-3442. The hotel is a luxurious establishment a few blocks from the opera house.

COMPANY STAFF AND REPERTORY

General/Artistic Directors. Day Thorpe (1956–1960); Bliss Herbert (1961–1963); Paul Callaway (music director, 1963–1967); Richard Pearlman (1968–70); Frank Marchlenski (business manager, 1970–72); Ian Strasfogel (1972–75); George London (1975–77); Gary Fifield/Frank Rizzo (acting, 1977–79); Martin Feinstein (1980–present).

World Premieres. (before Washington Opera); Jacobi's *Sybil* (December 27, 1915); Kern's *Show Boat* (November 15, 1927); Menotti's *The Unicorn, Gorgon and Manticore* (October 19, 1956).

American Premieres (before Washington Opera). von Winter's *The Peasant Boy* (Summer 1811); Puccini's *Madama Butterfly* (in English, October 15, 1906); Vaughan Williams's *Hugh the Drover* (February 21, 1928); Haydn's *L'isola disabitata* (in English as The Uninhabited Island, March 9, 1936)

World Premieres (Washington Opera). Menotti's *Maria Golovin* (revised version,

Opera House Entrance from Grand Foyer in JFK Center (Washington, D.C.)

January 22, 1965); Ginastera's *Bomarzo* (May 19, 1967); Ginastera's *Beatrix Cenci* (September 10, 1971); Menotti's *Goya* (November 15, 1986); Argento's *The Dream of Valentino* (January 15, 1994).

American/United States Premieres (Washington Opera). Schoenberg's *Erwartung* (first stage performance, December 28, 1960); Hindemith's *The Long Christmas Dinner* (March 18, 1963); Berlioz's *Béatrice et Bénédict* (in English, first stage performance, June 3, 1964); Cavalli's *Ormindo* (first professional performance, May 22, 1969); Delius's *Koanga* (December 18, 1970); Delius's *A Village Romeo and Juliet* (April 26, 1972); Monteverdi's *Il ritorno di Ulisse in Patria* (January 18, 1974); Jin Xiang's *Savage Land* (January 18, 1992)

World Premieres (Kennedy Center, other than Washington Opera). Bernstein's *Mass* (September 8, 1971).

American/United States Premieres. (Kennedy Center, other than the Washington Opera). Kovařovic's *Psohlavci* (April 1972); Cimarosa's *Il mercato di malmantile* (revision of La vanita delusa, October 5, 1974); Händel's *Poro* (January 8, 1978); Holliger's *Not I* (May 31, 1981); Dvořák's *Cert a Káča* (June 20, 1981); Menotti's *The Bride from Pluto* (children's opera, April 12, 1982); Glass's *The Panther* (June 1982); Skroup's *Dráteník* (March 5, 1983); Dvořák's *Král a uhlíř* (spring 1984); Bernstein's *A Quiet Place* (revised version, July 20, 1984); Händel's *Alessandro* (April 21, 1985); (Claude-Michel) Schönberg's *Les Misérables* (in English, revised, December 20, 1986).

Repertory (Washington Opera). **1956-57:** Die Entführung aus dem Serail, The Old Maid and The Thief/The Unicorn, The Gorgon and the Manticore. **1957-58:** Fidelio, Ariadne auf Naxos, Così fan tutte. **1958-59:** Le nozze di Figaro, The Rake's Progress, Falstaff, La favola d'Orfeo. **1959-60:** Don Giovanni, Pelléas et Mélisande, Otello. **1960-61:** Pikovaya dama (Queen of Spades), Erwartung/Le rossignol, Idomeneo. Carmen. **1961-62:** La traviata, Die Zauberflöte, L'heure espagnole/Oedipus Rex, Ariadne auf Naxos. **1962-63:** Così fan tutte, Gianni Schicchi/L'enfant et les sortilèges, Il barbiere di Siviglia. The Demon (ballet)/The Long Christmas Dinner. **1963-64:** Vanessa, Die Entführung aus dem Serail, Tosca, Béatrice et Bénédict. **1964-65:** Le nozze di Figaro, Maria Golovin, Madama Butterfly, Natalia Petrovna. **1965-66:** Faust, Die Zauberflöte, The Rape of Lucretia, El Retablo de Maese Pedro/El Amor Brujo. **1966-67:** L'infedelta delusa, Werther, Bomarzo. **1967-68:** no performances. **1968-69:** Amahl and the Night Visitors/The Medium, Manon Lescaut, Ormindo. **1969-70:** Le Comte Ory, The Turn of the Screw, La bohème. **1970-71:** Koanga. **1971-72:** Beatrix Cenci, Falstaff, A Village Romeo and Juliet. **1972-73:** Aufstieg und Fall der Stadt Mahagonny, Così fan tutte, The Rake's Progress, L'incoronazione di Poppea. **1973-74:** Macbeth, Il barbiere di Siviglia, Il ritorno di Ulisse in patria, Il tabarro/Gianni Schicchi, Manon. **1974-75:** L'incoronazione di Poppea, Die Walküre, Salome. **1975-76:** L'italiana in Algeri, Otello, Thaïs. **1976-77:** Attila, Madama Butterfly, Werther. **1977-78:** Die Zauberflöte, L'elisir d'amore, The Seagull, Tosca. **1978-79:** Die Entführung aus dem Serail, I Capuleti ed i Montecchi, Don Pasquale. **1979-80:** Der Schauspieldirektor/Abu Hassan, Postcard from Morocco, Christopher Columbus, Il furioso all'isola di San Domingo, Cendrillon, La traviata, Tristan und Isolde, Lucia di Lammermoor. **1980-81:** Un ballo in maschera, Semele, Il barbiere di Siviglia, Wiener Blut, Postcard from Morocco, Madama Butterfly, L'amore dei tre re. **1981-82:** La bohème, Macbeth, Die Zauberflöte, The Rake's Progress, L'elisir d'amore, Trial by Jury/Monsieur Choufleuri, Il barbiere di Siviglia. **1982-83:** Carmen, Falstaff, Tosca, La Cenerentola, The Turn of the Screw, Die Entführung aus dem Serail, Trial by Jury/Monsieur Choufleuri. **1983-84:** Così fan tutte, Rigoletto, La belle Hélène, Semele, L'elisir d'amore, The Telephone/The Medium, La Cenerentola. **1984-85:** La bohème, Die lustige Witwe, Le nozze di Figaro, La sonnambula, The Telephone/The Medium, L'italiana in Algeri, The Rake's Progress. **1985-86:** Don Giovanni, Eugene Onegin, Un ballo in maschera, La fille du régiment, Christopher Columbus. **1986-87:** Il trovatore, The Tsar's Bride, Goya, Il matrimonio segreto, Don Pasquale, Die Entführung aus dem Serail, Wiener Blut, L'incoronazione di Poppea. **1987-88:** Roméo et Juliette, Madama Butterfly, L'amico Fritz, Ruddigore, L'italiana in Algeri, The Consul, Fidelio, Cendrillon. **1988-89:** Tosca, La traviata, Il barbiere di Siviglia, Der Schauspieldirektor/Abu Hassan, The Postman Always Rings Twice, Pikovaya dama (Queen of Spades), La forza del destino. **1989-90:** Lucia di Lammermoor, Così fan tutte, Die lustigen Weiber von Windsor, Werther, The Aspern Papers, Aida, Die Fledermaus. **1990-91:** Salome, La bohème, Die Zauberflöte, King Arthur, The Saint of Bleecker Street, Manon, Rigoletto. **1991-92:** Don Carlo, Don Giovanni, Les contes d'Hoffmann, Agrippina, Savage Land, Cavalleria rusticana/I pagliacci, Der fliegende Holländer. **1992-93:** Otello, The Czar's Bride, Don Pasquale, Les pêcheurs de perles, La Cenerentola, Turandot, Příhody Lišky Bystroušky (The Cunning Little Vixen). **1993-94:** Anna Bolena, Tiefland, Le fille du régiment, Ariadne auf Naxos, The Dream of Valentine, Un ballo in maschera, Madama Butterfly.

Florida
─────────── FORT LAUDERDALE

• *Fort Lauderdale Opera* •

Gaetano Donizetti's *La fille du Regiment* was the inaugural work of the Fort Lauderdale Opera. Sung in English, the opera opened on April 17, 1991, in the Amaturo Theater of the Broward Center for the Performing Arts. After forty-seven years of presenting opera, the Fort Lauderdale Opera Guild began producing opera under the name Fort Lauderdale Opera.

Opera in Fort Lauderdale dates back to January 10, 1945, when Giuseppe

Broward Center for the Performing Arts (Fort Lauderdale, Florida).

Verdi's *Il trovatore*, sung in English, was staged at the Fort Lauderdale Central High School Auditorium. Three determined Fort Lauderdale women decided that their city needed opera and founded the Opera Guild to bring the Greater Miami Opera to their city. They persuaded Arturo di Filippi, the founder of the company (see Miami entry) to make the forty mile trek to Fort Lauderdale. Di Filippi, himself, sang Manrico in Verdi's *Il trovatore*. The production cost $750. During the next three seasons, Fort Lauderdale saw Charles Gounod's *Faust*, Giacomo Puccini's *La bohème* and *Madama Butterfly*.

The Opera Guild was incorporated in 1949, and the War Memorial Auditorium opened its doors the following year. During the next four decades, the Guild presented the Greater Miami Opera in the Auditorium. Many unforgettable performances took place. In 1956, Eleanor Steber sang Fiordiligi in Mozart's *Così fan tutte*, and the next year Cesare Siepi performed Méphistophélès in Charles Gounod's *Faust*. Risë Stevens appeared as Carmen in 1960, and Renata Tebaldi in Umberto Giordano's *Andrea Chénier* four years later. Fort Lauderdale witnessed Luciano Pavarotti and Joan Sutherland in Donizetti's *Lucia di Lammermoor* in 1965, and Pavarotti and Mirella Freni in Puccini's *La bohème* in 1978. Until 1967, the Guild presented one opera a season. At that time, they expanded the repertory to two works. A third opera was added in 1983, and a fourth in 1988. The next year, the Guild ventured into the world of producing opera. First there was a joint production of Franz Lehár's *Die lustige Witwe* with the Gold Coast Opera. Then, spurred by the opening of the Broward Center for the Performing Arts, the Guild hired Marvin David Levy as artistic director in 1990, signaling a permanent expansion of its producing role.

Levy opened his first season as artistic director on September 21, 1991, with

Gian Carlo Menotti's *The Saint of Bleecker Street*, testing the audience's and board's reaction to something new and contemporary (for Fort Lauderdale). *The Saint* was the first opera to grace the stage of the newly opened Au-Rene Theater at the Broward Center. One of Levy's goals is to cultivate a younger audience. This he feels would allow him to present more contemporary and experimental works. He is currently saddled with an aging audience and a board set in their ways, restricting experimentation and limiting production of contemporary operas to those that are "in a Romantic vein." His initial emphasis is on baroque, classic, and the *bel canto* repertory, which he makes "come alive in the twentieth century, but in a traditional way." Instead of updating the operas, they are made applicable through more subtle means. For example, the characters in the inaugural Donizetti's *La fille du régiment* parodied themselves in the absurdity of the opera.

The inaugural season of the Fort Lauderdale Opera was the swan song of the Greater Miami Opera visits to Fort Lauderdale. There was a disagreement between the two companies with the Greater Miami Opera insisting that Fort Lauderdale take all or none of their productions. Since Fort Lauderdale wanted only a couple, the visits ended. Instead, the Fort Lauderdale Opera and the Palm Beach Opera have formed a Florida Opera Consortium to share productions and cut production costs since both cities have new performing arts complexes. However, at the end of 1993, the Opera Guild of Ft. Lauderdale requested that the Greater Miami Opera manage their administrative activities.

The three-opera season offers mainstream repertory in the *stagione* system. The productions are traditional. Recent operas include Puccini's *La bohème*, Verdi's *Aida*, and Gioachino Rossini's *L'italiana in Algeri*. The company performs in the Broward Center for the Performing Arts.

Broward Center for the Performing Arts

A gala performance of Andrew Lloyd Webber's *Phantom of the Opera* inaugurated the Broward Center for the Performing Arts on February 26, 1991. Designed by Benjamin Thompson & Associates, the Center cost $54 million to build. Located in a former slum, the Center is part of a $100 million redevelopment project. The performing arts complex houses two auditoriums — Au-Rene Theater and the Amaturo Theater.

An imposing curved building of Italian Mediterranean-style, the complex is identified by BROWARD CENTER FOR PERFORMING ARTS in large bronze letters. Columnar textured stucco, glass, and wrought iron define the façade. The entrance foyer boasts Mexican marble and keystone, in which the aquatic fossils are visible. An expansive lobby curves gently around the building, soaring more than fifty feet to glass panels. The two-tier auditorium is horseshoe-configured. Cherry wood shutters and lattices conceal a system of absorptive draperies, banners, and reflective panels that allow the theater to be fine-tuned according to the acoustic requirements of the performance. Turquoise fabric orchestra and balcony seats contrast with the red fabric box and balcony seats. The lattice-style rattan proscenium frames a turquoise velvet curtain. The Au-Rene Theater seats 2,725. The Amaturo Theater holds a horseshoe-shaped auditorium of spruce wood and simulated stone. Red velvet plush seats contrast with purple velvet plush seats, and wood outlines a plain proscenium. The Amaturo Theater seats 595.

Practical Information. The Broward Center for the Performing Arts is at 201

Southwest Fifth Avenue. Tickets are available from the Fort Lauderdale Opera Guild offices, 333 Southwest Second Street between 9:30 A.M. and 5:00 P.M. weekdays, by telephoning 305-728-9700 during the above times, or by writing The Opera Guild, Inc., 333 Southwest 2nd Street, Fort Lauderdale, FL 33312. If you go, stay at the Hyatt, 400 S.E. Second Avenue, Miami, FL 33131; telephone 305-358-1234, fax 305-374-1728, reservations 1-800-233-1234. The Hyatt is a comfortable hotel offering magnificent views. It is a pleasant drive up I-95 to the Broward Center.

COMPANY STAFF AND REPERTORY

General/Artistic Director. Marvin David Levy (1990–present)

Repertory. 1990-91: Turandot (Greater Miami Opera production), Cavalleria rusticana/I pagliacci (Greater Miami Opera production), La fille du régiment, Le nozze di Figaro. 1991-92: The Saint of Bleecker Street, Otello (Palm Beach Opera production), Manon Lescaut (Greater Miami Opera production), Macbeth (Greater Miami Opera production). 1992-93: Aida, L'italiana in Algeri, La bohème.

FORT PIERCE

• *Treasure Coast Opera* •

Giacomo Puccini's *Madama Butterfly* inaugurated the Treasure Coast Opera Company at the Westwood High School Auditorium in April 1979. Puccini's *La bohème* and Pietro Mascagni's *Cavalleria rusticana* completed the first season. The tremendous need for cultural arts in the Fort Pierce area inspired Anne Abood, Patricia Hawkes and Carlos Battena to found the Treasure Coast Opera Society. Barrena organized the company and continued to act as general director.

Established talent and up-and-coming stars perform in the lead roles with local talent supporting them in secondary roles and the chorus. Recent productions include Verdi's *La traviata*, Romberg's *The Student Prince* and Puccini's *Madama Butterfly*. The three-opera season is presented in the St. Lucie County Civic Center.

Practical Information: The St. Lucie County Civic Center is located at 2300 Virginia Avenue. Tickets can be purchased by calling (407) 465-6204 or by writing the Treasure Coast Opera Society at 1309 Indiana Avenue, Fort Pierce, FL 34950.

MIAMI

• *Greater Miami Opera* •

The Miami Opera was born with a performance of Ruggero Leoncavallo's *I pagliacci* on February 14, 1942, in the Miami High School auditorium. It was the only opera offered during the inaugural season. The production, which cost $1,700, saw the cast singing in Italian and the chorus in English. Arturo di Filippi, who sang Canio (the obsessively jealous clown in Leoncavallo's *Pagliacci*), founded and guided the company for thirty years. Dr. Di, as he was affectionately called, was a voice teacher at the University of Miami when he decided that his students needed a place to perform and gave Miami an opera company.

Miami had seen some opera before 1942, when traveling troupes wanted sunshine and warm weather, but it was not until the formation of the Miami Opera that opera was performed regularly. For the first five years, the company staged one opera each season from the popular Italian and French repertory—Giuseppe Verdi's *La traviata* and *Il trovatore*, Georges Bizet's *Carmen*, and Charles Gounod's *Faust* among them. Dr. Di sang every year until 1946. Anthony Stivanello had joined the company the previous season as stage director, a position held for thirty years. The 1950s signalled growth for the company. Emerson Buckley was appointed resident conductor, and the company moved out of the Miami High School and into the Dade County Auditorium. Miami inaugurated its new home with Bizet's *Carmen* on February 24, 1952. The company also performed in the Miami Beach Auditorium and in Fort Lauderdale's War Memorial Auditorium. To reflect the larger area it served, Greater was added to its name.

Dr. Di's association with the Met brought star-studded casts and ushered in an era of unparalleled vocal splendor. Regina Resnik (*Cavalleria rusticana*), Eleanor Steber (*La traviata* and *Così fan tutte*), Licia Albanese (*Madama Butterfly*), Jussi Bjoerling (*Il trovatore*), Robert Merrill (*Il barbiere di Siviglia*), Cesare Siepi (*Faust*), Renata Tebaldi (*Andrea Chénier*), and Lucine Amara and George London (*Aida*) were some of the artists. The stars shone especially bright in 1962. Birgit Nilsson made her first Miami appearance as the ice princess in Giacomo Puccini's *Turandot*, and Richard Tucker and Phyllis Curtain sang in Verdi's *La traviata*. Tucker, however, was not scheduled to sing Alfredo. Dino Formichini was, but he came down with bronchitis a few hours before curtain time. Tucker was vacationing in Miami and Dr. Di found him sunbathing on the beach and saved the performance. History was made in Miami in 1965 when, as a result of a cancellation, Luciano Pavarotti made his American debut as Edgardo in Gaetano Donizetti's *Lucia di Lammermoor*. Joan Sutherland sang the title role. She received all the attention and money ($7,500)—until the curtain fell. Three years later another unknown tenor appeared in Miami, Plácido Domingo, who sang Riccardo in Verdi's *Un ballo in maschera*.

Dr. Di was willing to take chances on new performers; it was the new operas that he shunned. Although he occasionally staged rarely-performed works—Léo Delibes's *Lakmé* in 1964 and Ambroise Thomas's *Mignon* in 1967—the repertory maintained a conservative bias. It was the productions that were flamboyant. Di Filippi loved animals in his operas. Whenever the opera justified it, animals paraded, marched, or flew on stage with the singers. Some liked it so much, they did not want to leave. For example, the opening of Amilcare Ponchielli's *La gioconda* takes place in St. Mark's Square in Venice, where a festive crowd tosses doves skyward. For the company's production, di Filippi tried to import doves from Italy. When that proved impractical, he settled for Miami pigeons. All the birds flew upwards on cue. The problem came six weeks later when some of them were still ensconced in the rafters! That did not stop Dr. Di from using animals in Verdi's *Aida*. After the stage was tested with water-filled trucks, two small elephants arrived from Sarasota's Ringling Circus. Although the stage was strong enough, the stage door was not wide enough and one of the pachyderms could not fit through. Dr. Di ordered the overweight elephant on a crash diet and both elephants made their operatic debuts on schedule. It was a horse named Verdi, also in town for Verdi's *Aida*, that caused all the trouble. He was marching in *Aida*, and when startled by the strange surroundings, he created a nuisance in the midst of the stage. When an attendant come out to clean up the mess, the audience howled so long and hard that it ruined the rest of the performance.

After di Filippi's death in 1972, Lorenzo Alvary was named general director. He lasted six months. Robert Herman took the reins in 1973, and put the company on the national map. He ushered in an era that not only continued to feature star-studded casts, but also topnotch stage directors and designers. Under his reign, painted backdrops and balanced budgets became history. In his first season, the budget soared from $600,000 to $1.1 million. Since Herman could not change the 1974 season schedule, he put his stamp on the productions. Umberto Giordano's *Andrea Chénier*, featuring Gilda Cruz-Romo and Carlo Bergonzi, opened the season with Peter Hall–designed sets from the Dallas Opera. Robert O'Hearn designed the next production, Bizet's *Les pêcheurs de perles*, which Fabrizio Melano directed. Miami also staged its first contemporary American opera that season, Robert Ward's *The Crucible*. Although the house was sold out, the auditorium was only half full when the curtain went up. At the end of Act I, a quarter of those people had left. Miami was slow to accept new works.

During the next four seasons, operas that were standard fare in other companies were finally given their Miami premieres. The first German opera, Richard Wagner's *Der fliegende Holländer*, was mounted in 1975, and the first Russian opera, Modest Mussorgsky's *Boris Godunov*, graced the stage two years later. Verdi's Shakespeare trilogy—*Otello, Macbeth,* and *Falstaff* also arrived. The sudden wealth of unfamiliar operas took its toll on subscription renewals. The older, conservative, Miami audience was too set in its ways to enjoy unfamiliar works. For survival, the repertory reverted to the old standards. Nevertheless, an infrequently performed Verdi work, *Nabucco*, presented during the 1981 season was a smashing success. With Sherrill Milnes in the title role and a theme of enslaved Israelites, how could it not be!

That same season, Pavarotti sang Cavaradossi in Puccini's *Tosca*. Few who heard him knew of the rehearsal accident that almost canceled the production. In the final act, a firing squad shoots Cavaradossi for aiding the political prisoner Angelotti. This firing squad took their role seriously. They aimed directly at Pavarotti instead of at his side, as is usual. A piece of wadding hit him in the face and Pavarotti was fuming. The wadding, fortunately, had only grazed his cheek and the performance went on. The casts in Miami remained star-studded, and the roster read like the Met's: Franco Corelli (*Romeo et Juliette*), Jon Vickers (*Otello*), Teresa Zylis-Gara (*Otello, Adriana Lecouvreur* and *Manon Lescaut*), Teresa Stratas (*La Perichole*), Cesare Siepi (*Boris Godunov*), Plácido Domingo (*La fanciulla del West, Adriana Lecouvreur,* and *Andrea Chénier*), Mirella Freni (*La bohème*), Tatiana Troyanos (*Don Carlo*), and Beverly Sills (*Die Fledermaus*).

In 1974, Herman introduced a National Series to make opera accessible to a broader cross-section of the population and to showcase talented, young singers. The series paralleled the star-studded International Series, but the ticket prices were a fraction of the cost. The *coup d'état* of Herman's reign came in 1980 with

Jacques Offenbach's *Les contes d'Hoffmann*. The conductor, Antonio de Almeida, had recently discovered a portion of the original opera score believed lost in the fire that destroyed the Opéra Comique in 1887. It was incorporated into the opera and garnered national attention, and on January 14, 1980, the American premiere of the Fritz Oeser version of Offenbach's *Les contes d'Hoffmann* took place. Herman's biggest failure was the ill-fated New World Festival of the Arts. The Festival was designed to boost Miami tourism during the doldrums of June and to host contemporary arts. Under the auspices of the festival, Miami's first world premiere, Ward's *Minutes till Midnight*, took place on June 4, 1982. The work dealt with the moral dilemmas faced by scientists who have the knowledge to create weapons which can destroy society. Designed by Günther Schneider-Siemssen and directed by Nathaniel Merrill, the production featured Thomas Stewart and Evelyn Lear. Nevertheless, it failed. Criticized for a weak libretto and old-fashioned music, the opera has never been revived.

Robert Heuer took the helm in 1986 and tried to expand both the repertory and the operagoers' tastes. For a time he succeeded. The company introduced Richard Strauss's *Salome* and Thomas's rarely-staged *Hamlet*. Four Wolfgang Amadeus Mozart works then appeared in successive seasons — *Don Giovanni*, *Le nozze di Figaro*, *Idomeneo*, and *Così fan tutte*. Until then, only four Mozart operas had been seen in the first forty-five years! The provocative contemporary opera, Stephen Paulus's *The Postman Always Rings Twice*, rang for the first time in Miami, amid many protests, during the 1987-1988 season. That same season saw the American premiere of Alberto Rossini's *Bianca e Falliero*. This long-forgotten Rossini opera was world premiered at Teatro alla Scala on December 26, 1819. Revived in 1831, it disappeared from the stage for over a century until the Rossini Festival in Pesaro (Italy) revived it in 1986. The Miami Opera celebrated its fiftieth anniversary season with the same work that launched the company — Leoncavallo's *I pagliacci*. This *Pagliacci*, however, cost almost $700,000. During the golden anniversary season, the company tried to attract newcomers with a unique marketing approach. It offered a money-back guarantee to anyone who purchased a ticket to a Friday evening Verdi's *Falstaff* and was not satisfied. Two thousand attended and only four asked for refunds. Their reasons were suspect — "Falstaff was not jovial enough," said one couple. "The English surtitles caught me off guard," remarked another. "I was disappointed," stated a young man.

For the 1990s, Heuer's goal is a twentieth-century opera every other season and rarely performed gems during the alternate seasons. Launching the novelties in the 1990s was the world premiere of the revised version of Carlisle Floyd's *The Passion of Jonathan Wade*. To celebrate the Quincentennial of Columbus's voyage, Alberto Franchetti's *Cristoforo Colombo* followed, sailing into Miami on February 17, 1992. The production, a culmination of a ten year collaborative effort between Miami and the Franchetti family, took place amidst a "Voyage of Discovery Weekend." Budget problems forced the substitution of the planned productions of Strauss's *Elektra* and Mozart's *Die Zauberflöte* with Donizetti's *Lucia di Lammermoor*. Although Mozart's *Die Zauberflöte* was mounted the following season, Strauss's *Elektra* is still "on the boards." Miami's large Spanish-speaking population prompted the staging of Manuel de Falla's *El Retablo de Maese Pedro/El Amor Brujo/La Vida Breve* for the 1994 novelty. Stars are not so plentiful in Miami as before, prompting the discontinuation in 1994 of the "International" and "National" casts. (Not infrequently it was difficult to hear any difference between the

Dade County Auditorium (Miami, Florida).

two casts.) Although the emphasis is on quality ensemble casts, the results, with some uneven singing, have been mixed. Occasionally a "name" artist commits for the long required rehearsal periods and performs with the company. James Morris sang Wotan in Wagner's *Die Walküre* in 1989, and two years later, Sherrill Milnes portrayed his first Falstaff.

The growth of the Greater Miami Opera is hindered by its current home, the Dade County Auditorium. The performance hall is ill-suited for opera, and the voices get lost in the vast space. It is also acoustically transparent to airplane noise from nearby from Miami International Airport. Miami is planning to construct a $167 million Performing Arts Center on Biscayne Boulevard, and this would become the Greater Miami Opera's home for the twenty-first century.

The four-opera season offers the standard Italian and French repertory including one Verdi opera and one Puccini opera in a *stagione* system. There is an occasional novelty. Recent productions include Puccini's *La bohème* and *Tosca*, Verdi's *Rigoletto* and *La traviata*, Bizet's *Carmen*, and Mozart's *Die Zauberflöte*. The company performs in the Dade County Auditorium.

Dade County Auditorium

The Dade County Auditorium was erected in 1951. Designed by Steward and Skinner, Architects, the Auditorium was built by Cauldwell Scott for the County at a cost of more than $1 million. The Greater Miami Opera inaugurated the Auditorium in March 1951 with Bizet's *Carmen*. The building was completely refurbished in 1988, turning it into an Art Deco gem.

The Auditorium is a peach-painted concrete and glass building of the Art Deco Revival Style. DADE COUNTY AUDITORIUM in large silver letters across the top identifies the opera house. Palm trees flank the main entrance. The coral, baby blue, and pink lobby holds a bronze bust of di Filippi. The fan-shaped performance hall is painted twelve different shades of blue that reverberate around teal fabric seats. Midnight blue walls flank the proscenium, where a dark blue stage curtain hangs. The peach-colored rear wall and the white scalloped ceiling add contrast. One large balcony curves gently around the room. The Auditorium seats 2,438.

Practical Information. The Dade County Auditorium is at 2901 West Flagler. The ticket office is open from 9:30 A.M. to 6:00 P.M., Monday through Saturday. When there is a Sunday performance, it opens at 12:00 noon. Tickets are also available at the Greater Miami Opera, 1200 Coral Way, between 9:30 A.M. and 5:00 P.M. weekdays. Tickets can be ordered by telephoning 305-854-7890 or 1-800-741-1010, between the hours of 9:00 A.M. and 5:00 P.M. weekdays, by faxing 305-856-1042 twenty-four hours a day or writing: Greater Miami Opera, 1200 Coral Way, Miami, FL 33145-2980. If you go, stay at the Hotel Mayfair House, 3000 Florida Avenue, Coconut Grove, FL 33133; telephone 305-441-0000, fax 305-447-0173, reservations 1-800-223-6800. The hotel is so unique that it is a Coconut Grove landmark. Many rooms even boast pianos. It is convenient to the Auditorium.

COMPANY STAFF AND REPERTORY

General/Artistic Directors. Arturo di Filippi (1942–1972); Lorenzo Alvary (1972); Robert Herman (1973–1986); Robert Heuer (1986–present).

World Premieres. Ward's *Minutes till Midnight* (June 4, 1982); Floyd's *The Passion of Jonathan Wade* (revised version, March 18, 1991).

American/United States Premieres. Offenbach's *Les contes d'Hoffmann* (Oeser's critical edition, January 14, 1980); Rossini's *Bianca e Falliero* (December 7, 1987).

Repertory. 1942: I pagliacci. 1943: La traviata. 1944: Carmen. 1945: Il trovatore. 1946: Faust. 1947: La bohème, Il barbiere di Siviglia. 1948: Madama Butterfly, Rigoletto. 1949: Aida, Martha. 1950: Tosca, I pagliacci/Il segreto di Susanna. 1951: L'elisir d'amore, Carmen. 1952: Manon, Die Fledermaus. 1953: Gianni Schicchi/Cavalleria rusticana, La traviata. 1954: Madama Butterfly, Il trovatore. 1955: Il barbiere di Siviglia, Lucia di Lammermoor. 1956: Così fan tutte, La bohème. 1957: Faust, Don Pasquale. 1958: Aida, Tosca. 1959: Rigoletto, Un ballo in maschera. 1960: La gioconda, Carmen. 1961: Andrea Chénier, Martha. 1962: La traviata, Turandot. 1963: Manon, Madama Butterfly. 1964: Lakmé, L'elisir d'amore. 1965: Otello, Lucia di Lammermoor, Le nozze di Figaro. 1966: La bohème, Il trovatore. 1967: Tosca, Mignon, Cavalleria rusticana/I pagliacci. 1968: Un ballo in maschera, Die Fledermaus, Samson et Dalila. 1969: La gioconda, Faust, La forza del destino. 1970: La traviata, Rigoletto, Don Carlo. 1971: Ernani, Il barbiere di Siviglia, Les contes d'Hoffmann, Madama Butterfly. 1972: La Bohème, Manon Lescaut, Aida, Die lustige Witwe. 1973: La fille du régiment, Carmen, Werther, Il trovatore. 1974: Andrea Chénier, Lucia di Lammermoor, The Crucible, Les pêcheurs des perles. 1975: Roméo et Juliette, Der fliegende Holländer, L'elisir d'amore, Rigoletto. 1976: Otello, Don Pasquale, Thaïs, Tosca. 1977: Boris Godunov, La Périchole, Macbeth, La fanciulla del West. 1978: Falstaff, Die Entführung aus dem Serail, Adriana Lecouvreur, La bohème. 1979: Don Carlo, Il barbiere di Siviglia, Samson et Dalila, Madama Butterfly. 1980: Les contes d'Hoffmann, Mefistofele, Die Fledermaus (Rosalinda), Manon Lescaut. 1981: Nabucco, Die lustige Witwe, Carmen,

Tosca. **1982:** Simon Boccanegra, La traviata, Werther, Turandot. **1982:** New World Festival: Minutes till Midnight, Of Mice and Men. **1983:** Andrea Chénier, La Grande Duchesse de Gérolstein, Faust, Un ballo in maschera. **1984:** Lucia di Lammermoor, L'amore dei tre re, Così fan tutte, Il trovatore. **1985:** La gioconda, L'italiana in Algeri, Madama Butterfly, Ernani. **1986:** Rigoletto, La bohème, Of Mice and Men, Cavalleria rusticana/I pagliacci. **1987:** Bianca e Falliero, Salome, Hamlet, Le nozze di Figaro. **1988:** Tosca, Don Giovanni, The Postman Always Rings Twice, Otello. **1989:** Idomeneo, Il tabarro/Voix humaine, Die Walküre, La forza del destino, Les contes d'Hoffmann. **1990:** Turandot, Madama Butterfly, Il barbiere di Siviglia, Norma. **1991:** Passion of Jonathan Wade, Così fan tutte, Falstaff, Cavalleria rusticana/I pagliacci. **1992:** Lucia di Lammermoor, Cristoforo Colombo, Manon Lescaut, Macbeth. **1993:** La traviata, Tosca, Die Zauberflöte, Carmen. **1994:** La bohème, El Retablo de Maese Pedro/El Amor Brujo/La Vida Breve, Faust, Rigoletto.

——————————————————————— ORLANDO

• *Orlando Opera Company* •

The first full-length homegrown opera in Orlando, Giacomo Puccini's *La bohème*, graced the stage in 1963. The Orlando Opera was an outgrowth of gala benefits for the Florida Symphony Orchestra which began in 1958. During the first few seasons, concert arias were presented. Gradually entire staged opera scenes emerged until the first full-length opera was mounted. The Orlando Opera began its own productions in 1979.

Opera in Orlando dates back to 1927, when the La Scala Grand Opera Company paid a visit. They offered Giuseppe Verdi's *Aida* with Fidela Campigna, Gaetano Donizetti's *Lucia di Lammermoor*, Verdi's *Il trovatore*, Puccini's *Madama Butterfly*, Friedrich von Flotow's *Martha*, Charles Gounod's *Faust*, and Pietro Mascagni's *Cavalleria rusticana*/Ruggero Leoncavallo's *I pagliacci*. Other traveling troupes passed through town from time to time bringing primarily nineteenth-century Italian works. The first homegrown opera emerged with the symphony galas.

The second season of "symphony orchestra opera" saw Georges Bizet's *Carmen*. Successive seasons continued to offer one opera from the standard repertory — Verdi's *La traviata*, Puccini's *Madama Butterfly*, and Gioachino Rossini's *Il barbiere di Siviglia* among them. Plácido Domingo, Beverly Sills, and Norman Treigle highlighted the 1970 season with Jacques Offenbach's *Les contes d'Hoffmann*. With a season expansion to two works in 1971, the company mounted its first American piece, Carlisle Floyd's *Susannah*.

Donizetti's *Don Pasquale* started the Orlando Opera in the opera production business in 1979. The seasons quickly expanded from two to three offerings. The repertory remained in the popular vein. The year 1990 ushered in a new era when Robert Swedberg took the helm of the Orlando Opera. He inherited a conservative tradition which he is gradually changing by steering the company into more adventurous waters. He is creating a more balanced repertory — standard fare mixed with lesser-known works — and striving for ways to convert a community devoid of cultural history into opera-lovers, or at least operagoers.

The fall of 1991 saw the first Russian opera, Pyotr Il'yich Tchaikovsky's *Pikovaya*

Bob Carr Performing Arts Center (Orlando, Florida)

dama, performed in Orlando. A month later, Wolfgang Amadeus Mozart's *Die Zauberflöte* was given at the Lake Eola Amphitheater, an open-air theater located in a public park. Act II began and Sarastro informed the Priest of his plans. Then thousands of Haitians marched by, protesting the return of asylum-seeking Haitians to Haiti. There was no contest and the opera was stopped. When all the Haitians left, the act began over. The incident reinforced the Orlando Opera's most urgent problem — the lack of a good opera house in which to perform. Its current home, Bob Carr Performing Arts Center, is ill-suited for opera productions. The casts are composed of young American artists, and their voices get lost in the massive and acoustically poor auditorium. With the opening in 1993 of the 200-seat Dr. Phillips Center for the Performing Arts, the company was able to double its offerings, to include works suitable for small spaces, and to present a greater variety of operas.

The six-opera season offers a predominately standard repertory in a *stagione* system. These are one unusual piece and one musical. Recent productions include Verdi's *La traviata* and *Otello*, Donizetti's *Don Pasquale*, Rossini's *La Cenerentola*, Kurt Weill's *Die Dreigroschenoper*, Mitch Leigh's *Man of La Mancha*, and Bizet's *Carmen*. The company performs its grand operas in the Bob Carr Center for the Performing Arts.

Bob Car Performing Arts Center

The Bob Carr Performing Arts Center was born in 1926 as the Orlando Municipal Auditorium. Designed by Cruz and Parrish, Architects, and built by James

Peterson Construction Company, the Auditorium cost $175,000. The brick, steel, and concrete structure was erected in the classic revival style. In 1975, Thomas Price and Don Duer redesigned the building to serve as a theater/ concert hall. The remodeling cost $2.6 million, and Jerry Herman's *Hello Dolly* reopened the Auditorium on November 28, 1978.

The remodeled theater is identified by MAYOR BOB CARR PERFORMING ARTS CENTER, in large letters affixed to the building. A new façade of earth-tone brick and gray-tinted glass was built in front of the original façade, forming an outer "garden-lobby" with it. MUNICIPAL AUDITORIUM is etched above the arches and openings on the original façade. The fan-shaped auditorium is painted various shades of mauve, which lighten as they reach the rear of the room. The ceiling is black. One large balcony, shaped like the front of a sleek, modern train, curves gently around. Red velvet plush seats stretch in unbroken rows across the room. The auditorium seats 2,380.

Practical Information. The Bob Carr Performing Arts Center is at 401 West Livingston Street. The tickets are sold at the Orlando Arena box office on Revere Street in the Centroplex complex. The box office is open Monday through Saturday from 10:00 A.M. to 5:00 P.M. You can also purchase tickets directly from the Orlando Opera, 1111 North Orange, between 9:30 A.M. and 5:00 P.M. weekdays. The Bob Carr box office, to the left of the main entrance, opens one hour before curtain time. Tickets can be ordered by telephoning 1-800-336-7372 or 407-422-1700 during the above hours or by writing Orlando Opera, 1111 North Orange, Orlando, FL 32801. If you go, stay at The Peabody Orlando at Plaza International, 9801 International Drive, Orlando, FL 32819; telephone 407-352-4000, fax 407-351-0073, reservations 1-800-PEABODY (1-800-732-2639). It is famous for its March of the Royal Ducks and wonderful accommodations. It is convenient to the theater.

COMPANY STAFF AND REPERTORY

General/Artistic Director. Robert Swedberg.

Repertory. 1963: La bohème. 1964: Carmen. 1965: La traviata. 1966: Madama Butterfly. 1967: Il barbiere di Siviglia. 1968: Faust. 1969: Tosca. 1970: Les contes d'Hoffmann. 1970-71: Manon, Susannah. 1971-72: Rigoletto, Lucia di Lammermoor. 1972-73: La bohème, La rondine. 1973-74: La fille du régiment. 1974-75: Aida. 1975-76: Madama Butterfly. 1976-77: Carmen, Cavalleria rusticana/I pagliacci. 1977-78: Il trovatore, Il barbiere di Siviglia. 1978-79: Turandot, Roméo et Juliette. 1979-80: Don Pasquale. 1980-81: La traviata, Die lustige Witwe. 1981-82: Faust, Die Fledermaus. 1982-83: La bohème, Le nozze di Figaro, Noyes Fludde, Die Entführung aus dem Serail. 1983-84: Tosca, Les pêcheurs des perles, Porgy and Bess. 1984-85: Rigoletto, Die Zauberflöte, The Student Prince. 1985-86: Madama Butterfly, La traviata, Bitter Sweet. 1986-87: Der Rosenkavalier, Amahl and the Night Visitors, L'elisir d'amore, Susannah. 1987-88: Carmen, Il barbiere di Siviglia. 1988-89: Faust, Cavalleria rusticana/I pagliacci, Don Giovanni. 1989-90: Il trovatore, La bohème, L'italiana in Algeri, La nozze di Figaro. 1990-91: Les contes d'Hoffmann, Hänsel und Gretel, The Mikado. 1991-92: Pikovaya Dame, Die Zauberflöte, La fille du régiment, Rigoletto, Candide. 1992-93: Samson et Dalila, Otello, Madama Butterfly. 1993-94: Die Dreigroschenoper, La traviata, La Cenerentola, Carmen, Man of La Mancha, Don Pasquale.

———————————————————— PALM BEACH

• *Palm Beach Opera* •

Giuseppe Verdi's *La traviata* inaugurated the Palm Beach Opera (originally called the Civic Opera) on January 29, 1962, in the Palm Beach High School Auditorium. Paul Csonka was on the podium. A group of seven determined "godmothers," including Isabel Chatfield formed the company. The initial season also offered Johann Strauß's *Die Fledermaus*.

Although the company mounted two operas each season for the first two years, it was forced to scale back to one-opera seasons until 1972. The company follows a conservative philosophy, offering traditional productions of familiar repertory with established singers. The only exception was 1981, when the company offered Gian Carlo Menotti's *Amelia al ballo* and *The Medium*. Established singers perform with the company and have included Beverly Sills, Leona Mitchell, Ghena Dimitrova, and José Carreras.

The three-opera season offers primarily Italian standard repertory. Recent productions include Verdi's *Il trovatore* and Gioachino Rossini's *Il barbiere di Siviglia*. The company performs in the Kravis Center for the Performing Arts.

Kravis Center for the Performing Arts

A gala Night of the Stars opened the Kravis Center for the Performing Arts on November 28, 1992. Designed by Eberhard Zeidler, the Center cost $55 million to build. The idea for the Center was conceived almost forty years earlier, but it was not until the 1980s that the proposal came to fruition.

An imposing curved building in the Romantic Formalism style, the Center exhibits classical overtones. The soaring glass façade, interrupted with sea green metal supports, is topped by two levels of circular copper roofs. A sweeping lobby overflows with marble and boasts a grand staircase and majestic columns with gold torch-light capitals. The ivory and gold auditorium is horseshoe-shaped. Massive fluted pillars topped by golden torches circle the multi-tiered room. Maroon plush seats complement the multi-colored proscenium arch. A spider-like chandelier hangs in a center dome. There are 2,200 seats.

Practical Information. The Kravis Center for the Performing Arts is at 701 Okeechobee Boulevard. Tickets are available from the Palm Beach Opera box office, 415 South Olive Avenue, or by telephoning 407-833-7888, or by writing Palm Beach Opera, 415 South Olive Avenue, West Palm Beach, FL 33401. If you go, stay at the Ritz-Carlton Palm Beach, 100 South Ocean Boulevard, Manalapan, FL 33462; telephone 407-533-6000, fax 407-588-4202, reservations 1-800-241-3333. The Ritz-Carlton overlooks the Atlantic Ocean with magnificent views and accommodations. It is convenient to the Kravis Center.

————————————————————

COMPANY STAFF AND REPERTORY

General/Artistic Directors. Paul Csonka (1962–1983); Anton Guadagno (1984–present.

Repertory. 1962: La traviata, Die Fledermaus. 1963: La bohème, Manon. 1964: Les contes d'Hoffmann. 1965: Carmen. 1966: Madama Butterfly, Tosca. 1968: La traviata. 1969: Lucia di Lammermoor. 1970: Carmen. 1971: Rigoletto. 1972: Il barbiere di Siviglia, La bohème. 1973: Les contes d'Hoffmann, Faust. 1974: Madama Butterfly, Le nozze di Figaro, L'elisir d'amore. 1975: La traviata, Hänsel und Gretel. 1976: Die Fledermaus, Tosca, Cavalleria rusticana/I pagliacci, Il trovatore. 1977: La fille du régiment, Die lustige Witwe, Aida. 1978: Manon, Don Giovanni, Turandot. 1979: Il barbiere di Siviglia, Don Pasquale, Un ballo in maschera. 1980: La bohème, Rigoletto, Così fan tutte. 1981: Carmen, Amelia al ballo, La forza del destino, Norma, The Medium. 1982: I pagliacci, Gianni Schicchi, Adriana Lecouvreur. 1983: Lucia di Lammermoor, Il trovatore, Die Zauberflöte. 1984: Madama Butterfly, Tosca. 1985: La traviata, Nabucco, Samson et Dalila. 1986: La bohème, Faust, Manon Lescaut. 1987: Die Fledermaus, Il barbiere di Siviglia, Aida. 1988: Les contes d'Hoffmann, Carmen, L'elisir d'amore. 1989: Rigoletto, Andrea Chénier, Macbeth, La Cenerentola. 1990: Madama Butterfly, Tosca, Norma. 1991: Don Giovanni, Otello. 1992: La traviata, Aida, Don Pasquale. 1993: La bohème, Il trovatore, L'italiana in Algeri. 1994: Il barbiere di Siviglia, La forza del destino, Die Zauberflöte.

———————— POMPANO BEACH

• *Gold Coast Opera* •

Engelbert Humperdinck's *Hänsel und Gretel* inaugurated the Gold Coast Opera in 1980. Arthur Sullivan's *The Pirates of Penzance* completed the first season. Thomas Cavendish formed the Gold Coast Opera in May, 1979, as an ad hoc organization engaged to stage an opera for the 1979/80 Cultural Affairs Series of Broward Community College.

The company experienced some growth during the first three years, increasing the number of performances from one to two. The fourth season saw three operas, while also increasing the number of performances to four. The casts include both up-and-coming and established artists. Both Jerome Hines and Roberta Peters have performed with the company.

The three-opera season offers traditional fare and musical theater in a *stagione* system. Recent productions include Verdi's *La traviata* and Jerome Kern's *Showboat*. The company performs in three different venues, the 1,900-seat Broward Community College Omni Auditorium, the 1,500-seat Coral Springs City Center, and the 1,200-seat Bailey Concert Hall.

Practical Information. The Omni Auditorium is at 1000 Coconut Creek Boulevard. The City Center is at 2855 Coral Springs Drive, and the Bailey is at 3510 Southwest Davie Road. Tickets are available at the respective box offices or by writing Omni Box Office, 1000 Coconut Creek Boulevard, Pompano Beach, FL 33066, (telephone 305-973-2249); City Center Box Office, 2855 Coral Springs Drive, Coral Springs, FL 33065, (telephone 305-344-5990; Bailey Concert Box Office, Broward Community College, 3510 S.W. Davie Road, Fort Lauderdale, FL 33314, (telephone 305-475-6884). The Gold Coast Opera is at 1000 Coconut Creek Boulevard, Pompano Beach, FL 33066, telephone 305-973-2323. If you go, stay at the Ritz-Carlton Palm Beach, 100 South Ocean Boulevard, Manalapan, FL 33462; telephone 407-533-6000, fax 407-588-4202, reservations 1-800-241-3333. The

Ritz-Carlton overlooks the Atlantic Ocean with magnificent views and accommodations. It is convenient to the company's various performing venues.

COMPANY STAFF AND REPERTORY

General/Artistic Director. Thomas Cavendish (1980–present).
Repertory. **1980:** Hänsel und Gretel, Pirates of Penzance. **1981:** I pagliacci/Der Schauspieldirektor, Die Zauberflöte. **1982:** H.M.S. Pinafore, The Mikado. **1983:** Die Fledermaus, Il barbiere di Siviglia. **1984:** Carmen, Madama Butterfly, Oklahoma, Die lustige Witwe. **1985:** Don Pasquale, Kismet, The Desert Song. **1986:** Die Fledermaus, La traviata, L'elisir d'amore. **1987:** Carousel, La bohème, Man of La Mancha. **1988:** Gianni Schicchi, I pagliacci, Pirates of Penzance, The Student Prince. **1989:** Der tapfere Soldat, Die lustige Witwe, The New Moon. **1990:** La Cenerentola, Man of La Mancha, Naughty Marietta, Rigoletto. **1991:** Carmen, South Pacific, The Vagabond King. **1992:** Die Fledermaus, Madama Butterfly, Tosca. **1993:** Showboat, Camelot, Il barbiere di Siviglia. **1994:** Die Zauberflöte, La traviata.

SARASOTA

• *Sarasota Opera* •

Johann Strauß's *Die Fledermaus*, the first homegrown effort of the Sarasota Opera, opened the season in 1974. The Sarasota Opera, originally called the Asolo Opera Company, was an outgrowth of the chamber opera performances given in the Asolo State Theater. The first season balanced Christoph Gluck's eighteenth-century *Orfeo ed Euridice* with Francis Poulenc's twentieth-century *La voix humaine*. The company also staged Wolfgang Amadeus Mozart's *Così fan tutte*.

Opera in Sarasota dates back to December 27, 1926, when the San Carlo Opera Company visited. They presented Georges Bizet's *Carmen* and Friedrich von Flotow's *Martha* on the same day in the Edwards Theater. Two years later, the New York Grand Opera Company visited, staging Giuseppe Verdi's *Aïda* on February 13 and 14, 1928. An opera drought ensued until 1952, when the State of Florida purchased parts of the interior of an Italian playhouse from an antiques dealer, and constructed a tiny opera house in Gallery 21 of the Ringling Museum. The Asolo Theater, taking its name from the small hill-town in Italy where it was original built, was inaugurated with Giovanni Pergolesi's *La serva padrona* and Mozart's *Bastien und Bastienne*, performed by the New York City Center Opera Company. The theater received its own pink stucco building in 1957. A gala production of Mozart's *Die Entführung aus dem Serail* celebrated the event. In the audience that glorious evening was the widow of Josef Turnau, whose company brought professional chamber opera to small communities. The tiny Asolo Theater was the perfect setting for the Turnau Opera Players, and a wonderful partnership that lasted for fourteen seasons developed.

Turnau Opera Players opened their first season in 1960 with Mozart's *Così fan tutte*. Giacomo Puccini's *La bohème*, and a doublebill of Maurice Ravel's *L'heure espagnole* / Mozart's *Der Schauspieldirektor* followed. There were a total of fourteen performances. The second (and final season under the auspices of the Ringling Museum) saw mainly seventeenth- and eighteenth-century works— Claudio Monteverdi's *Il combattimento di Tancredi e Clorinda*, Henry Purcell's *Dido and Aeneas*, Mozart's *Le nozze di Figaro* and *Così fan tutte*—and Gioachino Rossini's *La Cenerentola*. The Asolo Opera Guild was formed in 1961 to ensure the continuation of the annual Turnau Opera Players seasons. The first Guild-sponsored season opened the following year with Strauß's *Die Fledermaus*. The schedule combined standard, classical, and twentieth-century operas. During their tenure at the Asolo, the Players performed some unusual works—Seymour Barab's *Chanticleer*, Claude Debussy's *L'enfant prodigue*, Carl Orff's *Die Kluge*, Vittorio Rieti's *Don Perlimplin*, Raffaelo de Banfield's *Lord Byron's Love Letters*, Lee Hoiby's *The Scarf*, and Gustav Holst's *The Wandering Scholar*. Two pianos accompanied the performances with the occasional use of other instruments—double string quartet, harpsichord, organ, piano, and guitar. An exception was Gluck's *Orfeo ed Euridice*, when a thirteen-piece orchestra played. The company mounted Verdi and Puccini operas, but only those that fit into a chamber concept—*La traviata*, *Rigoletto*, *Tosca*, *La bohème*, and *Madama Butterfly*.

The small size of the theater resulted in an "opera as theater" philosophy. One production caused such a scandal that it cast doubt on the future of the company. In 1977, Norman Walker produced Gluck's *L'incoronazione di Poppea* with all the overtones of Nero's Rome, including sexual acts of both men with women and men with men. It caused such an outrage that one board member resigned in horror and several journalists trashed the production. The incident had a happy ending. *Poppea* became the hottest ticket in town, and the remaining board members gave the green light to plan two seasons ahead, instead of the usual one. During the company's residence at the Asolo, two productions were mounted elsewhere. The 1967 production of Gluck's *Orfeo ed Euridice* was seen in the newly-built Neel Auditorium at Manatee Junior College, and the 1973 production of Carlisle Floyd's *Susannah* took place in the Van Wezel Performing Arts Hall. Floyd was in the audience for his opera that featured Johanna Meier in the title role.

In 1979, the Asolo Opera changed its name to the Sarasota Opera and purchased the Edwards Theater to renovate for its permanent home. It was not until five seasons later that the Sarasota Opera could performed in its new home. Victor de Renzi was hired in 1982 as artistic director to transform the Sarasota Opera from a semi-professional group to a noteworthy regional company. His first season was the final season at the Asolo Theater and featured Jacques Offenbach's *Orphée aux Enfers*, Gaetano Donizetti's *Don Pasquale*, Gluck's *Orfeo ed Euridice*, and Benjamin Britten's *The Turn of the Screw*.

The Sarasota Opera inaugurated its partially restored new home on January 21, 1984, with a gala performance of Pyotr Il'yich Tchaikovsky's *Eugene Onegin*. The larger theater and orchestra pit allowed expansion of the repertory. Since 1989, the company has introduced one rarely-performed or unusual opera into the repertory each season to garner national attention. Alfredo Catalani's *La Wally* took the honors in 1989, followed by Verdi's *Aroldo*, Bedřich Smetana's *Hubička* (The Kiss), and the original (1857) version of Verdi's *Simon Boccanegra*. *Boccanegra* was world premiered at La Fenice (Venice, Italy) on March 12, 1857, and had not been staged since 1880, when Verdi withdrew it for revision. The revised version appeared at La Scala (Milan, Italy) on March 24, 1881, and is the version commonly produced. The 1881 version introduced the powerful "Council Chamber" scene that replaced

Sarasota Opera House (Sarasota, Florida).

an unremarkable "Celebration" scene, and eliminated the "early Verdi" overture. To allow comparison of the two versions, two days after the company presented the original *Simon Boccanegra*, a dynamic and emotionally-charged production of the 1881 version was mounted.

DeRenzi is a traditionalist and sees the Sarasota Opera as an opera museum. The costumes in Verdi's original *Simon Boccanegra* were copies of the ones worn in the world premiere. The company upholds the old operatic tradition when music and singing were king, although the singers, fortunately, do not just stand on stage and sing as was the tradition at that time. They act in ensemble with sets and costumes true to the period of the opera and the country. The casts are made up of young artists at the beginning of their careers. Since Sarasota is a retirement area with an aging population and conservative tastes, the repertory is almost pure Romantic, with no contemporary operas, experimental works, or updated productions. It sometimes causes ennui.

The four-opera season, performed in repertory, balances a repertory favorite and a light opera against a lesser-known work and an obscure, "important" work. There is a Verdi opera every season. Recent productions have included Verdi's *Il trovatore* and *Les vêpres siciliennes*, Puccini's *Madama Butterfly*, Sergey Rakhmaninov's *Francesca da Rimini*, Pyotr Il'yich Tchaikovsky's *Iolanthe*, and Mozart's *Le nozze di Figaro*. The company performs in the Sarasota Opera House.

Sarasota Opera House

The Sarasota Opera House, originally known as the Edwards Theater, was named after its owner and Sarasota mayor, Arthur Britton Edwards. Designed by Lloyd A.

Benjamin and built by George A Miller, the theater cost $250,000 and the land an additional $100,000. The Edwards was primarily a showplace for silent movies and vaudeville. Eventually the theater experienced the decline common to the movie palaces of the 1920s and 1930s, hitting bottom in 1973. Six years later the Sarasota Opera Association purchased the theater, restoring it for $6 million dollars. The theater was renamed the Sarasota Opera House and became the company's permanent home.

The Mediterranean Revival style structure is covered with salmon-colored stucco. Coral red hipped roofs surround a central skylight. A large vertical forest-green-and-white neon sign blazons OPERA HOUSE in large white letters. Twin Ionic pilaster arches delineate an art-deco-style atrium lobby. A crystal chandelier, reportedly used in *Gone with the Wind*, is suspended from the center. The beige-and-white-stucco auditorium exudes a Mediterranean flavor with a single balcony sweeping across the rectangular hall. The seats are green tweed seats, and the plain proscenium is taupe. Ceiling spotlights complement the amber and white tiffany glass lamps that line the walls. The auditorium seats 1,033.

Practical Information. The Sarasota Opera House is at 61 N. Pineapple Avenue. The box office, to the left of the main entrance, opens on November 15. The hours are Monday through Friday 10:00 A.M. to 4:00 P.M. During the season (February–March) it remains open until curtain and opens on weekends three hours before the opera. Tickets can be ordered by telephoning 813-953-7030 during box office hours, or by writing The Sarasota Opera Assn., 61 N. Pineapple Ave., Sarasota, FL 34236. If you visit, contact the Sarasota Convention & Visitors Bureau, 655 North Tamiami Trail, Sarasota, FL 34236; telephone 813-957-7877, 1-800-522-9799 for hotel information.

COMPANY STAFF AND REPERTORY

General/Artistic Director. Victor de Renzi (1982–present).

American/United States Premiere. Verdi's *Simon Boccanegra* (1857 version, March 13, 1992).

Repertory. **1960:** Così fan tutte, Der Schauspieldirektor/L'heure espagnole, La bohème. **1961:** Il combattimento di Tancredi e Clorinda, Così fan tutte, Le nozze di Figaro, Dido and Aeneas, La Cenerentola. **1962:** Chanticleer, Trouble in Tahiti, L'enfant prodigue, The Medium, Le nozze di Figaro, Die Fledermaus. **1963:** L'enfant prodigue, Don Pasquale, L'heure espagnole, Il barbiere di Siviglia, La traviata. **1964:** Die Entführung aus dem Serail, The Rape of Lucretia, Il barbiere di Siviglia, Rigoletto. **1965:** Don Pasquale, Orfeo ed Euridice, La bohème, Sheherazade, Il turco in Italia. **1966:** Lord Byron's Love Letters, Così fan tutte, Rigoletto, La traviata. **1967:** Orfeo ed Euridice, I pagliacci, La serva padrona, Il barbiere di Siviglia. **1968:** Amahl and the Night Visitors, Madama Butterfly, Die Fledermaus, The Rake's Progress. **1969:** L'enfant prodigue, Don Pasquale, Faust, The Scarf, La bohème, La Cenerentola. **1970:** Così fan tutte, Die Kluge, Die Fledermaus, La traviata. **1971:** Susannah, Die Entführung aus dem Serail, La bohème, Il barbiere di Siviglia. **1972:** Le nozze di Figaro, Madama Butterfly, L'heure espagnole, Don Perlimplin, The Three Penny Opera, Il segreto di Susanna. **1973:** Don Pasquale, Susannah, Amahl and the Night Visitors, The Medium, La traviata. **1974:** Die Fledermaus, Orfeo ed Euridice, Così fan tutte, La voix humaine . **1975:** Tosca, Il barbiere di Siviglia. **1976:** Così fan tutte, La bohème, Rigoletto. **1977:** Don Pasquale, L'incoronazione di Poppea, Don Giovanni, Tosca. **1978:** Pelléas et Mélisande, The Wandering Scholar, I pagliacci, Il maestro di musica, Die Fledermaus. **1979:** The Rape of Lucretia, Martha, Die Entführung aus dem Serail, La traviata. **1980:** A Kékszakállú herceg vára (Duke Bluebeard's Castle), Il maestro di musica, Madama Butterfly, The Three Penny Opera. **1981:** Così fan tutte, El Capitan, Rigoletto. **1982:** She Loves Me, Ma Tante Aurore, Il barbiere di Siviglia. **1983:** Turn of the Screw, Don Pasquale, Orfeo ed Euridice, Orphée aux enfers. **1984:** Die Zauberflöte, La Périchole, Eugene Onegin, La traviata. **1985:** Fidelio, Lucia di Lammermoor, Die Entführung aus dem Serail, The Rake's Progress. **1986:** L'elisir d'amore, Hänsel und Gretel, Madama Butterfly, Falstaff. **1987:** Carmen, La fille du régiment, Cavalleria rusticana, Il tabarro. **1988:** Turn of the Screw, Die lustige Witwe, Le nozze di Figaro, Tosca. **1989:** La Wally, Don Giovanni, Die Fledermaus, Rigoletto. **1990:** Werther, Così fan tutte, La bohème, Aroldo. **1991:** Faust, Die Zauberflöte, Hubička (The Kiss), Un ballo in maschera. **1992:** Carmen, Martha, Il barbiere di Siviglia, Simon Boccanegra (1857, 1881 versions). **1993:** Il trovatore, Roméo et Juliette, Francesca da Rimini/Iolanthe, La fanciulla del West. **1994:** Madama Butterfly, Le nozze di Figaro, Prodaná nevěsta (The Bartered Bride), Les vêpres siciliennes.

Georgia ——————— ATLANTA

• *The Atlanta Opera* •

The Atlanta Opera, originally called the Atlanta Civic Opera, was formed in 1979, when the Atlanta Lyric Opera Company merged with the Georgia Opera. Thomas Pasatieri, the prolific opera composer (*Black Widow*, *The Seagull*, *Il Signor Deluso*, *The Trial of Mary Todd Lincoln*, and *The Penitentes* among others) was the head of the newly formed company. His *The Seagull* opened the first season on March 14, 1980, in the Fox Theater. Giuseppe Verdi's *La traviata* followed on March 28. Henry Purcell's *Dido and Aeneas*, Gian Carlo Menotti's *The Consul/The Medium*, and Gioachino Rossini's *La Cenerentola* were some of the operas performed during Pasatieri's tenure.

William Fred Scott replaced Pasatieri in 1985, taking the company in a different direction. The company's name changed to Atlanta Opera and all operas were presented in English. The season opened in the Alliance Theater with Giacomo Puccini's *Madama Butterfly* and concluded with Gaetano Donizetti's *La fille du régiment*. Since surtitles arrived during the second season, only comic operas are still sung in English. That season the company commissioned its own sets for Donizetti's *Lucia di Lammermoor*, and for Richard Strauss's *Ariadne auf Naxos* in 1988. The season expanded to three operas in 1987. The company's last performance in the Alliance Theater came with Rossini's *Il barbiere di Siviglia*, the second opera of the 1989 season. Symphony Hall hosted the final opera of the 1989 season, Puccini's *Madama Butterfly*. Symphony Hall held 1,000 seats more than the Alliance Theater, enabling the company to reduce the number of performances, which they hoped that would decrease costs. But the reverse occurred. That, combined with the surprisingly poor turn-out for Johann Strauß's *Die Fledermaus*, plunged the company into debt. (Atlanta is one of very few cities where the audience does not like operetta!) The company recovered, and has since become more daring in its repertory with productions of Benjamin Britten's *Albert Herring* and Verdi's *Stiffelio*. The absence of its own home has limited the expansion of the Atlanta Opera. The company's access to Symphony Hall is restricted

Robert W. Woodruff Arts Center (Atlanta, Georgia).

to Atlanta's hot, humid summer months. Finding a home of its own is one of the company's primary goals.

The three-opera season offers a standard repertory, with an occasional unusual piece in a *stagione* system. Some recent works include Puccini's *La bohème*, Verdi's *Macbeth*, Bellini's *Norma*, and Bizet's *Les pêcheurs des perles*. The company performs in Symphony Hall.

Symphony Hall

Symphony Hall is one of several theaters housed in the Robert W. Woodruff Arts Center, originally called the Atlanta Memorial Arts Center. Designed by the Atlanta firm of Toombs, Amisano, & Wells, the Center opened in 1968. It was built to honor the memory of 106 Atlanta arts patrons killed in an airplane crash at Orly Field in Paris, France, on June 3, 1962. The Atlanta opera's first home, the 784-seat Alliance Theater, is also located in the Center.

Terrazzo pillars, connected to the building by large horizontal beams, ring the contemporary, white concrete structure. The galleria, which acts as the lobby for both the Symphony Hall and Alliance Theater, is of columned concrete. The bronze-lettered inscription "DEDICATED TO ALL WHO TRULY BELIEVE THE ARTS ARE A CONTINUING EFFORT OF THE HUMAN SPIRIT TO FIND MEANING IN EXISTENCE, ORLY, FRANCE JUNE 3, 1962," is on one landing of the beige marble staircase that leads to the second level of the galleria. On the other is a bronze sculpture entitled *The Shade* by Auguste Rodin, which the French Government donated in memory of those killed at Orly. The entrance lobby of Symphony Hall sports muted-pink walls embellished with warm, dark wood. The two-tier, mauve-colored auditorium holds three shades of salmon-colored velvet plush orchestra seats that stretch continental-style across the room. The walls are columned concrete, and the space is illuminated by rows of lights that peek out between parallel beams. The Hall seats 1,762.

Practical Information. The Woodruff Arts Center is at Peachtree and 15th Street. The Atlanta Opera box office is at 1800 Peachtree St. N.W., Suite 620. It is open weekdays from 9:00 A.M. to 5:00 P.M. Tickets are for sale at the Woodruff box office beginning a few weeks before the performance. Box office hours are Monday through Friday, from 10:00 A.M. to 8:00 P.M., Saturday from 12:00 noon to 8:00 P.M., and Sunday from 12:00 noon to 5:00 P.M. The box office remains open until thirty minutes after curtain-time on performance nights. Tickets can be ordered by telephoning 404-355-3311, or by writing The Atlanta Opera, 1800 Peachtree St. N.W., Suite 620, Atlanta, GA 30309. If you go, stay at the Sheraton Colony Square Hotel, 188 14th Street (Peachtree at 14th Street) N.E., Atlanta, GA 30361; telephone 404-892-6000, fax 404-876-3276, reservations 1-800-325-3535. The Colony Square is part of a huge complex, one block from Symphony Hall.

COMPANY STAFF AND REPERTORY

General/Artistic Directors. Thomas Pasatieri (1979–1985); William Fred Scott (1985–present).

Repertory. **1985:** Madama Butterfly, La fille du régiment. **1986:** Lucia di Lammermoor, Die Entführung aus dem Serail. **1987:** Così fan tutte, La bohème, Rigoletto. **1988:** Tosca, Die lustige Witwe, Ariadne auf Naxos. **1989:** La traviata, Il barbiere di Siviglia, Madama Butterfly. **1990:** Die Fledermaus, Le nozze di Figaro, Rigoletto. **1991:** Tosca, Un ballo in maschera, L'elisir d'amore. **1992:** Lucia di Lammermoor, Carmen, Albert Herring. **1993:** Macbeth, Don Giovanni, La bohème. **1994:** Stiffelio, Les pêcheurs des perles, Norma.

AUGUSTA

• *Augusta Opera* •

Giacomo Puccini's *La bohème* inaugurated the Augusta Opera in 1967. A group of local residents founded the company, hiring Ian Strasfogel, who was stationed at nearby Fort Gordon, to direct the new-born organization. Puccini's *La bohème* was the sole offering of the inaugural season. Puccini's *Tosca* comprised the second season.

Beginning in 1974, the company expanded to three works, with some seasons also offering a musical theater piece. In 1980, Edward Bradberry was hired as general manager. He expanded the repertory by staging Bedřich Smetana's *Prodaná nevěsta* (The Bartered Bride) in 1982 and Marc Blitzstein's *Regina* three years later. Bradberry believes that nurturing young American artists' careers is the company's prime purpose, so most roles are filled by up-and-coming singers, the rest with established ones. Local talent comprises the chorus.

The three-opera season offers a mixture of traditional fare, contemporary works, operetta, and musical theater pieces. Recent productions include Puccini's *Tosca*, Cole Porter's *Kiss Me Kate*, and Arthur Sullivan's *H.M.S. Pinafore*. The company performs in the 819-seat Imperial Theater.

Practical Information. The Imperial Theater is at 745 Broad Street. Tickets are available from the Augusta Opera, Box 3865, Hill Station, Augusta, Georgia 30914, telephone 706-722-8341.

COMPANY STAFF AND REPERTORY

General/Artistic Directors. Ian Strasfogel (1967–?); Edward Bradberry (1980–present).

Repertory. **1967:** La bohème. **1968:** Tosca. **1969:** Il barbiere di Siviglia. **1970:** Carmen. **1971:** Madama Butterfly. **1972:** Don Pasquale. **1973:** La traviata. **1974:** Trouble in Tahiti/The Old Maid and the Thief, Così fan tutte, Il trovatore. **1975:** Lucia di Lammermoor, L'elisir d'amore, La cambiale di matrimonio. **1976:** A Hand of Bridge, The Medium, La bohème. **1977:** Susannah, L'italiana in Algeri, Die Fledermaus. **1978:** Le nozze di Figaro, H.M.S. Pinafore, Rigoletto. **1979:** La fille du régiment, Die lustige Witwe, Don Giovanni, Washington Square. **1980:** I pagliacci, Les contes d'Hoffmann. **1981:** The Fantasticks, The Pirates of Penzance, La traviata. **1982:** Carmen, Madama Butterfly, Prodaná nevěsta (The Bartered Bride), The Mikado. **1983:** La bohème, Il barbiere di Siviglia. **1984:** Tosca, H.M.S. Pinafore. **1985:** Regina, Die Fledermaus, Rigoletto. **1986:** Roméo et Juliette, Le nozze di Figaro, Side by Side by Sondheim. **1987:** Hänsel und Gretel, A Little Night Music, The Pirates of Penzance, La traviata. **1988:** West Side Story, S'Wonderful, S'Marvelous, S'Gershwin, I pagliacci. **1989:** Lucia di Lammermoor, Faust, Madama Butterfly, Oklahoma!. **1990:** Carmen, Cole, La bohème, South Pacific. **1991:** My Fair Lady, Die lustigen Weiber von Windsor, The King and I. **1992:** The Medium, The Telephone, Die Zauberflöte, Carousel, Il barbiere di Siviglia. **1993:** Don Giovanni, Kiss Me Kate, Tosca, H.M.S. Pinafore. **1994:** Rigoletto.

Hawaii ——————————— HONOLULU

• *Hawaii Opera Theater* •

In 1981, Giacomo Puccini's *La bohème* opened the first season of the Hawaii Opera Theater as an independent company. The company had been a division of the Honolulu Symphony for the first twenty years of its existence. The official separation took place on June 1, 1980, when the company named its own general manager. Gaetano Donizetti's *Lucia di Lammermoor* and Georges Bizet's *Carmen* rounded out that first independent season.

The second season continued in the grand opera tradition with Charles Gounod's *Faust*, Giuseppe Verdi's *Aida*, and Puccini's *Manon Lescaut*. The third season saw the first independently produced Russian opera, Pyotr Il'yich Tchaikovsky's *Eugene Onegin*. The fifth season was special. It was the Silver Anniversary of opera in Hawaii. The production of Wolfgang Amadeus Mozart's *Die Zauberflöte* took on a Hawaiian origin. Not only were all the costumes executed in Hawaii, but authentic local customs were recreated. The season's second opera,

Blaisdell Hall (Honolulu, Hawaii).

Puccini's *Madama Butterfly*, was co-presented with the Japanese Chamber of Commerce. The company also witnessed its first independently produced Wagnerian opera — *Der fliegende Holländer*. A David Hockney production of Igor Stravinsky's *The Rake's Progress* highlighted the sixth season. Although an artistic success, it was a box office failure. Pietro Mascagni's infrequently staged *L'amico Fritz* was the 1988-season novelty. The company boasted its first sold-out year in following year, and mounted a controversial Georges Bizet's *Carmen*. The abstract set combined with a return to Bizet's original score of spoken dialogue rather than the commonly used recitative caused the controversy. The 1990 season saw an authentically Hawaiian Mozart's *Così fan tutte* as *Pēlā No Ho'i Nā Wāhine*.

The three-opera season combines two grand operas (the tragic, emotional kind) with one piece on the lighter side. Recent productions include Johann Strauß's *Die Fledermaus*, Richard Strauss's *Der Rosenkavalier*, Verdi's *La traviata*, Puccini's *Madama Butterfly*, and Gounod's *Faust*. The company performs in Blaisdell Hall.

Blaisdell Hall

The Concert Hall is a stark, white-marble-faced rectangular structure. A large, gray stone overhang projects out from the façade, with NEAL S. BLAISDELL CONCERT HALL affixed in large bronze letters. The lush red and white grand foyer boasts a horseshoe-shaped, bronze-sculpted wall that follows the contour of the auditorium. A statue of Mayor Neal Blaisdell, the driving force behind the Hall's construction, resides in the center of the lobby. The red and white rectangular-shaped auditorium holds one balcony. The red velvet seats flow unbroken across the Hall in continental fashion. The theater seats 2,158.

Practical Information. The Blaisdell Hall is at 777 Ward Avenue. Tickets are available at the Hawaiian Opera Theater Offices, 987 Waimanu Street between 9:00 A.M. and 5:00 P.M. weekdays. You can order tickets by telephoning 808-537-6191 or writing Hawaii Opera Theater, 987 Waimanu Street, Honolulu, HI 96814. If you visit, stay at the Halekulani, 2199 Kalia Road, Honolulu, HI 96815, telephone 808-923-2311, fax 808-926-8004, reservations 1-800- 223-6800. The Halekulani was originally a private beachfront estate that was transformed into a luxurious hotel in 1917. It has been completely renovated and modernized. Its original charm is incorporated in the modern structure.

COMPANY STAFF AND REPERTORY

General Directors (as independent company). Marshall Turkin; J. Mario Ramos. *Repertory (as independent company).* **1981:** La bohème, Lucia di Lammermoor, Carmen. **1982:** Aida, Manon, Faust. **1983:** Rigoletto, Le nozze di Figaro, Eugene Onegin. **1984:** Norma, Il barbiere di Siviglia, La traviata. **1985:** Die Zauberflöte, Madama Butterfly, Der Fliegende Holländer. **1986:** Rake's Progress, Les contes d'Hoffmann, Tosca. **1987:** Un ballo in maschera, Les pêcheurs des perles, La bohème. **1988:** Turandot, Die Entführung aus dem Serail, L'amico Fritz/I pagliacci. **1989:** Die lustige Witwe, Don Giovanni, Carmen. **1990:** Otello, Prodaná nevěsta (The Bartered Bride), Così fan tutte. **1991:** Aida, Le nozze di Figaro, Candide. **1992:** Andrea Chénier, Il barbiere di Siviglia, Manon. **1993:** Samson et Dalila, Die Fledermaus, Madama Butterfly. **1994:** Der Rosenkavalier, Faust, La traviata.

Illinois
──────────── CHICAGO

• *Chicago Opera Theater* •

Wolfgang Amadeus Mozart's *Così fan tutte* inaugurated the Chicago Opera Theater, originally called the Chicago Opera Studio, in 1974, at the Jones Commercial High School. The chorus sang from the wings, because there was no money for costumes. The budget was $8,000. Alan Stone founded the Opera Studio the previous season to showcase Chicago's promising young operatic talent.

In 1976, the Opera Studio mounted its first two-opera season. Expansion to three operas took place three years later. By the end of the 1980s, the season reached four operas. The company established a reputation for performing American opera and rarely-performed works, and their production of Lee Hoiby's *Summer and Smoke* was televised nationally. It was renamed the Chicago Opera Theater in 1978. Christoph Willibald von Gluck's *Orfeo ed Euridice* highlighted the 1988 season with designs by the sculptor Louise Nevelson. Before the Chicago Opera Theater underwent major restructuring, suspending operations for the 1993-94 season, it had introduced more than a dozen operas to the Chicago area, among them Virgin Thomson's *The Mother of Us All*, Marc Blitzstein's *Regina*, and Robert Ward's *The Crucible*.

The four-opera season (before retrenchment) offered an unusual repertory emphasizing contemporary American works in a *stagione* system. Recent productions include Thomson's *Four Saints in Three Acts*, Puccini's *Madama Butterfly*, and Dominick Argento's *Postcard from Morocco*. The company performs in the Athenaeum Theater, which seats 925.

Practical Information. The Athenaeum is at South Port and Lincoln. Tickets are available at the Chicago Opera Theater box office, 20 East Jackson Boulevard, or by telephoning 312-663-0048, or writing Chicago Opera Theater, 20 East Jackson Boulevard, Chicago, IL 60604. If you go, stay at the Four Seasons, 120 East Delaware Place, Chicago, IL 60611-0142; telephone 312-280-8800, fax 312-280-9184, reservations 1-800-332-3442. The hotel, like the Civic Opera House, occupies several floors in a high-rise office building. It is a luxurious establishment with outstanding service and is convenient to the theater.

COMPANY STAFF AND REPERTORY

General/Artistic Directors. Alan Stone (1974–1991); Jean Perkins (interim, 1992–present).

Chicago Premieres. Thomson's *The Mother of Us All* (1976); Hoiby's *Summer and Smoke* (1977); Nicolai's *Die lustigen Weiber von Weiber* (1978); Britten's *Albert Herring* (1979); Offenbach's *La Périchole* (1980); Kurka's *The Good Soldier Schweik* (1981); Blitzstein's *Regina* (1982); Menotti's *The Consul* (1983); Ward's *The Crucible* (1985); Floyd's *Susannah* (1986); Rossini's *Il turco in Italia* (1986); Britten's *The Turn of the Screw* (1987); Smetana's *Dvě vdovy* (The Two Widows, 1987); Floyd's *Of Mice and Men* (1988); Mozart's *La finta giardiniera* (1989); Davies's *The Lighthouse* (1990); Argento's *Postcard from Morocco* (1991); Floyd's *Four Saints in Three Acts* (1993).

Repertory. **1974:** Così fan tutte. **1975:** Le nozze di Figaro. **1976:** Il barbiere di Siviglia, The Mother of Us All. **1977:** Die Entführung aus dem Serail, Summer and Smoke. **1978:** Don Pasquale, Die lustigen Weiber von Windsor. **1979:** Così fan tutte, Albert Herring, Les pêcheurs des perles. **1980:** La Périchole, L'italiana in Algeri, Summer and Smoke. **1981:** La Rondine, The Good Soldier Schweik, Le nozze di Figaro. **1982:** Die Entführung aus dem Serail, Regina, La fille du régiment. **1983:** Martha, The Consul, Il barbiere di Siviglia. **1984:** Don Giovanni, Prodaná nevěsta (The Bartered Bride), The Mother of Us All. **1985:** Les pêcheurs des perles, L'elisir d'amore, The Crucible. **1986:** Susannah, L'amico Fritz, Il turco in Italia. **1987:** Così fan tutte, The Turn of the Screw, Dvě vdovy (The Two Widows). **1988:** Orfeo ed Euridice, Don Pasquale, Of Mice and Men, La Cenerentola. **1989:** Where the Wild Things Are/Peter and the Wolf, La finta giardiniera, Albert Herring, Roméo et Juliette. **1990:** Die lustigen Weiber von Windsor, The Lighthouse, Lakmé, Carousel. **1991:** Where the Wild Things Are/Peter and the Wolf, Idomeneo, Madama Butterfly, Postcard from Morocco. **1992:** Le Comte Ory, La traviata. **1993:** Four Saints in Three Acts. **1994:** Don Giovanni (scheduled but not performed, operations suspended for season).

• *Lyric Opera of Chicago* •

On February 5, 1954, Wolfgang Amadeus Mozart's *Don Giovanni* became the "calling card" performance of the Chicago Lyric Theater, the Lyric Opera of Chicago's original name. The cast included Nicola Rossi-Lemeni, John Brownlee, Eleanor Steber, Léopold Simoneau, and Irene Jordan and was under the baton of

Nicola Rescigno. Founded by Carol Fox, Lawrence Kelly, and Rescigno, the company gave a repeat performance on February 7, 1954. The trio believed that opera could thrive again in this midwest city. As the program for Mozart's *Don Giovanni* explained, "With this 'calling card,' the Lyric Theater hopes you will invite them to call again this November."

More than one hundred years earlier, John Rice had arrived in Chicago, constructing a frame building on the corner of Dearborn and Randolph. The second floor housed a theater. Erected in six-weeks at a cost of $4,000, Rice's Theater opened on June 28, 1847, with a play, *The Four Sisters*. One month later, the first opera troupe arrived, staging Vincenzo Bellini's *La sonnambula* on July 29, 1850. The first performance was so successful that a second was scheduled for the following evening. Shortly after the second act had begun, fire raced through the theater. Although everyone escaped safely, everything except the curtain, costumes, and some scenery, was destroyed. Rice rebuilt his theater, and in October, 1853, an Italian company visited, mounting Gaetano Donizetti's *Lucia di Lammermoor*, and Bellini's *Norma*. Luigi Arditi conducted the performances with Rosa de Vries as the prima donna.

In 1857, James McVicker constructed a theater on Madison Street that boasted a parquet, boxes, and two galleries for $85,000. It was here that Durand English Opera Troupe opened on September 27, 1858, staging Giuseppe Verdi's *Il trovatore*, Daniel Auber's *Fra Diavolo*, Carl Maria von Weber's *Der Freischütz*, Michael Balfe's *The Bohemian Girl*, and Donizetti's *La fille du régiment*. Maurice Strakosch's Company visited two years later with Donizetti's *La favorita* and *Lucrezia Borgia*, Bellini's *I Puritani*, Mozart's *Don Giovanni*, Friedrich von Flotow's *Martha*, and Verdi's *La traviata*. Two addition troupes visited that same year. In 1863, Jacob Grau's Company performed at McVicker's Theater, offering Gioachino Rossini's *Mosè in Egitto*, Giacomo Meyerbeer's *Dinorah*, Fromental Halévy's *La Juive*, and Verdi's *Les vêpres siciliennes*. Grau returned the next year with the Chicago premiere of Charles Gounod's *Faust*. Leonard Grover arrived next with a German company, mounting Ludwig van Beethoven's *Fidelio* and Richard Wagner's *Tannhäuser*.

Chicago took a liking to opera and decided to erect a proper home for this sophisticated art form. The task fell to Uranus Crosby, a self-made millionaire, to build a Temple to the Muses. The Crosby Opera House was born on the north side of Washington Street between Dearborn and State in 1865. Designed by W. W. Boyington, it cost $700,000. Crosby scheduled the opening on April 17, 1865, but with the assassination of President Abraham Lincoln on April 15, the inauguration was postponed until April 20, 1865. For the inauguration, Maurice Grau's Italian Opera Company presented Verdi's *Il trovatore*. The next evening Donizetti's *Lucia di Lammermoor* with Clara Louise Kellogg graced the stage. Other works in the four-week season included Donizetti's *Poliuto*, *Lucrezia Borgia*, and *Don Sébastien*, Gounod's *Faust*, Mozart's *Don Giovanni*, Auber's *Fra Diavolo*, Flotow's *Martha*, and Bellini's *I Puritani* and *La sonnambula*. The season closed on Saturday, May 20 with a performance of Bellini's *La sonnambula*, followed by the Mad Scene from *Lucia di Lammermoor*. Grau's season was so successful that the company returned on June 5, with Gounod's *Faust*, the Chicago premiere of Verdi's *La forza del destino*, and Donizetti's *La fille du régiment*, among others. November saw Grau's Company back in Chicago offering the same fare with Donizetti's *L'elisir d'amore* added to the repertoire.

Opéra bouffe first came to Chicago on April 13, 1868, when Aline Lambele brought three pieces by Jacques Offenbach—*La Grande Duchesse de Gérolstein*, *La belle Hélène*, and *Orphée aux Enfers*. Christine Nilsson gave a concert at Crosby's in 1871. Then the fire begun by Mrs. O'Leary's cow devoured most of the city, including the opera house. When Colonel James Mapleson visited Chicago in 1878, his company performed at Hooley's Opera House, opening his season with Mozart's *Le nozze di Figaro*. Emma Abbott sang Ambroise Thomas's *Mignon* in 1879. Four years later, Henry Abbey's Company visited with Christine Nilsson and Marcella Sembrich, staging Donizetti's *Lucia di Lammermoor*, Wagner's *Lohengrin*, Gounod's *Faust*, Amilcare Ponchielli's *La gioconda*, Thomas's *Mignon*, and Meyerbeer's *Robert le Diable*. Mapleson also returned during the 1883-84 season with Adelina Patti and Etelka Gerster, offering Luigi Ricci's *Crispino e la Comare* and Meyerbeer's *Les Huguenots*, among his productions. In 1885, Walter Damrosch brought German opera to the city.

Around this time, Chicago was giving serious thought to constructing a permanent shrine to opera, and the Auditorium Theater became opera's next home. Construction began on June 1, 1887, on the American Romanesque building. Louis Sullivan was the architect and Dankmar Adler was in charge of the acoustics. The dedication ceremonies took place on Monday, December 9, 1889. The following evening, the Abbey-Grau Italian Grand Opera Company opened with Gounod's *Roméo et Juliette* with Patti and Perugini, under the baton of Sapio. The company's four-week opera season included Lillian Nordica in Verdi' *Aida*, Francesco Tamagno making his American debut in Rossini's *Guillaume Tell*, and singing a powerful *Otello*, and Patti in Rossini's *Il barbiere di Siviglia*. Patti returned the next year with the Abbey-Grau Italian Grand Company adding Donizetti's *Linda di Chamounix*, and Léo Delibes's *Lakmé* to her repertoire. Nordica and Tamagno were also featured in Meyerbeer's *L'Africaine*. Damrosch's German Opera Company visited the following month, opening with Wagner's *Tannhäuser*. Lilli Lehmann was Elizabeth. Wagner's *Die Meistersinger*, *Lohengrin*, and *Der fliegende Holländer*, along with Beethoven's *Fidelio*, Verdi's *Un ballo in maschera*, Bellini's *Norma*, and Peter Cornelius's *Der Barbier von Bagdad* rounded out the schedule. The Auditorium saw its first American premiere, Gounod's *Philemon et Baucis* (in English) on December 26, 1892. The premieres of André Messager's *La Basoche* (in English) and Jules Massenet's *Werther* followed. Damrosch brought Chicago its first *Tristan und Isolde* on April 17, 1895, with Max Alvary and Rosa Sucher in the title roles. After Henry Abbey died in the fall of 1896, Grau managed the company alone, bringing to the city Bizet's *Carmen*, Verdi's *Il trovatore*, Wagner's *Lohengrin* and *Siegfried* (with Jean de Reszke in the title role), and Massenet's *Le Cid*.

Chicago's first brush with a French Opera Company came in 1899, when a troupe from New Orleans visited for a week, offering Halévy's *La Juive*, and Gounod's *Reine de Saba*. A month later, Henry W. Savage's Castle Square Opera Company performed in Studebaker Hall staging Pietro Mascagni's *Cavalleria rusticana* and Ruggero Leoncavallo's *I pagliacci*, Ponchielli's *La gioconda*, Gounod's *Faust*, and Bizet's *Carmen*. The New Orleans troupe returned in 1900 with more novelties. The Castle Square Company also returned staging Wagner's *Lohengrin* one night and Ponchielli's *La gioconda* the next. Grau made his final Chicago visit in April 1903, opening with Donizetti's *La fille du régiment* and Leoncavallo's *I pagliacci*. Enrico Caruso and Marcella Sembrich appeared in Donizetti's *Lucia di*

Lammermoor, Caruso returned for Leoncavallo's *I pagliacci* and Ponchielli's *La gioconda*. Subsequently, Geraldine Farrar, Antonio Scotti, Leo Slezak, Emma Destinn, and Arturo Toscanini were all introduced to Chicago, the latter two on opening night 1909.

Chicago's first permanent opera company, Chicago Grand Opera Company, was born in 1910. Created from Oscar Hammerstein's Manhattan Opera, the new company inherited the Manhattan Opera almost intact—scenery, costumes, and most of its singers. Otto Kahn and his cohorts had bought out the indomitable impresario for $1.2 million in 1910 to eliminate the competition with the Metropolitan (see New York Metropolitan Opera entry). The Chicago Grand boasted Cleofonte Campanini as musical director, Andreas Dippel as artistic director, and Mary Garden as its prima donna, a role she played for twenty-one seasons. Verdi's *Aida* inaugurated the company on November 3, 1910, with Madame Korolewicz, Bassi, de Cisneros, and Campanini on the podium. The Auditorium was sold-out.

Garden made her debut in Claude Debussy's *Pelléas et Mélisande* on November 5, a role she created for the world premiere in Paris in 1902 and reprised for the American premiere at the Manhattan Opera House in 1908. Although Chicago loved Garden, they found the opera "difficult." Charpentier's *Louise* was the season's next novelty, again with Garden in the title role. The critics wrote favorably of the opera, as well as of Mary, "It is the song of youth and enthusiasm, of hope and courage.. Every tone of her voice, every subtle inflection she imparted to the grateful vocal part, every gesture was eloquent of youth." Richard Strauss's *Salome*, performed in French on November 25 was not so fortunate. The opera caused a volcanic eruption the next day over the role played by "art and morals" in the city. Garden also appeared in Massenet's *Thaïs* on December 6. During the ten-week inaugural season, John McCormack made his debut in Mascagni's *Cavalleria rusticana* on November 7, followed by appearances in Verdi's *Rigoletto* and *La traviata*, and Puccini's *La bohème*. Nellie Melba sang Mimi and Violeta, and Geraldine Farrar captivated the audience with her Madama Butterfly. Enrico journeyed to Chicago near the season's end for Canio in Leoncavallo's *I pagliacci* and Dick Johnson in Puccini's *La fanciulla del West*.

Camille Saint-Saëns's *Samson et Dalila* opened the second season on November 22, 1911. Several novelties were featured—Massenet's *Cendrillon* and *Le jongleur de Notre Dame*, Victor Herbert's *Natoma*, Ermanno Wolf-Ferrari's *Il segreto di Susanna*, and the first performance in Italian of his *I gioielli della Madonna* on January 16, 1912. The following year, the Auditorium hosted the American premiere of Frédéric d'Erlanger's *Noel* on January 8, 1913, and a Chicago novelty, Riccardo Zandonai's *Conchita*. On November 24, 1913, Puccini's *Tosca* with Garden in the title role opened the 1913-14 season. More than thirty different operas saw the stage during the season, including Leoncavallo's *Gli zingari*, with the composer himself on the podium. The novelties continued with Alberto Franchetti's *Cristoforo Colombo* and Wilhelm Kienzl's *Der Kuhreigen*, sung in French as *Le ranz des vaches*. By the end of the season, the deficit was $250,000. That, combined with dissension within the company, lead to the decision to declare bankruptcy. At the end of the season, Chicago's first homegrown effort, the Chicago Grand Opera Company, ceased to exist.

Harold McCormick purchased company's scenery, properties, costumes for $75,000, and formed a new company, the Chicago Opera Association, in the spring of 1915. McCormick guaranteed the company's debts for the next six years. He ran the company as if it were his private court opera. The productions were lavish, and the operas well-rehearsed. The McCormicks presented some of the best opera that Chicago has ever seen. The inaugural season opened on November 15, 1915, with Ponchielli's *La gioconda* featuring Emmy Destinn. The first week saw seven different operas—Charpentier's *Louise*, Wagner's *Tristan und Isolde*, Massenet's *Werther*, Puccini's *La bohème*, Henri Février's *Monna Vanna*, and Donizetti's *Lucia di Lammermoor*. A complete Ring Cycle and three premieres—Saint-Saëns's *Déjanire*, Massenet's *Cléopâtre*, and Simon Buchhalter's *A Lover's Knot*—were some of the season's highlights. A novelty opened the third season, the American premiere of Mascagni's *Isabeau*. *Musical America* wrote that the opera was "sumptuously staged and well sung." Rosa Raisa thrilled the audience in the title role. Four world premieres followed—Henry Kimball Hadley's *Azora*, Arthur Finley Nevin's *A Daughter of the Forest*, Sylvio Lazzari's *Le Sauteriot*, and Février's *Gismonda*. On January 17, 1919, the first production in America of Catalani's *Loreley* took place. The American premiere of Italo Montemezzi's *La Nave*, with Raisa and under the composer's baton, opened the 1919-1920 season. The scenery, designed by Norman Bel Geddes, was said to have cost $60,000. The opera survived two performances. Raisa also delighted with her Norma, Aida, and Suor Angelica that season. The company introduced Reginald de Koven's *Rip Van Winkle* to the world on January 2, 1920, a work Campanini had commissioned for the Chicago Opera. The opera was under-rehearsed, prompting the assigned conductor, Louis Hasselmans to relinquish the assignment to Alexander Smallens. Garden sang Montemezzi's *L'amore dei tre re* for the first time on January 9, 1920, along with Thaïs, Carmen, and Pelléas. Titta Ruffo performed in Thomas's *Hamlet*. The American premiere of Maurice Ravel's *L'heure espagnole*, and the United States premiere of Massenet's *Madame Chrysanthème* were other highlights. Campanini died a month after the season opened, and his funeral took place on the stage of the Auditorium, in a setting as dramatic and emotionally charged as any grand opera.

Gino Marinuzzi, a conductor and composer, took the helm. His *Jacquerie* opened the next season on November 17, 1920. The first German opera since the end of the war, Wagner's *Lohengrin* graced the stage. Camille Erlanger's *Aphrodite*, featuring Garden in the role of Chrysis, and the world premiere of Leoncavallo's *Edipo Re*, were the season's novelties. The 1921-22 season was McCormick's final year of patronage, and he wanted to go out in a "blaze of glory." McCormick felt that Garden had the *savoir-faire* to ensure a memorable last season and put her in charge. Garden not only contracted the largest number of singers in Chicago's history, but also paid them excessive fees. She even paid several not to sing. Garden claimed that McCormick told her the deficit could run as high as $600,000, but she left a much larger one. The season opened with Saint-Saëns's *Samson et Dalila*, followed by Raisa in Puccini's *Tosca*. In addition to her directorial role, Garden continued in her *prima donna* role appearing in Massenet's *Le jongleur de Notre Dame*, Bizet's *Carmen*, Montemezzi's *L'amore dei tre re*, Strauss's *Salome*, Debussy's *Pelléas et Mélisande*, Charpentier's *Louise*, Massenet's *Thaïs*, and Henri Février's *Monna Vanna*. The season's climax occurred on December 30, 1921, when the world premiere of Sergey Prokofiev's *Lyubov' k tryom apel'sinam* (The Love for Three Oranges) took place with Prokofiev, himself, on the podium. Inexplicably, the opera was sung in French, as *L'amour des trois oranges*, and many commented, "Quel désastre!" The production cost $100,000, the most expensive production ever produced by the company. Like Fox, the lady who ran the company a few decades later, Garden produced a deficit of over a million dollars in only twelve weeks. With the end of the season came the end of McCormick's patronage, and the end of the Chicago Opera Association. In the spring, the company was reorganized into the Chicago Civic Opera.

McCormick paid the deficit as promised and gave the Chicago Civic all of the costumes, scenery, and sets for ninety operas. The new company had no debt. Samuel Insull, a utilities magnate, was the company's president. He ran the company according to his motto, "One cannot ignore the dollar without getting into trouble." He also believed in democratization of the opera. The Civic Opera's first season opened on November 13, 1922, with Verdi's *Aida* in the Auditorium. Giorgio Polacco, the company's new musical director, conducted the performance with Raisa in the title role. Three days later, the season's first novelty, Nikolay Rimsky-Korsakov's *Snegurochka* was staged. It was highly praised. One critic wrote, "If the Chicago Civic Opera company does nothing else notable for the rest of the season . . . it would still have justified its right to exist from the manner in which it brought out Rimsky-Korsakov's *Snegurochka* at the Auditorium last night." The German repertory did not fare as well. The turnout for Wagner's *Parsifal* and *Die Walküre* was so poor that the scheduled *Tannhäuser* was canceled. Even the French operas were less in evidence. Garden was still very much in evidence, appearing in Bizet's *Carmen* and Montemezzi's *L'amore dei tre re*. Near the end of the season, the Civic introduced an American opera, Theodore Stearns's *Snowbird*. It received one performance. The Auditorium continued to host world premieres of operas by Americans, since the rage at that time was opera in English. The next novelty was Aldo Franchetti's *Namiko-San*. (Aldo Franchetti became an American shortly before the premiere.) William Harling's *A Light From St. Agnes* followed, and the next season saw Charles Cadman's *The Witch of Salem*.

Insull first unveiled his plans for what would eventually become the Civic Opera House on December 9, 1925. Since the 1926-27 season was the last that had a financial guarantee, Insull felt he had the perfect plan for supporting the Civic Opera. He intended to erect an enormous office building, where the lower levels would house a theater, and the upper levels would be divided into offices. The money from leasing the office space would pay for the running of the opera company. That was the dream, but the reality proved different. On October 29, 1929, the stock market crashed. Six days later, the Civic Opera House opened with a glorious *Aida*. A lively rendition of "The Star-Spangled Banner" preceded the opera. The next evening saw Mascagni's *Iris*. Gounod's *Roméo et Juliette*, Wagner's *Tristan und Isolde*, Verdi's *Il trovatore*, Bellini's *Norma* comprised the first week. Before Donizetti's *Lucia di Lammermoor* closed the season on February 1, the new opera house had seen thirty different operas, including Verdi's *Falstaff*, Montemezzi's *L'amore dei tre re*, Wagner's *Die Walküre*, Charpentier's *Louise*, Massenet's *Don Quichotte*, Halévy's *La Juive*, Zandonai's *Conchita*, and Debussy's *Pelléas et Mélisande*. Nevertheless, the days of Insull's enterprise were numbered. He had two more years before the company succumbed to the Depression. He opened the 1930-31 season with the American premiere of Ernest Moret's *Lorenzaccio*. The next evening witnessed the American debut of Lotte Lehmann as Sieglinde in Wagner's *Die Walküre*. The critics were unanimous in their praise—"She has one of the loveliest voices ever heard on the Chicago stage." In fact, Chicago heard several magnificent voices from the Civic stage. Then on December 10, 1930, the world premiere of Hamilton Forrest's *Camille* took place. Puccini's *Tosca* with Claudia Muzio opened the 1931-1932 season. For the company's last season, two novelties were staged—Max von Schillings's *Mona Lisa* and Franco Leoni's *L'oracolo*. Lehmann appeared in Wagner's *Lohengrin* and *Die Meistersinger*. Modest Mussorgsky's *Boris Godunov*, Bedřich Smetana's *Prodaná nevěsta* (The Bartered Bride), Saint-Saëns' *Samson et Dalila*, Wagner's *Tristan und Isolde*, Massenet's *Hérodiade*, and Halévy's *La Juive*, were among the other offerings. On January 29, 1932, the Chicago Civic Opera's last performance took place, Flotow's *Martha*. Then the company died.

The season after the collapse of the Civic Opera, the Chicago Stadium Grand Opera Company presented homegrown opera. They were simple productions of "standard fare" operas in the 12,000-seat Chicago Stadium. Between 1933 and 1946, several impresarios tried to breathe life into the defunct Civic Opera company, but none were successful for very long. Paul Longone was the general director of the first attempt, a company that took the name of Chicago's first opera company—Chicago Grand Opera Company. The company opened on December 26, 1933, with Maria Jeritza. On a shoestring budget, the Grand offered five weeks of familiar works. The only exception was the first Chicago staging of Puccini's *Turandot*. The second season was the last season of the Grand. Financial consideration caused the company's demise. The second attempt at resuscitation of opera came with the formation of the Chicago City Opera Company, again under the direction of Longone. Arrigo Boïto's *Mefistofele* inaugurated its first season on November 2, 1935. Premieres were again in evidence. The world premiere of Ethel Leginska's *Gale* took place on November 23, 1935, followed nine days later by the American premiere of Ottorino Respighi's *La fiamma*. During an arrangement with the Met, several of its artists sang in Chicago—Lily Pons, Lauritz Melchior, Helen Jepson, Giovanni Martinelli, Helen Traubel, Marjorie Lawrence, and Lawrence Tibbett among them. The company again reorganized, taking a new name, Chicago Opera Company. Eventually, Fortune Gallo, who had managed the San Carlo Opera Company took the reins. Familiar operas graced the stage. The only exception was Stanislaw Moniuszko's *Halka*. The company reorganized again in 1944, but did not change its name. Fausto Cleva ran the operation and conducted the season opener—Bizet's *Carmen*. During the company's brief existence (1944 to 1946), only popular fare was offered.

With the demise of the Chicago Opera, an eight-year opera drought ensued. Opera sprouted again in 1954, when the newly established Chicago Lyric Theater presented Mozart's *Don Giovanni*. The inaugural season opened on November 1, 1954, with Maria Callas causing a sensation with her American debut in Bellini's *Norma*. Two days later, Chicago heard Vittorio Giannini's *The Taming of the Shrew*. Callas returned for Donizetti's *Lucia di Lammermoor* on November, and Eleanor Steber assayed Puccini's *Tosca* three days later, with Giuseppe di Stefano as Cavaradossi, and Tito Gobbi as Scarpia. By the time Puccini's *Tosca* closed the season, the company had mounted sixteen performances of eight different operas. The operas were standard fare. It was the singers that made the season come alive. The 1955 season expanded and included two American premieres—Claudio Monteverdi's *Il ballo delle ingrate*, and Raffaelo de Banfield's *Lord Byron's Love Letter* (Tennessee Williams wrote the libretto). The singers were again the season's zenith. Not only did Callas return to open the second season, with Bellini's *I Puritani*, and to sing Verdi's *Il trovatore* and Puccini's *Madama Butterfly*, but Renata Tebaldi sang Verdi's *Aida* and Puccini's *La bohème* on alternate nights! The male artists were equally illustrious—Jussi Bjoerling, Gobbi, and di Stefano.

The financing of the company had changed from the McCormick era and box office revenue played an important role, forcing the company to emphasize popular operas with star-studded casts. At the end of the second season, a simmering bitter power struggle erupted between the founders—Fox, Kelly, and Rescigno—that resulted in nasty lawsuits and court battles. The fight revolved around who had final artistic authority. Fox felt as general director she did, but Rescigno believed as artistic director he did. Eventually Kelly backed Rescigno, and when the dust finally settled, Fox was victorious. Kelly and Rescigno departed for Dallas. They took Callas with them and established the Dallas Civic Opera (see Dallas entry). Fox renamed the company Lyric Opera of Chicago and continued her policy of popular repertory (with a strong Italian emphasis) and of hiring big-name stars. The Lyric Opera's first season opened with Steber, Mario del Monaco, and Gobbi in Puccini's *La fanciulla del West* on October 10, 1956. Ten days later, Birgit Nilsson offered an unforgettable Brünnhilde in Wagner's *Die Walküre*. Other highlights included Bjoerling and Tebaldi in Puccini's *Tosca* and Tebaldi and Richard Tucker in Verdi's *La forza del destino*. Chicago heard Leoš Janáček's *Jenůfa* for the first time in English on November 2, 1959, in a production borrowed from the Royal Opera House, Covent Garden. One critic found it "one of the dullest operas I have had the misfortune to encounter." The other critical flop was Leontyne Price cast in the title role of Massenet's *Thaïs*. More successful were Eileen Farrell and Tucker in Ponchielli's *La Gioconda*, Nilsson, Price, and di Stefano in Puccini's *Turandot*, and di Stefano, Nilsson, and Gobbi in Verdi's *Un ballo in maschera*. One of the most memorable performances took place the following season when Jon Vickers, Nilsson, Hans Hotter, and Christa Ludwig undertook Wagner's *Die Walküre*. Umberto Giordano's *Fedora* was the season's novelty.

The 1961 season heralded the company's first world premiere, Vittorio Giannini's *The Harvest*. The composer conducted his work, which was made possible with Ford Foundation money. Tucker and Joan Sutherland had opened the season in Donizetti's *Lucia di Lammermoor*. When the Lyric reached its tenth anniversary season, it became Chicago's longest surviving resident opera company. In 1964, Bruno Bartoletti, a conductor with the Lyric since 1956, was named co-artistic director with Pino Donati. The next year, Tito Gobbi made his directorial debut in Verdi's *Simon Boccanegra* and sang the title role. A nasty labor dispute with the musicians forced the cancellation of the 1967 season. Eleven years later, Krzysztof Penderecki's *Paradise Lost* was introduced to the world. The opera, based on John Milton's epic poem of the same name, was originally commissioned for the 1976 season as part of the Bicentennial celebrations. Its complex nature forced a two year postponement. Monumental in scope and exorbitant in cost, Penderecki's *Paradise Lost* was a spectacular but almost fatal achievement for the Lyric. The opera was six years in the making, $800,000 over budget, and poorly received by the critics. The work encompassed forty-four scenes, a chorus of 130 and required nine months of rehearsals. For the company's twenty-fifth-anniversary celebration, Fox assembled an astonishing array of vocal talent. The names were emblazoned in red and blue on a white background. Red carnations and floral displays blanketed the stage and proscenium. England's Princess Margaret sat in

Civic Opera House (Chicago, Illinois).

the audience while star after star paraded on stage. The climax was the appearance of Fox, amid bouquets thrown by the cast. She was greeted with a standing ovation from the audience. This spectacle lost over $1 million, and the souvenir book produced that same year, *Lyric Opera of Chicago* by Claudia Cassidy, did not sell because no review copies were offered to the critics. (All remaining copies of the book have mysteriously disappeared from the company.) Fox, who had been ill since 1975, managed to wipe out the Lyric's entire "rainy-day" endowment of $2.5 million in two years. This seriously threatened the Lyric's future, and everyone thought the end was near. Finally the board acted and ousted Fox.

Big-name-star casts that have been a Chicago tradition have continued, but the star wattage has dimmed considerably. The old style of the Lyric outbidding its competitors for the great singers is no longer possible. Instead, the Lyric has turned its attention toward filling the "holes" in its star vehicle, Italian-biased repertory. More American, German, French, Slavic, and Russian works are appearing during its seasons. Twentieth-century operas have also finally graced the stage. Among them are Luciano Berio's *La vera storia*, Dominick Argento's haunting *The Voyage of Edgar Allan Poe*, Sergey Prokofiev's *Ingrok* (The Gambler), Claude Debussy's *Pelléas et Mélisande*, and Samuel Barber's *Antony and Cleopatra*. The company even presented another world premiere on October 31, 1992, William Bolcom's *McTeague*.

The eight-opera season offers a mixture of standard, twentieth-century, and lesser known works. Recent productions include Puccini's *Tosca*, Verdi's *La traviata* and *Il trovatore*, Alban Berg's *Wozzeck*, Carlisle Floyd's *Susannah*, Rossini's *Otello*, and Massenet's *Don Quichotte*. The company performs in the Civic Opera House.

Civic Opera House

The Civic Opera Building was financed by Insull, the first president of Commonwealth Edison. Designed by the architectural firm of Graham, Anderson, Probst & White, the structure cost $30 million. Located in the mercantile district of the West Loop, the towering office-opera complex was nicknamed "Insull's Throne."

The massive structure exhibits a limestone- and terra cotta-clad façade with an intricately decorated colonnade. Flags from several nations flutter inside the peristyle. Flanked by Ionic columns, a black-and-white Civic Opera House sign hangs under the main pier arch. On a side wall, THE CIVIC OPERA HOUSE MCMXXVIII is etched. Music motifs—lyres and trumpets evoking Apollo—embellish the bronze entrance. Masks of Comedy and Tragedy ring a lofty grand foyer, illuminated with crystal-and-bronze Art Deco chandeliers. The Art Deco auditorium radiates with coral, turquoise, and gold. The fan-shaped room boasts three tiers that sweep across light mocha velvet seats. The walls and ceiling are intricately designed and carved in beige-and-gold. Lyres and trumpets infuse the hall with music motifs. Rows of gilded vines form a spectacular proscenium arch. The auditorium seats 3,450.

Practical Information. The Civic Opera House is on 20 North Wacker Drive at the Madison Street corner. The box office, inside the entrance foyer, is open daily from 9:00 A.M. until 6:00 P.M., and on performance days until 9:00 P.M. Tickets can be ordered by telephoning 312-332-2244, or writing Lyric Opera of Chicago, Box 70199, Chicago, IL 60673-0199. If you go, stay at the Four Seasons at 120 East Delaware Place, Chicago, IL 60611-0142; telephone 312-280-8800, fax 312-280-9184, reservations 1-800-332-3442. The hotel, like the Civic Opera House, occupies several floors in a high-rise office building. It is a wonderful establishment and convenient to the opera house.

COMPANY STAFF AND REPERTORY

General/Artistic Directors. Carol Fox (1956–1981); Ardis Krainik (1981–present).

American/United States Premieres (Crosby's Opera House). Offenbach's *La belle Hélène* (in English, September 14, 1867).

World Premieres (Chicago Grand Opera House). de Koven's *Robin Hood* (June 9, 1890); Herbert's *Babes in Toyland* (June 17, 1903).

American/United States Premieres (Chicago Grand Opera House). Offenbach's *Les braconniers* (November 29, 1887); Grieg's *Peer Gynt* (in English, October 29, 1906).

World Premieres (Chicago Auditorium). van Etten's *Guido ferranti* (December 29, 1914); Hadley's *Azora* (December 26, 1917); Nevin's *Daughter of the Forest* (January 5, 1918); Lazzari's *Le Sauteriot* (January 19, 1918); Février's *Gismonda* (January 14, 1919); de Koven's *Rip Van Winkle* (January 2, 1920); Leoncavallo's *Edipo Re* (December 13, 1920); Prokofiev's *Lyubov' k tryom apel'sinam* (in French as L'amour des trois oranges, December 30, 1921); Stearns's *Snowbird* (January 13, 1923); Franchetti's *Namiko-San* (December 11, 1925); Harling's *A Light From St. Agnes* (December 26, 1925); Cadman's *The Witch of Salem* (December 8, 1926).

American/United States Premieres (Auditorium). Gluck's *Orfeo ed Euridice* (first performance in Italian, November 11, 1891); Gounod's *Philemon et Baucis* (in English, December 26, 1892); Messager's *La Basoche* (in English, January 2, 1893); Massenet's *Werther* (March 29, 1894); Wolf-Ferrari's *I gioielli della Madonna* (January 16, 1912, first performance in Italian); D'Erlanger's *Noel* (January 8, 1913); Saint-Saëns's *Déjanire* (December 9, 1915); Massenet's *Cléopâtre* (January 10, 1916); Buchhalter's *A Lover's Knot* (stage premiere, January 15, 1916); Mascagni's *Isabeau* (November 12, 1917); Catalani's *Loreley* (January 17, 1919); Montemezzi's *La nave* (November 18, 1919); Ravel's *L'heure espagnole* (January 5, 1920); Massenet's *Madame Chrysanthème* (U.S. premiere, January 19, 1920); Marinuzzi's *Jacquerie* (November 17, 1920); Alfano's *Risurrezione* (December 31, 1925); Honegger's *Judith* (January 27, 1927); Handel's *Messiah* (stage presentation, March 20, 1933).

World Premieres (Civic Opera House). Forrest's *Camille* (December 10, 1930); Leginska's *Gale* (November 23, 1935); Giannini's *The Harvest* (November 25, 1961); Penderecki's *Paradise Lost* (November 29, 1978); Bolcom's *McTeague* (October 31, 1992).

American/United States Premieres (Civic Opera House). Moret's *Lorenzaccio* (October 27, 1930); Respighi's *La Fiamma* (December 2, 1935); Carrer's *Marco Bozzaris* (semi-staged scenes, January 21, 1940); Monteverdi's *Il ballo delle ingrate* (November 16, 1955); Banfield's *Lord Byron's Love Letters* (November 21, 1955).

World Premieres (Composer-in-residence program). Neil's *The Guilt of Lillian Sloan* (June 6, 1986); Goldstein's *The Fan* (June 17, 1989).

Repertory (Chicago Grand Opera Company). **1910-11:** Aida, Pelléas et Mélisande, Il trovatore, Cavalleria rusticana/I pagliacci, La bohème, Louise, Tosca, Carmen, La traviata, Faust, Salome, Rigoletto, Madama Butterfly, Lucia di Lammermoor, Thaïs, Les contes d'Hoffmann, Les Huguenots, La fanciulla del West, Otello, Un ballo in maschera. **1911-1912:** Samson et Dalila, Carmen, Lucia di Lammermoor, Le nozze di Figaro, Il trovatore, Cendrillon, La traviata, Thaïs, Hänsel und Gretel, Rigoletto, Cavalleria rusticana/I pagliacci, Il barbiere di Siviglia, Lakmé, Il segreto di Susanna/Le jongleur de Notre Dame, Natoma, Faust, Quo Vadis?, Die Walküre, Les contes d'Hoffmann, Lohengrin, I gioielli della Madonna, Tristan und Isolde. **1912-13:** Manon Lescaut, Carmen, Cavalleria rusticana/I pagliacci, Aida, Rigoletto, Cendrillon, La traviata, Il trovatore, Hamlet, I gioielli della Madonna, Das Heimchen am Herd, Faust, Les contes d'Hoffmann, Il segreto di Susanna/Hänsel und Gretel, Hérodiade, Tristan und Isolde, Mignon, Il segreto di Susanna/Le jongleur de Notre Dame, Louise, Lohengrin, Die Walküre, Il segreto di Susanna/Noel, La bohème, Tosca, Conchita, Le jongleur de Notre Dame/I dispettosi amanti. **1913-14:** Tosca, La gioconda, Don Quichotte, Madama Butterfly, Die Walküre, Aida, Natoma, Rigoletto, Samson und Dalila, La fanciulla del West, Cristoforo Colombo, I gioielli della Madonna, Carmen, La bohème, Der Kuhreigen, Hérodiade, Faust, Il barbiere di Siviglia, Don Giovanni, Zingari/I pagliacci, Fedora, Das Heimchen am Herd, Le jongleur de Notre Dame, Hänsel und Gretel, Il trovatore, Thaïs, Carmen, Les contes d'Hoffmann, La traviata, Lucia di Lammermoor, Parsifal, Manon, Louise, Monna Vanna, I dispettosi amanti, Martha.

Repertory (Chicago Opera Association). **1915-16:** La gioconda, Louise, Tristan und Isolde, Werther, La bohème, Monna Vanna, Lucia di Lammermoor, La traviata,

Tannhäuser, Das Rheingold, Tosca, Carmen, L'amore dei tre re, Il trovatore, Die Walküre, Déjanire, Madama Butterfly, Mignon, Siegfried, Götterdämmerung, I gioielli della Madonna, A Lovers' Quarrel, Parsifal, I pagliacci/La navarraise, Rigoletto, Faust, Aida, Roméo et Juliette, Cléopâtre, Thaïs, A Lovers' Knot, Tosca, Zazà, Don Giovanni. **1916-17:** Aida, Hérodiade, Andrea Chénier, Le Prophète, Carmen, Rigoletto, Hänsel und Gretel, Madeleine, Das Rheingold, Faust, Lucia di Lammermoor, Cavalleria rusticana/I pagliacci, Die Königskinder, Il trovatore, Die Walküre, La traviata, Manon, Siegfried, Madama Butterfly, Les contes d'Hoffmann, Götterdämmerung, Roméo et Juliette, Tosca, Parsifal, Falstaff, La bohème, Tannhäuser, Louise, Tristan und Isolde, Thaïs, Il barbiere di Siviglia, Le jongleur de Notre Dame, Francesca da Rimini, Lohengrin, Grisélidis. **1917-18:** Isabeau, Lucia di Lammermoor, Aida, Faust, Dinorah, Il trovatore, Roméo et Juliette, Tosca, La bohème, Carmen, Rigoletto, Les Huguenots, Manon, La traviata, Le jongleur de Notre Dame, I gioielli della Madonna, Cavalleria rusticana/I pagliacci, Louise, Il barbiere di Siviglia, Lakmé, Azora, Ernani, Daughter of the Forest, Monna Vanna, Sapho, Pelléas et Mélisande, Azora, Thaïs, Francesca da Rimini. **1918-19:** La traviata, Madama Butterfly, Il trovatore, Thaïs, Lucia di Lammermoor, Isabeau, Aida, Carmen, Guillaume Tell, Linda di Chamounix, Tosca, Roméo et Juliette, La bohème, Il barbiere di Siviglia, Faust, La Gioconda, Werther, Samson et Dalila, Cavalleria rusticana/I pagliacci, Manon, Crispino e la Comare, Dinorah, Monna Vanna, Rigoletto, Gismonda, Loreley, Cléopâtre, Le chemineau. **1919-20:** La nave, Madama Butterfly, Fedora, Un ballo in maschera, Norma, Lucia di Lammermoor, La bohème, Le Chemineau, Cléopâtre, Thaïs, Aida, Le jongleur de Notre Dame, Rigoletto, Il trittico, Carmen, La traviata, Tosca, Manon, Il barbiere di Siviglia, La sonnambula, Faust, Don Pasquale, Pelléas et Mélisande, Rip Van Winkle, Hérodiade, L'heure espagnole/I pagliacci, Monna Vanna, L'amore dei tre re, Le vieil aigle, Louise, Hamlet, Madame Chrysanthème, L'elisir d'amore. **1920-21:** Jacquerie, I gioielli della Madonna, Les contes d'Hoffmann, Cavalleria rusticana/I pagliacci, Tosca, Il trovatore, Le chemineau, Andrea Chénier, La bohème, La traviata, Rigoletto, Lucia di Lammermoor, Aida, Il barbiere di Siviglia, Gianni Schicchi, Roméo et Juliette, Edipo Re, Falstaff, Linda di Chamounix, Lakmé, L'elisir d'amore, Lohengrin, Otello, Aphrodite, Madama Butterfly, Monna Vanna, L'amore dei tre re, Manon, Die Walküre, Carmen, Faust, Mignon. **1921-22:** Samson et Dalila, Tosca, Madama Butterfly, Monna Vanna, Aida, Le jongleur de Notre Dame, Rigoletto, La bohème, Tannhäuser, Carmen, L'amore dei tre re, Otello, Faust, Roméo et Juliette, Lucia di Lammermoor, Manon, I gioielli della Madonna, Salome, Il barbiere di Siviglia, Lyubov' k tryom apel'sinam (The Love for Three Oranges), Thaïs, Pelléas et Mélisande, Lakmé, Tristan und Isolde, La fanciulla del West, Louise

Repertory (Chicago Civic Opera). **1922-23:** Aida, Carmen, La bohème, Snegurochka, L'amore dei tre re, I gioielli della Madonna, Parsifal, Tosca, Il trovatore, Madama Butterfly, Die Walküre, La fanciulla del West, Rigoletto, Cavalleria rusticana/I pagliacci, Lucia di Lammermoor, Mefistofele, Manon, La Juive, Il barbiere di Siviglia, Samson et Dalila, La forza del destino, Martha, Snowbird. **1923-24:** Boris Godunov, Samson et Dalila, Lucia di Lammermoor, Faust, La Juive, Mefistofele, Il trovatore, Siegfried, Snegurochka, L'Africaine, Manon, Andrea Chénier, Aida, Carmen, Rigoletto, Lakmé, Hänsel und Gretel, Martha, Monna Vanna, La traviata, Otello, Snowbird/Maître de chapelle/Cavalleria rusticana, La forza del destino, Il barbiere di Siviglia, Cavalleria rusticana/I pagliacci, Louise, Die Königskinder, Cléopâtre, Thaïs, Snegurochka, La jongleur de Notre Dame, La sonnambula. **1924-25:** La gioconda, Tosca, Le Prophète, Les pêcheurs des perles, Aida, Lucia di Lammermoor, Tannhäuser, Samson et Dalila, La bohème, Rigoletto, Cavalleria rusticana/I pagliacci, Il trovatore, Madama Butterfly, Aida, Thaïs, Werther, La traviata, Carmen, La Juive, Faust, Il barbiere di Siviglia, Mefistofele, Lakmé, I gioielli della Madonna, Le jongleur de Notre Dame, L'amore dei tre re, Fra Diavolo, Louise, Otello, Hänsel und Gretel, Les contes d'Hoffmann, Rigoletto, Martha, Boris Godunov, Roméo et Juliette, Pelléas et Mélisande. **1925-26:** Der Rosenkavalier, Manon Lescaut, Carmen, Un ballo in maschera, Rigoletto, La traviata, Martha, Aida, Cavalleria rusticana/I pagliacci, Il trovatore, Tosca, Samson et Dalila, Faust, Andrea Chénier, Otello, Madama Butterfly, Hérodiade, Die Walküre, Boris

Godunov, Lucia di Lammermoor, Namiko-San, Falstaff, Werther, A Light from St. Agnes, Risurrezione, Pelléas et Mélisande, Lohengrin, Louise, La Juive. **1926-27:** Aida, I gioielli della Madonna, La bohème, Risurrezione, Tristan und Isolde, Rigoletto, Il trovatore, Carmen, Lucia di Lammermoor, L'amore dei tre re, Le fille du régiment, La Juive, Samson et Dalila, La cena delle beffe, Il barbiere di Siviglia, Cavalleria rusticana/I pagliacci, La sonnambula, The Witch of Salem, Martha, L'elisir d'amore, Otello, Tiefland, La traviata, Don Giovanni, Tosca, Il trovatore, Der Rosenkavalier, Madama Butterfly, Boris Godunov, Faust, Hänsel und Gretel, Gianni Schicchi/Judith, Un ballo in maschera. **1927-28:** La traviata, Tannhäuser, Snegurochka, Il barbiere di Siviglia, Aida, Madama Butterfly, Loreley, Otello, Faust, La gioconda, Lucia di Lammermoor, Il trovatore, Martha, Gianni Schicchi/I pagliacci, Un ballo in maschera, Tosca, Falstaff, Cavalleria rusticana/I pagliacci, I gioielli della Madonna, Monna Vanna, Carmen, Linda di Chamounix, Louise, Rigoletto, Le jongleur de Notre Dame, Lohengrin, Die Fledermaus, Hänsel und Gretel, Roméo et Juliette, Sapho, Risurrezione, Samson et Dalila, The Witch of Salem. **1928-29:** Carmen, La bohème, Aida, Rigoletto, Lohengrin, Roméo et Juliette, Un ballo in maschera, Madama Butterfly, Aida, Otello, Faust, Samson et Dalila, Cavalleria rusticana/I pagliacci, Boris Godunov, Les contes d'Hoffmann, Il trovatore, Il barbiere di Siviglia, Die Walküre, Lakmé, Don Giovanni, La Juive, L'elisir d'amore, Der Rosenkavalier, Norma, Sapho, Le nozze di Figaro, L'amore dei tre re, Pelléas et Mélisande, Thaïs, Cavalleria rusticana/Judith, Don Pasquale. **1929-30:** Aida, Iris, La traviata, Roméo et Juliette, Tristan und Isolde, Il trovatore, Norma, Der Rosenkavalier, Falstaff, Faust, Tosca, L'amore dei tre re, Die Walküre, Louise, Le jongleur de Notre Dame, Don Quichotte, Tannhäuser, La Juive, Rigoletto, La forza del destino, Lohengrin, Don Giovanni, Conchita, Il barbiere di Siviglia, Lucia di Lammermoor, Thaïs, Fidelio, Pelléas et Mélisande, La gioconda, Carmen. **1930-31:** Lorenzaccio, Die Walküre, La forza del destino, I gioielli della, Madonna, Manon, Tannhäuser, L'amore dei tre re, Norma, Fidelio, Cavalleria rusticana/I pagliacci, Lohengrin, Madama Butterfly, Un ballo in maschera, Die Meistersinger, Otello, Mefistofele, La traviata, Camille, Der Rosenkavalier, Risurrezione, Il trovatore, Le Jongleur de Notre Dame, La navarraise, Prodaná nevěsta (Bartered Bride), Don Giovanni, Aida, Mignon, Tristan und Isolde, Pelléas et Mélisande. **1931-32:** Tosca, Die Zauberflöte, Aida, Rigoletto, Boris Godunov, Il trovatore, Lucia di Lammermoor, Prodaná nevěsta (Bartered Bride), La bohème, Samson et Dalila, Tristan und Isolde, Mona Lisa, Hérodiade, L'Oracolo, Gianni Schicchi, Die Meistersinger, Martha, Parsifal, La Juive, Il barbiere di Siviglia, Madama Butterfly, Mignon, Cavalleria rusticana/I pagliacci, La gioconda, Lohengrin, Carmen.

   Repertory (Chicago Grand Opera Company). **1933:** Tosca, Madama Butterfly, La bohème, Aida, Rigoletto, Carmen, Cavalleria rusticana/I pagliacci, Faust, Turandot, Manon, Il trovatore, Lohengrin, Samson et Dalila, La Gioconda, Le coq d'or, Martha, Mignon. **1934:** Turandot, Andrea Chénier, Tosca, Il trovatore, I pagliacci/Cavalleria rusticana, La. traviata, Aida, La bohème, La forza del destino, Lohengrin, Carmen, Salome/I pagliacci, Madama Butterfly, Martha, Tannhäuser, Manon, Tristan und Isolde, Don Giovanni, Faust, Rigoletto.

   Repertory (Chicago City Opera Company). **1935:** Mefistofele, Don Giovanni, Carmen, Martha, Cavalleria rusticana, Il trovatore, Thaïs, Lohengrin, La bohème, Der Rosenkavalier, Rigoletto, Turandot, Aida, Tannhäuser, Gale, Lucia di Lammermoor, La traviata, Madama Butterfly, La fiamma, Faust. **1936:** La fiamma, Thaïs, Martha, La traviata, Madama Butterfly, Mignon, Louise, Gianni Schicchi/Cavalleria rusticana, Jack and the Bean Stalk, L'elisir d'amore, Carmen, Faust, Il barbiere di Siviglia, Aida, Otello, Die Walküre, Lakmé, Mefistofele, La Juive, Prodaná nevěsta (The Bartered Bride), Lohengrin, Il trovatore, Tannhäuser, Samson et Dalila. **1937:** Aida, Samson et Dalila, Il trovatore, Madama Butterfly, Manon, Il barbiere di Siviglia, The Man without a Country, La traviata, Lucia di Lammermoor, Thaïs, Carmen, Tosca, L'amore dei tre re, Lohengrin, Norma, Tristan und Isolde, Cavalleria rusticana/I pagliacci, La gioconda, Lakmé, Otello, Faust, Die Walküre, La Juive, Hänsel und Gretel, Der Rosenkavalier, Rigoletto, Martha, La bohème, Mignon. **1938:** Otello, Aida, Die Meistersinger, La gioconda, Rigoletto, Samson et Dalila, Madama Butterfly, Les contes d'Hoffmann, Tosca, La bohème, Carmen, La traviata, Martha, Turandot, Tristan und Isolde, Lohengrin, Lucia di Lammermoor, Il barbiere di Siviglia, Die Walküre, Lakmé, Faust, Manon, Il trovatore, Hänsel und Gretel, Roméo et Juliette, Andrea Chénier, L'amore dei tre re. **1939:** Boris Godunov, Andrea Chénier, La traviata, Aida, Il barbiere di Siviglia, Louise, Faust, Mignon, La bohème, Cavalleria rusticana/I pagliacci, Carmen, Lucia di Lammermoor, Manon, Martha, Otello, Madama Butterfly, Tristan und Isolde, Tannhäuser, Lohengrin, Prodaná nevěsta (The Bartered Bride), Die Walküre, Tosca, Rigoletto, Il trovatore, Roméo et Juliette.

Repertory (Chicago Opera Company). **1940:** Aida, Tristan und Isolde, La traviata, Il trovatore, Madama Butterfly, Falstaff, Manon, Cavalleria rusticana/I pagliacci, Carmen, Rigoletto, Don Giovanni, L'amore dei tre re, Der Rosenkavalier, Die Walküre, I gioielli della Madonna, Martha, Salome, Hänsel und Gretel. **1941:** Un ballo in maschera, Carmen, Faust, La traviata, La fille du régiment, Il. barbiere di Siviglia, Otello, Aida, Lohengrin, Cavalleria rusticana/I pagliacci, Falstaff, Martha, La bohème, Il trovatore, Tosca, Madama Butterfly, Faust. **1942:** Aida, Rigoletto, Lucia di Lammermoor, Martha, Carmen, Faust, La traviata, Mignon, Il barbiere di Siviglia, Il trovatore, Halka, Manon, Otello, Cavalleria rusticana/I pagliacci, La bohème, Tosca, Les contes d'Hoffmann. **1943:** no season. **1944:** Carmen, La traviata, La bohème, Aida, Die Walküre, Il trovatore, Otello, Roméo. et Juliette, Pelléas et Mélisande, Faust, Rigoletto, Tosca. **1945:** Manon, Rigoletto, Il trovatore, Carmen, Tosca, Il barbiere di Siviglia, Parsifal, Cavalleria rusticana/I pagliacci, Faust, La forza del destino, Pelléas et Mélisande, Aida, Le nozze di Figaro. **1946:** Aida, La bohème, Amelia al ballo/The Emperor Jones, Tristan und Isolde, Rigoletto, Lucia di Lammermoor, Madama Butterfly, Tosca, Carmen, La Gioconda, Samson et Dalila, Lohengrin, Mignon, La traviata. **1947-1953:** no seasons.

Repertory (Lyric Opera of Chicago). **1954:** Il barbiere di Siviglia, La bohème, Carmen, Don Giovanni, Lucia di Lammermoor, Norma, Taming of the Shrew, Tosca, La traviata. **1955:** Aida, L'amore dei tre re, Il ballo delle ingrate, Cavalleria rusticana, Il tabarro, In ballo in maschera, La bohème, L'elisir d'amore, Faust, Lord Byron's Love Letter, Madama Butterfly, I Puritani, La revanche, Rigoletto, Il trovatore. **1956:** Andrea Chénier, Il barbiere di Siviglia, La bohème, Don Giovanni, Tosca, La traviata, Il trovatore, Die Walküre, La fanciulla del West, La forza del destino, Salome. **1957:** Adriana Lecouvreur, Andrea Chénier, In ballo in maschera, La bohème, Tosca, Cavalleria rusticana, Don Carlo, Lucia di Lammermoor, I pagliacci, La gioconda, Manon Lescaut, Mignon, Le nozze di Figaro, Otello. **1958:** Aida, Il barbiere di Siviglia, Boris Godunov, La traviata, Madama Butterfly, Falstaff, Rigoletto, Il trovatore, Tristan und Isolde, Gianni Schicchi, I pagliacci, Turandot. **1959:** In ballo in maschera, Carmen, Der fliegende Holländer, Così fan tutte, La Cenerentola, Jenůfa, La gioconda, Turandot, Thaïs, Simon Boccanegra. **1960:** Aida, La bohème, Carmen, Tosca, Madama Butterfly, Die Walküre, Fedora, Simon Boccanegra. **1961:** Andrea Chénier, Il barbiere di Siviglia, Don Giovanni, Lucia di Lammermoor, Così fan tutte, La forza del destino, Le nozze di Figaro, Fidelio, The Harvest, Mefistofele. **1962:** La bohème, L'elisir d'amore, Tosca, Rigoletto, Le nozze di Figaro, Orfeo ed Euridice, Prince Igor, Samson et Dalila. **1963:** In ballo in maschera, Il barbiere di Siviglia, Faust, Don Pasquale, Fidelio, Tannhäuser, Nabucco, Otello. **1964:** Ariadne auf Naxos, La bohème, Carmen, Don Giovanni, La Cenerentola, Don Carlo, Tosca, Il trovatore, La favorita. **1965:** Aida, La bohème, Carmina Burana, Madama Butterfly, Rigoletto, Mefistofele, Simon Boccanegra, L'heure espagnole, Wozzeck, Samson et Dalila. **1966:** Ognennïy angel (Fiery Angel), Boris Godunov, Cavalleria rusticana, La traviata, La gioconda, Otello, La giara, l'incoronazione di Poppea, Les pêcheurs de perles, Die Zauberflöte. **1968:** In ballo in maschera, Norma, Tosca, Falstaff, Salome, Manon Lescaut, Don Pasquale, Oedipus Rex, Le Rossignol **1969:** El Amor Brujo, Il barbiere di Siviglia, Cavalleria rusticana, Don Giovanni, Madama Butterfly, I Puritani, Der fliegende Holländer, Khovanshchina, Macbeth. **1970:** Billy Budd, A Kékszakállú herceg vára (Duke Bluebeard's Castle), Lucia di Lammermoor, La traviata, Madama Butterfly, Gianni Schicchi, Der Rosenkavalier, L'italiana in Algeri, Turandot. **1971:** Il barbiere di Siviglia, Don Carlo, Tosca, Rigoletto, Salome, Das Rheingold, Semiramide,

Werther. 1972: In ballo in maschera, La bohème, Così fan tutte, La traviata, Die Walküre, I due. Foscari, Pelléas et Mélisande, Wozzeck. 1973: La bohème, Carmen, Tosca, Manon, La fille du régiment, Maria Stuarda, Der Rosenkavalier, Siegfried. 1974: Madama Butterfly, Falstaff, Don Pasquale, Don Quichotte, La favorita, Götterdämmerung, Simon Boccanegra, Peter Grimes. 1975: Lucia di Lammermoor, La traviata, Le nozze di Figaro, Fidelio, Elektra, Otello, Orfeo ed Euridice. 1976: In ballo in maschera, La Cenerentola, Les contes d'Hoffmann, Tosca, Rigoletto, Khovanshchina, Lyubov' k tryom apel'sinam (The Love for Three Oranges). 1977: Il barbiere di Siviglia, L'elisir d'amore, Manon Lescaut, Idomeneo, Die. Meistersinger, Orfeo ed Euridice, Peter Grimes. 1978: Cavalleria rusticana, Madama Butterfly, La fanciulla del West, I pagliacci, Don Pasquale, Paradise Lost, Werther. 1979: Andrea Chénier, La bohème, Faust, Rigoletto, Tristan und Isolde, Simon Boccanegra, Lyubov' k tryom apel'sinam (The Love for Three Oranges). 1980: Attila, Un ballo in maschera, Boris Godunov, Don Giovanni, Lohengrin. 1981: L'elisir d'amore, Fidelio, Don Quichotte, Macbeth, Die lustige Witwe, Roméo. et Juliette, Samson et Dalila. 1982: Les contes d'Hoffmann, Così fan tutte, Tosca, Madama Butterfly, Tristan und Isolde, I pagliacci, Die Fledermaus, Luisa Miller, Rinaldo (concert version), La voix humaine. 1983: Aida, La bohème, La Cenerentola, The Mikado, Manon, Der fliegende Holländer, Ledi Makbet Mtsenskovo uyezda (Lady Macbeth of Mtsensk), Lakmé. 1984: Arabella, Il barbiere di Siviglia, Carmen, Eugene Onegin, Ernani, Die Entführung aus dem Serail, Die Frau ohne Schatten. 1985: Anna Bolena, I Capuleti e i Montecchi, La traviata, Madama Butterfly, Otello, Die Meistersinger, Samson et Dalila, La rondine. 1986: In ballo in maschera, La bohème, Lucia di Lammermoor, La gioconda, Kát'a. Kabanová, Die lustige Witwe, Parsifal, Orlando, Die Zauberflöte. 1987: Così fan tutte, Tosca, Faust, Il trovatore, La forza del destino, Le nozze di Figaro, L'italiana in Algeri, Lulu, Satyagraha. 1988: Aida, Don Giovanni, La traviata, Falstaff, Salome, La sonnambula, Tancredi, Tannhäuser. 1989: Il barbiere di Siviglia, La clemenza di Tito, Don Carlo, Tosca, Der Rosenkavalier, Die Fledermaus, Hamlet, Samson et Dalila. 1990: Alceste, Carmen, Lucia di Lammermoor, Rigoletto, La fanciulla del West, Eugene. Onegin, Die Zauberflöte, The Voyage of Edgar Allan Poe. 1991: Antony and Cleopatra, L'elisir d'amore, I Puritani, Le nozze di Figaro, Mefistofele, Igrok (The Gambler), Turandot. 1992: Otello (Rossini), Elektra, Prodaná nevěsta (The Bartered Bride), McTeague, Pelléas et Mélisande, Un ballo in maschera, La bohème. 1993: La bohème, Un ballo in maschera, Das Rheingold, Le Cid (concert version), La traviata, Don Quichotte, Susannah, Tosca, Così fan tutte, Die Walküre, Il trovatore. 1994: La traviata, Tosca, Il trovatore, Wozzeck.

Indiana ———————— INDIANAPOLIS

• *Indianapolis Opera* •

Gian Carlo Menotti's *The Telephone* with Bernice Fraction and Ted Wylie and Douglas Moore's *The Devil and Daniel Webster* with Gary Conway, Debra Lynne Hatfield, Neal Clark, Junior, and Samuel Hicks, inaugurated the Indianapolis Opera Company, the original name of the Indianapolis Opera, on March 5, 1976, at Ransburg Auditorium (on the campus of Indiana Central University). The double bill of the two contemporary operas was repeated March 6 and was the sole offering of the inaugural season. The company had been incorporated on October 1, 1975, by Miriam Ramaker.

The second season expanded to two operas, one in the contemporary vein, Carl Orff's *Die Kluge*, and one repertory favorite, Georges Bizet's *Carmen*. The

1979-80 season boasted four operas, three repertory favorites—Giacomo Puccini's *La bohème*, Bizet's *Carmen*, and Giuseppe Verdi's *Rigoletto*—and Leonard Bernstein's *Candide*, but the company had trouble sustaining four productions, and it was not until the 1989-90 season that a four-operas season had become the norm. The productions utilize an "opera as theater" philosophy, with rising young talent and established artists. Some of the emerging artists have carved out international careers. Richard Leech sang Tamino and Nemorino during the 1982-83 season, returning the following year for Alfred in Johann Strauß's *Die Fledermaus*. That same season, Ellen Shade assayed Desdemona and Kenneth Cox Méphistophélès in Charles Gounod's *Faust*. On April 18, 1986, Timothy Noble sang the title role in Verdi's *Falstaff*, and Cox returned in 1990 for Philippe II in Verdi's *Don Carlo*, with Priscilla Baskerville as Elisabeth de Valois.

The four-opera season offers a balanced repertory in the *stagione system*. There is usually a twentieth-century work, music theater piece, or operetta included each season. Recent productions include Verdi's *Il trovatore*, Puccini's *Tosca*, Donizetti's *L'elisir d'amore*, Camille Saint-Saëns's *Samson et Dalila*, and Douglas Moore's *The Ballad of Baby Doe*. The company performs in Clowes Memorial Hall.

Clowes Memorial Hall

Verdi's *Messa da Requiem*, with Ella Lee, Lili Chookasian, Walter Carringer, and Ezio Flagello inaugurated the Clowes Memorial Hall for the Performing Arts on October 20, 1963. Giacomo Puccini's *Madama Butterfly* and *La bohème*, Giuseppe Verdi's *La traviata*, and Wolfgang Amadeus Mozart's *Don Giovanni* were the initial operatic performances staged in the new house. The Hall was named after George Henry Clowes, who discovered the method for mass production of insulin. Most of the building cost of $3.5 million was donated by the Clowes family. Butler University owns and operates the theater.

Constructed of Bedford limestone and concrete, the nine-story structure overflows with vertical spaces. A six-story high lobby with full length windows forms a semi-circle around auditorium. The auditorium boasts a large open central area and shallow balconies, modelled after the seventeenth- and eighteenth-century Italian opera houses. But there is one major difference. The horseshoe-shaped tiers are raked, disconnected boxes, that allow excellent views of the stage. The theater seats 2,182.

Practical Information. The Clowes Memorial Hall is at 4600 Sunset Avenue. The box office, on the campus of Butler University, is open Monday through Saturday from 10:00 A.M. to 6:00 P.M. Tickets can be purchased by calling 317-921-6444 or 1-800-732-0804, or writing Indianapolis Opera, 250 East 38th Street, Indianapolis, IN 46205. For information call the Indianapolis Opera at 317-283-3470. If you go, stay at the Canterbury Hotel, 123 South Illinois Street, Indianapolis, IN 46225; telephone 317-634-3000, fax 317-685-2519, reservations 1-800-323-7500. The Hotel is a registered Historic Landmark, conveniently located downtown.

COMPANY STAFF AND REPERTORY

General Directors. Miriam Ramaker; Robert Driver; Durand Pope; Nando Schelle.
Repertory. **1975-76:** The Devil and Daniel Webster, The Telephone. **1976-77:** Carmen,

Die Kluge. **1978-79:** I pagliacci. **1979-80:** Candide, La bohème, Carmen, Rigoletto. **1980-81:** Aida, Il barbiere di Siviglia. **1981-82:** H.M.S. Pinafore, Madama Butterfly. **1982-83:** Il trovatore, Die Zauberflöte, L'elisir d'amore. **1983-84:** Die Fledermaus, Otello, Faust. **1984-85:** Aida, Le nozze di Figaro, The Mikado. **1985-86:** La bohème, Falstaff. **1986-87:** Carmen, Tosca, Ariadne auf Naxos. **1987-88:** Rigoletto, Il barbiere di Siviglia, Les contes d'Hoffmann. **1988-89:** La traviata, Hänsel und Gretel, La fille du régiment. **1989-90:** Die Zauberflöte, Anna Bolena, Don Carlo, Man of La Mancha. **1990-91:** The Pirates of Penzance, Don Giovanni, Orfeo ed Euridice, Faust. **1991-92:** Porgy and Bess, Madama Butterfly, Lucia di Lammermoor, Così fan tutte. **1992-93:** Il trovatore, Die lustige Witwe, Don Pasquale, Le nozze di Figaro. **1993-94:** Samson et Dalila, Tosca, L'elisir d'amore, The Ballad of Baby Doe.

Iowa
———————————— DES MOINES

• *Des Moines Metro Opera* •

On June 16, 1973, Giacomo Puccini's *La rondine* inaugurated the first season of the Des Moines Metro Opera. Defined by contemporary opera, the season included Benjamin Britten's *Albert Herring*, Gian Carlo Menotti's *The Medium*, and Arthur Benjamin's *Prima Donna*. Robert Larsen, a conductor and music professor at Simpson College, launched the Des Moines Metro Opera Summer Festival with a budget of $22,000. Larsen scheduled the unusual operas to garner national attention and to appeal to lovers of non-standard-repertory opera. He established the company, literally in the middle of the cornfields, because he felt "there was a reason for opera in the hinterlands." Twenty years later, the company is still very much Larsen's. Not only is he still the artistic director, but he directs and conducts almost every production.

Larsen believes in producing works as the composer intended, with realistic interpretation and traditional settings, especially since the audience are primarily opera neophytes. The emphasis remains on contemporary pieces and one has been mounted almost every season, including Robert Ward's *The Crucible*, Igor Stravinsky's *The Rake's Progress*, Carlisle Floyd's *Susannah*, Menotti's *The Consul*, Britten's *A Midnight Summer Night's Dream*, *The Turn of the Screw*, and *Peter Grimes*, Douglas Moore's *The Ballad of Baby Doe*, and Francis Poulenc's *Dialogues des Carmélites*. The company's first commissioned world premiere, Lee Hoiby's *The Tempest* took place on June 21, 1986. Based on Shakespeare's play, the opera was workshopped for two years before the premiere.

With more than three weeks of rehearsal for each opera, the company offers a good place for young American singers to perfect their craft, as well as a non-threatening location for the more established artists to try out new roles. A few years ago, Harry Dworchak assayed Boris Godunov for the first time in Indianola, and among the young singers making their debuts have been sopranos Jennifer Ringo and Laureen Flanigan, and baritone Robert McFarland. The Festival's productions place equal emphasize on the musical, visual, and dramatic aspects of the opera. All operas are performed in English.

The three-opera summer season offers a well-balanced schedule, emphasizing twentieth-century works, performed in repertory. The schedule includes a familiar

Blank Performing Arts Center (Indianola, Iowa).

"grand" opera, a twentieth-century piece, and a comedy. Recent productions include Giuseppe Verdi's *Un ballo in maschera*, Menotti's *The Saint of Bleecker Street*, Giacomo Puccini's *La fanciulla del West*, and Gaetano Donizetti's *Don Pasquale*. The company performs on the stage of the Pote Theater in the Blank Performing Arts Center.

Blank Performing Arts Center

The Blank Performing Arts Center opened in the spring of 1971. A special performance of Johann Strauß's *Die Fledermaus* produced by Simpson College inaugurated the structure. Charles Herbert & Associates designed the edifice, which was built at a cost of $1.5 million. Located on the campus of Simpson College, the Center is primarily a college performing venue.

The Center is reached by crossing a concrete bridge with A.H. & THEO BLANK PERFORMING ARTS CENTER in large bronze letters affixed to its concrete sides. The modern concrete and glass structure is geometric in shape. The glass and concrete carry into the lobby, where a huge "set piece" decorates the wall. The Pote Theater, one of two performing venues in the Center, offers a unique amphitheater-style house. Steeply raked, green-fabric seats form a semi-circle around the half-moon stage, bringing the singers close to the audience. The intimate space allows the audience to become more involved in the opera than is possible in larger halls. Dark-wood vertical boards clad the theater's front wall and also act as a proscenium arch. Brown-wooden slats cover the side walls. Acoustic squares alternate with spot-lights on the black ceiling. The auditorium seats 488.

Practical Information. Blank Performing Arts Center is at North D Street, on the campus of Simpson College in Indianola. Tickets can be purchased at the Des Moines Metro Opera, 106 West Boston Avenue, or by telephoning 515-961-6221 weekdays during business hours or by writing Des Moines Metro Opera Box Office, 106 West Boston Avenue, Indianola, IA 50125. If you visit, stay at the Apple Tree Inn, 1215 North Jefferson, Indianola, phone (515) 961-0551, fax (515) 961-0555. It is a comfortable inn, conveniently located to the theater.

COMPANY STAFF AND REPERTORY

General/Artistic Director. Robert Larsen (1973–present).
World Premieres. Hoiby's *The Tempest* (June 21, 1986); Paulus's *Harmoonia* (Opera Iowa educational touring troupe, February 23, 1991).
American/United States Premieres. Benjamin's *Prima Donna* (professional stage premiere, June 23, 1973); Spedding's *London's Burning* (children's opera, June 1982
Repertory. 1973: La rondine, The Medium, Prima Donna, Albert Herring. 1974: Madama Butterfly, The Crucible, Falstaff. 1975: Il trittico, Die Zauberflöte, The Rake's Progress. 1976: Il barbiere di Siviglia, Manon, Susannah. 1977: Così fan tutte, La traviata, Les contes d'Hoffmann. 1978: Carmen, La bohème, The Consul. 1979: Die Fledermaus, Rigoletto, A Midsummer's Night Dream. 1980: Il trovatore, Don Pasquale, Ariadne auf Naxos. 1981: Tosca, The Ballad of Baby Doe, Lucia di Lammermoor. 1982: Otello, L'elisir d'amore, Don Giovanni. 1983: Cavalleria rusticana/I pagliacci, Die lustige Witwe, La fille du régiment. 1984: Le nozze di Figaro, Dialogues des Carmélites, Aida. 1985: Faust, La Cenerentola, Of Mice and Men. 1986: Falstaff, The Tempest, Roméo et Juliette. 1987: La bohème, Der fliegende Holländer, The Turn of the Screw. 1988: Il barbiere di Siviglia, Turandot, Die Zauberflöte. 1989: Les contes d'Hoffmann, Die Fledermaus, The Crucible. 1990: Boris Godunov, Martha, La traviata. 1991: Peter Grimes, Die Entführung aus dem Serail, Madama Butterfly. 1992: Lucia di Lammermoor, Der Rosenkavalier, La fanciulla del West. 1993: Don Pasquale, Un ballo in maschera, The Saint of Bleecker Street.

Kentucky ———————————— LOUISVILLE

• *The Kentucky Opera* •

The doublebill of Gian Carlo Menotti's *The Medium / The Telephone* inaugurated the Kentucky Opera on February 5, 1953, in the Columbia Auditorium. The Kentucky Opera's founder, Moritz von Bomhard, was on the podium. Bomhard had been enticed to the area by some prominent local families who wanted him to establish a resident opera company. The seeds for a homegrown opera were planted four years earlier, when Bomhard visited Louisville with his traveling opera troupe. He had presented Wolfgang Amadeus Mozart's *Il nozze di Figaro* on December 7 and 8, 1949, at the University of Louisville.
James Caldwell, who had built the Camp Street and St. Charles Theaters in New Orleans (see the New Orleans entry), also owned a theater in Louisville. During the summer of 1836, he brought the Montressor Italian troupe, after its New Orleans season, to perform in Louisville. Other traveling opera companies followed

in the mid-nineteenth century, offering the city novelties like Ferdinand Raimund's *Der Alpenkönig und der Menschenfeind* and Jacques Offenbach's *L'Île de Tulipatan*. But there was no regular opera performed in the state until the birth of the Kentucky Opera.

The company garnered national attention soon after its establishment. Five world premieres were commissioned during its first six seasons, the result of Louisville's enterprising mayor, Charlie Farnesley. Farnesley had received a Rockefeller Foundation grant for $400,000 to commission five one hour, one-act works. The first world premiere, Peggy Glanville-Hicks's *The Transposed Heads* took place on March 28, 1954, and Richard Mohaupt's *Double Trouble* followed. The most successful of the group was Rolf Liebermann's *School for Wives*, first seen on December 3, 1955. This opera was repeated a decade late and incorporated into the repertory of several European houses. An additional world premiere, Lee Hoiby's *Beatrice*, was commissioned by George Norton, scion of a prominent Louisville family and first seen in 1959. During the 1950s, rarely-performed operas joined the world premieres in the repertory, including Maurice Ravel's *L'heure espagnole*, Emmanuel Chabrier's *L'éducation manquée*, Kurt Weill's *Street Scene*, and Igor Stravinsky's *L'histoire du soldat*. Repertory favorites, however, were not neglected. In the beginning, Bomhard not only conducted and directed, but also trained the singers and chorus, created and painted the sets, and even designed the brochures. The singers were imported from New York, with Tatiana Troyanos (Carmen) and Johanna Meier (Senta) among them. The artists available partially determined the repertory.

For the second decade, rarely performed works and contemporary pieces continued to find a home in Louisville. Carl Orff's *Carmina Burana* and *Die Kluge*, Weill's *Down in the Valley*, and Stravinsky's *Oedipus Rex* were staged alongside the standard repertory. Financial considerations brought a change in casting during the 1970s, when young talented singers replaced the experienced imported New York artists. The repertory remained adventurous and unique. Louisville saw two Leoš Janáček's operas—*Jenůfa* and *Kát'a Kabanová*—a decade before the composer's current popularity and two American operas—Carlisle Floyd's *Susannah* and Douglas Moore's *Ballad of Baby Doe*. As is inevitable in every opera company, there are some disasters that cannot be forgotten. One such event in Bomhard's reign took place during a performance of Mozart's *Don Giovanni*. Audrey Nossaman was halfway across the stage when she suddenly could not move any further. Her dress had caught on the scenery. She pulled and pulled and pulled until all the scenery collapsed—on her.

After thirty years at the helm, Bomhard stepped down in 1982. Thomson Smillie took the reins and continued to offer unusual works. Revivals of long-forgotten masterpieces—Christoph Gluck's *Alceste*, Henry Purcell's *Dido and Aeneas*, and Donizetti's *L'ajo nell'imbarazzo*—took their places along side contemporary works including Igor Stravinsky's *L'histoire du soldat*, Robert Ward's *Crucible*, and Philip Glass's *The Fall of the House of Usher*. Staged at the Macauley Theater on May 29, 1988, Glass's *The Fall of the House of Usher* was a joint commission with the American Repertory Theater in Cambridge. It was based on Edgar Allan Poe's tale of terror of the same name. The first world premiere in more than three decades came two years later when Daniel Dutton's *The Stone Man* was staged in the Bomhard Theater. The one act opera with a *divertissement* dealt with a surrealistic-type journey undertaken by a Dreamer through the mountains of

Kentucky. At the end he finds the reality of life balanced by the uncertainties of dream. The opera received a mixed reception. The casts are established international artists—and occasionally unique. The cast in a production of Bellini's *Norma* consisted of three sisters—Esther, Ruby, and Grace Hinds. The production of Bellini's *Norma* was also distinctive, with its symbolic and evocative scenery, prompting one patron to exclaim, "This is the strangest scenery I have ever seen!" Smillie has brought some of the adventure and flavor of European operagoing to Louisville with unusual operas and innovative sets.

The four-opera season offers a balanced repertory of grand opera and musical theater in a *stagione* system. Recent productions include Giacomo Puccini's *La bohème*, Benjamin Britten's *Turn of the Screw*, Verdi's *Rigoletto*, Andrew Lloyd Webber's *The Phantom of the Opera*, and Antonio Salieri's *Prima la musica e poi le parole*. The company performs in three different-size theaters, Whitney Hall and the Bomhard Theater in the Kentucky Center for the Performing Arts, and the Macauley Theater.

Kentucky Center for the Performing Arts

The Kentucky Center for the Performing Arts was inaugurated on November 19, 1983, with a gala program featuring Charlton Heston, Art Buchwald, Douglas Fairbanks Jr., and Jessye Norman. Designed by Caudill Rowlett Scott, Inc. the Center cost $23.5 million and took three-and-a-half years to build. The need for a cultural center dated back to 1967, when James Graham Brown, who owned the Brown Hotel and the Brown Theater, wanted to tear down the theater to build a parking garage for his hotel. Although Brown died a year later and the theater survived, the need for a performing arts center remained. The State of Kentucky realized the need and authorized the funds for construction of the performing arts center.

Located on the banks of the Ohio River, the Center is a striking structure of terra cotta brick, mirrored glass, and black-enamelled steel that rises like a giant wave. The lobby's modern decor includes walls of glass, white concrete, coffee-wood paneling, and mocha-colored brick. Whitney Hall (named after the Louisville Orchestra's founder, Robert Whitney) is a large, modern auditorium, boasting two shiny-white tiers. Tub-like boxes protrude from the coffee-wood side walls. Maroon velvet plush seats stretch uninterrupted across the room, and acoustic-cloud panels hang from the black grid-like ceiling. The Hall seats 2,479.

The Bombard Theater is identified by MORITZ VON BOMHARD THEATER in white letters on the smoked-glass entrance. The auditorium is fan-shaped with gray fabric seats. Its beige walls are sculpted like an accordion. The proscenium is black. The theater also boasts an unusual feature—a sound-proof cry room. Upset children are brought there until they calm down. The Bomhard seats 626.

Macauley Theater

The Macauley Theater was born as the Brown Theater on October 5, 1925. After major renovation in 1973, the theater was renamed. The Macauley Theater exhibits elegant and classic decor. The resplendent red, white, and gold lobby sparkles with beaded-glass and nugget-ribbon chandeliers. Gilded Grecian urns and mirrors

Kentucky Center for the Arts (Louisville, Kentucky).

flanked by Doric columns decorate the walls of the ivory-and-gold auditorium. White Corinthian columns surmounted by gold capitals define the proscenium. A single tier rises above the red fabric orchestra seats. The Macauley seats 1,453.

Practical Information. The Kentucky Center for the Arts is at 5 Riverfront Plaza (on Main Street between 5th and 6th Avenues). The ticket office is on the right side of the entrance lobby and is open Monday through Saturday from 9:00 A.M. to 5:00 P.M., Sunday from 12:00 noon until 5:00 P.M., and one half hour past curtain time on performance days. A drive-through box office is located behind the Kentucky Center at 5 Riverfront Plaza. Here you can purchase tickets without leaving your car. It is open Monday through Friday from 9:00 A.M. to 6:00 P.M. The Macauley Theater is at Broadway and Third Street. Its box office only opens an hour before curtain. All tickets are sold at the Kentucky Center ticket office at the above address. Tickets can be ordered by telephoning 502-584-7777, 502-584-4500 or 1-800-283-7777, or writing Kentucky Opera, 631 South Fifth Street, Louisville, KY 40202. If you visit, stay at the Seelbach Hotel, 500 Fourth Avenue, Louisville, KY 40202; telephone 502-585-3200, fax 502-587-6564, reservations 1-800-333-3399. The Seelbach was built in 1905 and is a historically significant building. It is decorated in period furnishings. Several American presidents—William Taft, Woodrow Wilson, Franklin Roosevelt, Harry Truman, John Kennedy, and Lyndon Johnson—have stayed at the hotel while visiting Louisville.

COMPANY STAFF AND REPERTORY

General/Artistic Directors. Moritz von Bomhard (1953–1982); Thomson Smillie (1982–present).

American/United States Premieres (before Kentucky Opera). Raimund's *Der Alpenkönig und der Menschenfeind* (May 7, 1854); Offenbach's *Le Violoneux* (possibly earlier elsewhere, July 6, 1860); Offenbach's *L'Île de Tulipatan* (March 10, 1876).

World Premieres (Kentucky Opera). Glanville-Hicks's *The Transposed Heads*

(March 28, 1954); Mohaupt's *Double Trouble* (December 10, 1954); Antheil's *The Wish* *(April 3, 1955); Liebermann's School for Wives* (December 3, 1955); Nabokov's *The Holy Devil* (April 16, 1958); Hoiby's *Beatrice* (October 30, 1959); Dutton's *The Stone Man* (January 6, 1990). *Repertory.* 1953: The Medium/The Telephone, La traviata. 1953-54: Transposed Heads, Die Entführung aus dem Serail, Tosca, L'heure espagnole. 1954-55: L'éducation manquée, I pagliacci, Double Trouble, Le nozze di Figaro. 1955-56: The Wish, School for Wives, Die lustigen Weiber von Windsor, Madama Butterfly. 1956-57: Faust, Così fan tutte, Street Scene. 1957-58: Don Giovanni, The Holy Devil, Die Fledermaus. 1958-59: Hänsel und Gretel, Orphée aux enfers, Rigoletto. 1959-60: Don Pasquale, Beatrice, Amahl and the Night Visitors, La bohème, L'histoire du soldat. 1960-61: Lucia di Lammermoor, Cavalleria rusticana, L'heure espagnole, La Cenerentola, Prodaná nevšta (The Bartered Bride). 1961-62: Carmina Burana, Tosca, Il barbiere di Siviglia, Aida, Down in the Valley. 1962-63: Die Zauberflöte, Die Kluge, Madama Butterfly, Il trovatore. 1963-64: Carmen, Die Entführung aus dem Serail, Gianni Schicchi, Rigoletto. 1964-65: Così fan tutte, Les contes d'Hoffmann, Die Fledermaus, Oedipus Rex. 1965-66: Faust, School for Wives, La bohème, Un ballo in maschera. 1966-67: Orfeo ed Euridice, I pagliacci, The Medium/The Telephone, Le nozze di Figaro, La traviata. 1967-68: Die lustige Witwe, Boris Godunov, Don Giovanni, Tosca. 1968-69: Die Zauberflöte, Prodaná nevěsta (The Bartered Bride), Ariadne auf Naxos, Il trovatore. 1969-70: The Rape of Lucretia, Lucia di Lammermoor, Roméo et Juliette, Madama Butterfly. 1970-71: Carmen, Manon, Il barbiere di Siviglia, Macbeth. 1971-72: L'elisir d'amore, Turandot, Die Fledermaus, Rigoletto. 1972-73: Don Pasquale, Jenůfa, La bohème, Aida, La traviata. 1973-74: Susannah, Die Entführung aus dem Serail, Tosca, Otello. 1974-75: Così fan tutte, Carmina Burana, Il tabarro, Der fliegende Holländer. 1975-76: Faust, Kát'a Kabanová, Le nozze di Figaro, Salome. 1976-77: The Ballad of Baby Doe, Don Giovanni, Madama Butterfly, Un ballo in maschera. 1977-78: Peter Grimes, Die Zauberflöte, Il barbiere di Siviglia, Macbeth. 1978-79: L'elisir d'amore, I pagliacci, Der Schauspieldirektor, La bohème, Rigoletto. 1979-80: Lucia di Lammermoor, Hänsel und Gretel, Die Fledermaus, Il trovatore. 1980-81: Carmen, Les contes d'Hoffmann, Tosca, The Crucible. 1981-82: Le nozze di Figaro, Prodaná nevěsta (The Bartered Bride), Ariadne auf Naxos, La traviata. 1982-83: Alceste, Così fan tutte, Madama Butterfly, Rigoletto. 1983-84: The Turn of The Screw, Don Pasquale, Don Giovanni, La bohème. 1984-85: Les pêcheurs des perles, Albert Herring, Turandot, L'italiana in Algeri. 1985-86: Fidelio, Trial By Jury, Die lustige Witwe, Die Entführung aus dem Serail, Dido and Aeneas. 1986-87: Porgy and Bess, Zolotoy petushok (The Golden Cockerel), Il barbiere di Siviglia, Aida. 1987-88: The Mikado, The Fall of the House of Usher, Salome, Il trovatore. 1988-89: Carmen, A Midsummer's Night Dream, Cox and Box, Trial By Jury, The Mikado, The Yeoman of the Guard, Falstaff. 1989-90: L'ajo nell'imbarazzo, The Stone Man, Die Zauberflöte, L'histoire du soldat, La traviata. 1990-91: Norma, The Pirates of Penzance, Il barbiere di Siviglia, Otello. 1991-92: My Fair Lady, Der Schauspieldirektor/Prima la musica e poi le parole, Lucia di Lammermoor. 1992-93: Madama Butterfly, Così fan tutte, The Turn of the Screw, Don Pasquale. 1993-94: La bohème, H.M.S. Pinafore, The Phantom of the Opera, Rigoletto.

Louisiana
———————————— BATON ROUGE

• *Baton Rouge Opera* •

Giuseppe Verdi's *Aida* inaugurated the Baton Rouge Opera in October, 1982, at the Centroplex. Henry Purcell's *Dido and Aeneas* completed the inaugural season.

Dolores Ardoyno and Donald Dorr founded the company. The second season expanded to three works. The company's first world premiere, William Still's *Minette Fontaine* took place on October 24, 1984. A second world premiere, Dinos Constantinides's *Antigone*, was presented on March 17, 1993. The cast is a mixture of up-and-coming stars and established artists, supported by local talent.

The three-opera season offers a mixture of traditional and contemporary works. Recent productions include Giacomo Puccini's *Tosca*, Jacques Offenbach's *Orpheus in the Underworld*, and Wolfgang Amadeus Mozart's *Die Zauberflöte*. The company performs in the Louisiana State University's 1,200-seat Union Theater.

Practical Information. The Union Theater is at the corner of Highland and tadium Streets. Tickets can be purchased at the LSU Union Theater Box Office at the above address, by calling 504-388-5128, or by writing LSU Union Theater Box Office, Box 25162, Baton Rouge, LA 70894.

COMPANY STAFF AND PREMIERES

General/Artistic Directors. Donald Dorr; Marioara Trifan.
World Premieres. Still's *Minette Fontaine* (October 24, 1984); Constantinides's *Antigone* (March 17, 1993).

───────── NEW ORLEANS

• *The New Orleans Opera* •

The inaugural performance of the New Orleans Opera, a double bill of Pietro Mascagni's *Cavalleria Rusticana* and Ruggero Leoncavallo's *Pagliacci*, took place in the open-air City Park stadium on June 11, 1943. The company called its efforts "Opera under the Stars." A group headed by Walter Loubat drew up a Charter that created the New Orleans Opera, so homegrown opera could again thrive in the city that boasted America's first permanent opera company, and for many years, its only opera company.

Tradition maintained that when New Orleans was under Spanish rule, Louis Tabary and his troupe performed "opera sketches" as early as 1791 in Le Spectacle de la Rue St. Pierre. Henry Kmen in his *Music in New Orleans* objects to this account, claiming that Tabary did not move to New Orleans until 1804. A group of refugees, however, did flee from Saint Domingue to New Orleans and performed comic opera, vaudeville, and drama at Le Spectacle. Louis Alexandre Henry built the theater on St. Peter Street, which opened on October 4, 1792. The first opera on record in New Orleans is the American premiere of André Grétry's *Sylvain* on May 22, 1796. Nicolas Dezède's *Blaise et Babet* followed on July 17, 1796, and three years later, the first performance in America of Nicolas Dalayrac's *Renaud d'Ast* took place on September 3, 1799. St. Pierre intermittently hosted operas until the city council ordered it closed due to structural defects on December 12, 1803. Jean Baptiste Fournier, a newly arrived actor, repaired the theater and reopened it around the end of 1804. Between June 1805 and February 1806, St. Peter witnessed sixteen different operas including several novelties, Giovanni Paisiello's *Il barbiere di Siviglia*, François Adrien Boieldieu's *Le Calife de Bagdad*, and Étienne Méhul's *Euphrosine*. The most popular composers were Dalayrac and Grétry. Tabary took over the directorship of the St. Pierre on March 1, 1806, and offered the American premiere of Pierre Monsigny's *La belle Arsène* later that year.

Opera had grown in popularity with the Creole population and a second opera house, Théâtre St. Philippe, opened on Saturday, January 30, 1808, with *Les fausses consultations* (French play) followed by Méhul's *Une Folie*. The "new" theater already had a "history." It was Bernardo Coquet's house on St. Philippe Street known as Salle Chinoise, where racially mixed dances took place. Before St. Philippe played the role of an opera house, Coquet had previously opened the Salle as Les Varietes Amusantes where he offered vaudeville and comedies. For a couple of years, this small town of 15,000 boasted two opera houses. One night Monsigny's *Felix* played at St. Pierre and the next night Grétry's *Richard, Coeur de Lion* played at St. Philippe. By alternating nights of shows, both theaters were able to survive harmoniously. But the harmony did not last long. On Sunday, April 24, 1808, both theaters scheduled programs at the same time: St. Philip offered the pantomime-ballet *Captain Cook*, and St. Peter presented Pierre Antoine della Maria's *L'opéra comique*. Two weeks later, both theaters again scheduled performances on the same day—May 8—with Monsigny's *Le deserteur* at St. Philip and Dalayrac's *Azémia* at St. Peter. The conflict came to a boil when both theaters scheduled Maria's *L'opéra comique* on the same day.

After the St. Philippe temporarily ceded defeat with an aptly named "heroic-tragic-comedy in prose, verse, and songs," *La mort de St. Philippe tué par St. Pierre* (The Death of St. Philip, killed by St. Peter), it closed its doors as an opera house and reopened under the name Winter Tivoli, reverting to its previous function of hosting racially mixed balls. That lasted only until May 31, 1809, when it reopened again as an opera house with another appropriately entitled piece, *Le resurrection de St. Philippe, ou le petit bonhomme vit encore* (The Resurrection of St. Philip, or the Good Little Man Lives Again). St. Philip was closed in December of that year and for most of 1810 while workmen virtually rebuilt it. The St. Pierre continued hosting opera until the St. Philippe was reopened. The swan song of the St. Pierre came on Sunday, December 9, 1810, with Philip Laroque's *Pauvre Jacques*. The theater was sold on Friday, December 28, 1810, and razed in 1821. With the demise of St. Peter, the first decade of opera in New Orleans came to a close. The city had seen more than three hundred performances of seventy-six operas by thirty-two composers. Méhul's *Une folie* was the most staged opera and Dalayrac the most popular composer. The St. Philippe became the anchor of opera in the city, reopening on December 20, 1810, with Grétry's *Sylvain* and Dalayrac's *Adolphe et Clara*. For the next five and a half years, it hosted forty-three novelties, including Boieldieu's *Ma Tante Aurore*, Luigi Cherubini's *Les deux journées*, Méhul's *Joseph*, and Nicolò Isouard's *Le billet de loterie*. A Spanish troupe from Havana mounted the final performances in January 1824, including the American premiere of Ferdinando Paër's *Le maître de chapelle*. The St. Philippe ended its life as the Washington Ballroom.

Back in 1806, Tabary had purchased a lot on Orleans Street between Bourbon and Royal. He hired the architect Hyacinthe Laclotte to build the Théâtre d'Orléans, but insufficient funds suspended the project. It took nine years before the Théâtre d'Orléans opened on October 19, 1815. Pierre Gaveaux's *Une quarte heure de silence* celebrated the event. The first season was a struggle. One disaster after another descended upon the theater before Henri Berton's *Ninon chez Madame de Sevigne* ended the season on June 6, 1816. During the sweltering summer, fire turned the ill-fated structure into a heap of ash. Cayetano Mariotini was in New Orleans with his circus when the Théâtre d'Orléans burned, so he decided to build a theater. The ballet, *La mort du Capitaine Cook*, inaugurated the Olympic Theater on February 22, 1817. Rodolphe Kreutzer's *Paul and Virginia* was the first opera to grace the stage a few months later. Cayetano mounted his last opera on April 20, 1817, and then went bankrupt. Although he died soon after, operas continued to be staged. The second season opened on December 14 with Gaveaux's *La jambe de bois*. Performances lasted until March. The Olympic was put up for sale in September.

Meanwhile, another impresario, John Davis, was determined to rebuilt the Théâtre d'Orléans. After several setbacks, the Orleans Theater opened on Saturday, November 27, 1819, with a performance dedicated to Davis. After an initial "Washington's March" overture, the curtain rose at half past six on Boieldieu's *Jean de Paris* followed by Berton's *Les maris garçons*. The beginning of 1820 saw the arrival of a Virginia Company headed by James Caldwell. Caldwell initially played at the St. Philippe, opening on January 8 with William Shield's *Rosina*. Henry Bishop's *Guy Mannering*, Gioachino Rossini's *La donna del lago* (in English as the Lady of the Lake) were among the five operas staged during his initial season. Caldwell soon left the St. Philippe and rented the Orleans Theater, presenting opera on the Monday, Wednesday, Friday, and Saturday nights when the French company was off. For a few years, the Orleans was home to both French and English opera. Caldwell became discontented with his rented quarters and constructed his own theater in the American part of town. Located on Camp Street, the theater was reminiscent of the Chestnut Street Theater in Philadelphia. The Camp Street Theater, also known as the Old American Theater, opened on January 1, 1824. The rivalry caused Davis financial problems that resulted in the temporary closing of his theater. On June 6, 1824, Boieldieu's *Le petit chaperon rouge* was the last opera staged at the Orleans for several months. During its first five years, the Orleans theater, with some help from the St. Philippe, hosted 140 operas by 50 different composers, including 52 novelties for a total of 462 performances. This was an impressive number in a city with under 30,000 inhabitants. Boieldieu was the favorite composer and his *Jean de Paris* was the favorite opera.

Davis reopened his theater and mounted the American premiere of Boieldieu's *La dame blanche* on February 6, 1827, only one year after its world premiere in Paris. Davis brought his troupe from France and had to pay them year-round, so he began making tours up north during the oppressive New Orleans summer to prevent the financial hardships that befell him in the past. His first was in the summer of 1827. During these tours he presented works in New York and Philadelphia that have erroneously been attributed as American premieres, when in fact almost all the operas had previously been staged in New Orleans. (By 1827, New Orleanians had witnessed more than one hundred premieres of "foreign language" opera.) Davis returned every December for the New Orleans season offering the usual French fare and some novelties. After his first northern tour, he opened the season with Boieldieu's *Jean de Paris*, and presented the America premiere of Gasparo Spontini's *La Vestale* on February 17, 1828. Hérold's *Marie* opened the 1829-30 season on Sunday, November 22.

Caldwell, meanwhile, exhibited an ambitious repertory, mounting over one hundred performances of opera between 1827 and 1833, including Rossini's *Il barbiere di Siviglia* (as The Barber of Seville), Mozart's *Le nozze di Figaro* (as The Marriage of Figaro), Boieldieu's *Jean de Paris* (as John of Paris), and Rossini's *La Cenerentola* (as Cinderella). The 1833-34 season witnessed the English singers Elizabeth Austin and John Sinclair, along with Auber's *Fra Diavolo* and *La muette de Portici* (Masaniello), Henry Bishop's *Guy Mannering* and *Rob Roy Macgregor*, John Gay's *The Beggar's Opera* and repeats from the previous season. Caldwell's greatest coup came on Monday, March 30, 1835, when he presented Meyerbeer's masterpiece *Robert le Diable* before the Théâtre d'Orléans (the French theater) did. Caldwell, however, had more ambitious plans — to build the largest and most resplendent opera house in the United States, and on May 9, 1835, construction began on the St. Charles Street Theater. The opera house cost $325,000 and had places for over 4,000 spectators. The theater opened on Monday, November 30, 1835, with the overtures to Auber's *La muette de Portici* and Weber's *Der Freischütz*. The first full opera, Mozart's *Le nozze di Figaro*, appeared the following evening. New Orleans now had three opera houses with a population of only 60,000! During the spring of 1836, it was possible to hear (Misses) Gibbs in Rossini's *La cenerentola* at the St. Charles, (Miss) Russell in Bellini's *La sonnambula* (in English as the Sleepwalker) at the Camp Street Theater, or Auber's *Le cheval de bronze* at the Orleans. In a single week in April, there were fourteen performances of nine operas. Caldwell imported the well-known Italian opera troupe of Montressor and expanded it with talent from the Havana Opera. They mounted the American premieres of numerous Italian works including Bellini's *Norma*, Rossini's *Semiramide*, and Donizetti's *Parisina*. English opera was not neglected during the Italians' visit: they sang Sundays, Wednesdays, and Fridays, and the Americans on the remaining nights.

In April 1837, financial factors and the shareholders forced Davis out of the theater he had built and controlled for almost two decades. He died two years later, on June 13, 1839. The Orleans continued to present French grand opera and introduce important works to America. Operas by Giacomo Meyerbeer, Fromental Halévy, and Auber dominated the repertory, and counted among the American premieres were Meyerbeer's *Les Huguenots* and *Le Prophète*, Rossini's *Guillaume Tell*, and Halévy's *La Juive*. Celebrated artists graced the stage. In five years beginning in 1836, the Orleans hosted almost four hundred performances of more than seventy different operas. Disaster struck the Orleans on February 26, 1854. A vaudeville show, *La petit fille de la grande armée*, was entertaining the Sunday matinee audience, when near the end of the second act the spectators heard a loud crack. They thought it was part of the show and paid no heed until they heard "crackling and crashing of timber, and the screams of women and shouts of men." The second and third galleries, under the weight of a sold-out crowd, separated from the wall and plunged toward the orchestra. Bedlam erupted and those that could escape ran screaming from the hall. The Orleans was quickly repaired and opera and vaudeville graced the stage again. It was the sale of the theater in 1859 to a new owner, Charles Parlange, that doomed it to a comprimario role in the New Orleans lyric world. Parlange lost no time in increasing the rental fee, and Charles

Boudousquié, who was the opera manager for the Théâtre d'Orléans, was so enraged that he decided to construct his own shrine to opera, the French Opera House. The demise of the Théâtre d'Orléans came on December 7, 1866, when a fire, begun in the wardrobe room, swallowed the structure.

Construction began in June at Bourbon and Toulouse Streets and in 233 days, the French Opera House was completed. Designed by James Gallier Jr., it cost $118,500. The theater was an impressive Italian-styled brick structure that towered over the neighboring buildings. Two steep and broad staircases led directly from the street into the gold, red, and creamy white, elliptical auditorium. There were seats for 1,600, which was later enlarged to 1,805, and standing room for 400 to 800 people. Rossini's *Guillaume Tell* inaugurated the new opera house on December 1, 1859. An overflowing crowd jammed into the theater to experience its splendor. Adelina Patti first appeared on the stage of the French on December 18, 1860, when she was only seventeen years old. She sang in Donizetti's *Lucia di Lammermoor* (December 18), Friedrich von Flotow's *Martha* (December 29), Rossini's *Il barbiere di Siviglia* (December 31), Giuseppe Verdi's *Il trovatore* (January 2), and *Rigoletto* (February 6), and created the title role in the American premiere of Meyerbeer's *Le pardon de Ploërmel* (March 4, 1861). She visited New Orleans frequently, always to a rousing reception.

On January 26, 1861, Louisiana seceded from the Union and eleven weeks later, the first shots were fired at Fort Sumter. Within a year, northerners occupied New Orleans, and the opera house remained dark during the Civil War. After Lee surrendered in 1865, three brothers, Charles, Marcelin, and Paul Alhaiza reopened the French. Charles and Marcelin sailed to France to recruit a new troupe, but they never returned. Marcelin died in France, and Charles with the entire company went down with the steamship *Evening Star* off the coast of Georgia. Paul, the sole surviving brother vowed to keep the theater in operation, and the Ghioni and Susini Italian Opera Company opened a short season at the French on Monday November 19, 1866. During their visit, Amelia Patti, Adelina's sister was introduced to New Orleans. Later in the season, the Grand Theatre of Mexico appeared.

By the 1870s, the seasons at the French Opera House lasted three months and like the Théâtre d'Orléans, the management hired all the performers and musicians from France. Grand opera occupied the stage Tuesday, Thursday, and Saturday nights. Light opera appeared on Sunday afternoon and operetta were heard Sunday evening. In 1885, James Mapleson brought Her Majesty's Opera Company with both Adelina and Emma Nevada. Nevada opened the engagement in Bellini's *La sonnambula* followed by Patti, who gave a electrifying performance in Verdi's *La traviata*. In fact, it was so spectacular, it was feared she had brought down the house. Patti had just finished "Alfredo, Alfredo, di questo core . . . io spenta ancora t'amerò" and applause of such force and magnitude followed that plaster began to fall from the ceiling. Bedlam erupted. Her fans remembered the Théâtre d'Orléans disaster and raced to the exits. The French had the glorious distinction of hosting dozens of American premieres during its lifetime, counted among them are Ambroise Thomas's *Mignon*, Ernest Reyer's *Salammbô*, and Jules Massenet's *Le Cid*, *Hérodiade*, and *Don Quichotte*. In 1909, the patrons of the French were treated to one of the most extraordinary vocal displays. The opera was Verdi's *Il trovatore* and Escalais had just finished Manrico's aria "Di quella pira" with its high C's ("Oteco almeno corro a morir") when the enthusiasm of the ovation prompted him to repeat the aria. He ultimately sang the aria five times, never missing any of the high C's. World War I cut off the theater's lifeblood, since no performing troupes or scenery could be imported. A storm on September 29, 1915, contributed to the theater's miseries, but a wealthy tobacco manufacturer came to the rescue of the opera house, paying to repair and restore it to its former glory. A resplendent theater reopened on November 11, 1919. On Tuesday, December 2, 1919, Meyerbeer's *Les Huguenots* graced the stage. The following evening saw rehearsals for Bizet's *Carmen*. Then in the early morning hours of December 4, 1919, the curse of all New Orleans theaters struck the opera house. The French went up in flames, and most opera activity in New Orleans went with it.

A twenty-four-year opera drought resulted. The only oases in the opera-desert were brief visits by Fortune Gallo's San Carlo Opera, the Metropolitan Opera, and Chicago Opera. The Chicago Opera inaugurated the Municipal Auditorium on March 5, 1930, with Jules Massenet's *Jongleur de Notre Dame* featuring Mary Garden. Donizetti's *Lucia di Lammermoor* followed the next evening. There were also five years of homegrown opera by Le Petit Opera Louisiana.

A professional resident opera company was re-established on February 18, 1943, four months before staging its first performance. The company planned the season as an annual summer event, modeled after the St. Louis Municipal Opera Association. (St. Louis presented summer seasons in the large Municipal Opera Theater.) The new company mounted four operas—the doublebill of Mascagni's *Cavalleria Rusticana*/Leoncavallo's *Pagliacci*, Bizet's *Carmen*, Verdi's *Il trovatore*, and Franz Lehár's *Die lustige Witwe*. But the productions were exposed to the trademarks of a New Orleans summer—heat, humidity, and showers—and were not successful. So the founders transformed the open-air summer season into a fall/spring season in the Municipal Auditorium. The Auditorium became the company's home for the next thirty years. Verdi's *Rigoletto* opened the first fall/spring season on October 29, 1943, in the Municipal Auditorium. Other works included Verdi's *La traviata*, Gounod's *Faust*, Bizet's *Carmen*, and Rudolf Friml's *Vagabond King*. The board hired Walter Herbert, a prominent German conductor and music director, as the company's first general director. He guided and nurtured the company for eleven years until friction with the board forced his departure in June 1954. During his tenure, he introduced Gian Carlo Menotti's *The Old Maid and the Thief*, Richard Strauss's *Der Rosenkavalier* and *Salome*, Wolfgang Amadeus Mozart's *Die Entführung aus dem Serail*, and Igor Stravinsky's *Petrushka* to New Orleans. Seven or eight productions, featuring renowned artists comprised the seasons. Victoria de los Angeles, Jussi Björling, Jerome Hines, Dorothy Kirsten, George London, Zinka Milanov, Jan Peerce, Eleanor Steber, Lawrence Tibbett, Richard Tucker, and Mario Lanza (his only operatic stage appearance) were some of the stars. The most important local artist to come from New Orleans during Herbert's reign, was the great bass Norman Treigle. He made his debut on October 23, 1947, in Gounod's *Roméo et Juliette*. At the time of his final appearance on October 3, 1968, as Escamillo in *Carmen*, he had given 117 performances of 36 roles with the New Orleans Opera.

Renato Cellini took the reins from Herbert, serving for a decade as music director until ill-health forced his retirement in 1964. Cellini opened his reign with Giacomo Puccini's *La bohème* on October 7, 1954. Cellini also introduced several works to New Orleans—Puccini's *Turandot* and *Manon Lescaut*, Strauss's *Elektra*, Floyd's *Susannah*, and Verdi's *Falstaff*, and resuscitated others to the New Orleans stage—Modest Mussorgsky's *Boris Godunov*, Italo Montemezzi's *L'amore dei tre re*,

Christoph Willibald Gluck's *Orfeo ed Euridice*, and Massenet's *Werther*. For a brief time, an Experimental Opera Theater of America functioned in New Orleans, giving young singers a venue to perfect their craft. Along with the repertory favorites, the Experimental Theater staged Bedřich Smetana's *Prodaná nevěsta* (The Bartered Bride), Menotti's *The Consul* and *Amelia Goes to the Ball*, John Gay's *The Beggar's Opera*, and Puccini's *Il trittico*. John Reardon, Mignon Dunn, and John McCurdy were among the young artists.

Knud Andersson succeeded Cellini as music director in 1964, and six years later, Arthur Cosenza joined him as general director. During Andersson's regime, the company presented its first world premiere, Carlisle Floyd's *Markheim*, on March 31, 1966. A gripping tale of evil and salvation, *Markheim* was written as a vehicle for Norman Treigle. Birgit Nilsson followed in Puccini's *Turandot*. Two seasons later, the company celebrated it twentieth-fifth anniversary in grand style. Among the highlights were Plácido Domingo and Montserrat Caballé in Verdi's *Il trovatore*, Beverly Sills and Treigle in Jacques Offenbach's *Les contes d'Hoffmann*, Joan Sutherland in Donizetti's *Lucia di Lammermoor*, and a new production of Gounod's *Faust*.

In 1973, Puccini's *Madama Butterfly* welcomed the company into its new home, the Theater of the Performing Arts. Massenet's *Thaïs* followed and was critically acclaimed. It also caused a scandal. Carol Neblett (Thaïs) disrobed at the end of Act I, and the city's strippers, of which there are many, picketed the performance. The strippers were protesting Neblett's nudity. They were prohibited from stripping naked: a law required them to wear pasties. With the 1973-1974 season in a more technically advanced theater, the company revived some French grand operas that had been standard fare at the French Opera House, but because of their complex nature, could not be staged in the Municipal Auditorium. These works included Massenet's *Hérodiade*, Meyerbeer's *Les Huguenots*, Donizetti's *La favorite*, and Halévy's *La Juive* with Richard Tucker as Eléazar. Andersson also introduced Verdi's *Attila* and *Nabucco*, and Strauss's *Arabella* and *Ariadne auf Naxos*.

Arthur Cosenza originally came to the company to sing in Umberto Giordano's *Andrea Chénier*. When given a choice of singing or stage directing, he chose the latter. During his reign, he has introduced Francesco Cilèa's *Adriana Lecouvreur*, Puccini's *La fanciulla del West*, and Verdi's *I Lombardi* to New Orleans, and revived Léo Delibes's *Lakmé*, Richard Wagner's *Tristan und Isolde*, Verdi's *Otello*, Mozart's *Die Entführung aus dem Serail*, and Rossini's *La Cenerentola*. The company continues to host international artists, including Siegfried Jerusalem, Gary Lakes, Ingvar Wixell, John Cheek, June Anderson, Catherine Malfitano, Stefka Evstatieva, and Edward Sooter. Cosenza believes the heyday of opera in New Orleans, with thirty operas a season, will remain history. Even the first few decades of the eight-opera season are gone. When voice was king and the scenery was painted backdrops, a few wealthy donors could pay the deficit. With the beginning of music theater — expensive productions, directors, lighting designers, set designers, and the like — the company can only afford to produce a few standard operas each season. The casts consist of established singers. Cosenza's immediate goal is to increase the number of performances of each opera.

The four-opera season offers a traditional repertory in a *stagione* system. Opera in New Orleans acts like the prelude and coda to Carnival. Recent productions have included Verdi's *Falstaff*, Puccini's *Tosca*, Donizetti's *Lucia di*

Lammermoor, Gounod's *Roméo et Juliette*, and Richard Wagner's *Tannhäuser*. The company performs in the Theater of the Performing Arts.

The Theater of the Performing Arts

A gala concert by the New Orleans Philharmonic inaugurated the Theater of the Performing Arts on January 9, 1973. William Bergman designed the hall, which took three years to build. Funded by a municipal bond, the theater was part of an urban renewal project.

The Theater of the Performing Arts is an imposing structure of concrete and glass located on its own plaza. Faced with aggregate stone, it rises like a giant rectangular box from the surrounding landscape. Evenly spaced concrete pillars divide the block-long glass façade into sections. The plush red and white grand foyer soars over fifty feet, restraining an enormous torch-shaped crystal chandelier pushing on the ceiling. Two perfectly symmetrical balconies overlook the open space. The auditorium swims in red. A single balcony curves gently across the plush red orchestra seats, connecting the side walls. The wall's accordion-like appearance breaks up the large space. The theater seats 2,316.

Practical Information. The Theater of the Performing Arts is at 801 North Rampart Street. Tickets are sold at the New Orleans Opera Office, 333 St. Charles Avenue, Suite 907, Monday through Friday, between 9:00 A.M. and 5:00 P.M. Tickets can be ordered by telephoning 504-529-2278, or writing New Orleans Opera Association, 333 St. Charles, Suite 907, New Orleans, LA 70130. If you visit, contact the Greater New Orleans Tourist and Convention Commission, 1520 Sugar Bowl Drive, New Orleans, LA, telephone 504-566-5011 for hotel information.

COMPANY STAFF AND REPERTORY

General/Artistic Directors. Walter Herbert (1943–1954); Renato Cellini (music director, 1954–1964); Knud Andersson (music director, 1964–1979); Arthur Cosenza (1970–present).

World Premieres. (Le Spectacle de la Rue St. Pierre); Laroque's *La jeune mère* (ca. 1808-10); Laroque's *Nicodème dans la lune* (ca. 1808-10); Laroque's *Pauvre Jacques.* (December 9, 1810).

American/United States Premieres (Le Spectacle de la Rue St. Pierre). Grétry's *Sylvain* (May 22, 1796); Solié's *Le Secret* (June 1800); Dalayrac's *Renaud d'Ast* (September 3, 1799); Devienne's *Les Visitandines* (June 11, 1805); Paisiello's *Il barbiere di Siviglia* (December 10, 1805); François Boieldieu's *Le Calife de Bagdad* (December 25, 1805); Grétry's *Richard, Coeur de Lion* (first performance in French, ca. November 1805-February 1806); Dalayrac's *Une heure de mariage* (ca. November 1805-February 1806?); Grétry's *Guillaume Tell* (ca. 1805-08?); Monsigny's *Félix* (1805-1808); Della Maria's *L'opéra comique* (1806-08); Candaille's *Pizarre* (1805-10); Dalayrac's *Camille* (1805-10?); Gaveaux's *Le petit matelot* (1805-10?); Della Maria's *Le prisonnier* (1805-10?); Dalayrac's *La jeune prude* (1805-10?); Dalayrac's *Gulistan* (1805-10?); Dalayrac's *Azémia* (January 2, 1806); Méhul's *Euphrosine* (February 15, 1806); Monsigny's *La belle Arsène* (October 29, 1806); Méhul's *Une Folie* (1806-07); Dalayrac's *Adolphe et Clara* (1806-10); Grétry's *Le jugement de Midas* (June 11, 1808); Isouard's *La ruse inutile* (1806-1808); Gaveaux's *L'amour filial* (December 31, 1809) ; Steibelt's *Roméo et Juliette* (August 6, 1810); Dalayrac's *Raoul, Sire de Créqui* (1810); Lemoine's *Les prétendus* (1810).

American/United States Premieres (Théâtre St. Philippe). Boieldieu's *Ma Tante Aurore* (1810); Cherubini's *Les deux journées* (March 12, 1811) ; Méhul's *Joseph* (April 21, 1812); Dalayrac's *Maison a vendre* (1812-15); Berton's *François de Foix* (March 9, 1813); Isouard's *Le billet de loterie* (1816); Gaveaux's *La jambe de bois* (1817); Rossini's *La donna del lago* (in English, 1820); Paër's *Le Maître de Chapelle* (January 1824).

American/United States Premieres (First Théâtre d'Orléans). Gaveaux's *Un quart heure de silence* (October 19, 1815); Grétry's *L'éprouvée villageoise* (1815); Gaveaux's *Le bouffe et le tailleur* (1815?); Grétry's *Les fausses apparences* (1815); Grétry's *La rosière de Salency* (1815); Dalayrac's *Gulnare* (1815); Duval's *L'Oncle-Valet* (1815); Méhul's *Le bion* (1815); Kreutzer's *Paul et Virginie* (first performance in French, 1815); Berton' *Ninon chez Madame de Sevigne* (1815-1816); Berton's *Les maris garçons* (1815-1816); Boieldieu's *Jean de Paris* (1815-16).

American/United States Premieres (Second Théâtre d'Orléans). Berton's *Aline, Reine de Golconde* (January 8, 1820); Isouard's *Le rendezvous bourgeois* (January 19, 1820); Gaveaux's *Le Diable en vacances* (1820-24); Isouard's *Joconde* (1820-24); Isouard's *Lully et Quinault* (1820-24); Hérold's *La clochette* (1820-29); Boieldieu's *La fête du village voisin* (1820-26); Bochsa's *La lettre de change* (first performance in French, 1824-27); Lebrun's *Le rossignol* (1820-26); Catel's *L'auberge de bagnières* (1820-26); Solié's *Le diable à quatre* (1820-26); Piccinni's *La maison en loterie* (1821-26); Boieldieu's *Le nouveau seigneur du village* (1821-1826); Boieldieu's *Le petit chaperon rouge* (January 1821); Rossini's *La gazza ladra* (in French as "La pie voleuse," 1821-23); Rossini's *Il barbiere di Siviglia* (in French as Le barbier de Seville, March 4, 1823); Castil-Blaze's *Les folies amoureuses* (1824-26); Auber's *Le maçon* (1825-1827); Fétis's *La vieille* (1826-27); Boieldieu's *La dame blanche* (February 6, 1827); Hérold's *Marie* (1827-29); Auber's *Fiorella* (1827-29); Carafa's *Le solitaire* (1828-29); Spontini's *La vestale* (February 17, 1828); Auber's *La fiancée* (1829); Rossini's *Le Comte Ory* (winter 1831); Auber's *Fra Diavolo* (1830-31); Hérold's *Zampa* (winter 1933); Auber's *Le philtre* (1831-33); Halévy's *Le dilettante d'Avignon* (1831-33); Auber's *La muette de Portici* (first performance in French, April 29, 1831); Hérold's *Le pré aux clercs* (1832-33); Adam's *Le chalet* (1834-36); Hérold's *La medicine sans médicin* (1834-36); Curto's *Le nouvel hermite* (May 16, 1834); Auber's *Lestocq* (February 10, 1835); Halévy's *L'éclair* (February 16, 1837); Auber's *Acteon* (1838); Auber's *Le domino noir* (1838); Auber's *L'ambassadrice* (1838); Auber's *Gustave III* (spring 1838); Adam's *Le brasseur de Preston* (1838-42); Prévost's *Cosimo* (January 1839); Prévost's *Bon garçon* (1839); Adam's *Le postillon de Longjumeau* (first performance in French, 1838-42); Meyerbeer's *Les Huguenots* (April 29, 1839); Donizetti's *Anna Bolena* (in French, November 1839); Bellini's *La sonnambula* (first performance in Italian, January 14, 1840); Thomas's *La double échelle* (January 1841); Auber's *Zanetta* (March 16, 1841); Donizetti's *Lucia di Lammermoor* (in French, December 28, 1841); Clapisson's *La perruche* (1841-42?); Prévost's *La esmeralda* (March 2, 1842); Auber's *Les diamants de la couronne* (1842); Donizetti's *Il furioso all'isola di San Domingo* (March 28, 1842); Rossini's *Guillaume Tell* (December 13, 1842); Donizetti's *La favorite* (February 9, 1843); Donizetti's *La fille du régiment* (March 2, 1843); Halévy's *La Juive* (February 13, 1844); Donizetti's *Don Pasquale* (January 7, 1845); Halévy's *La Reine de Chypre* (March 25, 1845); Auber's *La sirène* (1845); Auber's *Le cheval de bronze* (first performance in French, 1845-46); Donizetti's *Les Martyrs* (March 24, 1846); Halévy's *Charles VI* (April 22, 1847); Maillart's *Gastibelza* (November 1848); Auber's *Haydée* (1849); Verdi's *Jérusalem* (January 2, 1850); Meyerbeer's *Le Prophète* (April 1, 1850); Thomas's *Le caïd* (April 18, 1850); Halévy's *La fee aux roses* (January 1851); Thomas's *Le songe d'une nuit d'été* (January 1851); Limnander's *Les Monténégrins* (February 26, 1852); Meyerbeer's *Marguerite d'Anjou* (April 17, 1854); Meyerbeer's *L'étoile du Nord* (March 5, 1855); Adam's *Si j'étais roi* (April 10, 1856); Grisar's *Les amours du diable* (1858); Maillart's *Les dragons de Villars* (January 17, 1859).

American/United States Premieres (St. Charles Street Theater). Bellini's *Norma* (April 1, 1836) ; Rossini's *Zelmira* (April 24, 1836); Mercadante's *Donna Caritea* (April 26, 1837); Ricci's *Chiara di Rosembergh* (May 3, 1837); Rossini's *Semiramide* (May 19, 1837);

Caruso's *Monsieur de Chiffone* (February 19, 1837); Bellini's *I Capuleti e i Montecchi* (April 4, 1837) ; Bellini's *Beatrice di Tenda* (March 5, 1842) ; Mercadante's *Donna Caritea* (April 26, 1837); Donizetti's *Parisina* (June 4, 1837) ; Donizetti's *Marin Faliero* (February 22, 1842); Donizetti's *Lucia di Lammermoor* (first performance in Italian, February 27, 1842).

American/United States Premieres (Camp Street Theaters). Meyerbeer's *Robert le Diable* (first performance in French, March 30, 1835); Donizetti's *Lucrezia Borgia* (May 11, 1843).

American/United States Premieres (French Opera House). Offenbach's *Tromb-al-Cazar* (January 1860); Adam's *Le bijou perdu* (January 1861); Meyerbeer's *Le pardon de Ploërmel* (March 4, 1861); Offenbach's *La nuit blanche* (November 1861); Mermet's *Roland à Roncevaux* (1866-1891?); Gounod's *Faust* (first performance in French, November 12, 1866); Massé's *Galatée* (November 30, 1866); Meyerbeer's *L'Africaine* (first performance in French, December 18, 1869); Gounod's *Roméo et Juliette* (first performance in French, February 24, 1870); Thomas's *Mignon* (May 9, 1871); Donizetti's *Don Sébastien* (first performance in French, March 11, 1875); Bizet's *Carmen* (January 13, 1881); Massé's *Paul et Virginie* (first performance in French, January 31, 1881); Massenet's *La Roi de Lahore* (December 1883); Gounod's *Le tribut de Zamora* (January 12, 1888); Gounod's *La reine de Saba* (January 12, 1889); Lalo's *Le roi d'Ys* (January 23, 1890); Massenet's *Le Cid* (February 23, 1890; Reyer's *Sigurd* (December 24, 1891); Massenet's *Hérodiade* (February 13, 1892); Saint-Saëns's *Samson et Dalila* (first stage performance in French, January 4, 1893); Massenet's *Esclarmonde* (February 10, 1893); Massenet's *Manon* (first performance in French, January 4, 1894); Berlioz's *La damnation de Faust* (first performance in French, 1894); Bizet's *Les pêcheurs des perles* (first performance in French, 1894-95); Salvayre's *Richard III* (January 5, 1895); Diaz's *Benvenuto* (February 16, 1897); Reyer's *Salammbô* (January 25, 1900); Godard's *La vivandière* (December 29, 1900); Massenet's *Cendrillon* (December 23, 1902); Giordano's *Siberia* (in French, January 13, 1906); Mascagni's *Amica* (February 24, 1906); Cilèa's *Adriana Lecouvreur* (January 5, 1907); Léroux's *Le chemineau* (February 11, 1911); Massenet's *Don Quichotte* (January 27, 1912); Saint-Saëns's *Phryne* (February 3, 1914).

World Premieres (New Orleans Opera). Floyd's *Markheim* (March 31, 1966).

Roles Performed by Norman Treigle (New Orleans Opera). October 23 and 25—Duke of Verona in *Roméo et Juliette*; November 4 and 6, 1948—Lodovico in *Otello*; May 5 and 7, 1949—Dr. Grenvil in *La traviata*; October 13 and 15, 1949—King in *Aida*; November 10 and 12, 1949—Cappadocian & 1st Nazarene in *Salome*; December 1 and 3, 1949—Mathieu in *Andrea Chénier*; March 16 and 18, 1950—Innkeeper and Comte de Grieux in *Manon*; April 20 and 22, 1950—Samuele in *Un ballo in maschera*; May 4 and 6, 1950—Monterone in *Rigoletto*; October 19 and 21, 1950—King Henry in *Lohengrin*; November 16 and 18, 1950—Commendatore in *Don giovanni*; December 7 and 9, 1950—Notary & Commissioner of Police in *Der Rosenkavalier*; February 22 and 24, 1951—Bonze in *Madama Butterfly*; March 15 and 17, 1951—Colline in *La bohème*; April 19, 20, and 21, 1951—Zuniga in *Carmen*; October 11 and 13, 1951—Dr. Grenvil in *La traviata*; April 3 and 5, 1952—Monterone in *Rigoletto*; April 17 and 19, 1952—Innkeeper & Comte des Grieux in *Manon*; December 4 and 6, 1952—Colline in *La bohème*; March 12 and 14, 1953—Marquis in *La forza del destino*; October 8 and 10, 1953—Dr. Grenvil in *La traviata*; December 3 and 5, 1953—Cappadocian & 1st Nazarene in *Salome*; March 3 and 5, 1955—Monterone in *Rigoletto*; April 14 and 16, 1955—Plunkett in *Martha*; September 8 and 10, 1955—Escamillo in *Carmen*; September 22 and 24, 1955—Schicchi in *Gianni Schicchi*; November 10 and 12, 1955—Raimondo in *Lucia di Lammermoor*; April 13 and 14, 1956—Figaro in *Le nozze di Figaro* (in English); May 3 and 5, 1956—Pistola in *Falstaff*; April 25 and 27, 1957—Colline in *La bohème*; May 9 and 11, 1957—Escamillo in *Carmen*; December 5 and 7, 1957—Raimondo in *Lucia di Lammermoor*; March 19 and 21, 1959—Sparafucile in *Rigoletto*; April 16 and 18, 1959—Don Giovanni in *Don Giovanni*; November 12 and 14, 1959—Colline in *La bohème*; November 10 and 12, 1960—Comte des Grieux in *Manon*; March 15 and 17, 1962—Escamillo in *Carmen*; March 29 and 31, 1962—Olin Blitch in *Susanna*; November 29 and December 1, 1962—Méphisthophélès in *Faust*; November 14 and

16, 1963 — Schicchi in *Gianni Schicchi*; February 27 and 29, 1964 — Lindorf/Coppelius/Dappertutto/Dr. Miracle in *Les contes d'Hoffmann*; March 19 and 21, 1964 — Ramfis in *Aida*; March 11 and 13, 1965 — Le Père in *Louise*; March 17 and 19, 1966 — Escamillo in *Carmen*; March 31 and April 2, 1966 — Markheim in *Markheim*; April 25 and 27, 1968 — Lindorf/Coppelius/Dappertutto/Dr. Miracle in *Les contes d'Hoffmann* October 3, 1968 — Escamillo in *Carmen*.

Repertory (New Orleans Opera). 1943 **Summer:** Cavalleria rusticana/I pagliacci, Carmen, Il trovatore, Die lustige Witwe. **1943-44:** Rigoletto, Carmen, Cavalleria rusticana/I pagliacci, The Vagabond King, La traviata, Faust, Il trovatore. **1944-45:** Aida, La bohème, Tosca, La traviata, Martha, Faust. **1945-46:** La traviata, Il barbiere di Siviglia, Rigoletto, Hänsel und Gretel, Manon, Old Maid and the Thief, Carmen, Die Entführung aus dem Serail, Faust. **1946-47:** Madama Butterfly, La traviata, Aida, La bohème, Il trovatore, Carmen. **1947-48:** Les contes d'Hoffmann, Roméo et Juliette, Tosca, Rigoletto, Faust, Madama Butterfly, Samson et Dalila. **1948-49:** Lucia di Lammermoor, La bohème, Otello, Tristan und Isolde, Carmen, Il segreto di Susanna/I pagliacci, La traviata. **1949-50:** Aida, Il barbiere di Siviglia, Salome, Andrea Chénier, Manon, Un ballo in maschera, Rigoletto. **1950-51:** Lohengrin, Faust, Don Giovanni, Der Rosenkavalier, Madama Butterfly, La bohème, Carmen. **1951-52:** La traviata, Die Fledermaus, Tosca, Mignon, Rigoletto, Manon, Le nozze di Figaro. **1952-53:** Il barbiere di Siviglia, Samson et Dalila, Il trovatore, La bohème, Faust, La forza del destino, Lucia di Lammermoor, Die lustige Witwe. **1953-54:** La traviata, Don Pasquale, La Gioconda, Salome, Madama Butterfly, Thaïs, Carmen, The Student Prince. **1954-55:** La bohème, Otello, Tosca, Lakmé, Rigoletto Andrea Chénier, Martha, Die Fledermaus. **1955-56:** Aida, Manon, Lucia di Lammermoor, Elektra, L'amore dei tre re, La traviata, Le nozze di Figaro, Falstaff. **1956-57:** Madama Butterfly, Werther, Faust, La cenerentola, La bohème, Carmen. **1957-58:** Boris Godunov, Il barbiere di Siviglia, Tosca, Lucia di Lammermoor, Manon Lescaut, Il trovatore. **1958-59:** Turandot, La traviata, L'elisir d'amore, Hänsel und Gretel, Norma, Rigoletto. **1959-60:** Tannhäuser, Lakmé, La bohème, Aida, Madama Butterfly, Samson et Dalila. **1960-61:** La gioconda, Cavalleria rusticana/I pagliacci, Manon, Il trovatore, Don Giovanni, Andrea Chénier. **1961-62:** Un ballo in maschera, Il barbiere di Siviglia, Orfeo, Der Rosenkavalier, Carmen, Susanna. **1962-63:** Rigoletto, Le nozze di Figaro, Lucia di Lammermoor, Faust, Tosca, La traviata. **1963-64:** Roméo et Juliette, La bohème, La forza del destino, Cavalleria rusticana/Gianni Schicchi, Les contes d'Hoffmann, Aida. **1964-65:** Otello, La sonnambula, Werther, Il trovatore, Madama Butterfly, Louise, Don pasquale, Die Fledermaus. **1965-66:** Samson et Dalila, Rigoletto, La traviata, Tannhäuser, Andrea Chénier, Carmen, Markheim, Turandot. **1966-67:** Tosca, Lucia di Lammermoor, La bohème, Elektra, La Gioconda, Les pêcheurs des perles, Aida, Manon. **1967-68:** Faust, Madama Butterfly, Macbeth, Der fliegende Holländer, Lucia di Lammermoor, Il trovatore, Amelia Goes to the Ball/ I pagliacci, Les contes d'Hoffmann. **1968-69:** Carmen, La traviata, Il tabarro/Cavalleria rusticana, Fidelio, Rigoletto, Il barbiere di Siviglia, Manon Lescaut, Norma. **1969-70:** Attila, Don Pasquale, La bohème, Arabella, Tosca, Un ballo in maschera, The Medium. **1970-71:** Faust, Rigoletto, Madama Butterfly, La traviata, Salome, Carmen. **1971-72:** La bohème, Les pêcheurs des perles, Lucia di Lammermoor, Aida, Don Giovanni, Samson et Dalila. **1972-73:** Turandot, Roméo et Juliette, Tosca, Madama Butterfly, Thaïs, Il trovatore. **1973-74:** La Juive, Rigoletto, Faust, Carmen, Ariadne auf Naxos, La traviata. **1974-75:** Aida, Manon Lescaut, La bohème, Lohengrin, Tosca, Hérodiade. **1975-76** -Les Huguenots, Madama Butterfly, Macbeth, Der Rosenkavalier, Lucia di Lammermoor, Il tabarro/I pagliacci. **1976-77:** La favorite, Andrea Chénier, Rigoletto, Die Walküre; Il barbiere di Siviglia, La traviata. **1977-78:** Ernani, Don Pasquale, Carmen, La bohème, Il trovatore. **1978-79:** Nabucco, Tosca, Faust, Der fliegende Holländer, La fille du régiment. **1979-80:** Manon, Madama Butterfly, Die Zauberflöte, Salome, Macbeth. **1980-81:** Carmen, La traviata, Adriana Lecouvreur, Fidelio, La fanciulla del West. **1981-82:** Un ballo in maschera, Rigoletto, Lakmé, Elektra, Die Entführung aus dem Serail. **1982-83:** Samson et Dalila, La bohème, I Lombardi, Tristan und Isolde. **1983-84:** Cavalleria rusticana/I pagliacci, Il barbiere di Siviglia, Tosca, Madama Butterfly. **1984-85:** Aida, Carmen, La traviata,

Hänsel und Gretel. **1985-86:** Lohengrin, Les pêcheurs de Perles, La bohème, Lucia di Lammermoor. **1986-87:** Il trovatore, Madama Butterfly, Faust, Die Zauberflöte. **1987-88:** Otello, Tosca, Rigoletto, Samson et Dalila. **1988-89:** Turandot, Salome, Un ballo in maschera, Carmen. **1989-90:** Aida, La fille du régiment, La bohème, Der fliegende Holländer. **1990-91:** Norma, Madama Butterfly, La traviata, Le nozze di Figaro. **1991-92:** La forza del destino, Il barbiere di Siviglia, Faust, Fidelio. **1992-93:** Don Carlo, Tosca, L'elisir d'amore, Cavalleria rusticana/I pagliacci. **1993-94:** Lucia di Lammermoor, Falstaff, Roméo et Juliette, Tannhäuser.

-- SHREVEPORT

• *Shreveport Opera* •

Georges Bizet's *Carmen* with Ramon Vinay, Winifred Heidt, and Walter Cassel inaugurated the Shreveport Opera on December 12, 1949, at the Municipal Auditorium. Helen Ruffin Marshall, head of the voice department at Centenary College, founded the company. She had directed opera workshop productions in 1948 and 1949 that included Arthur Sullivan's *Patience*, Giovanni Battista Pergolesi's *The Music Master*, Gian Carlo Menotti's *The Old Maid and the Thief*, Wolfgang Amadeus Mozart's *Così fan tutte* and Engelbert Humperdinck's *Hänsel und Gretel*. These performances planted the seeds for the company's formation. Walter Herbert, director of the New Orleans Opera, (see New Orleans entry) conducted the inaugural production. It was the sole offering that first season.

The second season expanded to two standard works — Giuseppe Verdi's *La traviata* with Licia Albanese, Jan Peerce, and Robert Weede on November 23, 1950, and Giacomo Puccini's *Madama Butterfly* on February 27, 1951. The sixth season witnessed the first German opera, Richard Strauss's *Salome* on November 26, 1954, and the first Richard Wagner opera, *Die Walküre* was seen five seasons later, the only performance of the eleventh season. A less frequently seen French work, Léo Delibes's *Lakmé* was presented on April 26, 1963. The 1965-66 season offered a brief expansion into a four-opera season, but that was an exception. The 1980s ushered in some twentieth-century opera with the presentation of Ermanno Wolf-Ferrari's *Il segreto di Susanna* in 1980, Henry Mollicone's *Face on the Barroom Floor* in 1984, and Carlisle Floyd's *Willie Stark* the following year. Oscar Straus's infrequently performed *Der tapfere Soldat* was seen on November 18, 1988. The company presented their first world premiere on January 8, 1984, Carl Zytowski's *The Play of the Three Shepherds*. The cast is a mixture of up-and coming stars and established artists. Early in their careers, Beverly Sills, Plácido Domingo, Aprilo Millo, and Renée Fleming sang with the company.

The three-opera season offers primarily traditional works with the occasional unfamiliar piece. Recent productions include *Faust*, *Don Pasquale*, and *Zémire et azor* (Beauty and the Beast). The company performs in the Civic Theater with a seating capacity of 1,737. Some performances are given at the Strand Theater, a national historic landmark, which seats 1,626.

Practical Information. The Civic Theater is at Fant Parkway, between Crockett and Milam. Tickets can be purchased at the Shreveport Opera Offices, 212 Texas,

Suite 101, by calling 318-227-9503, or writing Shreveport Opera, 212 Texas, Suite 101, Shreveport, LA 71101-3249.

COMPANY STAFF AND REPERTORY

General Directors. Board Volunteers (1949–76); Mark Melson (1977–80); Robert Murray (1980–present),

World Premieres. Zytowski's *The Play of the Three Shepherds* (January 8, 1984).

Repertory. 1949: Carmen. 1950-51: La traviata, Madama Butterfly. 1951-52: Die Fledermaus, Rigoletto. 1952-53: Samson et Dalila, Faust. 1953-54: Il trovatore, The Student Prince. 1954-55: Salome, Carmen. 1955: La bohème. 1956-57: Le nozze di Figaro, Madama Butterfly, La traviata, La Cenerentola. 1957-58: Tosca, Manon. 1958-59: Rigoletto, Don Giovanni. 1959: Die Walküre. 1960: Un ballo in maschera. 1961-62: Faust, Lucia di Lammermoor. 1962-63: Die Fledermaus, Lakmé. 1963: Il trovatore. 1964: Otello. 1965-66: Rigoletto, Die Zauberflöte, Le nozze di Figaro, Don Giovanni. 1966-67: Aida, La traviata, Le nozze di Figaro. 1967: Cavalleria rusticana/I pagliacci. 1968: Les contes d'Hoffmann. 1969: Turandot. 1970: Lucia di Lammermoor, Tosca. 1971-72: 1776, La fille du régiment. 1972-73: Roméo et Juliette, L'elisir d'amore. 1974: La traviata. 1974-75: Madama Butterfly. 1976: Il barbiere di Siviglia, Carmen. 1977: Die lustige Witwe. 1977-78: La bohème, Die Fledermaus. 1978-79: El Capitan, Manon Lescaut. 1979-80: Il trovatore. 1980-81: Il segreto di Susanna, I pagliacci, Le nozze di Figaro. 1981-82: La traviata, Hänsel und Gretel. 1982-83: Tosca, Naughty Marietta. 1983-84: Les contes d'Hoffmann, The Play of the Three Shepherds, Lucia di Lammermoor, The Face on the Barroom Floor, The King and I. 1984-85: The Student Prince, Die Zauberflöte, La bohème. 1985-86: Willie Stark, Amahl and the Night Visitors. 1986-87: Rigoletto, Carmen (film), La traviata (film), The Medium. 1987-88: Otello (film), The Desert Song, Il barbiere di Siviglia, Madama Butterfly, Parsifal (film). 1988-89: Der tapfere Soldat, Hänsel und Gretel, Carmen. 1989-90: Die Fledermaus, Roméo et Juliette, La bohème. 1990-91: Tosca, Le nozze di Figaro, L'elisir d'amore. 1991-92: La traviata, Die Zauberflöte, Turandot. 1992-93: Don Giovanni, I pagliacci, Faust. 1993-94: Cavalleria rusticana, Don Pasquale, Zémire et azor (Beauty and the Beast).

Maryland   BALTIMORE

• *Baltimore Opera* •

The Baltimore Opera traces its formal beginnings to April 28, 1950, when the company staged Giuseppe Verdi's *Aida*, with Leigh Martinet on the podium. It was the only opera offered during the inaugural season. The roots of the Baltimore Opera, however, stretch back to May 10, 1927, when the Eugene Martinet School of Opera performed Arthur Sullivan's *H.M.S. Pinafore* in the Maryland Casualty Auditorium. Eugene Martinet was a conductor and voice teacher who needed a stage on which to give his students practical experience.

Baltimore heard opera as early as 1772, when the Old American Company visited, with Mister Wall as one of its performers. Wall returned nine years later. He joined forces with Adam Lindsay and built a new theater on East Baltimore Street. There the Maryland Company of Comedians performed. The troupe opened the new Baltimore Theater on January 15, 1782. During the company's first season, three operas were included in the schedule: Henry Carey's *Contrivances*, Charles Dibdin's *Padlock*, and I. Bickerstaffe's *Thomas and Sally*. The second season saw Dibdin's *Padlock*, Henry Fielding's *Mock Doctor*, Colley Cibber's *Flora*, John Pepusch's *The Beggar's Opera*, and two pantomimes, *Harlequin Landlord*, and *Witches*. Dennis Ryan then took the reins from Lindsay and Wall, continuing the season with pantomimes—*Witches*, *Harlequin Skeleton*, *Columbus*—and Fielding's *Mock Doctor*. For the 1784-85 season, Ryan's company staged Thomas Arne's *Love in A Village*, Pepusch's *The Beggar's Opera*, Bickerstaffe's *Thomas and Sally*, Fielding's *Virgin Unmasked*, William Boyce's *Chaplet*, and *Witches*. The next season was Ryan's last. He died in January 1786, leaving his widow and Wall to complete the season. It opened on September 7, 1785, and included Dibdin's *Padlock*, Carey's *Contrivances* and *The Honest Yorkshireman*, Bickerstaffe's *Thomas and Sally*, and Pepusch's *The Beggar's Opera*.

The operatic seasons continued in Baltimore with Lewis Hallam and John Henry's Old American Company from New York. They performed in a new theater built on Philpot's Hill that opened on August 17, 1786. Baltimore witnessed William Shield's *Rosina* and *Poor Soldier* during August and September of 1786. The Old American Company continued their visits and between 1787 and 1790 mounted Shield's *Poor Soldier*, Arne's *Love in A Village*, *Robinson Crusoe* (pantomime), Dibdin's *Deserter* and *Padlock*, Thomas Linley's *Duenna*, Shield's *Love in a Camp*, *Banditti*, and Samuel Arnold's *Dead Alive*. Opera performed in French arrived in the city on June 14, 1790, with a French Company of Comedians. They presented a "parody" of Giovanni Pergolesi's *La serva padrona* called *La servante maîtresse* by Père Golaise, which is considered the American premiere of Pergolesi's work. Then the well-established Philadelphia company, run by Thomas Wignell and Alexander Reinagle, began regular seasons in Baltimore.

In 1829, John Davis and his French troupe from New Orleans included Baltimore on the company's annual tour up north. They presented Gioachino Rossini's *La gazza ladra* (in French as La pie voleuse), *La donna del lago* (in French as La dame du lac), and Ferdinand Hérold's *Marie* during their season. Davis and his company returned the next year with more French operas. His final visit came in 1833. The Liederkranz presented Baltimore with German opera, including the first German performance of Wolfgang Amadeus Mozart's *Die Zauberflöte* in 1853. Three years later, the Liederkranz staged the American premiere of Franz Gläser's *Des Adlers Horst*. Other opera troupes visited as well, including Colonel James Mapleson's Opera Company with his two *prime donne*, Adelina Patti and Etelka Gerster, in tow. Baltimore preferred Patti.

The opera company that Martinet founded in 1927, adopted the name Baltimore Opera Company the following year. In January 1928, the Baltimore company mounted Sullivan's *Mikado*. Operating on a shoestring budget, the company found Martinet at the helm, on the podium, and behind the stage painting scenery. The Baltimore Opera changed its name to Baltimore Civic Opera by May 1932. During the 1930s, despite the meager resources available, the Civic Opera mounted several world premieres composed by Baltimore inhabitants— Emmanuel Wad's *Swing Low* (December 13, 1933) and Abram Moses's *Melody in I* (May 2, 1939) among them. The repertory, nevertheless, was primarily traditional Italian fare, including Giuseppe Verdi's *Aida*, *La traviata*, and *Otello*, Pietro Mascagni's *Cavalleria rusticana*, and Gaetano Donizetti's *L'elisir d'amore*. The popular French operas, George Bizet's *Carmen* and Charles Gounod's *Faust*, and the occasional German work, including Richard Wagner's *Lohengrin* with Bryson Tucker and Mary Lida Bowen, were also presented. Martinet's students sang most of the roles. When Martinet died in 1947, the Baltimore Civic Opera almost died with him.

Two years later Martinet's son, Leigh, resuscitated the company with a performance of Charles Gounod's *Faust* he conducted on May 20, 1949. The revived company gained sufficient support to incorporate in April 1950 as the Baltimore Opera. The Baltimore Opera hired a professional impresario, Anthony Stivanello, to provide orchestrations, scenery, and to direct the productions. The fledgling company got a boost when the legendary American soprano, Rosa Ponselle, who had retired from the stage and lived in Baltimore, took an active interest in the organization. Ponselle, officially the company's auditions director, turned her residence outside of Baltimore, Villa Pace, into the virtual home of the Baltimore Opera. There she auditioned and coached the singers, who during the 1950s, remained predominately local. There were exceptions. One was Beverly Sills, who on April 18, 1953, treated Baltimore to her Manon.

The 1960s ushered in a graceless ouster of Martinet. It was especially unfortunate, since he and his family had personally kept the company alive for the last few decades. No one even paid him the courtesy of a call after their unceremonious dumping. The company then turned more professional, engaging the Baltimore Symphony for performances, and hiring a professional staff. It also attracted several future big name artists. Sherrill Milnes made his major debut with the company in 1961 singing Gérard in Umberto Giordano's *Andrea Chénier*. That same season, Lili Chookasian appeared in Verdi's *Il trovatore* followed by *Aida* the next year and another *Il trovatore* during the 1964-65 season. The 1965-1966 season, however, was one of the company's more memorable. Birgit Nilsson, Teresa Stratas, and Sándor Kónya appeared in Puccini's *Turandot*, Sills and Norman Treigle sang in Mozart's *Don Giovanni*, Stratas in Puccini's *Madama Butterfly*, and Anna Moffo in Donizetti's *Lucia di Lammermoor*. Sills returned the following season for Jacques Offenbach's *Les contes d'Hoffmann* with Treigle, Plácido Domingo, and James Morris in the small role of Crespel. The cast of then "emerging talent" made it a legendary performance. Milnes returned for Verdi's *Rigoletto*, again with Morris. Gilda Cruz-Romo graced the Baltimore stage in several Verdi's operas—*Aida*, *Don Carlo*, *Il trovatore*, and *Messa da Requiem*. Evelyn Lear, Carol Neblett, Johanna Meier, Ruth Welting, Martina Arroyo, Aprile Millo, Ashley Putnam, and Richard Leech, all appeared with the company early in their careers. The Baltimore Opera acts as a springboard and showcase for young talented artists, who perform alongside established artists. "Big-name" artists also try out new roles there. For example, Morris assayed his first Wotan in Wagner's *Die Walküre* in 1985. He returned for Verdi's *Don Carlo* and *Macbeth*, giving spectacular performances.

The Baltimore Opera commissioned its first world premiere, Thomas Pasatieri's *Ines de Castro*, to celebrate the 25th anniversary of its incorporation. The opera, introduced on April 1, 1976, featured Morris, Chookasian, Richard Stilwell, and James Atherton. The 1980s saw Jay Holbrook at the helm. He tried to establish the Baltimore Opera as an outstanding regional company by presenting unusual works. Carlisle Floyd's *Susannah* staged during the 1980-1981 season, began the practice. Leoš Janáček's *Jenůfa*, Francis Poulenc's *Dialogues des Carmélites*, George Gershwin's *Porgy & Bess*, and three contemporary one act works called *American*

Lyric Theater Auditorium (Baltimore, Maryland).

Portraits: La Divina, The Stronger, and *The Italian Lesson* followed. Baltimore is a very traditional city and greeted the new works with coolness. Financial consideration forced the company to revert to the old standards.

Michael Harrison took the helm in 1989, mounting a successful Richard Strauss's *Salome* as his first production with the company. When he joined, he had hoped to expand the season, the repertory, and the operatic horizons of Baltimore. The recession forced retrenchment and company stabilization instead, so he turned his efforts to improving the quality of the operas currently in the repertory. He still plans to expand the season, and introduce lesser-known works by well-known composers, especially Verdi. *I due Foscari* and *I vespri siciliani* are "on the boards." Afterward he will pursue a more adventurous repertory by lesser-known composers. The foray will proceed cautiously in view of the unsuccessful attempt with a non-traditional scheduling in the early 1980s. He plans productions of Strauss's *Der Rosenkavalier,* Erich Korngold's *Die tote Stadt,* and Janáček's Věc Makropulos (The Makropulos Affair). Since the company is very dependent on ticket income, it must tread carefully in unfamiliar waters. Meanwhile, the company follows a "Verdi vein," offering a Verdi opera each season. They have included *Otello, Un ballo in maschera, Don Carlo, Macbeth,* and the Baltimore premiere of *Nabucco.* When the season expands to four operas, the fourth work will be a "challenge piece," like Alban Berg's *Wozzeck,* or a world premiere.

The three-opera season offers two popular works and one lesser-known (for Baltimore) piece in a *stagione* system. The Italian repertory is emphasized. Recent productions include Donizetti's *L'elisir d'amore* and *Lucia di Lammermoor,* Puccini's *La bohème,* Mozart's *Die Zauberflöte,* and Verdi's *Macbeth.* The company performs in the Lyric Theater.

Lyric Theater

The Lyric Theater was born as the Music Hall on October 31, 1894, with the Boston Symphony playing the gala opening concert. The renown Australian soprano, Nellie Melba, highlighted the inaugural program with her rendition of Handel's aria *Sweet Bird*. T. Henry Randall designed the building solely for symphonic performances. The theater was reconfigured in 1916, enabling opera and ballet to grace the stage. Beginning in 1979, the theater underwent a $14 million renovation, overseen by architect Richter Cornbrooks. Jerome Kern's *Showboat* reopened the Lyric on September 27, 1981.

The Lyric is an imposing structure harmoniously fusing the new tan brick-and-glass façade with the original rust-colored brick exterior. The russet brick exhibits Ionic and Corinthian pilaster embellishments. THE LYRIC in large silver letters rests above the entrance. A large painting of Rosa Ponselle in *La gioconda* inhabitants the soaring glass and terrazzo marble lobby. The cream-and-taupe rectangular auditorium exudes a baroque flavor. Supported by gently round columns, a single deep balcony with shallow side seating flows around the room. Plush red velvet seats sweep uninterrupted across the floor. Names of famous composers embellish golden transoms and twin gilded Ionic pilasters flank the proscenium. The theater seats 2,564.

Practical Information. The Lyric Theater is at 140 West Mount Royal Avenue. Tickets are purchased at the Baltimore Opera Box Office, 101 West Read Street, 6th Floor, Monday through Friday between 10:00 A.M. and 1:00 P.M., and from 3:00 P.M. to 5:00 P.M., or by telephoning 410-685-0692, or writing Baltimore Opera Box Office, 101 West Read Street, 6th Floor, Baltimore, MD 21201. If you go, stay at the Harbor Court Hotel, 550 Light Street, Baltimore, MD 21202, telephone 301-234-0550, fax 301-659-5925, reservations, 800-323-7500. The Harbor Court offers traditional red brick style architecture with oak, marble and brass interiors. It is on the inner harbor, convenient to the Lyric Theater.

COMPANY STAFF AND REPERTORY

General/Artistic Directors. Eugene Martinet (1927–1947); Operations suspended (1947–1949); Leigh Martinet (1947–1961); Rosa Ponselle, unofficial (1961–1970); Robert Collinge (1970–1980); Jay Holbrook (1980–1988); Michael Harrison (1989–present).

World Premieres (before Baltimore Opera). Herbert's *Sweethearts* (March 24, 1913); Kreisler & Jacobi's *Apple Blossoms* (September 29, 1919).

American/United States Premieres (before Baltimore Opera). Pergolesi's *La serva padrona* (June 14, 1790); Gläser's *Des Adlers Horst* (1856); Mozart's *Die Zauberflöte* (first performance in German, 1853).

World Premieres (Baltimore Opera). Bornschein's *The Willow Plate* (April 1933); Wad's *Swing Low* (December 13, 1933); Strube's *Ramona* (February 28, 1938); Moses's *Melody in I* (May 2, 1939); Pasatieri's *Ines de Castro* (April 1, 1976).

Repertory (Wignell & Reinagle). **1794:** Agreeable Surprise, Battle of Hexham, Castle of Andalusia, Comus (masque), Deserter, Flitch of Bacon, Forêt noire (pantomime), Highland Reel, Inkle and Yarico Lionel and Clarissa, Love in a Village, Maid of the Mill, No Song, no Supper, Padlock, Peeping Tom of Coventry, Poor Soldier, Prize, Robin Hood, Romp, Rosina, Spanish Barber, Spoiled Child, Surrender of Calais, Virgin Unmasked. **1795:** Agreeable Surprise, Beggar's Opera, Castle of Andalusia, Children in the Wood, Comus (masque), Devil to Pay, Duenna, Farmer, Flitch of Boston, Forêt noire (pantomime), Harlequin hurry-scurry (pantomime), Harlequin Shipwrecked (pantomime), Harlequin's Invasion (pantomime), Hartford Bridge, Haunted Tower, Highland Reel, Inkle and Yarico, Lionel and Clarissa, Love in a Camp, Love in a Village, Maid of the Mill, Midas, Miraculous Mill (pantomime), My Grandmother, Padlock, Poor Soldier, Prisoner, Prize, Purse, Quaker, Robinson Crusoe (pantomime), Romp, Son-in-law, Spanish Barber, Tom Thumb the Great, Two Misers, Waterman. **1796:** Children in the Wood, Comus (masque), Deserter, Deserter of Naples, Farmer, Harlequin hurry-scurry (pantomime), Harlequin Shipwrecked (pantomime), Harlequin Skeleton (pantomime), Harlequin Invasion (pantomime), Highland Reel, Inkle and Yarico, Love in a Village, Lucky Escape (pantomime), Mountaineers, My Grandmother, No Song, no Supper, Patriot, Peeping Tom of Coventry, Poor Soldier, Prisoner, Purse, Quaker, Robin Hood, Robinson Crusoe (pantomime), Romp, Sicilian Romance, Spoiled Child. **1797:** Adopted Child, Columbus, Dead Alive, Death of Captain Cook (pantomime), Forêt noire (pantomime), Harlequin Conqueror (pantomime), Highland Reel, Iron Chest, Lock and Key, Mountaineers, Poor Soldier, Prize, Purse, Waterman. **1798:** Shipwreck. **1799:** American True Blues, Castle of Andalusia, Children in the Wood, Columbus, Constellation, Death of General Wolfe (pantomime), Farmer, Mountaineers, Quaker, Robin Hood, Thomas and Sally, Waterm.

Repertory (Baltimore Opera). **1950:** Aida. **1950-51:** Cavalleria rusticana/I pagliacci, La traviata. **1951-52:** Carmen, Aida. **1952-53:** La bohème, Manon. **1953-54:** Madama Butterfly, Rigoletto, La traviata. **1954-55:** Il trovatore, Cavalleria rusticana/I pagliacci, Faust. **1955-56:** Aida, Le nozze di Figaro, Thaïs. **1956-57:** Die Fledermaus, La bohème, La forza del destino. **1957-58:** Madama Butterfly, Carmen, Il trittico. **1958-59:** Martha, Lucia di Lammermoor, Manon Lescaut. **1959-60:** Rigoletto, Faust, Tosca. **1960-61:** Il trovatore, La bohème, Andrea Chénier. **1961-62:** Aida, Le nozze di Figaro, Madama Butterfly. **1962-63:** Der Rosenkavalier, Cavalleria rusticana/I pagliacci, La traviata. **1963-64:** Rigoletto, Fledermaus, Carmen. **1964-65:** Il trovatore, Faust, Tosca. **1965-66:** Lucia di Lammermoor, Don Giovanni, Madama Butterfly, Turandot. **1966-67:** La bohème, Les contes d'Hoffmann, La forza del destino, La guerra/Gianni. Schicchi. **1967-68:** Boris Godunov, Salome, La traviata. **1968-69:** Manon Lescaut, Tosca. **1969-70:** Otello, Don Pasquale, Rigoletto. **1970-71:** Faust, Il barbiere di Siviglia, Madama Butterfly. **1971-72:** Manon, L'elisir d'amore, Un ballo in maschera. **1972-73:** Aida, The Saint of Bleecker Street, Andrea Chénier. **1973-74:** Carmen, L'elisir d'amore, Cavalleria rusticana/I pagliacci. **1974-75:** Der Rosenkavalier, Thaïs, Tosca. **1975-76:** Maria Stuarda, La Grande Duchesse de Gérolstein, Ines de Castro. **1976-77:** La bohème, Don Giovanni, Der fliegende Holländer, Falstaff. **1977-78:** Lucia di Lammermoor, L'Italiana in Algeri, Macbeth, Les contes d'Hoffmann. **1978-79:** Don Carlo, Madama Butterfly, Salome, La traviata. **1979-80:** Faust, Il barbiere di Siviglia, Eugene Onegin. **1980-81:** Turandot, Don Pasquale, Susannah, Il trovatore. **1981-82:** Carmen, Die Fledermaus, Jenůfa, Manon Lescaut. **1982-83:** Messa da Requiem, Così fan tutte, La bohème, La fille du régiment, Porgy & Bess. **1983-84:** Tosca, Die Zauberflöte, Die Walküre, Dialogues des Carmélites, Kismet. **1984-85:** Candide, La Cenerentola, American Portraits: La Divina, The Stronger, The Italian Lesson, Madama Butterfly, Rigoletto. **1985-86:** Aida, Lucia di Lammermoor, Cavalleria rusticana/I pagliacci. **1986-87:** La forza del destino, Roméo et Juliette, Turandot. **1987-88:** Norma, Martha, La traviata, Porgy & Bess. **1988-89:** Le nozze di Figaro, La bohème, Tosca, Les contes d'Hoffmann. **1989-90:** Faust, Salome, Il barbiere di Siviglia, Otello. **1990-91:** Carmen, Un ballo in maschera, Madama Butterfly. **1991-92:** Don Carlo, La fille du régiment, Die Zauberflöte. **1992-93:** Turandot, L'elisir d'amore, Nabucco. **1993-94:** Lucia di Lammermoor, Macbeth, La bohème.

Massachusetts ————— B O S T O N

• *Opera Company of Boston/* • *Boston Lyric Opera*

The Boston Opera Group, the original name of the Opera Company of Boston, presented Jacques Offenbach's *Le voyage dans la lune* in June 1958 as its inaugural work. Founded by Sarah Caldwell, the company offered the performance as part of the Boston Arts Festival. Giacomo Puccini's *La bohème* inaugurated the company's first official season in the Boston Fine Arts Theater on January 29, 1959.

Opera in Boston dates back more than two centuries. In 1750, two Englishmen and a few volunteers performed Otway's *Orphan*. *Orphan* so disgusted some inhabitants that an act was passed forbidding "public stage-plays, interludes, and other theatrical entertainment." Nevertheless, the farce *The Suspected Daughter* managed to be seen the next year, and Thomas Arne's *Love in a Village* was imported from London in 1762. Seven years later, in July and October, Boston again heard Arne's *Love in a Village* when it was "read in a large room." March 23, 1770, witnessed another "reading," that of John Gay's *The Beggar's Opera*.

Lewis Hallam and John Henry of the Old American Company requested permission to open a "real theater" in Boston in 1790, but permission was denied. This so enraged several powerful Bostonians that they began to defy the law. They opened a "New Exhibition Room" on August 16, 1792, with the pantomime *Bird Catcher*. Until Governor Hancock took legal action against the group in December, Boston saw several ballad operas and pantomimes, including C. Coffey's *Devil to Pay*, William Shield's *Rosina* and *Poor Soldier*, Arne's *Love in a Village*, I. Bickerstaffe's *Thomas and Sally*, Charles Dibdin's *Romp*, Thomas Linley's *Duenna*, Henry Fielding's *Virgin Unmasked* and *Mock Doctor*, *Birth of Harlequin*, *Bird Catcher*, *Harlequin Balloonist*, *Harlequin Skeleton*, *Old Soldier*, *Robinson Crusoe*, and *Two Philosophers*. Five pantomimes were performed for the first time: *Harlequin Doctor* (August 27, 1792), *Harlequin Supposed Gentleman* (August 29, 1792), *Two Woodcutters* (September 5, 1792), *Inkle and Yarico* (November 19, 1792), and *Bear Hunters* (November 26, 1792). When the decree was lifted in 1794, construction began at the corner of Franklin and Federal on the Federal Street Theater. It was completed a short time later, opening February 3, 1794. The next week Charles Powell's Boston Company performed the first opera, William Shield's *The Farmer*. The inaugural season boasted thirty-five performances of fifteen different operas, with Shield's *Poor Soldier* closing the season on July 4, 1794. Powell's second season opened on December 15, 1794, with Shield's *Rosina*. By the time the season ended in June 1795, Powell was almost bankrupt. Colonel Tyler replaced Powell and brought Hallam and John Hodgkinson's New York Company for the following season. Soon after the fifth season began, fire engulfed the theater, leaving only charred ruins. A second Federal Theater, designed by Charles Bulfinch, was erected on the same site. It remained a Boston landmark until 1852.

Powell, meanwhile, built a rival theater near the corner of Tremont and

Boylston in 1796. Known as the Haymarket, it initially hosted plays. Pantomimes and ballad operas first appeared with the premiere of *Mirza and Lindor* on December 26, 1796. The busiest year was 1797. Over fifty different operas and pantomimes were mounted, but not all of them by Powell's company. He disbanded his troupe in June 1797, and John Hodgkinson took over for the summer and fall seasons. Counted among the works were several novelties, including P.A. van Hagen's *Adopted Child*, Stephen Storace's *Three and the Deuce*, Victor Pélissier's *Launch*, and Arne's *Bourville Castle*. The company introduced numerous pantomimes as well, including *Deserter* (January 13, 1797), *Destruction of the Bastille* (May 26, 1797), *Galatea* (April 10, 1797), *Medea and Jason* (June 2, 1797), *Unfortunate Family* (July 10, 1797), *Harlequin Statue* (July 10, 1797), and *Love and Money* (October 10, 1797).

The Boston Theater was constructed on Washington Street, after the demise of the Federal Theater. The Boston, which seated 3,140, opened in 1854. The first opera appeared soon after, mounted by Louise Pyne's English Company. The company presented Vincenzo Bellini's *La sonnambula*, Daniel Auber's *Fra Diavolo* and *Les diamants de la couronne*, Michael Balfe's *The Bohemian Girl*, John Gay's *The Beggar's Opera*, and the Boston premiere of William Wallace's *Maritana*. In 1855, Giulia Grisi and Giovanni Mario with Luigi Arditi on the podium offered the an Italian season with Bellini's *I Puritani* and *Norma*, Gaetano Donizetti's *Lucrezia Borgia*, *Don Pasquale*, and *La favorita*, Gioachino Rossini's *Il barbiere di Siviglia* and *Semiramide*, and Wolfgang Amadeus Mozart's *Don Giovanni*. Then Adelina Patti sang her first Rosina in Boston and Pasquale Brignoli and Bertucca-Maretzek brought the city its first Rossini's *Guillaume Tell*. Colonel Mapleson brought his opera troupe in 1878, and Maurice Grau's French Company presented opera the next year. Maurice Strakosch's and Max Maretzek's troupes also visited, and Boston heard Clara Louise Kellogg and Anna Bishop. The Boston Ideals ignited "Pinafore fever" around the country with the American premiere of Arthur Sullivan's *H.M.S. Pinafore* on November 25, 1878. Sullivan's *Princess Ida* followed on February 11, 1884. Boston also witnessed several novelties, including Federico Ricci's *Corrado d'Altamura*, Arrigo Boïto's *Mefistofele* (in English), Edmond Audran's *La mascotte*, Julius Eichberg's *The Doctor of Alcantara*, Emilio Pizzi's *Gabriella*, and William Harling's *Alda*. During the 1860s, the theater briefly changed its name to Academy of Music, to be "associated" with the Academies of Music in New York and Philadelphia, which were built as opera houses.

The Boston Theater hosted the Theodore Thomas American Company, the Castel Square Company, and the newly established Metropolitan Opera, which Henry Abbey brought to Boston for its first out-of-town performances, during the 1880s and 1890s. Heinrich Conried brought the Met back to the Boston on April 1, 1905. The city was delighted with the debut of Geraldine Farrar, a Massachusetts native, and the presentations of Charles Gounod's *Faust* and Puccini's *Madama Butterfly* among others. Next Henry Russell brought his San Carlo troupe. Russell returned with the San Carlo in the winter of 1907, opening with Amilcare Ponchielli's *La gioconda* on December 9. When Russell returned to Boston the following year, it was to manage the Boston Opera Company, Boston's first resident grand opera company. To house the company in proper fashion, Eben Jordan Junior paid for the construction of the Boston Opera House. Designed by Parkman Haven, it was an impressive building of red brick, gray limestone, and white terra cotta. The gala opening night—November 8, 1909—found everybody from the president of Harvard University to Misses John Gardner in attendance. A spectacular Ponchielli's *La gioconda*, with Louise Homer and Lillian Nordica, inaugurated the new company and the new opera house. The first season ran from November 8 to March 24, and boasted twenty different operas. Operas by Giuseppe Verdi and Puccini—*Il trovatore*, *La traviata*, *Aida*, *Rigoletto*, *La bohème*, *Tosca*, and *Madama Butterfly*—took their places beside Boïto's *Mefistofele*, Donizetti's *Lucia di Lammermoor* and *Don Pasquale*, Pietro Mascagni's *Cavalleria rusticana*, Ruggero Leoncavallo's *I pagliacci*, Rossini's *Il barbiere di Siviglia*, Georges Bizet's *Carmen*, Léo Delibes's *Lakmé*, Giacomo Meyerbeer's *Les Huguenots*, Gounod's *Faust*, Richard Wagner's *Lohengrin* (in Italian), and Ferdinando Paër's *Le maître de chapelle*. The season's novelty was Act I of Sergey Rakhmaninov's *Skupoy rītsar* (TheMiserly Knight) sung in Russian on March 11, 1910.

The second season was no less spectacular with one world premiere—Frederick Converse's *The Sacrifice*—two American premieres, Claude Debussy's *L'enfant prodigue* and Raoul Laparra's *La habanera*, and Converse's *The Pipe of Desire*. (Converse's opera had received its world premiere in Boston on January 31, 1906.) The 1911-1912 season hosted several great artists. Camille Saint-Saëns's *Samson et Dalila* opened the season on November 27 featuring Giovanni Zenatello and Maria Gay. Gay and Zenatello returned for Bizet's *Carmen*. Gay appeared in Mascagni's *Cavalleria rusticana*, while Zenatello was in Leoncavallo's *I pagliacci*, and Verdi's *La traviata* and *Otello*. Luisa Tetrazzini sang Donizetti's *Lucia di Lammermoor*, Rossini's *Il barbiere di Siviglia* and Thomas's *Mignon*. Emmy Destinn assayed Aida and Cio-Cio-San. Nordica was Isolde, and Emma Eames portrayed Desdemona. The fourth season offered three novelties, Bizet's *Djamileh* and *L'Arlesienne*, and Louis Aubert's *La forêt bleue*. The Boston Opera Company's final season opened with Ermanno Wolf-Ferrari's *I gioielli della Madonna* on November 24, 1913. Lucien Muratore followed in Gounod's *Faust* and Mary Garden in Puccini's *Tosca*. Garden returned for Massenet's *Thaïs*. Margarete Matzenauer and Edoardo Ferrari-Fontana assayed Isolde and Tristan respectively, and Destinn was Gioconda. The novelty was Henri Février's *Monna Vanna*. During the company's extraordinary, but short life, fifty-one different operas were mounted, with as many as ninety performances a season. After a fateful trip to Paris, the company expired in 1914.

The Boston Opera Company was briefly reincarnated as the Boston Grand Opera Company, with Max Rabinoff at the helm. During its two season existence works as diverse as Italo Montemezzi's *L'amore dei tre re*, Christoph Willibald von Gluck's *Orfeo ed Euridice*, Daniel Auber's *La muette de Portici*, and Mascagni's *Iris* graced the stage. The city demolished the Boston Theater in the 1920s to construct the Keith Memorial, now called Opera House, the Opera Company of Boston's boarded-up home. Other homegrown opera was mounted by the Boston Civic Opera and the Fleck Grand Opera. In 1917, the Chicago Opera began annual visits which lasted until 1932. The previous year, the world premiere of George Gershwin's *Of Thee I Sing* took place on December 8, 1931, followed by the world premiere of his *Porgy and Bess* on October 10, 1935. The Met added Boston to its annual tour in 1934, and continued its visits until 1986. The Boston Opera House was demolished in 1958.

The current operatic era traces its roots to the New England Opera Theater, founded by Boris Goldovsky in 1946. It is best known for its splendid productions of operas by Gluck and Mozart, and the American premiere of Hector Berlioz's

Les Troyens (abbreviated version) on March 27, 1955. Boston witnessed other premieres: Alessandro Striggio's *Il cicalamento delle donne al bucato e la caccia* (concert version) on May 31, 1955, at the Museum of Fine Arts, Thomas Beveridge's *Dido and Aeneas* on February 14, 1958, at the Fogg Art Museum, and Mozart's *La finta semplice* (in English as The Clever Flirt) on January 27, 1961, in Jordan Hall.

Caldwell, a protégée of Goldovsky, established the Opera Group in 1958. (The name was changed to Opera Company of Boston in 1965.) The company was characterized by adventurous repertory and imaginative productions for which Caldwell was able to attract big name singers. In 1962, Beverly Sills made her company debut in Jules Massenet's *Manon*, and Joan Sutherland followed two years later in Bellini's *I Puritani*. Marilyn Horne, Tito Gobbi, Plácido Domingo, Nicolai Gedda, Renata Tebaldi, Régine Crespin, James McCracken, George London, Shirley Verrett, and Eva Marton have all sung under Caldwell's baton. After the Group's initial season at the Fine Arts Theater, it moved into the Donnelly Memorial Theater. This was home for the next nine years. Here Caldwell mounted the East Coast premiere of Alban Berg's *Lulu*, the original version of Modest Mussorgsky's *Boris Godunov*, the first American stage performance of Jean-Philippe Rameau's *Hippolyte et Aricie*, and the American premiere of Arnold Schoenberg's *Moses und Aron*. The Donnelly Theater (renamed Back Bay Theater in 1965) was demolished in 1968, forcing the company to find a new home. The Company then took up residence at the Shubert Theater for one season, a season which saw Sills in Donizetti's *Lucia di Lammermoor*. During the next two years, the most unlikely places — Kresge Auditorium, Rockwell Cage, Cousens Gymnasium, and the nineteenth-century Cyclorama Building — hosted the Company's performances. In 1971, grant money enabled the company to move into the Orpheum Theater, where it remained until November 1978. Bellini's *Norma* welcomed the company into its new home. The highlights of the Orpheum years included an uncut production of Berlioz's *Les Troyens*, Kurt Weill's *Aufstieg und Fall der Stadt Mahagonny*, the original French version of Verdi's *Don Carlos* and several novelties: Sergey Prokofiev's *War and Peace*, Roger Sessions's *Montezuma*, Mikhail Glinka's *Ruslan and Lyudmila*, and Berlioz's *Benvenuto Cellini* with Jon Vickers and John Reardon. Caldwell was on the podium for all the performances.

On November 1, 1978, the Company acquired the Savoy Theater on Washington Street and renamed it the Opera House. The Company finally had a permanent home. The next year the Opera House hosted the first of several American premieres, among them Michael Tippett's *The Ice Break* and Bernd Zimmermann's *Die Soldaten*. Caldwell introduced both Leoš Janáček's *Věc Makropulos* and Leonard Bernstein's *Mass* to Boston. The Company's first world premiere, Robert Di Domenica's *The Balcony* took place on June 14, 1990.

Caldwell presents opera as music theater, with the music igniting the theatrical elements. Theatrical components receive equal weight and attention as the musical ones, and their fusion defines Caldwell's productions. She tries to balance her seasons — new and old, eighteenth-, nineteenth-, and twentieth-century, standard and off-beat — feeling variety is important. She thoroughly researches the works she wants to do. The list of her favorites operas is eclectic — Puccini's *La bohème*, Schönberg's *Moses and Aron*, Donizetti's *Lucia di Lammermoor*, Berg's *Lulu*, and Wagner's *Der fliegende Holländer*. Caldwell's major problem is that her reach always exceeds her grasp; this has contributed to the current financial problems the company is experiencing. The future is uncertain. "There is a dire need to stabilize the financial problems, which have grown more acute with the drying up of federal funding and the recession," as Caldwell explains. She is searching for area universities that might be interested in collaborative efforts so her company can survive. She favors the European system, not only because heavy government subsidies would eliminate her money woes, but also because of its emphasis on the *Musiktheater* concept and longer rehearsal periods. Before the lack of money halted productions, the company offered a four-opera season, frequently with internationally known artists. For example, the 1989 season offered Siegfried Jerusalem in the Bernstein's *Mass*, Verrett and Giorgio Lamberti in Verdi's *Aida*, Gwyneth Jones, Tatiana Troyanos, and Siegfried Vogel in Richard Strauss's *Der Rosenkavalier*, and Teresa Stratas in Puccini's *La bohème*. Caldwell staged and conducted all the performances.

Posed to take the place of the Opera Company of Boston, should it not survive, is the Boston Lyric Opera. Having made peace, or at least a truce with its rival, the Boston Opera Theater, the Lyric is in a strong position to become Boston's main opera company. (The Boston Opera Theater presented a Peter Sellers production of Mozart's *Le nozze di Figaro* which left the company with a large debt the season before "the truce." When that is paid off, the 18-member board of the Boston Opera Theater will join the board of the Boston Lyric Opera.) The Lyric specializes in unusual repertory, featuring young American talent. One of the Lyric's goals is to promote American singers (who must also be good actors and actresses) and the American repertory. The standard repertory, which the company stages for "box office," takes on a "fresh appearance" with scenic designers like John Conklin conceiving the sets.

The Lyric was founded in 1976, and mounted its first production, Mozart's *Zaide*, in October 1977. Its repertory runs the gamut from Georg Friedrich Händel's *Agrippina* to Francis Poulenc's *Dialogues des Carmélites* and has included such rarely-seen works as Verdi's *Un giorno di regno* and Massenet's *Thérèse*. Since the cessation of performances by the Opera Company of Boston, the Lyric has experienced astronomical growth. The budget has jumped from $200,000 to $1.6 million in three years, and the season schedule has more than doubled to three performances of three operas. Further expansion to six performances of four operas is planned with operetta added to the repertory. Expansion throughout the greater New England is also envisioned. Stephen Lord, the company's music director, decides the repertory. He chooses only those works that he likes, since he "connects emotionally" to the operas which he conducts. He does not "interpret the music," but "reacts to the notes printed on the page."

The three-opera season offers one usual work in a *stagione* system. Recent productions include Stephen Paulus's *The Postman Always Rings Twice*, Gluck's *Orfeo ed Euridice*, and Bizet's *Carmen*. The Lyric performs in the Emerson Majestic Theater.

Emerson Majestic Theater

The Emerson Majestic began life in 1903 as the Majestic Theater. Designed in the Beaux Arts style by John Galen Howard, it was built by Eben Dyer Jordan. The theater hosted dramas, musicals, operettas, and vaudeville. After fifty-three years, the theater was sold to a local movie chain. Horror movies occupied the screen and the theater fell into deep decline. Emerson College bought the theater in 1983 and is ever so slowly restoring it.

The Beaux Arts style building boasts an splendid terra cotta façade. There are three stained-glass windows surmounted by painted lunettes, and four imposing Ionic columns. A russet-marble lobby boasts gilded stucco ornamentation. The ornately decorated auditorium holds two gently curving balconies that flow over bluish-green seats. Masks of Comedy and Tragedy reside overhead, and gilded stucco trumpet-vine wind around the room. The walls are covered with gilded lattice patterns holding rosettes. The theater seats 900.

Opera House

Puccini's *Tosca* inaugurated the Opera Company of Boston's new home, the Opera House, on November 8, 1978. Purchased only eight days earlier, the theater was hurriedly readied for the opening performance. The Opera House began life in 1928 as a memorial to Benjamin Franklin Keith, the founder of American vaudeville theater. Designed by Thomas Lamb, the Keith Memorial, or B.F. Keith Theater as it was commonly called, was built as a home for vaudeville. A short time later, motion pictures invaded the theater, and vaudeville was relegated to intermission entertainment. By the 1950s, only movies were shown. Sack Theaters took over the theater in the 1970s. The company had bought the opera house from Sack Theaters.

The Opera House façade is thin and narrow, sandwiched between two old buildings. Soaring above its neighbors, the façade displays KEITH'S on top. The Grand Lobby holds Corinthian marble columns and a sweeping grand staircase. The auditorium radiates in ivory, red, and gold splendor. A single tier rises above plush orchestra seats. Rectangular pillars flow into arches that support the balcony. Muses frolic in a heavenly environment in the ceiling dome. Unfortunately, decades of neglect — only one of which was attributable to the Opera Company of Boston — forced the Opera House to close in January 1991. The threat of the BayBank foreclosing on the building still looms in the distance and attack dogs patrol inside.

Practical Information. The Emerson Majestic Theater is at 219 Tremont Street. Tickets are purchased at the Boston Lyric Opera offices, 114 State Street, Monday through Friday between 10:00 A.M. and 5:00 P.M., by telephoning 617-248-8660 during the above business hours, by fax 24-hours a day at 617-248-8810 or by writing Boston Lyric Opera, 114 State Street, Boston, MA 02109-2402. If the Opera House is reopened, it is located at 539 Washington Street. The Opera Company of Boston can be reached by writing to P.O.B. 50, Boston, MA 02112. If you go, stay at the Ritz-Carlton, 15 Arlington Street, Boston, MA 02117; telephone 617-536-5700, fax 617-536-1335, reservations 1-800-241-3333. The Ritz-Carlton has been a Boston landmark since it was built in 1927, and is an architecturally important building. The hotel is luxurious, and the theaters are only a few blocks away.

COMPANY STAFF AND REPERTORY

General/Artistic Directors (Opera Company of Boston). Sarah Caldwell (1958–present).

General/Artistic Directors (Boston Lyric Opera). Janice Mancini del Sesto (managing, 1992–present).
American/United States Premieres (Federal Street Theater). Arnold's *Mountaineers* (April 6, 1795); Grétry's *Richard Coeur de Lion* (in English, January 23, 1796); Reeve's *The Sicilian Romance* (April 10, 1796); Shield's *Mysteries of the Castle* (April 15, 1796); Grétry's *Selima and Azor* (in English, March 31, 1797); Kelly's *Castle Spectre* (November 28, 1798) ; Dibdin's *Recruiting Sergeant* (March 15, 1799); Van Hagen's *Columbus* (February 17, 1800); Kelly's *Of Age Tomorrow* (January 31, 1806); Storace's *Lodoiska* (March 2, 1806); Woodward's *The Deed of Gift* (1822).
American/United States Premieres (Haymarket Theater). van Hagen's *Adopted Child* (March 15, 1797); Storace's *Three and the Deuce* (May 26, 1797); Pélissier's *Launch* (September 20, 1797); Arne's *Bourville Castle* (October 23, 1797); Attwood's *Smuggler* (May 13, 1799); Storace's *Cherokee* (June 24, 1799).
World Premieres (Boston Theater). Damrosch's *The Scarlet Letter* (February 10, 1896).
American/United States Premiere (Boston Theater). Offenbach's *Monsieur Choufleuri* (early 1869); Lecocq's *Giroflé-Girofla* (December 7, 1874); von Suppé's *Donna Juanita* (in English, May 12, 1881).
World Premieres (Boston Opera House). Converse's *The Sacrifice* (March 3, 1911).
American/United States Premieres (Boston Opera House). Rakhmaninov's *Skupoy rïtsar* (The Miserly Knight) (Act I, March 11, 1910); Claude Debussy's *L'enfant prodigue* (stage premiere, November 16, 1910); Laparra's *La habanera* (December 14, 1910); Debussy's *Le martyre de Saint Sebastien* (March 30, 1912); Bizet's *Djamileh* (February 24, 1913); Bizet's *L'Arlesienne* (first performance in French, March 6, 1913); Aubert's *La forêt bleue* (March 8, 1913); Février's *Monna Vanna* (December 5, 1913); Tchaikovsky's *Mazeppa* (December 14, 1922); Berlioz's *Les Troyens* (in English as The Trojans, abbreviated, March 27, 1955).
World Premieres(Opera Company of Boston). di Domenica's *The Balcony* (June 14, 1990).
American/United States Premieres (Opera Company of Boston). Rameau's *Hippolyte et Aricie* (first stage performance, 1966); Schönberg's *Moses und Aron* (November 30, 1966); Berlioz's *Les Troyens* (first uncut version, February 3, 1972); Prokofiev's *War and Peace* (first stage performance, May 8, 1974); Berlioz's *Benvenuto Cellini* (May 3, 1975); Sessions's *Montezuma* (March 31, 1976); Glinka's *Ruslan and Lyudmila* (in English, March 5, 1977); Tippett's *The Ice Break* (May 18, 1979); Zimmermann's *Die Soldaten* (January 22, 1982); Davies's *Taverner* (March 9, 1986); Shchedrin's *Myortvïe dushi* (Dead Souls, March 16, 1988).
Repertory (Federal Street Theater). **1794:** Agreeable Surprise, Farmer, Hunt the Slipper, Inkle and Yarico, Love in A Village, Midas, Mother Pitcher (pantomime), No Song, no Supper, Padlock, Poor Soldier, Quaker, Romp, Rosina, Son-in-law, Virgin Unmasked, Waterman. **1795:** Agreeable Surprise, Battle of Hexham, Bird Catcher (pantomime), Caledonian Frolic (pantomime), Children in the Wood, Deserter, Don Juan (pantomimeballet), Farmer, Haunted Tower, Highland Reel, Inkle and Yarico, Midas, Mock Doctor, Mountaineers, No Song, no Supper, Padlock, Poor Jack (pantomime), Prize, Quaker, Robinson Crusoe, Romp, Rosina, Sultan, Surrender Calais, Virgin Unmasked, Waterman. **1796:** Agreeable Surprise, Beggar's Opera, Children in the Wood, Cymon and Sylvia, Death of Captain Cook (pantomime), Deux Chasseurs, Devil to Pay, Farmer, Flitch of Bacon, Flora, Grateful Lion (pantomime), Harlequin Skeleton (pantomime), Harlequin's Invasion (pantomime), Highland Reel, Inkle and Yarico, Lionel and Clarissa, Love in a Camp, Love in a Village, Midas, Mock Doctor, Mountaineers, My Grandmother, Mysteries of the Castle, No Song, no Supper, Oscar and Malvina (pantomime), Patriot, Peep Behind the Curtain, Peeping Tom of Coventry, Prize, Purse, Quaker, Richard Coeur de Lion, Romp, Rosina, Sicilian Romance, Sultan, Tammany, Tom Thumb the Great, Virgin Unmasked, Witches (pantomime). **1797:** Adopted Child, Agreeable Surprise, American Heroine (pantomime),

Bird Catcher (pantomime), Castle of Andalusia, Children in the Wood, Death of Captain Cook (pantomime), Forêt noire (pantomime), Highland Reel, Iron Mask, Island of Calypso (pantomime-ballet), Lionel and Clarissa, Little Yankee Sailor (pantomime), Lock and Key, Maid of the Mill, Midas, Miraculous Mill (pantomime), Mountaineers, My Grandmother, No Song, no Supper, Oscar and Malvina, Padlock, Paul and Virginia, Peeping Tom of Coventry, Poor Soldier, Prisoner, Prize, Purse, Pygmalion, Romp, Rosina, Selima and Azor, Shipwrecked Mariner Preserved (pantomime), Son-in-law, Spanish Barber, Taste of Times (local pantomime), Two Philosophers. **1798:** Adopted Child, Agreeable Surprise, Castle Spectre, Double Disguise, Duenna, Highland Reel, Launch, Lock and Key, No Song, no Supper, Purse, Quaker, Rosina, Waterman. **1799:** Count Benyowski, Cymon and Sylvia, Double Disguise, Farmer, Gil Blas, Haunted Tower, Highland Reel, Inkle and Yarico, Mountaineers, No Song, no Supper, Oscar and Malvina, Poor Soldier, Prize, Purse, Recruiting Sergeant, Soldier's Frolic, Sicilian Romance, Siege of Belgrade, Siege of Quebec, Son-in-law. **1800:** Agreeable Surprise, American Volunteers (pantomime), Blue Beard, Columbus, Deserter of Naples, Garden of Love (pantomime-ballet), Harlequin Indian (pantomime), Harlequin's Wishing Cup (pantomime), Highland Reel, Inkle and Yarico, Mother Pitcher, Mountaineers, No Song, no Supper, Oscar and Malvina, Robinson Crusoe, Spanish Barber, Thomas and Sally, Waterman, Witches, (pantomime).

Repertory (Haymarket Theater). **1796:** Cooper (pantomime-ballet), Mirza and Lindor. **1797:** Adopted Child, Agreeable Surprise, Ariadne Abandoned, Archers, Battle of Hexham, Bourville Castle, Children in the Wood, Columbus, Deserter (pantomime), Destruction of the Bastille (pantomime), Don Juan (pantomime-ballet), Double Disguise, Fountainebleau, Galatea, Harlequin Doctor (pantomime), Harlequin Statue, Highland Reel, Inkle and Yarico, Launch, Lock and Key, Love and Money, Love in a Village, Medea and Jason, Midnight Wanderer, Milliners, Mirza and Lindor, Mountaineers, My Grandmother, New French Deserter, No Song, no Supper, Padlock, Poor Jack (pantomime), Poor Soldier, Prize, Purse, Quaker, Robinson Crusoe, Robin Hood, Romp, Rosina, Siege of Belgrade, Siege of Quebec (pantomime), Son-in-law, Spanish Barber, Three and the Deuce, Tom Thumb the Great, Touchstone of Truth, Two Hunters and the Milkmaid (pantomime), Unfortunate Family (pantomime), Waterman, Wood Cutters (pantomime), Zorinski. **1798:** Adopted Child, Agreeable Surprise, Padlock, Poor Soldier, Sicilian Romance, Thomas and Sally. **1799:** Birth of Harlequin (pantomime), Cherokee, Harlequin Restored (pantomime), My Grandmother, No Song, no Supper, Padlock, Poor Soldier, Romp, Shipwreck, Smuggler.

Repertory (Boston Opera Company). **1909-1910:** La gioconda, Aida, La bohème, Lakmé, I pagliacci, Cavalleria rusticana, Rigoletto, Don Pasquale, La traviata, Faust, Madama Butterfly, Il trovatore, Le Maître de Chapelle (Il Maestro di Capella), Lucia di Lammermoor, Mefistofele, Carmen, Les Huguenots, Skupoy rïtsar (The Miserly Knight), Tosca, Il barbiere di Siviglia. **1910-1911:** Mefistofele, Rigoletto, Otello, Tosca, Lucia di Lammermoor, Faust, L'enfant prodigue, I pagliacci, La bohème, Il barbiere di Siviglia, Aida, Tosca, La gioconda, Il trovatore, Madama Butterfly, Skupoy rïtsar (The Miserly Knight), Cavalleria rusticana, La Habanera, Carmen, Mefistofele, The Pipe of Desire, La traviata, La fanciulla del West, Hänsel und Gretel, Manon, Manon Lescaut, Lakmé, The Sacrifice, Don Pasquale. **1911-1912:** Samson et Dalila, Tosca, Aida, Carmen, Madama Butterfly, Thaïs, La bohème, Faust, Lucia di Lammermoor, Otello, Mignon, I pagliacci, Coppélia, Cavalleria rusticana, Pelléas et Mélisande, Rigoletto, La fanciulla del West, La traviata, Hänsel und Gretel, Il barbiere di Siviglia, Manon, Tristan und Isolde, Werther, Germania, Il trovatore, La Habanera. **1912-1913:** Les contes d'Hoffmann, La bohème, Madama Butterfly, Il trovatore, Tosca, Thaïs, Lucia di Lammermoor, Louise, La traviata, Aida, Hänsel und Gretel, Messa da Requim, Cavalleria rusticana, I pagliacci, Pelléas et Mélisande, Carmen, I gioielli della Madonna, Il barbiere di Siviglia, Otello, Tristan und Isolde, Don Giovanni, La fanciulla del West, Djamileh, Faust, La forêt bleue, Il segreto di Susanna, Martha. **1913-1914:** I gioielli della Madonna, Faust, Tosca, Tristan und Isolde, Lucia di Lammermoor, Monna Vanna, La traviata, Madama Butterfly, Aida, Thaïs, Il barbiere di Siviglia, Samson et Dalila, I pagliacci,

Cavalleria rusticana, Hänsel und Gretel, Il trovatore, Rigoletto, Les contes d'Hoffmann, La bohème, Louise, Die Meistersinger von Nürnberg, La gioconda, L'amore dei tre re, Carmen, Il segreto di Susanna, Martha, Don Giovanni, Otello, Roméo et Juliette, Manon.

   Repertory (Boston Grand Opera Company). 1915-1916: L'amore dei tre re, Orfeo et Euridice, Carmen, Madama Butterfly, Tosca, I pagliacci, La muette de Portici, Otello, La bohème, Faust, Cavalleria rusticana, Rigoletto, Hänsel und Gretel. 1916-1917: Andrea Chénier, Madama Butterfly, L'amore dei tre re, Faust, Iris, La bohème, Aida.

   Repertory (Boston Lyric Opera). 1977-78: Zaide, Die Kluge. 1979-80: Un giorno di regno. 1980-81: Amahl and the Night Visitors, The Consul, L'incoronazione di Poppea, La clemenza di Tito. 1981-82: Norma, Werther, Die Entführung aus dem Serail. 1982-83: Madama Butterfly, Ariadne auf Naxos, Il trovatore, Der Ring des Nibelungen. 1984-85: Der Schauspieldirektor/Prima la musica, e poi le parole. 1985-86: Agrippina, La voix humaine, Façade, Il barbiere di Siviglia. 1986-87: The Rake's Progress, Rigoletto. 1987-88: Maria Stuarda, The Turn of The Screw. 1988-89: Le portrait de Manon, Thérèse, Dialogues des Carmélites. 1989-90: Tosca, Der fliegende Holländer, La traviata. 1990-91: La fille du régiment, Ariadne auf Naxos, Regina. 1991-92: La Cenerentola, Lost in the Stars, Les contes d'Hoffmann. 1992-93: La bohème, Béatrice et Bénédict, Wuthering Heights. 1993-94: I Puritani, Carmen, The Postman Always Rings Twice.

Michigan ——————— DETROIT

• *Michigan Opera Theater* •

The Music Hall hosted the Michigan Opera Theater's inaugural season, which opened with Giacomo Puccini's *La rondine* in 1971. The world premiere of Andrew Lloyd Webber's rock opera *Joseph and the Amazing Technicolor Dreamcoat* followed on November 5, 1971. With the unusual inaugural repertory, it was apparent that this opera company would be unique. David DiChiera, associated with the music department at Oakland University, founded the company and has been its guiding force since its inception. Eight years earlier, DiChiera had begun the Overture to Opera series. Established as the educational/outreach arm of the Detroit Grand Opera Association (which brought the Metropolitan Opera to Detroit) the Overture to Opera led to the formation of the Michigan Opera Theater.

   Detroit hosted opera from the mid-1800s, when Luigi Arditi visited with an Italian company, offering Detroit its first taste of Italian opera. The troupe staged the *bel canto* repertory of Vincenzo Bellini, Gaetano Donizetti, and Gioachino Rossini. Other traveling opera companies—De Vries Company and the Pyne-Harrison Company—mounted the English and French repertory. Walter Damrosch brought his company with an impressive German schedule. The Metropolitan Opera also included Detroit in its touring schedule.

   Detroit saw its first homegrown opera company in 1928, when Thaddeus Wroński formed the Detroit Civic Opera. Six years later, the Civic joined forces with the Detroit Symphony Orchestra. Emphasizing twentieth-century and American operas, the company staged the American premiere of Lodovico Rocca's *Il Dibuk*

(May 6, 1936), Deems Taylor's *Peter Ibbetson* and Puccini's *La rondine* among others.

Beginning in 1963, the Overture to Opera group staged operatic scenes, which gradually gave way to rarely mounted one-act operas. In 1969, Italo Tajo joined the company for Gaetano Donizetti's *Il campanello di notte*. He returned in 1970 to direct and sing in the Overture to Opera's first full-length production, Rossini's *Il barbiere di Siviglia*. Performed in the Detroit Institute of Arts, Rossini's *Il barbiere di Siviglia* also featured the professional operatic debut of Maria Ewing. The following year marked the birth of the Michigan Opera Theater. Established to provide alternative works to the traditional grand opera presented by the Met visits, the company wanted opera to be accessible for everyone. The ticket prices were affordable and all productions were sung in English. When surtitles were introduced in the early 1980s, original language productions became the norm.

DiChiera's commitment to both revive and introduce contemporary operas, especially American works, is reflected in the twentieth-century bent of the repertory. The company combines unusual pieces, operatic favorites, and musical theater works for a balanced schedule. Musical theater pieces like Scott Joplin's *Treemonisha*, Jerome Kern's *Showboat*, Frank Loesser's *The Most Happy Fella*, Mitch Leigh's *Man of La Mancha*, and Stephen Sondheim's *Sweeney Todd*, shared the stage with the repertory favorites—Puccini's *Tosca* and *Madama Butterfly*, Wolfgang Amadeus Mozart's *Le nozze di Figaro* and *Die Zauberflöte*, and Verdi's *Aida* and *La traviata*. The company mounted its second world premiere, Thomas Pasatieri's *Washington Square* with Catherine Malfitano on October 1, 1976, and until the mid-1980s, almost every season offered a contemporary opera. Most were rarely-performed American works, including Victor Herbert's *Naughty Marietta*, Marc Blitzstein's *Regina*, Louis Gruenberg's *The Emperor Jones*, Carlisle Floyd's *Of Mice and Men* (with the composer directing), and Armen Tigranian's *Anoush*. The large Polish community around the Detroit area led to the mounting of two unusual Polish operas—Karol Szymanowski's *Król Roger* (King Roger) and Stanislaw Moniuszko's *Straszny Dwór* (The Haunted Castle).

The Michigan Opera Theater claims many memorable operatic moments during its more than two decade existence. Ghena Dimitrova made her North American opera debut in Giacomo Puccini's *Turandot*. Leona Mitchell made her professional debut in George Gershwin's *Porgy and Bess*, and Kathleen Battle made her debut in Rossini's *Il barbiere di Siviglia*. Malfitano sang her first Violetta in Detroit, and Joan Sutherland gave her last Norma there. Other renowned artists have performed with the company, including Phyllis Curtain in Puccini's *Tosca*, Jerome Hines in Modest Mussorgsky's *Boris Godunov*, Mignon Dunn in Pyotr Il'yich Tchaikovsky's *Orleanskaya deva* (Maid of Orleans), and Mariella Devia in Donizetti's *Lucia di Lammermoor*. Copland conducted his *The Tender Land* in a nationally televised broadcast, and actor Sal Mineo made his directorial debut and played Toby in Gian Carlo Menotti's *The Medium*. With the triumphs, a few disasters have befallen the company. Opening nights are especially susceptible. At 4:30 P.M. on the opening night of Puccini's *Tosca* in 1986, Charles Long, the Scarpia, lost his voice. Pablo Elvira, in town for Rossini's *Il barbiere di Siviglia*, was intercepted shopping, but did not know the role. So the indisposed Long pantomimed Scarpia on stage, and Elvira sang it from the side. Jerome Kern's *Showboat* was also struck. The scenery got caught on some wires and the cue system went

Masonic Temple Theater (Detroit, Michigan).

out. While moving scenery behind the singers, the drop curtain was inadvertently raised and the singers were prematurely placed in Chicago.

DiChiera feels each opera has its own aesthetic. "The production can be traditional, symbolic, or from another vein, if the interpretation flows naturally from the aesthetics of the work." DiChiera likes to expose his audience to the "incredible range of works that falls under the broad title of opera." Planning the repertory is like a jigsaw puzzle to DiChiera. It is necessary to fit a variety of operas together properly. According to DiChiera, some operas benefit from ensemble casting, but others need star quality. Consequently, the type of casts you hear depends on the opera.

The growth of the Michigan Opera Theater has been hindered by its nomad existence. The company performs its light-opera in the Fisher Theater and its grand-opera in the Masonic Temple. The halls lack the technical facilities necessary for "high-tech" opera productions, and the company's schedule must be planned around the theaters' availability. So a few years ago, the company purchased the old Grand Circus Theater, which it is restoring and transforming into the Detroit Opera House. A gala fund-raising concert with Luciano Pavarotti is planned for the reopening. The Opera House would be the company's permanent home and carry the Michigan Opera Theater into the twenty-first century. Once the company is in its new home, DiChiera plans to expand the current season to eight productions—four operas, one ballet, and three operettas—spaced throughout the season. The company is developing a ballet wing because ballet usually shares the stage in opera houses, and Detroit does not yet have a ballet company.

The four-opera season offers an interesting repertory mix that includes light, grand, and contemporary works, performed in the *stagione* system. Recent productions include Sondheim's *Side by Side by Sondheim*, Szymanowski's *Król Roger*, Rossini's *Il barbiere di Siviglia*, Puccini's *Turandot*, and Charles Gounod's *Faust*. The company performs in the Masonic Temple Theater and Fisher Theater.

Masonic Temple Theater

The Masonic Temple Theater is housed in the massive Masonic Temple building. Designed by George D. Mason, it was built as a home for the Masonic Order in Detroit. Ground breaking took place on Thanksgiving Day in 1920, and the cornerstone was laid on September 18, 1922. Four years later, the building was dedicated on November 25.

Constructed in the classic Gothic style and faced with Indiana limestone, the Temple looms like an old medieval castle over the surrounding area. MASONIC TEMPLE THEATER in large white letters is printed on the awnings. The lobby is honey-colored glazed concrete. Steep turquoise-painted concrete ramps lead into the auditorium. Decorated in Venetian Gothic style, the hall swims in gold, maroon, and turquoise. One enormous balcony curves around the hall with gilded masks decorating its parapet. Two bronze-and-glass art deco chandeliers that weigh one and a half tons each light the hall. The Masonic Temple seats 4,645.

Fisher Theater

The Fisher Theater is an integral part of the towering Fisher Building. It was the last of the great movie palaces built in Detroit. The seven Fisher brothers owned the building. Designed by Albert Kahn, the structure cost $9 million. The Fisher opened its doors in the fall of 1928. The Chicago firm of Graven and Mayger designed the theater's original interior in early Mexican and Indian style. As the era of movie palaces waned, so did the Fisher. The Fisher brothers modernized and remodeled the movie palace into a playhouse in 1961. After the renovation, the theater took on a different appearance.

The building's exterior is described as "American Vertical style" with windows grouped and recessed. Minnesota granite covers the first three stories and Maryland marble clads the rest. The theater is reached through an ornately decorated arcade. Heavy bronze doors lead into a cream-colored auditorium. Two tiers flow gently across dark gold-olive velvet seats. Dark wood paneling and rows of golden egg shapes on a cream-colored background cover the walls. A golden curtain hangs in the proscenium arch. The Fisher seats 2,089.

Grand Circus Theater

The future home of the Michigan Opera Theater began life as the Capital Theater on January 12, 1922. Inaugurated with vaudeville and the movie *Lotus Eater*, the theater was designed by C. Howard Crane in the Italian Renaissance style. The 3,384-seat vaudeville and moving picture theater was the fifth largest in the world at the time of its opening. The theater acquired the name Grand Circus Theater in 1960, and served as a movie house and a concert hall until 1985. That year its doors were shut and the theater abandoned. The Michigan Opera Theater purchased the building three years later. The company is restoring the theater under the guidance of Ray Shepardson, at a cost of $20 million. It is scheduled to reopen in September 1994.

Practical Information. The Masonic Temple Auditorium is at 500 Temple Avenue. The Fisher Theater is at 3011 West Grand Boulevard. All tickets are purchased from the Michigan Opera Theater Office at 6519 Second Avenue. The hours are 10:00 A.M. to 5:30 P.M., Monday through Friday. Tickets can be ordered by telephoning 313-874-7464 between 10:00 A.M. and 6:00 P.M., Monday through Friday, faxing 313-871-7213 twenty-four hours a day, or writing Michigan Opera Theater Ticket Office, 6519 Second Avenue, Detroit, MI 48202-3006. If you go, stay at the Ritz Carlton, 300 Town Center Drive, Dearborn, MI, 48126; telephone 313-441-2000, fax 313-441-2051, reservations 1-800-241-3333. The hotel offers an interesting collection of nineteenth-century artwork and antiques, wonderful accommodations, and is convenient to the theaters.

COMPANY STAFF AND REPERTORY

General/Artistic Directors. David DiChiera (1971–present).

World Premieres (before Michigan Opera Theater). Mayer's *The Conspiracy of Pontiac* (January 27, 1887); Romberg's *Nina Rosa* (October 22, 1929).

American/United States Premieres (before Michigan Opera Theater). Rocca's *Il Dibuk* (Masonic Temple Auditorium, in English as The Dybbuk, May 6, 1936); Dzerzhinsky's *The Quiet Don* (Masonic Temple Auditorium, May 25, 1945).

World Premieres (Michigan Opera Theater). Webber's *Joseph and the Amazing Technicolor Dreamcoat* (November 5, 1971); Pasatieri's *Washington Square* (October 1, 1976).

American/United States Premieres. (Michigan Opera Theater); Tigranian's *Anoush* (October 30, 1981).

Repertory. 1971-72: La rondine, Joseph and the Amazing Technicolor Dreamcoat, The Perfect Fool (Children's Series). 1972-73: Così fan tutte, Tosca, The Telephone/The Medium. 1973-74: Rigoletto, Madama Butterfly, Die lustige Witwe. 1974-75: La traviata, Boris Godunov, L'elisir d'amore, Die Fledermaus. 1975-76: Porgy & Bess, La bohème, Lucia di Lammermoor, Il barbiere di Siviglia. 1976-77: Washington Square, Madama Butterfly, Naughty Marietta, Die Zauberflöte. 1977-78: Regina, Carmen, The Student Prince, Amahl and the Night Visitors. 1978-79: Les pêcheurs des perles, Show Boat, La traviata, I pagliacci, The Emperor Jones, Madama Butterfly (Midland Festival), The Tender Land (Midland Festival). 1979-80: The Most Happy Fella, Il trovatore, La bohème, Orleanskaya deva (Maid of Orleans). 1980-81: Die Fledermaus, Of Mice and Men, Don Giovanni, Rigoletto, Les pêcheurs des perles (Midland Festival). 1981-82: Tosca, Carmen, Anoush, The Mikado, Porgy and Bess. 1982-83: Straszny Dwór (The Haunted Castle), Lucia di Lammermoor, Treemonisha, Le nozze id Figaro, The Sound of Music. 1983-84: La traviata, Faust, A Little Night Music, Anna Bolena. 1984-85: Die lustige Witwe, Die Zauberflöte, Sweeney Tod, Aida. 1985-86: Gianni Schicchi/I pagliacci, Martha, West Side Story, Turandot. 1986-87: Orpheus in the Underworld, Madama Butterfly, My Fair Lady, Tosca, Il. barbiere di Siviglia, Porgy and Bess. 1987-88: Falstaff, Man of La Mancha, Kismet, Il trovatore, Die Fledermaus, La bohème. 1988-89: The Ballad of Baby Doe, Follies, The Pirates of Penzance, Orlando, Norma, Le nozze di Figaro, Carmen. 1989-90: Les Misérables, Hänsel und Gretel, Don Giovanni, La traviata, Roméo et Juliette. 1990-91: Rigoletto, Show Boat, Ariadne auf Naxos, Die Zauberflöte, Madama Butterfly. 1991-92: Candide, The Mikado, Król Roger, Samson et Dalila, Lucia di Lammermoor. 1992-93: Side by Side by Sondheim, The Music Man, La bohème, Aida. 1993-94: Il barbiere di Siviglia, Die lustige Witwe, Turandot, Faust.

Minnesota

MINNEAPOLIS / SAINT PAUL

• *The Minnesota Opera* •

The Minnesota Opera, originally called the Center Opera, was born on November 22, 1963, with the world premiere of Dominick Argento's *The Masque of Angels*. Argento, a Minneapolis resident, was one of the company's co-founders. The Center Opera was affiliated with the Walker Art Center. The company became an independent entity six years later, and changed its name to Minnesota Opera in 1971.

Saint Paul's first opera season was performed in Melodeon Hall in 1859. After the Civil War, the city built its first opera house, the Grand Opera House. Constructed on the east side of Wabasha near the present Radisson Hotel on Kellogg Boulevard, the Grand opened in 1867. Several touring opera troupes performed there, as well as in the nearby Radisson Hotel. In fact, one of the city's world premieres, Willard Patton's *Pocahontas* (concert version), took place in the Radisson on January 4, 1911. The city built the Saint Paul Civic Theater in 1906. The Saint Paul Civic held a large, fan-shaped hall with 2,701 dark burgundy plush seats. The Civic served as home for the Saint Paul Opera, a small, homegrown opera company established in the 1930s. The company was a traditionally-oriented organization that offered standard fare with rented backdrops. During performances, the singers (all imported), frequently appeared anchored to the stage. During its final seasons, however, the Saint Paul Opera produced some novelties: Lee Hoiby's *Summer and Smoke*, Carl Nielsen's *Maskarade*, and Werner Egk's *Verlobung in San Domingo*. The Metropolitan Opera began annual visits in 1945 that lasted for forty-one years.

The Minnesota Opera was established as a small, progressive, "alternative" opera company that combined musical, dramatic, and visual elements in unified presentations. The company wanted to avoid competition with the traditionally-oriented Saint Paul Opera and the conservative Metropolitan Opera visits. All performances were sung in English with young singers. It emphasized new works and avant garde productions, the latter a result of the Walker affiliation. For example, the entire set of Wolfgang Amadeus Mozart's *Die Entführung aus dem Serail* consisted of two camp chairs about two stories high, one overturned and the other upright, and a coat rack and umbrella. The production of Robert Kurka's *The Good Soldier Schweik* displayed an enormous enema bag on stage for a group enema! The company resided at the Guthrie Theater, but rapid expansion of the Guthrie's own season forced the company to find other performing venues. After the spin off from the Walker, the team of John Ludwig (general manager), Wesley Balk (director), and Yale Marshall (composer) developed an ensemble of eight young singer-actors to perform experiment-oriented productions. The company performed at the Cedar Village Theater, staging eleven world premieres, including Marshall's *Oedipus and the Sphinx*, Paul Boesing's *The Wanderer*, John Gessner's *Faust Counter Faust*, and Susa's *Transformations*.

Ordway Music Theater (Minneapolis/Saint Paul, Minnesota).

In 1975, the Minnesota Opera merged with the ailing Saint Paul Opera, and the "new" Minnesota Opera adjusted its repertory to include traditional works alongside the novelties. A few years later, the company moved into larger performance spaces—O'Shaughnessy Auditorium and the Orpheum Theatre—and that precipitated a financial crisis. The crisis had grown so severe by 1982, that the company laid off all but two of its staff. Although the Opera was compelled to develop a strong standard operatic repertoire, it did not lose its primary goal—encouraging the composition and performance of new works by American composers. Several more world premieres graced the stage including Argento's *The Voyage of Edgar Allan Poe* and *Miss Havisham's Wedding Night*, Susa's *Black River*, Robert Ward's *Claudia Legare*, and Henry Mollicone's *The Mask of Evil*.

The American premiere of Lars Johan Werle's *Animalen* on January 10, 1985, welcomed the company into its new home, the Ordway Music Hall. Three months later, Argento's *Casanova's Homecoming* became the first world premiere to grace the Ordway stage. Directed by Arthur Masella and conducted by Scott Bergson, the witty and sophisticated opera buffa was based on the memoirs of one of history's most tantalizing libertines, Casanova. Ordway continued to see novelties; among them were Madsen's *Cowboy Lips*, William Harper's *Snow Leopard*, and Robert Moran's *From the Towers of the Moon*. Moran's opera dealt with the importance of love and respect as symbolized by the arrival on earth of a mysterious young girl. Although she eventually returned to her own people, she remained visible to the earthlings on the light from the towers of the moon to remind them of her message. The company has mounted over thirty world premieres.

The four-opera season offers standard fare with one new or unusual work in a *stagione* system. Recent productions have included Giuseppe Verdi's *Il trovatore*, Giacomo Puccini's *Madama Butterfly*, Franz Lehár's *Die lustige Witwe*, Georg Friedrich Händel's *Giulio Cesare*, and Hannibal Peterson's *Diary of an African American*. The company performs in the Ordway Music Center.

Ordway Music Center

A concert recital by Leontyne Price inaugurated the Ordway Music Theater on January 8, 1985. Two evenings later, the Minnesota Opera premiered Werle's *Animalen*. Benjamin Thompson designed the Center which cost $45 million and took a little over two years to build. The need for a cultural center dates back to 1970, when the Saint Paul Civic Center Theater was structurally deteriorating and in need of major improvements. A decade later, the theater was condemned and the city decided to construct a new performing arts complex.

Ordway Music Center is an imposing sculpted-shape building of red brick and glass, with undulating waves of glass radiating around the façade. The rust, blue, and gold auditorium fuses a warm, contemporary design into baroque ambiance. Three shallow balconies curve around the horseshoe-shaped room. Large wall sconces illuminate the space. The auditorium acts as a vibrating drum, bouncing and evenly distributing the sound off its sculpted, hard reflective surfaces. The theater seats 1,800.

Practical Information. Ordway Music Center is at 345 Washington Street, in Saint Paul. The box office is directly inside the Center's entrance. It is open Monday through Saturday from 10:00 A.M. to 5:30 P.M. You can order tickets by telephoning 612-224-4222 during the above box office hours or writing Ordway Music Theater Box Office, 345 Washington Street, Saint Paul, MN 55102. For information, contact the Minnesota Opera at 612-333-2700 (phone), 612-333-0869 (fax) or by writing The Minnesota Opera, 620 North First Street, Minneapolis, MN 55401. If you go, stay at the Radisson Hotel Saint Paul, 11 East Kellogg Boulevard, Saint Paul, MN 55101; telephone 612-292-1900, fax 612-224-8999, reservations 1-800-333-3333. It has a history of hosting opera performances and is convenient to the Center.

COMPANY STAFF AND REPERTORY

General/Artistic Directors. Dominick Argento/Yale Marshall (producers, 1963–64); John Ludwig (manager, 1964–74); Charles Fullmer (manager, 1974–83); Edward Corn (1983–85); Kevin Smith (1985–present).

World Premieres (Saint Paul Opera); Hoiby's *Summer and Smoke.* (June 19, 1971).

American/United States Premieres (Saint Paul Opera). Nielsen's *Maskarade* (June 23, 1972); Egk's *Verlobung in San Domingo* (in English as "The Betrothal in Saint Domingo," July 17, 1974).

World Premieres (Center Opera). Argento's *The Masque of Angels* (November 22, 1963); Stokes's *Horspfal* (February 15, 1969); Marshall's *Oedipus and the Sphinx* (November 29, 1969); Boesing's *The Wanderer* (February 28, 1970); Gessner's *Faust Counter Faust* (January 30, 1971); Marshall's *Christmas Mummeries/Good Government* (December 12, 1970); Dominick's *Postcard From Morocco* (October 14, 1971); Marshall's *The Business of Good Government* (January 21, 1972).

American/United States Premieres (Center Opera). Blitzstein's *The Harpies* (March 17, 1967); Birtwistle's *Punch and Judy* (January 30, 1970); Egk's *Siebzehn Tage und vier Minuten* (January 17, 1970).

World Premieres (Minnesota Opera). Susa's *Transformations* (May 5, 1973); Hodkinson's *Vox Populos* (December 1, 1973); Balk's *The Newest Opera in the World* (May 1974); Marshall's *Gallimaufry* (December 13, 1974); Blackwood's *Gulliver* (February 22, 1975); Susa's *Black River* (May 1975); Argento's *The Voyage of Edgar Allan Poe* (April 24, 1976); Ward's *Claudia Legare* (April 14, 1978); Stokes's *The Jealous Cellist* (February 2, 1979); Titus's *Rosina* (April 26, 1980); Argento's *Miss Havisham's Wedding Night* (May 1981); Mollicone's *The Mask of Evil* / Barnes's *Feathertop* (April 30, 1982); Mayer's *A Death in the Family* (March 11, 1983); Bach's *The Abduction of Figaro* (April 24, 1984); Argento's *Casanova's Homecoming* (April 12, 1985); Wargo's *The Music Shop* (September 25, 1985); McKeel's *Jargonauts, Ahoy!* (tour production, April 1988); Madsen's & Greene's *Cowboy Lips* (May 19, 1988); Hutchinson & Shank's *Fly Away All* (January 1988, revised version, May 19, 1988); Monk's *Book of Days* (May 1988); Shiflett's *Without Colors* / Sherman's *Red Tide* (March 23, 1989); Harper's *Snow Leopard* (November 9, 1989); Larsen's *Frankenstein, The Modern Prometheus* (May 25, 1990); Moran's *From the Towers of the Moon* (March 27, 1992).

American/United States Premieres (Minnesota Opera). Offenbach's *Christopher Columbus* (November 4, 1977); Werle's *Animalen* (January 10, 1985); Knussen's *Where the Wild Things are/Higglety Pigglety Pop!* (first stage performance, September 27, 1985).

Repertory. **1963-64:** The Masque of Angels, The Masque of Venus and Adonis, Albert Herring. **1964-65:** The Rape of Lucretia, Die Kluge. **1965-66:** Die Entführung aus dem Serail, The Good Soldier Schweik. **1966-67:** The Mother of Us All, Les malheurs d'Orphée, The Harpies, Socraties, Trois minute opéras. **1967-68:** Il mondo della luna, A Midsummer Night's Dream. **1968-69:** Così fan tutte, Horspfal, Die Kluge. **1969-70:** Oedipus and the Sphinx, Punch and Judy, Siebzehn Tage und vier Minuten, The Wanderer. **1970-71:** Christmas Mummeries/Good Government, Faust Counter Faust, L'incoronazione di Poppea, The Mother of Us All. **1971-72:** Postcard from Morocco, The Business of Good Government, The Good Soldier Schweik, Le nozze di Figaro. **1972-73:** Die Dreigroschenoper, Postcard from Morocco, Il barbiere di Siviglia, Transformations. **1973-74:** El Capitan, Transformations, Don Giovanni, The Newest Opera in the World. **1974-75:** Gallimaufry, Gulliver, Die Zauberflöte, Albert Herring. **1975-76:** Black River, El Capitan, Così fan tutte, The Voyage of Edgar Allan Poe. **1976-77:** Prodaná nevěsta (The Bartered Bride), The Passion According to St. Matthew, Candide, Aufstieg und Fall der Stadt Mahagonny. **1977-78:** Christophe Colomb, The Mother of Us All, Le nozze di Figaro, Claudia Legare. **1978-79:** Lyubov' k tryom apel'sinam (The Love for Three Oranges), The Jealous Cellist, The Passion According to St. Matthew, La traviata, The Consul, Viva la Mamma. **1979-80:** Die Entführung aus dem Serail, The Pirates of Penzance, La bohème, Rosina, A Christmas Carol. **1980-81:** Die lustige Witwe, Black River, Carmen, A Water Bird Talk, Miss Havisham's Wedding Night, Le nozze di Figaro, Die Dreigroschenoper. **1981-82:** Hänsel und Gretel, The Village Singer, Gianni Schicchi, Il barbiere di. Siviglia, Feathertop, The Mask of Evil, Hänsel und Gretel, Rosina. **1982-83:** Hänsel und Gretel, Lucia di Lammermoor, A Death in the Family, Kiss Me, Kate, Il barbiere di Siviglia, The Frog Who Became a Prince, Zetabet. **1983-84:** Hänsel und Gretel, Madama Butterfly, La Cenerentola, The Abduction of Figaro, The Boor, Chanticleer, Don Pasquale. **1984-85:** Animalen, Casanova's Homecoming, Die Zauberflöte, La bohème, Meanwhile, back at Cinderella's. **1985-86:** Where the Wild Things Are/Higglety Pigglety Pop!, La traviata, L'elisir d'amore, The King and I, Opera Tomorrow, The Fantasticks, Die Zauberflöte, The Music Shop. **1986-87:** Les pêcheurs des perles, The Postman Always Rings Twice, Ariadne auf Naxos, South Pacific, Hänsel und Gretel, Jargonauts, Ahoy!. **1987-88:** Die Fledermaus, Rigoletto, Rusalka, Cowboy Lips, Fly Away All, Book of Days, Oklahoma!, Carmen, Jargonauts, Ahoy!. **1988-89:** Don Giovanni, Salome, The Mikado, The Juniper Tree, Show Boat, Without Colors, Red Tide, Newest Little Opera in the World, La Cenerentola, Tintypes. **1989-90:** La bohème, A Midsummer

Night's Dream, Roméo et Juliette, Frankenstein, The Modern Prometheus, My Fair Lady, Snow Leopard, Madama Butterfly, Where the Wild Things Are. **1990-91:** Norma, The Aspern Papers, Carmen, Così fan tutte, Swing on a Star. **1991-92:** Tosca, Les pêcheurs des perles, Le nozze di Figaro, From the Towers of the Moon, Carousel, Die Zauberflöte. **1992-93:** Die fliegende Holländer, Armida, Madama Butterfly, The Pirates of Penzance. **1993-94:** Julius Caesar, Diary of an African American, Il trovatore, Die lustige Witwe, Don Giovanni.

Mississippi ————————— J A C K S O N

• *Mississippi Opera* •

The Mississippi Opera began under the auspices of the Jackson Opera Guild on November 27, 1945, with the presentation of Pietro Mascagni's *Cavalleria rusticana* in the Bailey Junior High School auditorium. One year later, Ruggero Leoncavallo's *I pagliacci* was performed. Mrs. John T. Caldwell founded the organization and was its president for the first decade. In 1970, there was a reorganization with the emergence of the Mississippi Opera.

One-opera seasons defined the company until 1965, along with an emphasis on contemporary works. The company staged its only world premiere, Lehman Engel's *The Soldier*, on November 24, 1958, in the Millsaps College Auditorium. Two years later, Beverly Sills sang Giacomo Puccini's *Tosca*. James Goolsby joined the company as artistic director in 1978, and converted the spring/fall season into a summer Mississippi Opera Festival of the South. The experiment survived only two seasons and left a $53,000 debt. Franklin Choset took the reins in 1982 and expanded the repertory by offering Richard Strauss's *Salome* and the first performance in the United States in thirty years of Raffaello de Banfield's *Lord Byrons Love Letters*. Banfield directed the opera. Nationally known artists, along with emerging and local talent comprise the casts.

The two-opera season offers standard fare, along with twentieth-century pieces, and musical theater in a *stagione* system. Recent productions include Giacomo Puccini's *Madama Butterfly* and Claude Debussy's *Pelléas et Mélisande*. The company performs in the Jackson Municipal Auditorium.

Jackson Municipal Auditorium

The Jackson Municipal Auditorium was constructed in 1968 at a cost of $6 million. The Auditorium also houses the offices of the Jackson/Hinds County/Arts Alliance. The theater seats 2,430.

Practical Information. The Jackson Municipal Auditorium is at 255 Pascagoula Street. Tickets are available by writing Mississippi Opera, P.O.B. 1551, Jackson, MS 39215, or telephoning 601-960-1528 between 9:00 A.M. and 5:00 P.M. weekdays.

COMPANY STAFF AND REPERTORY

General/Artistic Directors. Mrs. John Caldwell, Jr. (President, 1945–54); None (1955–1965); Richard Anderson (Resident Director, 1966–70); Barbara White Johnson (1970–77); James Goolsby (1978–82); Franklin Choset (1982–89); Barbara Johnson (General Manager, 1989–91); Frank Marion Johnson (1991–92); Carroll Freeman (1993–present). *World Premiere.* Engel's *The Soldier* (stage premiere, November 24, 1958) *Repertory.* 1945: Cavalleria rusticana. 1946: I pagliacci. 1948: Il trovatore, Carmen. 1949: Carmen. 1950: La traviata. 1951: Cavalleria rusticana/I pagliacci. 1952: Faust. 1953: Madama Butterfly. 1954: La bohème. 1955: Così fan tutte. 1956: Carmen. 1957: Lucia di Lammermoor. 1958: The Soldier/Malady of Love. 1959: Die Fledermaus. 1960: Tosca. 1961: La traviata. 1962: Madama Butterfly. 1963: Suor Angelica/Gianni Schicchi. 1964: Old Maid and the Thief. 1965–66: Rigoletto, Slow Dusk, Gallantry. 1966–67: La bohème, Trouble in Tahiti, Il segreto di Susanna, Cavalleria rusticana. 1967–68: Il trovatore, Aida. 1968–69: Andrea Chénier, La traviata. 1969: Carmen. 1970–71: Tosca, Hänsel und Gretel, Lucia di Lammermoor. 1971–72: Madama Butterfly, Il barbiere di Siviglia. 1972–73: Roméo et Juliette, La bohème. 1973–74: I pagliacci, Don Pasquale. 1974–75: Rigoletto, La fille du régiment. 1975–76: Faust, Die lustige Witwe. 1976–77: Il trovatore, Il tabarro, Gianni Schicchi. 1977–78: La traviata, Les contes d'Hoffmann. 1978–79: Help! Help! The Globolinks, Babes in Toyland, Tosca. 1979–80: Flower and Hawk, Carmen, Riders to the Sea, Curlew River. 1980–81: Hänsel und Gretel, La bohème, La Cenerentola. 1981–82: Alice in Wonderland, Don Giovanni, Die Fledermaus. 1982–83: Aida, Il barbiere di Siviglia, Let's Build a Town. 1983–84: Madama Butterfly, Carmen. 1984–85: La bohème, Salome, Lord Byrons Love Letters. 1985–86: Lucia di Lammermoor, La traviata. 1986–87: Tosca, Il trovatore. 1987–88: Rigoletto, The Consul. 1988–89: Falstaff, Roméo et Juliette. 1989–90: Die Fledermaus, Carmen. 1990–91: La traviata. 1991–92: La bohème, Amahl and the Night Visitors, Pelléas et Mélisande. 1992–93: Rigoletto, La Cenerentola. 1993–94: Madama Butterfly, The Pirates of Penzance.

Missouri
KANSAS CITY

• *Lyric Opera of Kansas City* •

Giacomo Puccini's *La bohème*, performed on the stage of the Rockhill Theater on September 29, 1958, opened the first season of the Kansas City Lyric Theater, the original name of the Lyric Opera of Kansas. Puccini's *La bohème* inaugurated a four-week repertory season that included Giovanni Pergolesi's *La serva padrona/* Ruggero Leoncavallo's *I pagliacci*, Wolfgang Amadeus Mozart's *Die Entführung aus dem Serail*, and Giuseppe Verdi's *Otello*. The predominately local cast sang twenty performances under the baton of Russell Patterson. The first season's budget was $34,000. Patterson and Morton Walker established the company. Patterson had done an apprenticeship with the Bayerische Staatsoper in Munich (Germany), and Walker had been associated with civic opera in Minneapolis and Fort Worth. Together they proposed to transplant the European concept of repertory opera-theater to Kansas City in America's heartland. The company's original name, Lyric Theater, reflected their emphasis on the theater aspect. The company's three goals were to establish a platform for American artists so they could develop their craft without having to go abroad, to present opera for American audiences by performing in English, and to stage American works.

The first five seasons offered a mainstream repertory with young American singers, and a series of amusing tales. The baritone singing Méphistophélès in Charles Gounod's *Faust* was in full costume and makeup on the way to the theater when he ran out of gas. After filling his car with gas, he turned to the gaping station attendants and asked, "Haven't you fellows ever served the devil before?" Then there was the all-enveloping mist for the third act of Puccini's *La bohème* that caused Patterson to cue a lamppost instead of the singer.

For the sixth season, the Ford Foundation gave the company a grant to mount a Spring Festival of American Opera in collaboration with the University of Missouri at Kansas City and the Conservatory of Music. Douglas Moore's *The Devil and Daniel Webster* opened the festival at the University Playhouse, followed by Gian Carlo Menotti's *The Medium* and Samuel Barber's *Vanessa*. The company continued in the American vein with Robert Ward's *The Crucible*, Vittorio Giannini's *The Taming of the Shrew*, Marc Blitzstein's *Regina*, Conrad Susa's *Transformations*, Virgil Thomson's *Mother of Us All*, and Lee Hoiby's *The Tempest* among the offerings. The company's first and only world premiere, Jack Beeson's *Captain Jinks of the Horse Marines*, took place on September 20, 1975.

The Rockhill Theater, a forty-year-old motion picture house for American and foreign art films, was the company's home for the first ten seasons. Located in a shopping mall, the theater seated 812. The auditorium was plain and the stage only thirteen feet deep, making opera production quite tricky. Nonetheless, the sightlines and acoustics were good. When fire destroyed the theater in 1967, the company moved into the Uptown Theater, also a home for motion pictures. It seated 2,000 and had a larger stage and orchestra pit. After two seasons at the Uptown, the company made its final move to the Capri Theater, subsequently renamed the Lyric.

The five-opera season offers two standard works, a lighter opera, a contemporary work, and an operetta/musical theater piece, in the *stagione* system. The singers are emerging American talent. Recent productions include Verdi's *Aida*, Puccini's *Madama Butterfly*, Gioachino Rossini's *La Cenerentola*, Menotti's *The Saint of Bleecker Street*, Arthur Sullivan's *The Mikado*, and Franz Lehár's *Die lustige Witwe*. The company performs in the Lyric Theater.

Lyric Theater

The Lyric Theater began life as the Ararat Shrine Temple in 1926. Local architects Owen, Sayler and Payson designed the Temple, which was constructed by Fogel Brothers at a cost of $1 million. In 1942 the Red Cross purchased the building. After the war, the building changed hands a few more times until the Lyric Opera bought it in May 1991 for $2.65 million. The company did extensive renovation on the theater to make it more suitable for opera performance.

The Lyric is build of Indiana limestone. Its classic façade boasts fluted Corinthian columns and ornamental reliefs. THE LYRIC in large brownish letters rests on a ledge. Gold embellishes the maroon and cream-colored lobby. The fan-shaped, shallow auditorium is mustard-colored with zigzag walls and clusters of acoustic pyramid-squares. Two massive Doric columns support the single steeply-

The Lyric (Kansas City, Missouri).

graded balcony. Ionic pilasters flank the black proscenium arch. The seats are red. The theater seats 1600.

Practical Information. Lyric Theater is at 11th and Central. The ticket office, inside the theater on the right, is open Monday through Friday between 10:00 A.M. and 6:00 p.m, and on performance-Saturdays at 12:00 noon. Tickets can be ordered by telephoning 816-471-7344 during box office houses, or by writing Lyric Opera of Kansas City, 1029 Central, Kansas City, MO 64105. If you go, stay at the Radisson Suite Hotel, Kansas City, 106 West 12th Street, Kansas City, MO 64105, phone 816-221-7000, fax 816-221-8902, toll free 800-221-3855. The art deco style Radisson is interesting architecturally and located only three blocks from the Lyric Theater.

COMPANY STAFF AND REPERTORY

General/Artistic Director. Russell Patterson (1958–present).

World Premieres. Beeson's *Captain Jinks of the Horse Marines* (September 20, 1975).

Repertory. **1958-59:** La bohème, La serva padrona/I pagliacci, Die Entführung aus dem Serail, Otello. **1959-60:** Tosca, Rigoletto, Il barbiere di Siviglia, Carmen. **1960-61:** Madama Butterfly, Don Pasquale, La traviata, Don Giovanni. **1961-62:** La bohème, Cavalleria rusticana/Gianni Schicchi, Le nozze di Figaro, La forza del destino. **1962-63:** Andrea Chénier, Faust, Così fan tutte, Il barbiere di Siviglia. **1963-64:** The Devil and Daniel Webster/The Medium, Vanessa, Tosca, Die lustigen Weiber von Windsor, L'elisir d'amore, Yeomen of the Guard, Otello. **1964-65:** La bohème, Le nozze di Figaro, Rigoletto, Gianni Schicchi/The Medium. **1965-66:** Vanessa, Les contes d'Hoffmann, Madama Butterfly, La traviata. **1966-67:** Ariadne auf Naxos, Il trovatore, Don Pasquale, Faust. **1967-68:** Un ballo in maschera, Il barbiere di Siviglia, Tosca, Don Giovanni. **1968-69:** The Crucible, L'elisir d'amore, Andrea Chénier, Carmen. **1969-70:** Taming of the Shrew, Rigoletto, Les contes d'Hoffmann, La bohème. **1970-71:** Of Mice and Men, Le nozze di Figaro, Cavalleria rusticana/I pagliacci, Otello. **1971-72:** Madama Butterfly, Il barbiere di Siviglia, Gianni Schicchi/Die Kluge, The Taming of the Shrew. **1972-73:** Aida, The Yeoman of the Guard, Die Entführung aus dem Serail, The Saint of Bleecker Street. **1973-74:** The Sweet Bye and Bye, Le Périchole, Der fliegende Holländer, Tosca. **1974-75:** Die Fledermaus, Transformations, The Crucible, Die Zauberflöte, La traviata. **1975-76:** Captain Jinks of the Horse Marines, Der fliegende Holländer, Le nozze di Figaro, La Périchole, La bohème. **1976-77:** The Ballad of Baby Doe, The Pirates of Penzance, Andrea Chénier, La traviata, Il barbiere di Siviglia. **1977-78:** Aida, The Mikado, Susannah, Les contes d'Hoffmann, Le nozze di Figaro. **1978-79:** Faust, La fanciulla del West, The Medium/Der Kluge, H.M.S. Pinafore, Ariadne auf Naxos. **1979-80:** Carmen, Don Giovanni, Christopher Columbus, Vanessa, Iolanthe. **1980-81:** Madama Butterfly, L'elisir d'amore, The Free Lance, Manon, La belle Hélène. **1981-81:** Regina, L'italiana in Algeri, Lucia di Lammermoor, Die lustige Witwe, Fidelio, The Goose from Cairo. **1982-83:** La bohème, Il barbiere di Siviglia, Rigoletto, The Ballad of Baby Doe, The Happy Time, The Mother of Us All. **1983-84:** The Most Happy Fella, Fidelio, La Périchole, Il trovatore, La cenerentola. **1984-85:** Candide, La traviata, Così fan tutte, Turandot, The Mikado. **1985-86:** Un ballo in maschera, Sweeney Todd, Faust, Die Dreigroschenoper, Martha. **1986-87:** Where the Wild Things Are/The Goose from Cairo, The Crucible, Tosca, Falstaff, The Pirates of Penzance. **1987-88:** Der Rosenkavalier, Madama Butterfly, Le nozze di Figaro, The Tempest, Die Fledermaus. **1988-89:** Tannhäuser, La fille du régiment, Don Giovanni, Carmen, Man of La Mancha. **1989-90:** Regina, La bohème, Don Pasquale, Les contes d'Hoffmann, The Yeoman of the Guard. **1990-91:** Samson et Dalila, L'elisir d'amore, Rigoletto, Die Walküre, H.M.S. Pinafore. **1991-92:** Lucia di Lammermoor, Il barbiere di Siviglia, Susannah, Siegfried, Die lustigen Weiber von Windsor. **1992-93:** Aida, The Mikado, Amahl and The Night Visitors, Tosca, Die lustige Witwe. **1993-94:** Die Zauberflöte, Madama Butterfly, Amahl and the Night Visitors, The Saint of Bleecker Street, La Cenerentola.

SAINT LOUIS

• *Opera Theater of St. Louis* •

On May 22, 1976, Gaetano Donizetti's *Don Pasquale* inaugurated the Opera Theater of St. Louis in the Loretto-Hilton Center. Only one hundred and thirty-seven seats were sold for opening night and the company appeared doomed. Wolfgang Amadeus Mozart's *Der Schauspieldirektor* and Gian Carlo Menotti's *The Medium* were performed next, but it was not until Benjamin Britten's *Albert Herring* played to a sold-out house that the company's future seemed brighter.

Opera was first heard in St. Louis in 1830. A local company presented Daniel Auber's *La muette de Portici* in English. Most of the American touring opera companies (discussed in several entries) visited St. Louis during the nineteenth century, including Colonel Mapleson and his company. The Metropolitan Opera made its first visit in 1884. The last was eighty-two years later. Homegrown opera appeared in 1919 with the establishment of the St. Louis Municipal Opera Association. The Association presented a summer festival of light opera, operetta, and musicals in the 11,476-seat outdoor amphitheater. In 1939, the company was reorganized as the St. Louis Grand Opera Association and Hungarian-born conductor László Halász became artistic and musical director. Richard Wagner's *Die Walküre* with Marjorie Lawrence, Irene Jessner, Lauritz Melchior, and Fred Destal inaugurated the reorganized company in the Municipal Auditorium on April 17, 1939. Internationally known singers—Giovanni Martinelli, Ezio Pinza, Rose Bampton, Kirsten Flagstad, and Grace Moore—sang with the company. Although this resulted in fine opera, it also resulted in huge fees, requiring a large private subsidy. When several of its supporters entered the armed forces in 1942, the company was forced to suspend operations.

The seeds for the Opera Theater were planted at a performance of Mozart's *Le nozze di Figaro* in June 1975. The Mississippi Valley Opera offered a two-week season at the Missouri Baptist College. The weather was hot. There was no air-conditioning, and money was in short supply. In fact, a collection was taken during intermission to pay the musicians so the performance could continue! Leigh Gerdine was at that performance. He was impressed with the stoicism and patience of the audience and decided to bring opera to St. Louis. Richard Gaddes was hired to run the newly-founded company and Gerdine guaranteed the first year's budget. Gaddes came from the Santa Fe Opera and modeled the fledgling company on his southwestern-opera company experience. Young American singers performed unusual operas in English. The formula worked. In its seventeen-year existence, numerous world and American premieres have been presented. Almost every season boasts a novelty. Among the world premieres have been three operas by Stephen Paulus—*The Village Singer*, *The Postman Always Rings Twice*, and *The Woodlanders*. A few neglected masterpieces are counted among the American novelties including Vicente Martín y Soler's *L'arbore di Diana*, Carl Maria von Weber's *Die drei Pintos* (completed by Gustav Mahler), and Rossini's *Il viaggio a Reims*, and rarely performed operas are also included in the repertory, Francis Poulenc's *Les Mamelles de Tirésias*, Hector Berlioz's *Béatrice et Bénédict*, and Ruggero Leoncavallo's *La bohème* among them. Other noteworthy productions include the six-opera Mozart Cycle that began with *Die Zauberflöte* in 1980, with *Così fan tutte*, *Don Giovanni*, *Idomeneo*, *Die Entführung aus dem Serail*, and *Mitridate, Re di Ponto* following. The Opera Theater often stages the lesser-known version of a work. For example in 1992, the company mounted the original version of Puccini's *Madama Butterfly*, the version that La Scala's opening night audience booed off the stage—and with good reason. It is in two acts, with the second act of Wagnerian length. In this production there was a loss of dramatic impact and some of the audience.

The Opera Theater of St. Louis presents singing theater—some funny, some serious—that happen to be operatic works. The budget is spent on singers, musicians, and importing critics. The productions are simple and only occasionally effective. The sets consist of a few props. There are no mood-setting lighting effects. The works are performed in English and only partially understandable. Although the quality of the singing and orchestra (St. Louis Orchestra) are commendable, that indescribable magic is missing, the magic that elevates opera above all other art forms, and creeps through you when the climactic moments are reached.

The four-opera season offers a mixture of popular, contemporary, and unusual works in repertory. The popular operas are usually the lesser known version of the work (if one exists). Recent operas include David Carlson's *The Midnight Angel*,

Benjamin Britten's *Billy Budd*, Massenet's *Cendrillon*, and Mozart's *Don Giovanni*. The company performs in the Loretto-Hilton Center.

Loretto-Hilton Center

The Loretto-Hilton Center is a college theater on the grounds of Webster University. Bronze letters blazon WEBSTER UNIVERSITY and LORETTO HILTON CENTER from two sides of a white-concrete marquee suspended on the brick and glass building. The auditorium exudes a brownish hue, filled with brown fabric seats that sweep around in a steeply graded semi-circle. Pop-up writing arms are attached to the rear section seats, reminding you that the auditorium doubles as a college lecture hall. The walls are dark wood paneled. There is no curtain and the back red brick wall serves as the universally present back drop. There are 924 seats.

Practical Information. The Loretto Hilton Center is at 130 Edgar Road, eight miles from St. Louis. The box office is inside the theater on the left. It is open 10:00 A.M. to 4:00 P.M., Monday through Friday. On performance days it remains open through the first intermission and opens Saturday at 10:00 A.M. and Sunday at 12:00 noon. You can order tickets by telephoning at 314-961-0644, or writing Opera Theater of St. Louis, P.O.B. 191910, St. Louis, MO 63119-7910. If you go, stay at the Ritz-Carlton, 100 Carondelet Plaza, St. Louis, MO, 63105; telephone 314-863-6300, fax 314-863-7486, reservations 1-800-241-3333. The Ritz-Carlton displays an outstanding art and antique collection and offers exquisitely furnished rooms. It is only a short drive to the opera theater.

COMPANY STAFF AND REPERTORY

General/Artistic Directors. Richard Gaddes (1976–1985); Charles MacKay (1986–present).

World Premieres (before the Opera Theater of St. Louis). Armstrong's *The Spectre Bridegroom* (1899); Moore's *Louis XIV* (February 16, 1917); Fink's *The Boor* (February 14, 1955).

American/United States Premieres (before the Opera Theater of St. Louis). Sullivan's *Patience* (July 28, 1881); Britten's *Let's Make an Opera* (children's opera, March 22, 1950).

World Premieres (Opera Theater of St. Louis). Paulus's *The Village Singer* (June 9, 1979); Paulus's *The Postman Always Rings Twice* (original version, June 17, 1982); Delius's *Margot la Rouge* (first stage performance, June 8, 1983); Miki's *Jōruri* (May 30, 1985); Paulus's *The Woodlanders* (June 13, 1985); Davis's *Under the Double Moon* (June 15, 1989); Carlson's *The Midnight Angel* (June 1, 1993); Touring Operas: White's *Love, Death and High Notes* (children's opera, October 1, 1988), Meyer's *Laclede's Landing* (children's opera, October 6, 1989).

American/United States Premieres (Opera Theater of St. Louis). Martin y Soler's *L'arbore di Diana* (in English as The Tree of Chastity, May 27, 1978); Weber/Mahler's *Die drei Pintos* (in English as The Three Pintos, June 6, 1979); Delius's *Fennimore and Gerda* (June 3, 1981); Miki's *An Actor's Revenge* (June 11, 1981); Prokofiev's *Maddalena* (in English, June 9, 1982); Rossini's *Il viaggio a Reims* (in English as The Journey to Rheims, June 12, 1986); Oliver's *La bella e la bestia* (in English as The Beauty and the Beast, June 11, 1987); Mozart's *Mitridate, Re di Ponto* (first stage performance, June 1, 1991); Weir's *The Vanishing Bridegroom* (June 2, 1992).

Repertory (St. Louis Grand Opera Association). **1939:** Die Walküre, Otello,

Loretto-Hilton Theater (St. Louis, Missouri).

Faust, Aida, La bohème, Amelia Goes to the Ball/I pagliacci, Siegfried. **1940:** Rigoletto, Carmen, Manon, Manon (Havana, Cuba), Cavalleria rusticana/I pagliacci (Havana, Cuba), La bohème (Havana, Cuba), Otello (Havana Cuba). **1941:** Don Giovanni, Manon, La traviata, Cavalleria rusticana/I pagliacci, Rigoletto (Havana, Cuba), Tosca (Havana, Cuba), Faust (Havana, Cuba), Madama Butterfly (Havana, Cuba), Martha, Martha (Evansville, Indiana), Tosca, Falstaf.
Repertory (Opera Theater of St. Louis). **1976:** Don Pasquale, Der Schauspiel-direktor/The Medium, Albert Herring. **1977:** Così fan tutte, Pygmalion, Gianni Schicchi, Le Comte Ory. **1978:** La bohème, Forever Figaro, L'arbore di Diana, Albert Herring, Madama Butterfly. **1979:** La traviata, Ariadne auf Naxos, Die drei Pintos, Gianni Schicchi, The Village Singer. **1980:** Die Zauberflöte, Falstaff, Spiel oder Ernst?, The Seven Deadly Sins, The Turn of the Screw. **1981:** Rigoletto, Le nozze di Figaro, Fennimore and Gerda, Il segreto di Susanna, An Actor's Revenge. **1982:** H.M.S. Pinafore, L'elisir d'amore, Così fan tutte, Maddalena, La Verbena de la Paloma, The Postman Always Rings Twice, The Beggar's Opera. **1983:** Pirates of Penzance, La traviata, Don Giovanni, Margot La Rouge, Les Mamelles de Tirésias, Béatrice et Bénédict. **1984:** Die Fledermaus, Die Zauberflöte, Madama Butterfly, Orfeo ed Euridice, Paul Bunyan. **1985:** The Mikado, The Beggar's Opera, Il barbiere di Siviglia, Jōruri, Idomeneo, The Woodlanders. **1986:** Les contes d'Hoffmann, Die Entführung aus dem Serail, A Death in the Family, Il viaggio a Reims, Curlew River. **1987:** The Gondoliers, Carmen, Alcina, La Cenerentola, La bella e la bestia, The Prodigal Son. **1988:** La bohème, Vanessa, La finta giardiniera, Oberon. **1989:** Die lustige Witwe, Werther, King Arthur, Under the Double Moon. **1990:** Peter Grimes, Le nozze di Figaro, La fille du régiment, Čert a káča. **1991:** Eugene Onegin, Mitridate, Re di Ponte, La bohème (Leoncavallo), Ariadne auf Naxos. **1992:** Madama Butterfly, Il turco in Italia, The Vanishing Bridegroom, A Midsummer's Night Dream. **1993:** The Midnight Angel, Cendrillon, Don Giovanni, The Very Last Green Thing, Billy Budd. **1994:** Candide, Falstaff, Iphigénie en Tauride, Black River: A Wisconsin Idyll.

Nebraska
OMAHA

• *Opera/Omaha* •

On January 19, 1959, Giacomo Puccini's *Madama Butterfly* marked the first production of the Omaha Civic Opera Society, the original name of Opera/Omaha. Cast with local talent, the opera took place in the Witherspoon Concert Hall of the Joslyn Art Museum. This single performance comprised the first season. It took so long for the amateur production to get off the ground that a five-month-pregnant soprano was singing Butterfly. The seeds for opera had been planted a year earlier, when conductor Richard Valente visited Omaha and inspired the creation of the Civic Opera Society. He believed that opera could survive in Nebraska.

The Society was a community organization in the early years with Valente as its musical director. Volunteers orchestrated the seasons of two familiar operas using local talent. Valente, who was also a composer, premiered his *Quivera* during the second season. Joseph Levine took over as music/artistic director in 1960. During his nine-year tenure, he hired Charles Peck, Leon Lishner, Glynn Ross, Arthur Schoep, and Ron Vaad to stage the mainstream works in a two-opera seasons. One of the company's first "major" productions was Douglas Moore's *The Ballad of Baby Doe*, mounted in 1967. Leo Kopp took the helm two years later and in 1971, expanded the season to three operas. The company also changed its name to Opera/Omaha. Several international artists have visited Omaha, including Regina Resnick, Richard Tucker, Norman Treigle, Dorothy Kirsten, Carol Neblett, Frederica von Stade, and Samuel Ramey. Beverly Sills captivated the city with her portrayal of Lucia during the 1974-75 season.

Mary Robert took the reins in 1980, and for seven years continued a three-opera season of familiar works. In the fall of that year, the company premiered an adventurous biennial festival that garnered both national and international attention. Benjamin Britten's *The Turn of the Screw* opened the first Fall Festival on September 18, 1987. Six days later, the world premiere of Michael Korie's *Where's Dick?* took place on September 24, 1987. Philip Glass & Robert Moran's *The Juniper Tree* concluded the festival. The company celebrated its thirtieth anniversary in style with the American premieres of Georg Friedrich Händel's *Partenope* and Udo Zimmermann's *Weiße Rose*. Novelties also highlighted the 1990 and 1992 Fall Festivals, including John Casken's *The Golem*, Gioachino Rossini's long neglected *Ermione*, and Hugo Weisgall's atonal work, *The Gardens of Adonis* (which took thirty years to complete). Plans for future Fall Festivals call for a continuation of new works, revivals of neglected European masterpieces, and "wild card pieces" — works that are "transitional between opera and music and offer a new approach to opera." Some of the "wild card pieces" have included Kurt Weill's *Stranger Here Myself* and Ricky Ian Gordon's *Autumn Valentine, a General Review of the Sex Situation*. The company transforms the stage of the Witherspoon Concert Hall (in the Joslyn Art Museum) into an opera house for the festival. The repertory concentrates on pieces that fit well into small places and can tolerate the orchestra seated behind a curtain because there is no orchestra pit. The company has plans to convert a former synagogue at 49th and Farnam into a performance

Orpheum Theater Auditorium (Omaha, Nebraska).

venue, to replace the unsatisfactory arrangement at the Witherspoon Concert Hall.

Robert follows a philosophy of making special the entire theater-going event. She also includes new works in the non-festival seasons to keep opera-going an "exceptional happening." She introduced this concept during the 1993 "Grand" Opera Season, when Andrew Lloyd Webber's *Requiem Variations* received its world premiere on June 2, 1993. The company mounts all new productions during the regular winter and spring seasons. To make this more financially viable, Opera/Omaha has formed a consortium with four other regional companies (Portland Opera/Edmonton Opera/Vancouver Opera/Minnesota Opera). This also allows major designers and directors to work on the productions. A blending of well-established artists with emerging talent comprise the casts.

The number of operas per season fluctuates between three and six, depending if there is a Fall Festival or not. During non-festival seasons, a musical joins two grand operas on the program. Recent main season productions have included Ludwig van Beethoven's *Fidelio*, Arthur Sullivan's *The Pirates of Penzance*, Puccini's *Tosca*, Jacques Offenbach's *Les contes d'Hoffmann*, and Richard Wagner's *Der fliegende Holländer*. The company performs the regular season at the Orpheum Theater.

Orpheum Theater

The Orpheum was born during the opulent era of the 1920s. Designed by Rapp and Rapp, the theater opened on October 9, 1927. It cost $2 million. Billed as the "golden palace," the Orpheum originally hosted vaudeville and live stage shows. During the 1950s, films replaced the stage shows. By 1971, the theater was in a terrible state of disrepair and on April 29, 1971, after a showing of Walt Disney's *A Barefoot Executive*, the theater shut its doors. The Knights of Ak-Sar-Ben purchased the Orpheum in 1972 and presented it as a gift to the city of Omaha. Architect Leo Daly was in charge of the $2.4 million renovation that restored the Orpheum to its former splendor. The theater reopened on January 17, 1975, as Omaha's Performing Arts Center.

The Orpheum resides on the lower floors of a towering beige-stone building. A marquee with ORPHEUM marks the entrance. The original gold-painted ticket booth remains in the rose and cream-colored lobby, filled with mirrors and marble. The ivory-and-gold auditorium offers an expansive orchestra, shallow loge and deep grand tier/balcony. Olive green seats harmonize with the gilded fleur-de-lis, imbrications, cartouches, garlands, vases, and flowers that decorate the hall. Exquisite glass and crystal chandeliers are suspended from the highly ornamented ceiling. The theater seats 2,870.

Practical Information. The Orpheum Theater is at 409 South 16th Street. The Witherspoon Concert Hall is in the Joslyn Art Museum at 2200 Dodge Street. Tickets for all performances are purchased at Opera/Omaha, 1613 Farnam Street, Suite 200, or by phoning 402-346-0357, faxing 402-346-7323, or writing Opera/Omaha, P.O.B. 807, Omaha, NE 68101. If you go, stay at the Radisson Redick Tower Hotel, 1504 Harney Street, Omaha, NE 68102, phone 402-342-1500, fax 402-342-5317. The Redick Tower is a splendidly restored art deco building dating from the 1920s. Interesting architecturally, it is located across the street from the Orpheum.

COMPANY STAFF AND REPERTORY

General/Artistic Directors. Richard Valente (1958–1960); Joseph Levine (1960–69); Leo Kopp (1969–74); Jonathan Dudley (1974–77); Martha Elsberry (1977–1980); Mary Robert (1980–present).

World Premieres. Valente's *Quivera* (May 5, 1960); Korie's *Where's Dick?* (September 24, 1987); Weisgall's *The Gardens of Adonis* (September 12, 1992); Gordon's *Autumn Valentine, a General Review of the Sex Situation* (September 16, 1992); Webber's *Requiem Variations* (June 2, 1993).

American/United States Premieres. Handel's *Partenope* (in English, September 10, 1988); Zimmermann's *Weiße Rose* (new version, in English as "The White Rose," September 14, 1988); John Casken's *The Golem* (September 15, 1990); Rossini's *Ermione* (September 11, 1992).

Repertory. **1958-59:** Hänsel und Gretel, Madama Butterfly, Oklahoma!, Tosca. **1959-60:** Carousel, Il pagliacci, Quivera. **1960-61:** Die Fledermaus, La traviata. **1961-62:** La bohème, Die lustige Witwe. **1962-63:** Carmen, La périchole. **1963-64:** Aida, Il barbiere di Siviglia. **1964-65:** Lucia di Lammermoor, Le nozze di Figaro. **1965-66:** Madama Butterfly, Rigoletto. **1966-67:** Il trovatore, The Ballad of Baby Doe. **1967-68:** La bohème, Tosca. **1968-69:**Carmen, La traviata. **1969-70:** Cavalleria rusticana/I pagliacci, Faust. **1970-71:** Aida, Die Fledermaus. **1971-72:** Madama Butterfly, Rigoletto, Les contes d'Hoffmann. **1972-73:** Roméo et Juliette, Un ballo in maschera, Tosca. **1973-74:** La bohème, L'elisir d'amore, Le nozze di Figaro. **1974-75:** La traviata, La périchole, Lucia di Lammermoor, Il barbiere di Siviglia. **1975-76:** Aida, Bilby's Doll, Manon. **1976-77:** Don Giovanni, Don Pasquale, Madama Butterfly, Die lustige Witwe. **1977-78:** Die Entführung aus dem Serail,

Il barbiere di Siviglia, Prodaná nevěsta (The Bartered Bride). **1978-79:**La bohème, Werther. **1979-80:** Die Fledermaus, La traviata, The Pirates of Penzance. **1980-81:** Così fan tutte, Rigoletto, Susannah. **1981-82:** La fille du régiment, Carmen, Die Zauberflöte. **1982-83:** Don Pasquale, Madama Butterfly, Faust. **1983-84:** Aida, Don Giovanni, Les contes d'Hoffmann. **1984-85:** Tosca, Falstaff, Gianni Schicchi/I pagliacci. **1985-86:** Turandot, Lucia di Lammermoor, Le nozze di Figaro. **1986-87:** La traviata, Il barbiere di Siviglia, Porgy and Bess. **1987-88:** The Turn of the Screw, The Juniper Tree, Where's Dick, La bohème, Carmen. **1988-89:** Oklahoma!, Partenope, The White Rose/The Diary of One Who Vanished, A Celebration of Bel Canto, Rigoletto, Manon. **1989-90:** Showboat, Madama Butterfly, Roméo et Juliette. **1990-91:** Carousel, Stranger Here Myself, Maria Padilla, Golem, Il trovatore, Die Zauberflöte. **1991-92:** My Fair Lady, Tosca, Don Giovanni. **1992-93:** Ermione, The Gardens of Adonis, Les contes d'Hoffmann, Der fliegende Holländer, Requiem Variations. **1993-94:** Requiem Variations, Fidelio, The Pirates of Penzance.

Nevada ———————————— RENO

• *Nevada Opera* •

Gioachino Rossini's *Il barbiere di Siviglia* inaugurated the Nevada Opera on July 18, 1968, in the Reno Little Theater. Merle Puffer, who directed the Voice-Music Department at the University of Nevada, founded the company. Giuseppe Verdi's *Rigoletto* was also performed during the inaugural season.

The second season expanded to three offerings, Johann Strauß's *Die Fledermaus*, Gaetano Donizetti's *Don Pasquale*, and Giacomo Puccini's *Madama Butterfly*. The sixth season saw the company's first American premiere, Ferruccio Busoni's *Doktor Faust* in January 1974. Another followed two seasons later, Pyotr Il'yich Tchaikovsky's *Orleanskaya deva* (The Maid of Orleans, in English). The company's first world premiere, Bern Herbolsheimer's *Mark Me Twain* took place on April 22, 1993. Young and emerging artists comprise the casts. Dolora Zajick and Evelyn de la Rosa are among the graduates.

The opera season varies between four and five works, offering a mixture of traditional fare, operettas, contemporary pieces, and musical theater in a *stagione* system. Recent productions include Verdi's *La forza del destino* and Johann Strauß's *Die Fledermaus*. The company performs in the 1,428-seat Pioneer Center for the Performing Arts.

Practical Information. The Pioneer Center for the Performing Arts is at 100 South Virginia Street. Tickets are available by writing Nevada Opera, P.O.B. 3256, Reno, NV 89505, or calling 702-786-4046.

COMPANY STAFF AND REPERTORY

General/Artistic Director. Merle Puffer (1968–present).
*World Premiere.*Herbolsheimer's *Mark Me Twain.* (April 22, 1993).
American Premieres. Busoni's *Doktor Faust* (January 25, 1974); Tchaikovsky's *Orleanskaya deva* (in English, May 13, 1976).
Repertory. **1968:** Il barbiere di Siviglia, Rigoletto. **1969:** Die Fledermaus, Don

Pasquale, Madama Butterfly. **1970:** La bohème, Die Dreigroschenoper, La Cenerentola. **1971-72:** The Student Prince, Tosca, Le nozze di Figaro. **1972-73:** Die lustige Witwe, Carmen, Don Giovanni, La traviata. **1973-74:** Cavalleria rusticana / I pagliacci, Doktor Faust, L'elisir d'amore. **1974-75:** Die Fledermaus, Madama Butterfly, Il barbiere di Siviglia. **1975-76:** La bohème, Falstaff, Orleanskaya deva. **1976-77:** The Pirates of Penzance, La fille du régiment, Rigoletto, Susannah. **1977-78:** Die Zauberflöte, Tosca, Il trovatore, H.M.S. Pinafore. **1978-79:** La Cenerentola, Faust, La traviata. **1979-80:** Carmen, Lucia di Lammermoor, Of Mice and Men. **1980-81:** Die lustige Witwe, Così fan tutte, La fanciulla del West. **1981-82:** Aida, Le nozze di Figaro, Madama Butterfly. **1982-83:** Die Fledermaus, Amahl and the Night Visitors, Macbeth, La bohème. **1983-84:** I pagliacci, Il barbiere di Siviglia, The Mikado. **1984-85:** Otello, Eugene Onegin, The Pirates of Penzance. **1985-86:** The Student Prince, Il trovatore, L'elisir d'amore. **1986-87:** Tosca, Cavalleria rusticana / The Medium, The Desert Song. **1987-88:** Rigoletto, Die Zauberflöte, Orleanskaya deva (The Maid of Orleans). **1988-89:** Carmen, Madama Butterfly, H.M.S. Pinafore. **1989-90:** Die lustige Witwe, Lucia di Lammermoor, Aida. **1990-91:** Show Boat, La traviata, Les contes d'Hoffmann. **1991-92:** Mame! Don Carlo, Hänsel und Gretel, La bohème, Le nozze di Figaro. **1992-93:** Annie Get Your Gun, Il barbiere di Siviglia, Hänsel und Gretel, Tosca, Mark Me Twain. **1993-94:** Gianni Schicchi / I pagliacci, Amahl and the Night Visitors, La forza del destino, Die Fledermaus.

New Jersey —————— LAWRENCEVILLE

• *Opera Festival of New Jersey* •

The Opera Festival of New Jersey opened with Wolfgang Amadeus Mozart's *Le nozze di Figaro* on June 15, 1984, at the Kirby Arts Center. The work was the Festival's only offering during the inaugural season. Peter Westergaard, Michael Pratt, and John Ellis founded the festival, which takes place on the campus of the Lawrence School. The second season saw an expansion to two operas. In 1993, to celebrate a decade of existence, a third opera was added to the schedule.

The Festival specializes in English-language productions and "intimate" operas, including works by Wolfgang Amadeus Mozart, Gioachino Rossini, and Benjamin Britten, ones that fit onto the thirty-six foot wide by forty-one foot deep stage. In 1992, the festival presented the 1904 Brescia version of Giacomo Puccini's *Madama Butterfly* and presented Maxwell Davies's *The Lighthouse* the following summer, the first professional production of the opera in eight years. The company witnessed its first world premiere, Peter Westergaard's *The Tempest*, on July 8, 1994. Young American singers comprise the casts.

The three-opera festival offers a mixed repertory of traditional and contemporary works. Recent productions include Mozart's *Die Zauberflöte*, Georges Bizet's *Carmen*, and Davies's *The Lighthouse*. The festival operas take place in the 890-seat Kirby Arts Center.

Practical Information. The Kirby Arts Center is on the campus of the Lawrenceville School. Tickets for the Opera Festival of New Jersey are available from the Opera Festival office, 55 Princeton-Hightstown Road, Suite 202, Princeton Junction, NJ 08550, telephone 609-936-1505, fax 609-936-0008.

COMPANY STAFF AND REPERTORY

General/Artistic Directors. James Dickson (1984–85); Steven Jordan (1986, General Manager); Michael Pratt (1987–1991); Deborah Sandler (1992–present).
World Premieres. Westergaard's *The Tempest* (July 8, 1994).
Repertory. 1984: Le nozze di Figaro. 1985: Albert Herring, Don Giovanni. 1986: La Cenerentola, Die Zauberflöte. 1987: Ariadne auf Naxos, Il barbiere di Siviglia. 1988: Così fan tutte, A Midsummer Night's Dream. 1989: Le nozze di Figaro, The Mikado. 1990: Don Giovanni, Die Fledermaus. 1991: Die Entführung aus dem Serail, Falstaff. 1992: Die lustige Witwe, Madama Butterfly. 1993: Die Zauberflöte, Carmen, The Lighthouse.

New Mexico ——————— S A N T A   F E

• *Santa Fe Opera* •

Giacomo Puccini's *Madama Butterfly* opened the inaugural season of the Santa Fe Opera on July 3, 1957. Founded by John Crosby, who was on the podium that evening, the company was established with $200,000 — paid for by Crosby's father. The idea of founding an opera company in Santa Fe in the mid-1950s was a bold venture. Santa Fe was a sleepy state capital far from any major metropolis. Besides, most American artists sang their summers away in Europe. But Santa Fe was hospitable to the arts, and the company made it their home.

The inaugural season boasted seven operas, including the world premiere of Marvin David Levy's *The Tower*. *The Tower* was not successful. Plagued by a poor libretto and threatening weather that almost toppled "the tower," it was also panned by the critics. The other highlight of the inaugural season, Igor Stravinsky's *The Rake's Progress* supervised by the composer, fared better. Stravinsky called the company's production "imaginative and daring in conception." It began an association that saw all of Stravinsky's works staged by Santa Fe before the mid-1960s, including *Oedipus Rex*, *Perséphone*, *Mavra*, *Renard*, and *Zolotoy petushok* (The Golden Cockerel).

The Santa Fe Opera is a mecca for contemporary-opera lovers. The company has pioneered a new path for American opera companies by offering a novelty every season. Among the world premieres are Carlisle Floyd's *Wuthering Heights*, Heitor Villa-Lobos's *Yerma*, and John Eaton's *The Tempest*. Most of the American premieres are operas by Germanic composers — Alban Berg, Arnold Schönberg, Aribert Reimann, Siegfried Matthus, Wolfgang Rihm, Paul Hindemith, Hans-Jürgen von Bose, and Hans Werner Henze. The company has also introduced works by Dmitry Shostakovich and Krzysztof Penderecki and a few neglected eighteenth-century masterpieces — Pier Francesco Cavalli's *L'egisto* and *L'Orione*. Richard Strauss and Wolfgang Amadeus Mozart works are "repertory staples." Strauss's operas have been performed every season since 1977, and only *Die Frau ohne Schatten* and *Guntram* have not been staged. Santa Fe has also seen Mozart works every season. But purists be warned, Crosby mercilessly cuts the Strauss and Mozart scores. Since the performances do not begin until nine in the evening (when the sun sets) the "abridged versions" are to avoid the operas' dragging on

Santa Fe Opera Theater (Santa Fe, New Mexico).

into the wee hours of the morning. The Achilles' heel of Santa Fe is the "seasoned classic" work. Singers endowed to do these masterpieces justice go where the money is—Salzburg. Santa Fe cannot afford to be a "star-seeking" company. Instead, it is a training ground and has been the starting point for many of today's leading artists—James Morris, Leona Mitchell, Sherrill Milnes, Ashley Putnam, Ellen Shade, and Samuel Ramey among them. Alumni willing to perform at a fraction of their usual fees make triumphant returns, and 1988 saw Morris assay a spectacular *Der fliegende Holländer*. A few "name-stars" willing to take a cut in pay have sung in Santa Fe. Tatiana Troyanos made her company debut in Georg Friedrich Händel's *Ariodante* in 1987. Three years later, Marilyn Horne undertook Christoph Gluck's *Orfeo ed Euridice*, and 1993 witnessed Frederica von Stade in the title role of Händel's *Xerxes*.

The five-opera season offers an interesting mix of works—an American or world premiere, a standard piece, a neglected masterpiece, a Strauss opera, and a Mozart opera—in a repertory system. Recent productions include Mozart's *Don Giovanni* and *Die Zauberflöte*, Strauss's *Der Rosenkavalier* and *Capriccio*, Puccini's *La bohème*, Händel's *Xerxes*, and Kurt Weill's *Der Protagonist* and *Der Zar läßt sich photographieren*. The company performs in the open-air Santa Fe Opera Theater.

Santa Fe Opera Theater

The first Santa Fe Opera Theater was built in 1957. Designed by John W. McHugh and Van Dorn Hooker, the outdoor structure was located in a magnificent hilltop bowl on the grounds of the San Juan resort ranch, more than seven thousand feet above sea level. By 1965, Crosby realized the outdoor facility hampered company growth, so he converted the theater to an "all-weather facility," but one that still lacked total protection from the elements. Of the 1,153 seats, almost half were exposed to the thunderstorms. The cost was $225,000. Two years later, fire turned the theater into charred ruins. The American premiere of Hindemith's *Cardillac* had graced the stage the previous evening. Now its sets were a pile of rubble. All the scores and costumes for the season were lost, except the costumes for Gioachino Rossini's *Il barbiere di Siviglia*, which were at the cleaners. The architectural firm of McHugh & Kidder was hired to rebuild the structure and eight months later, Santa Fe had a new opera house.

The structure is an imposing earth-colored building of cinder block, reinforced concrete, and steel, undulating with sweeping graceful lines that soar toward heaven. It overlooks the green-and-beige mesas, and purple-hued Jemez and Sangre de Cristo mountains. The theater has no sides. The wing-shaped roof is still open and ferocious electrical storms sweep through the mountains during the opera season, often competing in intensity with what transpires on stage, and drenching the audience. There are 1,797 seats, and almost half face the sky.

Practical Information. The Santa Fe Opera Theater is seven miles north of Santa Fe on Highway 84-285. The box office is on the theater grounds. It opens the end of May from 10:00 a.m. to 4:00 P.M., Monday through Saturday, and through the first intermission on performance days. Tickets can be ordered by telephoning 505-982-3855 during box office hours, or writing Santa Fe Opera Box Office, P.O.B. 2408, Santa Fe, NM 87504-2408. If you go, stay at the Eldorado Hotel, 309 W. San Francisco Street, Santa Fe, NM 87501; telephone 505-988-4455, fax 505-988-5376, reservations 1-800-955-4455. The hotel is built and decorated in Native Southwestern style, offering kiva fireplaces in many rooms. Include a visit to the Santa Fe Chamber Music Festival. For information write Santa Fe Music Festival, P.O.B. 853, Santa Fe, New Mexico 87504-0853 or call 1-800-962-7286 or 505-983-2075.

COMPANY STAFF AND REPERTORY

General/Artistic Director. John Crosby (1957–present).

World Premieres. Levy's *The Tower* (August 2, 1957); Floyd's *Wuthering Heights* (July 16, 1958); Berio's *Opera* (August 12, 1970); Villa-Lobos's *Yerma* (August 12, 1971); Rochberg's *The Confidence Man* (July 31, 1982); Eaton's *The Tempest* (July 27, 1985).

American/United States Premieres. Hindemith's *Neues vom Tage* (in English as "News of the Day," August 12, 1961); Berg's *Lulu* (Acts I, II, August 7, 1963); Henze's *König Hirsch* (August 4, 1965); Shostakovich's *Nos* (August 11, 1965); Hindemith's *Cardillac* (in English, July 26, 1967); Henze's *Boulevard Solitude* (August 2, 1967); Schönberg's *Die Jakobsleiter* (1968); Henze's *The Bassarids* (August 7, 1968); Menotti's *Help! Help! The Globolinks* (August 1, 1969); Penderecki's *Diably z Loudun* (August 14, 1969); Reimann's *Melusine* (August 23, 1972); Britten's *Owen Wingrave* (August 9, 1973); Cavalli's *L'egisto* (August 1, 1974); Rota's *Il cappello di paglia di Firenze* (July 6, 1977); Oliver's *The Duchess of Malfi* (August 5, 1978); Berg's *Lulu* (complete opera, July 28, 1979); Schönberg's *Von Heute auf Morgen* (American stage premiere, July 26, 1980); Strauss's *Der Liebe der Danae* (first professional performance, July 24, 1982); Cavalli's *L'Orione* (July 23, 1983); Henze's *We Come to the River* (July 28, 1984); Henze's *The English Cat* (July 13, 1985); Sallinen's *Kuningas lätee Franskaan* (The King Goes Forth to France) (July 26, 1986); Strauss's *Die*

Aegyptische Helena (Vienna version, July 19, 1986); Strauss's *Friedenstag* (first professional performance, July 23, 1988); Penderecki's *Die schwarze Maske* (in English, July 30, 1988); Weir's *A Night at the Chinese Opera* (July 29, 1989); Matthus's *Judith* (July 28, 1990); Rihm's *Oedipus* (July 27, 1991); von Bose's *The Sorrows of Young Werther* (August 1, 1992); Weill's *Der Protagonist* (July 31, 1993).

Repertory. **1957:** Madama Butterfly, Così fan tutte, La serva padrona/The Tower, Il barbiere di Siviglia, Ariadne auf Naxos, The Rake's Progress. **1958:** Wuthering Heights, Così fan tutte, La bohème, La Cenerentola, Capriccio, Falstaff. **1959:** Regina, Anna Bolena, Die Entführung aus dem Serail, Madama Butterfly, Il barbiere di Siviglia, Die Fledermaus. **1960:** Le nozze di Figaro, Gianni Schicchi, Tosca, La Cenerentola, Oedipus Rex, The Rake's Progress, The Gondoliers, La traviata. **1961:** Carmen, Neues vom Tage, The Ballad of Baby Doe, Le nozze di Figaro, La bohème, Der Rosenkavalier, Oedipus Rex, Perséphone. **1962:** Jeanne d'Arc au bûcher, Così fan tutte, Tosca, Salome, Mavra, Zolotoy petushok (The Golden Cockerel)/Oedipus Rex, Perséphone, The Rake's Progress, Renard, La traviata. **1963:** Lulu (Acts I,II), Jeanne d'Arc au bûcher, Don Giovanni, Madama Butterfly, L'enfant et les sortilèges, Die Fledermaus, Der Rosenkavalier, Zolotoy petushok (The Golden Cockerel). **1964:** Lulu (Acts I,II), Carmen, Le nozze di Figaro, La bohème, Gianni Schicchi, L'enfant et les sortilèges, Daphne, Rigoletto. **1965:** Lucia di Lammermoor, The Stag King, Le nozze di Figaro, Madama Butterfly, Il barbiere di Siviglia, Nos (The Nose), Arabella, La traviata. **1966:** Wozzeck, Don Giovanni, Dialogues des Carmélites, Tosca, La Cenerentola, Capriccio, The Rake's Progress, Rigoletto. **1967:** Carmen, Boulevard Solitude, Cardillac, Le nozze di Figaro, La bohème, Il barbiere di Siviglia, Salome. **1968:** L'elisir d'amore, The Bassarids, Die Jakobsleiter, Die Zauberflöte, Madama Butterfly, Der Rosenkavalier, Perséphone, La traviata. **1969:** Help! Help! The Globolinks, Così fan tutte, Die Zauberflöte, Diably z Loudun, Tosca, Salome, Zolotoy petushok (The Golden Cockerel). **1970:** Opera, Anna Bolena, Le nozze di Figaro, The Rake's Progress, Zolotoy petushok (The Golden Cockerel), La traviata. **1971:** Die Zauberflöte, Le nozze di Figaro, La Grande Duchesse de Gérolstein, Don Carlo, Yerma, Der fliegende Holländer. **1972:** Pelléas et Mélisande, Don Giovanni, La Grande Duchesse de Gérolstein, Madama Butterfly, Melusine, Salome. **1973:** Owen Wingrave, L'enfant et les sortilèges, Die lustige Witwe, Le nozze di Figaro, La bohème, Zolotoy petushok (The Golden Cockerel), Der fliegende Holländer. **1974:** Lulu (Acts I,II), L'egisto/L'enfant et les sortilèges, Die Zauberflöte, La Grande Duchesse de Gérolstein, La bohème. **1975:** Carmen, La Vida Breve, Příhody Lišky Bystroušky (The Cunning Little Vixen), Così fan tutte, Falstaff. **1976:** L'egisto, Le nozze di Figaro, Salome, The Mother of Us All, La traviata. **1977:** Pelléas et Mélisande, Fedora, Così fan tutte, The Italian Straw Hat, Falstaff. **1978:** The Duchess of Malfi, Tosca, Le Comte Ory, Salome, Eugene Onegin. **1979:** Lulu (complete opera), Lucia di Lammermoor, Die Zauberflöte, La Grande Duchesse de Gérolstein, Salome. **1980:** Die Zauberflöte, Erwartung, Von Heute auf Morgan, Die Jakobsleiter, Elektra, Zolotoy petushok (The Golden Cockerel), La traviata. **1981:** Neues vom Tage, La bohème, Il barbiere di Siviglia, Daphne, The Rake's Progress. **1982:** Le nozze di Figaro, The Confidence Man, Die Fledermaus, Die Liebe der Danae, Mignon. **1983:** Turn of the Screw, L'Orione, Don Pasquale, Orphée aux enfers, Arabella. **1984:** Il matrimonio segreto, Come to the River, Violanta, Die Zauberflöte, Intermezzo, Eine florentinische Tragödie. **1985:** The Tempest, The English Cat, Le nozze di Figaro, Orphée aux enfers, Die Liebe der Danae. **1986:** L'incoronazione di Poppea, Die Zauberflöte, Kuningas lätee Franskaan (The King Goes Forth to France), Die Fledermaus, Die Aegyptische Helena. **1987:** Ariodante, Le nozze di Figaro, Madama Butterfly, Nos (The Nose), Die schweigsame Frau. **1988:** Così fan tutte, Die schwarze Maske, Die Fledermaus, Feuersnot, Friedenstag, Der fliegende Holländer. **1989:** La calisto, Chérubin, Der Rosenkavalier, La traviata, A Night at the Chinese Opera. **1990:** Orfeo ed Euridice, Judith, Così fan tutte, La bohème, Ariadne auf Naxos. **1991:** La traviata, Le nozze di Figaro, La fanciulla del West, Die schweigsame. Frau, Oedipus, La fanciulla del West. **1992:** Fledermaus, Don Giovanni, The Beggar's Opera, Der Rosenkavalier, The Sorrows of Young Werther. **1993:** La bohème, Die Zauberflöte, Xerxes, Capriccio, Der Protagonist/ Der Zar läßt sich photographieren.

New York ——————— BINGHAMTON

• *Tri-Cities Opera* •

A program of opera excerpts, accompanied by a piano, inaugurated the Tri-Cities
Opera on April 20, 1950, at the Union-Endicott High School. The first complete
opera, also with piano accompaniment, was a double-bill of Gian Carlo Menotti's
The Medium/ The Telephone performed in November 1950. The first fully staged
production with orchestra, Pietro Mascagni's *Cavalleria rusticana*, arrived on May
24, 1951. Carmen Savoca and Peyton Hibbitt founded the company as a training
organization for up-and-coming singers.

By February 1952, the company was performing at the Masonic Temple with
orchestra, although it continued piano-accompaniment productions as well. A
decade later, the company mounted its first world premiere, Myron Fink's *Jeremiah* on May 25, 1962. It has since staged two additional world premieres, Darion
Laderman's *Galileo Galilei* on February 3, 1979, and Fink's *Chinchilla* on January 18, 1986. Beginning in 1975, the company moved to The Forum, which it calls
home.

The three-opera season offers primarily tradition productions in a *stagione*
system, although some contemporary operas are included. Recent works include
Giacomo Puccini's *La bohème*, Giuseppe Verdi's *Aida*, and Rossini's *L'italiana in
Algeri*. The company performs in the 1,500-seat Forum.

Practical Information. The Forum is at 236 Washington Street. Tickets are
available from the Tri-Cities Opera, 315 Clinton Street, Binghamton, NY 13905,
telephone, 607-729-3444, fax 609-797-6344.

COMPANY STAFF AND REPERTORY

General/Artistic Director. Carmen Savoca (1949–present).

World Premieres. Myron Fink's *Jeremiah* (May 25, 1962); Darion Laderman's *Galileo
Galilei* (stage premiere, February 3, 1979); Myron Fink's *Chinchilla* (January 18, 1986).

Repertory. **1951-52:** La traviata, The Medium/The Telephone. **1952-53:** Naughty
Marietta, Rigoletto. **1953-54:** Amahl and the Night Visitors, Madama Butterfly, La traviata.
1954-55: I pagliacci, Carmen. **1955-56:** Il trovatore, La bohème. **1956-57:** Il barbiere di
Siviglia, Faust. **1957-58:** Tosca, Les contes d'Hoffmann, Cavalleria rusticana. **1958-59:** Lucia
di Lammermoor, Un ballo in maschera. **1959-60:** Madama Butterfly, Die Fledermaus.
1960-61: Carmen, Il tabarro, Suor Angelica. **1961-62:** La traviata, La bohème, Jeremiah.
1962-63: Così fan tutte, Rigoletto. **1963-64:** Tosca, Faust. **1964-65:** Les contes d'Hoffmann,
Andrea Chénier. **1965-66:** Madama Butterfly, Samson et Dalila. **1966-67:** Un ballo in
maschera, Il barbiere di Siviglia. **1967-68:** Amahl and the Night Visitors, La bohème,
Eugene Onegin. **1968-69:** Rigoletto, Amahl and the Night Visitors, The Telephone, The
Old Maid and the Thief, Carmen, Dido and Aeneas. **1969-70:** Lakmé, Amahl and the
Night Visitors, La traviata. **1970-71:** Tosca, Roméo et Juliette. **1971-72:** Die Zauberflöte, An-
drea Chénier. **1972-73:** Madama Butterfly, Don Giovanni. **1973-74:** La bohème, Faust,
Gianni Schicchi/Cavalleria rusticana. **1974-75:** Il barbiere di Siviglia, Rigoletto, Die
Zauberflöte. **1975-76:** Die Fledermaus, Il trovatore, La bohème. **1976-77:** Un ballo in
maschera, Madama Butterfly, Lucia di Lammermoor. **1977-78:** Così fan tutte, La traviata,

Faust. **1978-79:** Carmen, Galileo Galilei, Il barbiere di Siviglia. **1979-80:** Die lustige Witwe, Il trovatore, Les contes d'Hoffmann. **1980-81:** Madama Butterfly, Andrea Chénier, Don Pasquale. **1981-82:** Rigoletto, L'elisir d'amore, Cavalleria rusticana. **1982-83:** Norma, Die Fledermaus, Jeremiah. **1983-84:** La bohème, Die lustige Witwe, Lakmé. **1984-85:** La traviata, Le nozze di Figaro, Lucia di Lammermoor. **1985-86:** Tosca, Chinchilla, Carmen. **1986-87:** Les contes d'Hoffmann, L'italiana in Algeri, Faust. **1987-88:** The Student Prince, Don Giovanni, Samson et Dalila. **1988-89:** Kismet, Il tabarro/Gianni Schicchi, Rigoletto. **1989-90:** Madama Butterfly, Roméo et Juliette, The New Moon. **1990-91:** Die Zauberflöte, Lakmé, Die Fledermaus. **1991-92:** La bohème, La traviata, Le nozze di Figaro. **1992-93:** L'elisir d'amore, Tosca, Carmen. **1993-94:** Il barbiere di Siviglia, H.M.S. Pinafore, Faust.
    Repertory. With piano or opera excerpts with orchestra. **1950-51:** The Medium/The Telephone. **1953-54:** Amahl and the Night Visitors. **1954-55:** Così fan tutte (excerpts). **1955-56:** Dido and Aeneas (excerpts). **1965-66:** Beauty and the Beast. **1966-67:** Die Zauberflöte. **1969-70:** Così fan tutte. **1970-71:** Rapunzel. **1978-79:** The Old Maid and the Thief. **1980-81:** A Christmas Carol. **1983-84:** Die Zauberflöte. **1984-85:** Beauty and the Beast. **1992-93:** Amahl and the Night Visitors.

BROOKLYN

• *Brooklyn Academy of Music* •

The Brooklyn Academy of Music began a new initiative in offering opera in the spring of 1989, following its success at presenting contemporary opera in the Next Wave Festival. Introducing seventeenth- and twentieth-century works and presenting European companies define the company's *raison d'être*. The productions are innovative, conceived by renowned directors like Peter Sellers, Robert Wilson, and Francesca Zambello.
    The opera season varies between two and four works, offering a repertory of lesser-known operas. Recent productions include Verdi's *Don Carlos* (French version), Marc-Antoine Charpentier's *Médée*, and Claude Monteverdi's *Il ritorno di Ulisse in Patria*. The performances take place in the 2,000-seat Brooklyn Academy of Music.
    Practical Information. The Brooklyn Academy of Music is at 30 Lafayette Avenue. Tickets are available from the BAM Opera, 30 Lafayette Avenue, Brooklyn, NY 11217-1486, telephone 718-636-4111, fax 718-857-2021. If you visit, stay at The Pierre Four Seasons at Fifth Avenue at 61st Street, New York, NY 10021; telephone 212-838-8000, fax 212-940-8109, reservations 1-800-332-3442. A New York hotel landmark for sixty years, the Pierre has been restored to its original grandeur and luxury.

REPERTORY

American/United States Premieres. Lully's *Atys* (May 17, 1989); Adams's *The Death of Klinghoffer* (September 5, 1991); Waits's *The Black Rider* (November 9, 1994); Charpentier's *Médée* (May 19, 1994).
    Repertory. **1989:** Das kleine Mahagonny, Atys, Falstaff (Welsh National Opera). **1990:** Dido and Aeneas, La finta giardiniera (Théâtre Royal de la Monnaie). **1991:** Hydrogen

Jukebox, The Death of Klinghoffer, Orfeo ed Euridice (Komische Oper). **1992**: Atys, Atlas. **1993**: A Kékszakállú herceg vára (Duke Bluebeard's Castle)/Erwartung, Castor et Pollux (concert version)/Les Indes Galantes (concert version), Il ritorno di Ulisse in Patria. **1994**: Orphée, The Black Rider, Don Carlos (Folkoperan), Médée (Les Arts Florissants).

BUFFALO

• *Greater Buffalo Opera Company* •

Giacomo Puccini's *Madama Butterfly* inaugurated the Greater Buffalo Opera in 1988 at Shea's Buffalo Center for the Performing Arts. Carlo Pinto and Gary Burgess founded the company when the Western New York Opera Theater and the Buffalo Lyric Opera merged to become the Greater Buffalo Opera Company in 1987. Gioachino Rossini's *Il barbiere di Siviglia* was also offered during the inaugural season.

The second season expanded to three offerings which included contemporary works with the favorites—George Gershwin's *Porgy and Bess*, Rogers & Hammerstein's *Carousal*, and Gaetano Donizetti's *Lucia di Lammermoor*. The fifth season introduced Karol Szymanowski's *Król Roger* (King Roger) to the East Coast. Both established singers, like Maurizio Mazzieri and Conchia Antunano, along with rising talent comprise the casts.

The three-opera season offers a range from traditional to contemporary in a *stagione* system. Recent productions include Richard Strauss's *Salome* and Ludwig van Beethoven's *Fidelio*. The company performs in the 3,182-seat Shea's Buffalo Center for the Performing Arts.

Practical Information. Shea's Buffalo Center for the Performing Arts is at 646 Main Street. Tickets are available from the Greater Buffalo Opera box office, 24 Linwood Avenue. It is open Monday through Friday 10:00 A.M. to 5:00 P.M. and Saturday from 10:00 A.M. to 2:00 P.M. You can telephone 716-852-5000, or write Greater Buffalo Opera, 24 Linwood Avenue, Buffalo, NY 14209.

COMPANY STAFF AND REPERTORY

General/Artistic Director. Gary Burgess (1988–present).
Repertory. **1988**: Madama Butterfly, Il barbiere di Siviglia. **1989**: Porgy and Bess, Carousal, Lucia di Lammermoor. **1990**: Cavalleria rusticana/I pagliacci, Turandot, Amahl and the Night Visitors. **1991**: Le nozze di Figaro, Rigoletto, Die Zauberflöte. **1992**: Tosca, Król Roger, Die lustige Witwe. **1993**: Otello, Il trittico, Il trovatore. **1994**: Salome, Fidelio.

CHAUTAUQUA

• *Chautauqua Opera* •

The first production of the Chautauqua Opera was Friedrich von Flotow's *Martha*, which took place in Norton Memorial Hall on July 22, 1929. Four additional works graced the stage during the inaugural season—Engelbert Humperdinck's *Hänsel und Gretel*, Christoph Gluck's *The May Queen,* Ermanno Wolf-Ferrari's *Il segreto di Susanna*, and Charles Gounod's *Faust.* The Chautauqua Opera was created as part of the Chautauqua Summer Music Festival, begun decades earlier. Albert Stoessel was the Opera's first general director. His appointment and the creation of a regular opera company marked a new era in Chautauqua's musical history.

Opera had been presented at Chautauqua previously, but not on a regular basis. A Rochester opera company had visited in 1926, presenting several works in English. This created a demand for more opera. When a suitable opera house opened in 1929, the Chautauqua Opera Association was born. The company was founded on the principals that opera should be performed in English, that promising young American singers should comprise the casts, that works by American composers should be promoted, and that equal emphasis should be given to singing and acting to ensure dramatic unity. Stoessel's philosophy reflected these tenets with his interest in contemporary music and a commitment to the American composer. But he did not neglect the classic repertory, offering popular operas and long-neglected eighteenth-century pieces as well.

His philosophy gave evidence in the first season with Christoph Gluck's *The May Queen* and Ermanno Wolf-Ferrari's *Il segreto di Susanna.* For his second season, Claude Debussy's cantata *L'enfant prodigue* was the season's novelty. Other works offered were Gounod's *Faust*, Engelbert Humperdinck's *Hänsel und Gretel*, Ruggero Leoncavallo's *I pagliacci*, Flotow's *Martha*, and Puccini's *Madama Butterfly.* In 1932, the company championed the cause of the American composer with three performances of Louis Gruenberg's *Jack and the Beanstalk.* (It had only recently been premiered on November 19, 1931, by the Juilliard School of Music.) Two opera buffa from the eighteenth-century Italian school were revived at Chautauqua during the 1933 season—Giovanni Pergolesi's *La serva padrona* and Domenico Cimarosa's *Il matrimonio segreto.* For *Il matrimonio segreto*, Stoessel wrote recitatives to replace the spoken dialogue. According to newspaper accounts, it was so skillfully done that it was "impossible to distinguish any change of style between Cimarosa's music and his."

The 1934 season ushered in the regular inclusion of light operas/operettas in the season's repertory. During this season, Arthur Sullivan's *The Mikado* and *The Pirates of Penzance* were heard, with Henry Hadley's *Bianca* as the season's contemporary American piece. The following season witnessed two American works, Robert Russell Bennett's *Maria Malibran* and Reginald de Koven's *Robin Hood.* Stoessel's opera *Garrick*, which had been premiered on February 24, 1937, at Juilliard, highlighted the 1937 season. The world premiere had attracted a stellar opera audience—Lauritz Melchior, Lawrence Tibbett, Kirsten Flagstad, Edward Johnson, and Walter Damrosch. Pauline Pierce and Donald Dickson sang the leading roles. There were seven offerings for the 1939 season, including Victor Herbert's *Naughty Marietta*, Sullivan's *Trial by Jury*, and Verdi's *Il trovatore.*

Douglas Moore's *The Devil and Daniel Webster* was given its first performance outside of New York City during the 1940 summer season. Other Chautauqua novelties that season included Ermanno Wolf-Ferrari's *Le donne curiose* and Bedřich Smetana's *Prodaná nevěsta* (The Bartered Bride). Oscar Straus's *Der tapfere Soldat*, previously seen in 1937, was repeated in 1941, along with Sullivan's *The Mikado*, Verdi's *La traviata*, Rossini's *Il barbiere di Siviglia*, and Mozart's *Le nozze di Figaro* among others. The company mounted Sullivan's *Cox and Box* for

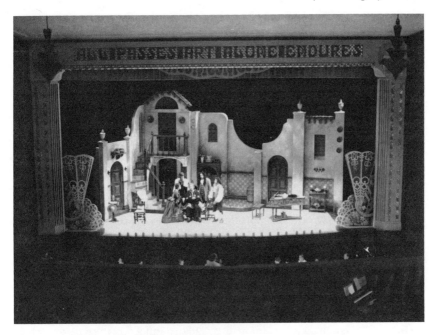

Chautauqua Opera (Chautauqua, New York).

the first time in 1942. When Stoessel died suddenly on May 12, 1943, while conducting the New York Philharmonic Orchestra, an era at Chautauqua died with him. Stoessel was the director of all musical activities at Chautauqua, including opera. After his death, there was a separation of responsibilities.

Alfredo Valenti, who sang principal bass in Chautauqua's opera performances, as well as being production director, became the opera's general director. The first season under his regime saw Gian Carlo Menotti's *The Old Maid and the Thief* as the contemporary American offering. The second company production of Moore's *The Devil and Daniel Webster*, under the supervision of the composer, took place in 1947, a season that saw Daniel Auber's *Fra Diavolo*, Camille Saint-Saëns's *Samson et Dalila*, Verdi's *La forza del destino*, Mozart's *Le nozze di Figaro*, Straus's *Der tapfere Soldat*, and Puccini's *Gianni Schicchi*. Two years later, Gluck's *Orfeo ed Euridice* made its first Chautauqua appearance. Alberto Bimboni's *In the Name of Culture* ushered in the 1950s. One reviewer wrote that "the libretto lacked sufficient focus for opera but that Bimboni's score bristles with spark in a style that might be described as a Mediterranean Richard Strauss." By the time the company celebrated its twenty-fifth anniversary in 1953, it had mounted sixty-six operas, including eight American operas. Many of its young American singers had gone on to sing at the Metropolitan Opera. Julius Rudel arrived in 1959 to head the opera company, but he survived only one season. As *The Chautauqua Daily* put it, "Rudel was cast in an unfortunate slot of trying to follow the beloved Valenti. He was innovative and brusque . . . He opened the door for greater appreciation of contemporary opera." Rudel had brought John Daggett Howell as his business manager, and Howell took over after Rudel's departure. He began staging musicals in the Amphitheater as part of the opera season. American musical theater became an integral part of the opera season through 1987.

Leonard Treash took over in 1966. During his tenure, the Chautauqua Opera Apprentice Program was started, since Treash felt that "professional training in America was not keeping pace with the growing opportunities in opera." He also enlarged the repertory and staged such grand operas as Verdi's *Otello*, Puccini's *Turandot*, and two Richard Wagner operas, *Der fliegende Holländer* and *Die Walküre*. Chautauqua saw its first world premiere on July 12, 1974, Seymour Barab's *Philip Marshall*. In 1981, Cynthia Auerbach took the helm, steering the company in a new direction. The number of offerings dropped to four from a high of seven operas a seasons only a few years earlier. The idea was that with fewer productions, there would be more preparation and rehearsal time, resulting in a better product. One of the more unique seasons took place in 1987, when every opera had a Shakespeare connection—Gounod's *Roméo et Juliette*, Benjamin Britten's *A Midsummer Night's Dream*, Cole Porter's *Kiss Me Kate* (based on *The Taming of the Shrew*), and Verdi's *Falstaff*.

Linda Jackson was appointed general director that same year. Jackson continues the company's mission, that of training young American singers. They take the comprimario roles in the performances, with established singers performing the leads. They are often company alumnae, who teach the young "student" artists. The productions use minimal scenery. The company's limited budget is spent on the principal artists and long rehearsal time. Opera is presented as a theatrical art form. Chautauquans are traditionalists, and that influences the repertory which is primarily nineteenth century Italian works. They are willing, however, to try contemporary opera, and the company staged a novelty on August 13, 1993, Richard Wargo's *A Chekhov Trilogy: Seduction of a Lady*, *Visit to the Country*, *Music Shop*. Operas are planned as part of the entire "Chautauqua Experience" and not for opera buffs who want to see three or four different operas in as many evenings.

The four-opera summer season offers one unusual work, two lighter pieces (comic or operetta), and one heavier work in a *stagione* system. The repertory is limited by the size of the stage and pit. Operas are always scheduled on Fridays and Mondays. Recent productions include Donizetti's *La fille du régiment*, Rossini's *Le Comte Ory*, Mozart's *Don Giovanni*, Sullivan's *The Mikado*, and Puccini's *Madama Butterfly*. The Chautauqua Opera performs in Norton Memorial Hall.

Norton Memorial Hall

Norton Memorial Hall opened on July 15, 1929. Construction began in the fall of 1928 and was completed in time for the 1929 summer festival. Designed by Architect Otis Floyd Johnson with Fred Torrey responsible for the facade's relief sculptures, the Hall was the first monolithic concrete structure built east of the Mississippi River. Several legends exist concerning the birth of the opera house. One contends that a member of the Norton family asked the Amphitheater audience (where performances then took place) whether they would like to hear opera indoors, sung in English. Apparently the answer was yes and the Norton family donated the $100,000 cost.

Norton Hall is a rectangular-shaped, art deco building that was originally grayish white. It acquired a delicate pink hue during restoration. The inner walls and ceiling of the loggia are covered with a deep magenta. "NORTON MEMORIAL HALL, DEDICATED TO MUSIC, LITERATURE, DRAMA" is carved in relief letters on the center of the façade. Original bronze-and-violet-glass lamps flank the entrance and hang from the loggia. The gray cinder-block-wall lobby holds the original pinkish-purple, petal glass lamps and a plaque commemorating the Norton family. The auditorium, exuding a pinkish-rose hue, finds a single balcony sweeping across contrasting orange-tweed seats. "ALL PASSES. ART ALONE ENDURES" crowns the proscenium arch. Original rose-colored, petal glass lamps illuminate the space. The theater accommodates 1,365.

Practical Information. Norton Hall is on Pratt Avenue (no number) in Chautauqua. The Chautauqua Opera box office is at the Main Gate of the Chautauqua Institution on Route 394. The Institution controls the town of Chautauqua and you must buy a gate ticket (in addition to the opera ticket) to enter the grounds. The ticket office is open Monday through Saturday from 9:00 A.M. to 9:00 P.M. Opera tickets can also be purchased by calling 716-357-6250, or writing Chautauqua Institution, Box 672, Chautauqua, NY 14722. For gate ticket information, call 716-357-6213, or write Chautauqua Institution, Operations Department, Chautauqua, NY 14722. If you go, contact the Chautauqua Accommodations Referral Service, Chautauqua Institution, Chautauqua, NY 14722, telephone 716-357-6204 for a list of available accommodations at the Institution.

COMPANY STAFF AND REPERTORY

General/Artistic Directors. Albert Stoessel (1929–1943); Alfredo Valenti (1944–1958); Julius Rudel (1959); John Daggett Howell (1960–1965); Leonard Treash (1966–1980); Cynthia Auerbach (1981–1987); Linda Jackson (1987– present).

World Premieres. Barab's *Philip Marshall* (July 12, 1974); Ching's *Who Killed Buoso Donati?* (July 1994).

American/United States Premieres. Wargo's *Seduction of a Lady/A Visit to the Country/Music Shop* (first professional performance, August 13, 1993).

Repertory. 1929: The May Queen, Martha, Hänsel und Gretel, Faust, Il segreto di Susanna. 1930: Madama Butterfly, Faust, L'enfant prodigue, Hänsel und Gretel, I pagliacci Martha. 1931: Les contes d'Hoffmann, Carmen, Il segreto di Susanna/I pagliacci, Madama Butterfly, Il barbiere di Siviglia. 1932: Martha, Jack and the Beanstalk, Carmen, The Mikado, Le nozze di Figaro. 1933: Les contes d'Hoffmann, H.M.S. Pinafore, Il segreto matrimonio, La serva padrona, Les cloches de Corneville, Cavalleria rusticana, H.M.S. Pinafore. 1934: La fille du régiment, La bohème, Pirates of Penzance, The Mikado, Gianni Schicchi, Bianca. 1935: Maria Malibran, H.M.S. Pinafore, Il barbiere di Siviglia, Robin Hood, Madama Butterfly, Yeoman of the Guard. 1936: Faust, Carmen, The Bohemian Girl, Die lustigen Weiber von Windsor, The Gondoliers, Pirates of Penzance. 1937: Iolanthe, Rigoletto, Der tapfere Soldat, Garrick, La bohème. 1938: Yeoman of the Guard, Roméo et Juliette, Patience, Die Entführung aus dem Serail, La traviata, Tosca. 1939: Don Pasquale, Madama Butterfly, Naughty Marietta, Les contes d'Hoffmann, Le nozze di Figaro, Trial by Jury, Il trovatore. 1940: Carmen, The Devil and Daniel Webster, Le donne curiose, Faust, The Gondoliers, Prodaná nevěsta (The Bartered Bride). 1941: La bohème, Il barbiere di Siviglia, Le nozze di Figaro, The Mikado, Pirates of Penzance, Der tapfere Soldat, La traviata. 1942: Cox and Box, Don Giovanni, H.M.S. Pinafore, Iolanthe, Manon, Rigoletto, Roméo et Juliette. 1943: Faust, Die Fledermaus, Martha, Le nozze di Figaro, Ruddigore, Tosca. 1944: Patience, La bohème, Les contes d'Hoffmann, L'elisir d'amore, Mignon, The

Old Maid and the Thief, I pagliacci. 1945: Il barbiere di Siviglia, Carmen, Cox and Box, Die Fledermaus, H.M.S. Pinafore, Lucia di Lammermoor, La traviata. 1946: Un ballo in maschera, The Gondoliers, Madama Butterfly, Rigoletto, Roméo et Juliette, La Rondine. 1947: The Devil and Daniel Webster, La forza del destino, Fra Diavolo, Gianni Schicchi, Le nozze di Figaro, Der tapfere Soldat, Samson et Dalila. 1948: La bohème, Carmen, Così fan tutte, Faust, Lucia di Lammermoor, The Mikado. 1949: Il barbiere di Siviglia, Les contes d'Hoffmann, Don Giovanni, Mignon, Orfeo ed Euridice. 1950: Cavalleria rusticana, Die Entführung aus dem Serail, Die Fledermaus, In the Name of Culture, Prodaná nevěsta (The Bartered Bride), Tosca, Il trovatore. 1951: Aida, Cox and Box, Iolanthe, Madama Butterfly, Le nozze di Figaro, I pagliacci, Rigoletto. 1952: Amahl and the Night Visitors, Lucia di Lammermoor, The Jumping Frog of Calaveras County, The Gondoliers, Martha, Lucia di Lammermoor, La traviata. 1953: La bohème, Carmen, Les contes d'Hoffmann, Don Giovanni, Don Pasquale, Faust, L'heure espagnol, Die lustige Witwe. 1954: Aida, The Mikado, Orfeo ed Euridice, Tosca, Die Zauberflöte. 1955: Amahl and the Night Visitors, Die lustigen Weiber von Windsor, Hänsel und Gretel, H.M.S. Pinafore, Madama Butterfly, Le nozze di Figaro, Il trovatore. 1956: Il barbiere di Siviglia, Cavalleria rusticana, Così fan tutte, Die Fledermaus, I pagliacci, Robin Hood, Rigoletto. 1957: La bohème, Carmen, Les contes d'Hoffmann, Lucia di Lammermoor, The Student Prince, La traviata. 1958: Don Giovanni, Faust, The Mikado, Susannah, Samson et Dalila, Tosca. 1959: Rigoletto, The Taming of the Shrew, Wuthering Heights, Prodaná nevěsta (The Bartered Bride), Madama Butterfly, Brigadoon, Rigoletto. 1960: La bohème, The Ballad of Baby Doe, Il barbiere di Siviglia, Carousel, Così fan tutte, La traviata. 1961: L'elisir d'amore, Die Fledermaus, Madama Butterfly, The Mikado, Rigoletto, South Pacific. 1962: The Apothecary, Hänsel und Gretel, The King and I, Lucia di Lammermoor, Pirates of Penzance, Tosca, Unicorn in the Garden. 1963: Aida, Don Pasquale, Faust, Die lustige Witwe, The Music Man, Le nozze di Figaro. 1964: Carmen, Cavalleria rusticana, Fantasticks, Gianni Schicchi, Martha, The Sound of Music, Il trovatore, Die Zauberflöte. 1965: Andrea Chénier, La bohème, Così fan tutte, Little Mary Sunshine, Eine Nacht in Venedig, Oklahoma, Samson et Dalila. 1966: Albert Herring, Il barbiere di Siviglia, Die Entführung aus dem Serail, L'heure espagnol, My Fair Lady, Rigoletto, Suor Angelica, Tosca. 1967: The Crucible, Falstaff, The Gondoliers, Lucia di Lammermoor, Madama Butterfly, Le nozze di Figaro, Showboat. 1968: Les contes d'Hoffmann, Don Giovanni, Gianni Schicchi, H.M.S. Pinafore, Kiss Me Kate, I pagliacci, Il tabarro, Susannah, La traviata. 1969: La bohème, Carmen, The Old Maid and the Thief, Pirates of Penzance, The Student Prince, Die Zauberflöte. 1970: Camelot, Così fan tutte, Faust, Fidelio, Die Fledermaus, Rigoletto. 1971: Aida, Angelique, Cavalleria rusticana, L'italiana in Algeri, The King and I, The Mikado, Der Rosenkavalier, Tosca. 1972: Otello, The Man of La Mancha, Der fliegende Holländer, Il barbiere di Siviglia, Prodaná nevěsta (The Bartered Bride), Le nozze di Figaro, A Midsummer Night's Dream, Le nozze di Figaro. 1973: Rape of Lucretia, Angelique, Carmen, Falstaff, L'heure espagnol, Madama Butterfly, Street Scene, Die Walküre. 1974: Philip Marshall, La bohème, La Cenerentola, Don Giovanni, Merry Mount, La traviata, West Side Story. 1975: Albert Herring, La bohème, Un ballo in maschera, Brigadoon, Hänsel und Gretel, Turandot, Die Zauberflöte. 1976: The Ballad of Baby Doe, Così fan tutte, Don Pasquale, La fanciulla del West, The Music Man, Die schweigsame Frau. 1977: Rigoletto, Tosca, Tannhäuser, Albert Herring, Hello Dolly, Les contes d'Hoffmann, Il barbiere di Siviglia, Rigoletto, Tosca. 1978: Faust, Eugene Onegin, Madama Butterfly, Le nozze di Figaro, The Sound of Music, La traviata. 1979: Ariadne auf Naxos, Die Entführung aus dem Serail, Falstaff, Lucia di Lammermoor, My Fair Lady. 1980: Carmen, La Cenerentola, Fiddler on the Roof, The Taming of the Shrew, Die Zauberflöte. 1981: La bohème, Les contes d'Hoffmann, Rigoletto, The Student Prince. 1982: Il barbiere di Siviglia, Regina, South Pacific, La traviata. 1983: Die lustige Witwe, Manon, Of Mice and Men, Le nozze di Figaro. 1984: The Man of La Mancha, Don Giovanni, Gianni Schicchi, Hänsel und Gretel. 1985: Carmen, Guys and Dolls, Madama Butterfly, Street Scene. 1986: La fille du régiment, The Mikado, The Rake's Progress, Il trovatore. 1987: A Midsummer Night's Dream, Falstaff, Kiss Me Kate, Roméo et Juliette. 1988: Così Fan tutte, The Desert Song, Susannah, Tosca. **1989:** The Gondoliers, Rigoletto, Turn of the Screw. **1990:** La bohème, Il barbiere di Siviglia, Faust, Pirates of Penzance. **1991:** Die Fledermaus, Le nozze di Figaro, Don Pasquale, The Crucible. **1992:** Madama Butterfly, Die lustige Witwe, Hänsel und Gretel, Le Comte Ory, Carmen. **1993:** Don Giovanni, The Mikado, La fille du régiment, A Chekhov Trilogy: Seduction of a Lady, Visit to the Country, Music Shop. **1994:** Who Killed Buoso Donati?/Gianni Schicchi, La traviata, L'italiana in Algeri.

COOPERSTOWN

• *Glimmerglass Opera* •

Giacomo Puccini's *La bohème* inaugurated the Glimmerglass Opera on July 10, 1975. Staged in the Nicholas J. Sterling Auditorium of Cooperstown High School before an audience new to opera, Puccini's *La bohème* was performed in English by young American singers. It was the only work given that inaugural season. Although the budget was a paltry $14,000, and the acoustics of the auditorium were disastrous, the three performances were successful. Peter Macris, the company's founder, was determined not to let his fledgling young company die. He incorporated Glimmerglass Opera as a non-profit institution and set about raising the necessary funds to "stay alive." The company took its name from James Fenimore Cooper's *Leatherstocking Tales*. During his four seasons at the helm, Macris presented a traditional repertory.

Paul Kellogg, who had been with the company since its inception, took the reins in 1979. Two years later, he expanded the season to three operas, with one unfamiliar work. The triple bill of Douglas Moore's *Gallantry* / Leonard Bernstein's *Trouble in Tahiti* / Wolfgang Amadeus Mozart's *Der Schauspieldirektor* inaugurated this practice. The company counts Hector Berlioz's *Béatrice et Bénédict*, Benjamin Britten's *Albert Herring*, Richard Strauss's *Intermezzo*, and Mozart's *Il re pastore* among its lesser-known offerings. Glimmerglass saw its first world premiere, William Schuman's *A Question of Taste* on June 24, 1989, performed with Schuman's *The Mighty Casey*, the only opera ever written about baseball. Schuman's *The Mighty Casey* played well in Cooperstown, the home of Baseball's Hall of Fame. Schuman's *A Question of Taste* was of an entirely different genre. A comical "music theater" piece set in the dining room of an elegant New York brownstone in 1910—the era of new money and the robber baron—the opera revolves around a bet. Can Phillisto Pratt, a wealthy oenophile, identify a certain wine of Mr. Schofield? At stake is half a million dollars and Mr. Schofield's daughter. Another novelty graced the stage during the 1993 season, David Carlson's *Midnight Angel*. It concerned a bored and arrogant Lady Neville who invited Death to her last and most lavish ball.

Kellogg has built Glimmerglass into one of the finest regional ensemble companies in the country, with casts comprised of gifted young American singers culled from national auditions. What makes Glimmerglass unique, however, is the exciting directors (Jonathan Miller and Mark Lamos) and designers (Robert Israel and John Conklin) who create intriguing and evocative productions. Puccini's

La bohème was reset in Soho, where the story of the four struggling artists unfolded. It purpose was to shed light on the problems today's artists experience — no money, searching for a mate, and losing friends to disease. Then it was consumption. Today it is drugs and AIDS. Another notable production was Mozart's *Il re pastore*. The opera maintained a child-like flavor while still appealing to adults. A chalk covered blackboard informed that the opera was conceived as "entertainment for the education of royal children." The production blended delightful props (white cardboard sheep, blue-cloth river), elegant eighteenth-century costumes, and pithy sayings from Thomas Jefferson, Voltaire and the like, in an imaginative and theatrical way to recreate the idealized land where this love-conquers-all tale that glorifies the monarchy with kingly magnanimity takes place. Crown-wearing youngsters were the stagehands as well as stage adornments. In fact, the repertory is partially decided by what operas these outstanding directors and designers want to mount. Every opera is a new production, and no works are repeated.

The company performed in English until 1992. With the introduction of surtitles and conversion to original-language productions, the aura of the festival changed, signalling the company's maturity. The Santa Fe Opera (see Santa Fe entry) and Glyndebourne Festival Opera also began with English-language productions. Glimmerglass is well on its way to attaining International Festival status, becoming the "Santa Fe" of the East.

The four-opera season offers a delightful mixture of both familiar, and new and unusual works, performed in repertory. Recent operas include Claudio Monteverdi's *L'incoronazione di Poppea*, Mozart's *Così fan tutte*, Leoš Janáček's *Příhody Lišky Bystroušky* (The Cunning Little Vixen), and Gioachino Rossini's *Le Comte Ory*. The company performs in the Alice Bush Opera Theater.

Alice Busch Opera Theater

Eugene Onegin's impassioned pleas for Tatiana to abandon her husband reverberated through the newly constructed Alice Busch Opera Theater. On June 28, 1986, Pyotr Il'yich Tchaikovsky's *Eugene Onegin* inaugurated Glimmerglass Opera's new opera house, the first opera house built in America in more than two decades. The occasion was not as auspicious as it should have been. Three days before the opening, workmen were still painting the proscenium arch, and that left no time for technical or dress rehearsals. The stage was steeply raked, and as *Eugene Onegin* progressed, so did Madame Larina's house and garden — toward the audience. No one had remembered to fasten the sets! Despite the inauspicious beginning, however, events have gone well for the company. The Alice Busch Opera Theater is one of the finest opera houses in the country. Hugh Hardy designed the theater, which cost $5.5 million. Mrs. Bradley Goodyear donated the land, and Mrs. Carl-Werner Gronewaldt gave enough construction money to warrant the theater's being named in memory of her mother.

Ensconced in the genteel countryside of the Catskill Mountains, the opera house looms over the pastoral landscape like a giant earth-colored barn. The building is of taupe-colored steel panels with a façade dressed in taupe-painted wood paneling. The rustic theater is actually a screened pavilion, transformed into an intimate opera house before each performance when its massive 16- by 24-foot steel doors roll shut. Although the outside world is visually shut out, it is not

Alice Busch Opera Theater (Cooperstown, New York).

acoustically sealed and the sounds of summer penetrate the walls, harmonizing with the opera.

Early nineteenth-century Italian opera houses inspired the multi-colored horseshoe-shaped auditorium that fuses the intimacy of this by-gone era with excellent sightlines. A single balcony rises around raspberry-colored-cloth orchestra seats. A teal-colored lattice, with circular, multi-colored patterns, covers the ceiling. Silver-bottom bulbs trace the patterns — the chandelier of the twenty-first century. "I hate going to the opera and sitting in the third balcony watching ant figures move on stage," remarked Kellogg, his reason for taking the financial risks associated with building a small theater. The opera house seats 920.

Practical Information. The Alice Busch Opera Theater is eight miles north of Cooperstown on route 80. The Glimmerglass Opera ticket office is in Cooperstown, at 20 Chestnut Street and opens June 1 from 10:00 A.M. to 6:00 P.M., Monday through Saturday. The theater box office, in front of the opera house, opens one and a half hours before the performance. Tickets can be ordered by telephoning 607-547-2255 beginning May 1, or writing Glimmerglass Opera Ticket Office, P.O.B. 191, Cooperstown, NY 13326, before May 1. Festival brochures are available in February. To obtain one, write Glimmerglass Opera at the above address or call 607-547-5704. If you go, stay at the Inn at Cooperstown, 16 Chestnut Street, Cooperstown, NY 13326; telephone 607-547-5756. The Inn was built in 1874 as the annex to the Fenimore Hotel and has hosted soprano Frederica von Stade and composer William Schuman.

COMPANY STAFF AND REPERTORY

General/Artistic Directors. Peter Macris (1975–1979); Paul Kellogg (1979–present).
World Premieres. Schuman's *A Question of Taste* (June 24, 1989).

American/United States Premieres Ford's *Mr. Jericho* (August 18, 1989); Mozart's *Il re pastore* (first professional stage performance, August 9, 1991).

Repertory. **1975:** La bohème. **1976:** La traviata, Cavalleria rusticana/I pagliacci. **1977:** Les contes d'Hoffmann, Tosca. **1978:** The Telephone/The Medium, Martha. **1979:** Die lustige Witwe, Il barbiere di Siviglia. **1980:** Der Zigeunerbaron, Le nozze di Figaro. **1981:** H.M.S. Pinafore, Manon Lescaut, Gallantry/Trouble in Tahiti/Der. Schauspieldirektor. **1982:** Die Fledermaus, Don Pasquale, Madama Butterfly. **1983:** Rigoletto, Die Entführung aus dem Serail, The Mikado. **1984:** The Student Prince, Ariadne auf Naxos, Carmen. **1985:** Prodaná nevěsta (The Bartered Bride), Così fan tutte, Falstaff. **1986:** La Cenerentola, The Mighty Casey/Gianni Schicchi, Les pêcheurs des perles. **1987:** Eugene Onegin, The Pirates of Penzance, A Midsummer Night's Dream. **1988:** Don Giovanni, La Grande Duchesse des Gérolstein, Béatrice et Bénédict. **1989:** A Question of Taste/The Mighty Casey, La traviata, Mr. Jericho/H.M.S. Pinafore, Albert Herring. **1990:** La bohème, Intermezzo, Albert Herring. **1991:** The Mikado, Il re pastore, Fidelio. **1992:** Die Zauberflöte, Il matrimonio segreto, The Turn of the Screw. **1993:** Le Comte Ory, Così fan tutte, The Midnight Angel, Werther. **1994:** L'incoronazione di Poppea, Příhody Lišky Bystroušky (The Cunning Little Vixen), Die Entführung aus dem Serail.

NEW YORK CITY

• *The Metropolitan Opera* •

Charles Gounod's *Faust*, sung in Italian, celebrated the opening of the Metropolitan Opera House on October 22, 1883. Highlighted by a stellar cast with Christine Nilsson as Marguerite and Italo Campanini as Faust, the performance lasted more than five hours. That did not matter since the audience was more interested in seeing who was there than in watching Gounod's *Faust*. The *Tribune* reported, "When the opening of the overture sounded through the house, there was a momentary hush, and then as if everybody had made his bow and done his duty by that, everybody turned to his neighbor and began to chat in the liveliest manner, or turned completely around in his seat to get a full view of the house. A more sociable gathering it would be hard to imagine." It is difficult today to imagine a society where the wife of a millionaire, denied a box of her choice at the opera, could cause another opera house to be built, but that is exactly what happened in the early 1880s when Mrs. William Vanderbilt could not get a box "from which to shine" at the Academy of Music, the fashionable home for opera at that time. Although her husband could have built an opera house himself, (having inherited $94 million in 1877), he banded together with other millionaires and formed the Metropolitan Opera House Company to erect the first Met.

The first work heard in New York was on December 11, 1732, when George Farquhar's *Recruiting Officer* "trod the boards" at "the New Theatre in the building of the Honorable Rip Van Dam, Esquire," according to Oscar Sonneck in his *Early Opera in America*. Soon, travelling opera troupes performed ballad-operas, which consisted of spoken dialogue interspersed with popular folk tunes. The Nassau Street Theater opened in another of van Dam's buildings on March 5, 1750, with Colley Cibber's version of the *Historical Tragedy of King Richard III*. The Nassau hosted several American premieres of ballad operas soon after its inauguration. First came Henry Fielding's *Mock Doctor* (April 23, 1750), followed by John Gay's *The Beggar's Opera* (December 3, 1750), Henry Carey's *Damon and Phillida* (February 18, 1751), and Fielding's *Virgin Unmasked* (April 16, 1751). Also in the repertory were C. Coffey's *The Devil to Pay* and Cibber's *Flora, or Hob in the Well*. The next season witnessed the American premiere of Carey's *Honest Yorkshireman* (March 2, 1752). Thomas Kean, Walter Murray, Charles Somerset Woodham, Nancy George, Miss Osborne, and Misses Taylor were some of the ballad-opera performers.

June of 1753 saw Lewis Hallam's London Company of Comedians arrive in New York. Finding the Nassau in a state of disrepair, Hallam promptly tore it down and built a new "very fine, large and commodious" theater on the same site. *The Conscious Lovers* followed by Carey's *Damon and Phillida* inaugurated the theater on September 13, 1753. The season ran until March 25, 1754, and included Fielding's *Virgin Unmasked*, Cibber's *Flora, or Hob in the Well*, Coffey's *Devil to Pay*, Gay's *Beggar's Opera*, and the pantomime *Harlequin Collector*. Dancing and singing entertained the audience between the acts. Hallam died in 1755, and his widow married David Douglass. Douglass arrived in New York in 1758 and finding the theater converted into a place of worship, constructed a new theater at Cruger's wharf. His company, known as the American Company (later Old American), inaugurated the Cruger Wharf Theater on December 28, 1758 with the play *Jane Shore* and Fielding's *Mock Doctor*. The season closed on February 7, 1759, with Carey's *Damon and Phillida*. When Douglass returned to New York for his 1761-62 season, he found the Cruger Wharf Theater had been deserted, so a new theater was constructed in Chapel Street that cost $1,625. The season opened with Carey's *Honest Yorkshireman* on November 26, 1761, and closed with Fielding's *Mock Doctor* on April 26, 1762. Carey's *Damon and Phillida*, Cibber's *Flora*, Coffey's *Devil to Pay*, Gay's *Beggar's Opera*, Fielding's *Virgin Unmasked* and *Harlequin Collector* were also part of the fare. In 1761, opposition to theater was so violent that Douglass and his company left New York. Soon after, the Chapel Street Theater was destroyed by mobs.

Douglass returned in 1767 and built the John Street Theater. It was a red frame building that cost $800 and seated 800 people. The season, which opened on December 7, 1767, and closed on June 2, 1768, saw the following operas among its offerings: Bickerstaffe's *Thomas and Sally*, Arne's *Love in a Village*, Carey's *Contrivances*, *Damon and Phillida*, and *Honest Yorkshireman*, Cibber's *Flora*, Coffey's *Devil to Pay*, and Boyce's *Chaplet*. On May 4, 1769, Douglass introduced Samuel Arnold's *Maid of the Mill* to America, followed by Dibdin's *The Padlock* twenty-five days later. On October 4, 1774. Congress passed the resolution "That we discourage every species of extravagance and dissipation, especially horse-racing and other expensive diversions and entertainment." This included theater. Douglass left for Jamaica on February 2, 1775.

New York first heard French opera on October 7, 1790, when the American premiere of Audinot's *Le Tonnelier* took place at the City Tavern. The premiere of John Jacques Rousseau's *Le Devin du Village* followed on October 21. The American Company returned to the John Street Theater for a few years until its new headquarters, the Park Theater (on Park Row) opened on January 29, 1798. Designed by Marc Brunel, the theater cost $42,375 to construct. The first Park Street Theater survived until fire claimed it in 1820. Rebuilt on the same site, the second Park Street Theater was devoured by fire in 1848. The Park became the first home in New York for foreign opera. Initially performed in English, the operas included the American premieres of Carl Maria von Weber's *Der Freischütz* and Wolfgang Amadeus Mozart's *Le nozze di Figaro* and *Don Giovanni*. *Don Giovanni* was introduced first in English and then in Italian. Dominick Lynch, a wealthy wine merchant, was responsible for the introduction of "original language" Italian Opera at the Park Theater in 1825. He persuaded the manager of the Park Theater, Stephen Price, to present an opera troupe headed by Manuel del Pópolo Vicente García, promising to pay any deficit. On November 29, 1825, the García troupe opened with Rossini's *Il barbiere di Siviglia* in Italian. Four Garcías participated in the American premiere production. Manuel was one of the great tenors in his day and had created the role of Almaviva at the Teatro Argentina in Rome (Italy). Although he was fifty and past his prime, García reprised the role for the New York premiere. His eighteen-year-old daughter Maria was Rosina, his son Manuel was Figaro, and daughter Joaquina was Berta. Nine Italian operas were in the repertory that initial season, all novelties: García's *La figlia dell'aria* and *L'amante astuto*, Rossini's *Il barbiere di Siviglia*, *Tancredi*, *Otello*, *Il turco in Italia*, and *La Cenerentola*, Mozart's *Don Giovanni* and Zingarelli's *Giulietta e Romeo*. García's company stayed almost a year before closing their season on September 30, 1826.

John Davis's New Orleans French troupe (see New Orleans entry) followed García, opening with Nicolò Isouard's *Cendrillon* on July 13, 1827. The French company remained three and a half months, offering a repertory of thirty operas, almost all of which Davis had previously performed in New Orleans. Ballad-opera was now considered too crass for social-climbing New Yorkers, who wished to emulate the sophistication of European musical centers, and who demanded European fare. The Park obliged and continued to host European novelties: Rossini's *La donna del lago*, Mozart's *Die Zauberflöte*, Vincenzo Bellini's *La sonnambula*, Donizetti's *L'elisir d'amore*, Ludwig van Beethoven's *Fidelio*, and Giuseppe Verdi's *Ernani* among them. Lorenzo da Ponte, the librettist for Mozart's *Le nozze di Figaro* and *Don Giovanni*, was a professor of Italian literature at Columbia University when García and his troupe visited the Park Theater in 1825 and 1826. He had harbored dreams of bringing Italian opera to New York and collaborated with the French tenor Montressor to mount opera at the Richmond Hill Theater, where on December 5, 1832, the American premiere of Bellini's *Il pirata* took place. After thirty-five performances, the season ended in failure, partly because of the location of the theater. Determined to continue, da Ponte convinced a group of wealthy opera-lovers to finance the construction of the Italian Opera House at Church and Leonard Streets, the first theater constructed specifically for opera. Rossini's *La gazza ladra* inaugurated the Italian Opera House on November 18, 1833. The season was ambitious with the world premieres of Carlo Salvioni's *Coriolanus Before Rome* (February 1, 1834) and *La casa da vendere* (March 22, 1834) and the American premieres of Domenico Cimarosa's *Il matrimonio segreto* (January 4, 1834), Bellini's *La straniera* (November 10, 1834), and Giovanni Pacini's *Gli arabi nelle Gallie* (January 20, 1834) among its offerings. The season closed with a $30,000 deficit, and with no one to guarantee Lorenzo da Ponte's Company, the company was forced to abandon performances after another year. A short time later, fire destroyed the Italian Opera House.

Next a successful opera-loving restaurant owner, Ferdinand Palmo decided to stage opera. He converted Stoppai's Arcade Baths on Chambers Street into the

Palmo Opera House with the hopes of democratizing opera. On February 3, 1844, Bellini's *I Puritani* inaugurated the Palmo Opera House. The Palmo hosted several premieres during its brief four-year existence including the first performance in America of a Verdi opera—*I Lombardi*—on March 3, 1847. Located in a bad section of town, the Palmo experienced financial problems, causing its demise the following year.

The next attempt to establish opera in New York was an opera house catering to the wealthy. Erected so that "society might enjoy opera in a refined environment," the Astor Place Opera House accommodated 1,800. The standard fare offered operas by Bellini, Donizetti, Rossini, and early Verdi, and included the premieres of Verdi's *Nabucco* and Donizetti's *Roberto Devereux*. Although the singing was acceptable, the acting was minimal and the sets usually were made of cardboard (and looked it). The performance, however, took a back seat to the lavish attire and the social role "a night at the opera" played. Despite the "high society" that frequented the theater, Astor Place soon faced mounting deficits, and William Niblo took over the theater and put popular entertainment on the stage. Niblo also ran Niblo's Gardens at the corner of Broadway and Prince Street. Niblo's Gardens hosted the first grand opera by an American on an American subject, George Frederick Bristow's *Rip Van Winkle* in 1855. Niblo's also witnessed numerous American premieres, among them Verdi's *Attila* and *Macbeth*, Donizetti's *La fille du régiment* (in Italian as La figlia del reggimento), and Friedrich von Flotow's *Martha*. Richard Wagner works were not performed in New York until 1855, when Wagner operas took up temporary residence for twelve nights at Niblo's. The event was not successful, neither financially nor with the public or critics, who accused the singers of "inexorable shrieking." The opera seasons were given by Shireff's English Company, New Orleans French Company, Havana Italian Company, and Strakosch's Opera Company.

Castle Gardens was the site of Jenny Lind's concert on September 11, 1850, when six thousand spectators, plus hundreds more bobbing in boats around the Gardens, thrilled to her "casta diva." Giulia Grisi also sang at Castle Garden offering an exciting Donizetti's *Lucrezia Borgia*. The Gardens hosted a few novelties, among them Xavier Boisselot's *Ne touchez-pas à la reine* and the first performance in Italian of Verdi's *Luisa Miller*.

Grisi with Giovanni Mario opened the New York Academy of Music at 14th Street and Irving Place with Bellini's *Norma* on October 2, 1854. Erected as the successor to Astor Place, the Academy reigned as New York's leading opera house for thirty years. During its reign, the Academy became not only a shrine to *bel canto* in America, but also the yardstick by which all other American opera houses were measured. Patterned after the fashionable Théâtre National de l'Opéra (Paris), the Academy emerged as the gathering place for the city's "old-money." By the Academy's second season, two of Verdi's great middle-period operas graced the stage for the first time in America—*Rigoletto* (February 19, 1855) and *Il trovatore* (May 2, 1855). In total, the Academy introduced ten Verdi operas: *La traviata*, *I vespri Siciliani*, *Un ballo in maschera*, *Aroldo*, *La forza del destino*, *Don Carlo*, *Aida*, and *Otello*. Premieres were not limited to Verdi operas. The Academy witnessed numerous novelties, including Gounod's *Roméo et Juliette*, Jules Massenet's *Manon*, Umberto Giordano's *Andrea Chénier*, and Wagner's *Die Walküre*.

In 1856, Elsie Hensler became the first American singer to perform at the

Academy. Three years later, on Thanksgiving Day, Adelina Patti made her debut in Donizetti's *Lucia di Lammermoor*. Although she was only seventeen, her phenomenal voice and "ideal art" made her the reigning prima donna. Clara Louise Kellogg, who claimed the title as the first American prima donna, followed in Patti's footsteps. She first assayed Gilda on February 27, 1861. The Academy had opened five weeks earlier with Mercadante's *Il giuramento*. A decade later, Christine Nilsson created the title role in Ambroise Thomas's *Mignon* and Italo Campanini appeared as Gennaro in Donizetti's *Lucrezia Borgia* in 1873. Lillian Nordica's first appearance came in 1882 as Marguerite. Four years earlier, Colonel James Henry Mapleson arrived at the Academy with his company. His presentation of the American premiere of George Bizet's *Carmen* (in Italian) on October 23, 1878, was unquestionable the highlight of that season. Minnie Hauk sang the title role, and claimed credit for the popularity of the opera. Mapleson then introduced Etelka Gerster on November 18 in Bellini's *La sonnambula*. Emma Juch's Academy debut came in 1881 as Philine in Thomas's *Mignon*. Sofia Scalchi graced the stage the following season. As wealth and pretension grew, so did the elaborateness of the Academy's opera productions and the galaxy of stars that shone from the stage.

Opera was first and foremost a social occasion, and the boxholders awaited the intermissions with more pleasure than the rising of the curtain. Since opera was considered one of the hallmarks of social and cultural acceptability, the *nouveau riche*, which included Mrs. Vanderbilt, "needed" boxes at the Academy. And that was the Academy's downfall—its paucity of boxes, ostensibly to keep these very people out. When Mrs. Vanderbilt could not obtain an appropriate box from which to exhibit her great wealth, her husband arranged with other millionaires to build their own opera house, which they called the Metropolitan Opera House. Designed by Josiah Cleaveland Cady, the Met cost slightly more than $1.8 million. Seventy stockholders (boxholders) paid $17,500 each. The rest was borrowed from the bank.

The Met's inaugural season was an Italian season. It did not mean that only Italian opera was given. It meant that every opera, even if it had been originally written in French or German was sung in Italian. For example, New Yorkers were treated to Giacomo Meyerbeer's *Il profeta* (Le Prophète) and *Gli Ugonotti* (Les Huguenots) among the offerings. There was no Metropolitan Opera Company as such, but the house was leased to an impresario who provided a season of opera. Henry Abbey managed the house the first season and his company presented the repertory—nineteen works. Among them were Rossini's *Il barbiere di Siviglia*, Verdi's *La traviata* and *Il trovatore*, Mozart's *Don Giovanni*, Bellini's *I Puritani* and *La sonnambula*, Wagner's *Lohengrin*, Bizet's *Carmen*, Donizetti's *Lucia di Lammermoor*, Arrigo Boïto's *Mefistofele*, Thomas's *Mignon* and *Hamlet*, and Meyerbeer's *Robert le Diable*, *Les Prophète*, and *Les Huguenots*. There was one novelty, the American premiere of Amilcare Ponchielli's *La Gioconda* on December 20, 1883.

An immediate rivalry resulted between the two houses—Mapleson at the Academy of Music downtown and Abbey running the Met uptown. Mapleson also opened his season on October 22, 1883, offering Gerster in Bellini's *La sonnambula*. He mounted Gounod's *Faust* with Nordica, and boasted of Adelina Patti on his roster. But his productions were mediocre, and by 1886, most of the Academy crowd had deserted to the Met. Mapleson was out of business, exclaiming, "I cannot fight Wall Street." Although the Academy held on for another decade, its days of glory were history. The Met lured the Academy's stalwarts with lavish sets, expensive costumes, and stellar casts. The stellar casts were lured with astronomical fees: Nilsson and Campanini were paid $1,000 per performance. The productions were the most lavish anywhere in America. Not surprisingly, Abbey ran up a deficit of $600,000, and his contract was not renewed. The Met stockholders did not want to absorb Abbey's losses and turned to German seasons. This did not mean that all operas performed were German, but that every opera staged was sung in German, including Fromental Halévy's *La Juive* (Die Jüdin), Daniel Auber's *La muette de Portici* (Die Stummerin von Portici), Rossini's *Guillaume Tell* (Wilhelm Tell), and Verdi's *Rigoletto*. Opera in German was cheaper to produce, because there was a large supply of German ensemble artists available on short notice, charging a fraction of what the Italian stars demanded. Leopold Damrosch agreed to undertake the German season for a salary of $10,000, with the stockholders absorbing any losses. Wagner's *Tannhäuser* with Anton Schott in the title role opened the Met's second season on November 17, 1884. Damrosch used an ensemble approach and effective staging. He conducted every performance as well as dealing with the artistic and administrative burdens of production. After an exhausting rehearsal one frigid early-February afternoon, he napped next to an open window and contracted pneumonia. His twenty-three-year-old son Walter took his father's place on the podium on February 11, 1885, so the performance of Wagner's *Tannhäuser* could go on. The younger Damrosch also conducted Wagner's *Die Walküre* the following evening. Three days later, the elder Damrosch was dead. His funeral was held on the stage of the Met, where every seat was taken, and everyone's eyes were filled with tears.

Edmund Stanton took over the managerial duties and Anton Seidl was appointed music director. His first season opened with Wagner's *Lohengrin* on November 23, 1885. Lilli Lehmann made her debut in Bizet's *Carmen*, and the American premieres of Karl Goldmark's *Die Königin von Saba* and Wagner's *Die Meistersinger von Nürnberg* took place. Lehmann also sang in the American premiere of Wagner's *Tristan und Isolde* conducted by Seidl. Lehmann and Seidl became the cornerstone of the remaining six German seasons, which saw Wagner's *Siegfried* and *Götterdämmerung* introduced to America on November 9, 1887, and January 25, 1888, respectively. With the American premiere of Wagner's *Das Rheingold* on January 4, 1889, the complete Ring Cycle was the staged. Italian and French opera continued to play a large role in the repertory, despite the fact that they were all sung in German. Gounod's *Faust* appeared so often that one critic dubbed the Met "Das Faustspielhaus."

The boxholders eventually tired of German opera, especially the seemingly eternal and complex Wagnerian ones, so in 1891, the directors asked Abbey to return. Abbey, along with his partners Maurice Grau and John Schoeffel staged a season of *bel canto* opera. The trio opened their first season on December 14, 1891, with Gounod's *Roméo et Juliette*. It was the first opera sung in French at the Met. The season opener boasted the American debuts of Emma Eames, and Jean and Édouard de Reszke, ushering in the Golden Age of singers. Jean de Reszke and Eames returned for Verdi's *Otello*, and Eames sang in the company's first *Cavalleria rusticana*. Lehmann appeared in Verdi's *Il trovatore*, and Nordica was seen in Meyerbeer's *Les Huguenots* and *L'Africaine*.

On August 27, 1892, a scenery painter dropped a cigarette into a can of paint thinner and fire swept the building. The damage was estimated at $300,000 of which only $60,000 was covered by insurance. The Metropolitan Opera House Company was dissolved, and the Metropolitan Opera and Real Estate Company was formed. There were now only thirty-five stockholders, nineteen of the original seventy stockholders plus sixteen newcomers. Each purchased $30,000 worth of stock and with it the ownership of one of the thirty-five parterre boxes that would soon appear in the rebuilt theater. (The boxholders also paid upwards of $4,500 annually for production expenses.)

When Gounod's *Faust* reopened the Met on November 27, 1893, the opera house was different. Electric lights were the biggest change, replacing the gas illumination. They caused the diamonds on the jewel-bedecked parterre box inhabitants to sparkle so brightly that the "golden horseshoe" was renamed the "diamond horseshoe." The Abbey/Grau/Schoeffel partnership continued to run the house, which was star driven. Besides Eames and the two de Reszke brothers in the opening *Faust* and several other operas, Nellie Melba made her debut in Donizetti's *Lucia di Lammermoor* on December 4, 1893, and Emma Calvé made hers in Pietro Mascagni's *Cavalleria rusticana*. Also on the roster was the noted bass Pol Plançon. The 1894-95 season heralded the debut of Francesco Tamagno. January 31, 1894, introduced the first *Le nozze di Figaro* seen on the Met stage, and two years after Verdi's *Falstaff* received its world premiere at La Scala, it opened at the Met on February 4, 1895. Wagner's *Tristan und Isolde* was now sung in German on November 27, 1895, with Jean de Reszke and Nordica in the title roles. Melba made the mistake of tackling Brünnhilde in Wagner's *Siegfried* on December 30, 1896, experiencing one of opera's great disasters.

After Abbey died on October 17, 1896, Grau leased the house alone with a hiatus of one year. During that time, the Damrosch-Ellis Company mounted a guest season. Grau's five seasons were defined by unparalleled vocal splendor and sloppy performances and poor physical productions. He introduced five works to America: Luigi Mancinelli's *Ero e Leandro*, Puccini's *Tosca*, Isidore de Lara's *Messaline*, Ignacy Jan Paderewski's *Manru*, and Ethel Smyth's *Der Wald*. Only Puccini's *Tosca* has stood the test of time. Several Met novelties also graced the stage: Puccini's *La bohème*, Donizetti's *La fille du régiment*, and Ernest Reyer's *Salammbô* among them. There were some tragedies as well. The baritone Armand Castelmary died on stage during a performance of Flotow's *Martha* on February 10, 1897, and Seidl died prematurely the following year on March 28, 1898, at the age of forty-seven. Another funeral was held on the opera house stage. Unexpected comedy also surfaced. The anvil would not break in Wagner's *Siegfried*, and in Wagner's *Lohengrin*, the Swan Boat collapsed during the triumphal entrance, unceremoniously dispatching the hero to the rear.

Heinrich Conried leased the Met after Grau, and brought both glory and controversy. The glory was opening the first season on November 23, 1903, with the debut of a nervous, young tenor named Enrico Caruso in Verdi's *Rigoletto*. The controversy came with the American premiere of Wagner's *Parsifal* on Christmas Eve in 1903, incurring the wrath of both Wagner's heirs and the clergy and with the scandalous American premiere of Richard Strauss's *Salome* on January 22, 1907. Olive Fremstad's Salome so thrilled and shocked that the Met stockholders banned it from the stage after the first performance. More glory came with Geraldine Farrar's debut as Juliette on November 26, 1906, and Gustav Mahler's conducting of Wagner's *Tristan und Isolde* on New Year's Day 1908. Mahler also conducted Wagner's *Die Walküre* and *Siegfried*, Ludwig von Beethoven's *Fidelio*, and Mozart's *Don Giovanni*, making them unforgettable experiences. Conried produced integrated performances, adding drama to the opera and making actors out of the singers. Feodor Chaliapin's portrayal in Boïto's *Mefistofele* on November 20, 1907, was so compelling that it was described as "bestiality incarnate." Conried preferred to mount new or unusual operas rather than showcase star-vehicles. Besides the controversial premieres of Wagner's *Parsifal* and Strauss's *Salome*, he introduced Giordano's *Fedora* with Caruso, Antonio Scotti, and Lina Cavalieri on December 5, 1906, and staged several operas new to the Met, among them Donizetti's *Lucrezia Borgia*, Mascagni's *Iris*, and Engelbert Humperdinck's *Hänsel und Gretel* with the composer himself present.

Gounod's *Roméo et Juliette* with Farrar opened the 1906-1907 season. Two days later, Farrar sang Marguerite in Hector Berlioz's *La damnation de Faust*. Puccini supervised the first Met performance of his *Manon Lescaut* on January 18, 1907, featuring Cavalieri, Caruso, and Scotti. February 11 saw Puccini's *Madama Butterfly* with the composer again at the Met. The cast included Farrar, Caruso, Scotti, and Louise Homer. But all was not well. One week after the Met opened its 1906-1907 season, Oscar Hammerstein opened his Manhattan Opera House with Bellini's *I Puritani*, and Conried's days were numbered. He opened his last Met season with Francesco Cilèa's *Adriana Lecouvreur* on November 18, 1907, featuring Caruso and Cavalieri. Less than two years later he was dead, and another body lay in state on the Metropolitan stage.

On December 3, 1906, Vincenzo Bellini's *I Puritani* inaugurated the Manhattan Opera House, starting an opera war in New York the likes of which had never before been seen. Founded by Oscar Hammerstein, the Manhattan Opera Company was the first to give the Metropolitan Opera serious competition. The company's opening night performance featured Alessandro Bonci, Regina Pinkert, and Mario Ancora under the baton of Cleofonte Campanini. Several months before, Oscar Hammerstein had announced his intentions to produce grand opera in direct competition with the Metropolitan Opera. He claimed the quality of opera that the Met was producing had deteriorated, and he wanted to raise operatic standards, as well as make the public more opera conscious.

Hammerstein's first opera house, the Harlem Opera House, opened on September 30, 1889. A short time later, the Emma Juch Grand Opera Company staged Gounod's *Faust*, Emil Kaiser's *Der Trompeter von Säckingen*, Thomas's *Mignon*, Michael Balfe's *The Bohemian Girl*, Bizet's *Carmen*, William Vincent Wallace's *Maritana*, and Weber's *Der Freischütz*. The performances were neither financially nor artistically rewarding. Hammerstein's second try at opera generated more success. On March 25, 1890, Lilli Lehmann opened in Bellini's *Norma* at the Harlem. Meyerbeer's *Les Huguenots* (in German) and Verdi's *Il trovatore* followed during a five-day opera spree. Counted among the singers were Paul Kalisch, Ida Klein, Conrad Behrens, and Sophie Traubmann. For the fall 1890 season at the Harlem, Hammerstein formed a troupe known as Hammerstein's English Opera Company, which opened on October 11 with Verdi's *Ernani*. Also in the repertory were Gounod's *Faust*, Thomas's *Mignon*, Verdi's *Il trovatore*, Balfe's *The Bohemian Girl*, Auber's *Masaniello*, and Bizet's *Carmen*. The opera season closed on November 1. Hammerstein built a second theater in Harlem called the Columbus Theater, where he continued his opera presentations with the Metropolitan English Opera Company on May 25, 1891. The season lasted until June 13, 1891, and offered Verdi's *Rigoletto* and *Il trovatore*, Balfe's *The Bohemian Girl*, Wallace's *Maritana*, and Weber's *Der Freischütz* (as The Free-shooter). The casts included Payne Clarke, Otto Rathjens, Louise Meisslinger, Thomas Guise, and Nina Bertini.

The first Manhattan Opera House opened on November 18, 1892. Situated on West 34th Street between Broadway and Seventh Avenue, the theater was located where Macy's was subsequently built. The Manhattan hosted Hammerstein's next operatic venture. His original plans called for opera in German, but insufficient financial support (too few subscriptions) forced a continuation of opera in English. The opera season opened on January 24, 1893, with a novelty, Moritz Moszkowski's *Boabdil*. Bizet's *Carmen*, Verdi's *Rigoletto* and *Il trovatore*, Balfe's *The Bohemian Girl*, and Ludwig van Beethoven's *Fidelio* followed.

Hammerstein scheduled the opening of his new Manhattan Opera House on November 19, 1906. The building, however, was not completed so the opening was postponed until December 3, when Bellini's *I Puritani* inaugurated the house. The production put more emphasis on the sets and customs than was customary during that era. Hammerstein felt the performances should be enjoyable not only aurally but also visually. That, combined with superb singers, garnered the venture good reviews. Verdi's *Rigoletto* followed on December 5, and introduced Maurice Renaud to New York. Although the baritone was experiencing vocal difficulties due to hoarseness, his performance received favorable reviews. Pinkert was Gilda and Bonci was the Duke. On Friday, December 7, New Yorkers had a choice of Fausts. Gounod's *Faust* played at the Manhattan, while Hector Berlioz's *La Damnation de Faust* was at the Met. Mozart's *Don Giovanni* entered the repertory during the second week, along with Bizet's *Carmen*. After *Carmen*, audiences increased in size. Although the critics had already noted that the performances were artistically outstanding and visually exciting, it took the audience a little longer to overcome their hesitation at trying something new.

In January 1907, Hammerstein added Verdi's *Il trovatore*, Donizetti's *L'elisir d'amore*, Meyerbeer's *Les Huguenots*, Rossini's *Il barbiere di Siviglia*, and Bellini's *La sonnambula* to his schedule. Melba made her long-awaited appearance at the Manhattan Opera in Verdi's *La traviata* on January 2, 1907. Tumultuous applause greeted her between acts and at the final curtain. When Hammerstein joined her on stage, "the enthusiasm of the audience passed all bounds, and for some minutes there was a deafening uproar, during which hundreds of people waved their handkerchief, and the younger members of the audience threw their floral buttonholes at her feet," as Agnes Murphy described it. Melba reprised Violetta and also sang Gilda and Lucia. In February, she added Marguerite to her repertoire. Head to head competition appeared with the Met on Saturday evening, February 9, 1907, when both houses offered Verdi's *Aida*. The Manhattan sold out, but the Met had many empty seats. In March, Puccini's *La bohème* finally graced the stage. The Met had tried unsuccessfully to keep Hammerstein from producing any of Puccini's operas, claiming that it had exclusive rights from Ricordi. Hammerstein took Ricordi to court and won. Melba made her final appearance for the season as Mimi on March 25, 1907. After the final curtain descended, she sang the mad scene from Donizetti's *Lucia di Lammermoor*, throwing the house into pandemonium. The ovation lasted forty minutes. Two days after Melba's departure, Calvé made her debut with the company in Bizet's *Carmen* on March 27.

The final weeks of the first season saw Verdi' *Requiem*, Auber's *Fra Diavolo*, and Flotow's *Martha* enter the repertory. Verdi's *Aida* closed the season on April 20, with Giannini Russ, Amadeo Bassi, Eleanora de Cisneros, Mario Ancona, and Campanini conducting. The future looked bright at the end of the first season. The net profit totaled $100,000 (whereas the Met showed a loss of $84,000), and Hammerstein had secured a loan of $400,000 from Frank Woolworth using the opera house as collateral. Meanwhile, both companies tried to raid the best singers of the other company. The Met succeeded in luring Bonci, but Hammerstein enticed Nordica to the Manhattan Company.

For his second season, Hammerstein embarked on an ambitious course of presenting novelties. Ponchielli's *La gioconda* opened the season on November 4, 1907, and before the end of the month, the first American premiere graced the stage — Jules Massenet's *Thaïs* on November 25, 1907, with Mary Garden in the title role. The premiere was originally scheduled for November 22, but was postponed because Garden was ill. Critics praised her acting ability but were not impressed with her vocal prowess. Regarding the opera itself, the reviews were mixed, with the *Herald* writing that the opera was "for the most part colorless and saccharine." The next American premiere, Gustave Charpentier's *Louise*, took place on January 3, 1908, with Garden again in the title role. This was both a musical and dramatic success. The *New York American* called it "an epoch at the Manhattan." The first performance in Italian of Giordano's *Siberia* followed on February 5, 1908, with one critic writing that it was "the best and the most promising demonstration of Giordano's talents."

On February 19, 1908, the long awaited introduction to America of Claude Debussy's *Pelléas et Mélisande* occurred. The reaction of the audience was one of "wonder and respect, rather than one of spirited approval." The critics were mixed. One wrote that "the work deserves repeated hearing; it is too unusual, too curious, too original in plan and execution for hasty judgement." Garden was praised for her interpretation. Even Debussy wrote to Hammerstein, expressing his appreciation at the introduction of his work to America and for aiding "the cause of French music." Luisa Tetrazzini had made her debut at the Manhattan in Verdi's *La traviata* on January 15, 1908. It was an unforgettable evening with accolades from both the public and the press. The success was especially satisfying because Conried had not exercised an option he had on Tetrazzini. Five days later she appeared in Donizetti's *Lucia di Lammermoor* with Giovanni Zenatello as Edgardo and Campanini conducting. January 29 saw her as Gilda and later in the season she sang in Meyerbeer's *Dinorah* and Luigi Ricci's *Crispino e la Comare*. On March 27, Giordano's *Andrea Chénier* which had not been heard in New York since 1896, graced the stage for a gala celebration in honor of Campanini. His wife, Eva Campanini, came out of retirement to sing Maddalena. Puccini's *Tosca* inaugurated the Manhattan's third season on Monday, November 9, 1908. Two days later, Garden reprised her role in Massenet's *Thaïs*. Garden also sang in the American premiere of Massenet's *Le jongleur de Notre Dame* on Friday, November 27, 1908, with Renaud and Hector Dufranne. Melba reappeared in Puccini's *La bohème*, and Verdi's *Otello*.

Before the opening of the regular 1909-1910 season, Hammerstein decided to mount popular-priced performances (50¢ to $2) to increase interest in opera so more New Yorkers would attend his regular season. Meyerbeer's *La Prophète* opened the preliminary season on August 30, 1909, with George Lucas as Jean de Leyde, Marguerite d'Alvarez as Fidès, and Madame Walter-Villa as Berthe under the baton of Giuseppe Sturani. Meyerbeer's *La Prophète* was one of three novelties of the season. Halévy's *La Juive* followed on September 9. The last new production of the season, Balfe's *The Bohemian Girl*, opened on October 20. The series of performances was unique, and occasionally the quality equalled that of the regular season. Hammerstein's fourth and last regular season at the Manhattan was nothing short of spectacular. Seven grand operas and *opéra comique* were added to the repertory. The Met, whose luster had been tarnished by Hammerstein's overwhelming success, also offered an ambitious season, not only at the opera house, but at the New Theater, on Central Park West, where it staged lighter works. During one week in New York, it was possible to see seventeen performances in six days. The Manhattan's season, which opened on Monday, November 8, 1909, with Massenet's *Hérodiade*, introduced two other Massenet works to America—*Sapho* on November 17, 1909, and *Grisélidis* on January 19, 1910. The second night of the season saw the debut of John McCormack opposite Tetrazzini in Verdi's *La traviata*. A young Irish tenor, McCormack became a favorite at the Manhattan and later at the Met. Charles Lecocq's *La fille de Madame Angot* heralded the presentation of *opéra comique* at the Manhattan. Edmond Audran's *La Mascotte*, Aimé Maillart's *Les dragons de Villars*, and Robert Planquette's *Les cloches de Corneville* were also mounted.

Hammerstein felt, according to the *New York Evening World Theater Section* that "opéra comique . . . is at once an antidote and a stimulant to grand opera." But after eight performances of the *opéra comique*, Hammerstein abandoned the experiment, sending the artists on an eleven-week tour of the United States and Canada. The *pièce de résistance* of his final season was the American premiere (in French) of Strauss's *Elektra* on Tuesday, February 1, 1910. It was an overpowering, almost shattering experience. As the final curtain fell, waves of shouts rolled over the auditorium. March 26, 1910, witnessed the season's final opera and Hammerstein's swan song—Donizetti's *Lucia di Lammermoor*. The memorable evening featured Tetrazzini as Lucia, McCormack as Edgardo with Oscar Anselmi conducting. Then on April 26, 1910, the Manhattan Opera ceased to exist. Arthur Hammerstein, using his father's power of attorney, sold Oscar Hammerstein's entire operatic empire to representatives of the Metropolitan. This included both opera houses (Manhattan and Philadelphia), the exclusive rights to several operas (Saint-Saëns's *Samson et Dalila*, Debussy's *Pelléas et Mélisande*, Strauss's *Salome* and *Elektra*, Massenet's *Thaïs*, Charpentier's *Louise*, and Massenet's *Le jongleur de Notre Dame*, *Sapho*, *Grisélidis*, and *Hérodiade*), the contacts of Tetrazzini, Garden, Renaud, McCormack, Charles Dalmorès, and Charles Gilbert, as well as all the scenery, stage furnishings, costumes, librettos, and scores. Hammerstein received $1.2 million and could not engage in the production of opera for ten years in New York, Philadelphia, Boston, or Chicago. The Metropolitan did not like the competition, and Hammerstein's success was thwarting its ambitions of absolute opera domination.

Before the opening of the twenty-fifth anniversary season at the Met, a permanent Metropolitan Opera Company was formed. Otto Kahn and William K. Vanderbilt bought Conried's opera producing company and brought Giulio Gatti-Casazza from Milan as its first salaried manager. One faction of the board led by John Pierpont Morgan objected to the appointment of Gatti-Casazza, preferring an American manager. So a compromise was struck. There would be a co-directorship with Gatti-Casazza dealing with the artistic side and the American (and former tenor) Andreas Dippel with administrative matters. The arrangement lasted two years. Dippel was then dispatched to the newly formed Chicago Grand Opera Company, which had been carved from the remains of Hammerstein's Manhattan Opera Company.

Gatti-Casazza reigned alone for twenty-seven years as the Met's general manager. Gatti-Casazza had previously managed Teatro alla Scala and brought Arturo Toscanini with him to conduct. Toscanini initially shared the podium with Mahler. Verdi's *Aida* with Emmy Destinn, Caruso, Scotti, and Homer under the baton of Toscanini ushered in Gatti-Casazza's reign on November 16, 1908. The inaugural season featured four Met novelties, Eugen d'Albert's *Tiefland*, Puccini's *Le Villi*, Alfredo Catalani's *La Wally*, and Bedřich Smetana's *Prodaná nevěsta* (The Bartered Bride). Mahler conducted Smetana's *Prodaná nevěsta* and a highly successful *Le nozze di Figaro* with Farrar, Eames, Scotti, and Marcella Sembrich. The following season, Mahler conducted the American premiere (in German) of Pyotr Il'yich Tchaikovsky's *Pikovaya dama* on March 21, 1910. It was the last performance he conducted. He returned to Vienna and died there on May 18, 1911.

The Met hosted its first world premiere, Puccini's *La fanciulla del West* on December 10, 1910, with Destinn, Caruso, Pasquale Amato, and Toscanini conducting. Puccini was in the audience. Eight years later, another Puccini work, *Il trittico: Gianni Schicchi/Suor Angelica/Il tabarro*, was seen for the first time anywhere on December 14, 1918. There were other world premieres by foreign composers—Humperdinck's *Königskinder* with Farrar, Homer, and Hermann Jadlowker, Giordano's *Madame Sans-Gêne*, Enrique Granados's *Goyescas* (the first opera in Spanish at the Met), and Albert Wolff's *L'oiseau bleu*. Although Gatti-Casazza did not speak English fluently, he developed American singers—Orville Harrold, Lawrence Tibbett, Grace Moore, Gladys Swarthout, and Rosa Ponselle among them—and championed the cause of the American composer (underwritten by Kahn). He presented the first American opera and the first opera in English seen on a Met stage, Frederick Converse's *The Pipes of Desire*, on March 18, 1910. He then showcased operas by American composers, mounting thirteen world premieres during his long tenure. Among them were Horatio Parker's *Mona*, Damrosch's *Cyrano*, Victor Herbert's *Madeleine*, Henry Hadley's *Cleopatra's Night*, and Deems Taylor's *The King's Henchman* and *Peter Ibbetson*. Only a few works met with any success.

Gatti-Casazza also staged fifty American premieres. He emphasized novelties more than star-vehicles, but he still had his share of stars. Although Sembrich and Eames retired soon after he took the helm, with Melba and Nordica following, he had Caruso and Farrar for over a decade. Caruso's last performance came on December 24, 1920, in Halévy's *La Juive*, and Farrar's on April 22, 1922, in Ruggero Leoncavallo's *Zazà*. Then Chaliapin returned in 1921 for eight seasons. As stars retired, more were introduced to take their places: Lucrezia Bori (November 11, 1912, Puccini's *Manon*), Frieda Hempel (December 27, 1912, Meyerbeer's *Les Huguenots*), Giovanni Martinelli (November 20, 1913, Puccini's *La bohème*), Claudio Muzio (December 4, 1916, Puccini's *Tosca*), Ponselle (November 15, 1918, Verdi's *La forza del destino*), Beniamino Gigli (November 26, 1920, Boïto's *Mefistofele*), Maria Jeritza (November 19, 1921, Erich Korngold's *Die tote Stadt*), Amelita Galli-Curci (November 14, 1921, Verdi's *La traviata*), Lotte Lehmann, (January 11, 1934, Wagner's *Die Walküre*), Tibbett (November 24, 1923, Modest Mussorgsky's *Boris Godunov*), Ezio Pinza (November 1, 1926, Gaspare Spontini's

La Vestale), Lauritz Melchior (February 17, 1926, Wagner's *Tannhäuser*), and Lily Pons (January 3, 1931, Donizetti's *Lucia di Lammermoor*.)

After the stock market crash on October 29, 1929, and the ensuing Depression, financial difficulties beset the company. There was a steep decline in subscriptions and box office income fell sharply. Then Kahn, who personally underwrote Gatti's novelties and paid the deficits, resigned from the board in 1931, and Company reorganized as a non-profit organization, underwritten by public funds. Everyone was now invited to become a Met patron. The 1932-33 season shrank to sixteen weeks and 1933-34 season went down to fourteen weeks. Taylor's *Peter Ibbetson* opened the season on December 26, 1933, the first American opera afforded the honor of opening night. Another American opera, Howard Hanson's *Merry Mount*, received its first stage performance on February 10, 1934. Kahn died March 29, 1934, and the March 30 performance of Wagner's *Parsifal* was dedicated to his memory. The 1934-35 season was Gatti-Casazza's last. Verdi's *Aida* opened the season, followed by the world premiere of Seymour's *In the Pasha's Garden* on January 24, 1935. The season's highlight was the debut of Kirsten Flagstad as Sieglinde, and the mounting of a complete Ring Cycle. With Gatti-Casazza's departure, an era had ended.

For a few weeks, the reins passed to Herbert Witherspoon, but he died of a heart attack in the opera house on May 10, 1935. Edward Johnson, the singer who created Peter Ibbetson at the Met, was the assistant general manager and took over. During his first season, Marjorie Lawrence made her debut in Wagner's *Die Walküre*. Two years later, the world premiere of Damrosch's *The Man Without a Country* took place on May 12, 1937, introducing Helen Traubel. That same season, the only American premiere of Johnson's reign took place, Hageman's *Caponsacchi* on February 4, 1937. The opera house was bought from its boxholders in 1940, and for the first time, the company that owned the opera house was the same company that produced the opera. The 1940s saw two world premieres, Gian Carlo Menotti's *The Island God*, and Rogers's *The Warrior*. Johnson ushered in a Mozart era with revivals of Mozart's *Le nozze di Figaro*, *Don Giovanni*, and *Die Zauberflöte*. New stars graced the stage—Zinka Milanov, Dorothy Kirsten, Eleanor Steber, Risë Stevens, Regina Resnik, Helen Traubel, Jussi Bjoerling, Jan Peerce, Richard Tucker, Leonard Warren, Jerome Hines, and Robert Merrill, and new conductors mounted the podium—Bruno Walter, Fritz Reiner, and Thomas Beecham.

Rudolf Bing took the helm in 1950, and steered the company in a new direction. He lured theater and movie directors to the opera house—Franco Zeffirelli, Alfred Lunt, Tyrone Guthrie, Cyril Ritchard, and Margaret Webster—transforming his productions into exciting theatrical as well as operatic experiences. Creative and imaginative sets occupied the stage, while fresh and stylish costumes dressed the singers. Webster staged the opening night *Don Carlo* with a cast mixing veterans with newcomers—Bjoerling, Hines, Merrill, Delia Rigal, Fedora Barbieri, Caesar Siepi, and Lucine Amara. Fritz Stiedry was on the podium. It was a strong ensemble production—a rare creature at the Met. Bing's first novelty, Igor Stravinsky's *The Rake's Progress*, arrived February 14, 1953. His next followed two years, Strauss's *Arabella*. In January 1955, Bing invited the first black soloist to sing at the Met, Marian Anderson. She made her debut on January 7, 1955, in Verdi's *Il trovatore*. Opening night of the 1956 season introduced Maria Callas in Bellini's *Norma*. She lasted two seasons at the Met before Bing fired her with the comment to the press that the Met was "grateful for her artistry for two seasons, but nevertheless also grateful that the association is ended." Bing attracted both foreign and American talent to the Met, including Rosalind Elias, George London, Giorgio Tozzi, Victoria de los Angeles, Renata Tebaldi, Leonie Rysanek, Mario del Monaco, Franco Corelli, Jon Vickers, Leontyne Price, Joan Sutherland, and Birgit Nilsson, whose debut made the front page of the *New York Times* and *Herald Tribune*. It was the second Golden Age. There was also sadness. Warren died on stage during the battle scene of Verdi's *La forza del destino* in 1960, and Tucker's death fifteen years later warranted the only on-stage funeral held for a singer at the Met. Bing also purged the conducting staff. Giuseppe Antonicelli, Pietro Cimara, Emil Cooper, Wilfrid Pelletier, and Jonel Perlea all departed, and Bruno Walter, Fausto Cleva, and Alberto Erede, among others, took their places.

The seventieth anniversary season featured the first world premiere under Bing's administration, Samuel Barber's *Vanessa*, on January 15, 1958. The first production of Verdi's *Macbeth* at the Met was the other highlight. At $109,626, it was the most expensive production to date. The old Met saw its last novelty on January 23, 1964, the American premiere of Menotti's *The Last Savage*. The building was outdated for opera production almost before it even opened. When Campanini (inaugural night tenor) was asked his opinion about New York's newest cultural jewel, he replied, "The house is no good for opera." The size and shape of the auditorium ordained it for grand opera, but more akin to Meyerbeerian "concerts in costume" that Wagnerian opera. So eighty-three years after the Met on 39th street opened, fifty-seven soloists and eleven conductors paid it a final tribute on April 16, 1966, and the great golden curtain fell for the last time.

On September 16, 1966, a snake slithered between Cleopatra's breasts and delivered a fatal poison as the world premiere of Barber's *Antony and Cleopatra* inaugurated the Met's new home in Lincoln Center. Taking two years to write, the world premiere was overpowered and buried by Zeffirelli's outrageous production. The presence of Jess Thomas and Price in the title roles and Thomas Schippers on the podium could not save the opera. With only eight performances, it was a resounding failure. (The Spoleto Festival resurrected it in 1983 and the Lyric Opera of Chicago in 1991, both with better success.) There was a second novelty that season, Marvin David Levy's *Mourning Becomes Electra*, but it met a similar fate. The opera, like its characters, was damned. Although briefly revived the next season, it had gasped its last breath at the Met.

With the opening of a new, technically advanced opera house, Bing could finally present the dramatic spectacles to which he aspired and for which the Met is famous. Seven additional new productions were staged that inaugural season, including a mesmerizing *Die Frau ohne Schatten*, where at one heart-stopping moment, the entire stage rose sixty feet into the flies and another fully set stage rose from below to replace it.

Probably one of the greatest productions of the era took place on November 18, 1971, when a magical Wagner's *Tristan und Isolde* of August Everding and Schneider-Siemssen transported the lovers and the audience to another world along with the heavenly strains of Nilsson in all her glory. Bing's final season opened as his first, with Verdi's *Don Carlo*. During his twenty-two-year tenure, eighty-seven operas received new dressing. Most were successes. A few were failures.

Göran Gentele took the reins from Bing, but was killed in a car crash in Sardinia

Metropolitan Opera House (New York City, New York).

seven weeks later. Schuyler Chapin took over, followed by Anthony Bliss in 1975, Bruce Crawford a decade later, and Hugh Southern in 1989. Southern survived only a short time, and with his departure, the title of general manager was temporarily retired. Joseph Volpe was named general director and James Levine artistic director, but in 1993, the Met revived the title general manager and bestowed it upon Volpe.

With the resounding failures of the Met's new works, it waited more than twenty years before again taking the risk. This time the works succeeded. John Corigliano's *The Ghosts of Versailles* was introduced on December 19, 1991, and Philip Glass's *The Voyage* on October 12, 1992. The Met commissioned Glass's *The Voyage* to celebrate the quincentennial of Columbus's voyage.

The building of the Met by a few wealthy men who became the stockholders and boxholders had precedent in Europe. Teatro alla Scala, Teatro la Fenice, and Royal Opera House, Covent Garden among others, were constructed the same way. The Met carries both their greatness and their stigma of elitism. It is probably the only opera house in America that has a rich operatic heritage where the majority still attend for social reasons. This, compounded with the absence of surtitles, has resulted in the audience behaving only marginally better than the 1883 inaugural crowd. The Met audience is the worse mannered in America, and one of the worst in the world. The house is star-driven, but the wattage is lower, although it is still one of the few houses that can afford the "astronomically-priced" superstars of the early 1990s — Luciano Pavarotti and Plácido Domingo. The philosophy is, bigger is better, and with a budget topping $110 million, and around $2 million earmarked for a new production, the results can be spectacular. Many of the older productions, however, are disappointing. Most are traditional, although the 1990s ushered in a modicum of adventure. With seven performances a week, the results are a few great evenings and (broadcast) matinees with an overabundance of mediocrity.

The twenty-one opera season (twenty-five in Ring Cycle seasons) offers a traditional schedule (notwithstanding the few novelties that have crept into the repertory in recent seasons — Britten's *Death in Venice* and Verdi's *I Lombardi* and *Stiffelio*) in a repertory-block system. Recent productions include Puccini's *Madama Butterfly*, *Tosca*, and *La bohème*, Verdi's *Aida* and *Otello*, Donizetti's *La fille du régiment* and *Lucia di Lammermoor*, Mozart's *Die Zauberflöte* and *Le nozze di Figaro*, Rossini's *Il barbiere di Siviglia*, and Berlioz's *Les Troyens*. The company performs in the Metropolitan Opera House.

Metropolitan Opera House

Almost from its inception, the old Met had been plagued with technical and physical inadequacies. By the 1950s the need for a new opera house took on a new urgency. The gold paint was peeling from the gilded tiers and the scenery from last night's opera waited on the sidewalk outside the theater, prey to the weather, until it was moved away. But it was not until Congress passed its urban renewal program that the plan for a new opera house took root. On May 14, 1959, twelve thousand people gathered for the ground-breaking ceremony, and on September 16, 1966, the new Met opened. Designed by Wallace K. Harrison, the opera house cost over $50 million. It was the centerpiece of Lincoln Center.

The Metropolitan Opera House is a concrete-and-glass building that rises boldly above the hustle and bustle of Manhattan. Posters of the operas and casts for the week stand perpendicular to the façade. Divided into five majestic glass arches, the façade reveals Marc Chagall's murals. Five tiers of gold, red-and-black faux marble splendor sweep around red plush seats of the horseshoe-shaped auditorium. The gold textured proscenium, crowned by an abstract sculpture frames the golden draped curtain. Small sunburst chandeliers form a semi-circle around the auditorium. Their slow rise toward the ceiling signals the performance is about to begin. The view and sound from the stage do not carry to all parts of the hall. The opera house seats 3,800.

Practical Information. The Met is on Lincoln Center Plaza, between Ninth and Tenth avenues at 63rd Street. The box office is inside on the right. It is open Monday through Saturday from 10:00 A.M. to 8:00 P.M. and on Sunday between 12:00 noon and 6:00 P.M. Tickets can be ordered by telephoning 212-362-6000 during box office hours or writing Met Ticket Service, Metropolitan Opera, Lincoln Center, New York, NY 10023. If you go, stay at The Pierre Four Seasons on Fifth Avenue at 61st Street, New York, NY 10021; telephone 212-838-8000, fax 212-940-8109, reservations 1-800-332-3442. Designed by architects Schultze and Werner in the Georgian style, The Pierre was financed by Kahn (owner of the Met's producing company), among others. Opened in 1930, the hotel has been restored to its original grandeur, offering luxurious accommodations. It is a New York landmark.

COMPANY STAFF AND REPERTORY

General Managers (Metropolitan Opera House). Henry Abbey (1883-1884); Leopold Damrosch (1884-1885, died February 15, 1885); Edmund Stanton (1886-1891); Henry Abbey/Maurice Grau/John B. Schoeffel (1891-1892); Henry Abbey/Maurice Grau/John B. Schoeffel (1893-1897, Abbey died October 17, 1896); Maurice Grau (1898-1903); Heinrich Conried (1903-1908).

General managers (Metropolitan Opera). Giulio Gatti-Casazza/Andreas Dippel (1908-1910); Giulio Gatti-Casazza (1910-1935); Herbert Witherspoon (1935, died May 10, 1935); Edward Johnson (1935-1950); Rudolf Bing (1950-1972); Göran Gentele (1972, died July 1972); Schuyler Chapin (acting, 1972-1975); Anthony Bliss (1975-1985); Bruce Crawford (1986-1989); Hugh Southern (1989-1990); Joseph Volpe (1991-present).

American/United States Premieres (Nassau Street Theater). Fielding's *Mock Doctor* (April 23, 1750); Gay's *The Beggar's Opera* (December 3, 1750); Carey's *Damon and Phillida* (February 18, 1751); Fielding's *Virgin Unmasked* (April 16, 1751); Carey's *The Honest Yorkshireman* (March 2, 1752).

World Premieres (John Street Theater). Hewitt's *The Patriot* (June 5, 1794); Carr's *The Archers* (April 18, 1796); Pélissier's *Edwin and Angelina* (December 19, 1796); Carr's *Bourville Castle* (January 16, 1797).

American/United States Premieres (John Street Theater). Arnold's *The Maid of the Mill* (May 4, 1769); Dibdin's *Padlock* (May 29, 1769); Arne's *Neptune and Amphitrite* (June 3, 1773); Shield's *Rosina* (April 19, 1786); Linley's *The Gentle Shepherd* (June 7, 1786); Dibdin's *The Two Misers* (July 17, 1786); Arnold's *The Castle of Andalusia* (April 21, 1788); Carey's *True Blue* (April 24, 1788); Arnold's *Inkle and Yarico* (July 6, 1789); Carter's *The Fair American* (November 9, 1789); Arnold's *Hunt the Slipper* (May 31, 1793); Bickerstaffe's *The Sultan* (May 3, 1794); Arne's *The Guard Outwitted* (May 7, 1794); Hook's *The Double Disguise* (April 29, 1795); Attwood's *Adopted Child* (May 23, 1796); Arnold's *The Battle of Hexham* (March 20, 1794); Storace's *The Siege of Belgrade* (December 30, 1796); Shield's *Abroad and at Home* (November 10, 1797).

World Premieres (Park Street Theater). Pélissier's *Sterne's Maria* (January 14, 1799); Hewitt's *Mysterious Marriage* (June 5, 1799); Pélissier's *Fourth of July* (July 4, 1799); Hewitt's *The Wild Goose Chase* (January 24, 1800); Hewitt's *Spanish Castle* (December 5, 1800); Hewitt's *Robin Hood* (December 24, 1800); Hewitt's *The Cottagers* (May 6, 1801); Pélissier's *The Good Neighbor* (February 28, 1803); Pélissier's *The Wife of Two Husbands* (April 4, 1804); Garcia's *L'amante astuto* (December 17, 1825); Garcia's *La figlia dell'aria* (April 25, 1826); Horn's *Dido* (April 9, 1828); Berkeley's *Rokeby* (May 17, 1830); Horn's *Nadir and Zuleika* (December 27, 1832); Horn's *Maid of Saxony* (May 23, 1842); Jones's *The Enchanted Horse* (September 30, 1844).

American/United States Premieres (Park Street Theater). Purcell's *King Arthur* (April 25, 1800); Dussek & Kelly's *The Captive of Spilberg* (March 25, 1801); Mazzinghi's *The Turnpike Gate* (June 8, 1801); Dalayrac's *Maison à vendre* (in English as A House to be Sold, May 25, 1803); Kelly's *Love Laughs at Locksmiths* (May 23, 1804); Mazzinghi's *The Exile* (April 27, 1810); Horn's *The Beehive or A Soldier's Love* (October 23, 1811); Bishop's *The Miller and His Men* (July 4, 1814); Braham's *The Devil's Bridge* (July 4, 1815); Bishop's *Brother and Sister* (January 5, 1816); Bishop's *The Slave* (July 4, 1817); Mozart's *Don Giovanni* (in English, Bishop's London version, November 7, 1817); Bishop's *Rob Roy Macgregor* (June 8, 1818); Braham's *The English Fleet* (April 26, 1819); Bishop's *The Barber of Seville* (May 3, 1819); Grétry's *Les événements imprévus* (in English as The Gay Deceivers, Kelly's London version, November 10, 1819); Bishop's *Clari, The Maid of Milan* (November 12, 1823); Bishop's *Maid Marian* (January 9, 1824); Mozart's *Le nozze di Figaro* (in English, May 10, 1824); Weber's *Der Freischütz* (in English as the Free-Shooter, March 2, 1825); Rossini's *Il barbiere di Siviglia* (November 29, 1825); Rossini's *Tancredi* (December 31, 1825); Rossini's *Otello* (February 7, 1826); Rossini's *Il turco in Italia* (March 14, 1826); Mozart's *Don Giovanni* (first performance in Italian, May 23, 1826); Rossini's *La Cenerentola*

(June 27, 1826); Zingarelli's *Giulietta e Romeo* (July 26, 1826); Weber's *Oberon* (September 20, 1826); Bishop's *Native Land* (January 12, 1827); Bishop's *Home, Sweet Home!* (May 25, 1829); Rossini's *Ivanhoe* (in English as The Maid of Judah, February 27, 1832); Mozart's *Die Zauberflöte* (in English as The Magic Flute, April 17, 1833); Meyerbeer's *Robert le diable* (in English, Lacy's London version, April 7, 1834); Auber's *Gustave III* (in English, Cooke's Covent Garden version, July 21, 1834); Barnett's *Mountain Sylph* (May 11, 1835); Vincenzo Bellini's *La sonnambula* (in English as the Sleepwalker, Nov 13, 1835); Balfe's *The Siege of Rochelle* (April 9, 1838); Donizetti's *L'elisir d'amore* (in English as The Elixir of Love, June 18, 1838); Beethoven's *Fidelio* (in English, September 9, 1839); Benedict's *The Gypsy's Warning* (April 20, 1841); Lacy's *The Israelites in Egypt* (October 31, 1842); Balfe's *The Bohemian Girl* (November 25, 1844); Verdi's *Ernani* (April 15, 1847); Balfe's *Maid of Artois* (November 5, 1847).

American/United States Premieres (Palmo's Opera House). Mendelssohn-Bartholdy's *Antigone* (April 7, 1845); Donizetti's *Linda di Chamounix* (January 4, 1847); Coppola's *Nina pazza per amore* (February 5, 1847); Verdi's *I Lombardi* (March 3, 1847).

World Premieres (Astor Place Opera House). Strakosch's *Giovanna prima di Napoli* (January 6, 1851).

American/United States Premieres (Astor Place Opera House). Mercadante's *Il giuramento* (February 14, 1848); Verdi's *Nabucco* (April 4, 1848); Donizetti's *Roberto Devereux* (January 15, 1849); Donizetti's *Anna Bolena* (first performance in Italian, January 7, 1850); Lortzing's *Zar und Zimmermann* (December 9, 1851).

World Premieres (Niblo's Garden). Bristow's *Rip Van Winkle* (September 27, 1855).

American/United States Premieres (Niblo's Garden). Montfort's *Polichinelle* (May 19, 1843); Donizetti's *Gemma di Vergy* (October 2, 1843); Verdi's *Attila* (April 15, 1850); Verdi's *Macbeth* (April 24, 1850); Auber's *La part du diable* (in English as The Devil's Share, May 10, 1852); Flotow's *Martha* (in English on November 1, 1852, and in German on March 13, 1855); Balfe's *The Devil's In It* (December 17, 1852); Donizetti's *La fille du régiment* (in Italian as La figlia del reggimento, January 10, 1853); Massé's *Les noces de Jeannette* (in English as The Marriage of Georgette April 9, 1855); Flotow's *Alessandro Stradella* (April 12, 1855); Balfe's *The Daughter of St. Mark* (June 18, 1855); Lortzing's *Undine* (October 9, 1856); Pacini's *Medea* (September 27, 1860); Balfe's *Satanella* (February 23, 1863); Offenbach's *Barbe-Bleue* (July 13, 1868).

American/United States Premieres (Terrace Garden). Offenbach's *Périnette* (in German as "Paimpol und Perinette," July 2, 1873); Offenbach's *Monsieur et Madame Denis* (July 16, 1873); Dittersdorf's *Doktor und Apotheker* (June 30, 1875); Brüll's *Das goldene Kreuz* (July 19, 1879).

World Premieres (Winter Garden). Mollenhauer's *The Corsican Bride* (June 15, 1863).

American/United States Premieres (Winter Garden). Verdi's *I masnadieri* (May 31, 1860); Gluck's *Orfeo et Euridice* (first performance as opera, in English, May 25, 1863).

World Premieres (Academy of Music). Hopkins's *Samuel* (May 3, 1877); Maretzek's *Sleepy Hollow* (September 25, 1879); de Konski's *Le Sultan de Zanzibar* (May 8, 1886).

American/United States Premieres (Academy of Music). Verdi's *Rigoletto* (February 19, 1855); Verdi's *Il trovatore* (May 2, 1855); Vaccai's *Giulietta e Romeo* (only famous finale, June 15, 1855); Verdi's *La traviata* (December 3, 1856); Mozart's *Le nozze di Figaro* (first performance in Italian, November 23, 1858); Verdi's *Les Vêpres Siciliennes* (in Italian as "I vespri Siciliani," November 7, 1859); Verdi's *Un ballo in maschera* (February 11, 1861); Petrella's *Ione* (April 6, 1863); Verdi's *Aroldo* (May 4, 1863); Peri's *Giuditta* (November 11, 1863); Donizetti's *Don Sébastien* (in Italian, November 25, 1864); Verdi's *La forza del destino* (February 24, 1865); Ricci's *Crispino e la Comare* (October 24, 1865);

Meyerbeer's *L'Africaine* (in Italian, December 1, 1865); Petrella's *Il carnevale di Venezia* (April 3, 1867); Gounod's *Roméo et Juliette* (in Italian, November 15, 1867); Offenbach's *Lischen et Fritzchen* (June 25, 1868); Cagnoni's *Don Bucefalo* (October 18, 1867); Offenbach's *Lischen et Fritzchen* (June 25, 1868); Wallace's *Lurline* (first stage performance, May 13, 1869); de Ferrari's *Pipele* (December 10, 1869); Thomas's *Mignon* (November 22, 1871); Thomas's *Hamlet* (in Italian, March 22, 1872); Verdi's *Aida* (November 26, 1873); Marchetti's *Ruy Blas* (October 14, 1874); Balfe's *The Talisman* (first performance in English, February 10, 1875); Flotow's *L'Ombre* (in Italian as "L'ombra," April 9, 1875); Wagner's *Der fliegende Holländer* (March 12, 1877); Berlioz's *Les Troyens* (in English as "The Trojans", Part II concert form, January 13, 1877); Wagner's *Die Walküre* (April 2, 1877); Verdi's *Don Carlos* (in Italian, Paris version, April 12, 1877); Wagner's *Rienzi* (March 4, 1878); Bizet's *Carmen* (in Italian, October 23, 1878); Offenbach's *Pomme d'Api* (May 20, 1880); Massenet's *Manon* (in Italian, December 23, 1885); Götz's *Der widerspenstigen Zähmung* (in English, January 4, 1886); Verdi's *Otello* (April 16, 1888); Giordano's *Andrea Chénier* (November 13, 1896).

   American/United States Premieres (Manhattan Opera House). Massenet's *Thaïs* (November 25, 1907); Charpentier's *Louise* (January 3, 1908); Giordano's *Siberia* (first performance in Italian, February 5, 1908); Debussy's *Pelléas et Mélisande* (February 19, 1908); Massenet's *Le jongleur de Notre Dame* (November 27, 1908); Blockx's *Die Herbergprinzessin* (in French as "La Princesse d'auberge," March 10, 1909); Massenet's *Sapho* (November 17, 1909); Massenet's *Grisélidis* (January 19, 1910); Strauss's *Elektra* (in French, February 1, 1910); Ganne's *Hans, Le joueur de flute* (in English as "Hans, The Flute Player," September 20, 1910).

   World Premieres (Metropolitan Opera, Metropolitan Opera House on Thirty-Ninth Street). Puccini's *La fanciulla del West* (December 10, 1910); Humperdinck's *Königskinder* (December 28, 1910); Parker's *Mona* (March 14, 1912); Damrosch's *Cyrano* (February 27, 1913); Herbert's *Madeleine* (January 24, 1914); Giordano's *Madame Sans-Gêne* (January 25, 1915); Granados's *Goyescas* (January 28, 1916); de Koven's *The Canterbury Pilgrims* (March 8, 1917); Cadman's *Shanewis* (March 23, 1918); Puccini's *Gianni Schicchi* (December 14, 1918); Puccini's *Suor Angelica* (December 14, 1918); Puccini's *Il tabarro* (December 14, 1918); Breil's *The Legend* (March 12, 1919); Hugo's *The Temple Dancer* (March 12, 1919); Wolff's *L'oiseau bleu* (December 27, 1919); Hadley's *Cleopatra's Night* (January 20, 1921); Taylor's *The King's Henchman* (February 17, 1927); Taylor's *Peter Ibbetson* February 7, 1931); Gruenberg's *The Emperor Jones* (January 7, 1933); Hanson's *Merry Mount* first stage performance, February 10, 1934); Seymour's *In the Pasha's Garden* (January 24, 1935); Damrosch's *The Man Without a Country* (May 12, 1937); Menotti's *The Island God* (February 20, 1942); Rogers's *The Warrior* (January 11, 1947); Barber's *Vanessa* (January 15, 1958).

   American/United States Premieres (Metropolitan Opera, Metropolitan Opera House on Thirty-Ninth Street). Ponchielli's *La gioconda* (December 20, 1883); Goldmark's *Die Königin von Saba* (December 2, 1885); Wagner's *Die Meistersinger von Nürnberg* (January 4, 1886); Wagner's *Tristan und Isolde* (December 1, 1886); Goldmark's *Merlin* (January 3, 1887); Wagner's *Siegfried* (November 9, 1887); Nessler's *Der Trompeter von Säckingen* (November 23, 1887); Weber's *Euryanthe* (December 23, 1887); Spontini's *Fernand Cortez* (in German, January 6, 1888); Wagner's *Götterdämmerung* (first stage performance, January 25, 1888); Wagner's *Das Rheingold* (January 4, 1889); Cornelius's *Der Barbier von Bagdad* (January 3, 1890); Franchetti's *Asrael* (in German, November 26, 1890); Smareglia's *Il vassallo di Szigeth* (in German, December 12, 1890); Ernest II's *Diana von Solange* (January 9, 1891); Bemberg's *Elaine* (December 17, 1894); Verdi's *Falstaff* (February 4, 1895); Massenet's *La Navarraise* (December 11, 1895); Mancinelli's *Ero e Leandro* (March 10, 1899); Puccini's *Tosca* (February 4, 1901); de Lara's *Messaline* (January 22, 1902); Paderewski's *Manru* (February 14, 1902); Smyth's *Der Wald* (March 11, 1903); Wagner's *Parsifal* (first stage performance, December 24, 1903); Giordano's *Fedora* (December 5, 1906); Strauss's *Salome* (January 22, 1907); d'Albert's *Tiefland* (November 23, 1908); Puccini's

Le Villi (December 17, 1908); Catalani's *La Wally* (January 6, 1909); Franchetti's *Germania* (January 22, 1910); Gluck's *Armide* (November 14, 1910); Dukas's *Ariane et Barbe-Bleue* (March 29, 1911); Thuille's *Lobetanz* (November 18, 1911); Wolf-Ferrari's *Le donne curiose* (January 3, 1912); Blech's *Versiegelt* (January 20, 1912); Mussorgsky's *Boris Godunov* (in Italian, March 19, 1913); Strauss's *Der Rosenkavalier* (December 9, 1913); Montemezzi's *L'amore dei tre re* (January 2, 1914); Charpentier's *Julien* (February 26, 1914); Wolf-Ferrari's *L'amore medico* (March 25, 1914); Leoni's *L'oracolo* (February 4, 1915); Borodin's *Prince Igor* (in Italian, December 30, 1915); Gluck's *Iphigénie en Tauride* (in German, November 25, 1916); Zandonai's *Francesca da Rimini* (December 22, 1916); Rabaud's *Mârouf, Savetier du Caire* (December 19, 1917); Mascagni's *Lodoletta* (January 12, 1918); Rimsky-Korsakov's *Zolotoy petushok* (in French as Le coq d'or, March 6, 1918); Leroux's *La Reine Fiammette* (January 24, 1919); Tchaikovsky's *Eugene Onegin* (in Italian, first stage performance, March 24, 1920); Weiss's *Der polnische Jude* (March 9, 1921); Korngold's *Die tote Stadt* (November 19, 1921); Rimsky-Korsakov's *Snegurochka* (in French, January 23, 1922); Mozart's *Così fan tutte* (March 24, 1922); Vittadini's *Anima allegra* (February 14, 1923); von Schillings's *Mona Lisa* (March 1, 1923); Riccitelli's *I compagnacci* (January 2, 1924); Janáček's *Jenůfa* (in German, December 6, 1924); Montemezzi's *Giovanni Gallurese* (February 19, 1925); Giordano's *La cena delle beffe* (January 2, 1926); Stravinsky's *Solovey* (in French as Le rossignol, March 6, 1926); de Falla's *La Vida Breve* (March 6, 1926); Puccini's *Turandot* (November 16, 1926); Korngold's *Violanta* (November 5, 1927); Alfano's *Madonna Imperia* (February 8, 1928); Puccini's *La rondine* (March 10, 1928); Strauss's *Die aegyptische Helena* (November 6, 1928); Respighi's *La campana sommersa* (November 24, 1928); Křenek's *Jonny spielt auf* (January 19, 1929); Pizzetti's *Fra Gherardo* (March 21, 1929); Rimsky-Korsakov's *Sadko* (in French, January 25, 1930); Mussorgsky's *Sorochintsy Fair* (in Italian, November 29, 1930); Lattuada's *Le preziose ridicole* (December 10, 1930); Weinberger's *Švanda dudák* (in German, November 7, 1931); Montemezzi's *La notte de Zoraima* (December 2, 1931); Verdi's *Simon Boccanegra* (January 28, 1932); Rossini's *Il Signor Bruschino* (December 9, 1932); Hageman's *Caponsacchi* (February 4, 1937); Stravinsky's *The Rake's Progress* (February 14, 1953); Strauss's *Arabella* (February 10, 1955); Menotti's *The Last Savage* (January 23, 1964).

World Premieres (Metropolitan Opera House, Metropolitan Opera, Lincoln Center). Barber's *Anthony and Cleopatra* (September 16, 1966); Levy's *Mourning Becomes Elektra* (March 17, 1967); Corigliano's *The Ghosts of Versailles* (December 19, 1991); Glass's *The Voyage* (October 12, 1992).

American/United States Premiere (Metropolitan Opera House, Metropolitan Opera, Lincoln Center). Britten's *Death in Venice* (October 18, 1974).

New Producations During Rudolf Bing's Tenure (Metropolitan Opera House on Thirty-Ninth Street). 1950-51: Don Carlo, Der fliegende Holländer, Der Fledermaus, Cavalleria rusticana/I pagliacci. **1951-52:** Aida, Rigoletto, Così fan tutte, Carmen. **1952-53:** La forza del destino, La bohème, The Rake's Progress. **1953-54:** Faust, Tannhäuser, Il barbiere di Siviglia. **1954-55:** Andrea Chénier, Arabella. **1955-56:** Les conte d'Hoffmann, Don Pasquale, Die Zauberflöte. **1956-57:** Ernani, La Périchole, La traviata. **1957-58:** Eugene Onegin, Don Giovanni, Vanessa, Madama Butterfly. **1958-59:** Cavalleria rusticana/I pagliacci, Macbeth, Wozzeck. **1959-60:** Il trovatore, La nozze di Figaro, Der Zigeunerbaron, Tristan und Isolde, Fidelio, Simon Boccanegra. **1960-61:** Nabucco, L'elisir d'amore, Alceste, Martha, Turandot. **1961-62:** In ballo in maschera. **1962-63:** Die Meistersinger, Ariadne auf Naxos, Adriana Lecouvreur, La sonnambula, Otello. **1963-64:** Aida, Manon, The Last Savage, Falstaff. **1964-65:** Lucia di Lammermoor, Samson et Dalila, Salome. **1965-66:** Faust, Pikovaya dama.

New Producations During Rudolf Bing's Tenure (Metropolitan Opera House, Lincoln Center). 1966-67: Antony and Cleopatra, La gioconda, La traviata, Die Frau ohne Schatten, Elektra, Lohengrin, Peter Grimes, Die Zauberflöte, Mourning Becomes Elektra. **1967-68:** Roméo et Juliette, Hänsel und Gretel, Die Walküre, Carmen, Luisa Miller. **1968-69:** Tosca, Das Rheingold, Der Rosenkavalier, Il trovatore. **1969-70:** Cavalleria rusticana/I pagliacci, Norma. **1970-71:** Orfeo ed Euridice, Parsifal, Fidelio, Werther. **1971-72:** Der Freischütz, Tristan und Isolde, Pelléas et Mélisande, La fille du régiment, Otello.

List of Selected Singers and Conductors Introduced During Bing's Tenure (Metropolitan Opera House on Thirty-Ninth Street). **1950-51:** Singers: Lucine Amara, Victoria de los Angeles, Roberta Peters, Mario del Monaco, Hans Hotter, Cesare Siepi. Conductors: Kurt Adler, Eugene Ormandy. **1951-52:** Singers: Brenda Lewis, George London. Conductors: Renato Cellini. **1952-53:** Singer: Erich Kunz. **1953-54:** Singers: Rosalind Elias, Charles Anthony, James McCracken, Theodor Uppman, Fernando Corena. **1954-55:** Singers: Renata Tebaldi, Marian Anderson, Giorgio Tozzi. Conductors: Dmitry Mitropoulos, Rudolf Kempe. **1955-56:** Singer: Tito Gobbi. Conductor: Thomas Schippers. **1956-57:** Singers: Maria Callas, Irene Dalis, Carlo Bergonzi, Wolfgang Windgassen, Conductor: Jean Morel. **1957-58:** Singers: Inge Borkh, Nicolai Gedda, Robert Nagy, Ezio Flagello. Conductor: Karl Böhm. **1958-59:** Singers: Martina Arroyo, Leonie Rysanek, Mignon Dunn, Cornell MacNeil. **1959-60:** Singers: Birgit Nilsson, Anna Moffo, Teresa Stratas, Elisabeth Söderström, Christa Ludwig, Giulietta Simionato, Jon Vickers, Walter Slezak. **1960-61:** Singers: Leontyne Price, Gabriella Tucci, Eileen Farrell, Franco Corelli. Conductors: Georg Solti, Leopold Stokowski. **1961-62:** Singers: Joan Sutherland, Ingrid Bjoner, Phyllis Curtain, Judith Raskin, Galina Vishnevskaya, Lili Chookasian, John Alexander, Sándor Kónya, George Shirley, Morley Meredith. Conductor: Nello Santi. **1962-63:** Singers: Régine Crespin, Rita Gorr, Janis Martin, Jess Thomas, John Macurdy. Conductor: Lorin Maazel. **1963-64:** Singers: Mary Costa, Shirley Love, Luigi Alva, William Dooley, Justino Díaz, Donald Gramm. Conductor: Leonard Bernstein. **1964-65:** Singers: Elizabeth Schwarzkopf, Bruno Prevedi. Conductor: Georges Prêtre. **1965-66:** Singers: Monserrat Caballé, Mirella Freni, Reri Grist, Pilar Lorengar, Renata Scotto, Grace Bumbry, James King, Alfredo Kraus, Sherrill Milnes, John Reardon, Thomas Stewart, Nicolai Ghiaurov. Conductors: Zubin Mehta, Alain Lombard.

List of Selected Singers and Conductors Introduced During Bing's Tenure (Metropolitan Opera House, Lincoln Center. **1966-67:** Singers: Karen Armstrong, Evelyn Lear, Patricia Welting, Walter Berry, Paul Plishka. Conductors: Richard Bonynge, Colin Davis. **1967-68:** Singers: Teresa Berganza, Fiorenza Cossotto. Conductor: Herbert von Karajan. **1968-69:** Singers: Teresa Zylis-Gara, Judith Forst, Shirley Verrett, Luciano Pavarotti, Plácido Domingo, Renato Bruson, Theo Adam, Martti Talvela. Conductor: Claudio Abbado. **1969-70:** Singers: Judith Blegen, Gilda Cruz-Romo, Gail Robinson, Marilyn Horne, Jean Kraft, Frederica von Stade. **1970-71:** Singers: James Morris, Ruggero Raimondi, Franco Bonisolli. Conductor: James Levine. **1971-72:** Singers: Jeannine Altmeyer, Anja Silja, Louis Quilico. Conductors: Christoph von Dohnanyi, John Pritchard.

Repertory (John Street Theater). **1787-92:** Agreeable Surprise, Banditti, Belle Dorothée, Bird Catcher, Birth of Harlequin, Columbine Invisible, Cymon and Sylvia, Darby's Return, Dead Alive, Deserter, Detection, Devil to Pay, Duenna, Elopement, Fairies, Flitch of Bacon, Flora, Harlequin Balloonist, Inkle and Yarico, King of Genii, Lord of the Manor, Love in a Camp, Love in a Village, Madcap, Magician of the Cave, Maid of the Mill, May Day in Town, Midas, Mock Doctor, Neptune and Amphitrite, Old Soldier, Padlock, Peep Behind the Curtain, Poor Soldier, Restoration of Harlequin, Rival Candidates, Rosina, Selima and Azor, True Blue, Two Misers, Two Philosophers. **1793-97:** Adopted Child, Agreeable Surprise, Alonzo and Imogen, Archers, Ariadne Abandoned by Theseus in the Isle of Naxos, Battle of Hexham, Beggar's Opera, Bird Catcher, Bourville Castle, Children in the Wood, Comus, Cooper, Cymon and Sylvia, Danaides, Darby's Return, Deaf Lover, Death of Captain Cook, Death of Harlequin, Demolition of the Bastille, Deserter, Devil to Pay, Don Juan, Duenna, Edwin and Angelina, Farmer, Flitch of Bacon, Flora, Fountainebleu, Forêt noire, Grateful Lion, Harlequin Fisherman, Harlequin Gardener, Harlequin's Animation, Harlequin's Restoration, Harlequin's Vagaries, Haunted Tower, Highland Reel, Hunt the Slipper, Huntress, Independence of America, Inkle and Yarico, Jeanne d'Arc, Lionel and Clarissa, Lock and Key, Love and Money, Love in a Camp, Love in a Village, Maid of the Mill, Midas, Midnight Wanderer, Mountaineers, My Grandmother, Needs Must, Nootka Sound, No Song, no Supper, Padlock, Patriot, Poor Jack, Poor Soldier, Poor Vulcan, Prisoner, Prize, Purse, Pygmalion, Quaker, Rival Candidates, Robin Hood, Robin Crusoe, Romp, Rosina, Rural Merriment, Selima and Azor, Shelty's Travels, Sicilian Romance, Siege of Belgrade, Siege of Gibraltar, Son-in-law, Sophia of Brabant, Spanish Barber, Sultan, Surrender of Calais, Tammany, Thomas and Sally, Tom Thumb the Great, Trick upon Trick, Two Huntsman and the Milk Maid, Two Misers, Two Philosophers, Tyranny Suppressed, Wapping Landlady, Waterman, Ways and Means, Wedding Ring, Whims of Galatea.

Repertory (Park Street Theater). 1798-1800: Adopted Child, Agreeable Surprise, Ariadne Abandoned by Theseus, Children in the Wood, Columbus, Constellation, Count Benyowsky, Cymon and Sylvia, Death of Captain Cook, Deserter, Doctor and Apothecary, Don Juan, Farmer, Federal Oath, Forêt noire, Fourth of July, Gil Blas, Harlequin's Frolic, Harlequin's Invasion, Harlequin's Vagaries, Haunted Tower, Highland Reel, Inkle and Yarico, Jubilee, King Arthur, Launch, Lock and Key, Love and Money, Midnight Wanderer, Mountaineers, My Grandmother, Mysteries of the Castle, Mysterious Marriage, Neptune and Amphitrite, No Song, no Supper, Old Soldier, Padlock, Patie and Roger, Poor Soldier, Prize, Purse, Quaker, Recruiting Sergeant, Richard Coeur de Lion, Robin Hood, Romp, Rosina, Sailor's Triumph, Selima and Azor, Shelty's Travels, Sicilian Romance, Siege of Belgrade, Siege of Quebec, Smugglers, Son-in-law, Spanish Barber, Sultan, Surrender of Calais, Three and the Deuce, Tom Thumb the Great, Touchstone of Truth, Two Philosophers, Waterman, Ways and Means, Whitsun Frolic, Wildgoose Chase, Zorinsky.

Repertory (Manhattan Opera House). 1906-07: I Puritani, Rigoletto, Faust, Don Giovanni, Carmen, Aida, Lucia di Lammermoor, Carmen, Il trovatore, La traviata, L'elisir d'amore, Les Huguenots, Il barbiere di Siviglia, La sonnambula, Cavalleria rusticana/pagliacci, Mignon, Dinorah, Un ballo in maschera, La bohème, Fra Diavolo, Martha, (Verdi) Requiem, La navarraise. 1907-08: La Gioconda, Carmen, Il trovatore, Aida, Les contes d'Hoffmann, Thaïs, La navarraise/ I pagliacci, Rigoletto, Faust, La Damnation de Faust, Un ballo in maschera, Don Giovanni, Louise, Cavalleria rusticana/I pagliacci, La traviata, Lucia di Lammermoor, Siberia, Pelléas et Mélisande, Dinorah, Crispino e la Comare, Andrea Chénier. 1908-09: Tosca, Thaïs, Samson et Dalila, Lucia di Lammermoor, Les Huguenots, Carmen, Le jongleur de Notre Dame, Il barbiere di Siviglia, Cavalleria rusticana/Le chair/ I pagliacci, Rigoletto, La traviata, La bohème, Les contes d'Hoffmann, Otello, Pelléas et Mélisande, Crispino e la Comare, Salome, Aida, La sonnambula, Louise, I Puritani, Il trovatore, La Princesse d'Auberge, La navarraise/I pagliacci. Preliminary Season (August–October 1909). Le Prophète, Aida, Carmen, Lucia di Lammermoor, La traviata, La Juive, Rigoletto, Cavalleria rusticana/I pagliacci, Tosca, Louise, Il trovatore, Faust, Les contes d'Hoffmann, The Bohemian Girl. 1909-10: Hérodiade, La traviata, Aida, Thaïs, Cavalleria rusticana/I pagliacci, Lucia di Lammermoor, La fille de Madame Angot, Sapho, La fille du régiment/I pagliacci, La Mascotte, Carmen, Tosca, Les Dragons de Villars, Le jongleur de Notre Dame, Les cloches de Corneville, Faust, Tannhäuser, Les contes d'Hoffmann, Grisélidis, La bohème, Samson et Dalila, Elektra, Louise, La navarraise/I pagliacci, Salome, Rigoletto, Lakmé.

Repertory (By Year of First Performance, Metropolitan Opera, Metropolitan Opera House on Thirty-Ninth Street). 1883: Faust, La gioconda, Il barbiere di Siviglia, Don Giovanni, Lohengrin, Lucia di Lammermoor, Mefistofele, Mignon, I Puritani, Robert le Diable, La sonnambula, La traviata, Il trovatore. 1884: Tannhäuser, Carmen, Fidelio, Der Freischütz, Guillaume Tell, Hamlet, Les Huguenots, Martha, La muette de Portici, Le prophète. 1885: Die Königin von Saba, La Juive, Rigoletto, Die Walküre. 1886: Tristan und Isolde, Die Meistersinger von Nürnberg, Aida, Das goldene Kreuz, Rienzi. 1887: Der Trompeter von Säckingen, Euryanthe, Siegfried, Merlin. 1888: Fernand Cortez, Götterdämmerung, L'Africaine. 1889: Das Rheingold, Un ballo in maschera. 1890: Der Barbier von Bagdad, Asrael, Il vassallo di Szigeth, Der fliegende Holländer, Norma. 1891: Diana von Solange, Cavalleria rusticana, Orfeo ed Euridice, Roméo et Juliette. 1892: Dinorah, Lakmé, Otello. 1893: I pagliacci, Philémon et Baucis. 1894: Elaine, Le nozze di Figaro, Semiramide,

Werther. **1895:** Falstaff, Navarraise, La favorita, Manon, Samson et Dalila. **1897:** Le Cid. **1899:** Ero e Leandro. **1900:** La bohème, Don Pasquale. Die lustigen Weiber von Windsor, Die Zauberflöte. **1901:** Tosca, Messa da Requiem, Salammbô. **1902:** Messaline, Manru, La fille du régiment. **1903:** Der Wald, Parsifal, Ernani. **1904:** La dame blanche, L'elisir d'amore, Lucrezia Borgia. **1905:** Die Fledermaus, Hänsel und Gretel. **1906:** Fedora, La damnation de Faust, Der Zigeunerbaron. **1907:** Salome, Adriana Lecouvreur, Iris, Madama Butterfly, Manon Lescaut. **1908:** Tiefland, Le Villi. **1909:** La Wally, Prodaná nevěsta (The Bartered Bride). **1910:** Germania, Armide, Königskinder, Alessandro Stradella, Fra Diavolo, The Pipe of Desire, Pikovaya dama. **1911:** Ariane et Barbe-Bleue, Lobetanz. **1912:** Le donne curiose, Versiegelt, Mona, Il segreto di Susanna. **1913:** Cyrano, Boris Godunov, Les contes d'Hoffmann. **1914:** L'amore dei tre re, Madeleine, Julien, L'amore medico. **1915:** Madame Sans-Gêne, L'oracolo Prince Igor. **1916:** Goyescas, Iphigénie en Tauride, Francesca da Rimini, Der widerspenstigen Zähmung. **1917:** The Canterbury Pilgrims, Mârouf, Savetier du Caire, Thaïs. **1918:** Lodoletta, Zolotoy petushok (The Golden Cockerel), Shanewis, Gianni Schicchi/ Suor Angelica/Il tabarro, La forza del destino, Oberon. **1919:** La Reine Fiammette, The Legend/The Temple Dancer, La fanciulla del West, L'oiseau bleu, Crispino e la Comare, L'italiana in Algeri, Mireille. **1920:** Eugene Onegin, Don Carlo, Zazà. **1921:** Der polnische Jude, Cleopatra's Night, Die tote Stadt, Andrea Chénier, Louise. **1922:** Snegurochka, Così fan tutte, Loreley, Le Roi d'Y's. **1923:** Anima allegra, Mona Lisa, L'amico Fritz. **1924:** I compagnacci, Jenůfa, La habanera, Le Roi de Lahore. **1925:** Giovanni Gallurese, I gioielli della Madonna, L'heure. espagnole, Pelléas et Mélisande, La vestale. **1926:** La cena delle beffe, Solovey (The Nightingale), La Vida Breve, Turandot. **1927:** The King's Henchman, Violanta. **1928:** Madonna Imperia, La rondine, Die aegyptische Helena, La campana sommersa. **1929:** Jonny spielt auf, Fra Gherardo, Luisa Miller. **1930:** Sadko, Sorochintsy Fair, Le preziose ridicole. **1931:** Peter Ibbetson, Švanda dudák, La notte de Zoraima, Boccaccio. **1932:** Simon Boccanegra, Il Signor Bruschino, Donna Juanita, Elektra. **1933:** The Emperor Jones. **1934:** Merry Mount, Linda di Chamounix. **1935:** In the Pasha's Garden, La serva padrona. **1936:** Caponsacchi. **1937:** The Man Without a Country, Il matrimonio segreto. **1938:** Amelia al ballo. **1941:** Alceste. **1942:** The Island God, Phoebus and Pan. **1946:** Die Entführung aus dem Serail. **1947:** The Warrior. **1948:** Peter Grimes. **1950:** Khovanshchina. **1953:** The Rake's Progress. **1955:** Arabella. **1956:** La périchole. **1958:** Vanessa. **1959:** Macbeth, Wozzeck. **1960:** Nabucco. **1962:** Ariadne auf Naxos. **1964:** The Last Savage.

Repertory (By Year of First Performance, Metropolitan Opera, Metropolitan Opera House, Lincoln Center). **1966-67:** Antony and Cleopatra, Mourning Becomes Electra, Die Frau ohne Schatten. **1973-74:** A Kékszakállú herceg vára (Duke Bluebeard's Castle), Les Troyens, I vespri siciliani. **1974-75:** L'assedio di Corinto, Death in Venice. **1976-77:** Dialogues des Carmélites, Esclarmonde. **1978-79:** Billy Budd. **1979-80:** Aufstieg und Fall der Stadt Mahagonny. **1980-81:** Les mamelles de Tirésias, L'enfant et les sortilèges. **1981-82:** Oedipus Rex. **1982-83:** Idomeneo. **1983-84:** Rinaldo. **1984-85:** La clemenza di Tito, Porgy and Bess. **1985-86:** Samson et Dalila. **1988-89:** Giulio Cesare, Erwartung. **1990-91:** Kát'a Kabanová. **1991-92:** The Ghosts of Versailles. **1992-93:** The Voyage. **1993-94:** Stiffelio, I Lombardi.

Repertory (1983-1994, Metropolitan Opera, Metropolitan Opera House, Lincoln Center). **1983-84:** Ernani, Francesca da Rimini, Rinaldo, Les Troyens, Dialogues des Carmélites, Tristan und Isolde, Hänsel und Gretel, Fidelio, La bohème, Aufstieg und Fall der Stadt Mahagonny, Macbeth, La traviata, Tannhäuser, Don Giovanni, Zolotoy petushok (The Golden Cockerel)/Oedipus Rex, Arabella, La forza del destino, Die Entführung aus dem Serail, Billy Budd, Don Carlo. **1984-85:** Il barbiere di Siviglia, Elektra, Porgy and Bess, Tosca, Simon Boccanegra, Les contes d'Hoffmann, La bohème, Otello, Rigoletto, Lulu, Wozzeck, Die Meistersinger, Ernani, Ariadne auf Naxos, Parsifal, Lohengrin, Così fan tutte, La clemenza di Tito, Eugene Onegin, Manon Lescaut, Aida. **1985-86:** Tosca, Jenůfa, Falstaff, Der Rosenkavalier, Khovanshchina, La traviata, Porgy and Bess, Cavalleria rusticana/I pagliacci, Le nozze di Figaro, L'italiana in Algeri, Lohengrin, Roméo et Juliette, Idomeneo, L'enfant et les sortilèges/Les mamelles de Tirésias, Samson et Dalila, Francesca da Rimini, Carmen,

Simon Boccanegra, Aida, Don Carlo, Parsifal. **1986-87**: Die Walküre, Aida, Manon Lescaut, Madama Butterfly, Le nozze di Figaro, Tosca, Der Rosenkavalier, Roméo et Juliette, I Puritani, Fidelio, Die Fledermaus, La bohème, Rigoletto, Tannhäuser, La clemenza di Tito, Manon, Carmen, Boris Godunov, Turandot, Dialogues des Carmélites, Samson et Dalila, Parsifal. **1987-88**: Das Rheingold, Siegfried, Il trovatore, Ariadne auf Naxos, La bohème, Così fan tutte, L'elisir d'amore, Die entführung aus dem Serail, Die Fledermaus, Les contes d'Hoffmann, Khovanschchina, Luisa Miller, Lulu, Macbeth, Manon, Otello, Pelléas et Mélisande, Tosca, La traviata, Turandot, Die Walküre, Werther. **1988-89**: A Kékszakállú herceg vára (Duke Bluebeard's Castle), Carmen, Billy Budd, L'elisir d'amore, Lucia di Lammermoor, Giulio Cesare, Hänsel und Gretel, I pagliacci, Cavalleria rusticana, Werther, Idomeneo, Le nozze di Figaro, La bohème, Madama Butterfly, Il barbiere di Siviglia, Erwartung, Die Fledermaus, Salome, Eugene Onegin, Aida, Don Carlo, Rigoletto, Il trovatore, Götterdämmerung, Das Rheingold, Siegfried, Die Walküre. **1989-90**: Don Giovanni, Faust, Der fliegende Holländer, Rigoletto, La traviata, Aida, Il barbiere di Siviglia, La bohème, Così fan tutte, Die Entführung aus dem Serail, Die Fledermaus, Die Frau ohne Schatten, La gioconda, Les contes d'Hoffmann, Manon Lescaut, Otello, Porgy and Bess, Samson et Dalila, Il trittico, Il trovatore, Turandot, Wozzeck. **1990-91**: Un ballo in maschera, Kát'a Kabanová, Parsifal, Semiramide, Die Zauberflöte, Andrea Chénier, La bohème, Boris Godunov, La clemenza di Tito, Don Giovanni, Faust, Fidelio, Die Fledermaus, Luisa Miller, Le nozze di Figaro, Porgy and Bess, I Puritani, Rigoletto, Der Rosenkavalier, Salome, Tosca, La traviata. **1991-92**: Don Giovanni, Un ballo in maschera, Die Zauberflöte, Idomeneo, La fanciulla del West, L'elisir d'amore, Aida, Così fan tutte, La traviata, Die Entführung aus dem Serail, The Ghosts of Versailles, La bohème, Der fliegende Holländer, Turandot, Fidelio, Tannhäuser, Il barbiere di Siviglia, Rigoletto, Don Carlo, Le nozze di Figaro, Parsifal, Elektra, Billy Budd. **1992-93**: Les contes d'Hoffmann, Un ballo in maschera, Madama Butterfly, Falstaff, The Voyage, Tosca, Semiramide, L'elisir d'amore, Lucia di Lammermoor, La bohème, Eugene Onegin, Die Walküre, Jenůfa, Die Meistersinger, Die Zauberflöte, Il trovatore, Der Rosenkavalier, Cavalleria rusticana, La fanciulla del West, Ariadne auf Naxos, La traviata, Das Rheingold, Siegfried, Götterdämmerung. **1993-94**: Madama Butterfly, Fidelio, Tosca, Die Zauberflöte, Stiffelio, La bohème, Rusalka, I Lombardi, Les Troyens, Il barbiere di Siviglia, Elektra, Lucia di Lammermoor, Aida, Le nozze di Figaro, Death in Venice, Le fille du régiment, Dialogues des Carmélites, Adriana Lecouvreur, Otello, Der fliegende Holländer, Ariadne auf Naxos.

• *New York City Opera* •

Giacomo Puccini's *Tosca* inaugurated the City Center Opera Company, the original name of the New York City Opera, on February 21, 1944, in the Mecca Temple. The previous year, Mayor Fiorello La Guardia had founded the City Center of Music and Drama, of which the City Opera was a part, to provide everything the Met did not—opportunity for American artists, affordable tickets, and opera as music theater. Mayor La Guardia selected Hungarian-born conductor László Halász, from sixty-three candidates, to head the newly-formed City Center Opera Company. Located at 133 West 55th Street, the company provided opera to the general public at ticket prices that were a throwback to the mid-1800s: 75¢ to $2. To keep costs down, Halász restricted the initial repertory to those operas for which he already had sets and costumes. He had previously headed the St. Louis Grand Opera Association, which went bankrupt shortly before the Center City Company was founded, and acquired the Grand Opera's scenery and costumes for a small fee. Halász, nevertheless, wanted to give the company an identity, so he presented one novelty each season, often in English.

The first season (winter 1944) lasted from February 21 to 27 and offered Puccini's *Tosca* (in Italian), Friedrich von Flotow's *Martha* (the novelty, in English), and Georges Bizet's *Carmen* (in French). The opening performance experienced some mishaps, including guns that did not fire for the Act III execution of Mario Cavaradossi. Cavaradossi obliged by dying of a heart attack instead. Overall the season was deemed a success, since the deficit was only $128 for the nine performances. The one sour note to the auspicious beginning was the loss to the Met of three of the company's better singers. (This problem still plagues the company, since they do not have the budget to compete with the Met.) The spring season (May 1–14) added Puccini's *La bohème* and the doublebill of Pietro Mascagni's *Cavalleria rusticana* / Ruggero Leoncavallo's *I pagliacci* to the repertory. One member of the cast of Leoncavallo's *I pagliacci* made history. On May 5, 1944, Todd Duncan became the first black artist to sing a leading role with a major American company. The season was not as successful as the first. Performances took place during an unseasonably hot May, and the Mecca Temple was not air-conditioned. In addition, there was competition. Fortune Gallo was in town with his San Carlo Grand Opera Company, playing at the air-conditioned Center Theater, and the New Yorkers preferred the cooler environment. The fall (third) season opened on November 9, 1944, with Puccini's *Manon Lescaut*, scheduled primarily as a vehicle for Dorothy Kirsten. Kirsten also sang Mimi. Johann Strauß's *Der Zigeunerbaron* (in English as The Gypsy Baron) was the novelty. Strauß's *Der Zigeunerbaron* replaced Flotow's *Martha*, which had lost its box office appeal. Julius Rudel, who became the company's fourth general director in 1957, made his conducting debut on November 25, 1944, in Strauß's *Der Zigeunerbaron*.

Although 1944 offered three distinct opera seasons, two seasons (spring and fall) emerged as the norm beginning in 1945 — one preceding the Met's opening, and one after the Met's season closed. Works added to the repertory during 1945 included Bedřich Smetana's *Prodaná nevěsta* (The Bartered Bride), Richard Wagner's *Der fliegende Holländer*, and Charles Gounod's *Faust*. The highlight of the 1946 season was the New York premiere of Richard Strauss's *Ariadne auf Naxos* with Ella Flesch in the title role, and Halász on the podium.

Premieres, including William Grant Still's *The Troubled Island*, Ermanno Wolf-Ferrari's *Quattro rusteghi* and David Tamkin's *The Dybbuk*, soon became the City Opera's trademark, and they began to grace the stage regularly. Music critic Olin Downes called Still's *Dybbuk* "one of the most brilliant and revealing [operas] that this enterprising company has given in any of its novelties." Tragedy also struck during the 1951 (fall) season. During the first act of Richard Wagner's *Die Meistersinger*, Oscar Natzka (Veit Pogner) suffered a heart attack. By 1951, the disagreements that had developed between the board and Halász, especially over the board's desire to cancel the world premiere of Tamkin's *The Dybbuk*, reached a boiling point. Halász, with the artistic staff behind him, won the battle for Tamkin's *The Dybbuk*, but eventually lost the war. He was dismissed "as threat to the prosperity and advancement of the City Center" one year before his contract ended. Halász sued the City Center Opera for $35,000. Although the court found that the City Center Opera had dismissed him with insufficient cause, the court did not award him the $35,000 he demanded, but only $15,000. Nevertheless, Halász felt vindicated.

Joseph Rosenstock took the helm in the spring of 1952. Rosenstock, who had been with the company since October 14, 1948, when he conducted Wolfgang Amadeus Mozart's *Le nozze di Figaro*, opened his first season conducting Strauss's *Der Rosenkavalier* on March 20, 1952. He also revived Tamkin's *The Dybbuk*, offered Béla Bartók's *A Kékszakállú herceg vára* (Duke Bluebeard's Castle), and Gian Carlo Menotti's *Amahl and the Night Visitors*. Since the company was experiencing severe financial difficulties that threatened its very survival, it made its first public appeal for funds. The response was heartening and over $140,000 was raised, enabling the American premiere of Gottfried von Einem's *Der Prozess* (in English), with the debut of Phyllis Curtain, to take place on October 22, 1953. The year 1954 witnessed the world premiere of Aaron Copland's *The Tender Land* on April 1, in an delightful season that opened on March 25 with Strauss's *Salome* with Curtin in the title role and Rosenstock on the podium. New York saw William Walton's *Troilus and Cressida* for the first time on October 21, 1955. Rosenstock was then besieged by "warfare," the likes of which had not been seen since Halász's era, and resigned at the ended of the 1956 spring season. Diverse repertory, ensemble singing, and novelties defined Rosenstock's reign.

The noted international conductor Erich Leinsdorf presided over the company for the fall of 1956. Although he introduced a revolving stage for set designs and several twentieth-century works, including the premieres of Frank Martin's *Der Sturm*, Carl Orff's *Der Mond*, and Carlisle Floyd's *Susannah*, attendance averaged only fifty-seven percent and eight of the scheduled thirty-nine performances had to be canceled. His grand plans for the revitalization of City Center Opera proved too expensive, resulting in the cancellation of the 1957 spring season. The financial situation had become so dire that consideration was given to converting the City Center Opera into an "Opéra Comique" run by the Metropolitan Opera! Leinsdorf never received payment for the season he presided over the company.

On January 17, 1957, the City Center board of directors appointed Julius Rudel as the company's fourth general director, a position he held for more than two decades. Puccini's *Turandot* with Rudel in the pit, opened the fall 1957 season, but it was the 1958 spring season that generated the excitement. With a grant from the Ford Foundation, the City Center mounted a season of American works that opened with Douglas Moore's *The Ballad of Baby Doe* on April 3, 1958, with Beverly Sills in the title role and Emerson Buckley on the podium. Mark Bucci's *Tale for Deaf Ear*, Leonard Bernstein's *Trouble in Tahiti*, Kurt Weill's *Lost in the Stars*, Vittorio Giannini's *The Taming of the Shrew*, Marc Blitzstein's *Regina*, Menotti's *The Old Maid and the Thief/ The Medium*, Floyd's *Susannah* and the world premiere of Robert Kurka's *The Good Soldier Schweik* on April 23, 1958, completed this first all-American season. Kurka had tragically died four months earlier of leukemia at age thirty-five, lending a somber note to the world premiere of his opera.

A second American opera season followed in the spring of 1959, opening on March 30, 1959, with Menotti's *Maria Golovin*. Weill's *Street Scene*, Moore's *The Ballad of Baby Doe*, Lee Hoiby's *The Scarf* (United States premiere)/ Moore's *The Devil and Daniel Webster*, Floyd's *Wuthering Heights*, Robert Ward's *He Who Gets Slapped*, Norman Dello Joio's *The Triumph of Saint Joan*/Menotti's *The Medium*, Blitzstein's *Regina*, and the world premiere of Hugo Weisgall's *Six Characters in Search of an Author* were in the repertory. Weisgall's work featured Beverly Sills and John Macurdy. Floyd's *Wuthering Heights* boasted Curtain, John Reardon and Patricia Neway with Rudel conducting. The second American season was more successful artistically and better received than the first, prompting one critic to write, "I shall be surprised if musical history does not record that American opera, as a movement, had its beginnings at the New York City Center in the spring seasons of 1958 and '59." The City Center Company finally had found an identity. The Ford Foundation grant enabled a large infusion of new American works into the repertory, and the continued staging of world premieres and other contemporary works. Operas introduced from the City Center stage between 1961 and 1965 included Moore's *The Wings of the Dove*, Ward's *The Crucible*, Abraham Ellstein's *The Golem*, Floyd's *The Passion of Jonathan Wade*, Jerome Moross's *Gentlemen Be Seated*, Hoiby's *Natalia Petrovna*, Jack Beeson's *Lizzie Borden*, and Ned Rorem's *Miss Julie*.

The American premiere of Alberto Ginastera's *Don Rodrigo* celebrated the company's move into its new home, the New York State Theater, on February 22, 1966. One critic wrote of the opera, "It was for all concerned a brilliant triumph. The most costly production in the company's history was lavished on one of the most stage-worthy new operas to be heard in New York in many season." Twentieth-century opera, featuring the American premiere of Gottfried von Einem's *Dantons Tod* on March 9, 1966, highlighted the season. Other works included Weill's *Street Scene*, Moore's *The Ballad of Baby Doe*, Francis Poulenc's *Dialogues des Carmélites*, Igor Stravinsky's *Oedipus Rex*/Carl Orff's *Carmina Burana*, Sergey Prokofiev's *Lyubov' k tryom apel'sinam* (The Love For Three Oranges), Menotti's *The Consul*, Strauss's *Capriccio*, and Dmitry Shostakovich's *Katerina Izmaylova*. Plácido Domingo, who made his company debut in Puccini's *Madama Butterfly* the previous season, created the title role in Ginastera's *Don Rodrigo*. Other renown artists who sang with the City Opera early in their careers were Shirley Verrett in 1958, Tatiana Troyanos in 1963, and Sherrill Milnes in 1964. That same year, Norman Treigle sang an electrifying Modest Mussorgsky's *Boris Godunov* propelling him to stardom, and two years later, Beverly Sills's appearance in Georg Friedrich Händel's *Giulio Cesare* launched her international career. One critic wrote that "her coloratura is unmatched by anyone's."

Vittorio Giannini's *The Servant of Two Masters* on March 9, 1967, marked another Ford Foundation–supported world premiere. It survived only one season. Sills as Queen of Shemakha and Treigle as King Dodon in Rimsky-Korsakov's *Zolotoy petushok* (The Golden Cockerel) highlighted the 1967 fall season. Spring of 1968 saw several more twentieth-century operas including Ward's *The Crucible*, Stravinsky's *Oedipus Rex*, Orff's *Carmina Burana*, and the New York premieres of Ginastera's *Bomarzo* and Moore's *Carry Nation*. The world premiere of Weisgall's *Nine Rivers from Jordan*, another Ford Foundation–supported work, was described by *Opera*, January 1969, as a "disaster," followed by the comment that "Proof has been offered one wearying time more that viable opera cannot be created by *fiat* or foundation grants." Notwithstanding the failure of Weisgall's work, another Ford Foundation–supported world premiere, Menotti's *The Most Important Man*, took place on March 7, 1971.

The repertory gradually included more seventeenth-, eighteenth-, and nineteenth-century operas. Sills assayed a series of memorable *bel canto* works—*Maria Stuarda*, *Roberto Devereux*, *Lucrezia Borgia*, and *Anna Bolena*, and no one who witnessed Treigle's portrayal of Mefistofele in Boïto's opera could ever forget it. Three of Claudio Monteverdi's operas, *Il ritorno di Ulisse in patria* (New York premiere), *La favola d'Orfeo* (New York stage premiere), and *L'incoronazione di Poppea* had entered the repertory and other early works, like Luigi Cherubini's *Medée*, and Wolfgang Amadeus Mozart's *Idomeneo* graced the stage. Twentieth century works, however, were not neglected. Leoš Janáček's *Věc Makropulos*, Benjamin Britten's *Albert Herring*, Hoiby's *Summer and Smoke*, Ginastera's *Beatrix Cenci*, Korngold's *Die tote Stadt*, Henze's *Der junge Lord*, the world premiere of Leon Kirchner's *Lily*, and the American premieres of Joseph Tal's *Ashmedai*, and Thea Musgrave's *The Voice of Ariadne* all graced the stage. Both Tal's *Ashmedai* and Kirchner's *Lily* were fiascos. With Tal's *Ashmedai*, half the audience did not return after the first intermission. During Kirchner's *Lily*, they did not even wait for the intermission.

Although the heavy emphasis of twentieth-century works of the Rudel era allowed several contemporary operatic composers to see their work produced, it discouraged many people from experiencing opera, resulting in poor attendance and box office receipts. Of the eighty-five works that Rudel introduced by the end of 1975, only half survived more than one season, heavily draining the budget. Consequently, after twenty-two years at the helm, Rudel was asked to step down to occupy a newly created position of principal conductor. His final season opened on February 22, 1979, with Giordano's *Andrea Chénier*. Rudel was on the podium for the only novelty of the season, the world premiere of Dominick Argento's *Miss Havisham's Fire* on March 22, 1979.

Sills took the helm on July 1, 1979, with the task to rescue the company from financial ruin. During her decade-long reign, she placed the company on sound financial footing and steered it into adventurous waters of a different kind — reviving neglected eighteenth-century masterpieces, and neglected works by famous composers. Counted among the offerings were Henry Purcell's *Dido & Aeneas*, Handel's *Alcina*, Mozart's *L'oca del Cairo*, Gioachino Rossini's *Le Comte Ory*, Giuseppe Verdi's *Il Lombardi*, *Nabucco*, and *Attila*, and the American premiere of Richard Wagner's *Die Feen*. Nevertheless, among her twenty productions each season, some new works appeared — a doublebill of Silverman's *Madame Adare/* Pasatieri's *Before Breakfast*, Anthony Davis's *The Life and Times of Malcolm X*, and Jay Reise's *Rasputin*. Musicals entered the repertory as well — Richard Adler and Jerry Ross's *The Pajama Game*, Rogers and Hammerstein's *The Sound of Music*, Stephen Sondheim's *A Little Night Music*, and Frank Loesser's *The Most Happy Fella*. Sills maintained a hectic schedule of six performances a week, leaving little time for rehearsal, and a decline in artistic standards ensued.

When Christopher Keene took over in 1990, he trimmed the schedule to fourteen works a season with three or four operas a week. The program reverted to "difficult" twentieth-century works — Arnold Schönberg's *Moses und Aron*, Bernd-Alois Zimmermann's *Die Soldaten*, Janáček's *Z mrtvého domu* (From the House of the Dead), and Ferruccio Busoni's *Doktor Faust* among them — but these did not draw sufficient box-office, and a planned Janáček's *Mr Brouček's Excursions* was canceled. More standard fare and musicals now populate the repertory, and these, unfortunately, are the company's Achilles' heel.

The company celebrated its Golden Anniversary in 1993 with a World Premiere Festival that included Ezra Laderman's *Marilyn*, Weisgall's *Ester*, and the 1988 version of Lukas Foss's *Griffelkin*. Future plans call for the long-delayed premiere of David Diamond's *The Noblest Game*. For over half a century, the New York City Opera has offered a stage for young American singers to perfect their art. Counted among the "graduates" are Samuel Ramey, Jerry Hadley, June Anderson, and Carol Vaness. You will see the stars of tomorrow, not today, at City Opera.

The fourteen-opera season offers "war horses," operetta, and musicals with one or two contemporary pieces in a repertory system. Recent operas include Mozart's *Le nozze di Figaro*, Puccini's *La bohème, Tosca, Turandot* and *La rondine*, Bizet's *Carmen*, Arthur Sullivan's *The Mikado*, and Richard Rogers *Cinderella*. The company performs in the New York State Theater.

New York State Theater

A showcase program inaugurated the New York State Theater on April 23, 1964. The program, which included the New York City Ballet dancing George Balanchine's *Allegro Brillante* and *Stars and Stripes* and the newly formed Music Theater (which folded in 1970) staging a scene from *Carousel*, was planned to demonstrate the theater's great versatility. The New York State Theater, designed by Philip Johnson, was the second building erected in Lincoln Center. The city of New York owns the theater.

The New York State Theater anchors the left side of Lincoln Center (viewed from Columbus Avenue). A rectangular building of white travertine stone, dark metal, and glass, it boasts a soaring portico that runs the length of the façade. The lobby provides a huge promenade area. The auditorium holds five tiers that soar toward a geometrically-patterned ceiling and sweep around red continental-style orchestra seats. A globe of headlights illuminated the hall. The theater seats 2,279.

Practical Information. The New York State Theater is on Lincoln Center Plaza, between Ninth and Tenth avenues at 63rd Street. The box office, in the center of the entrance lobby, is open Monday from 10:00 A.M. to 7:30 P.M., Tuesday through Saturday from 10:00 A.M. to 8:30 P.M., and on Sunday from 11:30 A.M. to 7:30 P.M. Tickets can be ordered by telephoning 212-496-0600, Monday through Friday between 10:00 A.M. and 5:00 P.M., by faxing 212-580-2545, or by writing New York City Opera, New York State Theater, 20 Lincoln Center, New York, NY 10023. If you visit, stay at The Pierre Four Seasons at Fifth Avenue at 61st Street, New York, NY 10021; telephone 212-838-8000, fax 212-940-8109, reservations 1-800-332-3442. A New York hotel landmark for sixty years, the Pierre has been restored to its original grandeur and luxury. The Pierre is a historically significant building.

COMPANY STAFF AND REPERTORY

General/Artistic Directors. László Halász (1944-1951); Joseph Rosenstock (1951-1956); Erich Leinsdorf (Fall 1956); Julius Rudel (1957-1979); Beverly Sills (1979-1989); Christopher Keene (1990-present)

World Premieres (Mecca Temple Auditorium, before New York City Opera). Weinberg's *Hechalutz.* (in Hebrew, November 25, 1934).

American/United States Premieres (Mecca Temple Auditorium, before New York City Opera). Stanislaw Moniuszko's *Straszny dwór* (The Haunted Castle, April 24, 1927); Mussorgsky's *Khovanshchina* (first performance in Russian, March 7, 1931); Rimsky-Korsakov's *Zolotoy petushok* (The Golden Cockerel, first performance in Russian, March 28, 1932); Lissenko's *Taras Bulba* (April 21, 1940).

World Premieres (New York City Opera). Still's *Troubled Island* (March 31, 1949); Tamkin's *The Dybbuk* (October 4, 1951); Copland's *The Tender Land* (April 1, 1954); Kurka's *Good Soldier Schweik* (April 23, 1958); Weisgall's *Six Characters in Search of an*

New York State Theater (New York City, New York).

Author (April 26, 1959); Moore's *The Wings of the Dove* (October 12, 1961); Ward's *The Crucible* (October 26, 1961); Ellstein's *The Golem* (March 22, 1962); Floyd's *The Passion of Jonathan Wade* (October 11, 1962); Moross's *Gentlemen be Seated* (October 10, 1963); Hoiby's *Natalia Petrovna* (October 8, 1964); Beeson's *Lizzie Borden* (March 25, 1965); Rorem's *Miss Julie* (November 4, 1965); Gianni's *The Servant of Two Masters* (March 9, 1967); Weisgall's *Nine Rivers from Jordan* (October 10, 1968); Menotti's *The Most Important Man* (March 7, 1971); Kirchner's *Lily* (April 14, 1977); Argento's *Miss Havisham's Fire* (March 22, 1979); Silverman's *Madame Adare*/Pasatieri's *Before Breakfast* (October 9, 1980); (Jan) Bach's *The Student From Salamance* (October 9, 1980); Davis's *The Life and Times of Malcolm X* (September 28, 1986); Reise's *Rasputin* (September 17, 1988); Laderman's *Marilyn* (October 6, 1993); Foss's *Griffelkin* (1988 version, October 7, 1993); Weisgall's *Ester* (October 8, 1993).

American/United States Premieres (New York City Opera). Wolf-Ferrari's *I quattro rusteghi* (in English as "Four Ruffians," October 18, 1951); von Einem's *Der Prozess* (in English, October 22, 1953); Martin's *The Tempest* (October 11, 1956); Egk's *Der Revisor* (in English, October 19, 1960); Prokofiev's *Ognennïy angel* (in English as "The Fiery Angel," September 22, 1965); von Einem's *Dantons Tod* (in English, March 9, 1966); Tal's *Ashmedai* (April 1, 1976); Musgrave's *The Voice of Ariadne* (September 30, 1977); Weill's *Der Silbersee* (in English as "Silverlake," March 20, 1980); Wagner's *Die Feen* (February 14, 1982); Janáček's *Z mrtvého domu* (first stage performance, in English as "From the House of the Dead," August 28, 1990).

Repertory (By Year of First Performance). **1944**: Tosca, Martha, Carmen, La bohème, Cavalleria rusticana/I pagliacci, La traviata, Manon Lescaut, Die Zigeunerbaron. **1945**: Der fliegende Holländer, Faust, Prodaná nevěsta (The Bartered Bride). **1946**: Rigoletto, The Pirates of Penzance, Madama Butterfly, Ariadne auf Naxos, Eugene Onegin. **1947**: Andrea Chénier, Salome, Werther, Il barbiere di Siviglia, Don Giovanni. **1948**: Pelléas et Mélisande, The Old Maid and the Thief, Amelia Goes to the Ball, Le nozze di Figaro,

Aida. 1949: Troubled Island, Les contes d'Hoffmann, The Medium, Der Rosenkavalier, Lyubov' k tryom apel'sinam (The Love for Three Oranges). 1950: Turandot, Die Meistersinger. 1951: Manon, The Dybbuk, I quattro rusteghi. 1952: Wozzeck, Amahl and the Night Visitors, A Kékszakállú herceg vára (Duke Bluebeard's Castle), L'heure espagnole, The Consul. 1953: La Cenerentola, Regina, Die Fledermaus, Hänsel und Gretel, Der Prozess. 1954: The Tender Land, Showboat, Falstaff. 1955: Don Pasquale, Die lustige Weiber von Windsor, Cherevichki, Troilus and Cressida. 1956: Il trovatore, The School for Wives, Der Schauspieldirektor, Orpheus in the Underworld, Mignon, Susannah, The Tempest, L'histoire du soldat, Der Mond. 1957: La Vida Breve/El Amor Brujo (ballet), Macbeth, Die lustige Witwe, Die Entführung aus dem Serail. 1958: The Ballad of Baby Doe, Tale for a Deaf Ear, Trouble in Tahiti, Lost in the Stars, The Taming of the Shrew, Good Soldier Schweik. 1959: Maria Golovin, Street Scene, The Scarf/The Devil and Webster, Wuthering Heights, He Who Gets Slapped, The Triumph of St. John, Six Characters in Search of an Author, Oedipus Rex/Carmina Burana, The Mikado, Così fan tutte. 1960: The Cradle Will Rock, La favola d'Orfeo, Il prigioniero, Der Revisor, The Inspector General. 1961: Il tabarro/Suor Angelica/Gianni Schicchi, The Wings of the Dove. 1962: The Golem, The Turn of the Screw, Porgy And Bess, Louise, The Passion of Jonathan Wade. 1963: A Midsummer's Night Dream, The Nightingale, Jeanne d'Arc au bûcher, Gentlemen Be Seated. 1964: Boris Godunov, Natalia Petrovna. 1965: Katerina Izmaylova, Die Dreigroschenoper, The Saint of Bleecker Street, Lizzie Borden, Ognennïy angel, Capriccio, Miss Julie. 1966: Don Rodrigo, Dialogues des Carmélites, Dantons Tod, Giulio Cesare, Die Zauberflöte. 1967: The Servants of Two Masters, Zolotoy petushok (The Golden Cockerel). 1968: Bomarzo, Carry Nation, Nine Rivers from Jordan. 1969: Prince Igor, Mefistofele, Lucia di Lammermoor, Catulli Carmina. 1970: Roberto Devereux, Věc Makropulos, Help! Help! The Globolinks. 1971: The Most Important Man, Un ballo in maschera, Albert Herring. 1972: Maria Stuarda, Summer and Smoke. 1973: L'incoronazione di Poppea, Beatrix Cenci, Der junge Lord, Anna Bolena, A Village in Romeo and Juliette, I Puritani. 1974: Medée. 1975: Idomeneo, Die tote Stadt, La fille du régiment. 1976: Il ritorno di Ulisse in Patria, Lucrezia Borgia, Ashmedai, La belle Hélène. 1977: Lily, La voix humaine, The Voice of Ariadne, La fanciulla del west. 1978: Naughty Marietta, Il turco in Italia. 1979: Miss Havisham's Fire, Dido and Aeneas, La Loca, Comte Ory, La clemenza di Tito. 1980: Silverlake, The Student Prince, Les pêcheurs de perles, Madame Adare, Before Breakfast, The Student from Salamance. 1981: Mary, Queen of Scots, Attila, Příhody Lišky Bystroušky (The Cunning Little Vixen), Song of Norway, Nabucco, Der Freischütz. 1982: Die Feen, L'amore dei tre re, I Lombardi, La Grande Duchesse de Gérolstein, Hamlet, Alceste, Candide. 1983: Cendrillon, Alcina, Of Mice and Men. 1984: La rondine, The Rake's Progress, Lakmé, Sweeny Todd, Akhnaten. 1985: Norma, Kismet, Casanova. 1986: Brigadoon, Don Quichotte, The New Moon, The Life and Times of Malcolm X. 1987: South Pacific, The Desert Song, L'oca del Cairo, Where the Wild Things Are. 1988: Rasputin. 1989: The Pajama Game. 1990: The Sound of Music, Z mrtvého domu (From the House of the Dead), A Little Night Music, Moses und Aron, L'enfant et les sortilèges. 1991: The Most Happy Fella, Die Soldaten, The Mother of Three Sons. 1992: 110 in the Shade, Doktor Faust, The Desert Song, Die Fledermaus. 1993: The Midsummer Marriage, Marilyn, Griffelkin, Ester, Cinderella.

SYRACUSE

• Syracuse Opera •

Charles Gounod's *Faust* was the first production of the Opera Theatre of Syracuse, the original name of the Syracuse Opera. Inaugurating the 1974-75 season at the

Regent Theater, the work shared the stage with three additional productions during the opening season. The Opera Theatre was conceived eleven years earlier as part of the Syracuse Symphony Orchestra and became independent in 1974.

Although the emphasis is on traditional productions, there have been some world premieres during the company's two decade existence, including Ross Dabrusin's *The Night Harry Stopped Smoking* and Michael Mautner's *Cartazan*. A combination of national and local professionals comprise the casts.

The two-or three-opera season offers tradition productions in a *stagione* system. Recent works include Puccini's *La bohème*, and Rossini's *L'italiana in Algeri*. The company performs in the 2,042-seat Crouse-Hinds Concert Theater in the John Mulroy Civic Center.

Practical Information. The Crouse-Hinds Concert Theater is at 411 Montgomery Street. Tickets are available from the Syracuse Opera box office, 620 Erie Boulevard West, Suite 210, Syracuse, NY, telephone 315-475-5915, fax 315- 475-6319.

COMPANY STAFF AND REPERTORY

General/Artistic Directors. Robert Porter (1974-1975); Robert Driver (1976-1987); Robert Swedberg (1987-1990); Richard McKee (1990-present).

World Premieres (Syracuse Opera). Dabrusin's *The Night Harry Stopped Smoking* (March 31, 1983); Mautner's *Cartazan* (May 17, 1988).

World Premieres (Youtheater). Israel's *Winnie the Pooh* (June 1, 1979).

Repertory. **1974-75:** Faust, Die Zauberflöte, La Cenerentola, Madama Butterfly. **1975-76:** Norma, La traviata, Zémire et azor. **1976-77:** Un ballo in maschera, Il barbiere di Siviglia, La Périchole. **1977-78:** Aida, Hänsel und Gretel, Le nozze di Figaro, Madama Butterfly. **1978-79:** Tosca, Hänsel und Gretel, Die Fledermaus, Rigoletto. **1979-80:** Cavalleria rusticana/ I pagliacci, Die Dreigroschenoper. **1980-81:** Lucia di Lammermoor, La bohème, Così fan tutte, Les contes d'Hoffmann. **1981-82:** La traviata, H.M.S. Pinafore, Il barbiere di Siviglia, Roméo et Juliette. **1982-83:** Il trovatore, Die Zauberflöte, L'elisir d'amore. **1983-84:** Die Fledermaus, Otello, Faust, Don Pasquale. **1984-85:** Aida, Le nozze di Figaro, Don Pasquale, The Mikado. **1985-86:** La bohème, Hänsel und Gretel, The Waterbird Talk/The Medium, Falstaff. **1986-87:** Carmen, Tosca, Man of La Mancha, Ariadne auf Naxos. **1987-88:** Rigoletto, Madama Butterfly, La traviata, Il barbiere di Siviglia. **1988-89:** Les contes d'Hoffmann, Porgy & Bess, Die Zauberflöte, La Cenerentola. **1989-90:** I pagliacci/Gianni Schicchi, La fille du régiment, Babes in Toyland, Fidelio. **1990-91:** Carousel, Turandot, Don Giovanni. **1991-92:** Die lustige Witwe, Lucia di Lammermoor. **1992-93:** La bohème, Babes in Toyland, Die Entführung aus dem Serail. **1993-94:** Aida, L'italiana in Algeri. Youtheater. **1978-79:** Winnie the Pooh, Christmas Carol. **1979-80:** Shepherdess & the Chimney Sweep. **1980-81:** Little Red Riding Hood. **1981-82:** Alice in Wonderland. **1982-83:** Il barbiere di Siviglia.

North Carolina —————— CHARLOTTE

• *Opera Carolina* •

In 1949, *Rosalind* (the English version of Johann Strauß's *Die Fledermaus*) inaugurated the Carolina Opera Association, the original name of Opera Carolina.

The Association paid $125 to purchase the rights to perform the inaugural operetta. The company's roots stemmed from the Charlotte Music Club. Volunteers formed the backbone of the organization. By the 1960s, they offered works like Charles Gounod's *Faust* and Jacques Offenbach's *Les contes d'Hoffmann* with artists imported from New York. The 1980s saw Camille Saint-Saëns's *Samson et Dalila* and Arthur Sullivan's *The Mikado*. The Opera Carolina performed in the 2,603-seat Ovens Auditorium until 1992 when the North Carolina Blumenthal Performing Arts Center opened.

The four opera-season offers a mainstream repertory in a *stagione* system. Recent productions include Giuseppe Verdi's *Il traviata* and Wolfgang Amadeus Mozart's *Così fan tutte*. The company performs in the North Carolina Blumenthal Performing Arts Center.

North Carolina Blumenthal Performing Arts Center

On November 20, 1992, a potpourri of entertainment inaugurated the North Carolina Blumenthal Performing Arts Center. Designed by Cesar Pelli & Associates, the Center took three years and $62 million to complete. The Center's location was decided when the Belk Brothers Company donated land in the heart of uptown Charlotte. The theater is part of a major complex with a glass enclosed public plaza.

The Belk Theater is a gently curving glass-and-stone structure. A bronze, glass, and fiber optic sculpture called Center-Light resides in the lobby. It is a modern, horseshoe-shaped, cream-colored space with classical overtones. Three tiers rise majestically around sea green seats. The three levels of side boxes add intimacy to the room. The hallmark of the auditorium is in the 2,400 points of light, most of which shine from a splendid ceiling dome. Other points of light run in a single line around the parapets. The Belk seats 2,100.

Practical Information. The North Carolina Blumenthal Performing Arts Center is located at 130 North Tryon. Tickets are available at the Center's box office or by phone at 704-372-1000. Opera Carolina's offices are located at 345 N. College Street, Suite 409, Charlotte, NC 28202, phone 704-332-7177.

COMPANY STAFF AND REPERTORY

General/Artistic Directors. Richard Marshall (1976–1982); Bruce Chalmers (1982–1988); James Wright (President, 1989–present).

World Premieres. Ward's *Abelard and Heloise* (February 19, 1982).

Repertory. **1948-49:** Die Fledermaus. **1949-50:** Prodaná nevěsta (The Bartered Bride), Les contes d'Hoffmann. **1950-51:** Blennerhassett, Sunday Costs Five Pesos, Martha, Der tapfere Soldat. **1951-52:** Le nozze di Figaro, La fille du régiment, Sweethearts. **1952-53:** La traviata, Desert Song, Cavalleria rusticana, Amelia al ballo. **1953-54:** Carmen, Taming of the Shrew, Die lustige Witwe. **1954-55:** La bohème, Così fan tutte, Les contes d'Hoffmann. **1955-56:** Madama Butterfly, Le nozze di Figaro, Aida. **1956-57:** Gianni Schicchi/Suor Angelica, Song of Norway, Die lustigen Weiber von Windsor, Faust. **1957-58:** Tosca, Il trovatore, Cavalleria rusticana/I pagliacci. **1958-59:** Carmen, Die Fledermaus, La traviata, Madama Butterfly. **1959-60:** Rigoletto, The King and I, Down in the Valley/The Medium,

North Carolina Blumenthal Performing Arts Center Auditorium (Charlotte, North Carolina).

La bohème. **1960-61:** Carousel, Il barbiere di Siviglia, Aida, La Périchole. **1961-62:** Die Zauberflöte, Kismet, Faust. **1962-63:** The Student Prince, Lucia di Lammermoor, Prodaná nevěsta (The Bartered Bride). **1963-64:** Die lustige Witwe, Tosca, Samson et Dalila. **1964-65:** Les contes d'Hoffmann, Most Happy Fella, Falstaff. **1965-66:** La bohème, La forza del destino, Evening with Rogers and Hammerstein. **1966-67:** Don Giovanni, Rigoletto, Annie Get Your Gun. **1967-68:** Faust, Così fan tutte, Tosca. **1968-69:** Madama Butterfly, Don Pasquale, Die Fledermaus. **1969-70:** La traviata, La Cenerentola, Cavalleria rusticana/I pagliacci. **1970-71:** Il trovatore, L'elisir d'amore, Carmen. **1971-72:** La bohème, Il barbiere di Siviglia, Les contes d'Hoffmann. **1972-73:** Aida, Roméo et Juliette, Lucia di Lammermoor. **1973-74:** Tosca, Un ballo in maschera, Faust. **1974-75:** Carmen, Le nozze di Figaro, Il tabarro/Cavalleria rusticana. **1975-76:** Madama Butterfly, L'italiana in Algeri, Daisy, Manon. **1976-77:** Rigoletto, Turandot, Die lustige Witwe. **1977-78:** La traviata, La Périchole, Don Giovanni. **1978-79:** Otello, Il barbiere di Siviglia, Der fliegende Holländer. **1979-80:** Aida, Die Zauberflöte, L'elisir d'amore. **1980-81:** Carmen, Così fan tutte, Porgy & Bess. **1981-82:** La bohème, Abelard and Heloise, Die Fledermaus. **1982-83:** Madama Butterfly, Fidelio, The Pirates of Penzance. **1983-84:** Tosca, Les contes d'Hoffmann, La fille du régiment. **1984-85:** Il trovatore, Samson et Dalila, The Mikado. **1985-86:** Willie Stark, Man of La Mancha, Manon Lescaut, Faust. **1986-87:** Gianni Schicchi/I pagliacci, A Little Night Music, Il barbiere di Siviglia. **1987-88:** La traviata, Kiss Me Kate, Lucia di Lammermoor. **1988-89:** Aida, L'elisir d'amore, Die Fledermaus. **1989-90:** Carmen, Rigoletto, Madama Butterfly. **1990-91:** Turandot, Don Giovanni, H.M.S. Pinafore. **1991-92:** La bohème, Il barbiere di Siviglia, Roméo et Juliette, Tosca. **1992-93:** Il trovatore, Die lustige Witwe, Die Zauberflöte, l'italiana in Algeri. **1993-94:** La traviata, Hänsel und Gretel, Cavalleria rusticana/I pagliacci, Così fan tutte.

—————————————————— DURHAM
• *Triangle Opera Theater* •

The 1984-85 season was the first for the Triangle Opera Theater (TOT), when "Street Opera" performances of Gian Carlo Menotti's *The Medium* and George Bizet's *Carmen* were staged, literally, in the street. The TOT was founded by composer Robert Ward and members of the Durham artistic community who felt there was a need for professional opera in the area. The Durham Arts Council supported the company for the first five years. During that time, Ward's *The Crucible*, Richard Wargo's *The Seduction of a Lady*, and James Legg's *The Informer* were the more unusual operas that were paired with familiar fare in a two-opera season. The company saw its first world premiere on June 9, 1993, wth the staging of Ward's *Roman Fever*.

The following year, the company moved into the newly renovated Carolina Theater, which they call home. Scott Tilley became artistic director and is heading the company in a more traditional direction to attract a wider audience base. He hopes to expand the season to three productions within a few years. The TOT also began original language productions. The casts are a mixture of established artists and up-and-coming talent. Most singers have connections to North Carolina.

The two-opera season pairs a "war-horse" with a more unusual piece in a *stagione* system. Recent productions include Verdi's *La traviata* and Christoph Willibald Gluck's *Orfeo ed Euridice*. The company performs in the Carolina Theater.

Carolina Theater

The Carolina Theater, originally called the Durham Auditorium, opened on February 2, 1926, with a show called Kiawian Jollies. Constructed by the City of Durham, it was designed by Frank Milburn. It housed a variety of entertainment until it was converted to a movie theater in 1929. The building was closed for renovations in 1988 and reopened in February 1994.

The Carolina is an impressive Beaux Arts building of dark yellow brick and terra cotta. The façade exhibits fluted Corinthian pilasters that support a band displaying DURHAM AUDITORIUM. The rectangular auditorium is richly ornamented with gilded carvings. The turquoise and ivory room holds two balconies. The theater seats 1,000.

Practical Information: The Carolina Theater is located at 309 Morgan Street. Tickets can be purchased by calling 919-560-3030 or writing the Triangle Opera Theater, 120 Morris Street, Durham, NC 27701.

COMPANY STAFF AND REPERTORY

General/Artistic Directors: Robert Ward (1984–1993; Scott Tilley (1993–present).
World Premiere: Ward's *Roman Fever* (June 9, 1993).
Repertory: **1984-85:** The Medium, Carmen. **1985-86:** The Crucible, I pagliacci. **1986-87:** Così fan tutte, The Seduction of a Lady, The Informer, Madama Butterfly. **1987-88:** Il barbiere di Siviglia, Die Zauberflöte. **1988-89:** Don Giovanni, L'elisir d'amore. **1990-91:** Die Dreigroschenoper, Faust. **1991-92:** Il nozze di Figaro, Street Opera Deja Vu. **1992-93:** Roman Fever, Der Schauspieldirektor. **1993-94:** Orfeo ed Euridice, La traviata.

GREENSBORO

• *Greensboro Opera Company* •

Giuseppe Verdi's *La traviata* inaugurated the Greensboro Opera on October 16, 1981, at the War Memorial Auditorium. It was the sole offering of the first season. A group of civic leaders finding inspiration from Peter Paul Fuchs, a former conductor with the Baton Rouge Opera, founded the company. The group felt that there was sufficient interest in the Greensboro area to establish an opera company.

The single opera seasons continue to the present, with an occasional visiting opera company supplementing the season's fare. In addition, the 1992 season saw an abbreviated version of Fuch's *White Agony*. Both up-and-coming and established singers fill the lead roles, supported by local talent.

The one-opera season offers traditional fare. Recent productions include Wolfgang Amadeus Mozart's *Die Zauberflöte* and Verdi's *Aida*. The company performs at the 2,400-seat War Memorial Auditorium.

Practical Information. The War Memorial Auditorium is located in the Greensboro Coliseum Complex at 1201 South Chapman Street. Tickets can be purchased at the Complex Box Office at the above address, by calling 910-373-7474 or writing Greensboro Opera Company, P.O.B. 29031, Greensboro, NC 27429-9031.

REPERTORY

Repertory. **1981:** La traviata. **1982:** Lucia di Lammermoor. **1983:** Rigoletto. **1984:** Tosca. **1985:** Il barbiere di Siviglia. **1986:** Madama Butterfly. **1987:** Carmen. **1988:** Don Giovanni. **1989:** La bohème. **1990:** Faust. **1991:** Il trovatore. **1992:** Les contes d'Hoffmann. **1993:** Die Zauberflöte.

WINSTON-SALEM

• *Piedmont Opera Theater* •

Giuseppe Verdi's *Rigoletto* inaugurated the Piedmont Opera Theater on September 15, 1978, at Reynolds Auditorium. It was the sole offering of the inaugural season. Norman Johnson founded the company and is still its general director.

The second season witnessed only one opera, Wolfgang Amadeus Mozart's *Don Giovanni*. The single opera season continued until the 1983-84 season, the same year the performances were moved to the Stevens Center. With the exception of the 1984-85 season, when three operas were mounted, the season has remained at two operas. The singers are up-and-coming talent in the leads supported by local talent. A new opera, based on *Ordinary People*, is being commissioned.

The two-opera season offers standard fare works in a *stagione* system. Recent productions include Mozart's *Così fan tutte* and Charles Gounod's *Faust*. The company performs in the Roger L. Stevens Center for the Performing Arts, which seats 1,380.

Practical Information. Roger L. Stevens Center for the Performing Arts is at 405 West Fourth Street. Tickets can be purchased at the Piedmont Opera Theater,

7990 North Point Boulevard, Suite 109, or by calling 919-725-2022, or writing Piedmont Opera Theater, 7990 North Point Boulevard, Suite 109, Winston-Salem, NC 27106.

COMPANY STAFF AND REPERTORY

General Director. Norman Johnson (1978–present).
Repertory. **1978-79:** Rigoletto. **1979-80:** Don Giovanni. **1980-81:** Les contes d'Hoffmann. **1981-82:** Prodaná nevěsta (The Bartered Bride). **1982-83:** Madama Butterfly. **1983-84:** La bohème. **1984-85:** Carmen, Amahl and the Night Visitors, Il barbiere di Siviglia. **1985-86:** La traviata, Don Pasquale. **1986-87:** Die Fledermaus, Die Entführung aus dem Serail. **1987-88:** Rigoletto, The Mikado. **1988-89:** Lucia di Lammermoor, Le nozze di Figaro. **1989-90:** Roméo et Juliette, Falstaff. **1990-91:** La Cenerentola, Madama Butterfly. **1991-92:** Die Zauberflöte, La fille du régiment. **1992-93:** Faust, L'italiana in Algeri. **1993-94:** La bohème, Così fan tutte.

North Dakota
—— FARGO

• *Fargo-Moorhead Civic Opera* •

Arthur Sullivan's *The Gondoliers* inaugurated the Fargo-Moorhead Civic Opera on April 17, 1969, at Festival Hall on the North Dakota State University campus. It was the sole offering of the inaugural season. A group of local residents who believed that there were many musical members of the community without an outlet for their talent organized the Fargo-Moorhead Civic Opera. They also felt that sufficient interest was present in the area to establish a light opera company.

The second season opened with a double-bill of Ermanno Wolf-Ferrari's *Il segreto di Susanna* and Arthur Sullivan's *Trial By Jury*. Sigmund Romberg's *The Student Prince* and Georges Bizet's *Carmen* completed the season, marking the company's expansion to three operas. Bizet's *Carmen* was the first production in which talent from outside the local area was employed. The 1974-75 season saw Carlisle Floyd's *Susannah* followed by Dominick Argento's *The Boor* during the 1976-77 season. The company's first foray into Russian opera ushered in the 1980s with Pyotr Il'yich Tchaikovsky's *Eugene Onegin*. The infrequently performed (in the United States) Albert Lortzing's *Zar und Zimmermann* saw the stage during the 1982-83 season. Douglas Moore's *The Ballad of Baby Doe* was offered at the end of the decade. The company features established, up-and-coming, and local talent for the lead roles.

The two- or three-opera season offers standard fare and some lesser-known works in a *stagione* system. Recent productions include John Gay's *The Beggar's Opera* and Bizet's *Carmen*. The company performs in the 877-seat Fargo Theater and 600-seat Moorhead Senior High School Auditorium.

Practical Information. Tickets are available by writing Fargo-Moorhead Civic Opera, 806 NP Avenue, Fargo, ND 58102, or calling 701-239-4558.

REPERTORY

Repertory. **1969:** The Gondoliers. **1969-70:** Il segreto di Susanna/Trial By Fire, The Student Prince, Carmen. **1970-71:** Hänsel und Gretel, The Most Happy Fella. **1971-72:** I pagliacci, The Mikado, Die Zauberflöte. **1972-73:** Trouble in Tahiti, Faust, Die lustige Witwe. **1973-74:** Il maestro di musica, La traviata, Die Fledermaus. **1974-75:** The Old Maid and the Thief/Chanticlear, Susannah, Il barbiere di Siviglia. **1975-76:** Don Pasquale, La bohème, The Pirates of Penzance. **1976-77:** The Boor/Comedy on the Bridge, Don Giovanni, Prodaná nevěsta (The Bartered Bride). **1977-78:** Amahl and the Night Visitors, Le nozze di Figaro, Showboat. **1978-79:** L'elisir d'amore, Un ballo in maschera, The Desert Song. **1979-80:** Madama Butterfly, Little Red Riding Hood, Fidelio, H.M.S. Pinafore. **1980-81:** Eugene Onegin, Rigoletto, Die Fledermaus. **1981-82:** Die Entführung aus dem Serail, Falstaff, Naughty Marietta. **1982-83:** Zar und Zimmermann, Tosca, The Gondoliers. **1983-84:** Die Zauberflöte, Die Freischütz, L'italiana in Algeri. **1984-85:** Requiem (Verdi), Hänsel und Gretel, Carmen. **1985-86:** The Consul, La bohème, The New Moon. **1986-87:** Le nozze di Figaro, Faust. **1987-88:** Madama Butterfly, Martha. **1988-89:** La traviata, Il barbiere di Siviglia, Die lustige Witwe. **1989-90:** Cavalleria rusticana, The Ballad of Baby Doe, The Pirates of Penzance. **1990-91:** L'elisir d'amore, H.M.S. Pinafore. **1991-92:** The Creation, Amahl and the Night Visitors, La Périchole. **1992-93:** I pagliacci, Il matrimonio segreto, The Desert Song. **1993-94:** The Beggar's Opera, Carmen.

Ohio ——————————— CINCINNATI

• *Cincinnati Opera* •

Friedrich von Flotow's *Martha*, under the baton of Ralph Lyford, inaugurated the Cincinnati Opera on June 27, 1920. Originally known as the Zoo Opera, the company was started as an attraction for Zoo visitors; they performed in the open-air pavilion at the Cincinnati Zoo. Not infrequently, singers found themselves competing with roaring lions, laughing hyenas, squealing seals, and yelping peacocks. Lyford, who headed the opera department at the Cincinnati Conservatory of Music, needed a place to give aspiring local singers experience. He approached Bertha Baur, the Conservatory's dean, and two wealthy women, Anne Sinton Taft and Mary Emery. With their financial backing, the company was born. Lyford had other ambitions as well. He wanted to set up a permanent professional opera company in Cincinnati that attracted outstanding artists. The Cincinnati Opera stages the oldest summer festival in the United States.

Opera was first heard in Cincinnati back in 1801, when an amateur group staged William Shield's *The Poor Soldier*. English-language productions of Wolfgang Amadeus Mozart's *La nozze di Figaro*, Vincenzo Bellini's *La sonnambula*, Gioachino Rossini's *Il barbiere di Siviglia*, and Carl Maria von Weber's *Der Freischütz* followed in the 1830s. Opera was initially offered in various halls built for purposes other than opera. Then the city's first opera house, Pike's Opera House, opened in 1859. Built by Samuel Pike, the theater was inaugurated on February 22, 1859, with a Grand Ball. Strakosch Italian Opera Company presented the first operatic performances seen in Pike's during a five week-opera festival. Flotow's *Martha* opened the festival that included Giuseppe Verdi's *La traviata*, *Il trovatore* and *Ernani*, Bellini's *Norma*, *La sonnambula* and *I Puritani*, Gaetano Donizetti's

La favorita, *La fille du Régiment*, *Lucrezia Borgia* and *Lucia di Lammermoor*, Rossini's *Il barbiere di Siviglia*, Mozart's *Don Giovanni*, and Giacomo Meyerbeer's *Robert le Diable*. In total, Strakosch's company mounted 25 performances.

The Music Hall opened in 1878. The premiere of Christoph Willibald Gluck's *Alceste* (concert excerpts) on May 14, 1878, was offered as part of the inaugural May Music Festival program. Touring companies continued to visit through the end of the nineteenth century and into the early part of the twentieth century. Among the city's most frequent guests were Damrosch Opera Company, Abbott English Opera Company, Maurice Grau's French Opera Company, Richings English Troupe, and Parepa-Rosa Opera Company. The Metropolitan began visits in 1895 that lasted nine years, and the Chicago Opera visited until 1924.

Four years earlier, Cincinnati had seen Flotow's *Martha*, the first production of the Zoo Opera. The opening night performance was not without incident. Samuel Wilson described it in the local newspaper as follows. "In response to Lady Harriet's cry for help, the noble women of the Queen's Hunt came charging out from the wings brandishing their spears at poor Lionel. One of them, abandoning herself to the spirit of the scene, dropped the point of her weapon a shade low and swung wide. The kinetic response of the huntress slightly to the northeast of her was instant and far more Minsky than Metropolitan." The first summer season saw seven weeks of popular opera, Rossini's *Il barbiere di Siviglia*, Donizetti's *Don Pasquale*, and Verdi's *Rigoletto* among the offerings. Lyford conducted every performance. The productions were threadbare — simple backdrops and time-worn costumes — and the casts were local people, but overflow crowds filled the four-hundred seat outdoor "opera house" for every opera. Lyford began importing singers for the principal roles by the second season, and stars like Natale Cervi, Francesco Curci, Cara Gina, Stella de Mette, Italo Picchi, Millo Picco, Joseph Royer, and Henrietta Wakefield, shone from the stage. In 1924, he further strengthened the singing quality by bring in twenty members of the Metropolitan opera chorus to act as a "core" for the local-singers chorus. The season increased to eight weeks, six operas a week, with up to fourteen operas on the schedule. The phenomenal growth of the Zoo Opera was proceeding respectably when Lyford, ill, exhausted, and dissatisfied with the management, resigned. Two years later, he suffered a fatal heart attack. That same year his opera, *Castle Agrazant,* received its world premiere, but not at the Zoo Opera.

It also appeared that the Zoo Opera might expire. There was no season in 1925. Only a single performance of Verdi's *Il trovatore* graced the stage. The company was reborn the next year with Isaac van Grove at the helm. He continued the eight-week season, offering fourteen popular works and the world premiere of his own opera, *The Music Robber*. The opera concerned the well-known incident in Wolfgang Amadeus Mozart's life when a stranger arrived at his home and offered him money to compose a mass. Three years later, *Enter Pauline*, an operetta by two Cincinnatians, Clark B. Firestone and Joseph Surdo, received its world premiere. Expansion continued with some seasons witnessing as many as eighteen different operas. In addition to the standard repertory, both contemporary and rarely performed works were performed, including Italo Montemezzi's *L'amore dei tre re*, Wolf-Ferrari's *I gioielli della Madonna* and *Il segreto di Susanna*, Franco Léoni's *L'oracolo*, Jules Massenet's *La Navarraise*, Giacomo Meyerbeer's *Dinorah*, and Fromental Halévy's *La Juive*. Van Grove also introduced German operas that were new to Cincinnati audiences.

During the Zoo Opera's early years, the wealthy families of the city—The Tafts, Emerys and Fleischmanns—paid the Zoo Opera's debt. With the Depression and the deaths of Mrs. Emery and Mrs. Taft in 1932, this was no longer possible and almost caused the company's demise (again). Attendance also began to fall. By 1933, only 600 spectators showed up at the performances, resulting in a shortened season. In 1934, the Zoo management banished the opera, and the company mounted its nine-opera season at the Nippert Stadium, where conditions were primitive. All operas were cut to run one and one-half hours. The auspicious happening of the season was the arrival of Fausto Cleva as music director. He remained with the company for twenty-eight years. (A dispute in 1962 with the newly arrived artistic director, Tito Capobianco, caused Cleva to resign.) The company incorporated as the Cincinnati Summer Opera Association in 1935, and returned to the Zoo. A newly renovated, roofed pavilion awaited them. Two years later, new parquet and balconies were added. The 1936 season offered some unusual works—Deems Taylor's *The King's Henchman* and Meyerbeer's *L'Africaine*—among its nineteen productions. But it was 1939 that heralded the arrival of the celebrated singers. Jan Peerce and Robert Weede gave a stirring *Rigoletto* (July 3, 1939), Gladys Swarthout a sultry *Carmen* (July 7, 1939), and Josephine Antoine a moving *Lucia di Lammermoor* (July 16, 1939). The next season, Giovanni Martinelli joined the Zoo Opera. He sang Manrico, Otello, Radames, and Samson, and Grace Moore performed her first Manon.

The 1941 season was the first one in twenty-one years that had no deficit. Meanwhile attendance had grown to 2,500 per performance. Cincinnati held virtually the only summer opera festival during World War II, so the stars continued to shine brightly. Among them were Zinka Milanov, Elizabeth Rethberg, Stella Roman, Bidu Sayao, and Dorothy Kirsten. Risë Stevens sang her first Carmen on July 13, 1943, and Mignon on July 20, 1943. Lawrence Tibbett and Martinelli starred in Verdi's *Otello*. The Silver Jubilee was celebrated with Italo Montemezzi conducting his *L'amore dei tre re* and four different divas—Lily Djanel, Coe Glade, Swarthout, and Stevens—singing Carmen. The next season, Marjorie Lawrence, stricken with polio on a trip to Mexico in 1941, sang a reclining Amneris.

The year 1948 marked the beginning of a new era in production. A subscription plan was begun that allowed memorable artists—Richard Tucker, Ezio Pinza, Astrid Varnay, and John Alexander (in his professional debut in Charles Gounod's *Faust*)—and monumental productions. The next season's productions, however, were too monumental and only a last minute contribution enabled the season to continue. By 1953, the audience had increased beyond capacity, so 300 new seats and standing room replaced an inadequate zoo-mezzanine. Six years later, an expanded stage proscenium was added, and Dino Yanopoulos and Wolfgang Roth introduced a "dramatic and simple stylization" method of mounting productions. Three dimensional units that used the available space more effectively replaced flat two dimensional sets. The 1960s ushered in more outstanding artists including Teresa Stratas in Giacomo Puccini's *La bohème* (both Mimi and Musetta in different performances), Sherrill Milnes in Puccini's *Tosca* (his first Scarpia) and Verdi's *Il trovatore* and *La traviata*, Martina Arroyo in Verdi's *Aida* (her first Aida), Plácido Domingo in Pietro Mascagni's *Cavalleria rusticana* and Georges Bizet's *Carmen*, Beverly Sills and Norman Treigle in Jacques Offenbach's *Les contes d'Hoffmann*, Elizabeth Schwarzkopf in Richard Strauss's *Der Rosenkavalier*, and Montserrat Caballé in Bellini's *Il pirata*. Some productions became more adventurous. For example, Donizetti's *L'elisir d'amore* was set in the Texas panhandle of the 1840s. By 1971, the Summer Opera had outgrown its Zoo habitat, and Cincinnati boasted a gem of a building suitable for opera, the 91-year old Music Hall. So Rossini's *Il barbiere di Seville* under the baton of James Levine marked the Zoo Opera's swan song at the Pavilion. The company opened their next season in the Music Hall. The Opera Pavilion was demolished.

Before leaving the Zoo Opera, a few "Zoo tales" are in order. The singers did not always sing alone at the Zoo, but were frequently joined by an "animal chorus." There was a pinniped that joined Sills one evening, leading to the morning headline, "Beverly Seals starred in [Verdi's] *La traviata*." There was a donkey that brayed while Caballé sang Bellini's *Il pirata*, sending the diva into stitches. The peacocks always voiced their opinion, before a high note, after a high note, and in the "pregnant pauses." They waddled up to the entrance and began screeching. The most famous peacock screech occurred during Gian Carlo Menotti's *The Medium*, right after Madame Flora called out, "Who's there?" The stories did not end with the "animal chorus." A skunk scurried across the stage during Wagner's *Die Meistersinger*. A moth flew into James Melton's mouth, and a baby llama followed a woman wrapped in white into the pavilion. The audience took it all in stride and looked back with nostalgia on the Zoo Opera days.

On June 24, 1972, a gala Arrigo Boïto *Mefistofele* inaugurated the renovated Music Hall. Treigle, John Alexander, and Carol Neblett performed under the baton of Julius Rudel. The season also witnessed Verdi's *La traviata* with Beverly Sills, Puccini's *Turandot* with Bernabe Marti (Caballé's husband), and Mozart's *Le nozze di Figaro* with Julian Patrick and Michael Devlin, among its highlights. Sills returned two years later for Donizetti's *Roberto Devereux* and Treigle assayed Modest Mussorgsky's *Boris Godunov*. James de Blasis's tenure began in 1974, and he began preparing for year-round activity. To reflect the company's new role, the Cincinnati Summer Opera dropped Summer from its name in 1975. Rarely-performed and contemporary works entered the repertory. Several acclaimed artists also tried out new roles with the company, including James Morris (Mefistofele), Neil Shicoff (Faust), and Richard Leech (Roméo). Although the company was no longer at the Zoo, it still experienced the unexpected. In Floyd's *Susannah*, the blond soprano forgot to pin her brown wig, and it slowly slipped offer her head. During the church scene in Gounod's *Faust*, no one taped a wire on the floor. Someone tripped and cut the power. The organist continued playing, the chorus continued singing, but no sound reached the audience. Then there was the night all the lighting cues in Offenbach's *Les contes d'Hoffmann* ending with the number seven went black.

During the early 1980s, the staging of three rarely performed *verismo* works— Franco Alfano's *Risurrezione*, Ruggero Leoncavallo's *Zazà*, and Jaromír Weinberger's *Švanda Dudák* garnered international attention. But large deficits and falling attendance plagued the company, forcing a retrenchment. The repertory turned to standard-fare. The season became a short summer one, and the number of productions was reduced. De Blasis's goal is to put the company on a more stable financial basis, and then reintroduce one unusual work each season.

The four-opera season offers a traditional repertory in a *stagione* system during a four-week summer season. Recent productions include Puccini's *Madama Butterfly* and *Tosca*, Verdi's *Rigoletto*, and Mozart's *Die Entführung aus dem Serail* and *Die Zauberflöte*. The company performs in the Music Hall.

Music Hall

The May Music Festival inaugurated the Music Hall in 1878. Samuel Hannaford designed the structure, which cost $296,000 to build. Reuben Springer paid most of the cost. The original Music Hall had no stage or proscenium. It was designed to accommodate a very large chorus and orchestra. When Reuben Springer died in 1884, he left a large sum of money for the "well-being" of the Music Hall, and the auditorium was remodelled, acquiring a stage, proscenium, and orchestra section. The Hall took on the appearance that it has today. Between 1969 and 1975, the Music Hall underwent another renovation, supervised by George Schatz and Associates. The project cost $12 million. A gala performance of Arrigo Boïto's *Mefistofele* reopened the Music Hall on June 24, 1972, with Treigle in the title role.

The Music Hall is a massive high Victorian Gothic style building of red brick and Ohio River sandstone. Multi-colored brick patterns weave an elaborate tapestry on the gable façade, while several symbolic stone-carved ornaments embellished the structure. Two great towers flank the building. The stately lobby of ivory, rose, and gold accommodates a larger-than-life statue of Reuben Springer. Italian Renaissance style defines the red, white, and gold horseshoe-shaped auditorium. Two cream-colored tiers supported by slender cast iron columns curve gently around the hall. A twenty-foot diameter crystal chandelier, weighing 1,500 pounds, hangs in the center. The auditorium accommodates 3,629.

Practical Information. The Music Hall is at 1241 Elm Street. The box office hours are 10:00 A.M. to 6:00 P.M. Monday through Friday, and from 12:00 noon to 5:00 P.M. Saturday. You can order tickets by telephoning 513-241-2742 or writing Cincinnati Opera, 1241 Elm Street, Cincinnati, OH 45210. If you go, stay at The Cincinnatian Hotel, Sixth & Vine Streets, Cincinnati, OH 45202; telephone 513-381-3000, fax 513-651-0256, reservations 1-800-323-7500. The Cincinnatian, with its Second Empire Victorian architecture, is listed on the National Register of Historic Places. It is convenient to downtown.

COMPANY STAFF AND REPERTORY

General/Artistic Directors. Ralph Lyford (1920–1924); Isaac van Grove (musical director, 1926–1933); Fausto Cleva (musical director, 1934–1964); Styrk Orwoll (manager, 1964–1973); James de Blasis (1974–present).

World Premieres (Cincinnati, before 1972); Tirindelli's *Blanc et Noir* (December 22, 1897); Floridia's *Paoletta* (August 29, 1910); Lyford's *Castle Agrazant* (April 29, 1926); Giannini's *The Taming of the Shrew.* (January 31, 1953).

American/United States Premieres (Cincinnati, before 1972). Rubinstein's *Der Turm zu Babel* (concert form, part II, June 1879); Rubinstein's *Das verlorene Paradies* (concert form part II, June 12, 1879); Britten's *Gloriana* (concert form, May 8, 1956).

World Premieres (Cincinnati Opera); van Grove's *The Music Robber* (July 7, 1926); Firestone & Surdo's *Enter Pauline* (Summer 1929).

Repertory. **1920:** Il barbiere di Siviglia, Don Pasquale, Il segreto di Susanna, Hänsel und Gretel, Martha, I pagliacci, Rigoletto. **1921:** Il trovatore, Rigoletto, Lucia di Lammermoor, Otello, Lohengrin, Hänsel und Gretel, Faust, Il barbiere di Siviglia, Aida. **1922:** Aida, Carmen, Cavalleria rusticana, Faust, Lakmé, Lohengrin, Manon, Mefistofele, Roméo et Juliette, Rigoletto, Samson et Dalila, Il segreto di Susanna, Il trovatore. **1923:** Tosca, La traviata, Samson et Dalila, Roméo et Juliette, Hänsel und Gretel, Fedora, La gioconda, Faust, Les contes d'Hoffmann,

Carmen, Aida. **1924:** Aida, Il barbiere di Siviglia, La bohème, Carmen, L'elisir d'amore, La gioconda, Lakmé, Lohengrin, Madama Butterfly, Manon, Martha, Mefistofele, Rigoletto, La traviata. **1925:** Il trovatore. **1926:** Aida, L'amore dei tre re, Carmen, Cavalleria rusticana, L'elisir d'amore, Falstaff, Faust, Lohengrin, Lucia di Lammermoor, Martha, The Music Robber, Rigoletto, Tannhäuser, La traviata, Il trovatore. **1927:** Aida, Il barbiere di Siviglia, The Bohemian Girl, Carmen, Faust, Hänsel und Gretel, I gioielli della Madonna, La Juive, Lohengrin, Mignon, The Music Robber, I pagliacci, Tannhäuser, Tosca, Die Walküre, Il trovatore. **1928:** The Bohemian Girl, Cavalleria rusticana, Die Fledermaus, La gioconda, La Juive, Lohengrin, Lucia di Lammermoor, Madama Butterfly, Martha, Die Meistersinger, Mignon, The Mikado, L'oracolo, Rigoletto, Il segreto di Susanna, Tannhäuser, Il trovatore, Die Walküre. **1929:** Aida, L'amore dei tre re, Carmen, Andrea Chénier, Dinorah, Enter Pauline, Lakmé, Madama Butterfly, Martha, Die Meistersinger, Otello, Parsifal, Rigoletto, Tannhäuser, Il trovatore. **1930:** Aida, Andrea Chénier, Carmen, Dinorah, Don Giovanni, Falstaff, Iris, Lakmé, Madama Butterfly, Martha, Mefistofele, Parsifal, Rigoletto, Samson et Dalila, Tannhäuser, Il trovatore. **1931:** Aida, Prodaná nevěsta (The Bartered Bride), Carmen, Don Giovanni, Iris, Fidelio, Lohengrin, Madama Butterfly, Mefistofele, Mignon, La navarraise, L'oracolo, Tosca, Rigoletto, Samson et Dalila, La traviata, Il trovatore. **1932:** Aida, Carmen, Faust, Fidelio, La forza del destino, Madama Butterfly, Der Zigeunerbaron, Martha, Mignon, Norma, Rigoletto, Tannhäuser, Il trovatore, Die Zauberflöte. **1933:** Aida, La bohème, Bolero, Carmen, Cavalleria rusticana, Der Freischütz, La fanciulla del West, Lohengrin, Madama Butterfly, I pagliacci, The Pirates of Penzance, Roméo et Juliette, Thaïs, Il trovatore. **1934:** Faust, Thaïs, Carmen, Lohengrin, Il trovatore, La traviata, Lucia di Lammermoor, Aida, La forza del destino. **1935:** Aida, Carmen, Cavalleria rusticana, Faust, La gioconda, Lohengrin, Martha, Norma, Il pagliacci, Rigoletto, Samson et Dalila, Tannhäuser, La traviata. **1936:** L'Africaine, Aida, Americans in Paris, La bohème, Bohemian Girl, Carmen, Cavalleria rusticana, Don Giovanni, Faust, La gioconda, The King's Henchman, Lohengrin, Madama Butterfly, Martha, Mignon, Otello, I pagliacci, Peter Ibbetson, Samson et Dalila. **1937:** Aida, Il barbiere di Siviglia, La bohème, Carmen, Cavalleria rusticana, Faust, Lohengrin, Lucia di Lammermoor, Madama Butterfly, Mignon, I pagliacci, Rigoletto, Il segreto di Susanna, Tannhäuser, Tosca, Il trovatore. **1938:** Aida, Il barbiere di Siviglia, La bohème, Carmen, Faust, La fanciulla del West, Hänsel und Gretel, Madama Butterfly, Norma, Otello, I pagliacci, La traviata, Il trovatore, Tosca, Thaïs, Tannhäuser, Rigoletto. **1939:** Aida, Il barbiere di Siviglia, La bohème, Carmen, Faust, Hänsel und Gretel, La traviata, Il trovatore, Lucia di Lammermoor, Madama Butterfly, Manon, Mefistofele, Mignon, I pagliacci, Rigoletto, Tannhäuser. **1940:** La bohème, Aida, Il barbiere di Siviglia, Lucia di Lammermoor, Faust, Carmen, Otello, Madama Butterfly, Manon, Rigoletto, Samson et Dalila, Tosca, Tannhäuser, La traviata, Il trovatore. **1941:** Aida, Il barbiere di Siviglia, La bohème, Faust, Carmen, Cavalleria rusticana, Manon, Lucia di Lammermoor, Madama Butterfly, Mignon, Otello, Rigoletto, I pagliacci, Samson et Dalila, Tosca, La traviata, Il trovatore. **1942:** La traviata, Il trovatore, Rigoletto, I pagliacci, Samson et Dalila, Manon, Mignon, Lucia di Lammermoor, Hänsel und Gretel, La gioconda, Faust, L'elisir d'amore, Carmen, La bohème, Aida, Il barbiere di Siviglia. **1943:** Carmen, la bohème, Aida, Il barbiere di Siviglia, Faust, Hänsel und Gretel, Lucia di Lammermoor, Martha, Mignon, I pagliacci, Rigoletto, Samson et Dalila, Tosca, La traviata, Il trovatore. **1944:** Carmen, La bohème, Aida, Il barbiere di Siviglia, Cavalleria rusticana, Faust, Hänsel und Gretel, Martha, I pagliacci, Rigoletto, Samson et Dalila, Tannhäuser, Tosca, La traviata, Il trovatore. **1945:** Aida, Il barbiere di Siviglia, La bohème, Carmen, Cavalleria rusticana, Don Pasquale, Faust, Martha, Mignon, Otello, I pagliacci, Rigoletto, Roméo et Juliette, Samson et Dalila, Tannhäuser, Tosca, La traviata, Il trovatore. **1946:** Aida, L'amore dei tre re, La bohème, Carmen, Cavalleria rusticana, L'elisir d'amore, Faust, Madama Butterfly, Mignon, Otello, I pagliacci, Rigoletto, Samson et Dalila, Tannhäuser, La traviata, Il trovatore. **1947:** Aida, L'amore dei tre re, La bohème, Carmen, Faust, Lohengrin, Madama Butterfly, Martha, Rigoletto, Samson et Dalila, Tannhäuser, Tosca, La traviata, Il trovatore. **1948:** Aida, Il barbiere di Siviglia, La bohème, Boris Godunov, Carmen, L'elisir d'amore, Faust, Lohengrin,

Madama Butterfly, Martha, Rigoletto, Der Rosenkavalier, Salome, Il segreto di Susanna, Tannhäuser, Tosca, La traviata, Il trovatore. **1949:** Aida, L'amore dei tre re, Andrea Chénier, La bohème, Carmen, Don Giovanni, Faust, Lohengrin, Madama Butterfly, Rigoletto, Salome, Samson et Dalila, La traviata, Tristan und Isolde, Il trovatore. **1950:** Aida, La bohème, Carmen, Die Fledermaus, Madama Butterfly, I pagliacci, Rigoletto, Der Rosenkavalier, Samson et Dalila, Tosca, La traviata. **1951:** Aida, Il barbiere di Siviglia, La bohème, Carmen, Don Giovanni, L'elisir d'amore, Faust, Die Fledermaus, Madama Butterfly, Die lustige Witwe, Rigoletto, La traviata, Il trovatore. **1952:** Aida, Il barbiere di Siviglia, La bohème, Carmen, Lucia di Lammermoor, Madama Butterfly, Manon, Die lustige Witwe, Rigoletto, Tosca, La traviata, Il trovatore. **1953:** Aida, La bohème, Carmen, Faust, Lucia di Lammermoor, Madama Butterfly, Die lustige Witwe, Rigoletto, Salome, Samson et Dalila, Il segreto di Susanna, La traviata. **1954:** Aida, Andrea Chénier, Il barbiere di Siviglia, Prodaná nevěsta (The Bartered. Bride), La bohème, Carmen, L'elisir d'amore, Faust, Lucia di Lammermoor, Madama Butterfly, Rigoletto, Tosca, La traviata. **1955:** Aida, La bohème, Carmen, Faust, Lakmé, Madama Butterfly, Manon, Martha, Rigoletto, Tosca, La traviata, Turandot. **1956:** Aida, La bohème, Carmen, Don Pasquale, Faust, Madama Butterfly, Martha, Le nozze di Figaro, Rigoletto, La traviata, Turandot. **1957:** Il barbiere di Siviglia, La bohème, Carmen, Faust, Lucia di Lammermoor, Madama Butterfly, Le nozze di Figaro, Der Rosenkavalier, Tosca, La traviata, Il trovatore. **1958:** La bohème, Boris Godunov, Carmen, L'elisir d'amore, Faust, Gianni Schicchi, Lucia di Lammermoor, Madama Butterfly, Manon Lescaut, Der Rosenkavalier, La traviata, Il trovatore, Le villi. **1959:** Aida, Andrea Chénier, Il barbiere di Siviglia, La bohème, Carmen, Madama Butterfly, Manon Lescaut, Susannah, Tosca. **1960:** Aida, La bohème, Carmen, Macbeth, Madama Butterfly, Peter Grimes, Salome, La sonnambula, La traviata. **1961:** Aida, Ariadne auf Naxos, Il barbiere di Siviglia, La bohème, Don Carlos, Don Giovanni, Macbeth, Manon, Das Rheingold, Rigoletto. **1962:** Aida, La bohème, Carmen, Madama Butterfly, Rigoletto, Salome, Tosca, La traviata. **1963:** Andrea Chénier, La bohème, La traviata, Tosca, Rigoletto, Cavalleria rusticana/I pagliacci, Madama Butterfly, Die Fledermaus, Così fan tutte, Carmen. **1964:** Aida, Il trovatore, La traviata, Susannah, Samson et Dalila, Cavalleria rusticana/I pagliacci, Manon Lescaut, Madama Butterfly, Die Fledermaus, Carmen. **1965:** Rigoletto, Il trovatore, Tosca, Aida, Il barbiere di Siviglia, La bohème, Carmen, Les contes d'Hoffmann, La forza del destino, Manon. **1966:** La bohème, Carmen, Cavalleria rusticana/I pagliacci, La traviata, Madama Butterfly, Faust, Don Pasquale, Così fan tutte, Les contes d'Hoffmann, La Cenerentola. **1967:** Andrea Chénier, Il barbiere di Siviglia, Carmen, Die Fledermaus, Faust, The Medium, Rigoletto, Der Rosenkavalier, Tosca, La traviata. **1968:** Carmen, Les contes d'Hoffmann, Don Pasquale, Lucia di Lammermoor, L'elisir d'amore, Manon, Madama Butterfly, Salome, La traviata, Il trovatore. **1969:** La bohème, Carmen, L'elisir d'amore, Faust, La forza del destino, Il pirata, Rigoletto. **1970:** Carmen, Cavalleria rusticana/I pagliacci, Madama Butterfly, Samson et Dalila, Tosca, La traviata, Il trovatore. **1971:** Il barbiere di Siviglia, La bohème, Carmen, Lucia di Lammermoor, Of Mice and Men, Rigoletto, Roméo et Juliette. **1972:** Mefistofele, Die Fledermaus, Madama Butterfly, Le nozze di Figaro, Turandot, La traviata. **1973:** Les contes d'Hoffmann, Hänsel und Gretel, Aida, Rigoletto, La rondine, La fille du régiment. **1974:** Boris Godunov, Roberto Devereux, La Périchole, La bohème, Manon Lescaut, Un ballo in maschera. **1975:** Faust, Il trittico, Der fliegende Holländer, Die lustige Witwe, Turandot, Il trovatore. **1976:** Carmen, Tosca, Così fan tutte, Aida, The Ballad of Baby Doe, Showboat. **1977:** Norma, Il barbiere di Siviglia, Madama Butterfly, Most Happy Fella, Don Giovanni, La traviata. **1978:** Les contes d'Hoffmann, Lucia di Lammermoor, Cavalleria rusticana/I pagliacci, Macbeth, La bohème, Die Walküre, The Student Prince. **1979:** Rigoletto, Adriana Lecouvreur, Le nozze di Figaro, Susannah, Attila, The Mikado. **1980:** La traviata, Die Fledermaus, Turandot, Manon, Fidelio, Il trovatore, Pirates of Penzance. **1980-81:** Carmen, Faust, Aida, Das Rheingold, Don Pasquale, Tosca, H.M.S. Pinafore, South Pacific. **1981-82:** La bohème, Cavalleria rusticana/I pagliacci, Otello, Il trittico, Salome, Roméo et Juliette, Die lustige Witwe, The Sound of Music. **1982-83:** Rigoletto, Madama Butterfly, Risurrezione, Die Meistersinger, Manon Lescaut, Così fan tutte,

Carousel, The Music Man. **1983-84:** L'elisir d'amore, Norma, Attila, La rondine, La traviata, Don Carlo, Oklahoma!, Eugene Onegin. **1985:** Zazà, Faust, Gondoliers, Carmen, Lucia di Lammermoor, Aida, Roberta. **1986:** Švanda Dudák, Der Rosenkavalier, Tosca, Die Zauberflöte, Il trovatore, La fanciulla del West. **1987:** Les contes d'Hoffmann, Zazà, Madama Butterfly, Il barbiere di Siviglia, Turandot. **1988:** Carmen, Susannah, Le nozze di Figaro, La bohème. **1989:** Don Carlos, Così fan tutte, La traviata, Roméo et Juliette. **1990:** Aida, Lucia di Lammermoor, Don Giovanni, Faust. **1991:** Manon Lescaut, Il barbiere di Siviglia, Carmen, Un ballo in maschera. **1992:** Madama Butterfly, Rigoletto, Die Entführung aus dem Serail, Les contes d'Hoffmann. **1993:** Tosca, Die Zauberflöte, Cavalleria rusticana/I pagliacci, Werther.

—————————————— CLEVELAND

• *Cleveland Opera* •

Giacomo Puccini's *Madama Butterfly* inaugurated the New Cleveland Opera Company, the original name of the Cleveland Opera, on October 22, 1976. Gioachino Rossini's *Il barbiere di Siviglia* concluded the two-opera season. Sung in English, both operas received two performances at Byron Auditorium in Shaker Heights. Although the auditorium offered admirable acoustics and sightlines, it lacked a place to put the orchestra. The maestro and his musicians sat backstage, and the singers followed the conductor via closed-circuit monitors placed strategically around the stage. David Bamberger founded the company and is still its director.

Cleveland heard its first opera in 1820, when a comic opera, *The Purse Won the Benevolent Tar*, was presented in Mowry's Tavern. The troupe also mounted Colman's *Mountaineers* during their week visit. In 1859, Cleveland heard Friedrich von Flotow's *Alessandro Stradella*. The Parepa Rosa Opera Company and Strakosch Grand Opera visited next, and in 1876, Kellogg's Grand English Opera Company staged Charles Gounod's *Faust*, Flotow's *Martha*, Michael Balfe's *Bohemian Girl*, and Richard Wagner's *Der fliegende Holländer*. In 1877, Gaetano Donizetti's *L'elisir d'amore* and Giuseppe Verdi's *Il trovatore* were mounted. Both Emma Abbott and her Grand English Opera Company and the Boston Ideals Opera Company visited during the 1880s. The Metropolitan Opera paid Cleveland its first visit in 1886. It was when the Metropolitan stopped their visits several decades later that Bamberger decided Cleveland needed homegrown productions to fill the opera-void.

During the summer of 1975, he staged as "calling cards," at the Greenbrier Commons in Parma Heights, the same operas he presented during his inaugural season. John Heavenrich, a Cleveland attorney and opera-lover, saw the performances and offered some financial backing. After three seasons, the company dropped New from their name. The first production of the fourth season, Gian Carlo Menotti's *The Consul* on October 14, 1979, was the company's last in the 1000-seat, suburban Byron Auditorium. Victor Borge, making his operatic conducting debut in Wolfgang Amadeus Mozart's *Die Zauberflöte* on November 28, 1979, welcomed the company into their home for the next five seasons, the 1,500-seat, downtown Hanna Theater. Although the Hanna had an orchestra pit, the acoustics were a problem. They were never intended for unamplified sound. The company celebrated its seventh season with a Verdi Festival, mounting *Un ballo in maschera*, *La traviata*, and *Falstaff*, and scenes from *Macbeth* and *Otello*.

A gala production of Johann Strauß's *Die Fledermaus* celebrated the company's move into its new home, the splendidly restored State Theater, on November 16, 1984. The next season saw a Cleveland novelty, Virgil Thomson's *The Mother of Us All*. Roberta Peters appeared in Franz Lehár's *Die lustige Witwe* in 1986, and Mozart's *Le nozze di Figaro* marked the final operatic appearance of John Reardon on February 21, 1988. The world premiere of rock superstar Stewart Copeland's *Holy Blood and Crescent Moon* highlighted the fourteenth season. It was a bold undertaking for the company. The first German-language production, Ludwig van Beethoven's *Fidelio*, took place on April 12, 1991, the same season that Justino Díaz starred in Mozart's *Don Giovanni*. Although some internationally-acclaimed have sung in Cleveland, the casts consist mainly of young singers about to appear on the national scene.

The five-opera season offers mainstream fare with emphasis on the Italian repertory in a *stagione* system. There is one light opera/operetta, one musical theater piece, and one contemporary work. Recent productions include Puccini's *Tosca* and *Madama Butterfly*, Verdi's *La traviata*, Arthur Sullivan's *The Yeoman of the Guard*, Andrew Lloyd Webber's *The Phantom of the Opera*, and Benjamin Britten's *Albert Herring*. The company performs at the State Theater

State Theater

The film, *Polly with a Past* starring Buster Keaton inaugurated the State Theater on February 5, 1921. Designed by Thomas Lamb, the State was constructed by Loew's Ohio Theater at a cost of $2 million. The State was built as a vaudeville and movie palace. During the 1960s, the theater fell victim to urban blight, and was slated for demolition. Ray K. Shepardson decided to save the theater and formed the Playhouse Square Association. Seven million dollars was spent renovating the building, and on June 11, 1984, Benjamin Britten's *Peter Grimes* reopened it. The Cleveland Opera mounted Strauß's *Die Fledermaus* on November 16, as its first production in the newly restored theater.

Built in a mixture of Roman, Greek, and European Baroque styles, the State boasts an incredibly long and opulent lobby embellished with murals by James Daugherty. The intricately decorated auditorium is fan-shaped. One deep balcony sweeps across the room. Two levels of boxes are stacked along the side wall. The theater seats 3,098.

Practical Information. The State is at 1519 Euclid Avenue. The box office, inside the theater lobby, is open between 10:00 A.M. and 5:00 P.M. Monday through Friday. You can order by tickets by telephoning 216-575-0900 or writing Cleveland Opera, 1422 Euclid Avenue, Suite 1052, Cleveland, OH 44115-1901. If you go, stay at The Ritz-Carlton, 1515 West Third Street, Cleveland, OH 44113; telephone 216-623-1300, fax 216-623-0515, reservations 1-800-241-3333. The Ritz is the focal point of downtown, and convenient to the theater.

COMPANY STAFF AND REPERTORY

General/Artistic Director. David Bamberger (1976–present).

World Premieres (before the Cleveland Opera). Freeman's *Valdo* (May 1906); Belcher's *The Legend of Ronsard and Madelon* (June 1918); Engel's *Brother Joe.* (May 28, 1953).

American/United States Premieres (before Cleveland Opera). Vaughan Williams's *Riders to the Sea* (February 26, 1950).
World Premieres (Cleveland Opera). Roy's *The Enchanted Garden* (children's opera, Cleveland Opera on Tour, September 2, 1983); Gooding's *The Legend of Sleepy Hollow* (Cleveland Opera on Tour, November 29, 1988); Copeland's *Holy Blood, Crescent Moon* (rock opera, October 10, 1989).
American/United States Premieres (Cleveland Opera). Britten's *The Little Sweep* (July 24, 1977).
Repertory. **1976-77:** Madama Butterfly, Il barbiere di Siviglia, The Little Sweep. **1977-78:** La traviata, Il barbiere di Siviglia, Le nozze di Figaro. **1978-79:** La bohème, La fille du régiment, Die Fledermaus. **1979-80:** The Consul, Die Zauberflöte, Lucia di Lammermoor, The Pirates of Penzance. **1980-81:** The Medium, The Student from Salamanca, Naughty Marietta, Madama Butterfly, A Little Love Music (Mall Opera). **1981-82:** Faust, Carmen, The Fantasticks. **1982-83:** La traviata, Il matrimonio segreto, Un ballo in maschera, Falstaff, Scenes from Macbeth, Otello, and Falstaff. **1983-84:** The Enchanted Garden, Don Giovanni, Il barbiere di Siviglia, Kiss Me, Kate. **1984-85:** Die Fledermaus, Aida, L'elisir d'amore. **1985-86:** Tosca, Faust, The Mother of Us All, The Mikado. **1986-87:** Die lustige Witwe, Lucia di Lammermoor, Les contes d'Hoffmann, Porgy and Bess. **1987-88:** Carmen, H.M.S. Pinafore, Le nozze di Figaro, Turandot, West Side Story. **1988-89:** La bohème, The Legend of Sleepy Hollow, Hänsel und Gretel, Rigoletto, Les pêcheurs des perles, My Fair Lady. **1989-90:** Holy Blood and Crescent Moon, The Pirates of Penzance, Madama Butterfly, Il trovatore, Showboat. **1990-91:** Don Giovanni, Don Pasquale, Aida, Fidelio, Carousel. **1991-92:** Cavalleria rusticana/I pagliacci, Il barbiere di Siviglia, Die Entführung aus dem Serail, The Ballad of Baby Doe, The Sound of Music. **1992-93:** Tosca, The Yeoman of the Guard, La traviata, Così fan tutte, The Phantom of the Opera, The Tale of Peter Rabbit. **1993-94:** Die Fledermaus, Madama Butterfly, Albert Herring, Fiddler on the Roof, Scenes from Russian Operas.

• *Lyric Opera Cleveland* •

Wolfgang Amadeus Mozart's *Die Zauberflöte* inaugurated the Lyric Opera Cleveland in the summer of 1974. Anthony Addison, head of the Opera Department at The Cleveland Institute of Music founded the company as the Cleveland Opera Theater Ensemble, an outgrowth of the Institute. During the first five years, the company produced both the standard fare and lesser known works, including Maurice Ravel's *L'heure espagnole*, Giovanni Battista Pergolesi's *La serva padrona*, and Gaetano Donizetti's *Il campanello*. The company's first American opera, Robert Ward's *The Crucible*, was also mounted during that time.
On March 2, 1985, the name Lyric Opera Cleveland was adopted in an effort to clarify the company's goals and to both identity and differentiate it from the other professional opera organizations in the area. Two years later, the Lyric Opera staged its first world premiere, Larry Baker's *Haydn's Head* on July 30, 1987. Six years later saw another world premiere, Libby Larsen's *Mrs. Dalloway*. The company continues to mount the familiar along with lesser known works, including Hector Berlioz's *Béatrice et Bénédict*, Pier Francesco Cavalli's *Calisto*, Claudio Monteverdi's *Il ritorno di Ulisse in patria*, and Giacomo Puccini's *La rondine*. The Lyric performs during the summer in a festival atmosphere with a mixture of established, up and coming, and local talent.
The three-opera summer season offers a repertory mix of early works and contemporary pieces from the standard and the lesser known repertories. Recent

productions include Gioachino Rossini's *Il barbiere di Siviglia*, Benjamin Britten's *The Rape of Lucretia* and Christoph Willibald von Gluck's *Orfeo ed Euridice*. The company performs at The Cleveland Institute of Music, Kulas Hall.

Practical Information. Kulas Hall is at 11021 East Boulevard. Tickets are available from the Lyric Opera Cleveland, P.O.B. 06198, Cleveland, Ohio 44106, or by calling 216-231-2910. If you go, stay at The Ritz-Carlton, 1515 West Third Street, Cleveland, OH 44113; telephone 216-623-1300, fax 216-623-0515, reservations 1-800-241-3333. The Ritz is the focal point of downtown, an elegant establishment, and convenient to the Institute.

COMPANY STAFF AND REPERTORY

General/Artistic Directors. Anthony Addison (1974–1979); Saul Feldman (1979–1982); Timothy Tavcar (1982–84); Michael McConnell (1984–present).

World Premieres. Baker's *Haydn's Head* (July 30, 1987); Larsen's *Mrs. Dalloway* (July 22, 1993).

Repertory. **1979:** H.M.S. Pinafore, The Old Maid and the Thief, Gianni Schicchi. **1980:** Die lustige Witwe, Il barbiere di Siviglia. **1981:** The Mikado, Der Zigeunerbaron. **1982:** A Ceremony of Carols, Amahl and the Night Visitors, Le nozze di Figaro. **1983:** La Périchole, Madama Butterfly. **1984:** Patience, Die Dreigroschenoper. **1985:** Albert Herring, La fille du régiment. **1986:** Béatrice et Bénédict, A Little Night Music. **1987:** Haydn's Head, The Medium, Così fan tutte. **1988:** The Pirates of Penzance, Calisto, Die Entführung aus dem Serail. **1989:** Turn of the Screw, Don Giovanni, La rondine. **1990:** She Loves Me, Die Zauberflöte, La Cenerentola. **1991:** Il ritorno di Ulisse in patria, Orpheus in the Underworld. **1992:** The Pirates of Penzance, The Rape of Lucretia, La finta giardiniera. **1993:** Mrs. Dalloway, Candide, Orfeo ed Euridice. **1994:** Oh, Boy!, Carmen, Il barbiere di Siviglia.

——————————————— COLUMBUS

• *Opera Columbus* •

Giacomo Puccini's *Tosca* inaugurated Opera Columbus on December 3, 1981, in the Ohio Theater. Lorna Haywood, Bill Justice, and Harry Thayard were in the cast. Giuseppe Verdi's *Il trovatore* and Wolfgang Amadeus Mozart's *Don Giovanni* also graced the stage that first season. Three-opera seasons remained the norm, (despite a brief expansion between the 1987 and 1990). The creation of Opera Columbus resulted from the combined efforts of the Columbus Symphony Orchestra, which had presented opera as part of its symphonic series, and a group of determined Columbus inhabitants.

The company presented its first world premiere, Thomas Pasatieri's *The Three Sisters*, on March 13, 1986, with Will Roy, Keith Olsen, Louis Otey, and Marvelle Cariaga, and briefly tested the Richard Wagner waters during the 1987-88 season with *Tristan und Isolde*, featuring Judith Telep-Ehrlich and George Gray in the title roles. Roberto Oswald (former artistic director of the Teatro Colón, Buenos Aires) staged the production. Another major event took place with the mounting of Modest Mussorgsky's *Boris Godunov* two seasons later. Emerging and local talent take the major roles.

The three-opera season offers both standard fare and twentieth-century works in a *stagione* system. Recent productions include Verdi's *La traviata* and Richard Strauss's *Ariadne auf Naxos*. The company performs in the Palace Theater.

Practical Information. The Palace Theater is at 34 West Broad Street. Tickets are available from Opera Columbus, 177 Naghten Street, Columbus, OH 43215, telephone 614-461-8101, fax 614-461-0806.

COMPANY STAFF AND REPERTORY

General/Artistic Directors. Michael Harrison (1983–1988); William Russell (1990–current).

World Premieres. Pasatieri's *Three Sisters* (March 13, 1986).

Repertory. **1981-82:** Tosca, Il trovatore, Don Giovanni. **1982-83:** La traviata, Les contes d'Hoffmann, Lucia di Lammermoor. **1983-84:** Cavalleria rusticana/I pagliacci, La Cenerentola, Rigoletto. **1984-85:** Un ballo in maschera, Roméo et Juliette, La bohème. **1985-86:** Il barbiere di Siviglia, Aida, The Three Sisters, Man of La Mancha. **1986-87:** Macbeth, L'elisir d'amore, Madama Butterfly, Porgy & Bess, Babes in Toyland. (Holiday show). **1987-88:** La traviata, Tristan und Isolde, La fanciulla del West, Die Fledermaus, Babes in Toyland (Holiday show). **1988-89:** Don Carlos, Tosca, Salome, Faust. **1989-90:** Carmen, Don Giovanni, Boris Godunov, Il trovatore. **1990-91:** Rigoletto, Der Rosenkavalier, Le nozze di Figaro. **1991-92:** Turandot, Die Zauberflöte, Die lustige Witwe. **1992-93:** Madama Butterfly, Fidelio, Così fan tutte. **1993-94:** Il barbiere di Siviglia, Ariadne auf Naxos, La traviata.

DAYTON

• *Dayton Opera* •

Giacomo Puccini's *Tosca*, performed in Memorial Hall on October 6, 1961, was the inaugural production of the Dayton Opera. Gioachino Rossini's *Il barbiere di Siviglia* and Giuseppe Verdi's *Rigoletto* completed the first season, which had a budget of $30,000. The Dayton Opera was founded by the joint efforts of the Rev. William Reiley, a Methodist minister, and Lester Freedman, general director of the Toledo Opera. Reiley had moved to Dayton from Toledo, where his wife sang in the opera chorus, and she yearned for another place to sing. Freedman, who had established the Toledo Opera, wanted a second opera company to share the costs of importing artists, sets, and costumes. These two men joined forces to form the company. Freedman directed the Dayton Opera for the first two decades.

Gaetano Donizetti's *Lucia di Lammermoor* opened the second season on October 13, 1962. Charles Gounod's *Faust* and Puccini's *La bohème* followed. The company staged three productions each season from the Italian and French repertory, with the occasional Russian or German opera. The tenth (1970-71) season was an exception. The first American opera, Robert Ward's *The Crucible*, graced the stage on January 30, 1971. Richard Wagner's *Lohengrin* followed on April 24, 1971 and remains the only Wagnerian opera mounted by the company.

Freedman's reign experienced several mishaps, some amusing, some painful. When Gounod's *Faust* was scheduled to open at 8:00 P.M. on December 8, 1962, neither the costumes nor the sets had arrived by curtain time. They were in a truck, stalled on a snowbound interstate. The curtain, nevertheless, went up on scenery that consisted of picnic tables and characters that wore make-shift attire. Faust put on a black top coat, muffler, and velvet beret as an old man and white tie and tails as a young man. Méphistophélès donned diplomat's attire. Only one patron requested a refund. Chorus members suffered the most mishaps. In Puccini's *La fanciulla del West,* one felt a horse stand on her foot. Another had a principal step on the train of her costume, causing her to almost walk out of it, and a third found his pants split during the moon-worshipping scene in Puccini's *Turandot,* treating the audience to a real "mooning." One principal made her entrance so grand that she almost knocked over the scenery.

Grand entrances are associated with New York artists and most singers were imported from the Big Apple. Plácido Domingo appeared in Puccini's *Tosca* on January 23, 1966. Mignon Dunn sang opposite Robert Moulson in Camille Saint-Saëns's *Samson et Dalila* in 1973, the same year that Rosalind Elias sang Carmen. Jules Massenet's *Manon* opened the thirteenth season with a star-studded cast—Mary Costa, Enzo Sordello, and Samuel Ramey. Robert Merrill then appeared in Verdi's *Rigoletto,* Jerome Hines and Johanna Meier in Gounod's *Faust,* and James McCracken in Verdi's *Il trovatore* and Ruggero Leoncavallo's *I pagliacci.* There was also Verdi's *La traviata* with Roberta Peters, Puccini's *Madama Butterfly* with Gilda Cruz-Romo, and Verdi's *Aida* with Martina Arroyo. Arroyo also sang her first *Tosca* with the company on May 3, 1980.

After twenty seasons, Dayton Opera broke with its past. Its founder and general director, Freedman, was asked to resign. David DiChiera, general director of the Michigan Opera Theater (see Michigan Opera Theater entry) was hired as artistic director. The star system and single performances upon which Dayton was built gave way to young rising stars and multiple performances. Grand opera mingled with operetta in the repertory, and an "opera theater" philosophy took hold. There was more rehearsal time. The stage directors were professional, and the theatrical and musical aspects of the productions were given equal weight. DiChiera's first season opened on October 3, 1981, with Verdi's *Rigoletto.* Two sold-out performances of George Gershwin's *Porgy and Bess* with Michael Smartt and Wilhelmenia Fernandez followed. Pamela South, Mary Jane Johnson, and Martina Arroyo sang with the company during DiChiera's tenure.

DiChiera resigned as artistic director at the end of the 1991-92 season. He not only ran the Michigan Opera Theater, but also took the helm of Opera Pacific in 1987 (see Costa Mesa, California, Opera Pacific entry). Running three opera companies was just too hectic. Jane Nelson, who had been the managing director, became general director and is continuing DiChiera's philosophy of strong ensemble casting and exciting visual productions. Dayton is a conservative town and the repertory is mainstream, although the company intends to introduce more adventurous works (for Dayton). A beginning was the world premiere of Michael Ching and Hugh Moffatt's *King of the Clouds* on January 18, 1993. *King of Clouds* is about the lives of real people and the issues one faces in daily living. She plans to improve the quality of the chorus and orchestra and expects to expand the season with summer performances of a fourth opera, which will take place in the Fraze Pavilion, an outdoor amphitheater seating 4,400.

The three-opera repertory is standard fare offered in a *stagione* system. Recent productions include Donizetti's *Don Pasquale,* Verdi's *La traviata,* Vincenzo

Memorial Hall (Dayton, Ohio).

Bellini's *Norma*, and Wolfgang Amadeus Mozart's *Die Zauberflöte*. The company performs in Memorial Hall.

Memorial Hall

Memorial Hall is a memorial to the veterans of the Civil War, dedicated in 1910. Designed by William Earl Ross in association with Albert Pretzinger, the Hall cost $250,000. Statues commemorating the Spanish-American War Soldier and World War I Doughboy were added in 1923. By 1950, the Hall was in a terrible state of disrepair and underwent renovation. An acoustically designed ceiling to improve sound quality and a graded orchestra level to improve sightlines were both installed. A gala celebration commemorated the reopening on September 13, 1956. A second renovation took place in 1990.

Memorial Hall is an imposing building of earth-colored brick. A steep granite staircase leads to a hexastyle portico. Pairs of memorial plaques pay homage to the soldiers. A somber granite foyer exhibits large paintings of battle scenes from the Civil and Spanish American War. The gray-and-white auditorium holds a single large balcony. Its parapet and proscenium are unadorned. Maroon seats complement the teal-colored curtain. The auditorium seats 2,489.

Practical Information. Memorial Hall is at 125 East First Street. The Dayton Opera box office is on the second floor (east mezzanine) of Memorial Hall. It is open Monday through Friday from 9:00 A.M. to 5:00 P.M. On performance days, the box office is open from 9:00 A.M. to 11:00 P.M. weekdays, from 12:00 noon to 11:00 P.M. Saturdays, and 12:00 noon until 6:00 P.M., Sundays. Tickets can be ordered by telephoning 513-228-7464 during box office hours, by faxing 513-228-9612, or by writing Dayton Opera Box Office, 125 East First Street, Dayton, OH 45402. If you go, stay at the Radisson Inn Dayton, 2401 Needmore Road, Dayton, OH 45414; telephone 513-278-5711, fax 513-278-6048, reservations 1-800-333-3333. The Radisson is a pleasant hotel convenient to Memorial Hall.

COMPANY STAFF AND REPERTORY

General/Artistic Directors. Lester Freedman (1960–1980); David DiChiera (1981–1992); Jane Nelson (1992–present).
World Premieres. Ching and Moffatt's *King of the Clouds* (January 18, 1993).
Repertory. **1961-62:** Tosca, Il barbiere di Siviglia, Rigoletto. **1962-63:** Lucia di Lammermoor, Faust, La bohème. **1963-64:** Il trovatore, Madama Butterfly, Boris Godunov. **1964-65:** Aida, Cavalleria rusticana/I pagliacci, La traviata. **1965-66:** Lucia di Lammermoor, Tosca, Carmen. **1966-67:** Die Fledermaus, Manon, Rigoletto. **1967-68:** La bohème, Don Giovanni, Turandot. **1968-69:** Il barbiere di Siviglia, Salome, Madama Butterfly. **1969-70:** Tosca, La gioconda, Lucia di Lammermoor. **1970-71:** Die Fledermaus, The Crucible, Lohengrin. **1971-72:** Faust, La traviata, Aida. **1972-73:** Die Zauberflöte, Samson et Dalila, Carmen. **1973-74:** Manon, Madama Butterfly, Il trovatore. **1974-75:** Tosca, Rigoletto, La fille du régiment. **1975-76:** Il tabarro/I pagliacci, Faust, La bohème. **1976-77:** Aida, Don Giovanni, La traviata, Lucia di Lammermoor. **1977-78:** Madama Butterfly, Roméo et Juliette; Don Pasquale, Un ballo in maschera. **1978-79:** Die Fledermaus, Carmen, Salome, Turandot. **1979-80:** La traviata, Don Carlo, Il barbiere di Siviglia, Tosca. **1980-81:** Samson et Dalila, Faust, La fanciulla del West, Il trovatore. **1981-82:** Rigoletto, Porgy and Bess, Madama Butterfly. **1982-83:** Lucia di Lammermoor, Le nozze di Figaro, H.M.S. Pinafore, La bohème. **1983-84:** La traviata, A Little Night Music, Faust, Il barbiere di Siviglia. **1984-85:** Die Zauberflöte, Tosca, Die lustige Witwe. **1985-86:** Gianni Schicchi/I pagliacci, Die Fledermaus, Turandot. **1986-87:** Madama Butterfly, My Fair Lady, Roméo et Juliette. **1987-88:** Falstaff, Kismet, Carmen. **1988-89:** The Ballad of Baby Doe, The Pirates of Penzance, Aida. **1989-90:** La bohème, Hänsel und Gretel, Don Giovanni. **1990-91:** Rigoletto, The Mikado, Les pêcheurs de perles, Der Schauspieldirektor/Prima la musica e poi le parole. **1991-92:** La Cenerentola, Candid, Madama Butterfly. **1992-93:** Norma, La traviata, Die Fledermaus. **1993-94:** Die Zauberflöte, Amahl and the Night Visitors/Gianni Schicchi, Don Pasquale.

TOLEDO

• *Toledo Opera* •

Giuseppe Verdi's *Aida*, performed in the Paramount Theater on October 6, 1959, inaugurated the Toledo Opera. Pietro Mascagni's *Cavalleria rusticana* and Giacomo Puccini's *Madama Butterfly* completed the first season. The Toledo Opera was formed by a group of community leaders earlier in the year. Lester Freedman was the company's general director.

Georges Bizet's *Carmen* opened the second season on September 27, 1960. Franz Lehár's *Die lustige Witwe* and Verdi's *La traviata* followed in the Rivoli Theater. The next season found the company performing in the Toledo Museum of Art Peristyle, which it called home for the next twelve years. The company staged three productions each season primarily from the Italian repertory, with some French and Russian operas included. The 1970-71 season was an exception, when the first American opera graced the stage, Robert Ward's *The Crucible* on January 23 and 24, 1971 in the Peristyle. After opening the 1973-74 season with Jules Massenet's *Manon*, the opera moved into the Masonic Auditorium where it still performs. Since the 1992-93 season, it has also added the Peristyle to its performing venues.

The three-opera season is standard fare, but the company also offers a Broadway series of musical theater. Recent productions include Charles Gounod's *Faust*, Verdi's *Aida*, Gaetano Donizetti's *La fille du régiment*, and Lloyd Webber's *Cats*. The company performs in the 2,400-seat Masonic Auditorium and the 1,710-seat Peristyle.

Practical Information. The Masonic Auditorium is at 4645 Heatherdowns. The Peristyle is at 2445 Monroe Street. Tickets are obtained from the Toledo Opera box office at 1700 North Reynolds Road, by telephoning 419-531-5511, or writing Toledo Opera, 1700 North Reynolds Road, Toledo, OH 43615. If you go, stay at the Radisson Hotel Toledo, 101 North Summit Street, Toledo, OH 43604; phone 419-241-3000, fax 419-321-2099. The hotel is located downtown, convenient to the theaters.

COMPANY STAFF AND REPERTORY

General/Artistic Directors. Lester Freedman (1959–1983); David Bamberger (acting, 1983–1985); Johann van der Merwe (1985–86); James Meena (1986–present).

Repertory. 1959-60: Aida, Cavalleria rusticana, Madama Butterfly. 1960-61: Carmen, Die lustige Witwe, La traviata. 1961-62: Tosca, Il barbiere di Siviglia, Rigoletto. 1962-63: Lucia di Lammermoor, Faust, La bohème. 1963-64: Il trovatore, Madama Butterfly, Boris Godunov. 1964-65: Aida, Cavalleria rusticana/I pagliacci, La traviata. 1965-66: Lucia di Lammermoor, Tosca, Carmen. 1966-67: Die Fledermaus, Manon, Rigoletto. 1967-68: La bohème, Don Giovanni, Turandot. 1968-69: Il barbiere di Siviglia, Salome, Madama Butterfly. 1969-70: Tosca, La gioconda, Lucia di Lammermoor. 1970-71: Die Fledermaus, The Crucible, Lohengrin. 1971-72: Faust, La traviata, Aida. 1972-73: Die Zauberflöte, Samson et Dalila, Carmen. 1973-74: Manon, Madama Butterfly, Il trovatore. 1974-75: Tosca, Rigoletto, La fille du régiment. 1975-76: Il tabarro/I pagliacci, Il barbiere di Siviglia, La bohème. 1976-77: Aida, Don Giovanni, La traviata, Lucia di Lammermoor. 1977-78: Madama Butterfly, Roméo et Juliette, Don Pasquale, Un ballo in maschera. 1978-79: Die Fledermaus, Carmen, Salome, Turandot. 1979-80: La traviata, Don Carlo, Il barbiere di Siviglia, Tosca. 1980-81: Samson et Dalila, Faust, La fanciulla del West, Il trovatore. 1981-82: La bohème, Aida, Die lustige Witwe, Suor Angelica/Cavalleria rusticana. 1982-83: Rigoletto, Carmen, Madama Butterfly, The Student Prince. 1983-84: Lucia di Lammermoor, Die Fledermaus, The Mikado, Le nozze di Figaro. 1984-85: Il barbiere di Siviglia, Aida, L'elisir d'amore, H.M.S. Pinafore. 1985-86: Don Pasquale, Faust, Pirates of Penzance. 1986-87: Carmen, La traviata, The Student Prince. 1987-88: La bohème, Die Fledermaus, Die Entführung aus dem Serail. 1988-89: Rigoletto, Die Zauberflöte, Madama Butterfly. 1989-90: Tosca, Die lustige Witwe, Fiddler on the Roof, Macbeth. 1990-91: Lucia di Lammermoor, Porgy & Bess, Roméo et Juliette, A Chorus Line, Peter Pan, The Fantasticks. 1991-92: Così fan tutte, Cats, Les Miserables. 1992-93: Madama Butterfly, La traviata, Guys & Dolls, Jesus Christ Superstar, Meet Me in St. Louis. 1993-94: Faust, Aida, Babes in Toyland, Cats, Evita, Love Letters. 1994-95: La fille du régiment, Hänsel und Gretel, Cavalleria rusticana/I pagliacci, Les Miserables, Will Rogers Follies.

Oklahoma ——————————————— TULSA

• *Tulsa Opera* •

Giuseppe Verdi's *La traviata* in "modern-dress" inaugurated the Tulsa Opera Club, the original name of the Tulsa Opera, on December 4, 1948, in a high school auditorium. Ralph and Ione Sassano sang Alfredo and Violetta respectively, and Mary Helen Markham was Flora. These three singers joined Bess Gowans, a piano teacher, and Beryl Bliss (a wealthy Tulsan opera-lover) in forming the "Club." The initial performance of Verdi's *La traviata* was so successful that the opera was repeated the following spring.

Opera in Tulsa dates back to 1904, when Charles Gounod's *Faust* graced the stage of the Epperson Opera House. Two years later a comic piece, *The Chaperones*, inaugurated the Grand Opera House, and touring companies began including Tulsa on their itineraries. The Boston Ideals Opera Company mounted Daniel Auber's *Fra Diavolo* in 1908, followed by the International Grand Opera's presentation of Verdi's *La traviata* the next year. The Ellis Grand Opera visited in 1916, with Georges Bizet's *Carmen*, featuring Mary Garden. After the Grand Opera House burned in 1920, opera performances moved to Convention Hall, which had opened in 1914. Tulsans continued to witness memorable performances. The Chicago Grand Opera returned with Garden in Jules Massenet's *Thaïs* and Frieda Hempel in Verdi's *La traviata*. Temaki Miura sang Giacomo Puccini's *Madama Butterfly*, and Feodor Chaliapin was Mefistofele in Arrigo Boïto opera. The Chicago Civic brought Rosa Raisa in Verdi's *Aida*, and Enrico Caruso gave a concert performance. The Metropolitan visited with Deems Taylor's *The King's Henchmen*. When the Depression hit, operatic activity in the city ground to a halt. It did not begin again until the founding of the Tulsa Opera Club.

In 1950, the Club offered Oscar Straus's *Der tapfere Soldat* and Sigmund Romberg's *The New Moon*. Romberg's work featured David Atkinson, the first professional singer hired by the group. The next year, the founders incorporated as the Tulsa Opera, striving to become a regional opera company. For monetary reasons, the company offered only light operas until 1953, when Puccini's *Madama Butterfly* introduced grand opera into the repertory. Renown artists began to grace the stage — Licia Albanese in Puccini's *Tosca*, Dorothy Kirsten in Puccini's *Madama Butterfly*, Jussi Bjoerling and Leonard Warren in Verdi's *Il trovatore*, Richard Tucker in Georges Bizet's *Carmen* and Verdi's *Aida*, Norman Treigle in Gounod's *Faust*, and Beverly Sills in Verdi's *La traviata* and Gaetano Donizetti's *Lucia di Lammermoor*. Brady Theater, a house with a small stage and limited seating capacity, was the company's performance venue.

In 1974, Edward Purrington became the company's first general director. He brought plans to broaden the company's standard repertory. Tulsans soon were treated to Douglas Moore's *Ballad of Baby Doe*, Jules Massenet's *Manon* and *La navarraise*, and Verdi's *Attila* and *Macbeth*. With the completion of a new performing arts center in 1977, the company was able to add "monumental" works to its repertory. The first Richard Wagner opera, *Die Walküre*, arrived during the 1979-80 season, and Modest Mussorgsky's *Boris Godunov* came the following season. Umberto Giordano's *Andrea Chénier* with Gilda Cruz-Romo and Ermanno Mauro ushered in the 1980s. Oklahoma natives Leona Mitchell and William Johns sang in Verdi's *Il trovatore* in 1982, a production conducted by Kurt Herbert Adler.

By the mid-1980s, Tulsa's once prosperous oil boom economy began to falter. Productions became more "economical," although the stars continued to shine — Samuel Ramey, Neil Shicoff, Diana Soviero, Richard Stillwell in Gounod's *Faust*, and Rosalind Plowright, Tatiana Troyanos, Samuel Ramey, Jerome Hines in Verdi's *Don Carlo*. Contemporary works entered the repertory beginning in 1988, and included Henry Mollicone's *Face on the Barroom Floor*, Carlisle Floyd's *Susannah*, and Philip Glass's *The Juniper Tree*. The 1989-90 season witnessed an updated production of Verdi's *La traviata* by John Conklin, but it was not popular with the Tulsa audience. The company's first premiere arrived in November 1990 when Verdi's *Le Trouvère* was mounted. Another premiere graced the stage two years later, Gioachino Rossini's *Armida*.

The three-opera season is standard fare in a *stagione* system. Recent productions include Verdi's *Rigoletto*, Puccini's *Tosca*, and Mozart's *Le nozze di Figaro*. The company performs in the 2,345-seat Chapman Music Hall in the Performing Arts Center.

Practical Information. The Chapman Music Hall is at Third and Cincinnati. Tickets are purchased at the Tulsa Opera box office, 1610 South Boulder, between 9:00 A.M. and 5:00 P.M. Monday through Friday, or by telephoning 918-587-4811, or writing Tulsa Opera, 1610 South Boulder, Tulsa, OK 74119-4479. If you go, stay at the Westin Hotel, William Center, 10 East Second Street, Tulsa, OK 74103; telephone 918-582-9000, fax 918-560-2261, reservations 1-800-228-3000. The Westin is located downtown, adjacent to the Performing Arts Center.

COMPANY STAFF AND REPERTORY

General/Artistic Directors. None (1948–1974); Edward Purrington (1974–1986); Bernard Uzan (1987); Nicholas Muni (1988–1993); Carol Crawford (1994–present).

American/United States Premieres. Verdi's *Le Trouvère* (November 3, 1990); Rossini's *Armida* (February 29, 1992).

Repertory. **1948:** La traviata. **1949:** La traviata, The Red Mill. **1950:** Der tapfere Soldat, The New Moon. **1951:** Irene, Die lustige Witwe, The Desert Song. **1952-53:** Rio Rita, The Prince of Pilsen, No, No, Nanette. **1953-54:** Madama Butterfly, Prodaná nevěsta (The Bartered Bride). **1954-55:** La traviata, La bohème. **1955-56:** Faust, Rigoletto. **1956-57:** Aida, Carmen. **1957-58:** Tosca, Lucia di Lammermoor. **1958-59:** Madama Butterfly, Il trovatore. **1959-60:** Un ballo in maschera, La bohème. **1960-61:** La traviata, Cavalleria rusticana/ I pagliacci. **1961-62:** Rigoletto, Il barbiere di Siviglia. **1962-63:** Carmen, Le nozze di Figaro. **1963-64:** Tosca, Lucia di Lammermoor. **1964-65:** Aida, Hänsel und Gretel, La bohème. **1965-66:** L'elisir d'amore, Hänsel und Gretel, Faust. **1966-67:** Turandot, Hänsel und Gretel, La traviata. **1967-68:** Madama Butterfly, Don Pasquale. **1968-69:** Rigoletto, Hänsel und Gretel, Die Fledermaus. **1969-70:** Aida, Il barbiere di Siviglia. **1970-71:** Tosca, Lucia di Lammermoor. **1971-72:** Otello, La bohème. **1972-73:** Carmen, Manon Lescaut. **1973-74:** Il trovatore, Roméo et Juliette. **1974-75:** Madama Butterfly, Rigoletto. **1975-76:** Tosca, Ballad of Baby Doe. **1976-77:** Manon, Macbeth. **1977-78:** Aida, I Puritani. **1978-79:** Don Giovanni, La traviata. **1979-80:** La navarraise/I pagliacci, Die Walküre, Die Fledermaus. **1980-81:** Boris Godunov, La bohème, La fille du régiment. **1981-82:** Andrea Chénier, Attila, Il barbiere di Siviglia. **1982-83:** Il trovatore, Der Rosenkavalier, Madama Butterfly. **1983-84:** Der fliegende Holländer, Lucia di Lammermoor, The Pirates of Penzance. **1984-85:** Carmen, Tosca, Die lustige Witwe. **1985-86:** Aida, Faust, Manon Lescaut. **1986-87:** Porgy & Bess, Le nozze di Figaro, Don Carlo. **1987-88:** Rigoletto, Les contes d'Hoffmann, The Mikado. **1988-89:** Suor Angelica/I pagliacci, Samson et Dalila, Roméo et Juliette, Face on the Barroom Floor, Susannah. **1989-90:** La bohème, Amahl and the Night Visitors, The Juniper Tree, La traviata, La Cenerentola. **1990-91:** Le trouvère, Amahl and the Night Visitors, Die Zauberflöte, Il barbiere di Siviglia, Madama Butterfly. **1991-92:** La fanciulla del West, Armida, Così fan tutte, H.M.S. Pinafore. **1992-93:** Carmen, Fidelio, Il barbiere di Siviglia. **1993-94:** Tosca, Rigoletto, Le nozze di Figaro.

Oregon ——————————— EUGENE

• *Eugene Opera* •

Giacomo Puccini's *La bohème* inaugurated the Eugene Opera as a professional company in 1982 at the Hult Center for the Performing Arts. Philip Bayles founded the company six years earlier as a community opera organization using local talent and performing in a high school auditorium. The initial season at the Hult Center also offered Johann Strauß's *Die Fledermaus* and Gaetano Donizetti's *Don Pasquale*.

Wolfgang Amadeus Mozart's *Die Zauberflöte* opened the second season that also saw Giuseppe Verdi's *La traviata*. Contemporary works also entered the repertory, including Gian Carlo Menotti's *The Medium* and *The Telephone*, and Henry Mollicone's *Face on the Barroom Floor*. The company uses young performers.

The three-opera season offers a mixture of traditional fare and contemporary musical theater. (One production is in concert form.) Recent works include Puccini's *Tosca* and Arthur Sullivan's *H.M.S. Pinafore*. The company performs in the 2,500-seat Hult Center for the Performing Arts.

Practical Information. Tickets are available by writing the Eugene Opera, P.O.B. 11200, Eugene, OR 97440, or telephoning 503-687-5000.

REPERTORY

Repertory. **1982-82:** La bohème, Die Fledermaus, Don Pasquale. **1983-84:** Die Zauberflöte, La traviata. **1984-85:** Faust, La Cenerentola, The Pirates of Penzance. **1985-86:** Carmen, Hänsel und Gretel, Madama Butterfly. **1986-87:** Il barbiere di Siviglia, Die lustige Witwe, The Medium, The Mikado. **1987-88:** Tosca, La fille du régiment, Tartuffe, Le nozze di Figaro. **1988-89:** La bohème, L'elisir d'amore, Così fan tutte. **1989-90:** Gianni Schicchi/I pagliacci, La Cenerentola. **1990-91:** Il barbiere di Siviglia, Rigoletto, Madama Butterfly. **1991-92:** Candide, Roméo et Juliette. **1992-93:** Der Schauspieldirektor, The Telephone, The Face on the Barroom Floor. **1993-94:** Cavalleria rusticana, Tosca, H.M.S. Pinafore.

─────────────────────────────────────── PORTLAND

• *Portland Opera* •

Giuseppe Verdi's *Aida* brought the Portland Opera Association, originally called the Portland Civic Opera, to life. The opera took place during the summer of 1950, in an amphitheater in Washington Park. Over 5,000 people gathered on a grassy slope to watch the *al fresco* production under the baton of Ariel Rubenstein. There were three additional performances.

Portland heard opera as early as 1867, when the Bianchi Opera Company visited. The company, a touring group of five singers with piano accompaniment, offered seven evenings of opera in the Oro Fino Theatre. Portland's first efforts at homegrown opera date back to 1917, when Roberto Corruccini established the first Portland Opera Association. The Portland Opera survived six years, offering a variety of operas never staged in the city. The company died when Corruccini did. The Civic Auditorium then hosted two world premieres—Franklin Peale Patterson's *The Echo* and Bruce Knowlton's *The Monk of Toledo*.

The next homegrown effort took permanent root. After the success of Verdi's *Aida*, Portland wanted their own indoor opera company. Verdi's *La traviata* inaugurated this effort. Rubenstein convinced Jan Peerce, a big name Met star, to sing Alfredo. Peerce recommended a then-unknown soprano, Beverly Sills, to sing Violetta, because her fee was low. As Violetta expired on an overstuffed couch, bravas greeted the sold-out performance. The box office receipts paid all the bills. Wolfgang Amadeus Mozart's *Don Giovanni* with Jerome Hines followed, but the remarkable feat of the box office receipts covering all the bills was not duplicated. By 1955, Rubstein had resigned and the company was mired in debt. The second homegrown opera effort in Portland was about to pass into oblivion when the city decided to go into the opera business. Eugene Fuerst took Rubenstein's place, and the company received a new name—Theatre Arts Opera Association. Although the annual outdoor productions in Washington Park drew large crowds, the company's indoor season played to half-empty houses in local high school auditoriums. The indoor season used local singers, directors, and designers.

The company was reorganized in 1964, changing its name to Portland Opera Association. That same year, Henry Holt succeeded Fuerst and began to improve the quality of the performances. His tenure in Portland, however, was short-lived. A combination of differences of opinion with the opera board and the lack of funding from the city prompted him to moved to the Seattle Opera. Two years later, Herbert Weiskopf's regime began. He propelled the company into the "big leagues" by casting big-name stars in grand Italian and French operas. The first season he presented Giacomo Puccini's *La bohème* with Jean Fenn and Giuseppe Campora and Georges Bizet's *Carmen* with Rosalind Elias and Justino Díaz. Two seasons later, Weiskopf offered James McCracken and Ramon Vinay in Verdi's *Otello*. Then came the fatal evening of March 22, 1970. A successful performance of Gaetano Donizetti's *Lucia di Lammermoor* had just finished. Giuseppe Campora and Anna Moffo took their final bows. Then Moffo brought out Weiskopf and the singers retired to allow Weiskopf to enjoy the enthusiastic ovation alone. The bow curtain closed, and Weiskopf started toward his dressing room. He did not get very far. Moments later he collapsed on stage, a victim of a heart attack from which he never recovered.

Stefan Minde took over the company, but his first season at the helm had been planned by Weiskopf—Verdi's *Un ballo in maschera*, Mozart's *Don Giovanni*, Ludwig van Beethoven's *Fidelio*, and a novelty, Puccini's *La rondine* with Mary Costa. Then he steered the company into German waters. He shifted from hiring a few big-name artists in otherwise mediocre casts to sing Italian operas to more balanced ensemble casting performing German works. His second season heralded the beginning of staging German novelties (for Portland). Among them were Richard Strauss's *Der Rosenkavalier* and *Ariadne auf Naxos*, Richard Wagner's *Tristan und Isolde*, and Carl Maria von Weber's *Der Freischütz*. The audience complained that the high costs of producing German opera resulted in second-rate, under-rehearsed casts for the Italian productions. Strauss's *Ariadne auf Naxos* was nick-named Ariadne Obnoxious. Nevertheless, the American premiere of Ernest Křenek's *Das Leben des Orest* took place in English as "Life of Orestes" on November 20, 1975. (The work had marked Minde's debut as an opera conductor in Wiesbaden.) The company was again restructured in 1982, with the appointment of Robert Bailey as general director. That same year saw the world premiere of Bernard Herrmann's *Wuthering Heights*. Eight years later, the company's first commissioned work and second world premiere, Christopher Drobny's *Lucy's Lapses*, was staged.

The four-opera season offers a mainstream repertory performed in a *stagione* system. Recent productions include Verdi's *Don Carlo*, Donizetti's *Lucia di Lammermoor* and *L'elisir d'amore*, Pyotr Il'yich Tchaikovsky's *Eugene Onegin*, and Johann Strauß's *Die Fledermaus*. The company performs in the Civic Auditorium.

Civic Auditorium

The Portland Civic Auditorium building dates back to 1917. The Auditorium was renovated in 1968, converting it into a modern performing arts theater. Although physically separated from the Portland Center for the Performing Arts, the Auditorium is considered part of the Performing Arts Complex.

The Portland Civic Auditorium is an imposing rectangular structure of white concrete, glass and steel. Soaring columns line the contemporary glass façade. The modern, fan-shaped auditorium holds two floating tiers. The sleek, white tiers hover over blood red seats. The hall seats 3,000.

Practical Information. The Portland Civic Auditorium is at SW Third Avenue between Clay and Market streets, seven blocks southeast of the Portland Center for the Performing Arts. The box office is at the new theater complex on the corner of Southwest Broadway and Main. Tickets can be ordered by telephoning 503-248-4496, or 503-241-1802 (Portland Opera), by faxing 503-241-4212, or by writing Portland Opera, 1516 SW Alder, Portland, OR 97205. If you go, stay at the Heathman Hotel, Southwest Broadway at Salmon, Portland, OR 97205, telephone 503-241-4100, fax 503-790-7110, reservations 1-800-323-7500. Dating from the "jazz era," the hotel is on the National Register of Historic Places. It is next to the Performing Arts Center.

COMPANY STAFF AND REPERTORY

General/Artistic Directors. Ariel Rubenstein (1950–1955); Eugene Fuerst (1955–1964); Henry Holt (1964–1966); Herbert Weiskopf (1966–1970); Stefan Minde (1970–1982); Robert Bailey (1982–present).

World Premieres (before Portland Opera). Patterson's *The Echo* (June 9, 1925); Knowlton's *The Monk of Toledo* (May 10, 1926); Bimboni's *Winona* (November 11, 1926).

World Premieres (Portland Opera). Bernard Herrmann's *Wuthering Heights* (November 6, 1982); Drobny's *Lucy's Lapses* (April 27, 1990).

American/United States Premiere (Portland Opera). Křenek's *Das Leben des Orest* (in English as "Life of Orestes," November 20, 1975).

Repertory. **1965-66:** Il barbiere di Siviglia. **1966-67:** Faust, Tosca, Madama Butterfly. **1967-68:** La bohème, La traviata, Carmen, Rigoletto. **1968-69:** Otello, Der fliegende Holländer, Manon, Il trovatore. **1969-70:** Aida, Il barbiere di Siviglia, Lucia di Lammermoor, Die Zauberflöte. **1970-71:** Cavalleria rusticana/I pagliacci, Fidelio, Un ballo in maschera, Don Giovanni. **1971-72:** La rondine, Le nozze di Figaro, Tosca, Der Rosenkavalier. **1972-73:** Carmen, Madama Butterfly, Hänsel und Gretel, Così fan tutte, Tristan und Isolde. **1973-74:** Les contes d'Hoffmann, La bohème, Don Pasquale, Ariadne auf Naxos. **1974-75:** Rigoletto, Der Freischütz, L'elisir d'amore, Salome. **1975-76:** La traviata, Das Leben des Orest, Il barbiere di Siviglia, Die Fledermaus. **1976-77:** The Consul, Werther, La Cenerentola, Die Meistersinger. **1977-78:** Carmen, Elektra, Die Zauberflöte, Falstaff. **1978-79:** Norma, Die fliegende Holländer, La fille du régiment, La bohème. **1979-80:** Madama Butterfly, Faust, Fidelio, Il trovatore. **1980-81:** Don Giovanni, Tosca, Die Walküre, Don Pasquale. **1981-82:** Rigoletto, Eugene Onegin, Die Entführung aus dem Serail, Manon Lescaut. **1982-83:** La traviata, Wuthering Heights, La fanciulla del West, Die Fledermaus. **1983-84:** Lohengrin, Così fan tutte, Lucia di Lammermoor, Prodaná nevěsta (The Bartered Bride). **1984-85:** Il barbiere di Siviglia, Carmen, Un ballo in maschera, Martha. **1985-86:** Les contes d'Hoffmann, Pagliacci/Gianni Schicchi, Le nozze di Figaro, Turandot. **1986-87:** La bohème, Der Rosenkavalier, Macbeth, Porgy and Bess. **1987-88:** Roméo et Juliette, Madama Butterfly, Andrea Chénier, Die Zauberflöte. **1988-89:** Tosca, Les pêcheurs des perles, Don Giovanni, Die lustige Witwe. **1989-90:** Aida, Faust, Don Pasquale, Lucy's Lapses, Show Boat. **1990-91:** Rigoletto, Salome, Manon, La favorita, Carousel. **1991-92:** Samson et Dalila, Falstaff, Hänsel und Gretel, La fille du régiment, My Fair Lady. **1992-93:** Eugene Onegin, L'elisir d'amore, Così fan tutte, La traviata. **1993-94:** Carmen, Lucia di Lammermoor, Man of La Mancha, Don Carlo, Die Fledermaus.

Pennsylvania
———————— PHILADELPHIA

• *Opera Company of Philadelphia* •

The first production of the newly formed Opera Company of Philadelphia, Charles Gounod's *Faust*, took place on September 30, 1975. The merging of the Philadelphia Grand Opera with the Philadelphia Lyric Opera created the Opera Company of Philadelphia. The inaugural season was the longest and most impressive season to date. The repertory encompassed seven works, including the world premiere of Gian Carlo Menotti's *The Hero*, introduced on June 1, 1976.

Philadelphia first heard opera during the spring of 1754. Lewis Hallam's London Company of Comedians staged Colley Cibber's *Flora, or Hob in the Wall* and the pantomime, *Harlequin Collector*, the latter seen on June 17, at Plumstead's Warehouse (a warehouse owned by Mayor William Plumstead). The season ran until June 27. When Hallam died the following year, his company disbanded. Hallam's widow married a certain David Douglass, who reorganized the company, renaming it the American Company. Douglass then received permission from Governor Denny to erected a wooden theater on "Society Hill" to offer ballad operas—Henry Fielding's *Virgin Unmasked* and *Mock Doctor*, Henry Carey's *Honest Yorkshireman*, John Gay's *Beggar's Opera*—and *Harlequin Collector*. The Quakers, German Lutherans, and Presbyterians then joined forces to outlaw what they viewed as immoral entertainment, passing the Blue Laws. But Douglass was determined to continue entertaining the Philadelphians and built a more substantial theater on South Street that he named Southwark Theater. Thomas Arne's *Thomas and Sally* inaugurated the Southwark on November 14, 1766. The 1766-1767 season repertory encompassed the following—Gay's *Beggar's Opera*, C. Coffey's *Devil to Pay*, Fielding's *Mock Doctor*, Carey's *Damon and Phillida*, Cibber's *Flora*, Arne's *Love in a Village*, *Harlequin Collector*, and two novelties—Carey's *Contrivances* and William Boyce's *Chaplet*. A planned new comic opera, Andrew Barton's *The Disappointment*, did not pass the censors and had to be canceled. It involved personal reflections deemed unsuitable for the stage. Fall of that year again saw ballad operas and pantomimes at the theater—Arne's *Love in a Village*, Coffey's *Devil to Pay*, Boyce's *Chaplet*, *Harlequin Restored*, and *Harlequin Collector*. The 1772-1773 season was very long, extending from October 28 to March 31. More than fifty-three different works were staged, among them a novelty, Charles Dibdin's *Lionel and Clarissa*. Other works included Dibdin's *Padlock*, Kane O'Hara's *Midas*, Samuel Arnold's *Maid of the Mill*, I. Bickerstaffe's *Thomas and Sally*, Gay's *Beggar's Opera*, Cibber's *Flora*, and Arne's *Neptune and Amphitrite*. During the season, some unsavory characters populated the gallery and subjected both the audience and the actors to offensive behavior—egg throwing! When the American Company returned to Philadelphia on November 1, 1773, their visit was cut short by vicious attacks on the theater published in the newspaper. "It is a matter of real sorrow and distress to many sober inhabitants of different denominations to hear of the return of those strolling Comedians, who are travelling through America, propagating vice and immorality."

The situation improved after the American Revolution. Philadelphia was the seat of the Federal Government and hosted a very active music center. The legislature repealed the anti-theater act on March 2, 1789, and the Southwark was called an Opera House, probably the first building in the United States that was so honored. The (Old) American Company, now under the leadership of Lewis Hallam (the son), was back in business, offering a broad repertory of comic operas and plays. Their last season in Philadelphia opened on September 22, 1794, with William Shield's *Robin Hood* and closed on December 4 with Arnold's *Children in the Woods*. Other works included Gay's *Beggar's Opera*, Dibdin's *Quaker* and *Wedding Ring*, Arne's *Love in a Village*, and James Hewitt's *Tammany*.

Thomas Wignell, a skilled actor with the Old American Company, had left the company to join with Alexander Reinagle, a composer and conductor, to build Philadelphia a new opera house. Richards, Reinagle's brother-in-law, designed the building which was located on Chestnut Street. Known as the New Chestnut Street Theater, it was commonly called the "old Drury," and claimed being the most technologically advanced theater of its day. On Monday evening, Feb. 17, 1794,

Arnold's *The Castle of Andalusia*, with Reinagle on the podium, inaugurated the house. Alongside the usual fare of ballad operas, Reinagle staged his own works — *Arabs of the Desert*, *Auld Robin Gray*, *Forêt noire*, *Gentle Shepherd*, *Italian Monk*, *Columbus*, *Savoyard*, *Shamrock*, *Sicilian Romance*, *Slaves in Algiers*, *Warrior's Welcome Home*, *Volunteers*, and *Witches of the Rock*. During December 1796 and January 1797, Wignell and Reinagle engaged a French Company of Comedians and offered Philadelphians the French opera, including André Grétry's *Le tableau parlant* and *Richard Coeur de Lion* (in English translation), Egidio Duni's *Les deux chasseurs et la laitière*, Alessandro Fridzeri's *Les souliers mordorés*, Nicolas Dezède's *Blaise et Babet*, Stanislaw Champein's *La mélomanie*, and Nicolas Dalayrac's *Les deux petits savoyards*.

John Davis brought his French company from New Orleans to the Chestnut Street Theater in 1827, opening on September 28. Many of the operas Davis introduced to Philadelphia have been called American premieres. This is incorrect. Davis had already performed the works in New Orleans, prior to touring. By the time the troupe departed Philadelphia on October 28, Davis had given sixteen performances, including Carl Maria von Weber's *Der Freischütz* (in French as "Robin des Bois"), Boieldieu's *La dame blanche*, Dalayrac's *Azémia*, and Michele Enrico Carafa de Colobrano's *Le solitaire*. Davis returned the following year, opening on September 16. During his season, the troupe presented the Philadelphia premieres of Étienne-Nicolas Méhul's *Joseph* (October 15), Gasparo Spontini's *La vestale* (October 30), and Auber's *Fiorella* (November 3). Davis's final tour came in 1833, when he brought Hérold's *Zampa*, Auber's *Philtre*, and Fromental Halévy's *Le dilettante d'Avignon* among others. The Havana Italian Opera Company presented Philadelphia with Italian opera, staging Giovanni Simone Mayr's *Che originali* and Rossini's *La gazza ladra* in 1829. Four years later, the Montressor Troupe presented Italian opera at the Chestnut Street Theater, which they dubbed the "Italian Opera House." Saverio Mercadante's *Elisa e Claudio* opened the run on January 23, 1833, followed by Vincenzo Bellini's *Il pirata* and Rossini's *L'italiana in Algeri*, *La Cenerentola*, and *Otello*. The 1843 season at the Chestnut was exceptional. On July 22, 1843, the American premiere of Bellini's *I Puritani* took place followed by the American premiere of Donizetti's *Belisario* on July 29, 1843. October then witnessed an interesting repertoire of French operas — Auber's *L'ambassadrice*, *Les diamants de la Couronne*, *Le domino noir*, and *Acteon*, Adolphe Adam's *Le postillon de Longjumeau*, A. Montfort's *Polichinelle*, Fromental Halévy's *L'éclair*, Antoine Clapisson's *La perruche*, Isouard's *La rendez-vous bourgeois*, Ferdinand Hérold's *Le pré aux clercs*, and Gaetano Donizetti's *La fille du régiment*. In November an Italian company staged a short season that included Bellini's *Norma* and *Il Puritani* and Donizetti's *Lucia di Lammermoor* and *Gemma di Vergy*. The following year, the season began on April 3 with Bellini's *La sonnambula*. Donizetti's *Anna Bolena* was heard as Anna Boleyn, translated into English by Joseph Fry, followed by Auber's *Gustave III* and Michael Balfe's *The Bohemian Girl* on December 30. The Chestnut hosted the world premiere of the first "American grand opera," William Henry Fry's *Leonora*, on June 4, 1845. The New Orleans troupe visited later in the year, mounting Halévy's *La Juive*, Giacomo Meyerbeer's *Robert le Diable* and *Les Huguenots*, Donizetti's *La favorite* and *La fille du régiment*, and Auber's *Le domino noir*, *La muette de Portici*, and *L'ambassadrice*.

The Walnut Street Theater, designed by Philadelphia architect John Haviland, also hosted opera. Visiting troupes performed Rossini's *Il barbiere di Siviglia* and several ballad operas back in 1822. September 1831 saw a short season of opera in English, including Wolfgang Amadeus Mozart's *Le nozze di Figaro* as "The Marriage of Figaro," and a truncated version of Rossini's *Tancredi* (condensed into one act). Gay's *The Beggar's Opera* appeared on January 6, 1832, followed by a "Rossinian" Cinderella (a *pasticcio* constructed from segments of *La Cenerentola, Maometto, Guillaume Tell*, and *Armida*) on January 16, 1832. Auber's *Masaniello* closed the season on September 10, 1832. Three years later, more operas were staged in English — Mozart's *Le nozze di Figaro* as The Marriage of Figaro and Rossini's *La Cenerentola* as Cinderella, and *Il barbiere di Siviglia* as The Barber of Seville. On January 31, 1846, the Walnut witnessed the world premiere of Balfe's *The Enchantress* followed by his *Bohemian Girl* and Fry's *Leonora*. The directors of the Italian Company from Havana announced a season at the Walnut for July / August 1847, that introduced Verdi's operas to the city. The season opened on the twelfth with Giovanni Pacini's *Saffo* followed by Verdi's *Ernani* on July 14, *I Lombardi* on July 17, and *I due foscari* on July 19. Five years later, the American premiere of Verdi's *Luisa Miller* (in English) took place with Caroline Richings and Anna Bishop. Two famous Italian singers, Giulia Grisi and Giovanni Mario, also performed at the Walnut, where the best seats for their performances sold for $3, when 10¢ to 50¢ was the norm.

The Academy of Music opened its doors on January 26, 1857. The first opera arrived on February 25, when the Academy hosted Verdi's *Il trovatore* with Marietta Gazzaniga and Pasquale Brignoli, and Max Maretzek on the podium. Donizetti's *Lucrezia Borgia* arrived three days later. Italian opera continued to predominate with Bellini's *Norma* and *I Puritani*, Auber's *La muette de Portici* (as Masaniello), Donizetti's *Linda di Chamounix*, and Verdi's *Luisa Miller* and *La traviata*. The second opera season offered only four works — Rossini's *Guillaume Tell*, Donizetti's *Maria di Rohan*, *La favorite* (as La favorita), and *L'elisir d'amore*. The Academy hosted the American premiere of Verdi's *Les vêpres siciliennes* on December 7, 1859, and the following evening saw a sixteen-year-old Adelina Patti make her debut in Donizetti's *Lucia di Lammermoor*. She performed in Bellini's *La sonnambula* later that week, and in Mozart's *Don Giovanni* at the end of the month. When the Prince of Wales (and future King Edward VII) visited the Academy, Patti entertained at his request. On October 10, 1860, Patti performed in Friedrich von Flotow's *Martha*. As was the custom, the program concluded with an act from another opera — the ballroom scene from Verdi's *La traviata*. Patti's association with the Academy spanned almost five decades.

During the Civil War and for a decade or so afterwards, the repertory consisted primarily of works rarely performed today — Konrad Kreutzer's *Das Nachtlager von Granada*, Méhul's *Joseph*, Boieldieu' *Jean de Paris*, Flotow's *Alessandro Stradella*, Adolphe's *Le postillon de Longjumeau*, Albert Lortzing's *Der Wildschütz* and *Zar und Zimmermann*, Auber's *Fra Diavolo* and *Le maçon et serrurier*, and Meyerbeer's *Le pardon de Ploërmel*. The Academy introduced Otto Nicolai's *Die lustigen Weiber von Windsor* to America on March 16, 1863, and Gounod's *Faust* (in German) on November 18, 1863. It saw its first world premiere, Fry's *Notre-Dame de Paris*, on May 4, 1864. The composer's brother, Joseph R. Fry, wrote the libretto. Sung in English, the opera was given seven performances. The American premiere of Gounod's *Mireille* arrived November 18, 1864. Boston had seen opera excerpts, but this was the first complete performance in America. For the centennial celebration, the Academy hosted the American premiere of Richard Wagner's *Der fliegende Holländer*, sung in Italian as Il vascello fantasma. The Academy celebrated its twentieth anniversary with *éclat*. The artists who had performed in the inaugural Verdi's *Il trovatore* (Gazzaniga and Brignoli) returned. Patti delighted on January 23, 1884, in Luigi Ricci's *La Crispino e la Comare*. The Metropolitan Opera Company gave its first performance in Philadelphia on April 14, 1884, beginning a tradition that lasted until the 1960s. The company, billed as "Mr. Henry Abbey's Grand Italian Opera Company from the Metropolitan Opera House," presented Meyerbeer's *Les Huguenots, Le Prophète*, and *Robert le Diable*, Gounod's *Roméo et Juliette*, Ambroise Thomas's *Mignon*, Wagner's *Lohengrin*, and Rossini's *Il barbiere di Siviglia*. Colonel Mapleson's company had a short season at the Academy in January 1885. It was also Patti's last season for a long time. Other *prime donne* filled the void—Sybil Sanderson, Emma Calvé, and Lilli Lehmann. Lehmann's debut was as Brünnhilde in Wagner's *Die Walküre* in January 1897. German operas had finally entered the repertory, including Weber's *Der Freischütz* and Wagner's *Tannhäuser, Die Meistersinger, Götterdämmerung*, and *Tristan und Isolde*. Pietro Mascagni visited with his company to conduct *Zanetto* and the American premiere of *Iris* on October 14, 1902. Patti gave her farewell performance on November 9, 1903, and Enrico Caruso made his Philadelphia debut in Verdi's *Rigoletto* on December 29. Geraldine Farrar followed in Gounod's *Roméo et Juliette* on December 4, 1906. The Philadelphia premiere of *Madama Butterfly* took place on February 14, 1907, and boasted an impressive cast—Farrar, Louise Homer, and Caruso.

Oscar Hammerstein first appeared on the Philadelphia opera scene in March 1908, responding to a formal invitation from several prominent Philadelphians. He challenged the supremacy of the Metropolitan in the Quaker city as he had in New York. The competition resulted in a rich operatic month of March at the Academy where both the Met and Hammerstein's Manhattan company performed. Hammerstein offered two productions, Donizetti's *Lucia di Lammermoor* (March 19) with Luisa Tetrazzini, Mario Sammarco, and Giovanni Zenatello, and Gustave Charpentier's *Louise* (March 26) with Mary Garden. The Met countered with Verdi's *Il trovatore* with Eames, Caruso, and Homer and *Aida* with Eames, Caruso, Scotti, and Plançon. Two days after the Academy's patrons cheered Hammerstein and Garden after the final curtain of Charpentier's *Louise*, Hammerstein's son, Arthur, broke ground for his Philadelphia Opera House. Completed in record time, the 4,000-seat theater was inaugurated with Bizet's *Carmen* on Tuesday, November 17, 1908, with Maria Labia, Charles Dalmorès, Andrés de Segurola, and Alice Zeppilli. Cleofonte Campanini was on the podium. That same evening, the Met opened its season at the Academy with Caruso in Puccini's *La bohème*. It was an evening Philadelphia opera-lovers never forgot. Many shuttled between the two theaters all evening, catching an act of Puccini's *La bohème* at the Academy and an act of Bizet's *Carmen* at the Philadelphia Opera House.

Hammerstein then mounted Saint-Saëns's *Samson et Dalila* on November 19 with Jeanne Gerville-Réache and Dalmorès, under the baton of Giuseppe Sturani. Hammerstein invited four hundred clergymen to attend the performance to demonstrate that it was possible to present operatic versions of biblical episodes that were not sacrilegious, since much criticism appeared in the newspapers of his proposed performance of Richard Strauss's *Salome*. *Salome* had already been banned at the Met. As in his Manhattan Opera House, Hammerstein emphasized the French repertory, staging Massenet's *Thaïs*, *Le jongleur de Notre Dame*, and *La navarraise*, Meyerbeer's *Les Huguenots*, Gounod's *Faust*, Debussy's *Pelléas et Mélisande*, and Charpentier's *Louise* among the traditional Italian fare. His first full season at the Philadelphia Opera House closed on April 3, 1909, with Donizetti's *Lucia di Lammermoor*.

At the beginning of the season, Hammerstein experienced problems securing a loan for the Philadelphia Opera House (because he refused to use the Manhattan Opera House as collateral). Then he announced on December 31, 1908, that if a loan was not forthcoming, he would either have to close the opera house or if he continued, use second-rate casts. Nellie Melba, who had appeared both at Hammerstein's Manhattan Opera House and his Philadelphia Opera House, pleaded his cause via the press. "Tell the people of Philadelphia that Melba says it would be a disgrace for them to sit idly by and see the splendid opera house closed. Tell them that I expect greater things of them, individually and collectively." Four days later, Edward Stotesbury personally took the $400,000 mortgage with only the Philadelphia Opera House as security.

An all-out opera war broke out during the 1909-1910 season. Both companies opened not only on the same night, November 9, 1909, but with the same opera—Verdi's *Aida*. At the Philadelphia House were Mariette Mazarin, Nicola Zerola, Marguerite d'Alverez, and Giovanni Polese, with Sturani conducting. A few blocks to the south at the Academy were Gadski, Caruso, Homer, and Amato, with Toscanini conducting. Hammerstein wanted a direct comparison between the two companies. Both houses were filled, with some patrons shuttling back and forth to catch both performances. The newspaper accounts were more concerned with the audience than with the performance. The *Public Ledger* wrote, "Socially considered, one audience was quite as brilliant as the other, the actual leaders in the city's fashionable set having so divided themselves as to give to neither house an advantage in this respect over the other." The fare was *opéra-comique* Monday evenings, and grand opera Tuesday, Thursday, Saturday evenings, and Sunday matinees. Massenet's *Hérodiade*, *Thaïs*, *La Navarraise*, *Le jongleur de Notre-Dame*, and *Sapho*, Edmond Audran's *La mascotte*, Claude Debussy's *Pelléas et Mélisande*, and Gustave Charpentier's *Louise* were some of his second season offerings. The Met mounted Ruggero Leoncavallo's *I pagliacci*, Wagner's *Die Walküre*, Verdi's *Falstaff*, and Mozart's *Le nozze di Figaro* among its presentations. It proved to be Hammerstein's final ruinous season. His Philadelphia Opera House had lost large sums of money and he could not continue. The Metropolitan was guaranteed $7,500 a performance, but Hammerstein had to rely on popular subscription. In addition, Otto Kahn and William Vanderbilt made large contribution to the Metropolitan Opera during the "opera war" so it could "sustain its losses without failing." On April 26, 1910, Arthur Hammerstein, with his father's power of attorney, sold Oscar Hammerstein's operatic interests which included the Philadelphia Opera House. The theater was renamed the Metropolitan Opera House, and the Academy lost its most faithful opera tenant for the next decade. (See New York Metropolitan Opera entry for more on the Hammersteins.)

On December 13, 1910, the Met opened with Wagner's *Tannhäuser* in the Metropolitan Opera House with Leo Slezak in the title role. The world premiere of Victor Herbert's *Natoma* followed on February 25, 1911. The Met also introduced Karl Goldmark's *Das Heimchen am Herd* (in English as The Cricket on the Hearth) and Alberto Franchetti's *Cristoforo Colombo*. Before the decade was over, the Philadelphia Orchestra had bought the Academy and called it home. The Metropolitan Opera House became a foreclosure victim that forced the Met to move back into the Academy. The Metropolitan celebrated its return to the Academy (1920-21 season) with Caruso and Ponselle in Fromental Halévy's *La Juive*. As in New York, Caruso's last appearance in Philadelphia was as Eléazar. Bizet's *Carmen* followed with Farrar, Martinelli, and Clarence Whitehill. In 1923, Maria Jeritza sang the title role in Massenet's *Thaïs* and appeared with Martinelli and Scotti in Umberto Giordano's *Fedora*. Feodor Chaliapin's marvelous voice also resounded through the Academy. The closing weeks of 1929 heralded the appearance of Marian Anderson, a city native.

A homegrown opera company, the Philadelphia Civic Opera (renamed the Philadelphia Lyric Opera Company in 1958) was established in 1923 with Alexander Smallens as the music director. The Civic Opera hosted several American premieres, including Erich Korngold's *Der Ring des Polykrates*, Richard Strauss's *Feuersnot* and *Ariadne auf Naxos*, and Eugene Goossens's *Judith*. Another homegrown opera company, the Philadelphia Grand Opera Company, was born in 1927 as the Pennsylvania Grand Opera Company and eventually developed into the Philadelphia La Scala Company. Leopold Stokowski frequently conducted there. The company presented both new productions of standard works and novelties, including the American premieres of Modest Mussorgsky's *Khovanschchina*, Arnold Schönberg's *Die glückliche Hand*, and Alban Berg's *Wozzeck*. The company mounted twenty performances during the 1931-32 season, including Wagner's *Tannhäuser* conducted by Fritz Reiner. One of the company's benefactors, Mrs. Bok, paid the deficit of $500,000, but she could not continue. The Depression was taking its toll. Opera continued at the Academy under the auspices of the Philadelphia Orchestra with productions that offered a full, rich orchestral sound. The Orchestra presented Bizet's *Carmen*, Strauss's *Der Rosenkavalier*, Engelbert Humperdinck's *Hänsel und Gretel*, Modest Mussorgsky's *Boris Godunov*, Verdi's *Falstaff*, and Debussy's *Pelléas et Mélisande*. Philadelphians also heard an uncut Wagner's *Die Meistersinger*, the first performance of the original score of Wagner's *Tristan und Isolde,* and more novelties, Igor Stravinsky's *Mavra*, Christoph Gluck's *Iphigénie en Aulide*, and Gian Carlo Menotti's *Amelia al Ballo*, in English as *Amelia Goes to the Ball*.

In 1938, the Philadelphia Opera Company was established, producing opera in English. One of their successes was Debussy's *Pelléas et Mélisande* with Maeterlinck (who wrote the libretto to Debussy's score) in the audience. A critic described the performance as "ambitious, enterprising, and even audacious." On February 9, 1942, the company introduced Deems Taylor's third opera, *Ramuntcho*, to the world. The production was called "the company's most notable undertaking and the fondest ambition of its four-year career." Two years later, the company signed a contract with Sol Hurok to go on a twenty-week cross-country tour of Franz Lehár's *Die lustige Witwe*. Without warning, it declared bankruptcy and disbanded.

Kirsten Flagstad's appearance after the war caused the worst disturbance that ever transpired either inside or outside the Academy walls. Flagstad's sympathies during World War II were not with the Allies, and that, understandably, disturbed many people. Protesters paraded placards reading "She sang for Goering in '42; tonight will Flagstad sing for you?." Hissing, whistling, and booing accompanied the concert. On January 7, 1955, Marian Anderson became the first black

Academy of Music (Philadelphia, Pennsylvania).

soloist ever to appear on the stage of the Metropolitan Opera House in New York (singing Ulrica in Verdi's *Un ballo in maschera*). Four days later, she returned to her native Philadelphia (with the Metropolitan Opera) and reprised her role. Herva Nelli, Richard Tucker, Leonard Warren, and Roberta Peters joined her in Verdi's *Un ballo in maschera* with Dmitry Mitropoulos making his Academy debut. During the 1960s, the Academy hosted many international artist—Jerome Hines, Leonard Warren, Renata Tebaldi and Richard Tucker, Birgit Nilsson, Joan Sutherland, and Nicolai Gedda. Plácido Domingo and Montserrat Caballé ushered in the 1970s with Verdi's *Il trovatore*. The Opera Company of Philadelphia was founded later in the decade.

A few years after the company's establishment, the board appointed Margaret Anne Everitt general director. During her decade-long reign, she brought international attention and acclaim to the company by combining outstanding voices, rarely performed operas, and innovative productions. Rossini's *Mosè in Egitto* was awakened from a 128-year sleep on October 13, 1981. Bizet's *Carmen* was reset in the Spanish Civil War. Jessye Norman made her American debut in Henry Purcell's rarely-performed *Dido & Aeneas* during the 1982-83 season. The following season, Vladimir Popov made his debut in Pyotr Il'yich Tchaikovsky's *Pikovaya dama*. James Morris also sang with the company. The 1983-84 season ushered in an unprecedented Faust trilogy—Gounod's *Faust*, Hector Berlioz's *La Damnation de Faust*, and Arrigo Boïto's *Mefistofele*. Benjamin Britten's *Death in Venice* graced the stage during the 1986-87 season, and Antonín Dvořák's *Rusalka* followed the next season. The first revival in the twentieth century of Rossini's *La gazza ladra*, along with Georg Friedrich Händel's *Ariodante*, and Menotti's *The Saint of Bleecker Street* highlighted the 1989-90 season. In February 1990, after a decade

at the helm, the board forced Everitt out. She did not offset her adventurous repertory with enough "war horses" to balance the books, leaving a $1 million deficit.
The company is retrenching, resulting in uninspired, hackneyed affairs under the
directorship of Robert Driver. He hails from a small regional-opera-company background and has been unable to steer the Opera Company of Philadelphia back to
national ranking. The glorious days of Everitt's tenure are history.

Philadelphia hosts the Luciano Pavarotti International Voice Competition,
which is alive and well. The competition started in 1980 with 500 singers from five
continents. Currently, it attracts more than 1,500 hopeful young artists from around
the globe. The Competition takes place over a twenty-six-month period, and the
winners perform with the competition's namesake, Pavarotti, in a nationally televised broadcast. Pavarotti has joined the competition winners in Donizetti's *L'elisir
d'amore*, Puccini's *La bohème*, and Verdi's *Un ballo in maschera*.

The four-opera season offers standard repertory in traditional productions in
a *stagione* system. Recent works include Bizet's *Carmen*, Puccini's *Tosca*, Mascagni's *Cavalleria rusticana*, Leoncavallo's *I pagliacci*, and Gounod's *Roméo et
Juliette*. The company performs in the Academy of Music.

The Academy of Music

The Philadelphian's passion for opera gave the city the oldest opera house still in
continuous use in America. The founding date for the Academy of Music is February 19, 1851. The original plans saw the Academy overshadowing the three
greatest opera houses of the time — Teatro di San Carlo in Naples, Teatro alla Scala
in Milan, and Her Majesty's Theater in London. Money considerations scaled down
this unrealistic dream. Gustav Rungé won the architectural competition and
designed the Academy. Private stock subscriptions paid the $250,000 price tag. A
Grand Inaugural Ball opened the Academy on January 26, 1857, to which the
cream of Philadelphia Society, dressed in their finest, came by carriage and foot.
The Academy did not disappoint.

The Academy looks very much today as it did when it opened. The building
displays an unassuming chocolate-brown concrete and reddish brick façade. Doric
pilasters separate tall arched windows, and cornices harmonize with the masonry
trim. Glass and wrought iron gas lamps flank the arched entrances. The grand
lobby boasts faux-marble ivory walls embellished with faux-marble Doric pilasters.
Delicately etched, glass-cup lights with Mercury poised on top flank the stairways.
Inspired by the Teatro alla Scala (Milan), the red, cream, and gilded horseshoe-
shaped auditorium boasts perfect acoustics. Three tiers of ivory splendor sweep
around the room, encircling it with slender columns. Muses inhabit the fresco-
ceiling. A gilded medallion of Mozart presides high above the proscenium arch,
flanked by massive pairs of fluted, gilded Corinthian columns. Clusters of
medallions, instruments, and urns embellish the parapets. The Academy seats
2,800.

Practical Information. The Academy of Music is at Broad and Locust Streets.
Tickets are purchased at the Opera Company of Philadelphia box office, at The
Graham Building, 20th Floor, One Penn Square West, Monday through Friday
from 9 A.M. to 5 P.M., by telephoning 215-981-1454 or writing Opera Company
of Philadelphia, The Graham Building, 20th Floor, One Penn Square West,

Philadelphia, PA 19102. If you go, stay at the Four Seasons Hotel Philadelphia, One Logan Square, Philadelphia, PA 19103; telephone 215-963-1500, fax 215-963-9506, reservations 1-800-332-3442. Faithful reproductions from Philadelphia's Federal period luxuriously decorate the hotel which offers elegant accommodations and superb service. (The Academy of Music itself is worth a visit.)

COMPANY STAFF AND REPERTORY

General/Artistic Directors (Opera Company of Philadelphia). Margaret Anne Everitt (1980–90); Jane Grey Nemeth (acting, 1990–92); Robert Driver (1992–present).

American/United States Premieres (Southwark Theater). Bickerstaffe's *Thomas and Sally* (November 14, 1766); Carey's *The Contrivances* (April 20, 1767); Boyce's *Chaplet* (June 4, 1767); O'Hara's *Midas* (November 24, 1769); Dibdin's *Lionel and Clarissa* (December 14, 1772); Arnold's *Agreeable Surprise* (January 27, 1787); Dibdin's *Deserter* (July 11, 1787); Grétry-Linley's *Selima and Azor* (July 28, 1787); Arnold's *Banditti* (November 5, 1788); Arnold's *Dead Alive* (February 19, 1790); Arnold's *Inkle and Yarico* (May 17, 1790); Arne's *Cymon and Sylvia* (May 20, 1790); Carter's *Rival Candidates* (July 13, 1791); Storace's *No Song, no Supper* (November 30, 1792); Pélissier's *The Danaides* (pantomime, October 8, 1794); Arnold's *The Children in the Wood* (November 24, 1794).

World Premieres (New Chestnut Street Theater). Reinagle's *Slaves in Algiers* (June 30, 1794); Reinagle's *The Volunteers* (January 21, 1795); Carr's *The Patriot* (May 16, 1796); Reinagle's *Columbus* (February 1, 1797); Reinagle's *The Savoyard* (July 12, 1797); Carr's *The American in London* (March 28, 1798); Taylor's *Buxom Joan* (January 30, 1801); Bray's *The Indian Princess* (April 6, 1808).

American/United States Premieres (New Chestnut Street Theater). Arnold's *Castle of Andalusia* (February 17, 1794); Dibdin's *Sultan* (May 19, 1794); Storace's *The Prize* (May 26, 1794); Shield's *Hartford Bridge* (May 30, 1794); Arnold's *The Spanish Barber* (July 7, 1794); Reeve's *The Purse* (additional music by Reinagle, January 7, 1795); Dibdin's *Poor Vulcan* (March 28, 1795); Arne-Markordt's *Tom Thumb the Great* (April 22, 1795); Storace's *My Grandmother* (April 27, 1795); Arnold's *Auld Robin Gray* (with new music by Reinagle, May 4, 1795); Shield's *The Noble Peasant* (May 8, 1795); Attwood's *The Prisoner* (May 29, 1795); Shield's *The Midnight Wanderers* (June 1, 1796); Dalayrac's *Deux petits savoyards* (January 14, 1797); Storace's *Iron Chest* (April 17, 1797); Arnold's *The Shipwreck* (March 2, 1798); Shield's *Marian* (April 21, 1798); Shield's *Rival Soldiers* (April 5, 1799); Kelly-Reinagle's *Castle Spectre* (April 2, 1800); Davy's *Spanish Dollar's* (1806-1807); Kelly's *Youth, Love and Folly* (1806-1807); Hook's *The Soldier's Return* (1807); Kelly's *The Young Hussar* (1807-1808).

World Premieres (Walnut Street Theater). Heinrich's *The Child of the Mountain* (February 10, 1821); Clemens's *Justina* (May 18, 1830).

American/United States Premieres (Walnut Street Theater). Barnett's *The Pet of the Petticoats* (March 7, 1835); Balfe's *The Enchantress* (January 31, 1846); Mercadante's *Il bravo* (in English as The Bravo, October 2, 1849); Wallace's *Maritana* (November 9, 1846); Adam's *Giralda* (in English, December 5, 1850); Verdi's *Luisa Miller* (in English, October 27, 1852).

World Premieres (Chestnut Street Theater). Fry's *Leonora* (June 4, 1845); Fairlamb's *Valerie* (December 15, 1869).

American/United States Premieres (Chestnut Street Theater). Weber's *Abu Hassan* (in English, November 21, 1827); Arne's *Artaxerxes* (December 28, 1827); Bishop's *The Fall of Algiers* (July 4, 1829); Weber's *Preciosa* (in English, October 31, 1829); Dalayrac's *Deux Mots* (in English as Two Words, May 18, 1839); Bishop's *Guy Mannering* (in English, November 30, 1840); Bellini's *I Puritani* (July 22, 1843); Donizetti's *Belisario* (July 29, 1843).

American/United States Premieres (Third Chestnut Street Theater): Millöcker's

Der Bettelstudent (in English as The Beggar Student, October 22, 1883); von Suppé's *Boccaccio* (in English, April 5, 1880).

World Premieres (Philadelphia Grand Opera House). Hinrichs's *Onti-Ora* (July 28, 1890).

American/United States Premieres (Philadelphia Grand Opera House). Mascagni's *Cavalleria rusticana* (September 9, 1891); Mascagni's *L'amico Fritz* (June 8, 1892); Leoncavallo's *I pagliacci* (June 15, 1893); Bizet's *Les pêcheurs de perles* (in Italian, August 23, 1893); Puccini's *Manon Lescaut* (August 29, 1894).

World Premieres (Metropolitan Opera House). Herbert's *Natoma* (February 25, 1911); Parelli's *I dispettosi amanti* (March 6, 1912); Heckscher's *The Rose of Destiny* (May 2, 1918).

American/United States Premieres (Metropolitan Opera House). Nouguès's *Quo Vadis?* (March 25, 1911); Goldmark's *Das Heimchen am Herd* (in English as The Cricket on the Hearth, November 7, 1912); Franchetti's *Cristoforo Colombo* (November 20, 1913); Kienzl's *Der Kuhreigen* (in French as Le Ranz des vaches, February 21, 1913); Gnecchi's *Cassandra* (February 26, 1914); Moniuszko's *Verbum Nobile* (February 28, 1916) ; Moniuszko's *Flis* (April 29, 1925); Korngold's *Der Ring des Polykrates* (February 10, 1927); Strauss's *Feuersnot* (December 1, 1927); Gluck's *Die Maienkönigin* (December 1, 1927); Mussorgsky's *Khovanshchina* (in English, April 18, 1928); Stravinsky's *Oedipus Rex* (first stage performance, April 10, 1931).

World Premieres (Academy of Music). Fry's *Notre-Dame de Paris* (May 4, 1864); Bonawitz's *Bride of Messina* (April 22, 1874); Bonawitz's *Ostrolenka* (May 3, 1874); Leps's *Andon* (concert form, December 22, 1905); Leps's *Hoshi-San* (May 21, 1909); Menotti's *Amelia al ballo* (in English as Amelia Goes to the Ball, April 1, 1937); de Senez's *Horus* (January 5, 1939); Taylor's *Ramuntcho* (February 10, 1942); Zimbalist's *Landara* (April 6, 1956); Menotti's *The Hero* (June 1, 1975).

American/United States Premieres (Academy of Music). Fioravanti's *Il ritorno di Pulcinella dagli studi di Padova* (one scene as Columella, April 4, 1857); Verdi's *Les vêpres siciliennes* (December 7, 1859); Massé's *Les noces de Jeannette* (in French, stage performance, October 25, 1861); Donizetti's *Betly ossia la capanna svizzera* (October 25, 1861); Massé's *Les noces de Jeannette* (first stage performance in French, October 25, 1861); Nicolai's *Die lustigen Weiber von Windsor* (March 16, 1863); Gounod's *Faust* (in German, November 18, 1863) ; Spohr's *Jessonda* (February 15, 1864); Gounod's *Mireille* (in German (Act I, Act II, November 17, 1864) ; Benedict's *The Lily of Killarney* (November 20, 1867); Wagner's *Der fliegende Holländer*, (in Italian as *Il vascello fantasma*, November 8, 1876); Mascagni's *Iris* (October 14, 1902); Strauss's *Ariadne auf Naxos* (November 1, 1928); Goossens's *Judith* (December 26, 1929) ; Schönberg's *Die glückliche Hand* (April 11, 1930); Berg's *Wozzeck* (March 19, 1931); Strauss's *Elektra* (first performance in German, October 29, 1931); Stravinsky's *Mavra* (in English, December 28, 1934); Gluck's *Iphigénie en Aulide* (February 22, 1935); Borodin's *Prince Igor* (first performance in Russian, December 23, 1935); Milhaud's *Le pauvre matelot* (April 1, 1937); Menotti's *The Old Maid and the Thief* (stage premiere, February 11, 1941); Rezniček's *Spiel oder Ernst?* (in English as Fact or Fiction, February 11, 1941.

Repertory (Southwark Theater). 1787–92 **(January through May):** Aesop in the Shades, Agreeable Surprise, Banditti, Bird Catcher, Birth of Harlequin, Columbine Invisible, Cymon and Sylvia, Darby's Return, Dead Alive, Deserter, Detection, Devil to Pay, Duenna, Dutchman, Flitch of Bacon, Flora, Fourth of July, Harlequin Protected by Cupid, Inkle and Yarico, King of Genii, Lord of the Manor, Love in a Camp, Love in a Village, Madcap, Maid of the Mill, Midas, Mock Doctor, Modern Love, Neptune and Amphitrite, Orpheus and Eurydice, Padlock, Patie and Roger, Poor Soldier, Return of the Laborers, Rival Candidates, Rosina, Selima and Azor, Thomas and Sally, Two Misers. **1792 (October through December) –1794:** Agreeable Surprise, America Discovered, Beggar's Opera, Bird Catcher, Birth of Harlequin, Children in the Woods, Danaides, Deserter, Devil to Pay, Don Juan, Farmer, Flitch of Bacon, Haunted Tower, Highland Reel, Hunt the Slipper, Lionel and Clarissa, Love in a Village, Maid of the Mill, Midas, No Song, No Supper, Padlock, Poor Soldier, Quaker, Rival Candidates, Robin Hood, Romp, Rosina, Tammany, Two Philosophers, Wedding Ring.

Repertory (New Chestnut Street Theater). 1794: Agreeable Surprise, L'Américain (pantomime), Battle of Hexham, Birth of Harlequin, (pantomime), Castle of Andalusia, Deserter, Duenna, Farmer, Female Heroism (pantomime), Flitch of Bacon, Forêt noire (pantomime), Fruitless Precaution (pantomime), Harlequin Shipwrecked (pantomime-pasticcio), Hartford Bridge, Highland Reel, Inkle and Yarico, Irish Lilt (pantomime), Lionel and Clarissa, Love in a Village, Maid of the Mill, No Song, no Supper, Peeping Tom of Coventry, Poor Soldier, Prize, Robin Hood, Robinson Crusoe (pantomime), Romp, La Rose et le bouton (pantomime), Rosina, Sailor's Landlady (pantomime), Scheming Clown (pantomime), Scheming Miners (pantomime), Selima and Azor, Slaves in Algiers, Son-in-law, Spanish Barber, Sultan, Surrender of Calais, Triumph of Mirth (pantomime), Virgin Unmasked, Waterman, Woodman. 1795: Agreeable Surprise, Les Amans d'arcade (pantomime), Auld Robin Gray, Beggar's Opera, La boiteuse (pantomime), Castle of Andalusia, Children in the Wood, Deserter, Deux Chasseurs (pantomime), Devil to Pay, Duenna, Flitch of Bacon, Flora, Forêt noire (pantomime), Harlequin Hurry-scurry (pantomime), Harlequin Shipwrecked (pantomime-pasticcio), Harlequin Invasion (pantomime), Hartford Bridge, Haunted Tower, Highland Reel, Inkle and Yarico, Irish Lilt (pantomime), Lionel and Clarissa, Love in a Camp, Love in a Village, Midas, Miraculous Mill (pantomime), My Grandmother, Noble Peasant, No Song, no Supper, Padlock, Peeping Tom of Coventry, Poor Soldier, Poor Vulcan, Prisoner, Prize, Purse, Purse, Quaker, Rival Harlequins (pantomime) Robin Hood, Robinson Crusoe (pantomime), Romp, Rosina, Rural Revels (pantomime), Sailor's Landlady (pantomime), Sailor's Return (pantomime), Scheming Miners (pantomime), Sicilian Romance, Spanish Barber, Surrender of Calais, Tom Thumb the Great, Travellers Preserved (pantomime), Tuteur trompé (pantomime), Two Misers, Volunteers, Waterman, Woodman. 1796: Agreeable Surprise, American Tar, La Boiteuse (pantomime), Castle of Andalusia, Children in the Wood, Deserter, Deux Chasseurs (pantomime), Deux soeurs (pantomime), Devil to Pay, Doctor and Apothecary, Duenna, Easter Gift (pantomime), Farmer, Flora, Forêt noire (pantomime), Harlequin, Dr. Faustus, Harlequin Hurry-scurry (pantomime), Harlequin Shipwrecked (pantomime-pasticcio), Harlequin Club (pantomime), Harlequin Invasion (pantomime), Irish Vagary (pantomime), Love in a Camp, Lucky Escape (pantomime), Maid of the Mill, Mélomanie, Merry Little Girl (pantomime), Miraculous Mill (pantomime), Mock Doctor, Motley Group (pantomime), Mountaineers, No Song, no Supper, Padlock, Patriot or Liberty Obtained, Peeping Tom of Coventry, Poor Soldier, Prisoner, Prize, Purse, Rival Knights (pantomime), Robin Hood, Robinson Crusoe (pantomime), Romp, La rose et le bouton (pantomime), Rosina, Rural Merriment (pantomime), Sailor's Landlady (pantomime), Shamrock (pantomime), Sicilian Romance, Souliers mordorés, Tom Thumb the Great, T'other Side of the Gutter, Valiant Officer, Warrior's Welcome Home (pantomime), Waterman, Witches of the Rock (pantomime), Woodman. 1797: Adopted Child, Alonzo and Imogen (pantomime), Blaise et Babet, Blue Beard (pantomime), Christmas Frolics (pantomime), Columbus, Dead Alive, Death of Captain Cook (pantomime), Deux petits Savoyards, Farmer, Flitch of Bacon, Forêt noire (pantomime), Highland Reel, Iron Chest, Lock and Key, Love in a Village, Mélomanie, Mountaineers, No Song, no Supper, Padlock, Peeping Tom of Coventry, Poor Soldier, Prize, Robin Hood, Sailor's Landlady (pantomime), Savoyard, Son-in-law, Sultan, Tom Thumb the Great. 1798: Abroad and at Home, Agreeable Surprise, Animated Statue (pantomime), Beggar's Opera, Children in the Wood, Columbus, Enchantress, Dead Alive, Death of General Wolfe (pantomime), Deserter, Devil to Pay, Forêt noire (pantomime), Gentle Shepherd (pantomime), Highland Reel, Italian Monk, Lock and Key, Love in a Camp, Marian, Padlock, Patriot or Liberty Obtained, Poor Soldier, Prisoner, Prize, Richard Coeur de Lion, Robin Hood, Robinson Crusoe (pantomime), Romp, Rosina, Shipwreck, Spoiled Child. 1799: Adopted Child, Arabs of the Desert, (pantomime), Battle of Trenton. (pantomime), Blue Beard (pantomime), Castle of Andalusia, Children in the Wood, Columbus,

Death of General Wolfe (pantomime), Deserter, Farmer, Highland Reel, Lock and Key, Magic Fire (pantomime), Mountaineers, Mysteries of the Castle, Padlock, Poor Soldier, Prize, Richard Coeur de Lion, Rival Soldiers, Robin Hood, Romp, Rosina, Shipwreck, Tom Thumb the Great, William Tell (pantomime). **1800:** Adopted Child, Agreeable Surprise, Blue Beard (pantomime), Castle Spectre, Columbus, Dead Alive, Double Disguise, Farmer, Harlequin Freemason (pantomime), Harlequin Shipwrecked (pantomime-pasticcio), Haunted Tower, Highland Reel, Lock and Key, Mountaineers, Naval Pillar, No Song, no Supper, Poor Soldier, Prisoner, Prize, Richard Coeur de Lion, Rival Soldiers, Romp, Rosina, Spanish Barber, Waterman, Zorinski.

Repertory (Academy of Music, first decade). 1857:
Il trovatore, Lucrezia Borgia, Lucia di Lammermoor, Norma, La traviata, I Puritani, Linda di Chamounix, Il barbiere di Siviglia, Luisa Miller, La sonnambula, Ernani, L'elisir d'amore, Masaniello, Der Freischütz, Fidelio, La Maçon, Martha. **1858:** Il barbiere di Siviglia, Semiramide, Rigoletto, Martha, Norma, I Puritani, L'Italiana in Algeri, Don Giovanni, Robert le Diable, Otello, Il trovatore, La favorita, La sonnambula, L'elisir d'amore, Don Pasquale, Maria di Rohan, Guillaume Tell, La traviata, Lucia di Lammermoor, La figlia del reggimento, Martha. **1859:** Le nozze di Figaro, La traviata, Les Huguenots, Robert le Diable, Don Giovanni, Don Pasquale, Martha, Norma, La favorita, Il trovatore, La figlia del reggimento, Il Poliuto, I vespri siciliani, Lucia di Lammermoor, Rigoletto, La sonnambula, Saffo, Die Zauberflöte. **1860-62:** Le chatte métamorphosée en femme, La sonnambula, Il trovatore, Die Freischütz, The Bohemian Girl, Il barbiere di Siviglia, La fille du régiment, Lucia di Lammermoor, I Puritani, I vespri Siciliani, Martha, Don Pasquale, La sonnambula, Lucrezia Borgia, La traviata, Norma, Ernani, Martha, La traviata, Mosè in Egitto, Il giuramento, La Juive, Linda di Chamounix, Un ballo in maschera, Betly, Dinorah. **1863:** Martha, Der Freischütz, Le Maçon, Fidelio, Die Zauberflöte, Der Wildschütz, Jean de Paris, La fille du régiment, Stradella, Il seraglio, Joseph, Le nozze di Figaro, Le postillon de Longjumeau, Merry Wives of Windsor, Fra Diavolo, Don Giovanni, Linda di Chamounix, Robert le Diable, La sonnambula, La Juive, Dinorah, Faust, Ione, La traviata, Lucrezia Borgia, Rigoletto, Macbeth, Un ballo in maschera, Il trovatore, Lucia di Lammermoor. **1864-66:** The Merry Wives of Windsor, Il templario, La dame blanche, Tannhäuser, Jessonda, Notre Dame of Paris, Robert le Diable, La Juive, Les Huguenots, Mireille, Martha, Faust, Robert le Diable, La Dame Blanche, Stradella, La forza del destino, Fra Diavolo, Ernani, La figlia del reggimento, L'Africaine, Il Poliuto, Martha, I Puritani, Lucrezia Borgia, Lucia di Lammermoor, Die Zauberflöte, Guillaume Tell, Les Huguenots, Maritana, Doctor of Alcantara, Crispino e la Comare, Il trovatore, L'étoile du Nord, L'elisir d'amore, Midsummer's Night Dream, Zampa, Le Maître de Chapelle, Les diamants de la couronne.

Repertory (Manhattan Opera Company).
Inaugural season (complete schedule, 1908-09): Carmen (November 17), Samson et Dalila (November 19), Il barbiere di Siviglia (November 21, matinee), Tosca (November 21), Thaïs (November 24), Lucia di Lammermoor (November 26), Samson et Dalila (November 28, matinee) Les Huguenots (November 28), Rigoletto (December 1), Le Jongleur de Notre Dame (December 3), Carmen (December 5, matinee), Cavalleria rusticana/I pagliacci (December 5), Lucia di Lammermoor (December 8), Les contes d'Hoffmann (December 10), Cavalleria rusticana/I pagliacci (December 12, matinee), Samson et Dalila (December 12), Le Jongleur de Notre Dame (December 15), La bohème (December 17), Il trovatore (December 19, matinee), La traviata (December 19), La traviata (December 22), Le Jongleur de Notre Dame (December 24), Cavalleria rusticana/I pagliacci (December 25), Tosca (December 26, matinee), Thaïs (December 26), La bohème (December 29), Tosca (December 31), Les Huguenots (January 1), Thaïs (January 2, matinee), Carmen (January 2), Cavalleria rusticana/I pagliacci (January 5), Rigoletto (January 7), La traviata (January 9, matinee), La bohème (January 9), Les contes d'Hoffmann (January 12), Otello (January 14), La bohème (January 16), Le Jongleur de Notre Dame (January 16), Samson et Dalila (January 19), Il trovatore (January 21), Crispino et la Comare (January 23, matinee), Otello (January 23), Rigoletto (January 26), Faust (January 28), Otello (January 30, matinee), La sonnambula (January 30), Tosca (February 2),

Crispino e la Comare/Cavalleria rusticana (February 4), La sonnambula (February 6, matinee), Il trovatore (February 6), Pelléas et Mélisande (February 9), Salome (February 11), Faust (February 13, matinee), Aida (February 13), Salome (February 16), Rigoletto (February 18), Aida (February 20, matinee), La bohème (February 20), Il trovatore (February 22), Otello (February 23), Thaïs (February 25), Tosca (February 27, matinee), Crispino e la Comare/Cavalleria rusticana (February 27), Salome (March 1), Aida (March 2), La sonnambula/Cavalleria rusticana (March 4), Lucia di Lammermoor (March 6, matinee) Un ballo in maschera (March 6), Lucia di Lammermoor (March 11), Un ballo in maschera (March 13, matinee) I Puritani (March 13), Le Jongleur de Notre Dame (March 16), Louise (March 18), Rigoletto (March 20, matinee), Faust (March 20), Louise (March 23), La Navarraise/I pagliacci (March 25), Il trovatore (March 27, matinee), Thaïs (March 27), Samson et Dalila (March 30), Aida (April 1), Le Jongleur de Notre Dame (April 3, matinee), Lucia di Lammermoor (April 3). **1909-10:** November 9-March 26: Aida, Hérodiade, Lucia di Lammermoor, Carmen, La fille de Madame Angot, La Mascotte, Sapho, Cavalleria rusticana/pagliacci, La fille du régiment, Les dragons de Villars, Il trovatore, La traviata, Le Jongleur de Notre Dame, Tosca, Samson et Dalila, Faust, Les contes d'Hoffmann, La bohème, Grisélidis, Elektra, Thaïs, Otello, La navarraise, Pelléas et Mélisande, Lakmé, Rigoletto. Final gala: I pagliacci (prologue), Les contes d'Hoffmann (Act III), Samson et Dalila (Act II), Roméo et Juliette (Act III), Hérodiade (Act I), Faust (Final Scene).

Repertory (Opera Company of Philadelphia). **1975-76:** Faust, Turandot, Anna Bolena, Madama Butterfly, La favorita, Un ballo in maschera, The Hero. **1976-77:** Tosca, Cavalleria rusticana/I pagliacci, Die Walküre, Il barbiere di Siviglia, Don Giovanni, La bohème. **1977-78:** Die fliegende Holländer, The Hero, Norma, Carmen, Lucia di Lammermoor, Attila. **1978-79:** Manon, Rigoletto, Die Fledermaus, Così fan tutte, La Cenerentola, Tosca. **1979-80:** Madama Butterfly, The Free Lance, Les pêcheurs de perles, La traviata, I pagliacci/L'heure espagnole, Die Zauberflöte. **1980-81:** Don Giovanni, Les contes d'Hoffmann, Falstaff, La fanciulla del West, Eugene Onegin, The Cunning Little Vixen. **1981-82:** Mosè, Il tabarro/Gianni Schicchi, Le nozze di Figaro, Il trovatore, La bohème, L'elisir d'amore. **1982-83:** La rondine, Dido & Aeneas/Oedipus, Don Pasquale, Simon Boccanegra, Carmen. **1983-84:** Pikovaya dama, La traviata, Faust, La Cenerentola, Werther. **1984-85:** La bohème, Macbeth, Il barbiere di Siviglia, La damnation de Faust, Manon Lescaut. **1985-86:** Ariadne auf Naxos, The Medium/Suor Angelica, Un ballo in maschera, La bohème. **1986-87:** Madama Butterfly, Death in Venice, Don Giovanni, Boris Godunov, Roméo et Juliette. **1987-88:** Tosca, Peter Grimes, Mefistofele, Così fan tutte. **1988-89:** Rusalka, Fidelio, Luisa Miller, L'elisir d'amore. **1989-90:** Lucia di Lammermoor, The Saint of Bleecker Street, Ariodante, La gazza ladra. **1990-91:** La nozze di Figaro, Madama Butterfly, Don Pasquale, Rigoletto. **1991-92:** Il barbiere di Siviglia, La traviata, Les pêcheurs de perles, Turandot. **1992-93:** Carmen, La favorita, Eugene Onegin. **1993-94:** Cavalleria rusticana/I pagliacci, Tosca, Die Zauberflöte, Roméo et Juliette.

• *Pennsylvania Opera Theater* •

Otto Nicolai's *Die lustigen Weiber von Windsor* inaugurated the Pennsylvania Opera Theater in 1975. The work was the season's sole offering. With painted cardboard scenery and an all-volunteer staff, the company mounted three performances on a budget of $15,000. Barbara Silverstein founded the company and is still its artistic director. The company was established as an alternative to the traditional, "star-related, big operas" of the Opera Company of Philadelphia. The repertory emphasizes new and lesser known works, sung in English by up-and-coming American talent. Silverstein conducts every performance. The company has mounted three world premieres and several local premieres.

The three-opera season offers one unusual work, a repertory favorite or musical, and one lighter piece in a *stagione* system. Recent productions include Gioachino Rossini's *Il viaggio a Reims*, Giuseppe Verdi's *Rigoletto*, Stephen Sondheim's *Sweeney Todd*, and Gaetano Donizetti's *La fille du régiment*. The company performs in various theaters, including the 1,700-seat Shubert Theater.

Practical Information. The Shubert Theater is at 250 South Broad Street. Tickets are purchased at the Pennsylvania Opera Theater offices, 1315 Walnut Street, Suite 1632, or by telephoning 215-731-1212, or writing Pennsylvania Opera Theater, 1315 Walnut Street, Suite 1632, Philadelphia, PA 19107. If you go, stay at the Four Seasons Hotel Philadelphia, One Logan Square, Philadelphia, PA 19103; telephone 215-963-1500, fax 215-963-9506, reservations 1-800-332-3442. Faithful reproductions from Philadelphia's Federal period luxuriously decorate the hotel which offers sumptuous accommodation and superb service.

COMPANY STAFF AND REPERTORY

General/Artistic Director (Pennsylvania Opera Theater). Barbara Silverstein (1975–present).

World Premieres. Garwood's *Rappaccini's Daughter* (May 6, 1983); Persichetti's *The Sibyl: A Parable of Chicken Little* (April 13, 1985); Pliska's *The Secret Garden* (March 2, 1991).

Repertory. **1975-76:** Die lustigen Weiber von Windsor. **1976-77:** La Cenerentola, Postcard from Morocco. **1977-78:** La Cenerentola, The Beggar's Opera. **1978-79:** Don Giovanni, Ormindo. **1979-80:** Il barbiere di Siviglia, La belle Hélène. **1980-81:** Le nozze di Figaro, Twelfth Night. **1981-82:** Le Comte Ory, Orlando Paladino, Candide. **1982-83:** Il furioso all'isola di San Domingo, Rappaccini's Daughter. **1983-84:** Die Dreigroschenoper, Così fan tutte. **1984-85:** The Sibyl, L'italiana in Algeri, Rigoletto. **1985-86:** Les contes d'Hoffmann, La Cenerentola. **1986-87:** Die Zauberflöte, The Turn of the Screw. **1987-88:** Il barbiere di Siviglia, The Fairy Queen, Le nozze di Figaro. **1988-89:** The Crucible, Candide, Don Giovanni. **1989-90:** La traviata, L'incoronazione di Poppea, La Grand Duchesse de Gérolstein. **1990-91:** Die Fledermaus, The Secret Garden, Carmen. **1991-92:** Die Zauberflöte, Tosca, Die Dreigroschenoper. **1992-93:** Il viaggio a Reims, Rigoletto, Così fan tutte. **1993-94:** Il viaggio a Reims, Sweeney Todd, Le fille du régiment.

PITTSBURGH

• *Pittsburgh Opera* •

Jacques Offenbach's *Les contes d'Hoffmann* inaugurated the Pittsburgh Opera, originally called the Pittsburgh Opera Society, on March 15, 1940. The performance took place in Carnegie Music Hall under the baton of Anthony Caputo. The season continued with Wolfgang Amadeus Mozart's *Le nozze di Figaro* and Pyotr Il'yich Tchaikovsky's *Eugene Onegin*. Several ambitious Pittsburgh ladies founded the Pittsburgh Opera Society the previous year and produced Pittsburgh's first homegrown opera—Arthur Sullivan's *Iolanthe*. A mixture of professional and amateur singers comprised the cast, led by Caputo.

Opera in Pittsburgh dates back to 1838, when the local inhabitants were treated to Gioachino Rossini's *Il barbiere di Siviglia*, staged by a touring company.

Over the next century, several visiting opera companies stopped in the Steel City and brought opera's famous stars with them—Adelina Patti, Lilli Lehmann, Emma Calvé, Nellie Melba, Jean and Édouard de Reszke, Mary Garden, John McCormack, Beniamino Gigli, Feodor Chaliapin, Titta Ruffo, and Frances Alda. In 1923, one of the German troupes produced a four-day Wagner Festival that included *Die Meistersinger* with Alexander Kipnis and Friedrich Schorr.

Two years after the founding of the Pittsburgh Opera, Richard Karp took the helm, steering the fledgling company into professional waters. (Karp was a Viennese violinist who had fled Nazi-dominated Europe.) His debut opera was Gaetano Donizetti's *Don Pasquale*. Three years later, Karp moved the company into the Syria Mosque, which became their home for more than two decades. He presented exciting productions of traditional operas with superstar casts, including Birgit Nilsson in Giacomo Puccini's *Turandot*, Beverly Sills in Donizetti's *Lucia di Lammermoor*, James McCracken in Giuseppe Verdi's *Otello*, and Montserrat Caballé in Verdi's *Il trovatore*. Eleanor Steber, Leonard Warren, Licia Albanese, Robert Merrill, Richard Tucker, and Norman Treigle also graced the Pittsburgh stage. Under Karp's leadership the Pittsburgh Opera experienced dynamic growth. In the fall of 1971, the company took up residence in Heinz Hall. Originally called Loews Penn Theater, the theater had been renovated as part of the development of a downtown cultural district. Verdi's *Aida* welcomed the Pittsburgh Opera into its new home. Karp's reign lasted more than three decades, ending with his death in 1977. Although the Pittsburgh Opera might not have survived without him, he had his quirks. One was reprimanding the audience about their lack of manners in the theater. (The opera world perhaps needs more people teaching the audience proper opera manners.)

After Karp's death his daughter, Barbara, took over the company. Although she was considered a brilliant and innovative artist, the situation did not work out. She resigned after two years and James de Blasis became the new artistic director. He was also the director of the Cincinnati Opera, and that company did not like sharing its director, so he resigned in 1982. The following year Tito Capobianco, who had sailed into troubled waters as head of the San Diego Opera, (see San Diego Opera chapter) took the reins. Capobianco knew Pittsburgh well since he had staged several operas there during the past two decades. In October 1987, the company moved into the Benedum Center with a lavish production of Puccini's *Turandot* featuring Gwyneth Jones in the title role. With a permanent home, the Pittsburgh Opera has been able to grow and mature.

The repertory remains traditional, with the company's only novelty coming in 1984, Verdi's *La battaglia di Legnano*. Capobianco champions the human voice, resulting in a notable absence of twentieth-century works in the repertory. He feels contemporary pieces do not do justice to the voice, but, instead "draw attention to themselves and exhibit the composer's knowledge of harmonies and composition." Capobianco aims to touch his audience with all the "feeling and passion that opera has to offer," and so picks operas that exhibit "real people experiencing real emotions." The 1991 production of Modest Mussorgsky's *Boris Godunov* was the original score, not the embellished Nikolay Rimsky-Korsakov version that is usually performed. His composer of choice is Verdi, and the season schedule usually includes one of his operas. In the productions, he tries to involve the audience emotionally so, as Capobianco says, "they do not think about unpaid bills or shopping lists."

Capobianco continued the star power tradition, and many renown artists have appeared on the Benedum Center stage, including Sherrill Milnes, José Carreras, Ghena Dimitrova, Joan Sutherland, Grace Bumbry, Vladimir Popov, Johanna Meier, and Justino Díaz. To celebrate the 50th anniversary of the company, Luciano Pavarotti was scheduled to sing the title role of Jules Massenet's *Werther* (in French)—and make history. He did not have time to learn the part and requested to sing Cavaradossi instead. Then Pavarotti took ill and canceled. Puccini's *Tosca* celebrated the company's golden jubilee, but *sans* Pavarotti. Financial considerations have limited the star wattage in recent years, with only "one name-star an opera to sell tickets" as Capobianco explained. The remaining roles are filled by talented young American singers, many of whom come from the Pittsburgh Opera Center at Duquesne, established in 1989. Several alumni have gone on to international careers, including Richard Leech, June Anderson, John Cheek, and Marilyn Zschau. Capobianco also plans expansion via the Opera Center and has scheduled the company's first world premiere there, Stephen Paulus's *The Gift of the Magi*. He feels the main season has reached its maximum.

The four-opera season offers the romantic repertory in traditional productions in a *stagione* system. Recent works include Verdi's *Il trovatore* and Puccini's *Turandot* and *La bohème*, Charles Gounod's *Faust*, and Georges Bizet's *Carmen*. The company performs in the Benedum Center for the Performing Arts.

The Benedum Center for the Performing Arts

The Benedum Center for the Performing Arts began life on February 27, 1928, as the Stanley Theater. The main inaugural event was the premiere of the silent film *Gentlemen Prefer Blondes*. The theater was built as "a movie palace version of Versailles" by James Bly Clark, and cost $3 million. The theater's opening marked the beginning of a golden era. For more than two decades, the finest in movie and stage entertainment took place, before decline set in. The road from being Pittsburgh's palace of amusement to becoming Pittsburgh's performing arts center began in 1984, when a gift of $14 million from the Claude Worthington Benedum Foundation launched the conversion project. Architect Albert Filoni and his associates were in charge of the renovation that cost $42 million.

The classic revival-style building boasts a movie palace façade decorated with ornate design patterns. A marquee announces the current show. BENEDUM CENTER FOR THE PERFORMING ARTS is etched in gold letters in multi-colored marble. The lobby is classic-revival decor. Elaborate ornamentation embellishes the rose, gold, and green auditorium. Urns rest on fluted, Corinthian columns in a room filled with vignettes, anthemia, tiny flowers, and mermaid-angels. A single balcony stretches across the auditorium and extends back, almost forever. A 50,000-piece, crystal-and-brass chandelier hangs from the ceiling. The original proscenium holds a crafted, adjustable, wood-panel "proscenium," created to improve the acoustics. It is adjusted according to the nature of the performance. The theater seats 2,885.

Practical Information. The Benedum Center is at 719 Liberty Avenue. Tickets for the opera are purchased at the Pittsburgh Opera box office, 711 Penn Avenue, between 9:30 A.M. and 5:00 P.M. weekdays. Tickets can be ordered by telephoning 412-456-6666 between 9:00 A.M. and 5:00 P.M. weekdays, or by writing Pittsburgh

Benedum Center for the Performing Arts (Pittsburgh, Pennsylvania).

Opera, 711 Penn Avenue, Pittsburgh, PA 15222. If you go, stay at the Westin William Penn, 530 William Penn Place (On Mellon Square) Pittsburgh, PA 15219; telephone 412-281-7100, fax 412-553-5239, reservations 1-800-228-3000. The William Penn Hotel, built by Henry Clay Frick in 1928-29, is an art deco treasure. Historically significant, the hotel was recently restored to its architectural splendor. It is only a five-minute walk to the Benedum Center.

COMPANY STAFF AND REPERTORY

General/Artistic Directors. Anthony Caputo (1940–42); Richard Karp (1942–77); Barbara Karp (1977–79); James de Blasis (1980–82); Tito Capobianco (1983–present).

Repertory. **1940:** Les contes d'Hoffmann, Le nozze di Figaro, Eugene Onegin. **1941:** La traviata, Martha, Il trovatore. **1942:** Die Zauberflöte, Carmen, Hänsel und Gretel. **1943:** Hänsel und Gretel, Un ballo in maschera. **1944-45:** Faust, Die Fledermaus. **1945-46:** Carmen, La traviata, Fidelio, La bohème. **1946-47:** Tosca, Fidelio, Rigoletto, Il barbiere di Siviglia, Die Zauberflöte. **1947-48:** Aida, Hänsel und Gretel, Le nozze di Figaro, Il segreto di Susanna/I pagliacci, Lohengrin, Il trovatore. **1948-49:** Carmen, Il barbiere di Siviglia, La traviata, La bohème, Rigoletto. **1949-50:** Faust, Madama Butterfly, Pinocchio, Prodaná nevěsta (The Bartered Bride), Don Pasquale, Tristan und Isolde. **1950-51:** Le nozze di Figaro, Tosca, Carmen, Rigoletto, La bohème. **1951-52:** L'elisir d'amore, Il trovatore, Lucia di Lammermoor, La traviata, Cavalleria. rusticana/I pagliacci. **1952-53:** Manon, Carmen, Tosca, Otello, Madama Butterfly. **1953-54:** La bohème, Faust, Il barbiere di Siviglia, Lohengrin, Don Giovanni. **1954-55:** Aida, Rigoletto, Lucia di Lammermoor, La traviata, Tosca. **1955-56:** Un ballo in maschera, Otello, Carmen, Le nozze di Figaro, Don Pasquale, Madama Butterfly. **1956-57:** Cavalleria rusticana/I pagliacci, La bohème, Rigoletto, La traviata, Faust. **1957-58:** Aida, La bohème, Les contes d'Hoffmann, Carmen, Il trovatore. **1958-59:** Madama Butterfly,

Susannah, Tosca, Così fan tutte, Lucia di Lammermoor. **1959-60:** Lohengrin, Aida, Il barbiere di Siviglia, La traviata, Carmen, Boris Godunov. **1960-61:** Lucia di Lammermoor, Un ballo in maschera, La bohème, Rigoletto. **1961-62:** Carmen, La traviata, Lakmé, Manon, Tosca. **1962-63:** La bohème, Turandot, L'elisir d'amore, Faust, Madama Butterfly. **1963-64:** Der fliegende Holländer, Aida, La forza del destino, Cavalleria rusticana/I pagliacci, La sonnambula. **1964-65:** La gioconda, Carmen, La traviata, Le nozze di Figaro, Il trovatore. **1965-66:** Don Carlo, La bohème, Lucia di Lammermoor, Faust, Andrea Chénier. **1966-67:** Tosca, Otello, Madama Butterfly, La traviata, Lohengrin. **1967-68:** Lucia di Lammermoor, Carmen, Aida, Lakmé, Il trovatore. **1968-69:** Rigoletto, Samson et Dalila, La bohème, Cavalleria rusticana/I pagliacci, Le nozze di Figaro. **1969-70:** Carmen, Il barbiere di Siviglia, Tosca, L'amore dei tre re, Faust. **1970-71:** Madama Butterfly, Un ballo in maschera, Boris Godunov, Il trovatore, Don Pasquale. **1971-72:** Aida, La traviata, Tannhäuser, La bohème, Roméo et Juliette, Lucia di Lammermoor. **1972-73:** Carmen, Rigoletto, Der fliegende Holländer, Tosca, Nabucco, Madama Butterfly. **1973-74:** Il barbiere di Siviglia, Faust, Don Giovanni, Il tabarro/I pagliacci, Fidelio, La traviata. **1974-75:** Otello, La fille du régiment, La traviata, La bohème, Manon Lescaut, L'elisir d'amore. **1975-76:** Les contes d'Hoffmann, Carmen, Lucia di Lammermoor, The Crucible, Madama Butterfly, Un ballo in maschera. **1976-77:** Tosca, Norma, Prodaná nevěsta (The Bartered Bride), Faust, Così fan tutte, Rigoletto. **1977-78:** Falstaff, Hänsel und Gretel, La bohème, Les pêcheurs des perles, Aida, Il barbiere di Siviglia. **1978-79:** Turandot, Die Zauberflöte, La traviata, Salome, Don Quichotte, Don Pasquale. **1979-80:** Die Fledermaus, Madama Butterfly, Don Giovanni, Il trovatore, L'elisir d'amore, Ariadne auf Naxos. **1980-81:** Susannah, Carmen, Attila, Der fliegende Holländer, Tosca, Le nozze di Figaro. **1981-82:** Cavalleria rusticana/I pagliacci, Les contes d'Hoffmann, La rondine, Die lustige Witwe, Lucia di Lammermoor, Otello. **1982-83:** Prodaná nevěsta (The Bartered Bride), Rigoletto, Die Entführung aus dem Serail, Faust, Fidelio, Manon Lescaut. **1983-84:** La bohème, Die Zauberflöte, Un ballo in maschera, Carmen, Roméo et Juliette, Il barbiere di Siviglia. **1984-85:** La battaglia di Legnano, Don Giovanni, Manon, Madama Butterfly, La traviata, Adriana Lecouvreur. **1985-86:** Norma, Tosca, Così fan tutte, La forza del destino, Rigoletto, La fille du régiment. **1986-87:** Macbeth, Faust, Lucia di Lammermoor, Il trovatore, Hamlet. **1987-88:** Turandot, Cavalleria rusticana/I pagliacci, Hänsel und Gretel, Don Giovanni, Carmen. **1988-89:** Aida, La bohème, Salome, Les contes d'Hoffmann, Die lustige Witwe, Tosca. **1989-90:** Madama Butterfly, Elektra, La traviata, Die Zauberflöte, Mefistofele. **1990-91:** Otello, Der fliegende Holländer, Die Fledermaus, Il barbiere di Siviglia, Eugene Onegin. **1991-92:** La Cenerentola, Boris Godunov, Samson et Dalila, Rigoletto, Un ballo in maschera. **1992-93:** Carmen, Tristan und Isolde, Il trovatore, Madama Butterfly. **1993-94:** Don Giovanni, Faust, Turandot, La bohème.

South Carolina ————— CHARLESTON

• *Spoleto Opera Festival USA* •

The noted opera composer Gian Carlo Menotti established the Spoleto Festival in 1977 as an American counterpart to the Festival of Two Worlds in Spoleto (Italy), which he had founded in 1958. The festival's purpose was to showcase promising young artists and present a broad range of new and neglected works, which is reflected in the eclectic array of operas that inhabit the repertory. Menotti's operas play an important role in the festival's opera presentations. His *The Consul* along with Pyotr Il'yich Tchaikovsky's *Pikovaya dama* were the inaugural season offerings.

Charleston claims the distinction of hosting the first opera performance in America—Colley Cibber's *Flora, or Hob in the Well* on February 12, 1735. The performance took place in a court room in Shepherd's Tavern. The first theatrical season in which Cibber's *Flora* was staged had opened on January 24, 1735. The second season opened on February 12, 1736, in the theatre on Dock Street, and among its offerings was the America premiere of C. Coffey's ballad opera *Devil to Pay* on March 16, 1736. Another performance of Cibber's *Flora* took place on November 23, 1736.

The American Company, originally called the Company of Comedians under Lewis Hallam, "till his death," visited Charleston in 1764, and again a decade later. The troupe presented numerous ballad operas—Thomas Arne's *Love in a Village*, Cibber's *Flora*, Henry Carey's *Honest Yorkshireman*, *Damon and Phillida*, and *Contrivances*, Charles Dibdin's *Lionel and Clarissa* and *Padlock*, John Pepusch's *Beggar's Opera*, Coffey's *Devil to Pay*, Kane O'Hara's *Midas*, and I. Bickerstaffe's *Thomas and Sally*. Dennis Ryan's American Company from Baltimore came to Charleston during the first half of 1785, opening the season on March 28, 1785. Two years later, a Mr. Godwin staged an unsuccessful season in which he offered Cibber's *Flora* on March 14 and 23, 1787, among others. Next the Virginia Company of Comedians under the management of Bignall and West played in Charleston. The company joined the effort to erect a new theater, the Charleston Theatre on Broad Street. It opened on February 11, 1793, with the American premiere of William Shield's *Highland Reel*. Samuel Arnold's *Agreeable Surprise*, Pepusch's *Beggar's Opera*, Coffey's *Devil to Pay*, Dibdin's *Padlock*, O'Hara's *Midas* and Arne's *Love in a Village* were among the many offerings that graced its stage. Bignall and West staged a second season which opened on January 22, 1794, with Shield's *Farmer*. Meanwhile some French comedians first took up residence at the City Theater on Church Street and afterward joined the Company of Comedians for a few seasons at the Charleston Theater. Bignall and West continued giving seasons at the Charleston Theater through 1796. Another company run by Mr. Edgar then played at the City Theater, opening their season on December 19, 1794. Dibdin's *Romp*, Henry Fielding's *Virgin Unmasked*, and Bickerstaffe's *Thomas and Sally* trod the boards. Next John Sollee brought his company from Boston to Charleston and performed several seasons of ballad opera and pantomime at the City Theater. During the nineteenth century, visiting companies supplied Charleston with the standard repertory and an occasional novelty—Moorehead's *The Cabinet* and Offenbach's *La rose de Saint-Flour*.

Now the Spoleto Festival offers Charleston novelties almost every season, along with repertory favorites. For example, during Spoleto's second season, Samuel Barber's *Vanessa*, Gaetano Donizetti's *Il furioso all'isola di San Domingo*, and Menotti's *Martin's Lie* and *The Egg*, were staged along with Giuseppe Verdi's *La traviata*. The repertory continues to remain unique. In addition to frequent presentations of Menotti works—*The Medium*, *Chip and His Dog*, *The Last Savage*, *Juana*, *La Loca*, *The Saint of Bleecker Street*, *Maria Golovin*, and *The Singing Child*, there is a curious mix of forgotten eighteenth-century pieces with twentieth-century works. Counted among the former are Domenico Cimarosa's *Il marito disperato*, Christoph Gluck's *L'Ivrogne Corrige*, Giovanni Pergolesi's *Il flaminio* and *Lietta e Tracolio*, Antonio Salieri's *Arlecchinata*, Georg Friedrich Händel's *Ariodante*,

Jean-Philippe Rameau's *Platée*, and Carl Graun's *Montezuma*. Dmitry Shosta-
kovich's *Ledi Makbet Mtsenskovo uyezda* (Lady Macbeth of the Mtsensk District),
Barber's *Anthony and Cleopatra*, Igor Stravinsky's *Renard*, Raffaelo de Banfield's
Lord Byron's Love Letter, Philip Glass's *The Hydrogen Jukebox*, and Alexander
von Zemlinsky's *Der Geburtstag der Infantin* represent the contemporary side.
Several were American or world premieres.

The number of operas fluctuates between two and three each festival. The
works are performed in repertory. Recent operas include Rossini's *Le Comte Ory*,
Strauss's *Elektra*, Claudio Monteverdi's *L'incoronazione di Poppea*, and Menotti's
The Singing Child. The Festival uses a variety of performing venues, including the
2,763-seat Gaillard Municipal Auditorium for grand opera, the 463-seat Dock
Street Theater, and two College of Charleston spaces—the 299-seat Albert Simon
Center and the 803-seat Sottile Memorial Auditorium.

Practical Information. The Gaillard Municipal Auditorium in on Calhoun
Street. The Spoleto Festival Box Office is at 14 George Street. It is open Monday
through Saturday from 10:00 A.M. to 8:00 P.M. during the festival and to 6:00 P.M.
before the festival opens. Tickets can be ordered by telephoning 1-800-255-4659
or 803-577-4500, Monday through Saturday from 8:00 A.M. to 10:00 P.M., faxing
803-723-6383, or writing Spoleto Festival U.S.A., P.O.B. 704, Charleston, SC
29402. If you go, stay at the Omni Charleston Place, 130 Market Street, Charleston, SC 29401; telephone 803-722-4900, fax 803-722-0728, reservations
1-800-843-6664. Located in the historic district, the Omni Charleston is a deluxe
hotel only minutes from the theaters.

COMPANY STAFF AND REPERTORY

General/Artistic Director. Gian Carlo Menotti (1977–present).

American/United States Premieres (before Spoleto Festival). Cibber's *Flora, or
Hob in the Well* (February 12, 1735); Coffey's *Devil to Pay* (March 16, 1736); Arne's *Love
in a Village* (February 10, 1766); Bickerstaffe's *Daphne and Amintor* (May 29, 1785); Shield's
Highland Reel (February 11, 1793); Shield's *Robin Hood* (February 16, 1793); Arnold's *Peep-
ing Tom of Coventry* (February 18, 1793); Dibdin's *Poor Vulcan* (February 22, 1793); Ar-
nold's *Son-in-Law* (March 8, 1793); Dibdin's *The Wedding Ring* (March 20, 1793); Storace's
Haunted Tower (April 24, 1793); Arnold's *Surrender of Calais* (April 29, 1793); Shield's
Woodman (May 13, 1793); Grétry's *Le tableau parlant* (June 17, 1794); Gluck's *Orfeo ed
Euridice* (June 24, 1794); Blaise's *Annette et Lubin* (July 16, 1794); Dèzede's *Blaise et Babet*
(July 23, 1794); Dalayrac's *Nina* (July 23, 1794); Grétry's *Zémire et Azor* (first performance
in French, August 6, 1794); Dalayrac's *L'amant statue* (August 11, 1794); Monsigny's *Le
Deserteur* (December 12, 1794); Shield's *Oscar and Malvina* (February 21, 1795); Shield's
Fountainebleau (March 9, 1795); Grétry's *La fausse magie* (June 1, 1795); Champein's *La
mélomanie* (June 16, 1795); Dèzede's *Alexis et Justine* (July 10, 1795); Champein's *Les dettes*
(July 21, 1795); Grétry's *La caravane du Caire* (August 3, 1795); Storace's *Doctor and
Apothecary* (April 26, 1796); Moorehead's *The Cabinet* (March 27, 1809); Offenbach's *La
rose de Saint-Flour* (March 5, 1860);

World Premieres (Spoleto Festival Opera). Anderson's *Empty Places* (June 8,
1989); Glass's *Hydrogen Jukebox* (May 26, 1990); Dresher's *Pioneer* (May 24, 1990); Menotti's
The Singing Child (May 31, 1993).

American/United States Premieres (Spoleto Festival Opera). Cimarosa's *Il
marito disperato* (in English as The Desperate Husband, May 25, 1979); Menotti's *Chip and
His Dog* (May 25, 1980); Pergolesi's *Il flaminio* (June 2, 1983); Rameau's *Platée* (May 24,

1987); Donizetti's *Il duca d'Alba* (first stage performance, May 27, 1992); Zemlinsky's *Der Geburtstag der Infantin* (May 29, 1993).

Repertory *(Charleston Theater—West & Bignall)*. **1793:** Agreeable Surprise, Beggar's Opera, Deserter, Devil to Pay, Farmer, Flitch of Bacon, Haunted Tower, Highland Reel, Inkle and Yarico, Love in a Village, Maid of the Mill, Midas, No Song, no Supper, Padlock, Peeping Tom of Coventry, Poor Soldier, Poor Vulcan, Quaker, Robin Hood, Romp, Rosina, Son-in-law, Surrender of Calais, Waterman, Wedding Ring, Woodman. **1794:** Agreeable Surprise, Battle of Hexham, Beggar's Opera, Castle of Andalusia, Cymon and Sylvia, Day in Turkey (pantomime), Death of Captain Cook (pantomime), Devil to Pay, Duenna, Farmer, Flitch of Bacon, Forêt noire (pantomime), Harlequin balloonist (pantomime), Highland Reel, Inkle and Yarico, Love in a Village, Maid of the Mill, Midas, Padlock, Peeping Tom of Coventry, Poor Soldier, Quaker, Robin Hood, Robinson Crusoe (pantomime), Romp, Rosina, Son-in-law, Surrender of Calais, Thomas and Sally, Waterman, Woodman. **1795:** Beggar's Opera, Cymon and Sylvia, Deserter, Devil to Pay, Duenna, Fountainebleu, Harlequin balloonist (pantomime), Haunted Tower, Highland Reel, Maid of the Mill, No Song, no Supper, Padlock, Poor Soldier, Rival Candidates, Rosina, Son-in-law, Surrender of Calais, Waterman. **1796:** Battle of Hexham, Cymon and Sylvia, Death of Captain Cook (pantomime), Death of Major André (pantomime), Deserter, Duenna, Fountainebleu, Hartford Bridge, Haunted Tower, Highland Reel, Inkle and Yarico, Ladies' Frolic, Mirza and Lindor, Mysteries of the Castle, Oscar and Malvina, Padlock, Prize, Quaker, Rejected Fool (pantomime), Romp, Rosina, Surrender of Calais.

Repertory *(City Theater—Sollee)*. **1795:** Castle of Andalusia, Double Disguise, Farmer, Highland Reel, Love in a Village, Poor Soldier, Romp. **1796:** Agreeable Surprise, American Heroine, Apotheosis of Franklin (pantomime), Children in the Wood, Doctor and Apothecary, Duenna, Farmer, Inkle and Yarico, Irish Taylor (pantomime), Midas, Mountaineers, My Grandmother (pantomime), No Song, no Supper, Old Soldier (pantomime), Peeping Tom of Coventry, Poor Soldier, Purse, Quaker, Recruit, Romp, Rosina, Son-in-law. **1797:** Adopted Child, Agreeable Surprise, Alcesta (pantomime), Belle Dorothée (pantomime), Children in the Wood, Coopers (pantomime), Cymon and Sylvia, Death of Captain Cook, Farmer, Highland Reel, Inkle and Yarico, Lock and Key, Love in a Village, Magic Chamber (pantomime), No Song, no Supper, Old Ground Young (pantomime), Padlock, Peeping Tom of Coventry, Poor Soldier, Princess of Babylon (pantomime), Purse, Pygmalion, Quaker, Romp, Rosina, The Servant Mistress, Sicilian Romance, Thomas and Sally, Two Woodcutters (pantomime), Virgin Unmasked. **1798:** Adopted Child, Agreeable Surprise, Children in the Wood, Harlequin Gentleman (pantomime), Harlequin Skeleton (pantomime), Harlequin Veteran, Highland Reel, Inkle and Yarico, Love in a Village, Mountaineers, My Grandmother (pantomime), Padlock, Peeping Tom of Coventry, Poor Soldier, Princess of Babylon (pantomime), Prisoner, Romp, Rosina, Sicilian Romance, Spanish Barber, Sultan, Telemachos in the Island of Calypso (pantomime), Thomas and Sally, Tom Thumb the Great. **1799:** Agreeable Surprise, Battle of Hexham, Children in the Wood, Coopers (pantomime), Death of Captain Cook, Echo and Narcissus (pantomime), Family Harlequin (pantomime), Farmer, Forêt noire, Harlequin Skeleton (pantomime), Highland Reel, Inkle and Yarico, Love in a Village, Men in the Iron Mask (pantomime), Mirza and Lindor (pantomime), Mountaineers, My Grandmother, No Song, no Supper, Oscar and Malvina (pantomime), Padlock, Poor Soldier, Purse, Quaker, Romp, Rosina, Sicilian Romance, Spanish Barber, Virgin Unmasked. **1800:** Adopted Child, Agreeable Surprise, American True Blues, Children in the Wood, Farmer, Flitch of Bacon, Genevieve of Brabant (pantomime), Harlequin Skeleton (pantomime), Highland Reel, Homeward Bound (pantomime), Mountaineers, No Song, no Supper, Padlock, Poor Soldier, Purse, Rinaldo and Armida (pantomime), Romp, Rosina, Spoiled Child.

Repertory *(Spoleto Festival Opera)*. **1977:** The Consul, Pikovaya dama. **1978:** Vanessa, La traviata, Il furioso all'isola di San Domingo, Martin's Lie/The Egg. **1979:** Il marito disperato, The Medium. **1980:** La sonnambula, Chip and His Dog, Le Docteur Miracle, Monsieur Choufleuri. **1981:** The Last Savage, The Mother/The Selfish Giant/

Harrison Loved His Umbrella, Monsieur Choufleuri, L'Ivrogne Corrige. **1982:** Ledi Makbet Mtsenskovo uyezda (Lady Macbeth of the Mtsensk District). **1983:** Madama Butterfly, Antony and Cleopatra, Il flaminio. **1984:** Die lustige Witwe, Juana, La Loca, Ariadne auf Naxos, Arlecchinata/Lietta e Tracolio. **1985:** La fanciulla del West, Ariodante. **1986:** The Saint of Bleecker Street, Lord Byron's Love Letter, Renard. **1987:** Salome, Platée. **1988:** Rusalka, Montezuma, Herod and the Innocents. **1989:** La straniera, Le nozze di Figaro, Empty Places. **1990:** Parsifal, Le nozze di Figaro, Hydrogen Jukebox, Pioneer, Tristan and Iseult. **1991:** Maria Golovin, L'incoronazione di Poppea, Les contes d'Hoffmann. **1992:** Il duca d'Alba, Elektra. **1993:** The Singing Child, Le Comte Ory, Der Geburtstag der Infantin.

Tennessee ————————— CHATTANOOGA

• *The Chattanooga Opera* •

Giuseppe Verdi's *Il trovatore*, performed on February 8, 1943, in the University Theater, was the inaugural production of the Chattanooga Opera. The opera, sung in English to piano accompaniment, was a resounding success with the opera-starved Chattanooga populace, and the company scheduled a second performance two days later. Dr. Werner Wolff, a refugee from Nazi Germany, was the founder and guiding force behind this fledgling new company.

The Metropolitan Opera, Chicago Opera, and some traveling opera companies had visited Chattanooga previously, but these visits were rare events. A Chattanooga "season" required large financial support from the Chattanooga business community, and this was not always possible in a small city. So Chattanooga welcomed a home-based opera company.

Wolff had been a well-established conductor at the Hamburg Opera when the Nazis took power. At the advice of his friend (and conductor), Walter Damrosch, he traveled to Tennessee where he joined the faculty of the Cadek Conservatory of Music at the University of Chattanooga. From the university, he nurtured the Chattanooga Opera until his retirement in 1959. His wife, Emmy Land Wolff, had been a successful operatic soprano in Europe. She trained the local singers when there was not enough money to import guest soloists from New York.

Bizet's *Carmen* opened the second next season on October 18, 1943. Engelbert Humperdinck's *Hänsel und Gretel* followed in January with a curious bonus on the same program: the second act of Richard Wagner's *Der fliegende Holländer*. The season closed on May 3, 1944, with Friedrich von Flotow's *Martha*. The company staged one performance of each opera in the Central High School auditorium, sung in English and performed by Chattanooga-area artists. During its third season the company found a home in Riverside High School, where it remained for the next eighteen years. Although Riverside High was not ideal, it held the only available auditorium suitable for opera. Pietro Mascagni's *Cavalleria rusticana* opened the third season, in which orchestral accompaniment replaced the piano. The season closed with Otto Nicolai's *Die lustigen Weiber von Windsor*.

As the company matured and the budget grew, it imported guest artists from the Met and New York City Opera. Claramae Turner sang Carmen, Astrid Varnay

Tivoli Theater (Chattanooga, Tennessee).

was Leonore in Ludwig van Beethoven's *Fidelio*, and Beverly Sills sang Donna Elvira in Wolfgang Amadeus Mozart's *Don Giovanni*. The 1956-57 season was the most outstanding to date, opening with Jon Vickers and Inge Borkh in Beethoven's *Fidelio* on December 4, 1956. It continued with Herva Nelli, Richard Cassilly, and Morley Meredith in Giacomo Puccini's *Tosca*, and concluded with the double bill of Mascagni's *Cavalleria rusticana* and Ermanno Wolf-Ferrari's *Il segreto di Susanna*. The sixteenth season was Wolff's last season, although nothing in the program indicated that Verdi's *Rigoletto* on April 21, 1959, was Wolff's swan song. There was no farewell celebration for the man everyone called "Mr. Opera" for sixteen seasons.

Siegfried Landau took the helm in 1960. Like his predecessor, he was German and came to America to escape Nazi persecution. He ushered in a new era and introduced several contemporary operas to Chattanooga. Carlisle Floyd's *Susannah* with Phyllis Curtain, Norman Treigle, and Richard Cassilly graced the stage on April 12, 1960, and Gian Carlo Menotti's *The Consul* was mounted the following season. The company celebrated their move into a new home, the Tivoli Theater, with a performance of Douglas Moore's *The Ballad of Baby Doe* on April 23, 1963. A double bill of Menotti's *The Medium*/Giovanni Pergolesi's *La serva padrona* followed in the autumn, and Menotti's *The Old Maid and The Thief* was staged four years later. The first Russian opera, Modest Mussorgsky's *Boris Godunov* received its Chattanooga premiere on April 26, 1966. The first Czechoslovakian opera, Bedřich Smetana's *Prodaná nevěsta* (The Bartered Bride), was first seen in Chattanooga on April 20, 1972. Landau also brought well-known artists to the city, including Rita Shane, Kenneth Riegel, and Eleanor Steber. Landau was a purist and mounted Mozart's *Le nozze di Figaro* and *Così fan tutte* uncut. This delighted other purists, but everyone else was unhappy. Landau resigned at the end of 1972-73 season and returned to Germany.

The Chattanooga Opera merged with the Chattanooga Symphony in 1985 with Don Andrews as managing director of the joint organization. The company spends its limited budget primarily on importing singers from New York and Europe. Painted backdrops define the scenery. The Chattanooga Symphony receives most of the funds. Andrews's goal of expanding the season to three operas was realized for the 1993-94 season when Puccini's *La bohème*, Beethoven's *Fidelio* (concert version), and Donizetti's *Don Pasquale* were staged. Chattanooga's first world premiere, Sorrel Hays's *The Glass Woman*, is planned for the 1995 season.

The three-opera season offers standard fare with traditional staging in a *stagione* system. Recent productions include Verdi's *La traviata*, Puccini's *La bohème*, and Mozart's *Die Zauberflöte*. The company performs in the Tivoli Theater.

Tivoli Theater

A concert by the Tivoli Symphony and a screening of Cecil Blount De Mille's *Forbidden Fruit* inaugurated the Tivoli Theater on March 19, 1921. Taking two years to construct, the Tivoli cost $750,000. Chattanooga architect R.H. Hunt designed the building in conjunction with Rapp & Rapp. Frank Fowler owned it. Built as an ornate movie palace, it also hosted vaudeville. The advent of television precipitated the end of the movie palace era, and in 1961, the Tivoli saw its last movie, *The Three Stooges*. The theater narrowly missed the wrecking ball. In 1976, the City of Chattanooga purchased the theater, and around a decade later, restored it. Robert A. Franklin was in charge. The Tivoli reopened on March 29, 1989, with a recital by Marilyn Horne.

The Tivoli took its name from the Tivoli in Italy and recalls many features of Italian style architecture. Tiles and terra cotta bricks cover the movie-palace façade. A large marquee hangs in front with TIVOLI in large letters. The beige and cream-colored lobby boasts a split grand staircase. A variety of medallions adorn the area. The art deco inspired auditorium radiates gold, silver, ivory, and rose, and holds rich red velvet plush seats. The fan-shaped space includes an orchestra level, one balcony, and twelve side boxes. Richly decorated with putti, cartouches, and fluorescent half-shells, it displays a lavishly embellished gold-and-silver proscenium, framing a rich red curtain. The Tivoli seats 1,686. *Practical Information.* The Tivoli Theater is at 709 Broad Street. Tickets are purchased at the Chattanooga Symphony and Opera Association, 630 Chestnut Street, or by telephoning 615-267-8583, or writing Chattanooga Symphony and Opera Association, 630 Chestnut Street, Chattanooga, TN 37402. The Tivoli box office, located in the middle of the entrance foyer, opens one hour before curtain. If you go, stay at the Radisson Read Hotel, Martin Luther King Blvd. and Broad St., Chattanooga, TN 37401-2165; telephone 615-266-4121, fax 615-267-6447, reservations 1-800-333-3333. Holabird and Roche build the Georgian style hotel which is an architectural landmark and prime example of period architecture and decorative art. Winston Churchill, Tallulah Bankhead, and Gary Cooper have been some of the guests. Restored to its original splendor, the hotel is one block from the Tivoli Theater.

COMPANY STAFF AND REPERTORY

Music/Artistic Directors (Chattanooga Opera). Werner Wolff (1943–1959); Siegfried Landau (1960–1973); Robert Carter Austin, Jr. (1974–83); None (1983–85).
Music/Artistic Directors (Chattanooga Opera & Symphony). Vakhtang Jordania (1985–92); Robert Bernhardt (1992-present).
World Premiere (before Chattanooga Opera). Lindsey's *Elizabeth and Leicester* (April 21, 1936).
World Premiere (Chattanooga Opera & Symphony). Hays's *The Glass Woman* (1995).
Repertory. **1942-43:** Il trovatore, Carmen (workshop). **1943-44:** Carmen, Hänsel und Gretel, Die fliegende Holländer (Act II), Martha. **1944-45:** Cavalleria rusticana, Hänsel und Gretel, Die Zauberflöte. **1945-46:** Cavalleria rusticana, Die lustigen Weiber von Windsor, La traviata. **1946-47:** Madama Butterfly, La traviata, I pagliacci. **1947-48:** Carmen, Die Fledermaus, La bohème. **1948-49:** Le nozze di Figaro, Madama Butterfly, Il trovatore. **1949-50:** Don Giovanni, Les contes d'Hoffmann, Rigoletto. **1950-51:** Tosca, Faust, Le nozze di Figaro. **1951-52:** Faust, Il barbiere di Siviglia, La bohème. **1952-53:** Un ballo in maschera, Fidelio, Carmen. **1953-54:** La traviata, Die lustige Witwe, Aida. **1954-55:** Don Giovanni, Die lustigen Weiber von Windsor, Il trovatore. **1955-56:** Madama Butterfly, I pagliacci/The Telephone, Rigoletto. **1956-57:** Fidelio, Tosca, Prodaná nevěsta (The Bartered Bride). **1957-58:** La bohème, Hänsel und Gretel, Cavalleria rusticana/Il segreto di Susanna. **1958-59:** Die Zauberflöte, La traviata, Rigoletto. **1959-60:** The Beggar's Opera, Susannah. **1960-61:** Così fan tutte, The Consul. **1961-62:** Madama Butterfly, Rigoletto. **1962-63:** Il barbiere di Siviglia, The Ballad of Baby Doe. **1963-64:** La serva padrona/The Medium, Les contes d'Hoffmann. **1964-65:** Don Pasquale, Carmen. **1965-66:** La traviata, Boris Godunov. **1966-67:** L'elisir d'amore, Le nozze di Figaro. **1967-68:** The Old Maid and the Thief/Cavalleria rusticana, Faust. **1968-69:** Die Entführung aus dem Serail, Il trovatore. **1969-70:** Tosca, Susannah. **1970-71:** Die Fledermaus, La bohème. **1971-72:** Madama Butterfly, Prodaná nevěsta (The Bartered Bride). **1972-73:** Così fan tutte, Die lustigen Weiber von Windsor. **1973-74:** Don Pasquale, La traviata. **1974-75:** L'elisir d'amore, Carmen. **1975-76:** Tosca, La Cenerentola, Le fille du régiment. **1976-77:** Madama Butterfly, Il barbiere di Siviglia, Die Fledermaus. **1977-78:** La traviata, Don Pasquale, Faust. **1978-79:** Rigoletto, Così fan tutte, Die lustige Witwe. **1979-80:** La Périchole, La bohème, Lucia di Lammermoor. **1980-81:** Don Giovanni, Il barbiere di Siviglia, The Devil and Daniel Webster. **1981-82:** Carmen, L'elisir d'amore, The Village Singer/Il Signor Bruschino. **1982-83:** La traviata, Madama Butterfly, Carmina Burana (concert). **1983-84:** Susannah, The Mikado, Don Pasquale. **1984-85:** Tosca,

Hänsel und Gretel, I pagliacci. **1985-86:** La bohème, La Cenerentola, Die lustige Witwe. **1986-87:** Carmen, La Périchole, Il trovatore. **1987-88:** La traviata, L'elisir d'amore, Die Fledermaus. **1988-89:** Aida, The Mikado. **1989-90:** Tosca, Il barbiere di Siviglia. **1990-91:** Don Giovanni, Rigoletto. **1991-92:** Un ballo in maschera, Madama Butterfly. **1992-93:** La traviata, Die Zauberflöte. **1993-94:** La bohème, Fidelio (concert version), Don Pasquale.

KNOXVILLE

• *Knoxville Opera* •

Giuseppe Verdi's *La traviata* inaugurated the Knoxville Opera in October, 1978, at the Bijou Theater. Verdi's great middle-period work was the sole offering of the inaugural season. The Knoxville Opera was incorporated in 1976 with the assistance of the Knoxville Council of Arts.

The second season expanded to two offerings with further expansion to three operas taking place during the sixth season. The first opera of that season, Johann Strauß's *Die Fledermaus*, marked the company's final presentation at the Bijou Theater. The double-bill of Pietro Mascagni's *Cavalleria rusticana* and Ruggero Leoncavallo's *I pagliacci* celebrated the company's move into its new home, the Tennessee Theater. The company witnessed its first world premiere, Kenton Coe's *Rachel* with Stella Zambalis and John Stevens, on April 7, 1989. The casts feature both up-and-coming and established singers in the lead roles, supported by local talent.

The three-opera season offers traditional works in a *stagione system*. Recent productions include Strauß's *Die Fledermaus* and Puccini's *Tosca*. The company performs in the 1,539-seat Tennessee Theater.

Practical Information. The Tennessee Theater is at 604 South Gay Street. Tickets can be purchased at the Knoxville Opera offices at 602 South Gay Street, by calling 615-525-1840, or writing the Knoxville Opera, P.O.B. 16, Knoxville, TN 37901.

REPERTORY

World Premiere. Coe's *Rachel* (April 7, 1989).
Repertory. 1978: La traviata. **1979:** Die lustige Witwe. **1980:** Carmen, Il barbiere di Siviglia. **1981:** Madama Butterfly. **1982:** La bohème. **1983:** Die Fledermaus, Cavalleria rusticana/I pagliacci, Hänsel und Gretel. **1984:** Tosca, Sound of Music, Lucia di Lammermoor, La Cenerentola. **1985:** Il trovatore, Faust. **1986:** Susannah, South Pacific, Rigoletto. **1987:** Roméo et Juliette, The Music Man, La bohème. **1988:** Le nozze di Figaro, Oklahoma, La traviata. **1989:** Rachel, My Fair Lady, Die Zauberflöte. **1990:** Aida, The King and I, Madama Butterfly. **1991:** Don Giovanni, West Side Story, Il barbiere di Siviglia. **1992:** Carmen, Man of La Mancha, Les contes d'Hoffmann. **1993:** Otello, Die Fledermaus. **1994:** Tosca.

MEMPHIS

• *Opera Memphis* •

Giuseppe Verdi's *La traviata* inaugurated the Memphis Opera Theater, the precursor of Opera Memphis, in 1956. Founded by Ike Myers with the help of the Beethoven Club and some friends, the company mounted only one production that inaugural season.

Memphis boasts a rich operatic heritage that dates back to at least 1850 when a New Orleans Burlesque Opera Troupe arrived, entertaining the city with a violin rendition of tunes from Gaetano Donizetti's *Lucia di Lammermoor*. Jenny Lind visited the next year. The Greenlaw Opera House was erected in the 1860s at a cost of $200,000, but fire claimed the building in 1883. During its existence, the Mozart Society presented operatic excerpts there. Memphis began construction on the Grand Opera House in 1898. A majestic four-story structure, the building was faced with Blue Bedford stone from Indiana. On September 22, 1890, Emma Juch and her Grand English Opera Company inaugurated the Grand with Giacomo Meyerbeer's *Les Huguenots*. The company offered six performances, including Charles Gounod's *Faust* and Georges Bizet's *Carmen* during its season at the Grand. Juch's company returned the following year, opening a four-performance opera season on November 2 with Wagner's *Tannhäuser* followed by *Lohengrin*. Grau's Opera Company paid a visit during the summer of 1893, and 1894 witnessed Adelina Patti in Friedrich von Flotow's *Martha*. The Boston Ideals brought Donizetti's *Lucia di Lammermoor*, Gounod's *Faust*, and Verdi's *Rigoletto* and *Il trovatore*.

After the turn of the century, the Metropolitan Opera visited in 1901. Homegrown opera sprouted with a troupe known as the Memphis Opera Company mounting a summer performance in 1920. Valentina Tumanskaya directed other productions. The Chicago Civic Opera visited in the mid-1920s, bringing Feodor Chaliapin. The San Carlo Opera Company offered Memphis Verdi's *Aida*, Gounod's *Faust*, and Bizet's *Carmen* during the 1920s and 1930s. The late 1940s saw the Met begin annual visits, stopping for three nights in May. One person, Ike Myers, personally underwrote the Met's annual visit for the first few seasons. Then in 1951, an Arts Appreciation Group formed to underwrite the Met's Memphis visit. The Met visits ended in 1984 when the company raised its guarantee price to $1.5 million for its three-day May visit. The Arts Appreciate Group felt the money was better spent on homegrown opera.

Meanwhile, in the mid-1950s, the Memphis Opera Theater began producing opera. The first five seasons saw only one production a season, including Giacomo Puccini's *Tosca*, Johann Strauß's *Die Fledermaus*, and Bizet's *Carmen*. The 1960s ushered in more adventurous fare with Douglas Moore's *The Devil and Daniel Webster*, Bedřich Smetana's *Prodaná nevěsta* (The Bartered Bride), and Leonard Kastle's *Deseret*, along with the repertory favorites. In 1971 George Osborne was hired as general director. He soon presented opera on a grand scale. The 1972 season witnessed Modest Mussorgsky's *Boris Godunov*, Camille Saint-Saëns's *Samson et Dalila*, Vincenzo Bellini's *La sonnambula*, and Carlisle Floyd's *Susannah*. In 1979, Verdi's rarely-performed opera *Attila* was mounted. In 1984, the company

Orpheum Theater (Memphis, Tennessee).

moved into the newly renovated Orpheum Theater, and Robert Driver took the helm. He also ran the Indianapolis Opera Company, never moving to Memphis. Under his leadership, therefore, the company was unable to address its mid-South constituency, preventing it from realizing its full potential. Michael Ching took the helm in 1992 and with his guidance, the company has broadened its audience base by adding a music theater piece to its repertory and by developing new American works in its National Center for Development of American Opera. There the company has given the workshop premieres of David Olney's *Light in August*, and John Baur's *The Vision of John Brown*, and the world premiere of Michael Korie & Stewart Wallace's *Hopper's Wife*.

The four-opera season offers one grand opera, one musical theater production, one revival, and one classical favorite performed in the *stagione* system. Recent productions have included Gounod's *Roméo et Juliette*, Bizet's *Carmen*, Allan Jay Lerner's *My Fair Lady*, Grétry's *Zémire et Azor*, Donizetti's *Don Pasquale*, and Puccini's *Tosca*. The casts are composed of established singers and emerging talent. Opera Memphis performs in the Orpheum Theater.

Orpheum

Construction of the Orpheum began in October 1927. Rapp & Rapp designed the theater as a home for the Orpheum Circuit, the largest vaudeville circuit in the United States. The Orpheum Circuit and members of the Memphis Theater and Realty Company paid the theater's $1.6 million price tag. On November 19, 1928, some of vaudeville's best shows inaugurated the showplace: *Money, Money, Money,*

The Blue Streak of Vaudeville, and *The Devil's Circus*. The Orpheum was part of the Keith-Albee-Orpheum Circuit and until the Depression, vaudeville was king. Eventually motion pictures became the primary attraction. On November 3, 1976, the Memphis Development Foundation purchased the building for $285,000, and the theater began hosting Broadway shows. On October 23, 1982, the theater closed for fourteen months, undergoing a $4 million restoration. When the Orpheum reopened in 1984, Opera Memphis called it home.

The Orpheum is an impressive beige brick building boasting both classical and movie palace features. The three arched windows hold winged maidens flanking vases in their transoms and four medallions are affixed overhead. A red, yellow and black marquee sparkling with tracer lights announces the shows. A huge vertical neon sign blazes ORPHEUM. The Italian-inspired auditorium swims with gold, taupe, and russet. Gilded fruit baskets (a Rapp & Rapp signature) and fleur-de-lis decorate the ceiling, walls and proscenium, and silver cartouches embellish the parapets. Fluted gilded pilasters flank the proscenium boxes. The hall boasts three tiers, the first one shallow, the others deep. The theater seats 2,643.

Practical Information. The Orpheum is at 203 South Main. Tickets are purchased at the Opera Memphis offices, located on the Memphis State University South Campus. You can also purchase tickets by telephoning 901-678-2706, faxing 901-678-3506, or writing Opera Memphis, Memphis State University Campus, Memphis, TN 38152. If you go, stay at the Peabody, 149 Union Avenue, Memphis, TN 38103, telephone 901-529-4000, fax 901-529-9600, reservations 1-800-323-7500. The Peabody was built in 1925 in an Italian Renaissance Revival architectural style. It is both an architectural landmark and a Mid-South institution. It is on the National Register of Historic Places and only a few blocks from the Orpheum.

COMPANY STAFF AND REPERTORY

General/Artistic Directors. George Osborne (1971–1984); Robert Driver (1984–1991); Michael Ching (1992–present).

World Premieres (National Center for Development of American Opera). Olney's *Light in August* (February 12, 1993); Baur's *The Vision of John Brown* (February 12, 1993); Korie & Wallace's Hopper's Wife (May 1994).

Repertory. **1956:** La traviata. **1957:** Tosca. **1958:** Die Fledermaus. **1959:** Carmen. **1960:** Der Schauspieldirektor. **1961:** The Devil and Daniel Webster, Prodaná nevěstra (The Bartered Bride), Cavalleria rusticana/I pagliacci. **1962:** Le nozze di Figaro, Rigoletto. **1963:** Don Giovanni. **1964:** La bohème, Madama Butterfly. **1965:** La traviata, Il barbiere di Siviglia. **1966:** Lucia di Lammermoor, Faust. **1967:** Deseret, Il travatore. **1968:** *Die Fledermaus, Otello.* **1969:** Aida, Rigoletto. **1970:** Faust, The Medium/The Telephone. **1971:** Don Giovanni, Gianni Schicchi/Carmina Burana, Turandot. **1972:** Boris Godunov, Samson et Dalila, La sonnambula, Susannah. **1973:** Tosca, Lucia di Lammermoor, Un ballo in maschera, Les contes d'Hoffmann. **1974:** La bohème, La forza del destino, Rigoletto, Salome. **1975:** La traviata, Carmen, L'elisir d'amore, Die lustige Witwe. **1976:** Madama Butterfly, Ariadne auf Naxos, Il travatore. **1977:** La fille du régiment, Cavalleria rusticana/I pagliacci, Il tabarro, Der fliegende Holländer, Faust, Turandot. **1978:** Il barbiere di Siviglia, Aida, Macbeth, Norma. **1979:** Tosca, Attila, Don Giovanni, Manon Lescaut. **1980:** La bohème, Die Fledermaus, Lucia di Lammermoor, La Périchole. **1981:** Madama Butterfly, La traviata, Rigoletto. **1982:** Il barbiere di Siviglia, Faust, Susannah. **1983:** La traviata, Carmen, Die Entführung aus dem Serail, Hänsel und Gretel. **1984:** Lucia di Lammermoor,

H.M.S. Pinafore. **1985:** La bohème, Madama Butterfly. **1986:** Aida, Carmen, Falstaff. **1987:** Il barbiere di Siviglia, Tosca, Rigoletto. **1988:** La traviata, Hänsel und Gretel, Les contes d'Hoffmann. **1989:** Anna Bolena, Le fille du régiment, Die Zauberflöte. **1990:** Don Carlo, Don Giovanni, Man of La Mancha, Pirates of Penzance. **1991:** Faust, Orfeo ed Euridice, Porgy and Bess, Madama Butterfly. **1992:** La bohème, Così fan tutte, Lucia di Lammermoor, My Fair Lady. **1993:** Don Pasquale, Roméo et Juliette, Zémire et Azor, Carmen. **1994:** Tosca, South Pacific, Hopper's Wife.

——————————————— NASHVILLE

• *Nashville Opera* •

Giacomo Puccini's *Madama Butterfly* marked the beginning of the Nashville Opera, originally called the Nashville Opera Guild, in 1981. The birth of the company is remarkable, considering Nashville is country and western territory. The Grand Ole Opry is considered the Grand Opera of Middle Tennessee.

Seeds for the opera company were planted by Thor Johnson, music director of the Nashville Symphony for ten years until his death in 1975. He bequeathed a sum of money to the Tennessee Performing Arts Foundation for operatic productions involving the symphony. Thor Johnson's successor, Michael Charry, asked a certain Mary Ragland to produce the operas. Ragland chartered the Nashville Opera Guild (to receive contributions to subsidize the opera productions) and opera took root. The first decade offered a one-opera season of predominately standard Italian fare. The exceptions were George Gershwin's *Porgy and Bess* and Arthur Sullivan's *The Mikado*.

In 1988, the Nashville Opera Guild became the Nashville Opera Association (another opera guild was formed to help support the organization), and Kyle Ridout joined the Association as its first general director. After a few years at the helm, Ridout believed that opera could grow in Nashville, and for the 1991-92 season, expanded the repertory to two works, one grand opera and one musical theater. The latter piece was to broaden the audience base. By the following season, the repertory offered two operas, one of which was one grand opera, Puccini's *Madama Butterfly*, and one a lighter work, Gioachino Rossini's *Il barbiere di Siviglia*. The Rossini piece was noteworthy — it carried a touch of verismo and a social message. The opera was set during the French Revolution and contrasted the sufferings of the underclass with the frivolity of the aristocracy. The storm scene became a vehicle for the first rebellious act of the people — Doctor Bartolo's house was blown up. The usually happy ending held a macabre twist as blood red lights flooded the stage and the underprivileged staged their uprising, pointing pistols and rifles at Almaviva, Rosina, and Doctor Bartolo. Ridout's immediate goal is to expand the season to three operas with long-range plans calling for a four-opera season: two grand operas, one light-comic opera, and one chamber opera.

The two-opera season offers standard fare in a *stagione system*. Recent productions include Gaetano Donizetti's *La fille du régiment*, Puccini's *Tosca* and *Madama Butterfly*. The company performs in Andrew Jackson Hall and Polk Theater in the Tennessee Performing Arts Center.

Tennessee Performing Arts Center (Nashville, Tennessee).

Tennessee Performing Arts Center

The Tennessee Performing Arts Center opened on September 9, 1980, but the idea for the performing arts center dates back eight years when the state was planning to build a new office tower on the site of the old Andrew Jackson Hotel. To make the performing arts center project financially feasible, it slipped in on the ground floor of the office tower. Designed by Taylor and Crabtree, the entire complex (State offices, State Museum, three theaters) cost $42 million. Although the project was not completed until 1980, this was Tennessee's celebration of the Bicentennial (it was originally scheduled to open on July 4, 1976) and a first step in helping Nashville change its image as a cultural desert.

The Center is an imposing white concrete and glass building that soars into Nashville's emerging skyline. A small gray-and-white sign, TENNESSEE PERFORM-ING ARTS CENTER, is affixed to the stone façade. The lobby is modern, yet rustic. A bronze bust of Andrew Jackson stands in the entrance of Jackson Hall. The functional auditorium is earth-colored, with sculpted concrete walls. Two free-form, snow-white tiers float above rust-colored velvet seats that stretch in unbroken rows across the room. Acoustic banners three shades of autumn — auburn, amber, and pumpkin — are suspended overhead. Andrew Jackson Hall seats 2,250.

JAMES K. POLK THEATER in large white letters identifies the theater's entrance. Warm wood striped panels cover the auditorium walls. A single sculpted, mocha-painted tier curves gently across the room, ending at the acoustic panels flanking the proscenium arch. Additional acoustic panels hang from the ceiling. The seats are coffee-colored plush. The Polk Theater seats 1,000.

Practical Information. The Tennessee Performing Arts Center is at 505 Deaderick Street. The box office, inside the Center on the left, is open from 10:00 A.M. to 5:00 P.M., Monday through Friday, and 10:00 A.M. to 4:00 P.M., Saturday. On performance days, the box office opens one and a half hours before the performance and closes after the last intermission. Tickets can purchased by telephoning Ticketmaster 615-741-2787, or writing Ticketmaster, P.O.B. 3406, Nashville, TN 37219. For information contact Nashville Opera, 1900 Belmont Blvd., Fidelity Hall, Suite 402, Nashville, TN 37212, telephone 615-292-5710. If you visit, stay at the Doubletree Hotel at 2 Sovran Plaza, Nashville, TN 37239; telephone 615-244-8200, fax 615-747-4894, reservations 1-800-528-0444. The Doubletree is across the street from the Tennessee Performing Arts Center.

COMPANY STAFF AND REPERTORY

General/Artistic Director. Kyle Ridout (1988–present).

Repertory. **1981:** Madama Butterfly. **1982:** Porgy and Bess. **1983:** Tosca. **1984:** La traviata. **1985:** Cavalleria rusticana/Pagliacci. **1986:** Il barbiere di Siviglia. **1987:** La bohème. **1988:** Il trovatore. **1989:** The Mikado. **1990:** Lucia di Lammermoor. **1991:** Rigoletto. **1991-92:** Carmen, Carousel. **1992-93:** Il barbiere di Siviglia, Madama Butterfly. **1993-94:** La fille du régiment, Tosca.

Texas
AUSTIN

• *Austin Lyric Opera* •

Wolfgang Amadeus Mozart's *Die Zauberflöte* inaugurated the Austin Lyric on January 9, 1987, at the University of Texas Performing Arts Center Concert Hall (renamed the Bass Concert Hall). The Mozart opera received three performances that inaugural season. Joseph McClain and Walter Ducloux founded the company in May 1985, since Austin was the only major city in Texas that could not boast an opera company or festival.

The second season expanded to two offerings, Charles Gounod's *Roméo et*

Juliette and Giuseppe Verdi's *Un ballo in maschera*. Three works became the norm in the 1989-90 season. The company's focus is to give "new life" to traditional works and has included the American premiere of Gioachino Rossini's *La pietra del paragone*. Both established and rising American artists comprise the casts.

The three-opera season offers standard fare in a *stagione* system. Recent productions include Donizetti's *Don Pasquale* and Giacomo Puccini's *Turandot*. The company performs in the 2,910-seat Bass Concert Hall.

Practical Information. The Bass Concert Hall is at 23rd and East Campus Drive on the University of Texas Campus. Tickets are available from the Austin Lyric Opera, P.O.B. 984, Austin, TX 78767-0984, telephone 512-472-5927. If you go, stay at the Omni Austin Hotel, 700 San Jacinto at Eighth Street, Austin, TX 78701, phone 512-476-3700, fax 512-320-5882. Located downtown, the hotel is convenient to the campus.

COMPANY STAFF AND REPERTORY

General/Artistic Director. Joseph McClain (1985–present).

American/United States Premieres. Rossini's *La pietra del paragone* (April 3, 1992).

Repertory. **1987:** Die Zauberflöte. **1987-88:** Roméo et Juliette, Un ballo in maschera. **1988-89:** La traviata, Die Fledermaus. **1989-90:** Carmen, Madama Butterfly, La Cenerentola. **1990-91:** Il trovatore, Don Giovanni, Il barbiere di Siviglia. **1991-92:** Aida, La bohème, La pietra del paragone. **1992-93:** Fidelio, Tosca, Die Entführung aus dem Serail. **1993-94:** Turandot, Le nozze di Figaro, Don Pasquale.

DALLAS

• *The Dallas Opera* •

Gioachino Rossini's *L'italiana in Algeri*, with Giulietta Simionato and Giuseppe Taddei and Nicola Rescigno on the podium, was the first stage performance of the Dallas Civic Opera, the original name of The Dallas Opera. It was the only opera staged during the inaugural season. Rescigno and Lawrence Kelly had lost a bitter power struggle with Carol Fox in Chicago (see Lyric Opera of Chicago entry) and came to Dallas to run the new company. The Dallas Civic was officially born a few weeks earlier, on November 21, 1957, when Maria Callas gave a gala inaugural concert in the State Music Hall. She sang arias from Wolfgang Amadeus Mozart's *Die Entführung aus dem Serail*, Giuseppe Verdi's *Macbeth* and *La traviata*, Vincenzo Bellini's *I Puritani*, and Gaetano Donizetti's *Anna Bolena*.

Dallas first heard opera on February 12, 1875, when Friedrich von Flotow's *Martha* was staged at Field's Theater. Arthur Sullivan's *Iolanthe* opened the Dallas Opera House on October 15, 1883. Several touring companies, including the Boston Ideals and Emma Abbott's Troupe stopped in Dallas in the late 1880s and 1890s, offering the standard repertory fare. The early 1900s saw the Olympic Opera Company and Henry Savage Company present several operas at the State Fairs. Max Rabinoff's Boston National Company visited in 1915 and 1916, and Fortune

Gallo brought his San Carlo Grand Opera Company as well. (During one of Fortune Gallo's productions, two donkeys tried to procreate in front of 4,000 opera lovers.) The Chicago Opera visited in 1913, bringing Donizetti's *Lucia di Lammermoor* with Luisa Tetrazzini, Jules Massenet's *Thaïs* with Mary Garden, and Richard Wagner's *Die Walküre*. The company performed in the 4,300 Fair Park Coliseum, almost filling it to capacity. Chicago returned in 1914, 1918, 1919, and 1920, but it was the 1923 visit that was outstanding. Dallas heard Feodor Chaliapin for the first time. The company's visit the next year was not as successful. Garden, who was making her last appearance, chose Richard Strauss's *Salome* as her farewell vehicle. She was forty-seven at the time, and it was reported that the Dance of the Seven Veils revealed only a middle-aged woman. The Metropolitan Opera visits began in 1939. Dallas had seen the Met once before in 1905, when Andreas Dippel sang the title role in Wagner's *Die Walküre*, but this was the Met's first visit in thirty-four years. It opened its brief tour with Massenet's *Manon*, featuring Grace Moore. Moore returned two days in Giacomo Puccini's *La bohème*, concluding the Met's visit. During the next few decades, the city heard most of the Met's great artists—Ezio Pinza, Lily Pons, Lawrence Tibbett, Jan Peerce, Richard Tucker, and Renata Tebaldi. Three years before the Dallas Civic was formed, the final scene of Strauss's *Capriccio* was staged at the Fair Park Auditorium on November 23, 1954. It was the first performance in German in America. Three years later, the Dallas Civic was founded.

Callas returned to open Dallas's second season in a Zeffirelli production of Verdi's *La traviata*. Rossini's *L'italiana in Algeri* followed on November 4, 1958, signaling the American debut of Teresa Berganza. Two days later, Callas gave her unforgettable performance in Luigi Cherubini's *Medée*. The opera, played out against the backdrop of the Palace of King Creon in the fifth century B.C., featured Jon Vickers in his United States debut opposite Callas. Callas opened the following season in Donizetti's *Lucia di Lammermoor* on November 6, 1959, and then reprised Medée. This time her Medea almost ended in disaster. Her sweeping cloak caught on a nail as she was making her dramatic climb up the temple stairs, preventing her from continuing. Callas, without missing a beat, tore her cloak from the nail, collected the ripped cloth, and continued as if nothing had happened. Although this was Callas's last appearance in Dallas, she had helped place Dallas on the world-opera map.

On November 16, 1960, the company introduced both Georg Friedrich Händel's *Alcina* and Joan Sutherland to the United States, to a half-empty house. Händel's *Alcina* began the company's foray into Baroque opera, including the premieres of Claudio Monteverdi's *L'incoronazione di Poppea*, Händel's *Samson* and Antonio Vivaldi's *Orlando furioso*. Another novelty of the 1960 season was Donizetti's *La figlia del reggimento* (the Italian version of his better-known *La fille du régiment*). The company borrowed the production from the Teatro Massimo (Palermo, Italy). A Franco Zeffirelli production of Mozart's *Don Giovanni*, featuring Sutherland as Donna Anna, Elizabeth Schwarzkopf as Donna Elvira, and Eberhard Wächter as Don Giovanni, was also mounted in 1960. The next year Dallas witnessed the American debut of Plácido Domingo as Arturo in Donizetti's *Lucia di Lammermoor*. Domingo wanted to return the following season for Cassio in Verdi's *Otello*, but Kelly, known for his elitist attitude, felt Domingo could not possibly be good enough to sing Cassio since he had sung Edgardo with the Fort Worth Opera. He did not hire Domingo. Domingo never forgot the insult and never again sang in Dallas. The company's first foray into the French repertory also came in 1961 with a Zeffirelli production of Jules Massenet's *Thaïs* and the American debut of Denise Duval in the title role. This was Zeffirelli's last production for Dallas. Sutherland also returned to Dallas in 1961 for Lucia, and Mario del Monaco arrived the following year for Otello and Canio.

The company's lowest point was the planned performance of Verdi's *Un ballo in maschera* on November 22, 1963, the day President John Fitzgerald Kennedy was assassinated in Dallas. (*Un ballo* re-creates the assassination of a ruler – King Gustav III or Riccardo, depending upon which version is staged.) Although the company postponed the opera to the following evening, it was one of the most difficult performances anyone could remember. The company found itself in severe financial straits the following year, reducing the number of performances to two. Montserrat Caballé brought her Violetta, and Renata Tebaldi brought her Tosca in 1965. Gwyneth Jones made her American debut in Verdi's *Macbeth* in 1966. An interesting triple bill graced the stage the next season – Domenico Cimarosa's *Maestro di Cappella*, Henry Purcell's *Faerie Queene*, and Puccini's *Suor Angelica*. A "Götterdämmerung" struck in 1970, and the company almost died. Experiencing a very severe financial crisis (worse than in 1964) Dallas bounced checks. This especially infuriated the Italian singers, who camped outside in protest. Then a disastrous Carl Orff's *Carmina Burana* was staged. Bertrand Castelli, who directed the opera, attempted a radical new approach, and his concept "bombed." Many of the company's generous patrons threatened to cancel their support.

Dallas's first German opera, Ludwig van Beethoven's *Fidelio*, arrived in 1971, with Helga Dernesch making her American debut. The next year, Alfredo Kraus revived the French repertory with Massenet's *Werther*. Jon Vickers kept up the Italian side with a moving portrayal of Andrea Chénier in 1973. Marilyn Horne sang her first Mignon under the baton of Sarah Caldwell in 1974. The first Wagnerian work staged in Dallas, *Tristan und Isolde*, arrived the following year. Set on a giant, raked, elliptical disc enveloped by clouds, Vickers and Roberta Knie (in her United States debut) portrayed the title roles. At one performance, persistent, loud coughing accompanied the prelude to the last act. This so incensed Vickers, who lay wounded behind a screen, that he rose from near death to deliver his immortal "Stop your damned coughing!" line. (The stage manager thought someone had requested coffee.) Vickers, nevertheless, returned for the title role in the American stage premiere of Camille Saint-Saëns's *Samson et Dalila* on November 5, 1976.

Plato Karayanis joined the company as general director in July 1977, with plans to enlarge the season and (slowly) expand the repertory. The company staged its first American opera, Douglas Moore's *The Ballad of Baby Doe* the next season. Benjamin Britten's *Peter Grimes* and Igor Stravinsky's *The Rake's Progress* followed, the latter with sets and costumes by David Hockney. Marilyn Horne sang the title role in Vivaldi's *Orlando Furioso*, the first opera by Vivaldi ever staged in the United States.

The Dallas Civic Opera became The Dallas Opera as the twenty-fifth season opened. A performance of Wagner's *Die Walküre* in 1981 introduced the *Ring* cycle (out of order) with *Das Rheingold* in 1982, *Siegfried* in 1984, and *Götterdämmerung* in 1985. The company initiated a spring season of chamber opera in the intimate Majestic Theater in 1984, and works like Britten's *The Rape of Lucretia*,

Gian Carlo Menotti's *Amelia Goes to the Ball* and *The Medium*, Mozart's *Die Ent-führung aus dem Serail*, Claudio Monteverdi's *La favola d'Orfeo*, and Rossini's *Il turco in Italia* were mounted. The spring season never caught on and died after a few years. Dallas presented its first world premiere, Dominick Argento's *The Aspern Papers*, on November 19, 1988, with Elisabeth Söderström, Neil Rosen-shein, Eric Halfvarson, Frederica von Stade, and Richard Stilwell, and Rescigno on the podium. John Conklin designed the production, which was directed by Mark Lamos. The end of the founder's era came when Rescigno resigned in January 1990, taking the company's "museum" philosophy with him. The relocation of the Dallas Symphony to its own hall allowed the opera to expand it season.

Karayanis has revitalized the company with a music theater philosophy — "Opera for the Twenty-First Century" — that involves the commissioning of new works, revivals of rarely-performed twentieth-century works, and a fresh look at the standard repertory. Contemporary operas grace the stage, including Samuel Bar-ber's *Vanessa*, Leoš Janáček's *Jenůfa*, and Argento's *The Dream of Valentino*. The star-driven system remains, but only singers with good theatrical skills now appear. Recent artists have included Carol Vaness, Renée Fleming, Marilyn Zschau, Ashley Putnam, Ruth Ann Swenson, Jerry Hadley, Gary Lakes, Richard Stilwell, and Timothy Noble.

The five-opera season offers a mixture of repertory favorites, lesser known pieces, and contemporary works in a *stagione* system. The first, third and final operas are well-known works with the lesser known pieces sandwiched between. Recent productions include Donizetti's *Lucia di Lammermoor*, Manuel de Falla's *La vida breve / El retablo del Maese Pedro / El amor brujo*, Verdi's *La traviata*, Pyotr Il'yich Tchaikovsky's *Eugene Onegin*, Mozart's *Così fan tutte*, Rossini's *Semi-ramide*, and Wagner's *Der fliegende Holländer*. The company performs in the Music Hall.

Music Hall

A lively performance of Sigmund Romberg's *The Student Prince* celebrated the opening of the Fair Park Auditorium, the original name of the Music Hall, on Oc-tober 10, 1925. The Auditorium accommodated 5,000 and cost $500,000 to build. A $5.5 million remodeling effort took place in 1972, the same year the building was renamed Music Hall.

The Music Hall is a massive, beige-brick, Spanish-Moor style structure with turrets and a deep red clay roof. A conglomeration of geometric shapes and forms delineates the façade. White-glazed concrete, cream brick, and wood trim defines the lobby. The auditorium is Texas-size — immense. A single huge balcony curves gently across the autumn-hue hall. Golden orange velvet seats harmonize with the taupe-painted concrete side walls that darken to mocha as they approach the pro-scenium. Geometric shapes sculpted into the wall break up its enormous area. Acoustic squares and rectangles are suspended on the ceiling. The Hall seats 3,420.

Practical Information. The Music Hall is at Fair Park on First Avenue. Tickets are sold at the Dallas Opera box office in the Centrum, 3102 Oak Lawn Avenue, Suite 450 between 9:00 A.M. and 5:00 P.M., Monday through Friday, and from 10:00 A.M. to 2:00 P.M. on Saturday. Tickets can also be ordered by telephoning 214-443-1000 or writing the Dallas Opera, The Centrum, 3102 Oak Lawn Avenue,

Music Hall at Fair Park (Dallas, Texas).

Suite 450, Dallas, TX 75219. If you go, stay at The Mansion on Turtle Creek, 2821 Turtle Creek Boulevard, Dallas, TX 75219; telephone 214-559-2100, fax 214-528-4187, reservations 1-800-323-7500. The Mansion on Turtle Creek, unquestionably one of the best hotels in the world, retains an architectural uniqueness from its days as a private mansion. It is filled with original artwork and antiques. The Mansion offers complimentary limousine service to the Music Hall.

COMPANY STAFF AND REPERTORY

General/Artistic Directors. Larry Kelly (1957–1974); Nicola Rescigno (music director, acting general director, 1974–1977); Plato Karayanis (1977–present).

World Premieres. Argento's *The Aspern Papers* (November 19, 1988).

American/United States Premieres. Händel's *Alcina* (November 16, 1960); Monteverdi's *L'incoronazione di Poppea* (first professional performance, 1963); Händel's *Samson* (November 5, 1976); Vivaldi's *Orlando furioso* (November 28, 1980).

Repertory. **1957:** L'italiana in Algeri. **1958:** Medée, L'italiana in Algeri, La traviata. **1959:** Medée, Lucia di Lammermoor, Il barbiere di Siviglia. **1960:** La figlia del reggimento, Alcina, Don Giovanni, Madama Butterfly. **1961:** Lucia di Lammermoor, Thaïs, La bohème. **1962:** I pagliacci/Suor Angelica, Il barbiere di Siviglia, Otello. **1963:** Carmen, L'incoronazione di Poppea, Un ballo in maschera. **1964:** Madama Butterfly, Samson et Dalila. **1965:** Giulio Cesare, Tosca, La traviata. **1966:** La bohème, Macbeth, Rigoletto. **1967:** Medée Il maestro di cappella/Suor Angelica, Le nozze di Figaro, Faerie Queene. **1968:** Anna Bolena, Orphée aux enfers, Otello. **1969:** Fedora, Don Giovanni, Aida. **1970:** Die lustige Witwe, Carmina Burana, Madama Butterfly, Rigoletto. **1971:** Fidelio, La favorita, Il tabarro, Samson et Dalila. **1972:** Lucia di Lammermoor, I pagliacci, Werther, Dido and Aeneas. **1973:** Andrea Chénier, Le nozze di Figaro, Zolotoy petushok (The Golden Cockerel). **1974:** I Puritani,

Lucrezia Borgia, Tosca, Mignon. **1975:** Anna Bolena, Les contes d'Hoffmann, Madama Butterfly, Tristan und Isolde. **1976:** Samson et Dalila, La bohème, Salome, La traviata. **1977:** I Capuleti e i Montecchi, Manon, Macbeth, Rigoletto. **1978:** The Ballad of Baby Doe, Il barbiere di Siviglia, Un ballo in maschera, Der fliegende Holländer. **1979:** Les pêcheurs des perles, Manon Lescaut, La Cenerentola, Aida. **1980:** Peter Grimes, Lakmé, Turandot, Orlando furioso. **1981:** Roméo et Juliette, Madama Butterfly, Ernani, Die Walküre. **1982:** Lucia di Lammermoor, I pagliacci/Gianni Schicchi, Der Rosenkavalier, Das Rheingold. **1983:** Carmen, La figlia del reggimento, The Rake's Progress, La forza del destino. **1984:** Amelia al ballo, The Medium, Così fan tutte, La traviata, Il trovatore, Siegfried. **1985:** Rape of Lucretia, Il maestro di cappella, La cambiale di matrimonio, Otello, L'elisir d'amore, La bohème, Götterdämmerung. **1986:** La sonnambula, Andrea Chénier, La favola d'Orfeo, Die Entführung aus dem Serail, La fanciulla del West, Mother of Us All, Rigoletto. **1987:** Porgy and Bess, Werther, Tosca, Turandot, L'italiana in Algeri, Il turco in Italia. **1988:** The Aspern Papers, Carmen, Die Zauberflöte, Don Carlo. **1989:** Don Pasquale, Die lustige Witwe, I pagliacci/Cavalleria rusticana, Madama Butterfly. **1990:** Prince Igor, Faust, Hänsel und Gretel, Les contes d'Hoffmann, Die Walküre. **1991:** Le nozze di Figaro, Aida, Gianni Schicchi/Suor Angelica/Il tabarro, L'elisir d'amore. **1992:** L'elisir d'amore, The Voyage of Edgar Allan Poe, Semiramide, Eugene Onegin, Così fan tutte. **1993:** Il barbiere di Siviglia, Jenůfa, La traviata, El Retablo de Maese Pedro/El Amor Brujo/La Vida Breve, Lucia di Lammermoor. **1994:** Vanessa, Der fliegende Holländer.

FORT WORTH

• *Fort Worth Opera* •

Giuseppe Verdi's *La traviata* inaugurated the Fort Worth Opera in November 1946. Former singers F.L. Snyder and August Spain founded the company to foster young artists and produce "in-house" productions of the standard repertory. Some early productions included Verdi's *Aida*, Johann Strauß's *Die Fledermaus*, and Giacomo Puccini's *Madama Butterfly*.

Plácido Domingo sang his first major role with the company in 1962 as Edgardo in Gaetano Donizetti's *Lucia di Lammermoor*. The performance also marked the last stage performance of Lily Pons. Beverly Sills also performed with the company. In the mid-1960s the company staged some less familiar works, along with the repertory favorites, including Franz von Suppé's *Die schöne Galatea* and Julia Smith's *The Shepherdess and the Chimneysweep*.

The three-opera season offers a mixture of standard and contemporary fare in a *stagione* system. Recent productions include Donizetti's *Don Pasquale* and Gian Carlo Menotti's *The Telephone/The Old Maid and the Thief*. The company performs in the 3,054-seat Tarrant County Convention Center.

Practical Information. The Tarrant County Convention Center is at 1111 Houston Street. Tickets are available from the Fort Worth Opera, 3505 West Lancaster, Fort Worth, TX 76107, or by telephoning 817-731-0200.

COMPANY STAFF AND REPERTORY

General/Artistic Directors. Rudolf Kruger (1954–1982); Dwight Bowes (1983–1985); Mario Ramos (1986–1989); William Walker (1990–present).

HOUSTON

• *Houston Grand Opera* •

The Houston Grand Opera made its debut with Richard Strauss's *Salome* in the Music Hall on January 19, 1956. Seven days later Cio-Cio-San (Madama Butterfly) was betrayed by B.F. Pinkerton and killed herself. So ended the company's first season, mounted with $25,000. Walter Herbert conducted both operas. His ambition to establish an opera company in Houston had been realized.

Opera in Houston dates back to 1867, when the first traveling opera troupes came to town. Giuseppe Verdi's *Il trovatore* and *La traviata*, Daniel Auber's *Fra Diavolo*, Wolfgang Amadeus Mozart's *Die Zauberflöte*, and Friedrich von Flotow's *Martha* were some of the offerings. Although the operas were not well received, opera companies and well-known singers continued to visit. Ilma di Murska gave a concert in 1875 and sang in Vincenzo Bellini's *Norma* three years later. Emma Abbott appeared in Ambroise Thomas's *Mignon* and Verdi's *Ernani*. A few theaters, called opera houses, sprang up in the city, but opera only occasionally, if at all, graced the stage. First came Gray's Opera House and then Perkins's Opera House. Perkins, which opened in 1866, was later renamed Pillot's. Twenty-four years later, Sweeney & Coombs Opera House began hosting performances. In 1901, the Metropolitan Opera paid its first visit to Houston. A single performance of Richard Wagner's *Lohengrin* with Emma Eames and Ernestine Schumann-Heink took place in the Winnie Davis Auditorium. The Winnie Davis, inaugurated in 1894, was named for the daughter of the former Confederate president. Although the Met returned in 1905 with Wagner's *Parsifal*, it did not reappear in Houston for forty-two years.

The City Auditorium opened in 1910. The spacious, well-proportioned hall boasted a grand proscenium arch, but also noisy wooden seats, no orchestra pit, and poor sightlines. The main floor was not graded and only the tallest in the audience could see the stage. Nevertheless, it hosted opera for fifty-three years, forty of which were the result of the efforts of one woman, Mrs. Edna W. Saunders. She brought opera's prominent artists and companies to town. In 1919, the Chicago Opera began annual visits that lasted for seven seasons. Mary Garden in Jules Massenet's *Thaïs* and Feodor Chaliapin in Modest Mussorgsky's *Boris Godunov* were among the legendary performances. The company returned in 1935 with Maria Jeritza performing Act II of Giacomo Puccini's *Tosca* in an evening of operatic excerpts. Enrico Caruso sang to a sold-out Auditorium in 1920, the same year the Boston Opera Company brought Puccini's *Madama Butterfly*. Antonio Scotti visited with his own company during the decade, and the German Grand Opera Company mounted an entire *Ring* in 1930. The 58-year-old Johanna Gadski assayed Brünnhilde. Fortune Gallo's San Carlo Opera Company also paid frequent visits, and a few decades later, the Charles Wagner Company brought Stella Andreva, Armand Tokatyan, John Alexander, and Beverly Sills to Houston.

There were homegrown efforts as well, but none sprouted roots. In the early 1920s and 1930s, a Houston soprano, Mary Carson, and a colorful singing teacher, Mrs. John Wesley Graham, staged several operas. Uriel Nespoli mounted an English-language Puccini's *Madama Butterfly* that featured Nancy Swinford as Cio-Cio-San. Swinford repeated the role for Houston Grand Opera's first season. Georges Bizet's

Carmen, produced by the Southern School of Fine Arts, was the most disastrous local attempt. The opera lasted so long that the management did not allow the tenor to sing the Flower Song. It was reported that this Carmen died from a mixture of exhaustion and embarrassment, not from Don José's knife! The Houston Symphony Orchestra entered the opera business during the 1942-43 season when it offered Act III of Verdi's *Aida* in concert form. The first full-staged performance came the following season with Puccini's *Tosca*. Although the 1944-45 season saw Verdi's *La traviata* and *Il trovatore* and Puccini's *La bohème*, no permanent Houston Symphony Opera materialized.

Walter Herbert's letter to Edward Bing on June 2, 1955, planted the first seeds for a permanent company. In his letter, he expressed his desire to establish an opera company in Houston. Herbert had previously nurtured the development of the New Orleans Opera (see New Orleans entry). With Bing's favorable response, Herbert visited Houston and Mrs. Louis G. Lobit signed him to a contract. Herbert almost did not return for a second season. A conflict arose with the board, and negotiations were terminated. Kurt Adler and Julius Rudel were considered as replacements, but Herbert did return. He staged Verdi's *La traviata*, Puccini's *Tosca*, and Gioachino Rossini's *La cenerentola*. Strauss's *Elektra*, directed by Herbert Graf, with Norman Treigle, Inge Borkh, and Regina Resnik highlighted the third season. Treigle frequently sang in Houston. His performances in Charles Gounod's *Faust*, Bizet's *Carmen*, and Jacques Offenbach's *Les contes d'Hoffmann* were a feast for both the eyes and ears.

The fifth season appeared jinxed. *Die Walküre*, the company's first Wagnerian work, was a disaster. It was reported that the production's most outstanding feature was the height of the three male leads—Noel Tyl 6'10", Jerome Hines 6'8", and Howard Vandenburgh 6'3". Bizet's *Carmen*, sung in English, followed, with two Don Josés. The first, Richard Cassilly, singing in English, became ill half way through the opera, and William Olvis replaced him. Olvis only knew the opera in French. The situation improved during the 1960/61 season. Puccini's *Turandot*, which opened the season on November 7, 1960, featured Richard Tucker in his first Calaf, and was a glorious production. Four years later, Jon Vickers appeared in Verdi's *Un ballo in maschera*, and Treigle followed in Nikolay's Rimsky-Korsakov's *Zolotoy petushok* (The Golden Cockerel). The last season in the Music Hall witnessed Johann Strauß's *Der Zigeunerbaron*. It was a production described as best forgotten. Strauß's *Der Zigeunerbaron* only came to life the evening a horse relieved itself on stage, and the singers performed elaborate acrobatics to avoid slipping in the mess. Some patrons felt the horse was merely commenting on the performance.

Verdi's *Aida*, with Richard Tucker and Gabriella Tucci, opened the company's first season in Jones Hall on October 5, 1966. Beverly Sills and Plácido Domingo appeared a short time later. The season's highlight, Hans Werner Henze's *Der junge Lord* on December 5, 1967, launched Herbert's excursion into modern opera. Douglas Moore's *The Ballad of Baby Doe* was mounted on February 17, 1970, Carl Orff's *Der Mond* followed on January 12, 1971, and Gian Carlo Menotti's *Help, Help, The Globolinks/The Medium* was offered on February 22, 1972. The 1971-72 season was Herbert's last. His seventeen years at the helm of the Houston Grand Opera are best summed up by Robert Giesberg in his booklet, *Houston Grand Opera: A History*. "Laboring under near crippling financial limitations, he gave Houston the best opera that he could for seventeen years. And while he made many mistakes, they were errors of judgement, not of slovenliness or lack of concern, and often they were forced on him by circumstances over which he had little or no control. If he was over-cautious in his choice of repertory, he knew the tastes of his public and the Board of the Houston Grand Opera. When he left, his most obvious legacy to his successor was a solidly based company and a loyal and growing audience that was ready for new things."

The audience was soon presented with "new things." The company's first world premiere, Thomas Pasatieri's *The Seagull*, was mounted on March 5, 1974. Two years later, Houston introduced Carlisle Floyd's *Bilby's Doll* on February 27, 1976. Floyd's second Houston world premiere, *Willie Stark*, took place on April 24, 1981. The formation of Opera New World in 1990 expanded the company's commitment to contemporary music theater. Underwritten by foundation grants, it commissioned Meredith Monk's *ATLAS: an opera in three parts* and Robert Moran's *Desert of Roses*. The company has also introduced unusual eighteenth- and nineteenth-century works, including André Grétry's *Zémire et azor*, Georg Friedrich Händel's *Rinaldo*, and critical editions of Rossini's *Tancredi* and *La donna del lago* among them.

Provocative productions have a home in Houston. On March 18, 1975, Frank Corsaro's interpretation of Alban Berg's *Lulu* caused an uproar. The activities in Berg's *Lulu* are gruesome enough. If you add large movie screens suspended above the stage projecting additional sexual activities—in larger-than-life images and full living color—you have a potential scandal. Letters to the local press called the production "an affront to decency." Then there was the disastrous 1985-86 season opening night of Puccini's *La bohème*. Domingo was scheduled to sing, but he canceled. His substitute, who shall best remain nameless, cracked on his high C. He stopped, looked at the conductor and said, "Excuse me maestro, let us start again." And they did. He fared better the second time.

On October 15, 1987, Domingo and Mirella Freni marched triumphantly in Verdi's *Aida* onto the stage of the Brown Theater in the Wortham Center, inaugurating the company's new home. Mozart's *Die Entführung aus dem Serail* opened the Cullen Theater. The Brown saw its first world premiere one week later, John Adams's *Nixon in China*. The next season witnessed more novelties, Philip Glass's *The Making of the Representative for Planet 8* and Michael Tippett's *New Year*. Although many big-name artists have graced the Houston stage in the past, only a few still visit. Money problems have restricted their number. Financial problems also caused a rapid fall from the glorious days of the 1990-91 and 1991-92 seasons, when twenty-three different operas were staged in the two seasons. Houston is retrenching and building a stronger financial foundation before attempting such a rapid expansion again.

The seven-opera season is a mixture of mainstream and lesser-known works, performed in the block system, with two works in the repertory at a time. Recent operas include Strauss's *Elektra*, Wagner's *Lohengrin*, Puccini's *Madama Butterfly* and *Turandot*, Verdi's *La traviata*, Kurt Weill's *Street Scenes*, and Noa Ain's *The Outcast*. The company performs in the Wortham Center.

Wortham Center

Within a decade after the opening of Jones Hall in 1966, there were calls for a new opera house in Houston. The Houston Lyric Theater Foundation, (later called the

Wortham Theater Foundation) was founded, and in March 1980, the City of Houston donated two vacant lots. Morris/Aubry Architects were chosen to design the structure which cost $70 million. Ground breaking took place in August 1984. Two years and nine months later a new performing arts center soared from the empty land. A gala program featuring Hildegard Behrens, Art Buchwald, Diahann Carroll, and Tony Randall, and Act II of Puccini's *La bohème*, performed by the Houston Grand Opera, inaugurated the Center on May 9, 1987.

The Wortham Center is a striking modern structure, set on its own plaza. The rose-colored Texas brick building, trimmed with Carmen-red granite, boasts a façade with a ninety-foot-high Romanesque entrance arch. GUS S. WORTHAM THEATER CENTER in brass letters runs along the top of the entrance. The "grand staircase" (an escalator) is flanked by multi-colored massive steel sculptures. They are designed as ornamental pylons with fluttering ribbons and banners, to recreate the pomp and pageantry identified with grand opera houses. Pure classical lines define the lobby, which is overlooked by four sculpted balconies. The horseshoe-shaped Brown Theater holds three tiers that curve around blood red seats. A single row of five-point Texas stars shine from the maroon-colored tiers. The walls are sculpted into semi-cylindrical shapes. The Brown Theater seats 2,176.

The Cullen Theater holds a single heavily sculpted tier of dark purple-gray. The seats are maroon. Small semi-cylindrical shapes are stacked on top of larger ones. They line the light and dark gray walls. The Cullen Theater seats 1,066.

Practical Information. The Wortham Theater Center is at 550 Prairie Street. Tickets can be purchased at the Houston Ticket Center at Wortham Center. The ticket center hours are 9:00 A.M. to 6:00 P.M. weekdays, and 10:00 A.M. to 5:00 P.M. Saturdays. On performance days, the Wortham Center ticket office remains open through the first intermission. Tickets can be ordered by telephoning 713-227-ARTS or 1-800-828-ARTS between the hours of 9:00 A.M. and 6:00 P.M. weekdays, and 12:00 P.M. to 6:00 P.M. Saturdays. If you go, stay at the Four Seasons Hotel, 1300 Lamar Street, Houston, TX 77010; telephone 713-650-1300, fax 713-650-8169, reservations 1-800-332-3442. The Four Seasons is a luxurious hotel that offers complimentary limousine service to the Wortham Center, ideally located in the heart of downtown.

COMPANY STAFF AND REPERTORY

General/Artistic Directors. Walter Herbert (1956–1972); David Gockley (1972–present).

World/American Premieres. Pasatieri's *The Seagull* (March 5, 1974); Floyd's *Bilby's Doll* (February 27, 1976); Floyd's *Willie Stark* (April 24, 1981); Bernstein's *A Quiet Place* (June 17, 1983); Adams's *Nixon in China* (October 22, 1987); Tippett's *New Year* (October 27, 1989); Monk's *ATLAS: an opera in three parts* (February 22, 1991); Moran's *Desert of Roses* (February 14, 1992).

American Premieres. Händel's *Rinaldo* (first stage performance, October 17, 1975); Glass's *Akhnaten* (October 12, 1984), Glass's *The Making for the Representative for Planet 8* (July 8, 1988).

Repertory. **1955-56:** Salome, Madama Butterfly. **1956-57:** La Cenerentola, Tosca, La traviata. **1957-58:** Aida, La bohème, Elektra. **1958-59:** Rigoletto, Der Rosenkavalier, Manon. **1959-60:** Die Walküre, Carmen, Die Fledermaus. **1960-61:** Turandot, La traviata, Les contes d'Hoffmann. **1961-62:** Faust, Lucia di Lammermoor, Boris Godunov. **1962-63:**

Wortham Center Grand Staircase (Houston, Texas).

L'elisir d'amore, Il trovatore, Il tabarro/I pagliacci, Die Meistersinger. **1963-64:** Il barbiere di Siviglia, La bohème, Otello, Don Giovanni. **1964-65:** Madama Butterfly, Un ballo in maschera, Roméo et Juliette, Zolotoy petushok (The Golden Cockerel). **1965-66:** Rigoletto, Tosca, Der fliegende Holländer, Samson et Dalila, Der Zigeunerbaron. **1966-67:** Aida, Hänsel und Gretel, Die Zauberflöte, La traviata, Faust. **1967-68:** Carmen, Der junge Lord, Manon Lescaut, Falstaff, Madama Butterfly. **1968-69:** La bohème, Salome, Il barbiere di Siviglia, Don Carlo, Don Quichotte. **1969-70:** Turandot, Rigoletto, Cavalleria rusticana/Gianni Schicchi, The Ballad of Baby Doe, Les contes d'Hoffmann. **1970-71:** Fidelio, Die Fledermaus, Der Mond/I pagliacci, Aida, Lucia di Lammermoor. **1971-72:** Carmen, Tosca, Boris Godunov, Help, Help the Globolinks/The Medium, Tannhäuser. **1972-73:** Madama Butterfly, Roméo et Juliette, La fille du régiment, Of Mice and Men, La forza del destino. **1973-74:** Macbeth, Le nozze di Figaro, La traviata, The Seagull, La Périchole, Mefistofele. **1974-75:** Manon, Il trovatore, Der Rosenkavalier, La bohème, Lulu, Lucrezia Borgia. **1975-76:** Rinaldo, Faust, Otello, Bibly's Doll, Don Giovanni, La fanciulla del West. **1976-77:** Rigoletto, Il barbiere di Siviglia, Peter Grimes, Andrea Chénier, L'incoronazione di Poppea, Salome. **1977-78:** Tancredi, Arabella, Aida, Falstaff, Die lustige Witwe, Tosca. **1978-79:** Norma, Jenůfa, Hänsel und Gretel, Werther, Der Rosenkavalier, La traviata, La Grande Duchesse de Gérolstein. **1979-80:** Otello, La Cenerentola, Madama Butterfly, Don Pasquale, Die Meistersinger, Regina. **1980-81:** Il trovatore, Die Zauberflöte, Carmen, Adriana Lecouvreur, Die Fledermaus, Un ballo in maschera, Hänsel und Gretel, Willie Stark, The Student Prince. **1981-82:** La donna del lago, La bohème, Kát'a Kabanová, La Périchole, Pikovaya dama, Treemonisha, Don Carlo, L'elisir d'amore, Show Boat. **1982-83:** Turandot, Wozzeck, Harlequin/I pagliacci, Rigoletto, La fille du régiment, Die lustige Witwe, Les contes d'Hoffmann, A Quiet Place/Trouble in Tahiti. **1983-84:** Il barbiere di Siviglia, Candide, Peter Grimes, Hänsel und Gretel, Simon Boccanegra, Tosca, Fidelio, Sweeney Todd. **1984-85:** Akhnaten, Der fliegende Holländer, Madama Butterfly, Die Zauberflöte, Eugene Onegin, La traviata. **1985-86:** La bohème, Faust, Don Giovanni, Le Comte Ory, Ariadne auf Naxos, Anna Bolena. **1986-87:** Boris Godunov, Orphée aux enfers, Porgy and Bess, Falstaff, Salome, Norma, Turandot. **1987-88:** Aida, Nixon in China, Die Entführung aus dem Serail, Così fan tutte, La rondine, Manon, Tannhäuser. **1988-89:** The Making of the Representative for Planet 8, Carmen, Le nozze di Figaro, Hänsel und Gretel, Show Boat, Un ballo in maschera, Dialogues des Carmélites, Otello. **1989-90:** Giulio Cesare, New Year, The Mikado, Hänsel und Gretel, Der Rosenkavalier, Rigoletto, Samson et Dalila, Madama Butterfly, Carousel. **1990-91:** Cavalleria rusticana/I pagliacci, Faust, Hänsel und Gretel, The Passion of Jonathan Wade, Tosca, ATLAS: an opera in three parts, Die Zauberflöte, La clemenza di Tito, Don Giovanni, Così fan tutte, Le nozze di Figaro, My Fair Lady. **1991-92:** Rusalka, La bohème, Babes in Toyland, Il trovatore, Parsifal, Desert of Roses, Zémire et azor, Mefistofele, Andrea Chénier, Annie Get Your Gun. **1992-93:** Lohengrin, Les contes d'Hoffmann, Aida, Il barbiere di Siviglia, Ariadne auf Naxos, A Midsummer Night's Dream, Frida. **1993-94:** Elektra, Madama Butterfly, Lucia di Lammermoor, Street Scene, La traviata, Turandot, The Outcast.

Utah
───────────── SALT LAKE CITY
• *Utah Opera* •

Giacomo Puccini's *La bohème*, performed in Kingsbury Hall in January 1978, inaugurated the Utah Opera. A second Puccini opera, *Tosca* completed the company's first season in May. Glade Peterson established the company to offer opera in his native Utah.

The second season opened with Giuseppe Verdi's *Otello* in the newly restored Capital Theater. A few months later, George Bizet's *Carmen* graced the stage. The number of performances was increased to three the following year, with a further permanent expansion taking place for the 1991-92 season. In December 1982, 1983, and 1984, there was an additional holiday performance of Gian Carlo Menotti's *Amahl & the Night Visitors*. The 1990s ushered in a holiday performance of Engelbert Humperdinck's *Hänsel und Gretel*. The repertory is predominately traditional Italian fare. Although some established stars have appeared with the company, including Martina Arroyo, Giorgio Tozzi, and Roberta Peters, the casts are primarily rising young talent, some of whom have gone on to international acclaim. Aprile Millo made her operatic debut with the company in Verdi's *Aida* in 1980.

The four-opera season offers a standard repertory of grand and comic operas in a *stagione* system. Recent productions include Puccini's *Madama Butterfly*, Verdi's *Macbeth*, Rossini's *L'italiana in Algeri*, and Wolfgang Amadeus Mozart's *Die Zauberflöte*. The company performs in the Capital Theater.

Capital Theater

The Capital Theater began life as the Orpheum in 1913. Designed by G. Albert Lansburgh, the theater cost of $250,000. It was built as a home for vaudeville. The Theater was renamed the Capital in 1927, when Louis Marcus purchased the building. Movies soon replaced vaudeville as the main attraction. In 1978, architect Steven Baird restored the Capital to its original splendor. A new chapter began for the theater when it reopened on October 18, 1978, as a performing arts center. The building displays a white terra cotta tile façade with a series of arches. The rectangularly-shaped, ivory and gold auditorium is ornately decorated. One large deep balcony holding side opera boxes sweeps across the deep burgundy velvet orchestra seats. A star-burst chandelier brightens the space. The Capital seats 1,900.

Practical Information. The Capital Theater is at 50 West 200 South. You can purchase tickets at the Utah Opera Offices at the above address between 10:00 A.M. and 5:00 P.M., Monday through Friday, or by telephoning 801-534-0888, or writing Utah Opera, 50 West 200 South, Salt Lake City, UT 84101. If you go, stay at the Perry Hotel, 110 West 300 South, Salt Lake City, UT; telephone 801-521-4300, reservations 1-800-331-0073. The Perry is an historic hotel only one block from the theater.

COMPANY STAFF AND REPERTORY

General/Artistic Directors. Glade Peterson (1978–1990, died April 21, 1990); Leslie Peterson Adams (acting, 1990–1991); Anne Ewers (1991–present).

Repertory. **1978:** La bohème, Tosca. **1979:** Otello, Carmen. **1979-80:** Madama Butterfly, Aida, Il barbiere di Siviglia. **1980-81:** La traviata, Amahl and the Night Visitors, Cavalleria rusticana/I pagliacci, Don Pasquale. **1981-82:** Lucia di Lammermoor, La fanciulla del West, Die lustigen Weiber von Windsor. **1982-83:** Rigoletto, Amahl and the Night Visitors, La bohème, Die Fledermaus. **1983-84:** Aida, Amahl and the Night Visitors, Tosca, Don Giovanni. **1984-85:** Faust, Amahl and the Night Visitors, Il trovatore, Die lustige Witwe. **1985-86:** Carmen, Madama Butterfly, L'elisir d'amore. **1986-87:** Turandot, Il barbiere di Siviglia, La traviata. **1987-88:** Die Zauberflöte, La bohème, I pagliacci/Gianni Schicchi. **1988-89:** Lucia di Lammermoor, Le nozze di Figaro, Die Fledermaus. **1989-90:** Les contes d'Hoffmann, Rigoletto, Don Giovanni. **1990-91:** Otello, Così fan tutte, Falstaff. **1991-92:** Samson et Dalila, Hänsel und Gretel, Tosca, La Cenerentola. **1992-93:** Un ballo in maschera, Hänsel und Gretel, Madama Butterfly, La belle Hélène. **1993-94:** Die Zauberflöte, Hänsel und Gretel, Macbeth, L'italiana in Algeri.

Virginia —— CHARLOTTESVILLE

• *Ash Lawn Opera Festival* •

Ash Lawn Opera Festival was founded in 1978, under the leadership of Priscilla Little. The first season offered two pre-twilight, one-act operas in English. The performances were free, underwritten by the Virginia Foundation for the Humanities. A piano accompanied a local cast. The performances took place outdoors, in the Boxwood Gardens of Ash Lawn-Highland, the Albemarle County home of James Monroe, fifth President of the United States. When it rained, the stage crew pushed the piano from the garden to the tent. Once the piano became so water-logged

Ash Lawn Summer Festival (Charlottesville, Virginia).

during its journey that it refused to offer any sound, and the performance had to be canceled.

The second season offered a similar schedule, but there was a small admission fee. The festival commissioned its first world premiere in 1981, a one-act opera by Judith Shatin, *Follies and Fancies* which took place on August 14, 1981. Shatin's *Follies* graced the stage for ten performances. The following season, Shatin's *Follies and Fancies* acquired a second act and multiple-act works began entering the repertory. Borrowed lights illuminated the stage, allowing performances after sunset. The 1986 season offered three operas, performed by nine local artists and accompanied by a six-member chamber orchestra.

The festival shed its amateur look in 1989 when it purchased an extensive lighting system and auditioned singers from Washington, D.C. and New York. The orchestra was seventeen strong. Ash Lawn staged a triple bill of three unusual pieces in 1990 — Giovanni Pergolesi's *La serva padrona*, Henry Mollicone's *The Face on the Barroom Floor*, and Gian Carlo Menotti's *The Telephone*. The results were disappointing. The unfamiliar works scared away the largely novice opera crowd. The next summer, Richard Rogers's *South Pacific* replaced the lesser known operas to help "balance the books." Rogers's *South Pacific* was the most successful of the season's offerings, which distressed general director Judith Walker. She prefers mounting an all "opera" season. Nevertheless, Walker now schedules one musical each season, hoping for a crossover of "broadway-musical people" into opera. Walker feels the absence of a permanent theater with reserved seats has hindered the festival's growth. The building of a permanent structure is a top priority. It will have a large stage and sheltered seating for five-hundred patrons. The structure will be open on all sides to allow people to sit on the lawn and picnic, so both the formally- and informally-inclined can enjoy the opera.

The festival spends its limited resources on singers, musicians, and directors. The productions are simple, yet clever. The curtain-less stage holds few sets and props. Operas whose scores can be reduced without compromising musical integrity define the repertory. All operas are sung in English, and the performances take place outdoors or under a tent if it rains. The large peacock population frequently screeches opinions, often during the quietest moments. The Ash Lawn–Highland Opera Festival is moving very slowly toward its goal—to become a regional opera company. But it does not want to lose sight of it primary purpose, that of attracting newcomers to the world of opera. It carries out its mission by offering understandable opera at low prices in a casual and intimate setting. The conductor explains the opera to the audience before the performance, and it could be one of the few "theaters" where you can still enter after the performance has started.

The three-opera festival offers a musical, a comic work, and one "heavier" piece in a repertory block system. (Two of the three operas are performed in repertory.) Recent productions include Wolfgang Amadeus Mozart's *Le nozze di Figaro* and *Don Giovanni*, Rogers's *Carousel*, and Gaetano Donizetti's *Don Pasquale*. The festival operas take place outdoors in the "Garden" Theater.

Ash Lawn Highland "Garden" Theater

The "open-air theaters" are nestled in the hills of Ash Lawn-Highland, at the end of a long, twisting, narrow road. The fair-weather theater is in the estate's Boxwood Gardens, behind Monroe's house. The sky and stars are the ceiling; the boxwoods form the walls; the grass is the floor. Folding metal chairs are set on the lawn around the stage, which consists of a large platform with a beige lattice backdrop. It is reminiscent of the late-seventeenth- and early-eighteenth-century European castle-garden theaters. When it rains, the performance takes place in the "inclement-weather theater," a blue and white tent with a small stage and several rows of folding metal chairs. If the rain begins during the production, the performance stops. Everyone and everything moves under the tent, and the show resumes, without missing a beat.

Practical Information. Ash Lawn–Highland Opera Festival is on County Route 795, near Interstate 64 and Route 250. The route from Charlottesville is clearly marked. Tickets go on sale mid-June at the box office, inside the main building at Ash Lawn-Highlands. It is open from 12:00 noon to 6:00 P.M. daily. On performance days it stays open until 7:00 P.M. Tickets can be ordered beginning mid-June by telephoning 804-293-8000 between the hours of 12:00 noon and 6:00 P.M., or by writing Ash Lawn–Highland, Route 6, Box 37, Charlottesville, VA 22902. For a Festival brochure telephone 804-293-9539. The seating is unreserved. If you go, stay at the Omni Charlottesville, 235 West Main Street, Charlottesville, VA 22901; telephone 804-971-5500, fax 804-979-1986, reservations 1-800-843- 6664. The hotel is a sustaining patron of the festival and can assist with tickets or brochure.

COMPANY STAFF AND REPERTORY

General/Artistic Directors. Priscilla Little; Judith Walker.
World Premiere. Shatin's *Follies and Fancies* (August 14, 1981).

"Professional" Repertory. **1988:** Le nozze di Figaro, L'elisir d'amore, La Cenerentola. **1989:** Così fan tutte, Il turco in Italia, Ormindo. **1990:** La fille du régiment, Die Zauberflöte, La serva padrona/The Face on the Barroom Floor, The Telephone. **1991:** Il barbiere di Siviglia, South Pacific, Hänsel und Gretel. **1992:** Le nozze di Figaro, Oklahoma! Die Fledermaus. **1993:** Don Giovanni, Carousel, Don Pasquale.

———————————————————————— NORFOLK

• *Virginia Opera* •

Giacomo Puccini's *La bohème* inaugurated the Virginia Opera on January 24, 1975. The performance took place at the Center Theater. It was sold out. A group of energetic women who wanted to introduce culture to Norfolk founded the company. Buoyed by the success of their first production, they hired Peter Mark as artistic director. He received $33,000 to mount a second work, Giuseppe Verdi's *La traviata.* Diana Soviero sang the title role, and Mark made his debut as an operatic conductor.

Opera in Norfolk dates back as early as the 1780s when Heard's Troupe performed ballad operas. Beginning in 1793, West and Bignall's company added Norfolk to its touring circuit, and during the next several seasons, the city witnessed a substantial number of operatic performances — Thomas Carter's *Rival Candidates,* Charles Dibdin's *Quaker, Romp,* and *Deserter,* Samuel Arnold's *Agreeable Surprise, Inkle and Yarico, Peeping Tom of Coventry, Children in the Wood,* and *Mountaineers,* William Shield's *Farmer,* John Pepusch's *Beggar's Opera,* Stephen Storace's *Doctor and Apothecary* and *No Song, no Supper,* William Reeve's *Purse,* John O'Keefe's *Highland Reel,* and Thomas Attwood's *Adopted Child.* Traveling opera troupes provided Norfolk with opera during the nineteenth century.

The Virginia Opera was the city's first homegrown operatic effort, and it took root immediately. All four inaugural season productions sold out, so the second season's budget jumped to $270,000, and the number of performances increased to nine. The season saw Ashley Putnam make her professional debut in the title role of Gaetano Donizetti's *Lucia di Lammermoor,* as well as Puccini's *Tosca* and Gioachino Rossini's *Il barbiere di Siviglia.* The third season boasted Diana Soviero, Putnam, and Jeannine Altmeyer. The company saw its first novelty with Thea Musgrave's *Mary, Queen of Scots.* (Musgrave is married to Mark.) It was a bold undertaking for the company, since the opera required several principal roles and a large chorus. Putnam sang the title role and Mark conducted. The company commissioned its first world premiere two years later, and Musgrave's *A Christmas Carol* was introduced on December 7, 1979. The company mounted a second world premiere by Musgrave, *Harriet, The Woman Called Moses,* on March 1, 1985. Despite a rehearsal accident that forced Cynthia Haymon (Harriet) to perform with crutches, the opera was critically acclaimed.

The 1991-92 season saw the company's third world premiere, Michael Ching's *Cue 67.* (Ching was then the Virginia Opera's associate artistic director.) The company commissioned *Cue 67* as a companion piece of Gian Carlo Menotti's *The Medium. The Medium* deals with the supernatural, seances, and charlatans, and *Cue 67* is a contemporary ghost story "performed in a crossover style."

Back during the 1983-84 season, posters advertising the company's updated production of Verdi's *Rigoletto* had bullet holes through the title. (The opera was set in Little Italy in the 1920s.) Some influential person of Italian descent felt offended and took the company to court. He perceived the posters as a slur on all Italians. These actions placed the company's future in jeopardy. Although the misunderstanding was eventually cleared up, it caused hardship and a large financial drain on the Virginia Opera. Another type of disaster almost struck the company in October 1990. It was during a performance of Richard Strauss's *Ariadne auf Naxos*, where there was a real fireworks display. Unfortunately, one lodged itself in the scenery. Smoke poured forth, while the backstage crew scrambled to find the fire extinguisher. The scene, fortunately, ended before the scenery went up in flames. On the lighter side, the 1989 production of Jacques Offenbach's *Les contes d'Hoffmann* included several nude bodies sprawled on the floor. The curtain rose, but stopped after four feet. There it remained for ten minutes and all the audience could see was nude bodies. Engelbert Humperdinck's *Hänsel und Gretel* also produced a few unexpected laughs. There was a flying witch in the production, but the mezzo singing the witch role was too hefty to ride her broomstick, so a thinner witch took to the air. The audience thought the witch's role was so strenuous that the mezzo instantly shed fifty pounds!

Mark's philosophy is one of music theater productions. The music and drama are integrated. Young, up-and-coming directors from the theater world are frequently hired as the stage directors. There are four weeks of rehearsal and it shows in the exactness and precision of the performance. Although the productions are not "high concept," some are clever reinterpretations of the composer's intent. The operas remain in a form "true to the art and true to the music." The casts are primarily young, emerging American singers, with local performers filling the supporting roles. Several "emerging" artists have returned after establishing successful careers—Putnam, Soviero, Altmeyer, and Lilli Chookasian among them.

The Virginia Opera is a statewide company, with a second headquarters in Richmond, and a third in Fairfax, at George Mason University. The identical productions are seen in all three cities. The small size of the orchestra pit in their main performing venue in Norfolk (the Center Theater seated forty-five) limited the repertory. With the conversion of the theater into the Harrison Opera House and the enlargement of the pit to accommodate sixty, Mark plans to expand the repertory to include grand Verdi works and small Wagner pieces, as well as mounting a spring or summer festival of light musicals or operetta.

The four-opera season offers a balanced repertory in a stagione system. There are comic operas, repertory favorites, musical theater, and twentieth-century pieces. Recent productions include Donizetti's *Don Pasquale*, Wolfgang Amadeus Mozart's *Don Giovanni*, Vincenzo Bellini's *Norma*, Puccini's *Turandot*, Leonard Bernstein's *West Side Story*, and Arthur Sullivan's *The Mikado*. The company performs in the Harrison Opera House.

Harrison Opera House

A gala operatic concert inaugurated the Harrison Opera House, originally called the Center Theater, on November 5, 1993. Built by the Navy in 1943, the theater was home for USO shows during World War II. After the war, the Navy gave the

Center Theater, now Harrison Opera House (Norfolk, Virginia)

theater to the city of Norfolk, which refurbished it for theatrical use. The Virginia Opera became a permanent resident. Beginning in 1991, the company performed a much-needed $10 million renovation on the theater, transforming it into an elegant opera house. The architectural firms of Graham Gund Associates and Williams, Tazewell & Associates were in charge of the renovation.

The original drab granite theater has been reconstructed into a majestic limestone and glass structure, framed by pairs of towers with Spanish clay-tiled roofs. There is a bright, spacious, three-story high grand lobby with floor to ceiling windows that replaced a dark, mustard-and-maroon concrete foyer. The plain, functional auditorium of maroon and white was converted into an elegant ivory and green auditorium with new boxes lining the cream-colored side walls. A single tier stretches across the hall. The auditorium accommodates 1,650.

Practical Information: The Harrison Opera House is at 160 Virginia Beach Road. The ticket office is open 10:00 a.m. to 5:00 p.m. weekdays. Tickets can be order by telephoning 804-623-1223 (Southside) or 804-877-2550 (Peninsula), or writing Virginia Opera, P.O.B. 625, Norfolk, VA 23501. Performances in Richmond take place at the Carpenter Center for the Performing Arts. Call 804-643-6004 for tickets and information. The performances in Fairfax take place at the Center for the Arts at George Mason University. Call 703-993-8888 for tickets and information. If you go, stay at the Omni Virginia Beach Hotel, 4453 Bonney Road, Virginia Beach, VA 23462; telephone 804-473-1700, fax 804-552-0477, reservations 1-800-843-6664. The Omni Virginia Beach is an Art Deco inspired hotel that is conveniently located between the opera house and the ocean resort of Virginia Beach.

COMPANY STAFF AND REPERTORY

General/Artistic Director. Peter Mark (1975-present).
World Premieres. Musgrave's A Christmas Carol (December 7, 1979); Musgrave's Harriet, the Woman Called Moses (March 1, 1985).
American/United States Premieres. Musgrave's *Mary, Queen of Scots* (March 29, 1978); Ching's *Cue 67* (January 24, 1992).
Repertory. **1975:** La bohème, La traviata. **1975-76:** Tosca, Lucia di Lammermoor, Il barbiere di Siviglia. **1976-77:** Rigoletto, Il trovatore, Der Schauspieldirektor/I pagliacci. **1977-78:** Madama Butterfly, Così fan tutte, Mary, Queen of Scots. **1978-79:** Carmen, La fille du régiment, Don Giovanni. **1979-80:** La bohème, A Christmas Carol, Don Pasquale, Les contes d'Hoffmann. **1980-81:** Porgy & Bess, Hänsel und Gretel, Werther, Roméo et Juliette. **1981-82:** Faust, La Cenerentola, La traviata, Die Zauberflöte. **1982-83:** Die Fledermaus, Amahl and the Night Visitors, Macbeth, L'elisir d'amore. **1983-84:** Norma, Gianni Schicchi/Suor Angelica, Rigoletto, La fanciulla del West. **1984-85:** Le nozze di Figaro, Amahl and the Night Visitors, Madama Butterfly, Harriet, The Woman Called Moses. **1985-86:** Un ballo in maschera, Hänsel und Gretel, Tosca, Die lustige Witwe. **1986-87:** Carmen, A Christmas Carol, Lucia di Lammermoor, Man of La Mancha. **1987-88:** Don Giovanni, La bohème, Manon, Cavalleria rusticana/I pagliacci. **1988-89:** Faust, Die Zauberflöte, Anna Bolena, La traviata. **1989-90:** Il trovatore, Les contes d'Hoffmann, Turn of the Screw, Il barbiere di Siviglia. **1990-91:** Ariadne auf Naxos, La Cenerentola, Roméo et Juliette, Così fan tutte. **1991-92:** Madama Butterfly, Le nozze di Figaro, The Medium/Cue 67, Porgy & Bess. **1992-93:** Carmen, Don Pasquale, The Mikado, Tosca. **1993-94:** Turandot, Norma, Don Giovanni, West Side Story.

——————————————— ROANOKE

• *Opera Roanoke* •

Gian Carlo Menotti's *The Consul* inaugurated the Southwest Virginia Opera Society, Inc., the original name of Opera Roanoke, in December 1976. It was the sole offering of the inaugural season. Two members of the Thursday Morning Music Club, Virginia Schricker and Tom Bailey, decided that there was enough interest in the Roanoke area to promote and produce opera.

The second season witnessed only one opera, Wolfgang Amadeus Mozart's *Le nozze di Figaro*, but the third season (1979) permanently expanded to two offerings, Johann Strauß's *Die Fledermaus* and Giacomo Puccini's *La bohème*. The first contemporary opera, Douglas Moore's *The Ballad of Baby Doe*, entered the repertory in 1980. The 12th season saw an usual work, Milton Granger's *The Proposal* in a one-act opera competition, along with the regular season. In 1989 the company amended its name to Southwest Virginia Opera, feeling Society denoted elitism. Two years later, they adopted the name Opera Roanoke to reflect their professional status. The company engages up-and-coming performers from across the United States and Canada, as well as local talent. Opera Roanoke is planning to mount the world premiere of Victoria Bond's *Travels* (an adaptation of the eighteenth century classic *Gulliver's Travels*) within the next couple of seasons.

The two-opera season combines one light opera or modern musical theater piece with a standard repertory work in a *stagione* system. Recent productions include Mozart's *Le nozze di Figaro*, Georges Bizet's *Carmen*, and Stephen Sondheim's *Sweeny Todd*. The company performs in Mill Mountain Theatre, which seats 358, and Olin Theater, which seats 404.

Practical Information. Tickets can be purchased by calling 703-982-2742, faxing 703-982-3601, or writing Opera Roanoke, P.O.B. 1014, Roanoke, VA 24005. The office is located at The Jefferson Center, 540 Campbell Avenue, Roanoke, VA 24016. If you go, stay at the Radisson Patrick Henry, 617 South Jefferson Street, Roanoke, VA 24011; telephone 703-345-8811, fax 703-342-9908, reservations 1-800-333-3333. The Hotel is a National Historic Landmark, conveniently located downtown.

REPERTORY

Repertory. **1977:** The Consul. **1978:** Le nozze di Figaro. **1979:** Die Fledermaus, La bohème. **1980:** La Cenerentola, The Ballad of Baby Doe. **1981:** Don Giovanni, Il trovatore. **1982:** Carmen, Rigoletto. **1983:** Madama Butterfly, Il barbiere di Siviglia. **1984:** La fille du régiment, Martha. **1985:** Così fan tutte, Die lustige Witwe. **1986:** Naughty Marietta, Tosca. **1987:** The Student Prince, La traviata. **1988:** Kismet, Gianni Schicchi/I pagliacci. **1989:** Yeoman of the Guard. **1989-90:** Die Zauberflöte, La bohème. **1990-91:** Die Fledermaus, Otello. **1991-92:** Il barbiere di Siviglia, Don Giovanni. **1992-93:** Carmen, Die lustige Witwe. **1993-94:** Sweeney Todd, Le nozze di Figaro.

VIENNA

• *Wolf Trap Opera* •

A Musical Theater Cavalcade inaugurated the Wolf Trap Opera company, originally christened the Wolf Trap Company, in 1971. Founded as an apprentice program to train and showcase promising young artists and technical staff, the company was comprised of opera singers, dancers, and technicians. The original company of 66 members rented the Madeira School, where the training classes took place. The singers performed as comprimario and in the chorus of Wolf Trap productions.

The second season ushered in an eclectic mix of opera and musical theater performances, including Wolfgang Amadeus Mozart's *Le nozze di Figaro*, Charles Gounod's *Roméo et Juliette*, Scott Joplin's *Treemonisha*, and Rogers and Hammerstein's *The King and I*. The company's first world premiere, Thomas Pasatieri's *Il signor Deluso*, on a double bill with his *Calvario*, took place at the Madeira School in July 1974. That same year Sarah Caldwell produced and conducted the company's Washington premiere of Sergey Prokofiev's *War and Peace*. Beverly Sills also appeared as guest artist beginning in 1974. She performed with Wolf Trap for three seasons and bestowed international recognition on the company. Wolf Trap's presentations of Gaetano Donizetti's *La fille du régiment* and *Roberto Devereux*, and Giuseppe Verdi's *La traviata* were telecast. These three seasons, despite their glory, were never repeated.

Frank Rizzo had joined the company in 1972 as artistic director, and he slowly revised the company's philosophy. The training of the singers became paramount, changing the company into a small pre-professional opera group with its members no longer singing only comprimario and in the chorus, but also the principal roles. To reflect the company's new role, "opera" was added to the company's name in 1977. The company presented a novelty that season, Ferruccio Busoni's *Doktor Faust*. Considered Busoni's most elaborate work, the piece had been neglected because of its complexity and musical challenge. Pier Francesco Cavalli's rarely-staged *L'egisto* was also mounted. The following season witnessed another world premiere, Stephen Douglas Burton's *The Duchess of Malfi*. The *Duchess* was part of Wolf Trap's commitment to produce American operas. Other important American works staged during the 1970s were Gian Carlo Menotti's *The Saint of Bleecker Street*, Robert Ward's *The Crucible*, and Vittorio Giannini's *The Taming of the Shrew*.

Sarah Caldwell was musical director for one glorious season, 1980, ushering in the decade with Verdi's *Falstaff* and Johann Strauß's *Die Fledermaus* (with Anna Moffo as guest star). Caldwell also staged operas by her Opera Company of Boston. One was a rare staging of Heinrich Marschner's *Der Vampyr*. During the decade an unusual mix of operas were in the repertory, including rarely performed seventeenth-, eighteenth- and twentieth-century works like Cavalli's *Ormindo*, Henry Purcell's *Dido and Aeneas*, Joseph Haydn's *Apothecary*, Igor Stravinsky's *L'histoire du soldat*, Prokofiev's *Lyubov' k tryom apel'sinam* (The Love for Three Oranges), Marc Blitzstein's *Regina*, Conrad Susa's *Transformations*, and Maurice Ravel's *L'enfant et les sortilèges*.

The recent absence of new works is a result of general director Peter Russell's belief that new works are not beneficial for young voices. (The company's role in past premieres was only a peripheral one.) This is also in keeping with the opera company's goal to become a leading Mozarteum like the one in Salzburg (Austria) by the year 2000. The repertory concentrates on the operas of Mozart and his contemporaries. Since the 1989 season, the schedule has included Mozart's *Le nozze di Figaro*, *Die Zauberflöte*, *Don Giovanni*, *La finta giardiniera*, and *La clemenza di Tito*, Gioachino Rossini's *Il turco in Italia*, and Domenico Cimarosa's *Il matrimonio segreto*. The productions are clever and ingenious, with imaginative use of the available space. Each year Russell discovers some of the most promising young singers in America for the Wolf Trap Opera program. The program teaches the singers the demands of a professional career and showcases their talents in the productions. Russell has turned the company into one of the outstanding "career-entry programs" for young singers in America. Many of Wolf Traps's alumni have carved out international careers, and the company retains an "honor roll" listing all the renown singers who sang with Wolf Trap Opera. They include Dawn Upshaw, Chris Merritt, Janice Hall, Allan Glassman, Warren Ellsworth, Tracy Dahl, and John Cheek.

The three-opera season offers late eighteenth- and early nineteenth-century works in a *stagione* system. There is an emphasis on Mozart operas and one offering is usually a rarely-performed piece. (The repertory is determined by the strengths and weaknesses of the singers chosen at auditions.) Recent productions include Mozart's *La clemenza di Tito*, *La finta giardiniera*, and *Le nozze di Figaro*, and Rossini's *Il turco in Italia*. The company performs in the Filene Center and the Barns. (Performances are in the original language and there are no surtitles in the Barns.)

Filene Center

The National Symphony Orchestra inaugurated the Filene Center on July 1, 1971, Julius Rudel conducting the gala concert. The New York architectural firm of Mac-Fadyen & Knowles designed the open-air theater, which was modeled after the Saratoga Performing Arts Center in New York. Wolf Trap is the first and only National Park for the Performing Arts in the United States. Its creation was the idea of Catherine Filene Shouse, who purchased the property known as Wolf Trap Farm in 1930 for $5,300. When development threatened her area, she wanted to preserve her property as "the only green spot in the area." After several organizations declined her offer of the property and money, President Lyndon Baines Johnson accepted the land and funds on behalf of the American people as a national park, including $1.75 million that Shouse donated to build an amphitheater.

The Center was constructed of fir and Oregon cedar to blend with the landscape, and eleven years later, on Sunday night, April 4, 1982, fire raced through the outdoor theater. The 1982 season went on in a modular auditorium that looked like an old-fashioned airplane hangar. The Center was rebuilt, reopening on July 30, 1984. Dewberry & Davis, John MacFadyen, and Joseph Boggs, were the architects and engineers who directed the rebuilding effort. They maintained the same basic design as the original theater. The cost was $26 million.

Wolf Trap is not only home to the Wolf Trap Opera, but hosts other opera companies as well. The inaugural season saw several productions by the New York City Opera, including Verdi's *La traviata*, Gounod's *Faust* with Norman Treigle and Donizetti's *Lucia di Lammermoor* with Sills. The Minneapolis's Center Opera Company followed with Virgil Thomson's *The Mother of Us All* and a hilarious opera parody, John Gessner's *Faust Counter Faust*. The Metropolitan Opera visited annually from 1974 to 1979, bringing noteworthy productions and casts, including Verdi's *Otello* with Jon Vickers, Cornell MacNeil, and Gilda Cruz-Romo, *Il trovatore* with Cruz-Romo, MacNeil, Carlo Bergonzi, and Mignon Dunn, and *Don Carlo* with Vasile Moldoveanu, Cruz-Romo, Jerome Hines, and James Morris. The company also mounted Giacomo Meyerbeer's rarely-performed *Le Prophète* with Marilyn Horne, James McCracken, and Hines. The Opera Company of Boston presented the original two-act version of Giacomo Puccini's *Madama Butterfly* on June 13, 1980, and a notable Richard Wagner's *Der fliegende Holländer* followed. But the scheduled performance of Verdi's *Aida* never took place. A ferocious thunderstorm caused the Park to lose electric power before the opening, forcing the performance to be canceled. A lawsuit was the result. In 1991, for its twentieth-birthday celebration, Wolf Trap Park hosted two outstanding Bolshoi Opera productions—Pyotr Il'yich Tchaikovsky's *Eugene Onegin* and Nikolai Rimsky-Korsakov's *Mlada*.

Opera at the Filene Center fuses with nature. The chirping birds, noisy crickets, and rustling leaves frequently blend with the singing and orchestra, giving the performance a true summer-festival ambiance. The exterior of the open-air theater is concrete and steel with chemically-treated, fire-resistant douglas fir siding. The fan-shaped auditorium contains southern yellow pine, and is slightly raked in the front and steeply raked in the rear. Uncushioned seats stretch across the space. Two rows of hexagonal acoustic panels are suspended from the soaring, wood-paneled ceiling. The Center seats 3,766 with room for 3,100 on the lawn.

The Barns of Wolf Trap (Vienna, Virginia).

The Barns

A Glenn Jacobson/Edward Mattos concert inaugurated the Barnes on October 4, 1981. The following summer the Wolf Trap Opera opened with an "Invitation to Opera" on July 1, 1982. Mozart's *Così fan tutte* followed fifteen days later. Set in the rolling countryside, the Barns of Wolf Trap joins together two genuine eighteenth-century barns, one Scottish and one German. Richard Babcock was the master builder who reconstructed the barns according to the architectural plans by Design Guild of Boston. The cost was $1 million.

The wooden barns were originally constructed in upstate New York. After the barns were moved to Vienna (Virginia), the exterior walls became the interior walls, and a new gray-stained exterior was constructed to protect the original structure. The roof is wood-shingled. The Scottish barn serves as a refreshment area and the German barn hosts the shows. Rough 200-year-old weathered wood form the walls and ceiling, with a loft-like area over the proscenium. One of the barn's features is its swing beam, which added support for the hayloft. For the theater, this means unobstructed views of the stage from every reddish beige seat. Lights are attached to the upper beams and stage lights are suspended from the cross beams. The barn seats 252 on the "threshing floor" and 98 in the "hayloft."

Practical Information. The Filene Center is in Wolf Trap Park, off exit 12 from Route 267, Toll Road West. The ticket office is in front of the theater. It is open from noon to 6:00 P.M., seven days a week on non-performance days, and from noon to 9:00 P.M. on performance days. The Barnes Box Office, at 1635 Trap Road, is open from 10:00 am to 6:00 P.M. Monday through Friday, and from noon to 5:00 P.M. Saturday and Sunday. The box office stays open until 9:00 P.M. on performance days. Tickets can be ordered by telephoning 202-432-0200, 301-341-WOLF, or 1-800-448-9009 between 10 A.M. and 10 P.M. seven days a week, by faxing 703-255-1989, or by writing Wolf Trap Ticket Service, 1624 Trap Road, Vienna, VA 22182. For season brochure call 703-255-1860. If you go, stay at the Ritz-Carlton, 1700 Tysons Boulevard, McLean, VA 22101; telephone 703-506-4300, fax 703-506-4305, reservations 1-800-241-3333. The Ritz-Carlton is a luxurious hotel convenient to Filene Center and the Barns.

COMPANY STAFF AND REPERTORY

General/Artistic Directors. Frank Rizzo (1972–79); Sarah Caldwell (1980); Adelaide Bishop (1981–82); Roger Brunyate (1983–84); Peter Russell (1984–present).

World Premieres. Pasatieri's *Il signor Deluso* (July 1974); Burton's *The Duchess of Malfi* (August 18, 1978).

Repertory. **1971:** Musical Theater Cavalcade. **1972:** The King and I, Roméo et Juliette, Treemonisha, Le nozze di Figaro. **1973:** The Most Happy Fella, The Saint of Bleecker Street, Don Pasquale. **1974:** Le fille du régiment, War and Peace, Calvary/Il Signor Deluso. **1975:** The Crucible, Kismet, Roberto Devereux, Albert Herring. **1976:** A Midsummer Night's Dream, La traviata. **1977:** Doktor Faust, L'egisto, Hänsel und Gretel, The Medium/The Telephone. **1978:** The Duchess of Malfi, The Gondoliers. **1979:** Kiss Me Kate, The Taming of the Shrew. **1980:** Falstaff, Die Fledermaus, Der Vampyr, Down in the Valley. **1981:** Le nozze di Figaro, The Rape of Lucretia. **1982:** Così fan tutte, The Apothecary/L'histoire du soldat, Regina. **1983:** L'ajo nell'imbarazzo, La calisto, Kurt Weill After Dark. **1984:** L'incoronazione di Poppea, Albert Herring, A Little Night Music. **1985:** Die Zauberflöte, Transformations, Il Signor Bruschino, Le convenienze e le inconvenienze teatrali. **1986:** Les contes d'Hoffmann, Le nozze di Figaro, Postcard from Morocco. **1987:** A Midsummer Night's Dream, Il barbiere di Siviglia, Ormindo. **1988:** Lyubov' k tryom apel'sinam (The Love for Three Oranges), Don Giovanni, The Rape of Lucretia. **1989:** Le nozze di Figaro, Dido and Aeneas, La Cenerentola. **1990:** Die Zauberflöte, Il viaggio a Reims, L'italiana in Algeri. **1991:** Il matrimonio segreto, Così fan tutte, Le nozze di Figaro. **1992:** Don Giovanni, La finta giardiniera, Die Zauberflöte. **1993:** Il turco in Italia, La clemenza di Tito, Le nozze di Figaro. Children's Theater-in-the-Woods. **1980:** Hänsel und Gretel. **1981:** L'enfant et les sortilèges, Rapunzel. **1982:** Doctor Miracle, The Apothecary. **1984:** The Bear, Rita. **1985:** Fleurette, The Island of Tulipatan. **1986:** Little Red Riding Hood, Cox and Box. **1987:** The Music Shop.

Washington
SEATTLE

• *The Seattle Opera* •

Giacomo Puccini's *Tosca* inaugurated the Seattle Opera on May 7, 1964. The first season also witnessed a jealous Don José stab Carmen. The Seattle Opera was created when the Western Opera Company merged with the Seattle Symphony on

January 23, 1964. Glynn Ross was at the helm, and he guided the company for almost twenty years.

Touring companies brought opera to Seattle during the nineteenth century, and the Metropolitan Opera visited in 1899 with Georges Bizet's *Carmen*. During 1910 and 1911, the Lombardi Grand Opera Touring Company gave seasons in the newly opened Moore Theater. The Chicago Grand Opera came to town in 1913 and 1914, bringing Gaetano Donizetti's *Lucia di Lammermoor*, Jacques Offenbach's *Les contes d'Hoffmann*, Richard Wagner's *Lohengrin*, and Giuseppe Verdi's *Aida*. Mary Garden was the high point of both seasons, singing Thaïs (1913) and Tosca (1914). Four years later, Fortune Gallo and his San Carlo Grand Opera Company visited, staging a week of Italian operas, primarily by Verdi and Puccini. The Scotti Opera Company and the Metropolitan Opera came to town in 1921. The Met offered John Gay's *The Beggar's Opera*. The year's highlight, however, was the arrival at the end of December of the Russian Grand Opera Company, under the direction of Leo Feodoroff. The company consisted of twenty-four major artists, a chorus of thirty-five, a corps de ballet, and a symphony orchestra. Feodoroff culled the principal singers from the best operas companies in Russia, who before World War I sang in Russia's leading opera cities—Petrograd, Moscow, and Odessa. The troupe presented the first performances in Russian of Pyotr Il'yich Tchaikovsky's *Pikovaya Dama* and Alexander Dargomïzhsky's *Russalka*.

Seattle's first homegrown operatic effort, the Standard Grand Opera Company, was launched in 1914. Composed exclusively of Seattle singers, the company mounted seven operas within a two-year period, including Charles Gounod's *Faust*, Verdi's *Un ballo in maschera*, Wagner's *Der fliegende Holländer*, Bizet's *Carmen*, Gioachino Rossini's *Il barbiere di Siviglia*, Ambroise Thomas's *Mignon*, and Otto Nicolai's *Die lustigen Weiber von Windsor*. World War I caused the demise of the company. The Seattle Civic Opera Company took center stage after the war, performing Verdi's *Il trovatore* and Friedrich von Flotow's *Martha*. The company reorganized into the Civic Opera Association of Seattle and presented Bizet's *Carmen* and Gounod's *Faust*. The Civic's crowning achievement was a grand scale production of Verdi's *Aida* at the University of Washington Stadium. After *Aida*, Seattle's opera-lovers turned to smaller scale productions. Opera Intime formed in 1927. Intime staged Ermanno's Wolf-Ferrari's *Il segreto di Susanna* and Giovanni Pergolesi's *La serva padrona* among others in the new Olympic Hotel. Karl Krueger was on the podium, and the singers were imported from Philadelphia and Chicago. Myron Jacobsen next produced Wolfgang Amadeus Mozart's *La finta giardiniera*, but his death in 1934 ended his plans for additional Mozart works for Intime. The company died two years later.

The Seattle Opera Society formed in 1929, and Gounod's *Faust* was its calling card. Headed by Madame Davenport Engberg, the group incorporated a couple years later as the Seattle Opera. The company staged an experimental performance of Wagner's *Tannhäuser*, followed by Wagner's *Lohengrin* in 1932. The productions were so successful that the company reorganized, and the Seattle Civic Opera Association was born the following year. Officially founded by Paul Engberg, Madame Engberg's son, the company mounted two operas each season in English at popular prices. Among its early productions were Thomas's *Mignon*, Karl Goldmark's *Die Königin von Saba*, Léo Delibes's *Lakmé*, Gounod's *Roméo et Juliette*, Donizetti's *Lucia di Lammermoor*, and Verdi's *La traviata* and *Un ballo in maschera*. The company staged operas through the 1950s. Gustave Charpentier's

Louise was the company's swan song. The Northwest Grand Opera Association came to life in 1952, but breathed only for a short time.

Seattle continued to host touring companies as well. Gaetano Merola brought his San Francisco Opera, mounting Verdi's *Rigoletto* and Massenet's *Manon*. La Scala Opera Company stopped over in 1938, and Fortune Gallo's San Carlo Grand Opera Company paid its last visit in 1942.

The Seattle Symphony's presentation of Verdi's *Aida* on June 7, 1962, as part of the World's Fair festivities, planted the seeds for a permanent opera company. The cast featured Gloria Davy, Irene Dalis, Sándor Kónya, and Robert Merrill. After the Symphony produced a second opera, Verdi's *La traviata*, it decided to go into the opera business. Meanwhile Seattle's newly formed Western Opera Company offered Engelbert Humperdinck's *Hänsel und Gretel* in December 1962. The next year performances of Puccini's *Madama Butterfly*, Johann Strauß's *Die Fledermaus*, Puccini's *La bohème*, and Rossini's *Il barbiere di Siviglia* took place. The two opera producing companies merged forming the Seattle Opera. The company's second season witnessed four works, including Gounod's *Faust* and Modest Mussorgsky's *Boris Godunov*. Star-studded performances followed. Franco Corelli sang the title role in Umberto Giordano's *Andrea Chénier* in 1966, and in Gounod's *Roméo et Juliette* two years later. Ross lured Giovanni Martinelli from retirement to be Emperor Altoum in Puccini's *Turandot* in 1967. Joan Sutherland sang her first Lakmé that same season and her first Olympia/Antonia/Giulietta in Offenbach's *Les contes d'Hoffmann* in 1970. Birgit Nilsson sang an unforgettable *Turandot* in 1970. Richard Tucker, Régine Crespin, Leonie Rysanek, and Sherrill Milnes also performed in Seattle. The symphony was on strike when Milnes was scheduled to appear in Mozart's *Don Giovanni* in 1979. Rather than cancel the production, two pianos accompanied the performance.

In 1966, the company developed a National or "silver" series, where opera was sung in English by young, emerging American talent. The series gave those singers a showcase for their talent. The series parallelled the International or "gold" series that offered the same operas with the star-studded casts. Since the "silver" series had no high-priced artists to jack up the cost, the price of tickets were a fraction of those for the "gold series," allowing those on limited budgets to experience opera for the first time.

The Seattle Opera's first world premiere, Carlisle Floyd's *Of Mice and Men*, took place on January 22, 1970. The critically acclaimed opera has since found its way into several American company repertoires. On April 28, 1971, Ross presented the professional stage premiere of The Who's rock opera *Tommy*, with Bette Midler. He was trying to attract more young people to opera. The production, which combined new techniques in design, staging, and film, was hailed by the press. Another novelty graced the stage on March 2, 1972, Thomas Pasatieri's *Black Widow*. The presentation pioneered a new process of film animation in opera. Three years later the West Coast premiere of Pasatieri's *The Seagull* took place. Ross put his company on the world opera map with the opening of the Pacific Northwest Wagner Festival in 1975. Two complete cycles of *Der Ring des Nibelungen* — one in English and one in German — played to Wagnerites from around the globe. For the next decade, the Ring became an annual ritual for Wagner-lovers, who flocked to "Bayreuth on Puget Sound." Ross, impassioned about his festival, stressed that he was the first to restore the Ring to its "mythic and picturesque nature" at a time when "ideological interpretations" were in vogue. The only problem with the venture was that after a couple of seasons of the summer Ring festival, most adventure and variety disappeared from the main season repertory. This, coupled with Ross's dream of The Northwest Park for the Performing Arts, caused a disagreement with the board. It culminated when the board asked Ross to leave two years before the completion of his contract in 1985, a year short of his twentieth season. In the program, only a full-page color photo of an unsmiling Ross, with "I'll miss you! Glynn Ross. May '83" written across the top, gave any hint that Seattle Opera's dynamic leader would not be back for the 1983-84 season. Even the customary salute of farewell in the program from the board of trustees was missing. When the final curtain fell on the last night of Ross's regime, only Jon Vickers was on stage to accept a tumultuous standing ovation for Benjamin Britten's *Peter Grimes*. Ross was six thousand miles away in Europe.

One of the more unnerving incidents to befall an opera company, a bomb threat, occurred in Seattle. The Rumanian soprano Mariana Nicolesco was singing Violetta in Verdi's *La traviata*. Some fanatical Iranians with a poor comprehension of English thought the Rumanian soprano was an Iranian soprano. Since this was an affront to their beliefs, they threatened to bomb the theater unless the Iranian (Rumanian) soprano canceled. Fortunately, neither happened. Speight Jenkins took the helm after Ross's departure and steered the company in a different direction — away from star-studded casts and into *Gesamtwerk* (ensemble work) productions. Opera in Seattle became a music-theater experience rather than a showcase for superstars. The company mounted several unusual works, including a revival of the Christoph Gluck's *Orphée et Euridice* and the baritone version of Jules Massenet's *Werther*. (Massenet created the baritone version for Mattia Battistini.) Jenkins's "music-theater" approach was most evident in the new Ring he forged for the 1986 Wagner Festival. The avant-garde, François Rochaix/Robert Israel production was a feast for the eyes, if not always for the ears. It boasted the largest fire ever set on an indoor stage and life-sized flying horses. The company repeated the cycle in 1987, and it resurfaces every four years. Since the Ring carries a $3 million dollar price tag, it is financially impossible to revive the Cycle annually.

The six-opera season offers a varied mainstream repertory with one contemporary piece in a *stagione* system. Some recent productions include Puccini's *Tosca*, Verdi's *Aida* and *Don Carlos*, Rossini's *Il barbiere di Siviglia*, Britten's *Turn of the Screw*, Claude Debussy's *Pelléas et Mélisande*, and Vincenzo Bellini's *Norma*. The company performs in the Seattle Opera House.

Seattle Opera House

The opera house was originally built as a civic auditorium, opening in 1927. For the Seattle World's Fair in 1962, Marcus Priteca and James Chiarelli remodelled the structure into the Opera House. A gala concert on April 21, 1961, inaugurated the renovated building. The program, which honored Igor Stravinsky on his 80th birthday, included Stravinsky's Symphony in Three Movements and his Suite from "The Firebird."

The Opera House is actually three shells — the original building, a modern brick façade encasing the original building, and an interior shell built within the original walls. The red brick building is embellished with slender, white columns.

Opera House (Seattle, Washington).

OPERA HOUSE in golden letters is affixed to the façade. The eclectically decorated lobby is defined by light russet marble pillars, golden rods, and amber walls. The multi-colored auditorium of white tiers, warm woods, and red velvet plush seats holds an orchestra section and two balconies. Honey-colored wood flanks the stage. Acoustic panels extend over the proscenium, directing the sound toward the audience. The auditorium seats 3,017.

Practical Information. The Opera House is at 301 Mercer Street. The ticket office, to the left of the main entrance, is open 9:00 A.M. to 5:00 P.M. weekdays. During performance periods, the ticket office opens Saturdays, between 10:00 A.M. and 2:00 P.M. Tickets are available at the Seattle Opera box office, 1020 John Street between 9:00 A.M. and 5:00 P.M. weekdays. Tickets can be ordered telephoning 206-389-7699, faxing 206-389-7651, or writing Seattle Opera, P.O.B. 9248, Seattle, WA 98109. If you go, stay at the Four Seasons Olympic Hotel, 411 University Street, Seattle, WA 98101; telephone 206-621-1700, fax 206-682-9633, reservations 1-800-332-3442. The hotel, built in 1924 in the Italian Renaissance style, was recently restored to its former glory. It is an architectural gem, making it a Seattle landmark and putting it on the National Register of Historic Places. The hotel is convenient to the theater.

COMPANY STAFF AND REPERTORY

General/Artistic Directors. Glynn Ross (1964-1983); Speight Jenkins (1983-present). *World Premieres (before Seattle Opera).* Moore's *Narcissa* (April 22, 1912); Tonning's *Blue Wing* (May 18, 1917); Johnson's *A Letter to Emily* (April 22, 1951); Verrall's *The*

Cowherd and the Sky Maiden (January 17, 1952); Kechley's *The Golden Lion.* (April 28, 1959).
   American/United States Premieres (before Seattle Opera). Tchaikovsky's *Piko-vaya Dama* (first performance in America in Russian, December 21, 1921); Dargomïzhsky's *Russalka* (December 23, 1921).
   World Premieres (Seattle Opera). Floyd's *Of Mice and Men* (January 22, 1970); Pasatieri's *Calvary* (April 7, 1971); Pasatieri's *Black Widow* (March 2, 1972).
   American/United States Premieres (Seattle Opera). The Who's *Tommy* (first professional stage performance, April 28, 1971); Massenet's *Werther* (baritone version, first performance in French, February 22, 1989).
   Repertory. **1964:** Tosca, Carmen. **1964-65:** Lucia di Lammermoor, Faust, Rigoletto, Boris Godunov. **1965-66:** La bohème, Samson et Dalila, Lohengrin, Madama Butterfly. **1966-67:** Il barbiere di Siviglia, Cavalleria rusticana/I pagliacci, Turandot, Lakmé, La traviata. **1967-68:** Otello, Roméo et Juliette, The Crucible, Fidelio, Don Giovanni. **1968-69:** Aida, Andrea Chénier, Der Rosenkavalier, Tosca, L'elisir d'amore. **1969-70:** Die Fledermaus, Turandot, Of Mice and Men, La forza del destino, Salome. **1970-71:** Madama Butterfly, Les contes d'Hoffmann, La nozze di Figaro, Don Carlos, Carmen. **1971-72:** La bohème, Un ballo in maschera, Der fliegende Holländer, Black Widow, Lucia di Lammermoor. **1972-73:** La Périchole, Faust, Manon Lescaut, Die Walküre, La traviata. **1973-74:** La fille du régiment, Rigoletto, Così fan tutte, Siegfried, Gianni Schicchi/I pagliacci. **1974-75:** Mefistofele, Il barbiere di Siviglia, Götterdämmerung, Manon, Il trovatore. **1975-76:** Der Ring des Nibelungen, Der Rosenkavalier, Eugene Onegin, The Seagull, Aida, Thaïs. **1976-77:** Der Ring des Nibelungen, Of Mice and Men, Werther, Otello, La Cenerentola, Tosca. **1977-78:** Der Ring des Nibelungen, Madama Butterfly, La Roi de Lahore, Boris Godunov, Die Zauberflöte, Falstaff. **1978-79:** Der Ring des Nibelungen, Norma, Carmen, Macbeth, Don Giovanni, La bohème. **1979-80:** Der Ring des Nibelungen, Lucia di Lammermoor, Faust, Pikovaya dama, Fidelio, La traviata. **1980-81:** Der Ring des Nibelungen, Les contes d'Hoffmann, Aida, Manon Lescaut, Tristan und Isolde, Don Pasquale. **1981-82:** Der Ring des Nibelungen, Die Fledermaus, Turandot, Rigoletto, Die Entführung aus dem Serail, Madama Butterfly. **1982-83:** Der Ring des Nibelungen, Il trovatore, Carmen, Il barbiere di Siviglia, La fanciulla del West. **1983-84:** Der Ring des Nibelungen, Le nozze di Figaro, Cavalleria rusticana/I pagliacci, La forza del destino, Elektra, La sonnambula. **1984-85:** Der Ring des Nibelungen, The Ballad of Baby Doe, Tannhäuser, L'elisir d'amore, La bohème, Jenůfa. **1985-86:** Die Walküre, Manon, Lucia di Lammermoor, Così fan tutte, Salome, Eugene Onegin. **1986-87:** Der Ring des Nibelungen, Tosca, Don Pasquale, Faust, Otello, Porgy and Bess. **1987-88:** Der Ring des Nibelungen, Carmen, Die Zauberflöte, Orfeo ed Euridice, Rigoletto, Die Fledermaus. **1988-89:** Satyagraha, La traviata, Roméo et Juliette, Der fliegende Holländer, Werther, Madama Butterfly. **1989-90:** Die Meistersinger, Il trovatore, Le nozze di Figaro, Dialogues des Carmélites, La fille du régiment, Les contes d'Hoffmann. **1990-91:** War and Peace, Cavalleria rusticana/Gianni Schicchi, Rusalka, Ariadne auf Naxos, Anna Bolena, Don Giovanni. **1991-92:** Der Ring des Nibelungen, La bohème, Fidelio, The Ballad of Baby Doe, Lucia di Lammermoor, Così fan tutte. **1992-93:** Aida, Il barbiere di Siviglia, The Passion of Jonathan Wade, Pelléas et Mélisande, Die lustige Witwe. **1993-94:** Don Carlos, Tosca, Hänsel und Gretel, Norma, The Turn of the Screw, Les pêcheurs des perles.

———————————————— TACOMA

• *Tacoma Opera* •

Johann Strauß's *Die Fledermaus*, the first production of the Tacoma Opera, originally the Tacoma Opera Society, took place in 1968. It was the only production that inaugural season. A few opera enthusiasts formed the Tacoma Opera Society to bring light opera to Tacoma. Until 1989, one-opera seasons defined the company, (except 1970-72), and a local university was home for the first fourteen years.

In 1980, Hans Wolf became the first permanent artistic director, steering the company into more professional waters. The group renamed themselves the Tacoma Opera to reflect their new status and in 1983 moved into the restored Pantages Theater in downtown Tacoma. A production of Jacques Offenbach's *Christopher Columbus* marked the opera's move into its new quarters. In 1991, a second, smaller performance venue, the Rialto Theater, joined the Pantages in hosting the company. The Tacoma Opera staged its first world premiere, Carol Sams's *The Pied Piper of Hamelin*, on November 6, 1993. The casts are a combination of established, up-and-coming, and local singers.

The two-opera season offers a mixture of lighter works, sung in English, in a *stagione* system. Recent productions include Gian Carlo Menotti's *Amahl and the Night Visitors* and Wolfgang Amadeus Mozart's *Le nozze di Figaro*. The company performs in the 1,165-seat Pantages Theater and the 750-seat Rialto Theater.

Practical Information. The Pantages Theater is at 901 Broadway and the Rialto Theater is at 310 South Ninth Street. Tickets are available from the Tacoma Opera, P.O.B. 7468, Tacoma, WA 98407, telephone 206-627-7789.

COMPANY STAFF AND REPERTORY

General/Artistic Directors. None (1968–1979); Hans Wolf (1980–present).
World Premiere. Sams's *The Pied Piper of Hamelin* (November 6, 1993).
Repertory. **1968:** Die Fledermaus. **1969:** Die lustige Witwe. **1970:** Vagabond King. **1971:** Il barbiere di Siviglia, Madama Butterfly. **1972:** Tosca, Le Périchole. **1973:** Der Zigeunerbaron, Madama Butterfly. **1974:** Student Prince. **1975:** Kismet. **1976:** Die lustigen Weiber von Windsor. **1977:** L'elisir d'amore. **1981:** Die Fledermaus. **1982:** La Périchole. **1983:** Christopher Columbus. **1984:** Der Zigeunerbaron. **1985:** Die Lustige Witwe. **1986:** Die Zauberflöte. **1987:** Prodaná nevěsta (The Bartered Bride). **1988:** Die Lustige Witwe. **1989-90:** Show Boat, Il barbiere di Siviglia. **1990-91:** Amahl and the Night Visitors, Die Fledermaus. **1991-92:** Amahl and the Night Visitors, Die Zauberflöte. **1992-93:** Amahl and the Night Visitors, Carmen. **1993-94:** The Pied Piper of Hamelin, Le nozze di Figaro. **1994-95:** The Pied Piper of Hamelin, La traviata.

West Virginia ——— CHARLESTON

• *Lilliput Opera Orchestra* •

The Lilliput Opera Orchestra was founded in 1979 by Donald and Suzanne Riggio, to promote awareness and appreciation of opera and musical theater in West Virginia. The company has no permanent home, but tours throughout the state. The company has been inactive during the past few years due to unfavorable economic conditions in West Virginia. When conditions improve, the company hopes to begin touring again.

Practical Information. For information contact Lilliput Opera Orchestra, 16 Terrace Road, Charleston, WV 25314, telephone 304-346-6095.

COMPANY STAFF AND REPERTORY

General/Artistic Director. Donald Riggio (1979–present).
Repertory. **1980-81:** Riverboat Man. **1981-82:** Riverboat Man. **1982-83:** The Medium.
1985-86: Opera, Archy & Mehitabel. **1986-87:** Così fan tutte, A Lot O'Taurus. **1987-88:** Così fan tutte, Riverboat Man. **1988-89:** Falstaff. **1989-90:** Hänsel und Gretel, 1776.

Wisconsin ——————————— MADISON

• *Madison Opera* •

Giacomo Puccini's *La bohème* inaugurated the Madison Opera, originally the Madison Civic Opera, in January 1963. Roland and Arline Johnson founded the company at the request of Madison area singers who wanted a stage on which to showcase their talents. The company is not an independent entity, but part of the Madison Civic Music Association, the umbrella organization for the opera, symphony, and chorus. Johnson also headed the Madison Civic Symphony.

It was not until 1980 that the company brought in professional talent—Lorna Haywood, Marvellee Cariaga, and Alan Crabb—for their production of Giuseppe Verdi's *Aida*. The reason was the company had a new home, the Oscar Mayer Theatre. The company presented its first world premiere, Daron Hagen's *Shining Brow* on April 21, 1993. The productions are traditional, and the casts are composed of local and regional talent.

The two-opera season offers standard, modern, and musical theater works in a *stagione* system. Recent productions include Giuseppe Verdi's *Aida* and Mitch Leigh's *Man of La Mancha*. The company performs in the Oscar Mayer Theater.

Oscar Mayer Theater

A concert by the Madison Civic Symphony inaugurated the Oscar Mayer Theater on February 23, 1980. The theater was born as the Capitol Theater in 1928, a movie palace gem of rococo pretensions. As early as 1954, a bond issue of $5.5 million had been voted for a Civic Center, but the project failed to gain support and languished. By 1974, the money had grown to $7 million, and Madison's mayor decided that the money should be used to restore the old Capitol Theater, since there was not enough funds for a new structure. Hardy, Holzmann, & Pfeiffer Associates were hired as the architects to do a "money-saving interpretive restoration." Oscar Mayer & Company donated $250,000, and the theater had its name.

With a soaring center façade and cupola, the theater meshes with the neighboring original Montgomery Ward Building converted into an art gallery, and the contemporary-style Isthmus Playhouse. Old stone cement fuses with the glass and metal. An aluminum sculpture entitled *Act* stands in front. The vertical lobby is multi-leveled, imparting an industrial atmosphere, with its gray cinderblock walls, marching gray carpeting, deep green heating vents, and fluorescent lighting. But there is also oak wood, and white and salmon colors. The auditorium, in Rapp & Rapp French style, swims in brown, terra cotta, and burgundy. The hall seats 2,200.

Practical Information. The Oscar Mayer Theater is on State Street. Tickets are available from the Madison Opera, 458 Charles Lane, Madison, WI 53711, telephone, 608-238-8085, fax 608-233-3431.

COMPANY STAFF AND REPERTORY

General/Artistic Director. Roland Johnson (1963–present).
World Premiere. Hagen's *Shining Brow* (April 21, 1993).
Repertory. **1963:** Noyes Fludde, La bohème. **1964:** La voix humaine. **1965:** Falstaff. **1966:** Tosca. **1967:** Die Fledermaus. **1968:** Jumping Frog/Calaveras City, Hänsel und Gretel. **1969:** The Ballad of Baby Doe. **1970:** Carmen. **1971:** Help! Help! The Globolinks. **1972:** Le nozze di Figaro. **1973:** Cavalleria rusticana/Gianni Schicchi. **1974:** Così fan tutte, Madama Butterfly. **1975:** La traviata. **1976:** The Ballad of Baby Doe. **1977:** Manon. **1978:** Die Fledermaus. **1979:** Faust, Amelia al ballo, Der Schauspieldirektor. **1980:** Hänsel und Gretel, Aida, La traviata. **1981:** Carmen, Amahl and the Night Visitors. **1982:** Turandot. **1983:** Prodaná nevěsta (The Bartered Bride), Der Zigeunerbaron. **1984:** La Périchole, La bohème. **1985:** The Stoned Guest. **1986:** Fidelio, Noyes Fludde, I pagliacci/Cavalleria rusticana. **1987:** Die lustige Witwe, Tosca, Side by Side by Sondheim. **1988:** Madama Butterfly, A Little Nightmare Music, A Little Night Music. **1989:** The Village Singer, Gianni Schicchi. **1990:** Carousel, Die Fledermaus. **1991:** Don Giovanni, Kiss Me Kate. **1992:** Man of La Mancha, Il barbiere di Siviglia. **1993:** Candide, Shining Brow. **1994:** Aida.

MILWAUKEE

• *Florentine Opera* •

Giuseppe Verdi's *La traviata* inaugurated the Florentine Opera at the Pabst Theater in the spring of 1951. The inaugural season also saw a double bill of Ruggero Leoncavallo's *I pagliacci* and Gian Carlo Menotti's *The Telephone*. The Florentine Opera was an outgrowth of the Italian Opera Chorus founded by John Anello in 1933. The Chorus performed scenes and arias from Italian operas at various locations around Milwaukee. When the United States declared war on Italy in 1942, the company changed its name to Florentine Opera Chorus. The Chorus celebrated the end of World War II with a Victory Opera Festival in the Lincoln High School Auditorium on May 25 and 26, 1945. For the Milwaukee Centennial celebration, the Chorus performed excerpts from Verdi's *Aida* in the Centurama on the Milwaukee lakefront. When the Chorus began producing complete operas in 1951, the Florentine Opera Company was officially born. Milwaukee, however, had been hearing opera for more than a century.

As early as 1850, traveling troupes visited Milwaukee, presenting opera to this midwest city. In fact, the company that gave Chicago its first taste of opera on

July 29, 1850, came from Milwaukee, taking a steamer down Lake Michigan to the Windy City ninety miles away. Since Milwaukee was inhabited predominately by German settlers, the city witnessed a heavy dose of German works, including the American premieres of Albert Lortzing's *Der Waffenschmied* on December 7, 1853, in Young's Hall and Johann Strauβ's *Der Karneval in Rome* at the Stadttheater in April 1878. The world premiere of the German-American composer Edward Sobolewski's *Mohega* took place on October 11, 1859, (in German) in Albany Hall.

After the Pabst Theater opened in 1895, it became home for visiting opera companies, in addition to its role as a home for spoken theater. On December 8, 9, and 10, 1898, performances of Arthur Sullivan's *Patience* and *Iolanthe* took place. The Chicago Grand Opera offered Gustave Charpentier's *Louise* on April 24, 1914, Giacomo Puccini's *La bohème* (matinee) on April 25, 1914, and in the evening on the 25th, Wagner's *Lohengrin*. The Boston Grand Opera Company came to town on May 1 and 2, 1916, bringing Italo Montemezzi's *L'amore dei tre re*, Puccini's *Madama Butterfly*, Christoph Gluck's *Orfeo ed Euridice*, and Puccini's *La bohème*. The Castel Square Opera Company followed, staging several works— Verdi's *Il trovatore* and *Aida*, Carl Maria von Weber's *Der Freischütz*, Wagner's *Lohengrin*, Gaetano Donizetti's *Lucia di Lammermoor*, Pietro Mascagni's *Cavalleria rusticana*, and Sullivan's *Pinafore*. The Pabst also saw several concerts by renown artists, including Geraldine Farrar (October 20, 1911 and October 7, 1921), Amelita Galli-Curci (May 18, 1917), Lotte Lehmann (January 29, 1934), and John McCormack (November 5, 1936).

Milwaukee welcomed the Russian Grand Opera Company under the direction of Leo Feodoroff in 1923. The company arrived in town on February 12, 1923, offering several Russian works, including Modest Mussorgsky's *Boris Godunov*, Pyotr Il'yich Tchaikovsky's *Eugene Onegin, Cherevichki*, and *Pikovaya dama*, Nikolay Rimsky-Korsakov's *Snegurochka* (The Snow Maiden), Anton Rubinstein's *The Demon*, and two non-Russian operas, Fromental Halévy's *La Juive* and Georges Bizet's *Carmen*. A few months later, the first performance in Polish of Stanislaw's Moniuszko's *Halka* took place on May 13, 1923. Next the American Opera Company presented, in English, Puccini's *Madama Butterfly*, Charles Gounod's *Faust*, Bizet's *Carmen*, and Wolfgang Amadeus Mozart's *Le nozze di Figaro*. Fortune Gallo brought his San Carlo Grand Opera Company on November 22, 1924, mounting Puccini's *Madama Butterfly* and Friedrich von Flotow's *Martha*. William Wade Hinshaw's *opéra comique* troupe offered Mozart's *Le nozze di Figaro* on March 11, 1926. The German Grand Opera Company visited in 1931, staging Eugen d'Albert's *Tiefland* on Wednesday, February 25. Fortune Gallo's San Carlo Grand Opera Company returned on Tuesday, January 31, 1950, with Verdi's *Aida* and *La traviata*.

Two years later, the second season of the Florentine Opera took place. The company's sole offering was Charles Gounod's *Faust* with Charles Curtis and Jerome Hines. The third season heralded the return to the two-opera season with Verdi's *Rigoletto* and Puccini's *Madama Butterfly*. Although the fifth and sixth seasons boasted three operas, it was not until the fifteenth season that the three-opera season became the norm. In addition to their regular season, the Florentine offered summer performances of light opera and musicals in Washington Park. The fifth season also witnessed an amusing incident. Walter Fredericks was singing Canio in Leoncavallo's *I pagliacci*. Fredericks was expressing his grief over Nedda's betrayal in "Vesti la giubba" when an agonized expression crossed his face. He grasped around his waist and horror filled his eyes in what colleagues and the audience felt was a spellbinding emotional performance. The reality was, he was losing his pants. Jan Peerce opened the 1960s with appearances in Puccini's *La bohème* and Verdi's *Rigoletto*. Midway through the decade, Plácido Domingo filled in at the last minute in Camille Saint-Saëns's *Samson et Dalila*. The only problem was, Domingo had last sung Samson in Israel in Hebrew. After a few intensive rehearsal days to put him in the "French mode," he offered an outstanding performance. The company also presented Richard Cassilly and Claramae Turner in Georges Bizet's *Carmen* and Richard Tucker in Verdi's *Aida*.

When Uihlein Hall opened in 1969, the company took up permanent residence. They inaugurated their new home with two scenes from Donizetti's *Lucia di Lammermoor*. The Florentine mounted its the first Wagner opera, *Lohengrin*, with John Alexander and Walter Cassel. That same season saw Sherrill Milnes and Kenneth Riegel in Rossini's *Il barbiere di Siviglia* and Carol Neblett, Nicholas DiVirgilio, and Louis Quilico in Verdi's *La traviata*. The 1972-73 season witnessed the first Richard Strauss work performed by the Florentine Opera, *Salome*. Milnes and Neblett returned for Verdi's *Il trovatore*, and James McCracken assayed Otello. The 1974-75 season counted Beverly Sills, Samuel Ramey, Nancy Shade, and Ezio Flagello among its artists. The following season witnessed Robert Ward's *The Crucible*, the first American work to grace the Florentine stage. Gilda Cruz-Romo also made her company debut in Verdi's *Un ballo in maschera* during the season. She returned for Puccini's *Madama Butterfly*, Amilcare Ponchielli's *La gioconda*, and Verdi's *Aida*. Sills returned for Donizetti's *La fille du régiment*, and McCracken sang the title role in Saint-Saëns's *Samson et Dalila*. June Anderson, Johanna Meier, Mary Jane Johnson, Justino Díaz, John Reardon, Richard Stilwell, Paul Plishka, and Valerie Popova have also sung with the Florentine Opera.

Although the repertory exhibits a traditional bent, the Florentine has not shied away from twentieth-century works, including Douglas Moore's *The Ballad of Baby Doe*, George Gershwin's *Porgy and Bess*, Strauss's *Ariadne auf Naxos*, and Menotti's *The Consul*. Dennis Hanthorn, Florentine's general director since 1989, plans to slowly expand the repertory by offering a more adventurous schedule "as money provides." He believes that "opera is great art and that a company must be able to pay for the art before buying it." The productions reflect the composer's intention, characterized as "authentic and pure." The casts are comprised of established artists in the principal roles, with up-and-coming regional artists in the secondary roles. The company aims to identify new talent. Occasionally "name" artists try out new roles with the Florentine since the company offers long rehearsal time and a supportive atmosphere.

The four-opera season offers a mixture of grand and comic opera, and a work never before performed by the company. The emphasis is on Italian opera. Recent productions include Verdi's *Otello*, Rossini's *La Cenerentola*, Donizetti's *Lucia di Lammermoor*, and Wagner's *Die Walküre*. The company performs in the Uihlein Hall of the Milwaukee Performing Arts Center and Pabst Theater.

Milwaukee Performing Arts Center

The Milwaukee Performing Arts Center raised its golden curtain for the first time on September 17, 1969. Harry Weese & Associates designed the Center, which

Milwaukee Performing Arts Center (Milwaukee, Wisconsin).

carried a $12 million price tag. First conceived near the end of World War II as a living memorial to Milwaukee County's War dead, the Center took a quarter of a century to become a reality. The building's original site was on the lakefront, but the $2 million cost of filling in the area forced the relocation to the banks of the Milwaukee River. The building officially became a memorial to veterans of all wars in dedication ceremonies held on August 17, 1969.

The Performing Arts Center is a large structure, formed by the fusion of various geometric shapes and housing three auditoriums—Uihlein Hall, Vogel Hall, and Todd Wehr Theater. It was originally faced with wheat-colored Italian travertine marble, but the stone cracked in the frigid Wisconsin winter. A $9.3 million project funded by Milwaukee County gave the building a new face of Biesanz stone (a dolomite limestone quarried in Minnesota) in 1993. The façade rises in layers, supported by massive pillars that frame glass entrances. The modern auditorium of Uihlein Hall is richly appointed with red velvet seats that stretch continental-style across the orchestra. There are three tiers, a small shallow box tier and two U-shaped balconies that stretch toward the stage with sleek white arms. A row of "dog-teeth" hang underneath each arm for acoustic purposes, and rectangular acoustic panels breakup the large wall space. A gold lame curtain weighing 2,800 pounds hangs in the proscenium arch. Uihlein Hall seats 2,189 for opera performances.

Pabst Theater

The Pabst Theater rose from the ashes of Das Neue Deutsche Stadttheater, originally called the Nunnemacher Grand Opera House. Frederick Pabst had purchased the theater from Jacob Nunnemacher in 1890. Fire claimed it on January 16, 1895. Pabst hired architect Otto Strack to design a new theater, and construction began on May 9, 1895. The theater was completed by October. A gala production of the German comedy *Zwei Wappen* inaugurated the Pabst on November 9, 1895. The first thirty years saw performances by Sarah Bernhardt, Enrico Caruso, and Ignace Padarewski. By 1928, its beauty had faded. Architects Dick & Bauer were in charge of the renovation that saw an Art Deco style imposed upon the theater's baroque elegance. Cool shades of green replaced the Victorian reds and the crystal chandelier gave way to a Tiffany-style glass dome. By 1967 the theater was in such a state of disrepair that it was closed. Conrad Schmitt Studios was commissioned to bring back the theater's original elegance, and the Pabst reopened on September 23, 1976.

The Pabst is an imposing Victorian building decorated in the baroque style. The mocha-colored brick façade is topped by PABST THEATER in gold letters. A wrought-iron balcony runs along the façade, acting as a covered walkway. The red-and-maroon, fan-shaped auditorium is accented with gold and silver. Two tiers weave across its burgundy red seats. PABST is intertwined in the ornamental grillwork of the gallery seats. Masks of comedy and tragedy and winged cherubs decorate gilded parapets. Great names from the arts circle the room, while Apollo holds a lyre above his head, crowning the proscenium arch. The Pabst seats 1,393.

Practical Information. The Uihlein Hall of the Performing Arts Center is at 929 North Water Street. The ticket office, in the middle of the entrance foyer, is open noon until 9:00 P.M. daily. Tickets can be ordered by telephoning 414-273-7206 between 9:30 A.M. and 9:00 P.M., Monday through Saturday, and 12:00 noon to 9:00 P.M., Sunday, or writing Florentine Opera, 735 North Water Street, Suite 1315, Milwaukee, WI 53202-4106. The Pabst Theater is at 144 East Wells Street. The box office, on the left of the entrance foyer, is open 12:00 noon to 5:30 P.M., Monday through Friday, and 10:00 A.M. to 4:00 P.M., Saturday. You can telephone the Pabst box office at 414-278-3663. If you go, stay at The Pfister Hotel, 424 East Wisconsin Avenue, Milwaukee, WI 53202; telephone 414-273-8222, fax 414-273-0747, reservations 1-800-323-7500. The Pfister was built in 1893 and recently celebrated its centennial. Restored to its original splendor, the hotel is a Milwaukee landmark. The architecturally significant hotel offers the ambiance of that gilded age. It is a few blocks from the theaters.

COMPANY STAFF AND REPERTORY

General/Artistic Directors. John David Anello, Senior (1933–75); Alan Bellamente (manager, 1976–78); Robert Caulfield (manager, 1978–80); John Gage (1980–89); Dennis Hanthorn (1989–present).

Repertory. **1951:** La traviata, I pagliacci/The Telephone. **1952:** Faust. **1953:** Rigoletto, Madama Butterfly. **1954:** Carmen, Lucia di Lammermoor. **1955-56:** La traviata, Hänsel und Gretel, Cavalleria rusticana/I pagliacci. **1956-57:** La bohème, Hänsel und Gretel, Il trovatore. **1957-58:** Rigoletto, La bohème. **1958-59:** Madama Butterfly, Tosca. **1959-60:** La traviata, Carmen. **1960-61:** Faust, Lucia di Lammermoor. **1961-62:** La bohème, Il trovatore. **1962-63:** Rigoletto, Die lustige Witwe. **1963-64:** Cavalleria rusticana/I pagliacci, Madama Butterfly. **1964-65:** Carmen, Die Fledermaus. **1965-66:** Samson et Dalila, Hänsel und Gretel, La traviata. **1966-67:** Les contes d'Hoffmann, Rigoletto, La bohème. **1968-69:** Madama Butterfly, L'elisir d'amore, Don Giovanni. **1969-70:** Lucia di Lammermoor (2 scenes), Aida, Don Pasquale,

Pabst Theater (Milwaukee, Wisconsin).

Manon. **1970-71:** Lohengrin, Il barbiere di Siviglia, Roméo et Juliette, La traviata. **1971-72:** Turandot, Così fan tutte, Faust, La bohème. **1972-73:** Carmen, Madama Butterfly, Salome, Rigoletto. **1973-74:** Il trovatore, Tosca, Otello, Cavalleria rusticana/I pagliacci. **1974-75:** Aida, L'elisir d'amore, Lucia di Lammermoor, Manon Lescaut, Les contes d'Hoffmann. **1975-76:** La traviata, Der fliegende Holländer, The Crucible, Un ballo in maschera. **1976-77:** La Cenerentola, La bohème, Don Giovanni, Faust. **1977-78:** Il trovatore, Madama Butterfly, Le fille du régiment. **1978-79:** Die Zauberflöte, Manon, Rigoletto. **1979-80:** Macbeth, Tosca, Die Fledermaus. **1980-81:** Carmen, Don Pasquale, La gioconda. **1981-82:** Lucia di Lammermoor, Le nozze di Figaro, La traviata. **1982-83:** La bohème, Fidelio, Samson et Dalila. **1983-84:** Salome, Il barbiere di Siviglia, Madama Butterfly. **1984-85:** Aida, Die Entführung aus dem Serail, Die lustige Witwe. **1985-86:** Cavalleria rusticana/I pagliacci, Les pêcheurs des perles, Rigoletto. **1986-87:** Tosca, Don Giovanni, Les contes d'Hoffmann. **1987-88:** Il trovatore, The Ballad of Baby Doe, Turandot. **1988-89:** Carmen, Manon Lescaut, Faust. **1989-90:** Porgy and Bess, Un ballo in maschera, Die Zauberflöte. **1990-91:** Ariadne auf Naxos, La traviata, Le nozze di Figaro, Die Fledermaus. **1991-92:** Il barbiere di Siviglia, La bohème, Eugene Onegin, Roméo et Juliette. **1992-93:** La Cenerentola, Die Walküre, Madama Butterfly, Aida. **1993-94:** The Consul, Carmen, Lucia di Lammermoor, Otello.

• *Skylight Opera Theater* •

An Evening with Gilbert & Sullivan performed in an "attic theater" brought the Skylight Comic Opera, the original name of the Skylight Opera Theater, to life in 1959. Jim Keeley and Ray Smith comprised the entire cast of this original work. Clair Richardson, a local "gifted eccentric" who loved opera and Gilbert & Sullivan, conceived and founded the company. The second production of the inaugural season, which offered a total of seven works, was Wolfgang Amadeus Mozart's *Così fan tutte*. *Così* was another bare-bones production featuring three East Coast free-lance singers — Merle Puffer, Jim Billings, and Leslie Loosli — that Richardson had lured to Milwaukee. Named the Boston Comic Opera-in-residence-at-the-Skylight, they sang all the performances with piano accompaniment. The in-augural season continued in a "coach yard theater," which offered an awning as sole protection from the elements and the neighbor's garbage. Here Gaetano Donizetti's *Il campanello di notte*, Ermanno Wolf-Ferrari's *Il segreto di Susanna*, Johann Strauß's *Die Fledermaus*, and Arthur Sullivan's *The Mikado* were staged.

When the cold weather arrived, Richardson needed a different performing venue so he converted a vacant tire recapping garage into a 249-seat theater, which became Skylight's home for the next thirty-three years. Sullivan's *H.M.S.Pinafore* inaugurated the theater on November 22, 1960. A clever production of Sullivan's *The Gondoliers* followed, featuring a motorized gondola entering under its own steam. The cast dropped to the stage from the ship's rigging. The Sullivan pieces formed the backbone of the repertory, with works by Robert Kurka, Carl Orff, Gian Carlo Menotti, Jerome Kern, Ermanno Wolf-Ferrari, Victor Herbert, Sigmund Romberg, and Franz Lehár, among others, sharing the stage. The practice of mixing late eighteenth-century works (Alessandro Scarlatti's *Il trionfo dell'onore*, Paisi-ello's *Il barbiere di Siviglia*, Pier Francesco Cavalli's *La Calisto*, and Pergolesi's *La serva padrona*) and twentieth-century pieces (Marc Blitzstein's *Regina*, Orff's *Die Kluge*, Wolf-Ferrari's *Il segreto di Suzanne*, Thomas Pasatieri's *The Black Widow*, and Benjamin Britten's *Albert Herring*) with operettas and musicals made for in-teresting repertory. The company consciously avoided similarity or competition with the larger Milwaukee opera company, the Florentine Opera, and never staged the same works. Richardson's philosophy was to avoid comparison with his peers and do the best job with the least money. The sparse budget led to some disasters, like the time baritone Kurt Ollmann plunged with such force into a chair in Doni-zetti's *Le convenienze e le inconvenienze teatrali* that he had to be rescued from it. It was also embarrassing when a cardboard tree collapsed during a Sullivan *Pirates of Penzance* performance.

In 1969, the Milwaukee Performing Arts Theater opened (see Florentine Opera entry, immediately above) with the Skylight staging a summer operetta festival. Richardson attempted to make the festival authentically international by hiring a Polish ballet company, stars from the Volksoper Wien and acquiring scenery from Sormaini Scenografia, Milan (Italy). One production, Franz Lehár's *Die lustige Witwe*, allegedly opened without rehearsal of the last act, and the imported Vien-nese cast discovered that the door through which they planned to exit was painted on the canvas. Another operetta featured a group of military officers marching back and forth across the stage. The jackets were too small for the larger officers so they were slit open in the back. These men were condemned to marched back and forth without being able to turn around. The festival was not successful and died after three summers.

After Richardson's death in 1981, the company turned more professional. Stephen Wadsworth and Francesco Zambello directed the 1981-82 season produc-tion of Claudio Monteverdi's *L'incoronazione di Poppea* and the 1982-83 pro-duction of Leoš Janáček's *Věc Makropulos* (The Makropulos Affair). They also served as artistic directors for a time. The company continued to emphasize the dramatic aspect of a work and intimate involvement with the audience. Skylight finally came of age on October 6, 1993, when the company moved into a new "eighteenth-century" opera house, their home for the twenty-first century.

The five-opera season offers a peculiar blend of opera, operetta, and musicals with almost a total absence of the popular, nineteenth-century romantic repertory. The works are eighteenth-century pieces, operetta, and contemporary musicals. Recent productions include Wolfgang Amadeus Mozart's *Die Zauberflöte*, Georg Friedrich Händel's *Semele*, Sullivan's *The Mikado*, Tom Jones's *110 in the Shade*, and Stephen Sondheim's *In the Woods*. The company performs in the Skylight Theater.

Skylight Theater / Broadway Theater Center

The Skylight Theater was a former tire recapping plant, described as "being in a state of advancing decrepitude." A large black-painted room filled with frayed red seats and black poles served as the auditorium. It was reminiscent of off-off broadway theaters. Skylight's new home, known as the Broadway Theater Center, opened October 6, 1993. Designed by Beckley/Myers Architects, the theater was constructed at a cost of $5.9 million. Three groups call the space home: Skylight Opera Theater, Milwaukee Chamber Theater, and Theater X.

The new opera theater is housed in a brick-and-glass, three-story building. Large sheet-metal rings hang between columns of brick on the theater building. A glazed terra cotta ceramic entrance-way joins it to an existing six-story brick warehouse that was renovated for support space. The auditorium is modeled after eighteenth-century Italian opera houses, with proscenium boxes and three shallow tiers curved like lyres. Midnight blue walls and wood-tone painted pillars contrast with the mustard-colored parapets which are embellished with the names of the Muses and their "props." The Muses, themselves, surround mother "Memory" on the high ceiling. The theater is intimate and offers splendid views—unfortunately of the other people. This was the custom in the eighteenth-century, when it was more important to see and be seen than to watch the happenings on stage. The theater seats 372.

Practical Information. The Skylight Theater is at 158 North Broadway. The box office is inside the theater and is open weekdays from 9:00 A.M. to 5:00 P.M., except on performance days when it stays open until the first intermission. Tickets can also be ordered by telephoning 414-271-8815 or by writing Skylight Opera Theater, 158 North Broadway, Milwaukee, WI 53202. If you go, stay at The Pfister Hotel, 424 East Wisconsin Avenue, Milwaukee, WI 53202; telephone 414-273-8222, fax 414-273-0747, reservations 1-800-323-7500. The Pfister was built in 1893 and recently celebrated its centennial. Restored to its original splendor, the hotel is a Milwaukee landmark. The architecturally significant hotel offers the ambiance of the gilded age. It is a few blocks from the theaters.

COMPANY STAFF AND REPERTORY

General/Artistic Directors. Clair Richardson (1959–1981); Various (1982–1988); Chas Rader-Shieber (1989–present).

Original Works. An Evening with Gilbert & Sullivan (1959–1960); Operetta Holiday (1959–1960); An Evening with Brecht & Weill (1962–63); Gentlemen Be Seated (1964–65);

Husband at the Door (1981–82); John J. Plenty/Fiddler Dan (1981–82); The Young Visitors (1982–83); Holiday Punch (1983–84); Son of Holiday Punch (1983–84); Beertown Burlesque (1984–85); Dark Pony (1985–86); Bath Tub Gin Revue (1985–86); Bernstein Revued (1986–87); Night! Youth! Paris! and the Moon! (1987–88); Oh, Coward! (1988–89); Edith Piaf Onstage (1988–89); Cole Porter with a Twist (1989–90); Camille: La traviata (1989–90); Close Harmony Holidays (1989–90); Broadway Cabaret (1991–92).

Original Versions of American Premieres. Orontea (1987–88); Mario and the Magician (1988–89); Ba-ta-clan (1988–89); The Jewel Box (1992–93).

Repertory. **1959-60:** Così fan tutte, Il campanello, Il segreto di Susanna, The Mikado, Die Fledermaus, Operetta Holiday, An Evening with Gilbert & Sullivan. **1960-61:** Don Pasquale, H.M.S. Pinafore, La vie Parisienne, The Pirates of Penzance, Iolanthe, Patience, Trial by Jury, The Gondoliers, Madama Butterfly, Il barbiere di Siviglia. **1961-62:** Leave It To Jane, Trouble in Tahiti, The Mikado, Ruddigore, Mademoiselle Modiste, Das Land des Lächelns, Le nozze di Figaro, La serva padrona, The Desert Song. **1962-63:** Der Zigeunerbaron, Così fan tutte, Trial by Jury, Little Mary Sunshine, The Mikado, H.M.S. Pinafore, The Sorcerer, The Yeoman of the Guard, An Evening with Brecht & Weill. **1963-64:** Die Entführung aus dem Serail, Die Zauberflöte, La finta giardiniera, The Pirates of Penzance, Ariadne auf Naxos, Die Dreigroschenoper, Trial by Jury, An Evening with Gilbert & Sullivan. **1964-65:** Little Mary Sunshine, The Medium, The Telephone, Albert Herring, The Pirates. of Penzance, Knickerbocker Holiday, Gentlemen Be Seated. **1965-66:** Oh Boy!, Die Kluge, La bohème, Iolanthe, The Good Soldier Schweik. **1966-67:** Oh Lady, Lady, Dialogues des Carmélites, Ruddigore, Così fan tutte, Madama Butterfly. **1967-68:** Les pêcheurs des perles, Very Good Eddie, Lyubov' k tryom apel'sinam (The Love for Three Oranges), Il barbiere di Siviglia, La traviata, Lost in the Stars. **1968-69:** Salad Days, Die Zauberflöte, Lost in the Stars, Orfeo ed Euridice, Werther, Die Dreigroschenoper. **1969-70:** La bohème, The Streets of New York, Patience, Falstaff, The Mother of Us All, Die lustige Witwe, Die Fledermaus, Das Land des Lächelns. **1970-71:** The Amorous Flea, The Gondoliers, Wozzeck, Rigoletto, Die lustige Witwe, The Student Prince, Gasthof des weißen Pferdes, Your Own Thing. **1971-72:** Le nozze di Figaro, Oh, Boy!, The Devil and Daniel Webster, Down in the Valley, The Mikado, The Turn of the Screw. **1972-73:** Obrucheniye v monastïre (Betrothal in a Monastery), H.M.S. Pinafore, Le jongleur de Notre-Dame, Aufstieg und Fall der Stadt Mahagonny, La Cenerentola. **1973-74:** Der Freischütz, Der Bettelstudent, The Student Prince, Die lustige Witwe, Eugene Onegin, Madama Butterfly, The Pirates of Penzance, Les pêcheurs des perles, Die Dreigroschenoper. **1974-75:** El Capitan, Iolanthe, Il barbiere di Siviglia, The Good Soldier Schweik, Die Zauberflöte. **1975-76:** The Fashionable Lady, Naughty Marietta, Leave It To Jane, I Do, I Do, The Saint of Bleecker Street, Trial by Jury, Black Widow, An Evening with Gilbert & Sullivan. **1976-77:** The Gondoliers, Blossom Time, Le nozze di Figaro, Susannah, Die Fledermaus. **1977-78:** Il barbiere di Siviglia (Paisiello), Die lustige Witwe, The Mikado, The Student Prince, Il trionfo dell'onore, The Free Lance. **1978-79:** La cambiale di matrimonio, Il cappello di paglia di Firenze, Ruddigore, La finta giardiniera, Il Re Teodoro in Venezia, The Red Mill. **1979-80:** The Beggar's Opera, Hotel for Criminals, H.M.S. Pinafore, Oh Lady, lady, The Vagabond King, Le convenienze e le inconvenienze teatrali, The Stronger, La serva padrona, Flower and Hawk, Un mari a la porte, The Daughter of the Duke of Dingle. **1980-81:** Orphée aux Enfers, Regina, The Pirates of Penzance, Happy End, The Rake's Progress, The Ballad of the Bremen Band, Eine Nacht in Venedig. **1981-82:** The Medium, Livietta e Tracollo, The Mikado, Iolanthe, The Fantasticks, L'incoronazione di Poppea, Candide, John J. Plenty, Fiddler Dan, Un mari a la porte. **1982-83:** Die Dreigroschenoper, Iolanthe, Il matrimonio segreto, Oh, Kay, Věc Makropulos (The Makropulos Affair), A Little Night Music, Cox and Box, A Night with Noel Coward, The Young Visitors, Le mariage aux lanterne. **1983-84:** Trial by Jury, Turn of the Screw, H.M.S. Pinafore, La Calisto, The Student Prince, The Jumping Frog of Calaveras County, Holiday Punch, Tintypes, A Night with Cole Porter. **1984-85:** Charlotte Sweet, Jacques Brel is Alive and Well, The Egg, Favola d'Orfeo, The Pirates of Penzance, Griffelkin, Anything Goes, Beertown Burlesque, The Egg, Son of

Holiday Punch, Don Pasquale, Cox and Box, A Night with Irving Berlin. **1985-86:** Little Me, Side by Side by Sondheim, Xerxes, Patience, Tintypes, Postcard from Morocco, The Desert Song, Don Giovanni, Dark Pony, Bath Tub Gin Revue. **1986-87:** The Cradle Will Rock, The Mikado, At the Drop of a Hat, Ain't Misbehavin', Così fan tutte, Sweeney Todd, Bernstein Revued. **1987-88:** Irma La Douce, Le nozze di Figaro, H.M.S. Pinafore, Orontea, West Side Story, Albert Herring, Night! Youth! Paris! and the Moon!, A Propos de Paris, Working. **1988-89:** Die Fledermaus, Il ritorno di Ulisse in patria, L'incoronazione di Poppea, Favola d'Orfeo, The Fantasticks, Die Dreigroschenoper, Oh, Coward!, Edith Piaf Onstage, Mario and the Magician, Ba-ta-clan. **1989-90:** The Mikado, Cabaret, The Telephone, La voix humaine, Pacific Overtures, Edith Piaf Onstage, Close Harmony Holidays, Camille:La traviata, Cole Porter with a Twist. **1990-91:** El Capitan, The Gondoliers, Harriet, The Woman Called Moses, Girl Crazy, Carmen, Die Entführung aus dem Serail, Man of La Mancha. **1991-92:** Lady in the Dark, Werther, The Cocoanuts, L'italiana in Algeri, Gypsy, Candide, Cole Porter with a Twist, Broadway Cabaret. **1992-93:** Oklahoma!, I pagliacci, Dames at Sea, Pelléas et Mélisande, Into the Woods, The Jewel Box. **1993-94:** Die Zauberflöte, The Mikado, Ain't Misbehavin', Semele, 110 in the Shade.

Selected Bibliography

Alberti, Luciano. *Music of the Western World*. New York, 1974.

Anderson, Marian. *My Lord, What a Morning*. New York, 1956.

Armstrong, W.G. *A Record of the Opera in Philadelphia*. Philadelphia: AMS Press, Inc., 1884.

Barlow, Harold, and Sam Morgenstern (eds.). *A Dictionary of Musical Themes*. New York: Crown, 1948.

*Becker, Ralph E. *Miracle on the Potomac: The Kennedy Center from the Beginning*. Silver Spring: Bartleby Press, 1990.

Berson, Misha. *The San Francisco Stage: From Gold Rush to Golden Spike 1849–1869*. San Francisco, 1989.

_____. *The San Francisco Stage: From Golden Spike to Great Earthquake 1869–1906*. San Francisco, 1992.

Bing, Rudolf. *5000 Nights at the Opera*. New York, 1972.

*Bloomfield, Arthur. *The San Francisco Opera, 1922–1978*. Sausalito, CA, 1978.

Blum, Daniel. *Opera World*. New York, 1955.

_____. *A Pictorial Treasury of Opera in America*. New York, 1954.

Blumenson, John. *Identifying American Architecture*. New York: Norton, 1981.

Briggs, John. *Requiem for a Yellow Brick Brewery*. Boston, 1969.

Brockway, Wallace, and Herbert Weinstock. *The Opera: A History of Its Creation and Performance, 1600–1941*. New York, 1941.

Budden, Julian *Verdi*. New York: Random House, Inc., 1987.

Burk, Cassie, Virginia Meierhoffer, and Claude Anderson Phillips. *America's Musical Heritage*. New York, 1942.

Carson, William. *St. Louis Goes to the Opera*. St. Louis, 1946.

Cassidy, Claudia. *Lyric Opera of Chicago*. Chicago, 1979.

*Chandler, Mary Voelz. *The Greater Miami Opera: From Shoestring to Showpiece 1941–1985*. Miami, 1985.

Chase, Gilbert. *America's Music: From the Pilgrims to the Present*. Urbana, IL: University of Illinois Press, 1987.

Cone, John Frederick. *Oscar Hammerstein's Manhattan Opera Company*. Norman, OK, 1966.

Cooper, Grosvenor W. *Learning to Listen*. Chicago: University of Chicago Press, 1957.

*Coote, Albert. *Four Vintage Decades 1930–1970*. Hartford, 1970.

Crichton, Kyle. *Subway to the Met: Risë Stevens' Story*. Garden City, NY, 1959.

Cross, Milton, and David Ewen. *Milton Cross' Encyclopedia of Great Composers and Their Music*, volumes I and II. Garden City, NY: Doubleday, 1962.

Curtis, John. *One Hundred Years of Grand Opera in Philadelphia,* 7 volumes unpublished, Philadelphia.

da Ponte, Lorenzo. *Memoirs of Lorenzo da Ponte*. New York, 1967.

Davis, Ronald. *A History of Music in American Life*, volumes I, II, III. Malabar: Krieger Publishing Co., Inc., 1982.

_____. *A History of Opera in the American West*. Englewood Cliffs, NJ, 1965.

_____. *Opera in Chicago*. New York: Irvington Publishers, Inc., 1966.

Dembsky, Stephen, et al. *International Vocabulary of Music*. New York, 1979.

Dowley, Tim. *Schumann — His Life and Times*. New York: Paganiniana Publications, 1982.

Eaton, Quaintance. *The Boston Opera Company*. New York: Da Capo Press, Inc., 1965.

_____. *The Miracle of the Met*. New York: Da Capo Press, Inc., 1968.

_____. *Opera Caravan*. New York: Da Capo Press, Inc., 1957.

_____ (ed.). *Musical U.S.A.* New York, 1949.

Estavan, Lawrence (ed.). *The History of Opera in San Francisco*. Works Progress Administration, San Francisco, 1939.

Ewen, David. *Complete Book of the American Musical Theater*. New York, 1958.

_____. *Encyclopedia of the Opera*. New York, 1963.

_____. *Music Comes to America*. New York, 1947.

Gagey, Edmond M. *The San Francisco Stage: A History*. New York: Greenwood Press, Inc., 1950.

Garden, Mary, and Louis Biancolli. *Mary Garden's Story*. New York: Ayer Company Publishers, 1951.

Gatti-Casazza, Giulio. *Memories of the Opera*. New York: Riverrun Press, 1941.

Gerson, Robert A. *Music in Philadelphia*. Philadelphia, 1940.

*Giesberg, Robert I. *Houston Grand Opera: A History*. Houston, 1981.

Gill, Brendan. *John F. Kennedy Center for the Performing Arts*. New York, 1981.

Glass, Philip. *Music By Philip Glass*. New York: Harper & Row, 1987.

*Glasser, Alfred (ed.). *The Lyric Opera Companion*. Kansas City, 1991.

Graf, Herbert. *The Opera and Its Future in America*. New York, 1941.

_____. *Producing Opera for America*. New York, 1940.

Grout, Donald Jay. *A Short History of Opera*. New York: Columbia University Press, 1963.

Grun, Bernard. *The Timetables of History*. New York, 1979.

Hackett, Karleton. *The Beginning of Grand Opera in Chicago*. Chicago, 1913.

Hamilton, David (ed.). *The Metropolitan Opera Encyclopedia*. New York, 1987.

Hammett, Ralph. *Architecture in the United States*. New York, 1976.

Harewood, Earl of. *The Definitive Kobbé's Opera Book*. New York, 1987.

Harris, Kenn. *Renata Tebaldi*. New York, 1974.

Hipsher, Edward. *American Opera and Its Composers*. Philadelphia: Da Capo Press, Inc., 1927.

Hitchcock, Wiley, and Stanley Sadie. *The New Grove Dictionary of American Music*. New York, 1986.

Holderness, Marvin. *Curtain Time in Forest Park*. St. Louis Municipal Theater Association, St. Louis, 1960.

Hornblower, Arthur. *A History of the Theater in America*. Philadelphia: Ayer Company Publishers, 1919.

Howard, John Tasker. *Our American Music*. New York, 1930.

Hume, Paul. *Verdi*. New York: Dutton, 1977.

*Irwin, Alfreda. *Three Taps of the Gravel: Pledge to the Future*. Chautauqua, NY, 1987.

Jellinek, George. *Callas: Portrait of a Prima Donna*. New York: Ayer Company Publishers, 1960.

*Johnson, Charles A. *Opera in the Rockies: A History of the Central City Opera House Association 1932–1992*. Denver, 1992.

Jones, Howard Mumford. *America and French Culture*. Chapel Hill, NC, 1927.

Kennedy, Michael. *The Oxford Dictionary of Music*. New York: Oxford University Press, 1985.

Kline, Peter. *Enjoying the Arts/Opera*. New York: Rosen Group Co., Inc., 1977.

Kmen, Henry. *Music in New Orleans: The Formative Years 1791–1841*. Baton Rouge, LA: Books Demand UMI, 1966.

Knight, Ruth Adams. *Opera Cavalcade: The Story of the Metropolitan*. New York, 1938.

Kolodin, Irving. *The Metropolitan Opera, 1883–1939*. New York, 1940.

Lahee, Henry. *Annals of Music in America*. Boston: AMS Press, Inc., 1922.

_____. *Grand Opera in America*. Boston, 1910.

Lang, Paul Henry (ed.). *One Hundred Years of Music in America*. New York: Da Capo Press, Inc., 1961.

Lawrence, Marjorie. *Interrupted Melody*. New York, 1949.

Lawrence, Robert. *A Rage for Opera*. New York, 1971.

Lehmann, Lilli. *My Path Through Life*. New York: AMS Press, Inc., 1914.

Lehmann, Lotte. *My Many Lives*. New York: Greenwood, 1948.

Leinsdorf, Erich. *Cadenza*. Boston, 1976.

Leiser, Clara. *Jean de Reszke and the Great Days of Opera*. London, 1933.

Lesznai, Lajos. *Bartók*. London, 1961.

Lindsey, Edwin S. *Achievements of the Chattanooga Opera Association, 1943–1978*. Chattanooga, TN, 1978.

Lucie-Smith, Edward. *Cultural Calendar of the 20th Century*. Oxford, 1979.

McCracken, James and Sandra Warfield. *A Star in the Family*. New York, 1971.

MacMinn, George R. *The Theater of the Golden Era in California*. Caldwell, ID, 1941.

*Marion, John Francis. *Within These Walls: A History of the Academy of Music in Philadelphia*. Philadelphia, 1984.

Martin, George. *The Opera Companion*. New York: Dodd, 1961.

_____. *The Opera Companion to Twentieth-Century Opera*. New York, 1979.

Massenet, Jules. *My Recollections*. Boston: Ayer Company Publishers, 1919.

Mattfeld, Julius. *A Handbook of American Operatic Premieres, 1731–1962*. Detroit, 1963.

_____. *A Hundred Years of Grand Opera 1825–1925*. New York, 1925.

Matthews, Thomas. *The Splendid Art: A History of the Opera*. London, 1970.

Matz, Mary Jane. *A Hundred Years of Grand Opera 1825–1925*. New York, 1925.

_____. *Opera: Grand and Not So Grand*. New York, 1966.

Mayer, Martin. *The Met: One Hundred Years of Grand Opera*. New York, 1983.

Melba, Nellie. *Melodies and Memories*. London: AMS Press, Inc., 1925.

Merkling, Frank, John W. Freeman, and Gerald Fitzgerald. *The Golden Horseshoe: The Life and Times of the Metropolitan Opera House*. New York, 1965.

Merrill, Robert and Sandford Dody. *Once More from the Beginning*. New York, 1965.

Moore, Edward. *Forty Years of Opera in Chicago*. New York: Ayer Company Publishers, 1930.

Mordden, Ethan. *Opera Anecdotes*. New York: Oxford University Press, 1985.

_____. *Opera in the Twentieth Century*. New York: Oxford University Press, 1978.

Mountfield, David. *Tchaikovsky*. New York, 1990.

Murphy, Agnes. *Melba: A Biography*. New York: AMS Press, Inc., 1909.

Naylor, David. *American Picture Palaces*. New York, 1991.

O'Connell, Charles. *The Victor Book of the Opera*. Camden, NJ, 1936.

Odell, George. *Annals of the New York Stage*. New York: AMS Press, Inc., 1927.

Osborne, Charles. *The Complete Opera of Verdi*. New York: Da Capo Press, Inc., 1987.

_____. *The World Theater of Wagner*. New York: Macmillan, 1982.

Osborne, Richard. *Rossini*. Boston, 1986.

*Patterson, Russell. *A View from the Pit*. Kansas City: Lowell Press, 1987.

Pavarotti, Luciano. *Pavarotti, My Own Story*. Garden City, NY: Warner Books, 1981.

Peltz, Mary Ellis. *The Magic of Opera: A Picture Memoir of the Metropolitan*. New York, 1960.

Pleasants, Henry. *The Great Singers*. New York, 1981.

Pugnetti, Gino. *Life and Times of Beethoven*. New York, 1967.

_____. *Portraits of Greatness — Verdi*. New York, 1984.

Rich, Alan. *The Lincoln Center Story*. New York, 1984.

Rich, Maria (ed.). *Central Opera Service Directories*. New York, 1969, 1975, 1980, 1990.

Rosenthal, Harold, and John Warrack. *The Concise Oxford Dictionary of Opera*. Oxford: Oxford University Press, 1989.

Sachs, Harvey. *Music in Fascist Italy*. New York: Norton, 1987.

_____. *Toscanini*. New York: Harper & Row, 1987.
Sadie, Stanley. *Handel*. New York: Riverrun, 1968.
_____ (ed.). *History of Opera*. New York, 1990.
_____. *The New Grove Dictionary of Music and Musicians*. Washington, DC: Grove, 1980.
_____. *The New Grove Dictionary of Opera*. New York & London: Grove, 1992.
*Scott, Eleanor. *The First Twenty Years of the Santa Fe Opera*. Santa Fe, NM, 1976.
Shaw, George Bernard. *The Perfect Wagnerite*. New York: Dover Publications, Inc., 1967.
Sheean, Vincent. *Oscar Hammerstein I*. New York, 1956.
Sills, Beverly. *Bubbles: A Self Portrait*. Indianapolis, 1976.
Slonimsky, Nicolas (ed.). *Baker's Biographical Dictionary of Musicians*. New York: Macmillan, 1984.
_____. *Lectionary of Music*. New York: McGraw-Hill, Inc., 1989.
Sokol, Martin L. *The New York City Opera*. New York: Macmillan, 1981.
Sonneck, O.G. *Early Opera in America*. New York, 1914.
Thomson, Virgil. *American Music Since 1910*. New York, 1971.
Turnbull, Robert. *The Opera Gazetteer*. New York, 1988.
Upton, George P. *Musical Memoirs*. Chicago, 1908.
Vickers, Hugh. *Great Operatic Disasters*. New York: St. Martin's Press, Inc., 1979.
Virga, Patricia. *The American Opera to 1790*. Ann Arbor, MI: Books Demand UMI, 1981.
Watson, Margaret G. *Silver Theater: Amusements of Nevada's Mining Frontier*. Glendale, CA, 1964.
Wells, L. Jeanette. *A History of the Music Festival at Chautauqua Institution from 1874 to 1957*. Washington, DC, 1958.
Willis, Eola. *The Charleston Stage in the XVIII Century*. Columbia, SC: Ayer Company Publishers, 1924.
*Young, Toni. *The Grand Experience: A History of the Grand Opera House*. Wilmington, DE, 1976.
Zietz, Karyl Lynn. *Opera! The Guide to Western Europe's Great Houses*. Santa Fe, NM: John Muir Publications, Inc., 1991.

Opera Company and Opera House Booklets and Pamphlets

American History Through American Opera Lecture/Performance Series. Wilmington, DE, 1989.
The Barns at Wolf Trap, Richard W. Babcock, Vienna, VA, 1982.
Boettcher Concert Hall. Denver, 1978.
Broadway Theater Center. Milwaukee, 1992.
Central City Opera: Looking Back over Sixty years 1932–1992. Denver, 1992.
The Collection of the Kentucky Center for the Arts. Louisville, KY, 1990.
The Detroit Opera House. Detroit, 1990.
Glimmerglass Opera. Cooperstown, NY, 1990.
The Historical Hotel Jerome. Aspen, CO, 1989.
History of Opera in New Orleans: A Sketch, Edward Alexander Parsons. New Orleans, 1959.
Masonic Temple, Detroit. Detroit, 1926.
Master Plan for Historical Renovation of the Wheeler Block. Chicago, 1979.
Masterwork: The Virginia Opera Campaign for the Renovation of the Norfolk Center Theater. Norfolk, VA, 1990.
The Music Center. Los Angeles, 1976.
Music Hall. Dallas, 1972.
Opera in New Orleans, Jack Belsom. New Orleans, 1993.
Opera Pacific: A Major Success Story. Costa Mesa, CA, 1990.

Performing Arts Center. Milwaukee, 1969.
Pittsburgh Cultural Trust. Pittsburgh, 1989.
*Wheeler Opera House—A History. Aspen, CO, 1984.
*Wolf Trap: Celebrating the Past, Looking to the Future. Vienna, VA, 1991.

*Those books or booklets marked with an asterisk are available directly from the opera company gift shops and are recommended for more detailed information about the opera company or house.

Opera Company and Opera House
Magazines and Newsletters

Adventures. Long Beach, CA: Long Beach Opera.
Aria. Honolulu: Hawaii Opera Theater.
Aspen Music Festival. Aspen, CO: Aspen Music Festival.
The Atlanta Opera News. Atlanta: Atlanta Opera.
Bis! New Orleans: New Orleans Opera.
Bravi! Milwaukee: Florentine Opera.
Bravo! Detroit: Michigan Opera Theater.
Bravo. Omaha: Opera Omaha.
Center Stage. Nashville: Tennessee Performing Arts Center.
Central City Opera. Central City: Central City Opera.
The Chautauquan Daily. Chautauqua, NY: Chautauqua Institution.
Cincinnati Opera Newsletter. Cincinnati: Cincinnati Opera.
The Dallas Opera Magazine. Dallas: Dallas Opera.
Dayton Opera. Dayton: Dayton Opera.
DCA Scenes. Miami: Dade County Auditorium.
Encore. Seattle: Seattle Opera.
Fanfare. Baltimore: Baltimore Opera.
Filene Center Lines. Vienna, VA: Wolf Trap Foundation for the Performing Arts.
Glimmerglass Opera News. Cooperstown, NY: Glimmerglass Opera.
Kennedy Center News. Washington, DC: The Kennedy Center for the Performing Arts.
Kentucky Center Presents. Louisville: Kentucky Center for the Performing Arts.
Kentucky Opera News. Louisville: Kentucky Opera.
Keynotes. Nashville: Nashville Opera.
Il Libretto. Miami: Greater Miami Opera.
Libretto. Sarasota, FL: Sarasota Opera.
Lyric Opera News. Chicago: Lyric Opera of Chicago.
Metro News. Indianola, Iowa: Des Moines Metro Opera.
Milwaukee PAC News. Milwaukee: Milwaukee Performing Arts Center.
Mobile Opera. Mobile: Mobile Opera.
On Stage. Costa Mesa, CA: Opera Pacific.
Opera Cleveland. Cleveland: Cleveland Opera.
OperaCue. Wilmington: OperaDelaware.
Opera L.A.. Los Angeles: Los Angeles Opera.
Opera News. New York: Metropolitan Opera Guild.
Opera San José. San José: Opera San José.
Opera Voice. Norfolk: Virginia Opera.
Ovation. Hartford, CT: The Bushnell.
Ovation. Minneapolis: Minnesota Opera.
Pabst Theater Collection. Milwaukee: Pabst Theater.
Performing Arts Magazine. San Diego: San Diego Opera.
Recitative. St. Louis: St. Louis Opera Guild.

Renaissance. Pittsburgh: Pittsburgh Opera.
San Francisco Opera Magazine. San Francisco: Theater Publications, Inc.
Santa Fe Opera. Santa Fe: Santa Fe Opera.
Utah Opera. Salt Lake City: Utah Opera.
The Voice. Philadelphia: Philadelphia Opera Guild.
The Washington Opera. Washington, DC: Washington Opera Guild.

Selected Opera / Music Magazines

Musical America. New York
Musica Viva. Milan
L'Opera. Milan
Opera. London
Opéra International. Paris
Opera Monthly. New York.
Opera Now. London
The Opera Quarterly. Durham, NC.
Das Opern Glas. Hamburg
Opernwelt. Zurich
La rivista illustrata del Museo Teatrale alla Scala. Milan

In addition to the above, newspaper and magazine articles, opera company programs, press releases, annual reports, and chronicles too numerous to list were used as source material.

Index